FROM BIBLE BELT TO SUNBELT

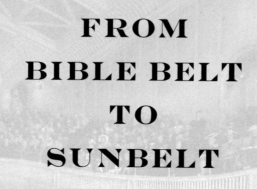

FROM BIBLE BELT TO SUNBELT

◆ ◆ ◆

Plain-Folk Religion,
Grassroots Politics, and the
Rise of Evangelical Conservatism

DARREN DOCHUK

W. W. NORTON & COMPANY
NEW YORK LONDON

Portions of chapter 4 were adapted from Darren Dochuk, "Christ and the CIO:
Blue-Collar Evangelicalism's Crisis of Conscience and Political Turn in Early
Cold War California," *International Labor and Working-Class History* 74
(Fall 2008), published by Cambridge University Press.

Manufacturing by RR Donnelley, Harrisonburg
Book design by Lovedog Studio
Production manager: Anna Oler

Library of Congress Cataloging-in-Publication Data

Dochuk, Darren.
From Bible belt to sunbelt : plain-folk religion, grassroots politics,
and the rise of evangelical conservatism / Darren Dochuk. — 1st ed.
p. cm.
Includes bibliographical references (p.   ) and index.
ISBN 978-0-393-06682-1 (hardcover)
1. Christian conservatism—California, Southern—History—20th century.
2. Evangelicalism—California, Southern—History—20th century.
3. California, Southern—Church history—20th century. I. Title.
BR555.C2D63 2011
277.94'9082—dc22

2010032740

W. W. Norton & Company, Inc.
500 Fifth Avenue, New York, N.Y. 10110
www.wwnorton.com

W. W. Norton & Company Ltd.
Castle House, 75/76 Wells Street, London W1T 3QT

1 2 3 4 5 6 7 8 9 0

For Debra

CONTENTS

III. SOUTHERN SOLUTIONS

IV. SOUTHERN STRATEGIES

SOUTHERN CALIFORNIA, CIRCA 1980

San Bernardino Mountains

San Bernardino

ROUTE 66

Riverside

San Bernardino County

Los Angeles County

San Diego County

Riverside County

Orange County

Glendora

El Monte

Whittier

Brea

Fullerton

Anaheim

Disneyland

Santa Ana

Huntington Beach

Costa Mesa

Laguna Hills

Newport Beach

Pasadena

Bell Gardens

Maywood

Downey

Norwalk

Buena Park

Knott's Berry Farm

Long Beach

Pacific Ocean

San Gabriel Mountains

Burbank

Glendale

Hollywood

Downtown

South Central

South Gate

Watts

Bellflower

Lakewood

Compton

Terminal Island

Torrance

Griffith Park

Inglewood

San Fernando Valley

Van Nuys

Beverly Hills

Northridge

Santa Monica

Pacific Palisades

Malibu

Ventura County

Los Angeles

0 5 10
miles

City Limits

San Diego

Miramar

La Jolla

El Cajon

La Mesa

North Park

Downtown

Coronado

N

INTRODUCTION

"AT HOME WITH THE ANGELS"

O N A BRILLIANT, SUNNY AFTERNOON IN LATE SEPTEMBER 1969, fifty thousand Californians wrestled unseasonable heat and anticipation while waiting to hear southern preacher Billy Graham deliver the old-time gospel. The occasion was the first Sunday meeting of the evangelist's Southern California Crusade, a ten-day religious revival held in Anaheim's "Big A" baseball stadium. After the preliminaries of worship and prayer, the lanky cleric emerged from behind the large carved-oak pulpit at the front of the flower-banked stage straddling second base. With his tanned skin, piercing blue eyes, and wavy golden hair, he looked all California, but the moment he began speaking he was pure North Carolina. Graham skillfully blended the intimidating gesticulations of a Baptist preacher with the inviting lilt of a Presbyterian minister, the passion of a Pentecostal with the straightforwardness of a Methodist. With refulgent eyes demanding attention, his right arm chopped at the pulpit repeatedly with index finger outstretched as if to physically prick listeners' consciences, and his voice drew the masses into spiritual submission. Having arrived hours earlier to take their seats in the sunshine, it took but a few minutes for Graham's audience to be convinced by the performance.

It was the substance of Graham's message that truly drew them to his words. For this occasion Graham chose to speak on the Second Coming of Christ, a subject foundational to evangelical doctrine. As he had done countless times before, Graham laid out the basics of his eschatology— that Christ would return suddenly, without warning, in a time of chaos— before presenting evidence of this impending doom. "And there shall be signs in the sun, and in the moon, and in the stars," Graham declared, with reference to Luke 21. "And upon the earth there will be distress of nations . . . the sea and the waves roaring . . . men's hearts failing them for fear." To see that men's hearts were failing them, Graham warned, Californians needed only to look to nearby university campuses where student militants, inspired by reckless utopian visions, were promising to destroy America and the democratic political system it held dear. To see the distress of nations, Californians needed only to ponder communism's troubling advances in lands just across the Pacific. To see the unhealthiness of their environs—"the sea and the waves roaring," Graham rose to a crescendo—Californians needed only to look out their car windows at the concrete landscape that surrounded them. Once a rustic paradise that smelled of orange blossoms and citrus, Southern California was now a giant "strip-city" overrun by freeways, overcome by smog, and blighted by violent neighborhoods.

Graham asked, What path should Christians take out of this hopeless situation? Not to the vestibules of federal power, he insisted, because even the most honest, well-meaning politician faced the immovability of big government. "You see, we've built such a bureaucratic machine in this country and a monster, nobody can control it. It's feeding upon itself and growing by leaps and bounds and it's become like an octopus reaching into every home and life in America, a gigantic monster bureaucracy, and no man can control it. It's out of hand. Nobody knows how to reverse it; nobody knows how to stop it; nobody knows how to cut it." Wanting to bring his jeremiad to a gentler close, Graham then offered the true path to resolution. He asked Californians to respond not with fear to the trials of this world but with hope that, through a personal commitment to Christ, they would experience the fullness of divine blessing in this moment of crisis. With their heads bowed and eyes closed and the soft melody of "Just as I Am" humming through the stadium's sound system, Graham beckoned his audience forward to realize their salvation. As if waiting all their lives for this moment, thousands answered the call.[1]

Graham, too, seemed to have been waiting for this moment. A consummate professional known for his impassioned sermons, he nevertheless preached in the Big A with a depth of feeling not sensed before. To be sure, the evangelist never spoke glibly about the apocalypse. Still, in Anaheim he broached this subject with newfound urgency. In this context Graham delivered his ultimatum not as a prophet from a distant shore but rather as one of the rebuked who shared blame and carried a personal burden for California's well-being. The public glimpsed this sincerity in each of the crusade's nightly sermons as he railed against the onslaught of secular humanism that battered every demographic in his audience— young and old, male and female, black and white, student and soldier. But his vulnerability was also witnessed in a telling moment at a press conference that followed the campaign. Beaming at reporters, he rhapsodized about the miraculous convergence of human effort and divine blessing that made this revival so special. Truly, he proclaimed, this was the "high point of his career." Then, with surprising candidness, he went a step further: "I feel more at home here than any place I've ever been."[2]

Clearly the southern evangelist had approached the Southern California Crusade with special purpose, yet why such a heartfelt, personal response? Graham, of course, had experienced a career-defining moment in Southern California once before—in 1949, when he held his first evangelistic rally in Los Angeles—so returning there always elicited his deepest emotions. Anaheim was no different, in this respect. The stunning statistical triumph of the Big A's crusade offered yet another reason for his elation. The campaign's ten-day attendance was 384,000, the highest daily average for any Graham event held on American soil. Of these people, 20,336 had made decisions for Christ, a number that was more than three times that produced by his 1949 Los Angeles meetings. Graham's post-crusade ebullience can also be chalked up to the many high-profile guests who supported his campaign. His wife, Ruth Graham, made a rare public appearance at a pre-crusade luncheon hosted by California's First Lady, Nancy Reagan, and attended by eleven thousand women (making it the largest sit-down meal ever served west of the Mississippi). During the crusade, meanwhile, Graham's team assembled a "who's who" inventory of prominent citizens for special seating on stage. John Wayne and Gene Autry (owner of the Big A) occupied privileged positions on this list, as did other Hollywood denizens like Christian crooner Pat Boone. Many civic leaders joined them. Santa Ana's mayor, Anaheim's vice mayor, Brig. Gen. Henry W. Hise, commander of the El Toro Marine Corps Air Station, and Reverend E. V. Hill, a leading black evangelical pastor and city commissioner from Watts, all watched from the infield as Graham preached. So did Ronald Reagan, who opened proceedings by expressing his admiration for Orange Countians and his deep respect for Graham, his friend.[3]

Graham's jubilation can also be attributed to the astounding community support he received. At the height of pre-crusade planning, a forty-three-member Executive Committee oversaw a pyramid of subcommittees reaching out to neighborhoods as far as sixty miles away. The middle layer of this mammoth structure included the Council of Ministers, Laymen's Council, and Youth Council, each consisting of nine hundred members. Centering the base, meanwhile, was the Prayer Committee, comprised of several coordinating divisions, none larger than the division that monitored local industries like the McDonnell Douglas plant in Long Beach, home to seventeen different prayer groups. The organizational sophistication of these committees impressed Graham, but it was the earnestness of their ground troops that garnered his highest commendation. With still over a month to go in their preparations and an estimated 200,000 "man-hours" yet to be performed, officials reported that 10,000 people had already volunteered 60,636 hours, representing $781,908 in the California labor market (or many times that, they joked, had workers belonged to "some kind of 'Crusade Union Local 103'"). The crusade register calculated that housewives had performed 8,636 hours of work, an impressive number that did not account for the "Emergency-On-Call-Workers," fifty "elite" women who were "known to cancel beauty shop appointments and evenings out to stuff envelopes and type." Equally impressive was the contribution by youth. By this point students from six colleges and twenty-four high schools had already worked with Billy Graham's planning team. "With their long straight hair, cut-off blue jeans, sandals, football jerseys, mini-skirts, and bell-bottom slacks," these raw recruits contrasted starkly with "elderly women in hats and executives in pin-striped blue suits," organizers admitted, but their presence was welcomed as a sign of unabashed Christian zeal. Young and old, loosely clad and tightly wound—all types were on hand for the team's final triumph, when, following morning services on Sunday, September 21, 175,000 "walking workers" carried out a door-to-door advertising campaign that reached every corner of Orange County.[4]

The combination of all these factors made Graham feel exceedingly comfortable in Southern California, yet there was something more basic to his sense of belonging. When this famous southern evangelist spoke of this place as home, or in the next breath decried its precipitous decline, he did so not as an eminent preacher grateful for his high-powered friends and devout following but as the southerner fully committed to the ideals implanted in its cultural soil. Having grown up in the Old South, Graham preferred a setting where the simple truths of the Gospel were revered, small-town values encouraged, and revival summoned on a regular basis. As the ambassador of an emerging New South he drew energy from an atmosphere where Christians were called forth through modern media, mass marketing, and cultural engagement to become custodians of their neighborhoods and nation. On both counts Graham found precisely this kind of environment in Southern California, which is why he so passionately claimed it as his own. As evident in their extraordinary dedication to his cause, Southern Californians returned the affection by claiming him as their champion.

THIS BOOK EXPLAINS WHY Southern California proved so welcoming to Graham and nurturing of his worldview. More specifically, it describes and assesses the ways in which this evangelist's style of southern plain-folk religion—uprooted and relocated to the West Coast by monumental social changes begun in the late 1930s—reoriented Southern California evangelicalism toward the South by the late 1960s. *From Bible Belt to Sunbelt* also tells the analogous story of how transplanted southern evangelicalism, itself revitalized and recreated in the Golden State, moved from the margins of the southern Bible Belt to the mainstream of America's first Sunbelt society.

Graham's own biography bears witness to this remarkable transformation, yet it does not fully explain it. For a more complete rendering of southern evangelicalism's rise in the West we need to look to the southern people who ensured that this religious system took root there. Our starting point is the seismic population shift that saw these citizens leave their home region for new beginnings elsewhere. Over the course of three generations—between 1910 and 1970—a multitude of people left the South to find work in other parts of the country. The most intense interval transpired between the late 1930s and the late 1960s, when over six million southerners relocated from the South's small towns and farms to industrial centers like Detroit and Los Angeles. As a result of this and earlier waves of migration, by 1970 11 million southerners—7.5 million whites, 3.5 million blacks—lived outside their home states. Although it is a national story, southern migration redefined Southern California like no other region. At the moment Billy Graham appeared in Anaheim to lead his ten-day revival, more southern-born residents, 2.5 million (1.7 million white, 0.8 million black), lived in the Golden State than in any other single non-southern state. By 1969, California claimed more southern residents than Arkansas. Although Graham's team of coordinators may not have recognized it, when they established a sixty-mile radius for pre-crusade activities they in fact drew a circle around the core of California's southern settlement. More southerners lived within this orb than resided in Little Rock and Oklahoma City combined.[5]

These statistics only hint at more elusive but ultimately pervasive ways in which southern people transplanted their religion to the California coast. *From Bible Belt to Sunbelt* captures such momentous change in a second way, through the life experiences of those who filled rail cars on the Santa Fe line during World War II or drove west on Route 66; those who sat in folding wooden chairs on a sawdust floor during Graham's tent revival in 1949 and stationed themselves on concrete and plastic at the Big A for his crusade in 1969. There are too many individual biographies to tell, of course, but we can start with people like Marie Koenig, a Louisianan who moved to Los Angeles in 1944 in hopes of a fulfilling career. When Graham made his breakout appearance in 1949, Koenig was there to witness history. So was Marie Allen, a Texan who moved west with her children in 1941 so that her husband could work in a defense plant. In 1969 Marie and Clifford Allen were working and worshipping in Orange County and more eager than ever to throw support behind their favorite evangelist. Eleanor Vandruff missed the 1949 gathering but made sure to attend Graham's religious meetings twenty years later. An Oklahoman who made her way to Southern California via Detroit in the 1940s, Vandruff lived in a neighborhood that could be seen from the top deck of the Big A. It was a neighborhood designed by her husband, Jean, another Oklahoman whose fundamentalist convictions and leadership within his independent Baptist church prevented him from participating in Graham's ecumenical affair, yet whose theological (and political) proclivities he shared.[6]

Through these life stories we gain access to vital dimensions of southern evangelicalism's ascent in Southern California, but it is in the middle ground between demographics and personal dramas, in the realm of institutions and ideology—the primary focus of this book—that we truly learn how this religious system flourished on the West Coast. As they left home, Oklahomans, Arkansans, Texans, Missourians, and Louisianans carried their churches with them, then replanted them on California terrain. By doing so they redrew the region's religious map in quick and stunning fashion. Organized in 1940, the Southern Baptist General Convention of California (SBGCC), for example, claimed a dozen congregations at its infancy. By 1970 it claimed over a quarter of a million members, making it the third largest Protestant body in California. In 1990 the SBGCC was the largest, with half a million members. Other institutions with ties to the evangelical South—Pentecostal, Foursquare, Nazarene, Church of Christ, fundamentalist Baptist—grew at a similar pace and with the same resolve. Scores of independent-minded pastors and parishioners from the South, meanwhile, built and staffed Southern California's largest nondenominational churches, parachurch ministries, and schools, all of which had a multifaceted and profound effect on this region's Protestant establishment.[7]

Southern evangelicals also had a distinctive disposition that they imposed on the Golden State. Like all other evangelicals, they held fast to certain core tenets—the primacy of individual conversion, the inerrancy and infallibility of the Bible, and the scriptural injunction to witness for Christ—but it was the way they upheld them that set them apart. One could say that they exuded "Texas theology." Certain of the absolute rightness of their doctrine, unwilling to compromise this doctrine but always open to new ways of proselytizing it, and dedicated to strong, single-minded leaders, southern evangelicals displayed a gritty determination and a spirit of pragmatism that distinguished them in California's religious climate. Unlike mainline liberal Protestants, they possessed little patience for urbane sensibilities. In comparison to Southern California's resident evangelicals, who turned "serious, quiet, intense, humorless, sacrificial, and patient" in the peak religious experience, these southern sojourners were always "busy, vocal, and promotional" and "task-oriented." Postwar Southern California provided the ideal proving ground for this temperament. Its decentralized and deregulated suburban layout was perfectly suited to Texas theology's emphases on congregational autonomy and neighborhood witness. And its Hollywood culture and competitive marketplace of ideas, resources, and influence drew out this faith's innate inventiveness and combativeness. Granted, a cosmopolitan Southern California imposed itself on southern evangelicalism too by compelling it to trim some of its harder-edged tendencies—its racial views, for instance, and resistance to interdenominational cooperation. Over time, southern evangelicalism embraced this requisite, in part to remain viable in the competition for converts. The bottom line, though, is that Texas theology's encounter with a Southern California style forged a vigorous cultural force, one that melded traditionalism into an uncentered, unbounded religious culture of entrepreneurialism, experimentation, and engagement—in short, into a Sunbelt creed.[8]

Tellingly, Texas theology was already apparent in the "crossing myth" of southern evangelicals, hinting at what their faith was about to become. Until now historians of the South have described this region's out-migration by using Old Testament allegories. While black migration has been portrayed in terms of exodus, the fleeing of an oppressed group from captivity to freedom, the parallel migration of white southerners has been told in the context of exile, the forced abandonment of home for a foreign land. Yet southern evangelicals moving to Southern California had a different biblical narrative in mind, one that conjured up notions of empowerment. This was especially true for white migrants, the principal subjects of my study, who chose to say that they were on an "errand," like the Apostle Paul journeying from Jerusalem to Macedonia—and the Puritans from England to North America—commissioned by God to evangelize the wilderness in hopes of saving it and the people they left behind. To be sure, hardship accompanied this group of migrants too. Yet for these Christian citizens, "Steinbeckian pathos" was a rare affliction. Confident of their religious heritage, they preferred New Testament rather than Old Testament allegory, and envisioned themselves on a mission rather than forced egress. The choice of metaphor was important, for it not only enabled them intellectually, it also made them active participants in the seismic social transformations of the period. Galvanized by the process of migration, emboldened by the challenges and freedoms allowed them by their new environment, and determined to carry out their task of Christianization, southern evangelicals thus carried with them a mandate to make their religion count—to be champions of a cause, not the victims of circumstance.[9]

FROM NEW DEAL TO NEW RIGHT

This errand also inspired its pathfinders to make their politics count. Just as Billy Graham so easily transitioned his end-times sermon from prophecy to punditry, southern evangelicals who moved west brought a faith blended with politics. In the world from which they came, the distinction in fact was a false one; as custodians of their culture, evangelicals were expected to govern with a Christian conscience and vote in accordance with core Christian values. Now, in a society like California's, derailed, in their minds, by progressive thinking, the need for an engaged Christian citizenry seemed all the more urgent. They knew that the stakes were high. If trendsetting Californians were to reach the horrible end predicted by their preachers, surely all of civilization would suffer a similar fate. And so at the same time they sought to remake postwar California's religion, southern evangelicals also set out to recast its politics. They did, at every level, and the nation felt its effects.

This book's second major thrust is to show how southern evangelicalism's ascent on the West Coast coincided with the beginning of a conservative revolution that gathered momentum in Southern California during the early cold war period before breaking through nationally in the 1970s. The convergence was no coincidence. At the point of their arrival, white southern evangelicals helped exacerbate tensions within the New Deal Democratic coalition—of which they were part—and then played an increasingly important role in constructing a political counteroffensive against this liberal establishment. By the early 1950s transplanted southern evangelicals were lobbying for "A New Age, Not a New Deal." By the mid-1960s they had helped remake California politics, and within another decade they were looking for ways to spread their success eastward across the South. In 1980, roughly forty years after their first purposeful steps, southern evangelicals celebrated with fellow conservatives the election of their favored son Ronald Reagan to the Oval Office.

To highlight this end point of national power as if it was predestined, however, is to ignore the crises of conscience that marked southern evangelicalism's transformation. Southern evangelicals did not see the conservative revolution as an inevitability but rather as a daily struggle, animated by competing values and complicated by the clash of self-interests. We can extract drama from these contingencies in four chronological stages, each of which frames separate sections of the book.

Part I, "Southern Errand," charts plain-folk evangelicalism's relocation from the western South to the West Coast. It shows it to be a religious movement awakened by encounters with migration, but also as a political system stirred to action by the mobilization for war. The principles of this system were rooted in early nineteenth-century American populism: the efficacy of pristine capitalism, unbridled optimism about the freedom and power of the individual conscience, a belief in the rightness of government by popular consensus, and, most importantly, a commitment to the sanctity of the local community. These Jeffersonian precepts came wrapped in a package of Christian, plain-folk Americanism, an all-encompassing worldview that gave white southerners especially a sense of guardianship over their society. Fully committed to these ideas and the rights and privileges they prescribed, southern evangelical plain folk, preachers, and entrepreneurs assumed responsibility for protecting their communities and country from those who would undermine them. Their responsibility grew heavier as they made their way west. Faced with a fragmented culture, in which their beliefs seemed at odds with dominant liberal viewpoints, southern evangelicals began constructing an alternative system of churches and schools, and proclaiming their brand of Christian nationalism as a counterweight to progressive notions of citizenship. In doing so they aggravated an already tense political situation and forced ideological divisions within the New Deal coalition.[10]

Part II, "Southern Problem," examines the clash of cultural views that resulted from southern evangelicalism's West Coast sojourn. Wary of expanding southern influences, California's New Deal Social Democrats set out to curtail them, especially as they were taking root in Los Angeles' blue-collar suburbs. This led to open political combat in the late 1940s. In question for both parties—Social Democrats on one hand, southern evangelical populists on the other—was the status of organized labor, the future of California's Democratic Party, and ultimately the legacy of New Deal liberalism. Disillusioned by their bitter, partisan defeat, rank-and-file southern evangelicals began shifting out of the Democratic fold and into the Republican Right, where they joined other middle-class citizens and corporate activists in dreaming about a conservative insurgence.

Following the tumult of the late 1940s, and increasingly agitated by the polarized climate of cold war California, southern evangelical plain folk, preachers, and entrepreneurs forged a powerful political front on behalf of the emerging conservative movement. Part III, "Southern Solutions," describes how this potential was first contemplated in the pew and then exercised in the community. From their pulpits southern evangelicals learned that California's precipitous slide to secularism meant American patriots needed to marshal their energy against a liberal establishment that assailed congregational and personal sovereignty in matters of faith as easily as it undermined the autonomy of neighborhood and nation state in matters of governance. The effect of this soul searching was profound, for in the process of adjusting old-time ideals to new political realities these citizens not only mobilized their own but also generated activism on multiple levels. Convinced that they occupied the front line in a fight against liberalism, they demanded diligent counteraction in church, precinct, and government. Meanwhile, the most industrious preachers and entrepreneurs among them constructed an elaborate network of schools, interdenominational organizations, communication systems, and associations, from which a united conservatism could emerge. This phalanx of institutions threw its full weight behind Barry Goldwater's presidential run of 1964.

Part IV, "Southern Strategies," shows how this evangelical front helped win the governorship for Ronald Reagan in 1966, the South for Richard Nixon in 1972, and ultimately the country for Reagan's Republican Party in 1980. Indeed, what is implicit in the first three sections is foregrounded in this one; namely, that developments within the West Coast's evangelical subculture did not unfold in isolation but rather transpired within the context of an emerging Sunbelt. Though always present during the early cold war years, religious interchange between Southern California and the South gained importance on a national scale in the late 1960s and 1970s as preachers and politicians sought ways to undo the Democratic Party's "Solid South." In this context of political upheaval, California precedents became pedagogy for others. At the presidential level, California's network of evangelical ministries played a critical role in bringing Nixon and especially Reagan into national power. Lessons learned by activists working in California's suburban trenches, meanwhile, were transmitted through widening institutional channels to the uninitiated in the South, who then proceeded to Republicanize their precincts. All of these endeavors completed what had been a long-standing crusade by southern evangelicals who, in keeping with their errand, wanted not only to conquer their new frontier but also to redeem those they had left behind.

By tracking these contingencies, southern evangelicalism comes alive as one of the most sweeping, dynamic political forces in post-Depression America. To date, historians have barely glimpsed it in parts. We know a bit about the role white southern evangelical migrants played in the collapse of the New Deal order outside the South. And, thanks to recent scholarship, we are learning more about how southern evangelicalism and its strong prejudices for decentralized governance and traditional values helped fracture the Democratic Party's Solid South from within. The same holds true when we turn from the New Deal's fall to the New Right's rise. Few subjects have received more scholarly treatment lately than modern conservatism, and rightfully so. Whereas a previous generation of historians assumed liberal consensus in post–World War II America, the current one sees a contested political climate in which conservatism occupies a central role. Local studies of its activists, biographies of its leaders, analyses of its core ideas, and appraisals of its partisan maneuvers have all brought this diffuse and complicated movement into clearer focus. Yet, with few exceptions, these studies have cordoned off evangelicalism as an interest that nudged politicians and inflected politics only sporadically as a voice of protest from the periphery. In part this has to do with Jerry Falwell and Pat Robertson's so-called Religious Right, which seemed to acquire power overnight in the late 1970s. Because of its continued salience, scholars have expended inordinate energy trying to understand why these men and their movement struck in this particular moment. Such single-minded concern, however, has helped reify the popular notion that evangelicalism affects the political arena only haphazardly and episodically in contexts of crisis. This plays into a general tendency in political history to treat religion as an historical agent that pops up for a short time, makes some noise, surprises some people and scares others, but then suddenly disappears again to wait for its next release.[11]

From Bible Belt to Sunbelt will challenge this notion and help fill these gaps by demonstrating how southern evangelicalism was, from the very beginning, aligned with the forces that created the Sunbelt and embedded in the political processes that upset this region's Democratic allegiances and constructed its Republican Right. When historians focus solely on Falwell and Robertson's Religious Right they miss a good deal of this story; in the taxonomy of postwar religious politics they see only one species of a much larger genus. Though varied in their intentions and level of influence, the evangelical actors in this book had no desire to operate on the margins. As power brokers and rank-and-file citizens, mediators and activists, they were invested in a much larger project to create a moral geography—a Sunbelt landscape attuned to all of their scriptural truths about self, community, government, money, and society. And so, in Southern California's blue- and white-collar suburbs, they entered into grassroots combat at the very moment of resettlement. Thereafter they sustained a keen political interest in virtually every political matter that affected their livelihood, those that affected home and hearth certainly, but also ones that affected pensions and employment practices, zoning and housing policies, disarmament and right-to-work legislation, race relations and tax relief—areas few historians have considered relevant to religious folk. California's polarized political climate and popular democratic system of ballot initiatives and movement politics, moreover, kept them highly charged, always on edge, always ready for the next fight. On a grander scale, the southern evangelical elite helped lay the foundation for a major shift in the nation's political economy. Through migration chains and institutional channels, they cemented the southern power base of defense, aerospace, technology, electronics, and oil and gas extraction industries, and they constructed cultural agencies to match this capitalist system, all the while putting their accumulated wealth to work for right-wing political endeavors. Together, southern evangelicals of each social stratum fashioned a distinctively Sunbelt "creative conservatism," animated by free market and family politics, racial moderation and youthful zeal, and a determination to defend the autonomy of their churches, neighborhoods, and nation.[12]

When we stretch our vision to include this full array of affairs, therefore, we find a religious system layered with political imperatives and a sophisticated apparatus of power rooted in a long history. Rather than an invention of Falwell and Robertson's Religious Right, evangelicalism's politicization was a product of an earlier time made possible by an earlier generation, a generation that came of age on the West Coast during Roosevelt's time, not Reagan's.

THE ERRAND BEGINS

Southern evangelicals who began their errand in the California wilderness amid the specter of war and the Depression set this history in motion, and so it is here that we begin our story. Part I of the book suspends time in order to capture this errand in three separate segments. At first it turns to the southern plain folk who moved west to find work in Southern California's defense plants. Drawing from a powerful legacy of pioneering and pilgrimage, these sojourners set out to re-create the church-centered communities they left behind. We turn next to southern preachers. While the lesser-known prophets among them spurred their congregants on to aggressive evangelism in the local neighborhood, higher-profile preachers framed their errand as a defense of traditional Christianity against the liberalization of Protestantism and the waywardness of California culture. Finally, we discover the third dimension of the southern evangelical errand in boardrooms and classrooms where a small but influential group of entrepreneurs worked quietly behind the scenes to build a network of schools from Southern California to South Carolina. Meant to instill Christian values in young Americans, these institutions were also conceived as conservative counterweights to state-sponsored colleges, which evangelical entrepreneurs held responsible for the New Deal's state-controlled economy and society's slide toward secularism. Motivated by religious convictions, these three dimensions of the southern errand were politically subversive. In isolation, each threatened the principles underlying the New Deal; together they tested the power by which the New Deal ruled.

I

SOUTHERN ERRAND

Restless tides of humanity ... have swept west-ward until the blue waters of the Pacific seem to say, "Thus far shalt thou come and no farther." Here the brown-skinned men from the Island Empire work in the flower and vegetable gardens of the rich or sell their produce at corner stands. Children of Spanish descent comment glibly in Mexican theaters, using the latest American slang. Far-away Russia and mys-terious China have sent from their numbers vast throngs to mingle with the multitudes. And to the voices of the past, when covered wagons rolled west-ward over the plains and crept over lofty mountain passes in the days of the gold rush, new voices have been added—the voices of Southern Baptists, bring-ing the glad news of salvation and saying to the thou-sands of lost people, "California, here we come."

—*SOUTHERN BAPTIST HOME MISSIONS*, 1946

1

PLAIN FOLK

You don't find proud people on farms. They are humble, common folks and have an inherent knowledge of, and dependence on, the Lord. They may not be Bible scholars, but they know there is a God and they try to live close to him.[1]

—JEAN VANDRUFF

YOUNG JEAN VANDRUFF HATED STANDING STILL. A PRECOCIOUS child with an insatiable need to "figure out an easier, faster, better way to do everything," Jean's childhood often proved the proverb that "foolishness is bound in the heart of a child." At the age of four he discovered fire. Impressed by his brother's fire-making abilities but determined to outdo him, Jean set a large pile of dry hay ablaze in his father's large storage shed. Within minutes the flames had engulfed the entire edifice, leaving him scrambling to the farmhouse for safety. Horrified by the inferno he had somehow ignited, the panicked boy ran to his mother's side and blurted, "I matched the barn."

Returning from town, where he had just purchased a new stove for his wife, Jean's father, Rollie Vandruff, watched with mounting horror as tufts of smoke on the horizon evolved into an ominous cloud above his property. By the time he arrived home, the charred frame of a once impressive structure was beyond salvage, as were its smoldering, uninsured contents: a brand-new Chevrolet, farm equipment, and bales of harvested grain, hay, and cotton. Aware of the trouble he had caused, but oblivious to its severity, Jean stood watching the fire next to the farm's watering tank, upwind from the barn, "with my dad at my side, his hand on top of my head, and wondering why he wasn't beating me to death."

The emotional trauma of this episode taught Jean that life is fragile and a secure wage rare. Because of the devastating conflagration, Jean's father was forced to abandon his land, move his family into town, and assume the undignified role of tenant farmer. Once the most successful sodbuster in the area, he closed his career by working for neighbors, using his mules to build roads, ponds, and terraces—ridges across sloped land that helped catch "the run-off water and hold it in place to soak into the ground." But in observing his father's stoicism Jean absorbed a second, more important truth: Hardship was inevitable but defeat was not. Through undying faith in "God's plan," Jean's father reminded him, generations of Vandruffs had refused to bow to life's many trials. On the contrary, it was their triumphs over adversity that had made the Vandruffs true Oklahomans. The importance of standing steadfast in the face of difficult circumstances was a fundamental precept of the pioneering ethic. Rollie dared not abandon it; Jean dared not forget it.

Jean not only remembered these lessons, he carried them with him to Southern California. After graduating from high school in Hominy, his hometown of 1,500 people, situated northwest of Tulsa, he began looking for work. Jean's mother watched her son "flounder around" in part-time shifts at the local theater and funeral home, and finally encouraged him to join his older brother Lindsey on a job-hunting mission to Los Angeles. Jean secured a loan for $250 from the local banker and, in 1941, headed to California. Within days he and Lindsey were living in an apartment on Figueroa Street near Olympic Boulevard, enjoying employment at Douglas Aircraft in El Segundo, ready access to idyllic beaches, and regular dining at Clifton's Cafeteria on Broadway, "an easy walk of about eight blocks, where they had beautiful singing waitresses." By the time the Japanese bombed Pearl Harbor in December, Jean was feeling at home in Los Angeles, working on the assembly line and worshipping in a local church.[2]

JEAN VANDRUFF GREW UP in a society that could not stand still. At the moment he began his trip west, fifteen million other Americans (12 percent of the national population) were on the move. Sojourners like Vandruff, who steered their way to Los Angeles just prior to World War II, traveled in search of decent jobs at the city's automobile, airplane, and rubber factories. The 320,000 newcomers who made their way to Los Angeles in 1941 alone were greeted by employment opportunities in these same mammoth plants, which now functioned as armories generously funded by the federal government. Already in 1940 Washington was pumping $1.3 billion per year into California's economy, and by 1945 this number would rise nearly 600 percent to $8.5 billion. The manufacturers, of course, reaped rewards, but so did the workers. The wages the federal government disbursed through its investments in the state increased tenfold during the war from $216 million in 1940 to $2.1 billion in 1945, allowing Californians' personal incomes to double. Blessed by their region's favor with Washington, Southern Californians' wallets expanded the quickest. When Vandruff awoke early each morning to take his spot on the assembly line, he was among the 40 percent of Los Angeles' residents whose paychecks were signed by Uncle Sam.[3]

Many joined them on the journey, but what makes Vandruff and his fellow southern migrants special is the way they interpreted the drama that unfolded around them. Whether as young men and women yearning for independence, middle-aged males fleeing farms for steady factory work, or families looking for stability, they came west with notable optimism and resolve. Their connection with the powerful pioneering legacy of their forebears—romanticized through time, yet still tangible and real in their minds—sustained them as they looked to re-create their supportive southern communities in the modest suburbs that grew up around Los Angeles' booming factories. For many of these self-identified "plain folk," such hope was fortified by a powerful sense of mission conveyed to them from the pulpits of their churches. Rooted in a popular narrative long embraced by white Anglo-American Protestants, and accentuated by the experiences of their own trailblazing grandparents who had first settled territory west of the Mississippi River, these white southern evangelicals envisioned themselves as pilgrims carrying out their own "errand into the wilderness."[4]

Theirs, of course, was a modern sort of frontier and an unusual kind of wilderness, but it was a borderland just the same that called forth the urge to civilize. Aided by their unassailable confidence, as well as Los Angeles' decentralized and unregulated layout, they found freedom to graft their notions of Christian individuality and community onto the land. In the process they served notice to their neighbors that they had come west not looking for salvation but to impart it.

LIVING A PIONEERING LEGACY

As with all migrants, it is impossible to understand what white southern evangelicals brought with them to California without appreciating the
world from which they came. Just like the Vandruffs after Jean's experiment with fire, many families in the western South during the 1920s and
1930s had been forced to move abruptly because of unforeseen crisis or
unanticipated opportunity. Such upheaval was not new for this region and
its people. These farming families had been on the move for four generations, stretching back to pre–Civil War years. Seeking land for crops
and cattle, independent-minded yeomen in the 1830s forced the southern
frontier west across the Mississippi plains and over the Ozark–Ouachita
highlands. While Arkansas and Oklahoma proved most welcoming to
transplants from the highlands of Tennessee and Kentucky, Texas greeted
an equal number of homesteaders and planters from the Upper and Lower
South. Regardless of origins, those who carved out new lives amid the
foothills and forests of eastern Texas and Oklahoma, or on the treeless
plains that followed the Red River west to the Panhandle region, forged
an inspiring legacy for their descendants. Jean's family, in this way, saw
his journey to California as not so different from his grandfather's move
from Virginia to Indian Territory in the 1880s. Both men left home in
search of self-discovery and a better life.[5]

The social system of movement that shaped existence in the western
South was certainly a product of a venerated ancestral past, but it was
also a consequence of the present. Beginning in the early twentieth century but accelerating in the 1920s, small landowners and tenant farmers abandoned the rural hinterland for nearby towns and cities. Although
diversified to a far greater extent than in the Deep South, farming in the
western South had, by the early twentieth century, become tied to two
of Dixie's enduring economic conventions: cotton and tenant farming.
In times of economic boom like the immediate aftermath of World War
I, when high demand and prices helped stimulate record yields, cotton
proved to be the ultimate boon for family farms. But increasing dependency on this crop proved disastrous, as abundant harvests led invariably
to market gluts, depreciating prices, and, in turn, misguided attempts to
increase profits by increasing acreage, a cyclical phenomenon repeated
throughout the 1920s that resulted in eroded soil and the institutionaliza-
tion of tenancy. Once an ideal arrangement whereby poorer farmers were

able to climb the economic ladder to full ownership of their own estates, tenancy by the late 1920s had become a dead end, with debt a permanent feature of life on the land. Driven off the soil by a combination of economic and ecological forces, the more fortunate independent husbandmen sold their depreciating property and relocated to cheaper and fresher terrain in the western reaches of Oklahoma and Texas. The much larger percentage of this region's yeomanry looked to nearby towns and cities for employment in the trades, service sector, or expanding extractive industries like oil and mining. Others, meanwhile, simply remained trapped on the land, forced to eke out a living. Neither the most fortunate nor indigent, Jean Vandruff's father followed a well-traveled path when he gave up cotton farming for alternative employment and life in a nearby town.[6]

As the fortunes of cotton farmers continued to plummet, the more daring left the western South altogether, striking out to the growing labor markets of Southern California. In truth, Southern California had always appealed to white southern migrants, even as early as the gold rush days. Then, fortune hunters were known to pick up the Oregon–California trail in Missouri or the Santa Fe Trail running parallel to the south, and follow them to their terminuses in the Far West. Later, during Reconstruction, other southerners from Texas, Arkansas, and Oklahoma followed the more southerly route in search of land on which to begin rebuilding family estates lost during the Civil War. Twentieth-century California's favorite berry farmer, Walter Knott, came from a family borne to the Golden State on this early wave of southern migration. Knott's maternal grandparents had left their plantation in Virginia in the early 1840s and guided their covered wagon to Texas, where they built a contented life. But during Reconstruction, as Knott himself would later recount, "the carpetbaggers came down South and disenfranchised every Southerner that had been in the war." With wagons loaded once again, Knott's grandparents embarked on a four-month trip west to Southern California and, upon arrival in spring of 1868, established a new home in El Monte, a town just east of Los Angeles that soon became a known sanctuary for southern expatriates.[7]

Knott's celebrated heritage notwithstanding, Southern California looked all the more enticing for southerners as the economic troubles that began plaguing Oklahoma, Arkansas, Texas, and pockets of Missouri and Louisiana in the 1920s hit endemic proportions in the late 1930s. During the 1920s nearly 250,000 natives of these states traveled west to California to chase material dreams of better living. Some in this generation parlayed economic opportunity into extraordinary wealth, but far more common were stories of blue-collar solidity like Dyer Bennett's. Born in the Ozark Mountains, Bennett moved west in 1926 to take a job at Union Oil, which he vastly preferred to the alternatives back in Arkansas. Life in the company town of Brea, located north of Fullerton and southeast of Los Angeles, proved comfortably oriented to the same routines of home: hard daily labor, revelry on Friday evenings, company ball games on Saturday, and church on Sundays.[8]

Those in the 1930s who followed Bennett's path altered the demographic profile of white southern migration, but only slightly. If somewhat poorer than their predecessors, they were not destitute. The popular joke circulating in the Panhandle during the late 1930s and early 1940s, that "the 'rich 'uns' had pulled up and gone to California to starve" while "the 'poor folks' just stayed hungry where they were," contained much truth. A number of penniless peripatetics came to California during the dust bowl days and turned north at Barstow toward California's Central Valley, where a few lived lives that mirrored the Joads', John Steinbeck's fictional family in *The Grapes of Wrath*. But more prominent were semi- and unskilled laborers and proprietors from towns and cities—comfortably working-class folk, no longer tied to the land, who followed Route 66 to Los Angeles to work in the city's industrial sector. Then there were some, like Roscoe Crawford, who experienced the entire gamut of this migration. Driven off his cotton farm in the 1920s, Crawford moved to the large town of McAlester, in the southeastern section of Oklahoma, where he opened a tackle shop and general store. Having heard about jobs in California from family members already living there, Crawford packed his belongings and, out of curiosity as much as necessity, traveled to the West Coast. After stints as a fruit picker in the Central Valley, Crawford eventually made his way to Southern California, where he settled for good in the early 1940s.[9]

By the time Jean Vandruff made his move, then, Southern California had already become a logical destination for job hunters and homesteaders like him. They had heard stories about their grandparents leaving the Upper South for land west of the Mississippi, seen their parents vacate the countryside for towns and their cousins and brothers go west. Now they themselves possessed the means (however limited) and motivation to take advantage of well-traveled highways that pointed west. Historical and existing social patterns of movement, in short, paved Vandruff's way.

LIVING A POPULIST LEGACY

Vandruff and his fellow modern-day pioneers came from the western south, a region centered at the intersection of the borders of Arkansas, Texas, and Oklahoma but also extending westward along the Oklahoma–Texas Panhandle and north-south between Missouri and Louisiana. South meets West here, so naturally this land produced a distinctive hybrid culture that combined the steely persistence and principles of the South with the rugged impatience and pragmatism of the West. By the early twentieth century the western South showed patterns of this fusion in architecture, land use, speech, diet, recreation, and even musical tastes, as the guitar replaced the banjo and hillbilly music gave way to country and western. Behind popular tastes, however, was a distinct South-meets-West blend of populist Americanism.[10]

This political ideology was a dynamic and malleable one that drew its cues from precepts of "herrenvolk" democracy deeply embedded in small southern towns east of the Mississippi. As it first cohered there in the early nineteenth century, this loose doctrine stood for equal representation and an expanded male suffrage, rule of the majority, and states' rights. Grounded in life experience on the geographical fringe, it exhibited a general hostility toward any aristocracy of "wealth, privilege, or political preferment" seemingly flaunted by elites in cities, as well as an ingrained assumption of white racial superiority and the blessedness of small government and the "common man." Inspired by the mythologized ideal of Thomas Jefferson's virtuous yeoman farmer, nineteenth-century southern plain folk preferred a contained world in which the local community met all of their essential needs. Distant and potentially dangerous, the federal state's only acceptable roles, in their mind, were to provide security for hearth and home and spread the "Empire of Liberty" through the perpetuation of democratic ideals and the conquest of "free land."[11]

A product of frontier thinking, Jeffersonian democracy naturally found fertile cultural soil west of the Mississippi. Yet there, as it became dominant by the late nineteenth century, this political system became more powerful than anything seen east of the Mississippi in the Upper and Lower South, where economic and racial inhibitors worked against the populist imperative. Tenuously perched on the social rung immediately above blacks, white plain folk living on the east side of the Mississippi could not extend the ideals of egalitarianism too far for fear of jeopardizing their racial privileges. At the same time, they faced pressure from paternalistic landholders and new urban elites who demanded white citizens' compliance and depended on race solidarity for control of the Democratic South. For both reasons, white commoners in the Upper and Lower South felt compelled to sacrifice some of the inventive possibilities and intense fervor found in their Jeffersonian ideals. This did not mean they stopped talking in revolutionary tones. With mounting intensity after World War I, they joined movements led by "voices of protest" like Georgia's Eugene Talmadge and Mississippi's Theodore Bilbo, all of whom articulated familiar complaints about unrestrained capital (the "silk hat crowd") and Democratic elites. But in essence these movements functioned as outlets of frustration for a class of citizens browbeaten by the Solid South's economic order yet too heavily invested in the system of segregation to look for political alternatives.[12]

In the western South, the relative absence of such top-down authority permitted a purer populist doctrine that combined a radical individualism, experimentalism, and egalitarianism with a willingness to unite in protection of their interests. Those self-reliant men and women who settled there embraced new techniques and technologies and became forward-looking producers who searched out ways to maximize profit. When they felt trapped by someone else's terms they responded ferociously, refusing to comply or even compromise. In rapid succession through the late nineteenth and early twentieth centuries, as corporate capitalism placed them under the unscrupulous power of creditors and the banks, rank-and-file citizens of the western South condemned the inequities and banded together to lobby for reforms. At times they entertained wild conspiracies about the wealthy, bureaucrats, and professional elites, and sometimes they advocated unworkable restructuring plans. But as evidenced in the way William Jennings Bryan's relatively modest proposals enlivened them, they usually acted within a long-running tradition in American politics by using conventional political processes to correct imbalances and reassert principles of popular democracy and the sovereignty of "the people."[13]

The political dynamics of race also figured differently in the western South. A thinner black population clustered in fewer concentrated areas, coupled with the realities of a slightly more diffuse and diverse racial landscape, meant that the average white citizen could imagine living his or her life in this place beyond the pale of segregationist divide. This revised outlook did not come as a result of benevolence. In many ways, the lack of a rigid, codified racial and economic order intensified the power struggle between white and nonwhite. Violent incidents of lynching and a resurgent Ku Klux Klan that gained more power in the western South than anywhere else during the 1920s were just some of the more conspicuous signs that a more "egalitarian" society did not necessarily mean a less racially charged one. Quite the opposite: The white yeoman's republic was always in need of protection. Still, though racial conflict flared up in this region, often in the most brutal outbursts imaginable, generally it was not as overtly or consistently politicized as elsewhere in the South; nor did it need to be. Unlike their counterparts in the Deep South who remained shackled to ghosts of the Confederacy and romantic notions of the Lost Cause, western southerners could and did seize opportunities to worry about matters other than race and their racial heritage. This was a false peace created by a prejudiced society that drew subtler lines of exclusion, but white plain folk living in the western South had reason to believe they lived in an environment where the strengths of belief and merits of hard work, not the color of skin, defined one's existence.[14]

This attitude gave these citizens and their politicians the courage to cut against the grain of the Democratic Party's Solid South. Oklahomans and Arkansans were not Georgians and Mississippians when it came to party allegiance; they were small-d Democrats at best, and always remained open to other possibilities, both at the state and federal level. Of course they often gravitated toward charismatic leaders who barnstormed under the banner of the Democratic Party in the Deep South, men like Talmadge and Bilbo. And in many ways the "fiddle-and-banjo-thumping, foot-stomping" campaigning of politicians like Jeff Davis, the "Wild Ass of the Ozarks," W. Lee "Pass the Biscuits, Pappy" O'Daniel of Texas, and Louisiana's Huey Long mesmerized them in the same fashion Talmadge and Bilbo captivated voters east of the Mississippi. But citizens in the western South always expected more than coarse race baiting from their dynamic politicians. Indebted to "the people," these leaders thus delivered a fuller vision of Jeffersonian democracy. As far as voters were concerned, this meant that a broader range of political visions could be assessed openly. Independents, Republicans, and even socialists vied for power in this vigorously contested realm, though prior to World War II such openness more commonly translated into spirited debate within the Democratic Party itself.[15]

Regardless of their affiliation or vote, citizens like Marie King felt empowered by the politics of popular democracy that enlivened their region. Born in New Orleans in 1919, Marie's family history was even more wrenching than Jean Vandruff's. When she was three her mother died of pneumonia; her father, a hardworking steamboat engineer, passed away three years later. Marie's maternal grandparents, James Rufus and Lulu Kapley King, assumed responsibility for her and her two siblings. Like her father, Marie's grandparents were from Tennessee and claimed a lineage that went back to Andrew Jackson. In the mold of his forebears, James King was a rugged man who worked as a lumberman, though by the time Marie and her sister and brother had moved in to his New Orleans house, King had retired because of heart trouble. Thanks to her grandmother's thrift, however, the family continued to live in relative comfort throughout the late 1920s and early 1930s. Lulu King was an accomplished musician and teacher, but she was also pragmatic and knew how to make a dollar. It must have stung her to sell off the family's library to stretch their savings, but she performed the task with grace, keeping the King household solvent during the Depression.

The years Marie spent in her grandparents' house were tough but they were by no means grim. Weekly attendance at First Methodist Church and involvement in the congregation's Epworth League for young people were two sources of excitement; another was politics. Early in life Marie got her first taste of participatory democracy and it never left her. Under the influence of her grandfather, who held key leadership positions within Huey Long's organization, Marie became one of the governor's youngest and most dedicated supporters. By four she spoke fondly of "Hupey Long" and by eight she performed her first official task for his movement. With her grandfather's help she crafted a speech in tribute to the Kingfish that she delivered in front of a large gathering of ward officials and support-ers. At the age of nine she sat on her grandfather's lap on stage at New Orleans's Athenaeum while Long delivered a rousing speech against his impeachment. Later, when practicing for a play in which she shared the spotlight with Rosemary Long, Huey's daughter, Marie even had a chance to visit her hero's home.

For Marie, as for so many other Louisianans, politics was a way of life, an all-encompassing concern and activity. Indeed, to be a true Jefferso-nian Democrat, as she so proudly labeled herself, one had to be vigilant in the defense of community and passionate about the betterment of society. Marie and her grandfather were dedicated to grassroots reform and the protection of representative and responsible government, regardless of the cost. This personal investment in local affairs left her all the more devastated when, in 1935, Long was assassinated in the state capitol. Her commitment to Long's agenda, however, did not end with this tragedy. By the time she was twenty Marie had gotten a job in Baton Rouge as secretary to the state attorney of Louisiana. Energized by her close proximity to political power, and further invigorated by the wartime activity that swept New Orleans in the early 1940s, Marie had no desire to leave, nor ever imagined doing so. But greater opportunity called. In 1944 she followed her sister's lead and moved west to Los Angeles to take advantage of its booming economy. She brought her politics with her.[16]

Marie King and Jean Vandruff were the last of a long line of pioneers. Linked but not chained to the southern plain-folk ethic, enraptured but not overwhelmed by the freedom of the western frontier, they carved out an identity that they believed was quintessentially American. The dialectic of being southern and western, of wanting to preserve and create, defend and advance, not only motivated them in their personal quests for fruitful lives, but led them to believe collectively that they and their plain-folk Americanism held the keys to a better society.

JEFFERSON AND JESUS

The commanding influence of evangelicalism assured them of this conviction. At the core of their political culture was an unwavering faith that conflated the doctrines of Jefferson and Jesus. Shaped by the conservatism and communalism of southern evangelicalism, but radicalized by their encounter with the boundless frontier, Christian citizens living west of the Mississippi believed their true calling was to advance the Christian heritage passed down to them from their Anglo-Saxon or Scotch-Irish ancestors, not simply preserve it. Plain-folk pioneers thus became pilgrims burdened with the responsibility of evangelizing and civilizing, initially on the godless borderland of the western South, then in the dark, secular reaches of Southern California.[17]

The region Vandruff and King left behind can be described as the "burned-over district" of southern evangelicalism. Just as the fiery gospel of evangelist Charles Finney swept across upstate New York in the early nineteenth century, recasting its religious culture during the Second Great Awakening, equally talented and passionate preachers set the

Upper South ablaze with their own proselytizing. With increasing fervor after the 1830s, these "saddlebag saints" carried their message deeper into the new territory west of the Mississippi, where they found a cultural climate perfect for sustaining a high-energy faith. The western South thus entered the twentieth century burned over by revivalist religion but still not burned out. Southern Baptists dominated this scorched landscape, reporting membership numbers over four times greater than the next largest religious group, but they faced stiff competition from the Methodist Episcopal Church, South, and to a lesser extent from smaller denominations like the Church of Christ. Within its own ranks, meanwhile, the Southern Baptist Convention (SBC) had to contend with dissident Baptists aligned with Landmarkism, whose radically anti-establishment sympathies dominated the entire Baptist orb in western Arkansas. Southern Baptist officials in Nashville viewed this "sectarian" movement as an irritant, but for the western South it was yet another stimulant, a centrifugal force set on democratizing religion.[18]

Pentecostalism and Baptist fundamentalism performed similar functions in the early twentieth century. Neither was native to the western South, but both helped ensure that religion there kept its radical edge. Initially a compilation of ideas that emphasized the personal experience of God through baptism in the Holy Spirit and the exercise of spiritual gifts like speaking in tongues, Pentecostalism took plain-folk evangelicalism to a new level. At the beginning of the twentieth century, in a period of widespread religious experimentation, Pentecostalism's eccentricity allowed it to gain a footing through spontaneous revivals in California, Texas, Kansas, and North Carolina. Under the inspiration of men like Charles Parham, a Methodist minister who taught at a Bible school in Kansas before moving to Houston, and the leadership of preachers like William J. Seymour, an African American trained by Parham in Houston before moving to Los Angeles, the Pentecostal phenomenon quickly gathered momentum. Following the 1906 Azusa Street Revival in Los Angeles, led by Seymour, the phenomenon spread back across the South, leading to the formation of several denominations. The largest of these was created in 1914 when veterans of the Pentecostal revival gathered in Hot Springs, Arkansas, and soon thereafter formed the Assemblies of God.[19]

While plain folk affiliated with the Assemblies of God sought solutions to modern crises in the miraculous outpourings of the Holy Spirit, a cohort of southern "fundamentalists" found answers in the defense of biblical truth. Prior to the 1910s, calls for a return to the fundamentals of the faith seemed redundant to most southerners. Unlike their cousins to the north, whose empire was already rent with theological division, southern evangelicals remained relatively unified in their defense of orthodoxy. However, in the 1910s, factionalism began filtering down from the North. Small cracks became schisms in the 1920s when court proceedings in Dayton, Tennessee, challenged core beliefs of the conservative order. In the wake of the Scopes trial of 1925, during which southern evangelicals saw their belief in creationism and their champion William Jennings Bryan ridiculed by East Coast sophisticates like famed journalist H. L. Mencken, religious communities proclaimed fundamental biblical orthodoxy as an organizing tenet of their convictions. Soon thereafter many of these citizens—now self-identified fundamentalists—began storming courthouses, legislatures, and Southern Baptist and Methodist institutions, demanding militancy on behalf of their truths. The burned-over district of the western south saw the most forceful demonstrations.[20]

Through succeeding waves of revival and reform, and the fierce competition for converts and power, the western South thus carved out a vibrant religious system all its own and became the buckle of the Bible Belt. By the 1930s, evangelical churches of all kind claimed higher membership levels in this hub than anywhere else in the country, including the Deep South. Yet the true measure of this religion's hegemony was its pervasive influence over the lives of its people. Plain-folk evangelicalism acquired authority in this region by empowering its disciples. Through conversion, a profoundly existential experience triggered by a personal encounter with the Holy Spirit, its doctrine held that all persons enjoyed direct access to heaven and therefore equal status in Christendom. But ideally the individual's transformation did not end there. Rebirth in turn promised a life of religious "devotion, moral discipline, and missionary zeal." To be saved represented just one vital step in a progression toward holiness. And in the cosmic struggle between good and evil, one's salvation gained ultimate meaning only when followed by complete dedication to the soul-winning cause and a desire to see family, friends, and all of society aligned with God.[21]

By advancing a heavenly kingdom in which all were equal before God, evangelicalism also created a powerful sense of community down below. It leveled distinctions between farmer and oil worker, educated and uneducated, parsons and parishioners, and in turn created unity based on shared religious experience in the local congregation. Here too individuals had the last say. Unwilling to bow to aristocrats and the federal government, plain folk were just as resistant to ecclesiastical types in denominational headquarters. While some were more willing than others to abide by church guidelines, most preferred to work out on their own the meanings of their faith. Such democratic passions left the church vulnerable to prevailing prejudices and excesses. Yet as long as they were allowed to associate and worship freely, as a community of equals bound voluntarily by conviction rather than formal decree, evangelicals believed that excess would be limited and its effects more easily contained.[22]

Their commitment to personal liberty and congregational autonomy did not, however, preclude a commitment to social order. True freedom, evangelicals believed, could only be realized in a society attuned to Christian values. Plain-folk evangelicalism thus carried with it a social ethic as well, one that surfaced often in campaigns for stricter legal codes on moral concerns like prostitution, divorce, and alcohol, and the teaching of evolution, the last of which energized citizens like no other. Other political interests, however, also captured evangelicals' imagination. During the late 1920s and 1930s Christian voters in the western South were known to rally behind issues that spanned the entire political spectrum. Recognizing the power of the sacred, politicians like Huey Long even enlisted preachers to help bring faith to bear on legislative and electoral drives for income redistribution and economic restructuring. Religion and politics worked hand in hand in Long's country.[23]

In fact, distinctions between the two ultimately held little meaning there. Although its resident evangelicals claimed the principle of church-state separation, they rejected the notion that religious influence should be cordoned off from the state. As products of dissenting traditions they remained adamant that all denominations enjoy the freedom to operate on their own terms beyond intrusion from government. And they recoiled when any formal religious body (Catholicism especially) seemed to acquire special access to power. Yet at no point did they ever allow for the separation of Protestant faith from the public or political realm. In evangelicalism's estimation true religious liberty was dependent on a common set of rules provided by the Protestant tradition, on which the nation itself was founded. Any group or agenda that threatened to undermine this system by taking the logic of church-state separation to its unintended consequences of secularization was immediately suspect in the evangelical mind and targeted for a political response. Although they claimed to be "apolitical" in their rejection of state-sponsored religion or a church-sanctioned state, plain-folk evangelicals were therefore never unpolitical or antipolitical; to the contrary. Their myth of the spiritual church notwithstanding, they always knew "how to play political hardball when the prayer meeting let out." Quite often political maneuvers began long before their final "amen."[24]

Driven by a sense of guardianship over their culture, and energized by the universal potential of personal conversion, evangelicals in the western South folded the teachings of Jesus and Jefferson into a formula for participatory politics. Unlike evangelicals in the Deep South who fashioned themselves the last great bulwark of Christian democracy, they looked confidently upon themselves as its last great vanguard. Both saw themselves in exceptional terms, as protectors of this sacred political ideal. But whereas evangelicals east of the Mississippi remained seared in their faith and politics by the "knowledge of human limitations"—"Christ haunted" in Flannery O'Connor's memorable phrase—their counterparts to the immediate west relished possibility; theirs was a "Christ enchanted" society. By the late 1930s the West Coast beckoned as a new frontier on which enchantment with Christian democracy was just beginning to flourish.[25]

WITH FRIENDS AT THE OLD COUNTRY CHURCH

Like so many other journeyers during this time, southern evangelicals hoped simply to find jobs and homes in Southern California, but building strong churches weighed just as heavily on their minds. In the blue-collar suburbs of Los Angeles they found plenty of space for both.

Bell Gardens was one such suburb. In the late 1930s Bell Gardens was known as a squatters' paradise, a last refuge for human castoffs from the dust bowl plains; critics called it "Billy Goat Acres" and "Shanty Town." Though derisive, labels of this sort were, in truth, not entirely misapplied. A test case for sociologists during the Depression, Bell Gardens had a quaint, open, country feel, as did the people who lived there. Walking the community's oiled streets (so as to keep the dust down), one attentive social scientist shorthanded: "Trim little gardens. Protruding water spigots. Rows of growing vegetables. . . . Sway-back autos that don't require

garages. . . . A group of kids with a dog. They're 'rushing' the barefoot season. The boys need haircuts. I could pick 50 for Mark Twain." The citizens were aware of their peculiarities; in fact, they seemed fond of them.
Speaking of his youth as a Bell Gardens resident, John Allard recalls:

> There was just barely a designated downtown street—which afterward
> folded entirely. . . and a few small businesses, and a few sprinklings
> of homes. It worked out pretty good for those that were from a farm
> because many of the people had chickens and geese. There were some
> cattle and hogs, but not many to speak of. . . . There was no particular
> standard that had to be met, and so people were just building whatever
> they needed to, and they were making out with it.[26]

It was industry and cheap housing, not the chance to graze farm ani-
mals on crabgrass, however, that brought Allard and a majority of his
neighbors to Bell Gardens, and it was these economic offerings combined
with its rural feel that connected it to a much wider phenomenon of metropolitan growth in the late 1930s and early 1940s. Home to no more than
7,500 residents in 1938 and 30,000 by 1947, Bell Gardens was a relatively
tiny community in a larger constellation of working-class suburbs scattered along Los Angeles County's industrial corridor. Like Bell Gardens,
those communities occupying the basin between Los Angeles and Long
Beach—neighboring cities like South Gate, Maywood, Huntington Park,
Compton, and Norwalk—owed their livelihoods to the growth of heavy
industry in the 1920s and 1930s, a dramatic process, culminating in the
mobilization for war in the 1940s, that turned the region into the second
largest industrial area west of Chicago. Between 1940 and 1950 close to
eight hundred thousand new jobs were created in Southern California,
most of these in the six hundred plants scattered throughout southern
Los Angeles County.[27]

Boosters called this industrial belt the Detroit of the West. Unlike
Detroit, however, Los Angeles' manufacturing zone was distinctively
non-urban, with its large factories and small homes interspersed almost
randomly among dairy farms and pea patches. Residents throughout the
region enjoyed both rural pastimes and urban amenities. Wage laborers by
day, they returned home to comfortable rural routines, growing vegetables
and raising small livestock in backyards. By transforming their domestic
property into sites of production, workers in this way found alternative

means for family sustenance and, in the process, ensured that their communities would be at once country and city. Local culture, too, revealed the transitional nature of this industrial corridor. The city of Maywood, Bell Gardens' neighbor to the north, grappled for years with its overlapping rustic and industrial heritages. Within two months of each other in 1937, for example, Maywood's residents put on their two most anticipated annual fetes: "Pioneer Days" and the Industrial Fair. Even as late as 1949, commemorating the silver jubilee of their town, residents "organized a gigantic parade, followed by a rip-snorting rodeo to get the crowded program underway" and, as a sign of solidarity, encouraged all willing and able men to sprout "chin whiskers by way of calling attention to the coming jubilee." The town's re-creation of its glorious frontier past, meanwhile, was threatened by more modern concerns, such as anticipated labor unrest at local plants and a much-publicized scandal involving the acting chief of police, Clarence Paramenter. Charged with using police cars to "hunt rabbits in Maywood bean fields, firing shots from the cars during predawn hours" (acts he admitted doing "just to break the monotony at night"), Paramenter was reprimanded but nevertheless later sworn in as the city's top cop.[28]

Less heavily industrialized than their counterparts in Los Angeles County, similarly modest communities like Van Nuys in the valley and Santa Ana in Orange County, meanwhile, entered the 1940s with similar struggles to define their spatial layouts. Orange County had seen its economy evolve during the last three decades from one based on cattle ranching to one diversified slightly by oil, but defined especially by agribusiness and citrus farming. With industrial expansion encroaching in the 1930s, Orange County's elite rezoned the region to permit defense bases like the El Toro Marine Corps Air Station and U.S. Air Corps Cadet Replacement Training Center, both located just outside Santa Ana, but not heavy manufacturing or defense plants. Their plan to circumvent the type of industrialization seen in Los Angeles and preserve their pastoral paradise would gain traction in the 1950s, but the flurry of defense mobilization resulted in an environment not so different from that of the other industrial suburbs in the early 1940s, one characterized by blurred boundaries between places of work, home, and production, and an inability to reconcile with the modern city. Though they evolved at different paces, communities like Bell Gardens, Maywood, South Gate, and Santa Ana all faced the realities of an exploding population and economy and an incoherent urban topography in need of definition. Ultimately, they would succumb to a "post-modern" pattern of sprawl.[29]

Funneling into this fragmented frontier, hundreds of thousands of white southerners encountered a centerless grid, a milieu that allowed them to adjust to urban life without abandoning their cultural rituals. Yearning for familiarity, they began constructing churches and establishing congregations that reflected the demographics of their towns in the South. Since blue-collar suburbia allowed groups of migrants to settle in the same neighborhoods, entire communities quickly sorted themselves by faith. It was not unusual for churches to gain reputations for being "Arkie" or "Okie," and entire neighborhoods to become classified as Pentecostal, Baptist, or Church of Christ hotbeds. Newspaper advertisements, directory listings, and radio all helped facilitate this clustering, but the flock gathered mostly through word of mouth.[30]

In April 1939, for example, six families with common roots in southern Oklahoma and the Texas Panhandle founded Southern Missionary Baptist Church in Santa Ana, then set out to recruit friends from these same sections of the South. Marie and Clifford Allen were two of their earliest recruits. Natives of Dodson, Texas, a small farming community perched on the southeastern edge of the Texas Panhandle, just west of the Oklahoma border, the Allens followed the same westerly route as Jean Vandruff in 1941. Married with two young girls, Clifford and Marie decided that Clifford should abandon his day-labor job on a nearby cotton farm and travel to Los Angeles. After securing work in the shipbuilding industry on Terminal Island, near Long Beach, he called for Marie and the kids to join him. In the fall of 1941 they boarded the train in Amarillo and two days later stepped off the platform at Los Angeles' Union Station. The move to Santa Ana was difficult for Marie because it uprooted her from the only world she knew. Yet just like her grandmother, who had relocated to the Panhandle from East Texas, she saw the journey as a test of faith. And faith is what allowed her and Clifford to weather the difficulties of trying to connect with their new community. Regular attendance at Dodson's Second Baptist Church had set the pace for their weekly routine back in Texas, so Clifford and Marie started looking for a similar house of worship in Orange County. They found it in Southern Missionary Baptist. Quick to make new friends among the fellow Oklahomans and Texans who shared their pew, the Allens soon encouraged family and old friends following their westerly path to join them at their fledgling congregation.[31]

The sense of community the Allens found in this congregation was deeper than anything found in Dodson. Theirs was not an uncommon experience. During the last stages of the Depression, southern evangelicals relied heavily on their churches for support of all kind. After moving from Oklahoma to Compton in the 1930s, Melvin Shahan, for instance, saw his parents falling into debt, even with his own weekly ten-dollar paycheck from Goodyear helping out. In response, the Shahans' church organized a "pounding," a ritual that saw congregants stock the pantry of a needy and unsuspecting friend with canned goods, preserves, and smoked meat. Melvin would later recall that such acts of kindness were facilitated in part because his neighbors lived so nearby, something he did not experience in Oklahoma:

> So many of the people there at Guymon [Oklahoma] came from neighboring farmhouses out around town. When they came into town for the services, it was farther for them to drive than it was here [Compton] where people lived right in the immediate area of their church.

For the Shahan family, the intimacy of the country church often idealized by those from the South was a reality not enjoyed until after arriving in Southern California. The same applied to the Allens. When wartime conditions forced fathers to the front and mothers to work, the congregants of Southern Missionary leaned especially hard on each other. Since women constituted a majority of church membership during these years, the onus for community building fell on them. Churchwomen not only organized drives to increase Sunday attendance but also made sure that neighborhood families were provided with child care, transportation, and, when needed, financial support. For Marie Allen, whose family's livelihood depended on her full-time work at a local defense plant, such neighborly assistance proved financially critical. More importantly, it strengthened the bonds of Christian sisterhood and her ties to the church family.[32]

It was out of a desire to formalize such bonds that southern evangelicals soon looked to acquire or construct permanent church structures. Southern Missionary found an older church building in Santa Ana to purchase, but other southern religious bodies often had to worship in members' homes, garages, and temporary shacks. Money was always a concern. Prior to the guaranteed loans denominational agencies made available in the 1950s, congregations were forced to rely on primitive fund-raising measures like the ceremonial "march around the barrel," during which congregants dropped cash in a wooden drum. The limitations of such homespun rituals meant congregants were usually forced to construct their own sanctuaries. Throughout blue-collar suburbia, bands of determined men and women, having perhaps taken time off from building their own homes, gathered their energy to raise cheap, practical meeting-houses. Sometimes this meant only one day of concentrated labor by the entire church family. Gathered on a clear fall day, the men of First Fundamental Baptist Church of Bellflower, for example, managed to erect their 20 x 40 foot rectangular building with minimal costs in a matter of hours; they only stopped for lunch "served by the ladies on a table placed in the middle of the street" of their new residential track.[33]

Building a church was rarely a one-day affair, however, especially where paperwork was involved. Southern evangelicals often grew flustered and impatient with the drawn-out process of securing land permits. Often they took matters into their own hands. In Bellflower, a "disorganized building office" informed First Fundamental Baptist that it had made an error in zoning classification and that the congregation's structure was subject to stricter restrictions. Rather than waste more time or adjust their plans, church members simply purchased land just across the city line on a lot that was surrounded by a dairy farm but slated for single-family houses. They would have liked to build a fine church on a prominent downtown corner, but they had neither the funds nor the bureaucratic fortitude to make it happen. First Fundamental Baptist's experience was not atypical. With a keen sense of future growth and a unwavering resolve to be embedded in the community, southern congregations established themselves on lots already tucked away in the middle of neighborhood streets or on open land ready for new housing development. Nestled in the domestic fold, they proceeded to organize—not simply occupy—their dwelling space.[34]

Their haste led to mixed blessings. Committed to a pay-as-you-go approach, southern congregations built quickly and cheaply, always wanting to incur minimal levels of debt. But within a year or two, poorly planned growth often necessitated new space. Unprepared for the war-time expansion of the early 1940s, members of First Assemblies of God Fellowship in Bell Gardens, for instance, had not even finished one building before they were forced to begin another. The aesthetics of the add-on became a familiar sight in blue-collar suburbia, and it did not please southern denominational leaders. The "monstrosities and glaring amateurish buildings" migrants built in fact embarrassed them. Bold enough to proclaim that "the future of California and even the nation may depend in large measure on the extent to which California is reached for Christ," critics warned that such a glorious future would not be realized unless local churches were better-looking and removed from the obscurity of the neighborhood to the "corner lot on a main street." In truth, churchgoers themselves felt some angst too. For those reared in large Protestant cathedrals in southern cities, calling a slapdash, clapboard hut a church often proved challenging. Trying to reassure his fellow urbanites that there was indeed much more to true religion than stained glass and soft pew cushions, one transplanted Southern Baptist wrote in the district paper:

> I did not come to California because of its beautiful and commodious church buildings, well-trained choirs and mellow-toned pipe organs. I came with the realization that my cathedral would likely be an old store building or a tent, or at best a modest church building. My choir would consist in many instances of persons who had met for the first time, but who had the same song in their hearts and a kindred longing in their souls to serve Christ; the only musical instrument, a simple piano. I simply came to answer the call of God.

This exhortation, part of an extended essay about the price of Christian humility, intimated a satisfaction the author shared with his cohort that the kingdom of God was being expanded by industrious common folk just like them, one nail and one splinter at a time.[35]

Of course Southern California was "not quite heaven yet" for southern evangelicals, a sentiment often repeated by those on the West Coast. Though impressed with their ability to lay claim to Southern California soil, southern migrants were mystified at the ease with which other communities—ethnic, racial, religious—did the same. "In a section of the country where cults of every kind, both foreign and domestic . . . are enjoying a phenomenal growth," one layman lamented, Southern California had become a turbulent sea of pluralism. Faced with this cultural tumult, southern evangelicals entered into a program of evangelism. In its initial stages, carried out by local people, the program was modest but it laid the groundwork for things to come.[36]

Their first evangelistic strategy focused on one-on-one relationships with neighbors. "Collective witness," as this method was called, encompassed a wide array of on-the-ground tactics. Visitation, canvassing, and social interactions of various types—poundings, potlucks, and day schools among them—all helped local congregations ensure that those in the immediate vicinity were not only made aware of but also attracted to their allotment of cradle-to-the-grave ministries. These programs' initial, stated purpose was to draw in displaced southerners who happened to reside in the area; "collective witness" was, in this sense, a quest for organic community among those who yearned for the neighborliness of the small-town South. Over time, however, as local congregations grew in size and confidence, "collective witness" came to mean no-holds-barred proselytization of the "unsaved." Like their brethren in other parts of the country, southern evangelical parishioners in California initiated intense and well-orchestrated door-to-door campaigns in hopes of drawing interested—but "spiritually lost"—neighbors into their new buildings.[37]

Their second evangelistic strategy was more ambitious: the annual revival. Its purpose was twofold. The simplest was to provide regular opportunity for spiritual renewal within the congregation. Southern evangelicals in California welcomed any opportunity to revisit favorite pastimes, and it was in this nostalgic mode that raising a revival tent each summer gained added meaning. Among the first pieces of business each year for the Allens' Southern Missionary congregation was laying the groundwork for its annual season of revival. Planning for a series of meetings that sometimes continued for five weeks straight was a labor of love for church members like Marie Allen. Sitting uncomfortably on a rough wooden bench with the sound of gospel singing reverberating off the canvas walls and the smell of the fresh sawdust floor, Allen could—for at least a few moments each year—convince herself that she was back in Texas.[38]

But the ultimate success of a church's revival was judged by how many new converts were brought into the fold. In their quest for influence, southern evangelicals made sure that their tents were the biggest and the worship led by the best preachers. For the typical congregation, the best meant the cheapest. Personal service ads placed by preachers in district newspapers helped churches locate candidates with this most important credential. "Evangelist A. F. Johnson of Oklahoma City and Detroit will be glad to contact churches here in need of the services of an Evangelist," one advertisement read, before noting that the speaker asked only for a small donation in return. "It was my pleasure to have Brother Johnson

in a revival in Oklahoma," an endorsing third party added to this commendation of cost-effective evangelistic work. "He is a real preacher of
the word, a forceful speaker [and] will be a fine helper to any pastor and
church." Just in case the bright tents and bold preaching failed to do the
job, southern evangelicals also employed special enticements to attract
their fellow citizens. Evangelism committees advertised their events in
giant-print layouts in the local paper, which for added effect often shouted
out sermon themes that resonated with the latest political developments,
as if to confirm revivalism's relevance to all of America's problems. More
daring southern churches sometimes turned their revival into something
of a carnival; hot dog and candy stands were not a strange sight next to
their canvas cathedrals.[39]

Regardless of how far they were willing to go in marketing their revival's meetings, southern evangelicals were determined to awaken every
Southern Californian to their gospel message. Nothing underscored
this more, perhaps, than the letter-writing campaigns they undertook
in anticipation of their revivals, campaigns that often targeted the city's
most esteemed residents, including the mayor of Los Angeles. A favorite
among Protestants for his commitment to moral reform, Fletcher Bowron
topped the invitation list of any church that sought legitimacy for its particular religious cause, even for events as routine as a weekly meeting of
the Women's Christian Temperance Union or Temple Baptist Men's Club.
No more common in the steady stream of invitations Bowron opened
were those from southern evangelists and churches seeking his presence
at upcoming revivals. James Alley's request for Bowron to greet delegates
at the Bell Gardens Church of Christ tent revival was typical for its rever-
ential tone. Others, like Ralph Michelson, who scribbled a letter to Bowron, skipped formalities to get to the point: "Dear Sir—You are invited to
attend services at the Irwin Church of Christ when it is convenient. Virgil
Fox minister. Come and hear the Gospel. P.S. Are you a Christian?"[40]

Neither Alley nor Michelson was privileged with a response.

WHETHER ACKNOWLEDGED OR NOT, southern evangelicals like Alley
and Michelson were resolved to bring all Californians into unison with
their spiritual designs. They took pride in fulfilling providence in the way
expected of them by their ancestors and commanded of them by scripture. Faced with an existential burden forced on them by difficult social

and economic conditions, southern evangelicals who traveled west to Southern California nevertheless shouldered it as a mark of authenticity, a concrete connection to earlier generations. The sense of mission that animated their move west only added to the righteousness of this responsibility. It helped these once independent farmers and townsfolk now working assembly lines in colossal manufacturing and defense plants to know that they were assisting a divine plan. This concept of Christian servitude was psychologically soothing, but such vivid spiritual imagination was more than a coping mechanism. It also served as a blueprint for civic engagement and a public declaration that they would not be isolated in their blue-collar suburban enclaves. Their errand, just begun, had to reach farther.

A large army of southern preachers, now on its way west to fill the pulpits of the new local churches, would help them get organized and win attention from powerful people like Fletcher Bowron. Motivated by their own grander version of the southern errand, these modern-day "saddle-bag saints" began to wrap the plain-folk ethic in a powerful narrative of southern exceptionalism and American patriotism. Prescriptive by design, it was a narrative that would urge people in the pews to look beyond their neighborhoods and invest in a much larger struggle for their region and nation. Having achieved the sense of community desired by Jefferson and Jesus, they next would strive to extend the empire of Christian democracy championed by both.

2

PREACHERS

Prophets of God have always found the way of Truth with bleeding feet in a path hedged about with thorns and bitter misunderstanding.[1]

—JONATHAN PERKINS

You recall that I told you the hope of the situation was in the revolt of the old solid South. I have held great meetings in every state in the South. . . . There is indeed a great awakening, and the swing is back to conservatism in politics, business, and most important in religion.[2]

—J. FRANK NORRIS

IN THE SUMMER OF 1937, SIXTEEN SOUTHERNERS AND C. L. GUTTERY, A small-town preacher from Arkansas, decided it was time to plant a church in Bell Gardens. Their strategy was simple. They would sweep their neighborhood with door-to-door canvassing, then begin holding morning worship in local homes, until they had built the momentum to construct a church. Complete revival would follow. Local residents and city authorities did not appreciate First Baptist Bell Gardens' enthusiasm, however, especially when gospel singing and preaching awakened them at ungodly hours, so they circulated a petition asking the southerners to learn to abide by the rules of civic propriety or leave.

Spurned but undaunted, First Baptist congregants secured a new location for their church on Florence Avenue, one of the city's major arteries. There, First Baptist's handful of men pooled their supplies and began constructing a meetinghouse. "A little building perhaps thirty feet long by twenty feet wide, perched on concrete piers and unsealed inside [with] benches made of plain boards with backs nailed precariously in place," the finished structure hardly compared to the large tabernacles in Dallas and Tulsa, but in their minds nothing evoked the sacrificial life more than an unassuming edifice and unforgiving pew. While relocation signified a fresh beginning for these parishioners it did not, to their dismay, bring an end to trouble. In their haste, they had failed to apply for a land-use permit. City officials ordered First Baptist to halt construction. At one point they threatened punitive repercussions, and even jail time. Unyielding to such threats, in fact seemingly revitalized by them, First Baptist's cocksure handymen "bowed their necks, paid no attention to the nettling, and kept on driving nails and sawing lumber." Rebuffed, city officials quietly let the matter drop, realizing that the rules of civic propriety were no match for southern evangelical fervor.[3]

FAR FROM AN ISOLATED CASE, First Baptist's determination to claim its space was repeated throughout Southern California, as was its eagerness to inspire others with its David-versus-Goliath tale. Indeed, First Baptist members not only survived their run-in with local authorities, they retold it in church annals as an edifying example of southern evangelicalism's pioneering spirit. Throughout the early 1940s other churches joined the chorus, publicizing their own versions of the same story. Wrapped in the specifics of their location, these narratives reiterated the theme of plain-folk initiative overcoming the odds for the sake of Christian truth, freedom, and the American way.

First Baptist's story points to a second dimension of the southern errand. While local people in the pews worked hard to transplant the values of Jefferson and Jesus in their neighborhoods, a cadre of southern preachers undertook their own errand to bring their Christian American-ism to Southern California. Their influence was felt on two levels. At the grass roots, maverick prophets like C. L. Guttery mobilized their congregants behind "collective witness" campaigns that could bring displaced southerners back into the fold and win other citizens to their faith. As Guttery's activities suggest, these initiatives did not always sit well with neighbors, including religious-minded ones. These brash campaigns, in fact, incited a turf war with leaders of Southern California's Protestant establishment. The controversy worried church executives watching from a distance in the South, but a second class of local southern clerics—district chairmen, church-paper editors, and high-profile celebrity pastors—celebrated these grassroots developments. They made sure that inspiring stories like Guttery's were published to remind their constituents that God's will, not man's, was their only guide. Over time, they would tap their constituents' sense of chosenness and use their influence to marshal a broader conservative assault on Southern California's Protestant order, which they saw as growing dangerously liberal. They would also articulate a new vision for transplanted southern evangelicalism that melded Bible belt religion with the militaristic priorities of Los Angeles' emerging gun-belt. In their calculations, amid mobilization for war, California's southern transplants now shouldered a providential burden for all Americans. They were the nation's new protectors, forerunners of freedom and sound belief, called by God to be pioneers, pilgrims *and* patriots.

HEROES OF THE CROSS

In the late 1930s and early 1940s, an influx of plain-folk pulpiteers suggested that Southern California Protestantism would never be the same. As residents of Bell Gardens discovered, when preachers like C. L. Guttery appeared on the scene the peace was often shattered, and as church executives in the South learned, that brought trouble.

The legacy of clerical power in the western South set the stage. In Texas, Oklahoma, and Arkansas the preacher assumed a prestige that placed him at the center of public life. Novelist and minister's son Erskine Caldwell once wrote that a clergyman in the Deep South "was frequently called upon to act as a social welfare worker, a marriage counselor, a financial advisor, an arbitrator between feuding families, a psychiatric consultant, and as a judge to decide what was and what was not moral conduct." Across the Mississippi, on the South's western fringe, the minister shouldered this same burden and acquired the same power but also assumed greater risks and reaped greater rewards. Here he was to focus less on the nurturing of community and more on readying the masses for salvation. Self-proclaimed heirs to the revivalists of the early nineteenth century, preachers who excelled in this culture did so less for their counseling skills than for their magnetism, single-mindedness, and ability to mobilize constituents for action. The best of them became famous.[4]

Each of this region's Protestant traditions had star preachers whom they advertised as models for young aspirants to follow. For Southern Baptists the list of luminaries started with George Truett, venerated pastor of First Baptist Church, Dallas, and Mordecai Ham, a "hog jowl and turnip green" parson from First Baptist Church, Oklahoma City. Like Truett, Ham was a descendant of several generations of preachers whose roots went back to the Appalachians, but he achieved more success as a traveling evangelist than as a pastor. One of Ham's proudest accomplishments came out of a revival in North Carolina where a young Billy Graham responded to his word and walked the "sawdust trail" to salvation. In the Church of Christ, meanwhile, a tradition with no clerical office and few accessories for worship (such as no musical instrumentation), preaching became an even more democratic and vital activity. With their movement's founders Barton Stone and Alexander Campbell as their benchmarks, Church of Christ lay preachers had high standards to meet. None carved out a more impressive legacy than Foy E. Wallace Jr. Born on a farm near Belcherville, Texas, northwest of Dallas, Wallace was baptized in 1909 at the age of thirteen and delivered his first sermon three years later. The young prodigy would carry the nickname "The Boy Preacher" proudly into adulthood and into a position of unquestioned authority in the 1930s and 1940s.[5]

John R. Rice and J. Frank Norris carried the mantle for Baptist fundamentalists. Whereas the former wore the look of a statesman, the latter was a scrapper. Known for his strident Texas theology, Norris cut a reputation that transcended all others. Born in east-central Alabama, he moved with his family to Hubbard, Texas, in the late 1880s when he was eleven. He lived a harsh adolescence there, informed by the poverty of sharecropping and the abuse of an alcoholic father. To those (like his own wife) who would chastise him later in life for being too harsh with others, Norris would say he could not help it because his childhood made him this way:

> I was born in the dark of the moon, in the dog-fennell season, just after a black cat had jumped upon a black coffin. My diapers were made from wheat sacks, and they rubbed the hide the wrong way. . . . Where I came from they praised mostly mules, race-horses, and coon-dogs.

By the 1910s, such exposure to tough living had hardened Norris into a fierce fighter. At six foot one and one hundred ninety pounds, he commanded respect, with a voice like William Jennings Bryan's that could "run the gamut of human emotions" "night after night in the open air with no ill effects." Famous for his pulpit attacks on liberals, and infamous for being tried for murder (his claim of self-defense led to acquittal), Norris was eventually expelled from the Southern Baptist Convention in 1923. Thereafter the "Texas Tornado" remade himself as southern fundamentalism's most accomplished subversive by forming a separate association of independent Baptist churches, establishing his own Bible college, and simultaneously pastoring two of the largest churches in America: First Baptist Church, in Fort Worth (his home base), and Temple Baptist Church, in Detroit.[6]

For every celebrity preacher, however, there were countless more contenders who never ascended to the top tier. They faced stiff odds from the very beginning. Surrounded by a cult of toughness that encouraged outward displays of masculine bravado, an inexperienced preacher boy had to bring high energy and supreme confidence to the ministry. In small-town Oklahoma and Texas this was often enough to get a young man behind the pulpit of a local church. Parishioners expected nothing more or less than comprehensible, extemporaneous preaching that coupled simple, inductive logic and basic biblicism with raw, unrehearsed emotion. Meant to console the heart without troubling the mind, cast light rather than stir doubt, express rather than expound, plain-folk evangelicalism provided plenty of room for the entry-level cleric. But in order to rise through the ranks, the novice needed instruction in scripture and opportunity to sharpen his skills. Those determined to make the next cut had to go to a denominational Bible school. The most ambitious and talented of this crew attempted yet a third step: training at a seminary. Prior to the 1930s, most graduating collegians and seminarians could expect to be recruited by an established city church.[7]

During the Depression and war years, however, the system stalled. With churches in the hinterland closing because of out-migration and poor finances, entry-level clerics no longer found guaranteed work. And the few who managed to locate and fill a pulpit, with dreams of climbing to higher rungs of respectability, now faced a steeper ascent to ultimate success: command of a large congregation and reputation. By the late 1930s the market in the western South for metropolitan ministers was saturated, meaning that many proven pastors who wanted to become the next Norris, Truett, or Wallace packed their Bibles after Bible school or seminary and, like some of their own grandfathers had done, looked for untilled spiritual soil on the frontier. These eager graduates were joined on their journey by a mass of other hopefuls, those who had not had the privilege of schooling, or because of past failures simply wanted a fresh start. All of these peripatetic saints believed in the promise of California and drew assurance from the knowledge that thousands of displaced southern church folk looked forward to their arrival.

Many of them were also buoyed by rare testimonies of West Coast success like Bob Shuler's. A proudly unrefined product of Virginia's Blue Ridge Mountains, Shuler proved southern preachers could reach stardom in California. Born in 1880, Shuler spent his childhood in a small cottage, raised by a couple of "illiterate mountain whites" who, as he liked to tell others, said "'this here' and 'that there' and 'climming trees' and 'toting water' and 'kivering ingerns' and other quaint things." When Bob was eight, his father, J. W. Schuler, felt a calling to preach and decided to become a Methodist circuit rider. With five children and a wife in tow, he harnessed his horses ("old Bet" and "old Bird," Bob Shuler recalled fondly) to the covered wagon and crossed over Iron Mountain to begin training at Emory & Henry College. J. W. Shuler finished his schooling in just two years and began service on the Bluff City Circuit in East Tennessee. An exceptional orator, and blessed with a financially savvy wife, he quickly rose through the ranks from rural circuits to urban ones. In 1913, after his wife had passed away and he had secured his legacy as one of southwest Virginia's most popular Methodists, J. W. relocated to Texas, where he ministered for fifty more years (he lived to 102).[8]

Bob Shuler followed his father into the ministry and out to the West. By his early twenties the young man was a successful merchant of revival, known in Methodist circles for his sharp wit and silvery tongue. This combination of traits secured him a position at the largest Methodist congregation in Paris, Texas, where he served briefly as minister before moving to Trinity Methodist Church of Los Angeles, a struggling congregation located in the heart of the city. In 1920 Trinity hired the thirty-year-old upstart as its senior pastor in hopes of resuscitating this once-proud flagship of the Methodist Episcopal Church, South. During his first two decades there, "Fighting Bob," as he became known, launched attacks against profligate priests, Hollywood celebrities, and city officials. Facilitated in part by the acquisition of a radio station in 1929, his political activities increased, as did his reputation for controversy. In 1930 he used his radio program to prevent judiciary candidates he thought corrupt from getting elected to the State Supreme Court. Flustered with the cleric, the Los Angeles Bar Association, which promoted these candidates, requested that Shuler be held in contempt. Fighting Bob served twenty days in prison for his actions but emerged even more eager to wage war for his moral objectives. During the 1930s he helped recall Los Angeles' mayor and ran for United States senator on the Prohibition ticket (resulting in a narrow defeat). During this period, his life was threatened, his church bombed, and his radio station silenced by the federal government. Each setback only solidified his reputation as champion of the common man and further endeared him to a congregation that by the late 1930s had grown swiftly to five thousand believers.[9]

For their part, denominational leaders encouraged the type of ambition Shuler embodied by issuing their call for west-going preachers in epic terms. Anxious to meet the religious needs of displaced church members, denominational executives in Nashville, Fort Worth, and Springfield constantly urged pastors throughout the South to consider helping "the cause" by committing their labor to church growth, either as "John the Baptist types" willing to clear the way for new congregations or as "Barnabas types" able to help nascent church bodies mature. As if to dare young preachers to be like the cowboy saints of yesteryear, widely circulated petitions called for only the most "virile and self-sacrificing of men" to serve on the West Coast. "Would-be leaders who maintain that 'born-tired' feeling and who desire to keep soft white hands seem not to thrive in this section of the Master's vineyard," one publication declared to its readers. "Those who love publicity and cheap praise ought never to come here," added another. By challenging the manliness of their constituency, denominational leaders hoped to spark the interest of seminarians who seemed intent on practicing their craft in cozier settings. They got more than they bargained for.[10]

While some seminarians did indeed answer the call, a steadier supply of underqualified and overzealous "John the Baptist types" dominated the flood of clerics. Assemblies of God executives were the first to confront this situation. During the late 1930s Arthur (A. G.) Osterberg, the superintendent of the Southern California District Council of the Assemblies of God, pestered national leaders in Springfield, Missouri, to help corral the brethren who come . . . with their broken down automobiles, their wives and large families together with their washboards and washtubs, billy goats and bedding, their chicken coops and their lice with the information that God in Heaven sent them to take up a pastorate here.

Reporting to his superiors at war's end, Osterberg's successor, F. C. Woodworth, decried the overabundance of would-be clerics on the West Coast and the strain this placed on administration. Convinced that the problems he faced were unprecedented, Woodworth wrote: "We have about 175 churches and about 650 preachers on our roll; consequently, you can see somewhat of the task we have here." Although sympathetic to Woodworth's predicament, Assemblies of God general secretary J. Roswell Flower's response could not hide his frustration: "With 650 preachers and 175 churches, all the churches of southern California ought to have the best preachers and Heaven help the rest of them. If they weren't so determined to live in the paradise of southern California, some of them might be able to find a ministry in other sections of the country."[11]

TENT MAKERS AND PROPHETS

Quality and not quantity of leadership thus became the central concern for denominational officials. Indeed, as the Depression gave way to World War II, the real concern was not that they had too few recruits but that this infantry refused to fall in line. They had only themselves to blame. Playing on the dreams of men hungry for glory, they marketed the west as a place for true "heroes of the cross." There were a great number of genuine, serious, and talented preachers who made the transition to California, but just as often the collection of men—young and old—who moved west came out of sincere purpose but with limited means, or with questionable intentions and unquenchable drive. Much to the consternation of church elders, it was the industrious part-time clerics and ambitious self-proclaimed prophets who seemed to adapt quickest to the volatile conditions of California and began to flourish.

Logistics dictated this trend. Barely capable of paying rent, let alone the salary of a full-time pastor, small congregations like First Baptist Bell Gardens usually tried to find self-supporting candidates. These part-time clerics—or "tent makers," as the Apostle Paul was known in the New Testament—could readily be found among the bloated ranks of bivocational pastors on the West Coast: those working shifts in defense plants, driving trucks, loading ships, or working as door-to-door salesmen. A Southern Baptist church in Riverside, for instance, lured veteran George H. Woodward to its pulpit in 1941. Prior to accepting the pastorate in Riverside, congregants boasted, he had been a miner and railroad man in Kentucky, a church planter in Missouri, a farmer in Arkansas, and most recently a retailer for Sears in Arizona. At the time this congregation preferred (and could only afford) a seasoned salesman to a seminarian.[12]

As logical as candidates like Woodward seemed for the people in Southern California's pews, the bivocational pastor raised immediate concerns for denominational officials, the lack of training being one. Those who filled tent-making pastorates typically operated outside the expectations for education. As late as 1950, when the Assemblies of God's Southern California district officials instituted a reading test as part of licensing requirements, the average level of schooling attained by those transferring into the district remained the eighth grade. Proper instruction in basic church doctrine was another shortcoming. Denominations had trouble forcing tent-maker preachers to subscribe to a formal system of belief, because many of these clerics had neither the background nor occasion to follow doctrinal codes; some were in the West because they refused to toe the theological line back home. Not that advanced education or doctrinal training would have solved every problem. Even better-trained tent-making pastors had to sacrifice scriptural study when splitting time between their church and job. No matter how one broached the concern, moonlighting pastors were, in other words, far from an ideal.[13]

A second class of clerics worried officials even more. While the tent maker often failed to meet expectations, he usually did so out of misunderstanding. The prophet, on the other hand, did so because of ulterior motives. Fervid in their belief, these preachers cherished independence over all else. In one sense they represented the potential for excess that always existed in plain-folk evangelicalism. In California, where congregations were distanced from their superiors, prophets used personal charisma and the freedom of self-expression to construct and control their flock. Church officials in the South tried to disassociate and excommunicate the perpetrators, but at every point they had to tread lightly. Even the subtlest attempts to assert central control were met with skepticism from believers in California who almost always trusted their own preacher over any denominational executive that delivered orders from a faraway place.

Not all prophets operated with the same proclivities, and so Pentecostal and Baptist officials faced distinct challenges. Within Pentecostal circles, where a man could claim divine inspiration and easily obtain a ministerial license, officials faced an assortment of enigmatic types. Prone to conspiratorial thinking and bouts of exaggeration in the name of self-promotion, these prophets usually suffered most from a spiritual ardor that manifested itself in chronic anti-institutional behavior. Their circular logic read as follows: To be a true prophet one had to stand against society's grain no matter the cost; the greater the cost (and controversy), the truer the prophet.[14]

In the eyes of Assemblies of God executives, Jonathan Perkins was the worst of the lot. Born in 1889 to an Ohio family with roots in Maryland and Methodism, Perkins spent his early years living in a log cabin on a quarter section (160 acres) of land tilled by his father but owned by his grandfather. By the time he turned fourteen his father had lost all the family's savings, forcing Perkins into "the world by rude circumstances to earn my living." Perkins's hardship contributed to a lifelong quest for quick-fix schemes, but it was the sudden death of his father when he was eighteen that had a more profound spiritual impact, shocking him, as he described it, out of the "dark paths of trouble" into a dour state of introspection. Together, these two experiences—one of economic dislocation, the other of intense spiritual crisis—predisposed Perkins to a blend of reactionary politics and warped Pentecostalism that grew more intemperate with time. There were signs of this future early on. As a youth, Perkins wanted to be like his grandfather, a Methodist circuit rider who was known to discipline "rowdies" in his audience by "taking them by the nap of the neck and the seat of the pants [wrapping] them unceremoniously about a tree." Determined to match his grandfather's toughness but surpass him in intellect, Perkins set off to school, first Southwestern College in Kansas, and then for a short stint at Moody Bible Institute in Chicago.[15]

After deciding he could not accept Moody's "Calvinist doctrine," Perkins returned to his roots in the holiness branch of evangelicalism and rose quickly within Pentecostalism. By the late 1920s he had reached the highest echelon in the Assemblies of God, thanks principally to his pen. A talented writer, whose commonsense eloquence made for highly readable prose, Perkins earned his stripes as associate editor of the *Pentecostal Evangel*, the Assemblies of God's denominational paper, and as a published author. His book *The Brooding Presence and Pentecost* became a best-seller in Pentecostal circles and reached a fourth edition with an estimated fifty thousand copies printed. Perkins built on this renown by becoming pastor of one of the oldest churches in the denomination, Tulsa's Central Assembly of God. It was here that his eccentricities nudged him toward antinomianism, the belief that certain sanctified saints operated above human-made canons of faith. "Rejecting the idea of Apostles" was one of the great failures of "modern Church life," Perkins once said. He had no doubt that he was an apostle, and though this designation meant a life of hardship, he welcomed the tribulation. It was in Tulsa, also, that Perkins slid into a racist doctrine of the kind advocated by his cousin, fundamentalist radio personality Gerald Winrod, who spread a message of white supremacy and anti-Semitism. Perkins aspired to the same level of influence, and almost reached it. Under his leadership Central added members at an unprecedented rate and constructed a new building at the then unimaginable cost of fifty thousand dollars. At the same time, he allowed his church to become the headquarters for the local Ku Klux Klan.[16]

Following his stay in Tulsa, which grew increasingly problematic for the Assemblies of God, Perkins packed his wife, children, and belongings into an automobile, and traveled west to Los Angeles. Once settled there in the early 1930s he assumed the pastorate of a church and a routine of agitation that saw him take on virtually all of Los Angeles' most prominent religious leaders. Usually these clashes transpired on theological grounds, with Perkins accusing the defendants of doctrinal laxity, but politics also entered the mix. In 1935, Perkins wrote a slanderous article about Sister Aimee Semple McPherson and her assistant, Rheba Crawford, in which he accused Crawford of misconduct while working as the state's social welfare director. Crawford and McPherson responded with a lawsuit, which led to a judicial—and very public—showdown. The trial was dramatic and filled a courtroom with local tabloid reporters, who gave the case and its victorious (Crawford and McPherson) and vanquished (Perkins) combatants front-page attention. Perkins's relationship with his denominational hierarchy grew more tenuous with each disquieting episode. By the end of the decade the once-promising orator was banned from the denomination, was reduced to irregular shifts at General Motors, and was preaching in a small storefront church in a run-down neighborhood of Los Angeles. Yet Perkins remained relevant. Nicknamed "Ichabod Crane" for his wiry frame and pointy features, the apostle still had his readers and continued to earn their trust with his lucid and witty prose. While his wife slept in the bedroom of their apartment in Griffith Park, he wrote religious and political tracts late into the night that spoke to his followers' most pressing anxieties. At World War II's end, Perkins' writings would help resurrect his career.[17]

Whereas Assemblies of God officials struggled to defrock preachers with loose doctrine, officials in the SBC contended with clerics whose doctrine seemed too unyielding. Their creed was Landmarkism. Like their allies, who exercised significant authority in Arkansas, Texas, and Oklahoma, California Landmarkists believed that Baptists needed to maintain fixed standards of community based on strict codes of baptism, communion, church membership, worship style, and clean living. No Southern Baptist took theology lightly, yet in the South, where the SBC enjoyed a comfortable, majority status, there at least remained space in the pews for the repentant backslider and wayward soul. In California, where Southern Baptists felt alienated from the mainstream and defensive of their faith, breeches of doctrine were viewed as grounds for immediate expulsion. A powerful band of Landmarkist prophets took control of the expulsions. These preachers had little patience for denominational authority and they believed that only heavy-handed, local pastoral control could correct the slippage in doctrine that had occurred in California under the watch of other Baptists, particularly those affiliated with the Northern Baptist Convention (NBC), the state's largest and most powerful Baptist body.[18]

Were it simply a matter of fine-tuning internal mechanisms of governance, Baptist and Pentecostal authorities might easily have solved their problems with prophets. But their constituency's fierce independence threatened to upset a tentative balance in California Protestantism. The issue manifested itself differently for Pentecostals than it did for Southern Baptists. In the case of the former, the most pressing issue was the negative impressions intemperate pastors gave off. Assemblies of God officials desperately wanted acceptance, by other evangelicals and mainstream culture generally, and would spend the 1940s ridding their ranks of renegades. SBC officials faced a more immediate crisis. Their preachers' self-directed attempts to set things right on the West Coast promised to ignite a turf war between newcomers and native Californians—between southern Landmarkists who considered themselves orthodox and Northern Baptists whom they looked upon as heretical. Were this to happen, SBC executives worried, North and South would surely fight again.

STORMING THE WEST, SAVING THE SOUTH

True to form, Landmarkists triggered this territorial battle by championing the ideals of popular democracy. In 1936 a family of cotton farmers from Oklahoma founded the Orthodox Missionary Baptist Church of Shafter in the Central Valley, and soon thereafter commissioned a pastor from Paragould, Arkansas to be their leader. Upon his arrival in California, Sam Wilcoxon organized a handful of southern-based independent Baptist churches in Central California into the San Joaquin Valley Missionary Baptist Association. Meanwhile, other congregations in the Los Angeles area began petitioning SBC headquarters in Nashville for the right to adopt Sunday School material and officially call themselves Southern Baptist. Under long-standing territorial agreements, drafted in the nineteenth century, the SBC promised to refrain from organizing churches in California, leaving the NBC in charge. Out of respect for their counterparts in the NBC, and a history of peaceful cooperation, SBC officials thus ignored Southern Californians' request for affiliation. In 1940, an Oklahoma evangelist named Robert Lackey decided to force the issue by preaching a ten-day revival at First Baptist in Bell Gardens, after which the church unilaterally declared its alignment with the SBC. Lackey returned to the Central Valley to continue his agitation. In fall of 1940, Lackey and Wilcoxon helped organize the Southern Baptist General Convention of California (SBGCC), a mutinous affront to the national organization. Of this momentous occasion Lackey later recalled, "Some cried, some shouted for joy, all were happy. The long looked for day had come. Southern Baptists now face the future with a zeal and determination, the like of which we had never seen before."[19]

Assisted by fellow Landmarkists in the SBC's hierarchy, and after a year of intense wrangling, Lackey and the SBGCC eventually earned official recognition by the national body. As SBGCC executive secretary, Lackey announced that this decision was not a "question of territory" as much as it was an acknowledgement that SBC members no longer felt comfortable in NBC churches. In his mind, the NBC was compromised because it endorsed open communion, alien immersion, and "other grosser forms of modernism." No longer willing to enforce the most important boundaries of pure Christianity, Northern Baptists had also failed in the Christians' calling to spread the good news of salvation. Faced with the prospect of having to join a denomination run by "radical liberals" and fraternizing ecumenicists, therefore, southern folk had only two options: "either sell out and move out of California all together, or else organize churches of real Baptist faith." That they followed the latter course was, in Lackey's opinion, a credit to their courage.[20]

Their orthodoxy under attack, California's NBC leaders coordinated their own offensive. Articles in the NBC's leading national journals lambasted SBC agitators for the offenses committed against well-meaning brethren. In the estimation of one irate author, Southern Baptists had not only stolen property from the NBC by "forcing" well-established congregations to align with the southern branch but, more distressingly, had damaged the cause of Christian witness on the West Coast. Other churchmen's barbs were sharper. One individual compared Southern Baptist justifications for moving into California to Hitler's policy of conquering countries because Germans lived there. As to the charges leveled against his denomination, NBC spokesman W. Earle Smith replied, "Anybody who knows anything about the [Northern] Baptist position in California knows full well that Baptist churches are universally evangelistic, aggressively missionary and thoroughly conservative in theology." The problem with Southern Baptist accusations, however, was not that they were initiated out of ignorance—though there seemed to be plenty of that to go around, Smith suggested—but that they were manufactured by a band of delinquent pastors who had escaped to California from questionable pasts, and who saw moonlighting in "feeble," storefront churches as a chance to supplement their wages from factory work.[21]

Not surprisingly, Smith's words did little to bridge barriers, yet this was perfectly fine with Lackey, who loved the controversy. Amid this tension Lackey was now easily able to spur California's Southern Baptists on to a grander quest, one that spun internecine quarrels with the NBC into a contest between the liberal North and conservative South for control of the nation's soul. Lackey wasted no time articulating this vision. Having already become California's Southern Baptist power broker as executive secretary, he also gained sway within his new church community as editor of its only mouthpiece, the *California Southern Baptist*. Through his regular editorials and vetting of news, Lackey rallied his readers behind the notion that their Christian work in Southern California would have serious consequences. In the process of saving the West, this prophet cried out, Southern Baptists would also awaken the South to the perils of liberal Protestantism and the desperate need for a strong conservative response. "God's noblest ministers, poor in purse but rich in an experience of Grace . . . and [cast] in the highest type of Christian manhood," Lackey announced, were ready to lead the charge.[22]

No one who knew Lackey would have called his words hyperbole. Short and stocky, Lackey not only possessed the proven Baptist credentials but also exuded all of the manly qualities he celebrated and expected from his charges. Those who questioned them were corrected, usually with a biting tongue but at times also with a rock-solid fist. This toughness served him well in his role as SBGCC executive secretary. Often sleeping in his car on cross-state business trips, Lackey acted decisively and sometimes offensively in the protection of Baptist belief. He predicted Baptist conquest, vigorously and routinely, and, throughout the war years, delivered this message through razor-sharp analyses of current events, lengthy treatises about Baptist polity and politics, and on-the-ground coverage of local church growth. This last approach was perhaps the most powerful, for it took local stories—like that of First Baptist Bell Gardens' run-in with authorities—and turned them into parables for uplift and motivation. As editor of the *California Southern Baptist*, Lackey sought to fulfill a prophetic role. He believed his chief task was to convince transplanted Southern Baptists that their response to social and cultural circumstances in the West had direct bearing on the future of the South. He urged them to be active agents, enabled and determined to shape two regions' destinies.[23]

But what did this mean? For Lackey it meant standing up to cultural and political liberalism. One particularly sinister force, in Lackey's mind, was the Federal Council of Churches (FCC). Since its founding by liberal Protestants in 1908 as an organization to hasten Christian unity and coordinate social reform, conservatives had viewed the FCC with deep suspicion as a cover for socialistic thinking. Prior to the 1930s, southern evangelicals saw little reason to worry about its impact on their daily lives; a northern creation, the FCC was also a northern problem. This changed during the Depression as the FCC began asserting itself in the South through support of religious programs meant to offset economic crisis. Like other parallel New Deal programs coming from the federal government, FCC initiatives were tolerated in the South as short-term responses to overwhelming economic stress. Yet by the early 1940s southerners began to see the FCC as a permanent feature in the South and a constant threat to the region's religious values. The FCC encouraged pulpit sharing between men of different religious traditions and asked local church bodies to meet regularly in federated church councils. Southern evangelicals thought that this undermined the very foundations of Christian democracy. Lackey and many others argued that individual religious expression and conscience quickly fell away when such thinking penetrated local congregations. A northern imperialist force with insidious religious and political motivations, the FCC was, in short, out to "unionize" southern churches and ensure that they were no longer the "Problem Child of Protestantism." For the good of southern society, Lackey said, the FCC could no longer be left to its own devices.[24]

As Lackey relayed it, then, the mission for his West Coast brethren was clear: to emancipate the South from northern aggression by providing an inspiring model of strong religion. But there was more to the plan. By taking the fight out of the South and into the West, they would have the chance to offset the moves being made by their religious competitors. Tired of being colonized, in other words, white southern religious folk would now be the colonizers. Lackey urged individuals to organize themselves in vibrant congregations that might testify to the vitality of Baptist principles and the feebleness of liberal ecumenism. They were to carry out collective witness in their communities with such verve and efficiency that they would jar Christians in the South out of their spiritual stagnation.[25]

Lackey's editorial agenda also included commentary on liberal notions of statehood. Already anticipating the domestic fight that would ensue in the postwar period, the *California Southern Baptist* predicted that Americans would long wrestle with the implications of a managerial state created by the New Deal. In response, Lackey and his associates implored individuals to be "very jealous" of their Baptist values of individualism and localism. At the same time, they implored their constituents to commit wholeheartedly to the military effort. Through their involvement in the armed forces, Southern Baptists would open up new channels for Christian democracy, especially into the countries ruled by Fascists and Communists. Meanwhile, by proving themselves in the trenches overseas and on the assembly lines of California's factories, southern migrants would show that their resolve for Christ translated easily into a passion for American liberty. Viewed by liberal Protestants as an obstacle to the nation's progress, California's Southern Baptists wanted to prove the opposite. Writing in 1944, a pastor in Fresno, expressed clearly what he, Lackey, and district leaders were thinking:

> The future for Southern Baptists of California is as bright as the noon-day sun. . . . All eyes are focused upon Southern Baptists in California: not just the Southland of Baptists, but every denomination in California is watching us. We have already influenced many churches of other faiths to attempt greater things for God.

Meant to encourage migrants in times of adjustment, such words, of course, displayed a heightened sense of self that did not entirely mesh with reality. But this was not empty rhetoric. From Lackey down to the pew, Southern Baptists were certain that their actions in the West would have a direct bearing on cultural developments in the South. Like the Puritans, to whom they looked for inspiration, they believed that their errand in the wilderness was, first and foremost, for the ultimate good of those they left behind.[26]

STIRRING THE NATION, SAVING THE WORLD

Had it been particular to Southern Baptists, the notion that southern transplants in California could help save the South might have seemed far-fetched, the product of an isolated people seeking solace in their condition. But the energy and activism this vision encouraged was infectious. Cheering California's Southern Baptists on in their fight against the NBC, other southern preachers from other denominations attached themselves to Lackey's ambitious agenda. Together, they proclaimed, southern evangelicals would shape California into an arsenal of Christian democracy, a marshaling zone for the spread of true religion throughout the country and across the globe.

Not surprisingly, Bob Shuler led the pack. Though a dyed-in-the-wool Methodist, he expressed heartfelt admiration for his Baptist brethren. He followed the SBC-NBC fight closely, and offered congratulations to California's Southern Baptists after their triumph. In a brief editorial with broad commentary on the state of the SBC titled "Thank God for the Baptists," Shuler wrote: "The Southern Baptists are spreading themselves like a green bay tree and their number is increasing miraculously. There is a reason. They stand for something." Naturally, his own struggles within

California Methodism roused his praise for the competition. Since his arrival in Los Angeles, Shuler had fought liberal trends in his own church family and constantly butted up against its most progressive and powerful clergy, notably G. Bromley Oxnam. Born and raised in California, Oxnam was an earnest liberal in every sense of the word. After studying at the University of Southern California (USC), one of Methodism's proudest academies, he became a minister and was assigned to a run-down parish in Los Angeles, which he transformed into a multicultural center of worship called Church of All Nations. Inspired by Walter Rauschenbusch's social gospel of reform, Oxnam focused his energy on eradicating poverty. "Someday," he announced, "I'm going to help lead the church against the slums, their causes . . . and smash them forever." His commitments made him a natural leader in ecumenical Protestantism, and in 1936, at the age of forty-four, he was elected bishop in the Methodist Church. Eight years later he began a two-year term as president of the FCC.[27]

Oxnam's antithesis in every way, Shuler chafed at submitting to rules this progressive activist helped draw up for California Methodism and the nation's liberal Protestant establishment. After his radio station was shut down in the early 1930s, due to what the Federal Communications Commission deemed inappropriate political activity by a preacher, he started the *Methodist Challenge* as a way to keep California's conservative Methodists in touch with other evangelicals and their brethren in the South. Convinced that the Baptist schism signaled a power shift toward evangelical orthodoxy in California Protestantism, he covered the story extensively in hopes it would inspire local Methodists to support this trend. Meanwhile, he heralded the actions of breakaway groups outside the state. At mid-decade a few southern discontents formed the Evangelical Methodist Church. Led by Reverend J. H. Hamblen, from Abilene, Texas, the Evangelical Methodist movement captured Shuler's imagination. His glowing review of Hamblen's church outlined his disgust with his own church environment:

They believe in the New Birth and that a man must be born again. They oppose the substituting of social, educational or any other variety of cultural salvation. . . . The Evangelical Methodists permit the local congregations to own their own property and select their own pastors. They have the advantage of thus warding off that despotism and autocratic power that have practically made of the great Methodist

Church an ecclesiastical machine, second only to the Roman Catholic church. . . . Another advantage lies in the fact that the Evangelical Methodists are unanimously loyal to the American way of life. There is no taint of socialism or communism in that bunch. They are sound in doctrine and sound in patriotism. They are democratic and free. They are spiritual and soundly pious. They are strictly fundamental in faith and practice.

In Shuler's mind, Evangelical Methodists were true Methodists and the only hope for the church's future.[28]

As supportive as he was of these dissenting voices, Shuler was also a pragmatist and recognized that leadership within his father's revivalist tradition had passed to other southern faiths. Besides Southern and fundamentalist Baptist, Shuler also praised the Pentecostals. In an article published shortly after the war, he bashed the "high-brow Methodist preachers with . . . university degrees and [a] new social gospel," and asserted that plain-folk preachers now carried the mantle of orthodoxy:

The great Methodist Church, once the burning evangel of two centuries, is now barren and without spiritual fruit. Her altars are empty. Many of them have been destroyed. . . . The same thing has happened to the Northern Baptists, the Presbyterians and other great ecclesiastical bodies. They are engaged in large enterprises looking to world movements. The fires have gone out on their altars. They are cold, lifeless, formal, dead.

In comparison, Shuler pointed out, the "Pentecostals and others like them" were "building little churches everywhere," growing, and stirring revival throughout the land. And rather than dismiss them as unlearned and uncouth, Shuler reprimanded his Methodist colleagues, Pentecostals deserved respect, for they were the "poor and lowly" led by "fiery prophets" who leaned heavily on God and expected miracles in return. They were the people that had America on the verge of a spiritual redemption.[29]

Shuler, more than anyone else, anointed southern plain-folk preachers as the vanguard of a national turn toward orthodox faith, but it was J. Frank Norris who helped orient southern evangelicals' wider global perspective. What Lackey, Shuler, and officials in the SBC and NBC learned through denominational infighting Norris saw through outside observation: The westerly advancement of southern evangelicalism was radically altering the nation's religious map. Urged on by his followers, he began scheduling regular West Coast swings. One of his first visits occurred on December 9, 1941, two days after the attack on Pearl Harbor. By late fall that year, Norris had visited with J. Edgar Hoover in Washington, preached in the Texas and Georgia legislatures, and marched through the Deep South on an evangelistic crusade. Norris's visit to Los Angeles garnered less media attention because of the sudden outbreak of war, but in many ways it marked the Texan's greatest triumph. Sponsored by the Christian Broadcasters' Fellowship and coordinated by a growing coterie of southern clergymen trained in his Fort Worth Bible college, Norris's two-day stay was highlighted by a standing-room-only rally in the seven-thousand-seat Shrine Auditorium. Behind the scenes, meanwhile, he met with old colleagues and young ministerial apprentices and took a personal tour of a Baptist seminary in South Gate. Certainly the most rewarding session during this brief two-day visit, however, was the gathering of pastors to discuss his World Fundamental Baptist Fellowship. For Norris, the meeting was "a joy, it was refreshing . . . it was a little bit of heaven on earth to look in the face of this fine body of strong, vigorous, consecrated pastors." For his apprentices—representing churches spread along Route 66 between Los Angeles and Amarillo, and clustered in Southern California's blue-collar suburbs—the meeting provided a sense of unity. Norris left Los Angeles convinced his fellowship was "growing in every direction."[30]

Norris returned often to Los Angeles during World War II and on these occasions continued to speak of Southern California's increasing importance to the South. Helping his home region escape from the expanding reach of northern liberalism was real motivation for the Texas fundamentalist, and it was his exposure to the militarization of Southern California that, in part, allowed him to see an opportunity for the South in wartime mobilization. And, like Shuler, he was determined to use all of his media capabilities to force a "great revolt" that would swing the South and the nation to conservatism in politics, business, and religion. Norris went a step further than most of his contemporaries, however, by also recognizing Southern California's potential in the spread of southern religion across the Pacific. Like others within their religious orb, independent Baptists were proud of their enlisted men, but especially pleased with the role their chaplains were performing on the European and Asian fronts.

Through the bravery of his clerics, Norris hoped, Baptist fundamentalism would be true to the codes of southern honor and masculinity. More
importantly, he believed that through such displays of valor, southern
evangelicals would demonstrate to the rest of the nation that they were
no longer the poor cousins that liberals claimed them to be but rather
the standard-bearers of a new, confident Americanism. Norris thus recognized in World War II the chance for southern fundamentalism, the
South, and American defense to be fused in one common mission.[31]

No one blended the interests of southern fundamentalism and American nationalism more than Norris's ultimate hero of the cross, John Birch.
This southern preacher boy hit every chord Norris wished to strike with
his constituents, especially on the West Coast, where the young man's
journey out of the South seemed so familiar. Born to missionary parents
stationed in India, Birch returned to the United States to spend the better
part of his adolescence in his father's native Georgia. At the age of seventeen, he entered Mercer University, in nearby Macon, where he majored
in religion and gained practical training serving as pastor of a small Baptist church. In January 1939, this young zealot went to hear Norris speak
during one of the preacher's forays into the Deep South. Convicted by
Norris's message on conditions in the Far East, Birch left the rally with
China "on his heart."[32]

Imbued with the same fiery dogmatism of his new mentor, Birch finished his last semester at Mercer University, graduated magna cum laude,
and immediately began seminary training at Norris's Fundamental Baptist Bible Institute in Texas. After spending the summer of 1939 preaching in Baptist churches across the country, including Norris's in Detroit,
Birch arrived in Fort Worth already a much-ballyhooed warrior for fundamental Christianity. During his year of study at the institute, and under
Norris's careful nurturing, Birch channeled his militancy into a passion
for missions. One of the institute's first graduates, he completed studies in
the spring of 1940, then boarded a freighter from California for mainland
China. Upon arrival there, Birch immediately found himself in one of
the world's most heated geopolitical zones, with invading Japanese forces
controlling the coastal cities, Chinese nationalists and communists occupying the interior, and U.S. interests pinned in between. Commanded by
the U.S. State Department to evacuate China, Birch nevertheless continued on, accelerating his study of the language and becoming bolder in
his evangelism of Chinese villagers scattered behind Japanese lines. On

one of these ventures, Birch was led to Lt. Col. James H. Doolittle and his crew of "Doolittle's Raiders," who had been forced down by enemy fire during an attack on Japan. Birch guided them through enemy lines to safety, then proceeded to rescue another forty fliers. For his heroism, Doolittle introduced Birch to Gen. Claire Chennault, commander of the China Air Task Force (formerly the American Volunteer Group known as the "Flying Tigers"), who offered Birch the position of intelligence officer and second lieutenant. Later, in 1944, at Chennault's urging, the young hero received the Legion of Merit award, one of the nation's highest awards for military service. Of Birch's qualifications for the award, Chennault wrote that the young missionary did more "than any other man to win the war against Japan in China."[33]

Secretive though these operations might have been, Birch's stories of espionage (minus classified details) found their way into Norris's newspaper and into the homes of fundamentalists throughout Southern California and the South. From the moment he departed for Asia, Birch remained in close contact with his mentor, writing Norris as frequently as his own family. Norris, in turn, published these letters, hoping that their contents would inspire other preacher boys to follow Birch's example. As they were presented to the public, Birch's letters read as the struggle of a young man to conquer Asia for the sake of Christ and country. Writing in April 1944, Birch mused that the Far East would "play a rising part in the affairs of the post-war world—a world that should be more ripe for the Gospel than ever before." In this same letter, in language that surely resonated deeply with California's southern migrants, he revealed his vision for the Christianization of Asia:

> As for my own future activities, as soon as this war ends in victory and I can make a trip home, and if God leads, I should like to push westward, possibly in an effort to storm the mountainous Buddhist citadel of Tibet, or else to move through Lanchow to little-reached Chinese Turkistan and some day to load with the Word of God and itinerant native preachers the camel caravans and eventual airships of Continental Asia!

While war continued, however, Birch remained on the Japanese–Chinese border. He worked hard to establish an outpost for future evangelism, even attempting to broker a deal so Norris could purchase local property owned by the Bible Institute of Los Angeles (BIOLA).[34]

Birch's legacy, however, would be as a martyr. Fluent in the language and knowledgeable about the terrain, Birch quickly proved a valuable intelligence officer who could probe the backcountry for critical military information. Absent from his home base for weeks at a time, Birch would take the opportunity of his secret reconnaissance to preach sermons to Chinese churches and, when possible, evangelize Chinese soldiers through one-on-one contact and the distribution of Christian literature (including his mentor's own newspaper, the *Fundamentalist*). It is in this context that Birch reconciled his sacred and secular vocations. Convinced that Christianity itself was at stake in the war over China, Birch saw it as his duty to fight the army's battles for the sake of greater eternal reward—for the lost souls of China especially but also for his own edification. In August 1945, while on a mission to retrieve American prisoners of war behind Japanese lines, Birch and his commandos were detained by a unit of Chinese Communist soldiers. Birch questioned the actions of the Chinese officer in command. Insulted in front of his men, the officer had him bound and shot. Though its details would be shrouded in mystery for the next five years, news of Birch's death made its way to Norris and his other admirers. Within months of his death, public and military officials were pushing for Birch to receive a hero's commendation. At a formal gathering at Norris's college in Fort Worth to rename a new campus building "John Birch Hall," one general recounted:

> He preached at every occasion to the American forces in China when time permitted receiving far greater numbers of acceptances to The Kingdom than the regular chaplains. He was a constant example to all and the biggest single inspiration to my life.[35]

Long before they saw a legend to be embraced, however, Norris and his followers found Birch a model to be followed. During World War II, the young man who acted so bravely in the field embodied all of the traits the fundamentalist patriarch sought to cultivate. No doubt Norris saw a piece of himself in John Birch and mourned deeply when his protégé was taken from him so abruptly. But in Birch, Norris also found the ultimate marketing device for his ministry. By reading and hearing about

Birch, Norris expected, other young men would come forward and follow a similar path from the South to California and then on to the front line in Asia. For those in the pews, meanwhile, Norris used the stories about Birch and other brave chaplains to prove their exceptionalism as the only true defenders of Christian America.

So IT WAS THAT, in wartime Southern California, the tale of expanding horizons within white southern evangelicalism was blended into the unfolding saga of American nationalism. For those who lived through it, the transition seemed epochal, and in many ways it was. Led by an army of stout clerics, transplanted southern evangelicals succeeded not simply at altering power relations within California Protestantism but also at connecting Southern California to the South through new institutional channels. Thanks to the rhetoric of a few celebrity preachers, these linkages between Southern California and the South assumed a consciously political tone. Preachers like Robert Lackey, Bob Shuler, and J. Frank Norris made it the priority of the West Coast's southern migrants to help their home region regain its faith and rebuild. Tired of "carpetbag liberals" descending on their home turf, they took the fight outside the South in a quest to democratize a nation they feared lost to collectivist thinking. They pledged their commitment to war efforts abroad, sacralized militancy in the defense of Christian liberty, and commissioned followers to embrace their new status as protectors of the state. It would be left up to a third group of southern evangelicals to ground this flourish of patriotism in real political capital.

3

ENTREPRENEURS

Southern California is . . . a mission field. Here is gathered almost every sort and kind of people that can be imagined. Los Angeles, with its suburbs, contains over two million people. The Churches of Christ are small in number, but strong in faith and fighting hard. Christians are looking to George Pepperdine College as the greatest power and influence for good that has ever come to this section.[1]

—BATSELL BAXTER

ON A RAKED PATCH OF DIRT A FEW MILES DUE WEST OF FIRST Baptist Bell Gardens, on a bright sunny afternoon in September of 1937, a wealthy businessman began his own errand. The occasion was the official opening of Pepperdine College in South Central Los Angeles. The ceremony's two thousand attendees, many dressed in their Sunday best, sat before a raised stage in front of the college's only completed edifice, a blue stucco "streamlined-modern" administration building. The gleaming façade clashed with the solemn economic times, but the crowd was there to celebrate new hopes and dreams, and for a moment forget the false ones that had recently plagued their country. Clad in dark suits and ties, school president Batsell Baxter and California governor Frank Merriam both took time at the speaker's platform to congratulate George Pepperdine for acting with such Christian charity.[2]

Following a heartfelt ovation, the college's founder stood next and, with quiet dignity, declared the moment the "mountain peak" of his life and career. He then outlined his school's primary objectives: "First, we want to provide first-class, fully accredited academic training in the lib-

eral arts. . . . Secondly, we are especially dedicated to a greater goal—
that of building in the student a Christ-like life, a love for the church
and a passion for the souls of mankind." His college, he explained, would
offer study in the liberal arts but also in vocational training, "which shall
prepare young men and women for . . . diversified activities in the business world." It would also ensure that students secured employment so
as to offset their tuition and, just as importantly, internalize economic
principles founded on scriptural truth and social responsibility. Guiding
this process would be a faculty "composed of devout Christians, men and
women who will give careful attention to safeguarding and deepending
[*sic*] the faith of students, increasing their loyalty to Jesus and their zeal
for saving souls." At Pepperdine College, mind, body, and spirit were to
receive equal care.[3]

GEORGE PEPPERDINE'S SPEECH INAUGURATED a third dimension of
the southern errand. The goal was still to evangelize the Golden State
with the southern gospel, but this facet of the mission displayed a wider
range of objectives and involved a more select cast of characters, all of
whom wielded a degree of power that few within local pews and pulpits
could match or even fathom.

At the center of the action were self-made men like Pepperdine whose
evangelical commitments extended beyond their local communities into
the world of high finance and higher education. These businessmen were
politically more shrewd than plain folk and preachers but no less serious, and the common dictates of Jefferson and Jesus continued to be
their guide. Convinced that an overbearing, bureaucratic New Deal state
threatened their belief in the primacy of individualism and local community, these entrepreneurs worked to create a network of institutions
that could begin reversing the trend. Through the construction of private
colleges, they hoped to rescue the next generation of southerners and
Southern Californians from northern liberal philosophies that, in their
mind, privileged secular rationalism and fostered intellectual elitism over
spiritual development and respect for the supernatural. There was more
to their pedagogy than book learning, however. Attuned to the financial
crisis of the Depression and aware of economic possibilities in wartime,
these entrepreneurs-turned-educators organized their schools around
a comprehensive doctrine that blended Christ and capitalism. "Head,

Heart, and Hand," as this philosophy was known, combined Bible study and the liberal arts with vocational training and wrapped all three in a formula for increased production and profit that would benefit the South and the entire nation. By imbuing young people with faith in the free market, a New South would emerge, primed for economic advancement and ready to lead the nation away from the precipice of collapse.

California was critical to this collaborative effort. Incapable of financing their schools alone, evangelical entrepreneurs turned to friends in the corporate sector. Impressed by the politics behind Head, Heart, and Hand, California donors welcomed these overtures and opened their checkbooks with the expectation that the schools they supported would remain true to the capitalist cause and dedicated to building a conservative counterrevolution against an ascendant New Deal state. Evangelical colleges responded in kind by readying their students to lead the charge.

HEAD, HEART, AND HAND

George Pepperdine's educational philosophy was the product of a rising trend in southern higher education begun after the Scopes trial of 1925. In the eyes of many southern Protestants, this cataclysmic court decision proved that modernist pedagogy prevalent in the North had pierced the shield of theological orthodoxy that once protected their society. With fears of secularization rapidly mounting and faith in state schools diminishing, southern evangelicals began shoring up their church colleges and looking to vocational schools as a necessary alternative.

One response to Scopes came in the form of the independent Bible school. A groundbreaking evangelist from Alabama set an example for this approach when, in 1927, he started Bob Jones College. Bob Jones's lofty ambition was to combat "all atheistic, agnostic, pagan . . . adulterations of the Gospel" through traditional Bible teaching and create the "greatest interdenominational, orthodox educational center in the world." In 1933, Jones moved the school to Cleveland, Tennessee, where it would be stationed for the next fourteen years before relocating again to Greenville, South Carolina. In the process of these moves, Jones expanded his school's curriculum to encompass degrees in religion and speech, and courses in English, mathematics, biology, and history. Wanting to combat stereotypes of fundamentalists as people who "had greasy noses, dirty fingernails, baggy pants and never shined their shoes," Jones committed his students to cultural refinement. Art and classical literature, drama and music became central to the college experience, as did lessons in courtship. Summing up his philosophy, Jones once declared that "here at Bob Jones we believe in educating the whole person. It is just as important for a man to know how to get in and out of a lady's parlor as it is for him to have book learning."[4]

A concern for spiritual and intellectual development—and cultural caché—enlivened new Bible institutes like Bob Jones's, but during the 1930s, financial considerations began to enter the classroom as well. Fearful of bankruptcy, a cohort of evangelical clerics and lay leaders forged another educational strategy that blended the ideals of the Bible college with those of the vocational institute. Their inspiration came from two related sources. Some drew on extant models already operational in the South, like Berea College in Kentucky and Tuskegee Institute in Alabama. Evangelical educators adopted these schools' programs for work-study in agriculture, home economics, and trades and blended them with inculcation in scripture. Both students and administrators benefited. While the former were allowed to practice their skills in day-to-day assignments and reduce their tuition costs, the latter were able to lower their institutional overhead. Other evangelical educators borrowed a second style of vocational training implemented in the North. Since the nineteenth century, wealthy businessmen like Henry Parsons Crowell (head of Quaker Oats in Chicago), and Charles L. Huston (head of Lukens Steel Company in Pittsburgh) had seen education as a way to prepare young people for a life centered on business and the Bible. They wanted their youth trained for evangelism overseas, but also equipped with technical managerial skills for the manufacturing sector at home. Again, the relationship was considered reciprocal: students were offered spiritual and economic advancement while corporate leaders were supplied with a devout, well-trained, compliant workforce.[5]

No one did more to export this second brand of vocational training to the South than Robert (R. G.) LeTourneau. LeTourneau owned a land-moving company in Illinois, which designed and built equipment impressively advanced for its day. With business booming, the self-trained engineer and self-proclaimed fundamentalist was able to siphon profits into a charitable foundation for religious ministry. In the late 1930s, he started a technical institute, which, overnight, became a vital part of his evangelical outreach. At this same time he grew tired of government regulation and labor unions, and decided to relocate to the South. Boosters from the town of Toccoa, in northeast Georgia, offered him virgin land to test his equipment and access to the community's unskilled laborers. In July 1939 the *Atlanta Constitution* announced LeTourneau's arrival: "Toccoa factory is dedicated to principles of Christianity—guidance of God is implored for a $2,000,000 plant; Big gathering of friends and employees cheer dedication in revival-like atmosphere." Vicksburg, Mississippi, was next to welcome LeTourneau's industry, then Longview, Texas. Consolidated in the last stages of World War II, the Longview plant proved to be LeTourneau's most important. He had long wished for a plant that could produce steel to forge the heaviest pieces of his machinery. Invited by civic leaders to check out East Texas, he not only found a failed company in the Lone Star Steel Company, but he also discovered that an adjacent government-owned hospital was now up for sale. Within weeks he secured Lone Star's property, began building a steel mill, and presented plans to turn Harmon Hospital into LeTourneau Technical Institute. For property valued at $870,000, LeTourneau paid the federal government a token price of one dollar, opened his engineering school, and began training youth to advance a new Christian, capitalist order.[6]

LeTourneau's burgeoning enterprise in the South was part of a much larger phenomenon in educational philosophy and politics. Devastated by the Depression, the South desperately needed men like LeTourneau to provide industry, capital, and the skilled workforce of a modern economy. In 1938, President Roosevelt helped underscore the urgency of the moment when he declared the South "the Nation's No. 1 economic problem." Long reliant on decentralized manufacturing in textiles, hosiery, and lumber, the South's industrial capabilities in the 1930s were antiquated and abysmal. Employing on average 18 percent more workers than their rivals outside the region, southern plants realized 18 percent less output. Only low labor costs helped compensate for this disparity, but this too raised other glaring deficiencies in the system. On average, the South's vast pool of unskilled laborers—women and children included—worked longer hours than their counterparts in other regions but earned two-thirds of their annual wage. Underdeveloped and impoverished, the South, in Roosevelt's judgment, was a colonial economy still woefully dependent on the North, mired in pre-industrial stasis, and desperately in need of federal assistance.[7]

An emerging class of southern businessmen and politicians agreed with

Roosevelt and saw the needs and possibilities of a New South, but they disagreed with the president on how to address them. In bald terms, they welcomed Roosevelt's financial assistance but insisted that local authorities manage it. The issue of race and civil rights figured into this arrangement. Although eager to make the South less wedded to the exploitive and explosive policies of Jim Crow, which, in crass fiscal terms, prohibited effective recruitment of capital, they still wanted states to be able to dictate the terms of their social relations, with no federal strings attached. The bottom line, though, is that they wanted to turn the region into a bastion of free market capitalism, autonomous from the federal state. They were happy in the short term to take federal funds through New Deal relief measures and wartime defense contracts, but in the long term they wanted to build a new economy by attracting businesses through guarantees of low taxes and open (union-free) shops and a trained workforce that was devoted to conservative economics and primed for progress in a post–World War II, postindustrial economy. Enterprising evangelical educators were ready to equip the South with such a workforce and the South's boosters recognized it. At Christian training institutes like LeTourneau's, the next generation of southerners would not only internalize an entrepreneurial ethic and by extension pro-business mindset but also acquire the perfect skill set needed to advance a developing economy.[8]

Jesse H. Jones was a leading visionary who saw immediately what LeTourneau's Head, Heart, and Hand pedagogy could do for his region. Jones was a "corporate populist" from Texas who decried the hegemony of industrial giants yet idealized the pristine qualities of capitalism and entrepreneurship. Like the Populists of William Jennings Bryan's day, he advocated federal investment in the economic infrastructure—transportation, irrigation, agriculture, and finance—insofar as it could allow small-scale farmers and economic actors on the nation's periphery to compete on an even playing field with the corporate lords of the urban North. He brought this philosophy with him to Washington, D.C., as head of the Reconstruction Finance Corporation and as Roosevelt's secretary of commerce, through which he had the authority to distribute billions of federal dollars to industry. Though he pledged his commitment to Roosevelt, he remained anti–Wall Street, anti–big government to the core, and concerned with the exploitation of southern resources. Nevertheless, as a discerning realist, Jones preached patience to his fellow southerners, urging them not to bite the hand that fed them until they were able to feed themselves. All the while he worked behind the scenes to support local enterprises like LeTourneau's in hopes of finally achieving economic and political self-sufficiency for his beloved South.[9]

With help from men like Jones, evangelical educators struck a deal: in exchange for aid in building their institutions they would train a New South. West of the Mississippi River, where the Christian, capitalist impulse flourished, alliances like LeTourneau and Jesse Jones's would become common, their joint promotion of vocational training a staple of economic life. Others in LeTourneau's cohort found that a similarly vibrant relationship between Christian education and corporate populism could be struck in Southern California and harnessed for institutional gain. Three trendsetters laid the groundwork for this exchange.

THE ARKANSAS TRAVELER

John Brown embodied the Head, Heart, and Hand philosophy like no other in his generation. He was also the first among his peers to count on Californians' help in implementing this pedagogy across the South. Brown first introduced himself to California in the 1910s as a traveling Methodist evangelist. Paired with musical talent C. P. Curry to form the Dynamic Dixie Team, he rivaled Billy Sunday in the minds of Southern Californians as America's premier evangelist. But by the 1930s Brown's work in California began to change. Although maintaining primary residency in Siloam Springs, a small town tucked away in the foothills of Arkansas' Ozark Mountains, he came to view Los Angeles as a second home and appeared regularly for preaching duties at area churches. Trinity Methodist Church was the congregation he frequented most. To "Brother Brown," Bob Shuler's wife would say, "You are the only man that comes to Trinity Church that can hold Bob's crowds."[10]

Even as he continued to captivate crowds as an evangelist, Brown spent the interwar years honing his skills as an educator and entrepreneur. Of these appellations, the proudest held was the first. Schooled only to the fifth grade, Brown was deeply insecure about his lack of learning. He expressed this timidity in regular correspondence with his wife, who usually remained in Siloam Springs while Brown ministered in Los Angeles. This angst inspired him to work so that other country boys and girls would never have to struggle with the same "tragic lack of education." In 1919, he decided to parlay his new evangelistic fame into a school of his own, the Southwestern Collegiate Institute, soon renamed John Brown College. John Brown College grew steadily until, in 1934, it became John Brown University (JBU), comprising a preparatory school and three colleges: John E. Brown College, the Siloam School of the Bible, and the John E. Brown Vocational College. Despite this promising start, JBU quickly slipped into financial difficulties. Located in the heart of rural Arkansas, Brown's constituency was rich in "pure Americanism," as Bob Shuler liked to say, but poor in the pocket. Moreover, Brown was adamant that his practical training remained free; in fact, no student was admitted who was able to pay his or her way, because "schools for young people of means" were plentiful. Instead, students earned their keep in one of the college's cottage industries: automobile repair, plumbing, carpentry, blacksmith and electrical shops, brush and furniture factories, a canning department, a five-hundred-acre farm with twenty-seven dairy cows, and the "largest publishing plant in northwest Arkansas." As a result of his students' industriousness, Brown was able to boast that he could educate each one of them for merely one hundred dollars a year. "Nowhere in the world," he declared, "will a little money go as far in the building of character and the training of mind as here in this school." This was only partially true.[11]

As much as its apprentices offset operational costs, JBU still required outside assistance. Like Bob Jones, Brown first raised money through his evangelism. Early on, monies generated by his religious rallies (estimated at a half-million dollars by 1941) flowed constantly. Middle-class Californians affected by Brown's speaking were the most eager to fill his offering plate to support his Arkansas school. Touched by their generosity, Brown built his school's most impressive dormitory in California Mission style and designated it "California Hall." All the while he courted local donors as well, rich oilmen like Murray Sells, founder of Sells Petroleum Company, based in Gladewater, Texas. One day, while checking on his rigs, Sells found his radio tuned to Brown's preaching. After stopping his vehicle to listen, he decided that Brown had "the right idea for training the youth of our nation" and warranted his support. Millions of dollars in donations followed this auspicious pause.[12]

By far the most important of Brown's local benefactors was Jesse H. Jones, the same man who endorsed his friend R. G. LeTourneau. It had been Brown who had helped trigger Jones's passion for Christian charity in the first place. Counseled by Brown into a personal religious experience after a chance meeting in Houston in 1905, Jones repaid his spiritual mentor by becoming JBU's most generous supporter. From the very beginning, Jones's support for Brown's school rested on strong political prescriptions, not just financial handouts, as hinted at in the commencement address he gave at JBU in 1938. Speaking directly to students from Arkansas, Missouri, Louisiana, Texas, and Oklahoma, "states so similar in interest that no economic boundaries separate them," Jones said:

> It is my opinion that no section of the country offers as great opportunities, present and future, as this, our section. And no part of the country so badly needs young people to do its work now, and to train for leadership in solving its problems of the future. This great Southwest will need pioneers in the 40's, 50's and 60's of this century as badly as it did in the same years a century ago. Not pioneers to clear the wilderness, but pioneers to develop and use the great natural resources that are here.

Although speaking as a Washington insider, Jones challenged Brown's students to think of the day when politicians would once again take a backseat to pastors and parents in the management of their society. It was the message of a man who yearned for a redeemed South and saw Brown's campus as one place to begin achieving this dream.[13]

Even with men like Sells and Jones subsidizing his cause, Brown was always stretched thin. Enter Brown the entrepreneur. By the early 1930s he resolved to tap the business world to guarantee his institution's endowment. After establishing his own College Bank and Savings Corporation in Arkansas, Brown warmed to the investment potential of Southern California, where he now spent on average half a year. His first venture was a chain of gasoline service stations, purchased in 1931. Borrowing from a southern tale about a whimsical journeyman playfully outwitted by a fiddling local, Brown sought to translate Ozark folklore into big-city profit by calling his franchise "The Arkansas Traveler." Over the course of the next five years Brown invested business profits in new ventures. He acquired a hotel in Long Beach, which he advertised as a place where friends journeying to the Coast could stay. At the same time he purchased radio time on KMPC in Beverly Hills and began broadcasting a daily half-hour program called *God's Half Hour*, in part to market his ministry. Los Angeles' airwaves would figure prominently in his plans for the late 1940s, but in the late 1930s his crowning communications achievement was the purchase of Arkansas station KUOA from the Fulbright family. From this station's headquarters, moved to his campus in 1936, Brown reached thousands in the western South with "spiritual inspiration, practical education, and wholesome entertainment."[14]

During the Depression, Brown discovered additional investment opportunities on the West Coast. Facing difficulties, a number of Southern California evangelicals agreed to transfer their equities to the John Brown schools if Brown would in turn refinance their properties. To do so, he established the John E. Brown College Corporation, "a self-perpetuating, non-denominational, non-profit, educational organization," and incorporated it under the laws of the State of California. In 1937 the corporation acquired two highly regarded but financially strapped preparatory schools and renamed them the Brown Military Academy for boys (located in San Diego), and the Brown School for Girls (situated in Glendora). These schools quickly became self-supporting and convinced Brown that the "California enterprise" needed to assume priority within his entire institutional network.[15]

In late spring of 1940 Brown unveiled this new phase of his ministry in a speech to his cadets in the Gothic-style granite chapel on the grounds of the Brown Military Academy. Southern California would henceforth assume primary importance in generating money and enthusiasm for his university. As he articulated it, investment in his Arkansas school now was not simply an act of charity but an act of political reciprocity. By helping his students rebuild the South, he explained, Californians would also allow America to reclaim its Christian democratic heritage, the kind quietly supported by his patron Jesse H. Jones and loudly demanded by his friend "Fighting Bob." Moreover, by lending him their financial assistance, Californians would gain the allegiance of a region primed for growth. Just imagine the energy that could be unleashed by a reawakened South, Brown intoned. Just imagine the lasting consequences for the nation, provided Californians were generous enough. Strong rhetoric indeed, meant to sway well-to-do friends and raise capital, but it was a rhetoric backed by clear economic prerogatives and true, political potential.[16]

THE MISSIONARY PATRIOT

Every bit as earnest as Brown, George Benson, the president of a small church college located on Mississippi basin land two hundred miles east of Siloam Springs, made his way to Christian higher education from a very different background. Both were comfortable in the countryside, but whereas Brown often carried himself like an urbane executive, Benson was raw frontier to the core. His brand of education reflected this heritage, as did his persistent efforts to court the corporate world.

Benson was born in 1898 to Scotch-Irish parents who migrated with the first wave of homesteaders into eastern Oklahoma. Homesteading was the sum of their existence. Later Benson recalled that he had "never seen people anywhere who were more contented or happier than were the people of those frontier days when neighbors joined freely to solve one another's problems and stood firmly behind one another." Through to the eighth grade Benson attended a one-room school, after which he transferred to the U.S. Government Indian School one hundred miles east in Claremore. Working as a janitor to pay his way, he excelled at school but struggled with finances and was forced to go back home. In fits and starts he chipped away at high school and finally, at the age of twenty-one, earned his diploma. After farming for two more years he decided to attend Harper College, a junior college in Kansas supported by the Church of Christ. Older than most of his fellow students, he assumed a leadership role on campus, even serving on the college's finance committee under President J. N. Armstrong. He viewed this as a prelude to his true calling—missionary work in China—which he pursued seriously after transferring to Harding College, a small Church of Christ school in eastern Arkansas. After earning his degree and marrying his college sweetheart, Sally Ellis Hockaday, in July 1925, he and his new wife skipped a honeymoon and left immediately for Asia.[17]

The Bensons' first impressions of China never left them. In spring 1926, they vacated their base in Canton and traveled five hundred miles up the West River to the city of Kwei Hsien, in Kwangsi province, where they began language training. This was a period of escalating warfare between local warlords and Communist-led forces, which under the auspices of the Kuomintang (Chinese Nationalist Party) sought to centralize the southern region of the country. Trapped, the Bensons struggled for several perilous months as the Kuomintang gradually gained control of the area and, in an effort to rally citizens behind a new nationalism, spread antimissionary sentiments. The Bensons barely made it back to Canton, where rising antiforeign violence forced them to flee to Hong Kong. After three years conducting missionary work there and in the Philippines, the Bensons returned to Canton in 1929, but finding antimissionary sentiments had hardly softened, they assumed a less conspicuous tack and began teaching English to Canton's high society. After gaining the support of elites, they gradually eased their students into Bible study and then full-blown evangelistic training. By 1934 their newly formed Canton Bible School was offering comprehensive instruction in history, mathematics, and scripture, and training nationals to establish similar institutes elsewhere. The Bensons, however, did not stay long enough to see the fruits of this labor. In the fall of 1936 they returned to Arkansas, at the request of their troubled alma mater.[18]

In 1936 Harding College, now located in the town of Searcy, was headed for financial collapse. Its aging president, J. N. Armstrong, to whom Benson had grown close while at Harper College (now merged with Harding), was set to retire. Asked by Armstrong to step in as his successor, Benson only agreed out of obligation, but gradually he grew confident that Harding could be salvaged. Between 1936 and 1942 he drew on his missionary experience to revamp Harding's fund-raising. When Depression-starved local Church of Christ congregations came up short in their giving, Benson turned to wealthy friends. Clinton Davidson was the first. Reared in Kentucky, Davidson attended the state's tiny Church of Christ-affiliated Potter Bible College, where he studied under its two strongest teachers, James Harding and J. N. Armstrong. Davidson eventually made his way to New York City and began selling life insurance, catering to wealthy industrialists who seemed drawn to his personality as much as his product. His two consulting firms soon managed clients with a combined wealth of three billion dollars. Convinced that Benson was the man to reinvigorate his mentors' college, Davidson became its first distinguished donor, with a gift of ten thousand dollars.[19]

While he courted the well heeled, Benson also attended to Harding's financially strapped—its students and faculty. Harding's undergraduates typically arrived in Searcy with little money and few prospects. Having been himself an impoverished student, Benson looked for ways to impart the lessons of toil and forbearance to his students through vocational training. Over time, Benson purchased fifteen hundred acres of farmland, a concrete-block plant, and a campus laundry and dry-cleaning plant that serviced the local area. By 1941, sixty percent of Harding's students were employed in one of its operations; all were able to offset their costs and some worked hard enough to pay for tuition, room, board, and books. New graduates had opportunities with companies that now actively recruited them for their usable skills. This same year—just four years after facing collapse—Harding formally dissolved its debt and Benson proudly forecasted a future of surplus.[20]

Even as he took pride in Harding's economic recovery, Benson realized that his strategy could be used effectively for politics, too. Through Davidson's connections, Benson was introduced to lobbyists in Washington, D.C., who, in May 1941, invited him to testify before the House Ways and Means Committee on the New Deal. He was witness number 147 and offered his testimony after 146 others had proposed their own economic remedies. One of the first witnesses was Secretary of the Treasury Henry Morgenthau, whose appearance set a contentious tone. Confirming recent reports that the federal government had operated the previous year with a deficit of over three million dollars, Morgenthau recommended tax increases and cuts to "non-defense expenditures." This proposal infuriated critics who had been trying to convey to the voting public that expenditures "grafted onto government" now registered over $7 billion dollars. Rather than reduce these expenditures, the federal government seemed set on spending its way out of the Depression, and by doing so, detractors argued, it was only making the national economy worse.[21]

Counting himself among the New Deal critics, Benson appeared before the committee on May 15 ready to reprimand Roosevelt's man and help the president find a way to balance the budget. A no-name schoolmaster who wore no official title and boasted no formal training, his presence caused an extraordinary stir. Beginning with a passionate account of his state's poverty and its residents' courageous thrift, Benson described the ways Harding had erased its spiraling debt. If humble Americans and a poor church college could reduce their spending, so could the state. Benson then shifted from anecdote to the facts, which in his eyes read like a clear condemnation of government mismanagement. Proving that he was there not simply to complain, the Arkansan offered a formula for recovery that hinged on the elimination of bureaucracy. By pruning programs like the Civilian Conservation Corps, National Youth Administration, and Works Progress Administration, he pointed out, government would save two billion dollars. After suggesting a further hundred million dollars in savings, the witness concluded with a nod to history and the divine:

To me, the questions involved are extremely serious and the danger very real. We can avoid inflation and the evils which follow it, provided the first steps are taken before the House passes the 1941 tax bill that you are planning to recommend. We are at the crossroads—where will we be five or ten years from now? That depends upon whether we continue drifting toward the . . . disastrous steps I have pictured or whether we change our course. In all seriousness I say, "May God help you."

At the end of his speech, the crowd broke into applause, and House Ways and Means chairman Robert L. Doughton ordered Benson's testimony inserted into the *Congressional Record*. One ranking Republican called Benson's statement the most illuminating yet and, the day following, offered Congress a detailed recounting of it.[22]

With his name in the national press, Benson accepted speaking invitations for the next few months from all over the country. Besides repeating his plea for government restraint, he reminded his listeners that Harding College was setting the pace for the next generation of Americans and therefore deserving of their support. Quickly, with Davidson's help, Benson's barnstorming began to generate interest from high-powered people. Just as they bought Davidson's insurance, leading conservative businessmen purchased Benson's educational plan as a way to bankroll their nation's future. They wanted it to be a capitalist one, and Benson assured them he would prepare America's young people for it. Gradually the message made its way onto the desks of executives at companies like Eastman Kodak, DuPont chemical, General Motors, and Sun Oil (now Sunoco). His courtship of J. Howard Pew, president of Sun Oil, was typical. Pew learned of Benson through his nephew in Dallas, who saw Benson speak at a special meeting of the Dallas Petroleum Club. Intrigued, Pew—at his nephew's advice—awaited the Arkansan's petition and soon received it. In an introductory letter to the oil baron, Benson explained that he had come to be an ardent defender of free enterprise after encountering communism in China and then, upon his return home, seeing his country's frontier spirit subdued by socialist panaceas. He followed this with a list of concrete accomplishments meant to instill confidence in his agenda. Pew did not offer any money at this point, but he was clearly sold on Benson.[23]

Besides his evangelical faith, what appealed to Pew was the combination of Benson's plain-folk allure and big-time ambition. Pew, himself an evangelical, welcomed regular communication with the educator and wrote other businessmen to spread the word about Harding College. In one letter, he laid out Benson's promise (as well as persistence):

> I have run into Dr. Benson . . . two or three times over the last few months and have discussed the general problems in which we are all so vitally interested. While Dr. Benson was full of ardor and enthusiasm to do something, I found that he had an awful lot to learn about the problem before he could hope to accomplish the things he had in mind. On the other hand, he is a natural and should be encouraged; but if anything is to be done, we should put him in a position to get all of the necessary basic material. I am wondering whether we could open a door for Dr. Benson.

Pew's associates did help open doors and expand Benson's donor list and speaking schedule. By 1943 he was averaging two hundred speeches per year. On one midwestern jaunt he spent his days talking to businessmen in boardrooms and clubs before hosting large evening rallies for war-plant workers; gatherings with fellow educators and Christians were squeezed in between. In all these settings Benson stuck to his stump speech on free enterprise, constitutional government, and Christian citizenship. Benson's script read fresh every time, as if it were a proverb drawn from the profoundest experiences of his life, which it was.[24]

More than his salesmanship, this ability to communicate passionately "as one commoner to another" was what made Benson so attractive to such a wide audience of businessmen, farmers, and working Americans. By the time he first contacted Pew, Harding's president had in fact already begun reaching out to residents in America's rural heartland with the message of free enterprise. "Thousands of men and women without a college education are faced with vital problems of public policy which require a sound background of scientific knowledge and the discipline of clear, orderly thinking furnished by higher education," he explained. Whether about economics or social policy, rural Americans needed to make informed decisions, and colleges like Harding needed to be there to help them along. Through extensive mass communications, placed under the direction of Harding's National Education Program (NEP), Benson hoped to "move public opinion at the grassroots in the direction of godliness and patriotism" and rally average Americans to reverse "pernicious" government policies restricting markets and states' rights. The NEP produced booklets that could be purchased by industrial and civic organizations for distribution in the workplace and local neighborhood. Yet a third outlet for Benson's message was his syndicated column, Looking Ahead, in which he provided readers with commentary on political developments. By 1944 these editorials were published regularly in 2,500 small-town and city newspapers in 46 different states.[25]

Among all the people who read these columns and purchased educational material from Harding College, few did so with more dedication than Southern Californians. From the moment he began reconstructing Harding, Benson looked west for some of his most vital support. He often traveled to Los Angeles, and even when he was not present in the city his presence was felt. Angelenos could expect to find the latest installment of Looking Ahead, either on the first or second page of their local paper, next to Benson's picture; when breaking for lunch in their factory they would not be surprised to see literature published in Searcy displayed nearby; when gathering for a meeting of their local Chamber of Commerce they could assume someone had read one of Benson's booklets before arriving ready to speak. This was just as Benson's wealthier West Coast supporters wanted it. Convinced by this zealous missionary patriot, they welcomed him to the Golden State on frequent occasion to speak at seminars sponsored by the Los Angeles Chamber of Commerce and Merchants and Manufacturers Association. More often, they sent their money to northeast Arkansas to bolster Harding's free enterprise educational programs. It is no wonder Benson came to see California as a rich financial field he needed to till.[26]

THE AUTO SUPPLY SALESMAN

George Pepperdine was one of the many Californians who sent Benson his money. The relationship between these two men, having begun when Pepperdine funded Benson's missionary work, was closer than any other Benson maintained in the West. Shortly after Benson returned to Arkansas, Pepperdine pledged twenty-five thousand dollars to Harding College, dwarfing even Clinton Davidson's own sizable donation. Though never stated as such, in return for his pledges, Pepperdine wanted Benson's help in bringing Head, Heart, and Hand pedagogy to Southern California. Pepperdine saw this educational philosophy as the only viable way to raise a generation of Americans shielded from (and mobilized against) the sinister influences of New Deal liberalism and bridge the political spheres of plain-folk and silk-stocking conservatives who together feared big government.[27]

Pepperdine grew up near the town of Parsons, in southeastern Kansas, just a few miles from the intersection of Oklahoma and Missouri's current state lines. As a young boy he imbibed his parents' fervor for revivalist religion and populist politics, both of which grew out of intense conversion experiences. Shortly after moving to Kansas, his parents, John and Mary Pepperdine, attended a revival nearby, led by a Church of Christ minister, where they were baptized into the Christian faith. Later, in 1896, when George was just ten, his parents were swept up in the mania of William Jennings Bryan's Populist movement. Joining farmers from around the county, George and his father attended political rallies, including a colorful parade in their village that illustrated Bryan's "16-to-1" "free-silver" slogan by having sixteen young women dressed in shiny silver walk proudly while one slumped forward in gold. Yelling "Hurrah for Bryan," the Pepperdine men were transfixed by the moment. It even got George wondering whether politics or the ministry could be his calling.[28]

Recognizing as a young man that business was a healthy compromise between religion and politics, and better suited to his demeanor, Pepperdine moved to Kansas City in 1907, at the age of twenty-one, to take an accounting job at an automobile repair shop. He was hired to balance the office's books but found the grimier work outside in the garage far more interesting. In 1908, after quitting his job to protest his boss's shady financial dealings, Pepperdine decided to combine his skill and new curiosities and start his own auto parts retail store. Considering the tenuousness of his personal finances, the move was courageous, if not foolish, but it worked. At the time of Pepperdine's decision, automobiles left factories looking like steel wagons. They moved but they had no style; although functional, that is all they were, sold without even basic equipment like tops, windshields, bumpers, horns, and headlamps. Anticipating the need—and desire—of the consumer to purchase these parts, Pepperdine founded the Western Auto Supply Company. Through walk-up retail and mail-order sales, Western Auto expanded rapidly as the supreme supplier of car accessories in Kansas City. Just as his company was taking off, however, Pepperdine contacted tuberculosis and was urged by his doctor to relocate to a dryer climate. In 1916 he moved to the City of Angels, determined to get healthier and corner its market. He achieved both goals. By 1920, his two Los Angeles stores boasted sales of $700,000. A year later he began aggressive expansion, opening 25 new stores per year. Five years later, he had 150 branch stores operating in San Francisco, Phoenix, Seattle, and major centers in eleven western states.[29]

Western Auto was soaring as it entered the 1930s. When asked by fellow businessmen to explain his success, Pepperdine pointed to the character of his employees, all of whom were expected to demonstrate Christian disciplines of humility and honesty. Western Auto's general manager, Hal Baker, explained this mantra to managers at a general meeting, reminding them that "we, as executives of this organization, are just plain, ordinary, every-day folks, and that is what we want you boys to be. You should serve as a leader to the men under you and set examples for them. Your business conduct should at all times be above reproach." At the same company convention, Pepperdine elaborated in a pep talk of his own:

> Regardless of the size to which "Western Auto" may grow, we want always to maintain a warm, human relationship . . . and continue to build the spirit of our Western Auto Family. . . . We want everyone who is a part of the "Western Auto Family" to be clean in his personal life and in his contact with the people. We want him to treat people in such a way that he will be regarded by the public as a wholesome person.

Pepperdine meant what he said. Potential employees at Western Auto were exhaustively screened to make sure they maintained a clean-cut appearance and positive attitude. Provided they made the grade, aspiring managers faced a litany of tests on intelligence, their cooperative spirit, leadership potential, and most importantly their desire to serve.[30]

If character development was Pepperdine's stated pathway to prosperity, his anti-unionism was a less mentioned route. By the time Western Auto reached its zenith, Los Angeles was known as the capital of the open shop, a place where pro-business sentiment stoked fierce anti-labor politics. Pepperdine flourished here. Within his company he encouraged a civil but firm approach to unionization. Eager to see capital and labor function "as friends," he worked diligently to keep employees happy with bonuses, stock options, profit sharing, and picnics. Although these perquisites were not uncommon corporate strategies in his day, meant to build company loyalty and subdue workers' solidarity, Pepperdine stood out among peers as unusually generous in his offerings. As a leading member of the Chamber of Commerce, meanwhile, he gave numerous public talks and radio addresses, including a memorable exhortation titled "Los Angeles, The Heart of the World":

> Right here we shall some day see the heart and center of human activity, the climax and mountain peak of American and world civilization. Right here we shall some day see the ultimate accomplishments in education, literature, art and music, as well as scientific discovery and spiritual advancement. Right here we shall some day see the world's greatest center of manufacturing and industrial progress, with the entire commercial universe vibrating in response to our activities and with every nation on earth paying financial tribute. . . . Right here, my friends, we shall some day see Los Angeles the greatest city of the greatest country, the real, "Heart of the World."

Quiet and reserved in person, Pepperdine openly gushed about his city whenever a public opportunity arose. He even dabbled in poetry. One of his odes was titled "Praise God for California," and it closed with a promise: "I shall love California forever, / All the years of my life here I'll spend, / And I'll praise Him who is the Great Giver, / For the generous gift from his hand." Considering his own journey west into affluence, it is not hard to see why Pepperdine's imagination ran wild with enthusiasm for God, city, and capital.[31]

During the 1930s, when societal crisis seemed to demand heavy sacrifice, Pepperdine's generosity paid off. Even with the Depression chipping away at its profit margin, Western Auto continued to operate in solvency. The chief executive credited the "complete co-operation on the part of all employees of the 'Western Auto Family.'" In cruder terms, the employee handouts Pepperdine had doled out in times of prosperity now helped shield him against labor unrest during cutbacks and store closures. Western Auto workers also seemed impressed by the fact that their boss forfeited much of his annual salary, even as he dealt with the tragic loss of Mrs. Pepperdine, the company's beloved matriarch, to a rare disease. These trials not only strengthened bonds of community within the company but also encouraged Pepperdine to honor the memory of his wife by focusing his energies on charity work. Already giving to missions and church growth, Pepperdine established the George Pepperdine Foundation to handle his rapidly expanding empire of charitable agencies. Under the leadership of his second wife, Helen Louise, this organization funneled funds from Western Auto and income accrued from various real estate holdings into benevolent initiatives like the Pacific Lodge Boys' Home and Helen Louise Girls' Home. In the late 1930s, Pepperdine decided to sell his company and focus entirely on philanthropy. After thirty years spent building a network of two hundred stores and a thousand employees, the decision was a difficult one, but any second-guessing was dampened by the dream of what he could do with its tremendous financial yield.[32]

Pepperdine's greatest dream was to build a school. Too often, he lamented, he "had seen young people go off to college with strong Christian faith and after four years of training under the guidance of cynical and materialistic professors, return home minus their spiritual nature . . . and faith in God." Pepperdine was deeply anxious that young people were losing their work ethic. Just like Pew and R. G. LeTourneau, he was convinced that the American educational system had been co-opted by labor leaders, sympathetic liberals, and socialist doctrines. Prior to the 1930s these business leaders and their allies had in fact worked closely with state school administrators and actively supported their educational system, which remained geared largely to training in the trades. Amid difficult economic times, however, a chasm grew. Struggling with recession, business reduced its financial support for public education and, through the Chamber of Commerce and National Association of Manufacturers (NAM), called for a reduction in school taxes and budgets. At the same time, a new class of liberal educators criticized corporate giving and vocational training as a ploy to create docile workers. A propaganda and policy war erupted. Conservative organizations like NAM began monitoring textbooks and demanding loyalty oaths, while business leaders began looking to private schools as a countermeasure to the public system. On the other side of the spectrum, liberal educators championed a curriculum that allowed for critiques of capitalism, condemned right-wing surveillance as censorship, and worked within New Deal power structures to shore up their control of the public educational system. Pepperdine rushed to build a school that would serve as a conservative institutional counterweight.[33]

"Rush" describes Pepperdine's actions mildly. He first thought of it in 1937, and soon became convinced that Los Angeles needed a college designed in the Head, Heart, and Hand mold. Southern California already contained more Bible institutes than most states in the country, and southern schools like Bob Jones College and John Brown University were recruiting the West Coast's young people into their classrooms. As far as Pepperdine was concerned, however, this was not enough. And so he turned for help first to Hugh Tiner, a supervisor for Los Angeles County schools, who had attended Abilene Christian College in Texas. Pepperdine next took an extended tour to six different southern colleges, primarily Church of Christ schools like Abilene, Harding, and David Lipscomb. Moving quickly, he called his old friend George Benson for advice. Always eager to talk education, in person, Benson got in his Plymouth and drove from Searcy to Los Angeles, where he recommended Batsell Baxter as Pepperdine College's first president. Baxter had worked in Searcy before moving to David Lipscomb, and even now remained invested in Harding (he would continue to be a speaker in its Division of Popular Education during the 1940s), so Benson knew him well.[34]

In February of 1937, during an evening-long conference, Pepperdine, Tiner, and Baxter hashed out curricula. They decided that their school would be a four-year "institution of higher learning where any worthy boy or girl, regardless of his religion, or financial standing" could get an education in an academically and spiritually sound environment. Pepperdine College would not require its students to subscribe to any specific doctrine but would require them "at least to be in sympathy with [its] policy of Christian ideals and willing to give some of your time to the study of the Bible." This subtlety reflected Pepperdine's own low-church theology, which, in accordance with Church of Christ teachings, placed no firm demands on followers for membership and resisted any declarations of compliance with church authority; the Bible alone was to serve as their supreme guide. But Pepperdine's nuance was not moderation. He insisted that "all instruction" at his school be conducted "under conservative, fundamental Christian supervision." His theology informed financial arrangements as well. Rather than depend on any other denominational support, Pepperdine vowed to fund his school's entire operation, beginning with a two-million-dollar start-up fund and one-million-dollar endowment. He pledged to use his foundation's earnings to offset any budgetary needs or deficits in subsequent years.[35]

With philosophical issues resolved, Pepperdine and his two advisors next turned to practical matters, and here Tiner and Baxter received a jolt. Excited about Pepperdine's plan to build a college, and ready to join his staff, they asked their future boss when he expected his school to open. Fall of the same year was his answer. The exacting entrepreneur that he was, Pepperdine saw no reason why a fully functioning institution of higher learning could not be completed in six months. Too shocked to argue, Tiner and Baxter began scurrying to find a campus, hire a staff, design a curriculum, recruit faculty, and enroll students. Unfazed by such daunting logistics, the auto supply salesman and his advisors went out the next morning searching for property and soon found a suitable thirty-four-acre tract of land southwest of downtown Los Angeles. The property had once been ranch land centered by a beautiful eighteen-room mansion, but now it was overgrown and decayed and nestled tightly in a suburban tract of small, single-family homes. As far as Pepperdine was concerned, it was ideal. The mansion would become the presidential house; more importantly, the location would provide students with the security of the suburb but also access to the city center, where he intended most of them to find part-time work and business experience. After purchasing the land, Pepperdine hired an architect to design an administration building, dining hall, and two residence halls. Art Deco–inspired, with straight lines, rounded corners, and wide expanses of glass, the buildings seemed perfectly suited to their time and setting.[36]

Pepperdine and his associates spent the next several months generating publicity and gathering students and staff for their school. From their rented office in Los Angeles' Chamber of Commerce Building, the three men began building a faculty. Although they desired a national reputation, these administrators narrowed their search to Church of Christ people who personified its core principles. Making it clear to church folk that Pepperdine College's "wholesome atmosphere" was guaranteed to please "parents and students who are looking for constructive and ennobling training," school officials also asked for transfer students from the South's Christian colleges. "Good Christian boys and girls" were needed, they said, "especially the first year . . . when the ideals of the student body are in the making." To prove they meant business, they also hired Martha Middlebrooks away from David Lipscomb College to be dean of women and gave her special treatment in promotional literature. Middlebrooks brought with her years of experience in Georgia's public school system and several vocational institutes in Tennessee. As the college's catalogue said, she was perfectly qualified to "provide capable and worthy leadership and guidance" for the school's impressionable coeds. All of these assurances worked. Anchoring the school's first student body of 160 were 19 transferees from David Lipscomb, 9 from Abilene, and 6 from Harding; its handful of seniors were all transfers from these three institutions. In addition, 17 of the college's 22-member faculty hailed from the South, with 15 listing Church of Christ schools on their vitae. All subscribed to the school's theological codes, which confirmed orthodox belief in "the virgin birth, the deity, the miracles of Christ, and the Biblical account of creation."[37]

Whether they subscribed to this theological code or not, Los Angeles' businessmen heralded the bootstrapping ethic that was ensconced in Pepperdine College's program of study. In a stylish pamphlet distributed just prior to the college's opening, school officials catered to these corporate boosters by emphasizing that students would be trained for ministry, teaching, engineering, medical, and law careers, but that their schooling would see consistent emphasis "placed upon Business Administration and preparation for commercial life." Designed to be a "school of workers," all undergraduates would complete courses in the Department of Business Administration and Economics, the largest on campus, and be provided with internships at major companies in the area. Men would be encouraged to specialize in finance, while women would be steered into secretarial training or a division of the Home Economics Department, like Family and Child Welfare or Household Administration. Pepperdine College identified family values as a vital part of the biblical blueprint for economic growth, and the maintenance of separate spheres as key to the nation's spiritual recovery. So while it would teach its men how to succeed in the business world through drive and self-discipline, its women were to learn how to be managerial stalwarts in the home. This struck Los Angeles' business leaders as exceptionally timely. At last, the city had a school run by one of their own, an institution able to prove that even in its darkest time, capitalism still held the keys to better families, stronger communities, and a brighter future for church and state.[38]

To celebrate, they showed up in numbers, along with political leaders and church people, on September 21, 1937, to witness Pepperdine College's official opening. The impressively large and diverse audience represented the culmination of Baxter and Tiner's hard work and the fulfillment of George Pepperdine's dream. Though frenzied, the six-month campaign to get their school up and running actually proved to be empowering for its administrators. Forced into an aggressive marketing approach, they succeeded at generating attention on a national scale; even *Time* magazine covered the opening ceremonies. For Pepperdine, meanwhile, the public event confirmed the power of personal faith. Late in life he would publish a memoir, *Faith Is My Fortune.* "More than just another story of a farm boy who was blessed," he intended the book to "teach some eternal principles that would benefit young people" and to "give clear reasons why strong faith in God is worth more to us than all the treasures of earth; more than any fortune man can acquire." Standing before his guests in 1937, Pepperdine spoke with the evidence rising around him.[39]

FAITH'S FORTUNE SEEMED TO shine on Helen Mattox, too, as she listened to Pepperdine's inaugural address. Mattox was a quintessential child of the western South, raised in a family of plain folk and preachers, and precisely the type of individual evangelical entrepreneurs hoped to reach. The sixth of seven children, she was also the granddaughter of an illustrious Church of Christ preacher from Texas and the daughter of a struggling cotton merchant from Oklahoma. This heritage, in many ways, dictated her future course to Pepperdine College. Mattox's father was adamant that all of his children attend a Church of Christ school. As each of his kids reached college age, he sold off parcels of his last piece of land in western Oklahoma. When Helen's turn came, more was sold to offset her tuition at Harding College. Even with this money, Mattox worried about finances; in a letter home during her second semester, she wrote "My books are costing a lot: $.50 rent on psy. Book, $1.00 trig book, .60 work book in psy., $3.00 Soc. Book. Do you suppose I'm worth it?"[40]

In the fall of 1937, Mattox transferred as a sophomore to Pepperdine College, near where her sister lived. Thrilled by the move, she soon enrolled in a number of social clubs, joined the pep squad, and found a part-time job. And, like the majority of her classmates, she got part-time work, though on campus acting as an assistant to Dean Middlebrooks. None of these commitments, however, stole time from her studies. She wanted to finish a degree in business administration quickly so that she could attend graduate school at the University of Oklahoma and ease her family's financial troubles. Her plans changed, though, because of a man. Early in her studies she met M. Norvel Young, a history professor from Tennessee. Unlike Mattox, Young came from an established family that had helped shape the cosmopolitan Church of Christ culture of Nashville. His polish as a preacher and professor impressed Pepperdine College students, especially Mattox. On August 31, 1939—her twenty-first birthday—Mattox married Norvel in Oklahoma City. When looking back on her college days, Mattox would see her marriage as the clearest extension of her faith and good fortune. But even two years earlier, when this moment still lay in the unknown future, she was convinced that God had led her into a special situation. Sitting in front of the administration building on September 21, 1937, listening to California's governor praise her school's founder, Los Angeles' wealthiest businessmen offer their heartiest congratulations, and local church folk and students clap, sing, and pray, she knew that this was something unprecedented and new. She sensed it was something important, too.[41]

Mattox, of course, did not know how significant Pepperdine College was or would become politically. Nor did she recognize how much her own life was already fused with politics. The same held true for most other plain folk, preachers, and entrepreneurs who brought the South to Southern California in the Depression and early years of World War II. Focused on creating new lives for themselves—finding jobs and homes, churches and communities—these sojourners did not yet have a collective sense of where they stood in their nation's rapidly changing political order. There were clues but not yet clear political imperatives in their errand. Among them evangelical entrepreneurs like Brown, Benson, and Pepperdine certainly possessed the clearest outlook. Triggered by twists and turns in their personal lives, professions, and theology, they approached the postwar period aligned with a cadre of powerful but still marginalized conservative businessmen who sought to challenge the New Deal order. In the coming years, these Christian capitalists would help build a movement strong enough to roll back the New Deal legacy. Over the next decade, their objectives would become more consciously political, their strategy more concretely partisan.

During the late 1940s, southern plain folk and preachers would begin to see their politics clarified too, though mostly in oppositional terms to liberal citizens native to California. As proud progressives and protectors of the New Deal, these activists looked to carry out their own errand for the nation. In stark contrast to the southern evangelical mission, their mandate called for Californians to extend the Social Democratic principles of Roosevelt's vision. The collision of these two missions would prove scarring for southern evangelicals and set them loose from their political moorings. It would also create a crisis of conscience. Thinking they were the solution for America, southern evangelicals would find themselves categorized as its biggest problem.

II

SOUTHERN PROBLEM

The members of our churches are threaded into the life of our land. The church life through these members is woven into the whole fabric of our social, economic, political and industrial life, like the warp is threaded into the woof of the garment. Let church members take their religion seriously, let them make it a matter of daily living, let them translate it hourly into conduct, character and conversation and this land of ours will be filled with the glad tidings of salvation.

—SOUTHERN BAPTIST STAMINA, 1941

In the opinion of the writer, the southernizing of California is becoming a real factor. . . . By this I mean that California is becoming a state as southern in influence as the states largely contributing to its population; namely, Texas and Oklahoma. On all sides can be sensed a general change of attitude toward the Negro, due to the impress of this southern influence on almost every activity within the community.

—FLOYD COVINGTON,
LOS ANGELES URBAN LEAGUE, 1940

4

LABOR WARS

We now have Roosevelt Democrats, Wallace Democrats, Truman Democrats, Regular Democrats, Liberal Democrats, American Democrats, and Russian Democrats. All are yelling at the top of their voices, saying different things at the same time. Their only unity is in noise.[1]

—BOB SHULER
Methodist Challenge, 1946

WHITE SOUTHERN EVANGELICALS FOUND TWO STRIKINGLY different sides to Southern California, one bright, glittery, and exhilarating, and the other dark, dull, and foreboding. During the volatile war years, they concluded that liberal progressives, earnest New Dealers, and radicals represented the region's ominous side. Liberal progressives had a very different view of things. To them, southern evangelicalism promised damnation for their region, not its salvation.

No one was more wary of his region's split personality—or southern evangelicalism's deleterious effects—than its most famous resident chronicler, Carey McWilliams. Trained as a lawyer, he began moonlighting as a writer in the early 1920s under the tutelage of America's foremost muckraker, H. L. Mencken. Following his mentor's lead, he set out to expose the "quacks and swindlers, fools and knaves" that seemed to roam freely in California's Southland. With wit and irreverence, McWilliams peeled back layers of Southern California to expose its dark side—those he believed to be its corrupt corporate bosses, crazy cultists, and rabble-rousers. Of his home's array of undesirable denizens he wrote memorably in 1946, "I hated . . . the big, sprawling, deformed character of the place. I loathed the crowds of dull and stupid people that milled around the downtown sections dawdling and staring, poking and pointing, like villagers visiting a city for the first time. I found nothing about Los Angeles to like and a great many things to detest." Yet, "in all the world," he admitted reluctantly, there would never be "another place like the City of the Angels. Here the American people were erupting, like lava from a volcano; here, indeed, was the place for me—a ringside seat at the circus."[2]

Although already accomplished as a lawyer and essayist by the late 1930s, McWilliams hit his stride in the early 1940s as an activist. Like Mencken, who became a national figure for his coverage of evangelical "buffoonery" during the Scopes trial in 1925, McWilliams found his reputation on the rise once he set his sights on the South. Whereas his tutor had to travel to Tennessee to find Dixie, McWilliams discovered it in his own backyard. Convinced that the southern plain folk, preachers, and entrepreneurs settling in his home region represented an ultimate threat, one that could no longer be approached lightly with just the pen, he joined the fray as an impassioned crusader for progressive liberalism. The culture clash that followed was not his doing, but McWilliams's involvement lent it color and intensity, and most certainly attention.

SOUTHERN EVANGELICALS OF JEAN VANDRUFF and Helen Mattox's generation began arriving in Southern California at a politically tumultuous time. Much of the chaos centered around one grand political question: To what extent would Franklin D. Roosevelt's New Deal be extended philosophically and politically after America's last battles abroad had been won? In the main, southern evangelicals' responses to this vexing issue remained unresolved heading into the post–World War II years, though many still believed that Roosevelt's Democratic coalition best served the political interests of Jefferson and Jesus.

Yet new circumstances brought on by postwar economic turmoil triggered a crisis in their politics. Prior to World War II, while rallying behind independent-minded Democrats like Huey Long, these citizens had simultaneously protested corporate capitalism and the bureaucratic state. Their defense of local institutions and determination to "pull down the rich" and "raise up the spiritual state of the nation" were absolute. Simplistic and at times incoherent, this agenda nevertheless fit loosely within a New Deal Democratic coalition that made equal room for commitments to class and Christian creed. In the political tumult that surfaced after the war, southern plain folk witnessed the swift dissolution of this vision. The point of contention between California Democrats was the degree to which an emboldened labor movement would set the party's future course. A Huey Long–style movement called Ham and Eggs fanned this debate and, in fact, elicited bloody clashes over the workplace, housing, and race reform. For those on the Democratic Left, Ham and Eggs illustrated the damage done to industrial unionism and social democracy by popular religion. For those on the Right, Social Democrats' furious response to Ham and Eggs offered further proof that organized labor and its accomplice, the centralized state, had become political leviathans that threatened a free America. Caught in the middle, southern evangelical plain folk, along with their tent-making pastors and prophets, looked for an alternative path that maintained their notions of individualism, economic security, racial privilege, and Christian community. By the time the labor wars came to an end, they realized that this third way—Huey Long's way—was neither efficacious nor possible.[3]

THE SOUTHERN PROBLEM

For Social Democrats, wartime demographic change had already left little doubt that the evangelical populists from the South were a problem. Progressives like McWilliams dreamed of an illustrious future for California inspired by the New Deal's reformist spirit, in which government would actively facilitate racial tolerance, economic equality, religious ecumenism, cultural pluralism, and international cooperation. In general terms, they aspired to a liberal cosmopolitanism that shunned parochialism of any kind. So with intensifying panic they watched southern "provincials" settle around them, growing anxious that the "world city" they wanted Los Angeles to become was turning whiter and more Protestant and prejudiced than it had ever been. In the southern evangelical errand they glimpsed a foreboding future.[4]

In one way or another, all Californians wanted to keep their communities safe from the seedier sort they imagined arriving from the South. Besides stigma and prejudice, southern migrants faced "bum blockades" (security checkpoints at the state line), police harassment, and political initiatives designed to forestall their settlement in the Golden State. One of the architects of an "anti-Okie" petition drive was Thomas McManus, who summarized California's devastating view of southern sojourners: "No greater invasion by the destitute has ever been recorded in the history of mankind . . . they will soon control the political destiny of California. We must stop this migration or surrender to chaos and ruin." California's liberal progressives were therefore not alone in their worry about southern migrants. Yet, as people who desperately wanted their state to be a paragon of inclusiveness, they approached this issue with questions peculiar to their politics: How might a nation aspiring to be more tolerant, ecumenical, and internationally aware seek to instill these values in a constituency driven by extreme prejudice for tradition, individualism, and autonomy? For impatient iconoclasts like McWilliams, the issue was even simpler: When would American society finally shed its racism, redneckism, and revivalism and enter the modern age?[5]

The seeds of this anxiety had been planted in the 1920s, as southerners began to migrate north and west, yet for McWilliams and fellow progressives, the fear of southernization intensified considerably during World War II as migrants poured into Los Angeles' defense industries and blue-collar suburbs. Worried observers became certain that white southerners clustering on Los Angeles' poorly regulated, peripheral space would remain maladjusted and would be able to turn their unsupervised neighborhoods into communities full of foul religion and racism. A 1940 government study by McWilliams fed this apprehension. Using findings from his fieldwork in Bell Gardens, he called on the State to overhaul its planning and welfare systems in this "unincorporated," "unplanned," and unpleasant "marginal area." The précis read like a stern warning: Should policy not change on assimilating this southern subculture, the consequences would be grave. Throughout the war years, other researchers issued similar cautions. In these suburbs, where "hundreds of square miles of land fringing agricultural and industrial centers alike have been chipped up into mean, disorderly and insanitary [sic] developments," one official lamented, there existed a "potential civic problem" of enormous proportions. A matter of blighted land use certainly, this "problem" was also a political one that promised to "make any exercise of eminent domain much more complex," whether it be in terms of zoning policies or race restrictions. Meanwhile, a few grassroots activists stressed behavioral problems over poor planning when assessing the crisis. In 1942, one anxious reformer attributed the "danger of outright segregation" in Los Angeles' outlying areas to "the southernizing of attitudes and conditions." Regardless of their particular point of view, in the early 1940s it already seemed possible—even likely— to liberal progressives that unplanned sprawl was allowing the worst traits of Dixie to flourish in Southern California.[6]

In one way these assumptions were grounded in fact; in another way, they were overstated. Nevertheless, they got serious traction in civic politics. Racism did accompany southerners to Southern California, and it would stay with them, not soon (and in some cases never) to be expunged from their worldview. Threaded through their errand was a presumption of white superiority that manifested itself in several concrete ways. Besides supporting race restrictions in housing and labor, for instance, southern evangelicals also deemed it paramount that white and nonwhite parishioners worship under separate ministries. This was a belief entrenched in a segregationist complex buttressed by a Christian folklore of white privilege. It was also a well-formed Protestant theology that said each racial group had to internalize Christ's teachings on its own terms. In keeping with this belief system, southern evangelicals demanded mission churches for racial minorities—African American, Japanese American, Latino, and Chinese—yet saw no contradiction in celebrating them as evidence of "multicultural cooperation" within their faith community. Racial assumptions also punctuated the Head, Heart, and Hand philosophy, which envisioned Christian vocational training as a means of uplift for the South's poorest white people, that last stronghold—as Bob Shuler once told John Brown University students—of "pure Anglo-Saxon blood." Pepperdine College acted on this assumption. For a decade after its founding in 1937, it allowed black students to enroll in school programs but not to live on campus, meaning the South Central Los Angeles campus stood as a bastion of whiteness.[7]

At the same time, liberal activists often glanced over the nuances of local southern culture and ignored their own ingrained prejudices. In truth, white southerners acted out a range of racial biases, all of which were destructive but few of which prescribed lynch-mob violence; while some fire-breathing preachers like Shuler employed an overtly offensive racist language to evoke pride in white Americanism, most southern evangelicals exhibited racist attitudes and behavior forged from a lack of exposure to multiracial environments and perpetuated by the homogeneity of their institutions. Moreover, liberal activists spent little time trying to understand the belief system that undergirded this community, or wrestling with some of the deeper socioeconomic challenges that plagued its

members as well. White southerners were subjects to study and a people
to pathologize, not citizens with whom to sympathize. By pinning a great
deal of the social problems that surfaced during the early 1940s on southern whites, Southern Californians overlooked other core values of community fastened to in this citizenry's conscience. They also found an easy
catchall for their anxieties about Los Angeles' other structural injustices
and bigotries, which flowed in multiple directions. Indeed, while ready to
condemn white southerners for their intolerance, California liberals, like
other native residents, displayed ample impatience of their own. Unfair
generalizations and disparaging stereotypes flowed freely through local
discourse about the strange "Okies" and "Arkies" in their midst.[8]

Whether aware of it or not, rank-and-file southern evangelicals fell
under close watch as their presence in California increased. The heaviest
scrutiny came from the region's spirited, left-leaning custodians of California liberalism. This constituency's singular approach to the southern
problem stemmed from a distinctive set of concerns rooted in social experience, as well as a firm belief that it had the most to lose by an ascendant white South. Driving the Social Democratic movement was a cadre
of activists who had found their political voice in California's vibrant
Popular Front, a movement generated by radical labor activists under
the auspices of the Congress of Industrial Organizations (CIO). Helping mobilize this constituency were men like Philip "Slim" Connelly, the
communist firebrand who acted as secretary-treasurer of the Los Angeles
CIO Industrial Union Council and inspired the CIO's left-leaning Political Action Committee (CIO-PAC). Providing its public face, meanwhile,
were celebrity figures like actor Orson Welles and state Attorney General
Robert Kenny, independent leftists who helped promote sweeping racial
and social reform and support the Popular Front's and CIO-PAC's campaigns on behalf of civil liberties and labor rights.[9]

This core constituency benefited from the support of several other
communities. Middle-class Social Democrats were suspicious of the political radicalism seen in the Popular Front, but they exhibited the same
devotion to ideals of pluralism. These dedicated New Dealers were confident in the ability of an educated bureaucracy to reform society. John
Anson Ford, a Methodist and a member of the Los Angeles County Board
of Supervisors, brimmed with this type of self-assurance. One of his
proudest achievements was the formation in 1943 of the County Human
Relations Commission, the primary governmental organ for combat-

ing intolerance in Southern California. Ford's activities were supported by ecumenically minded clerics affiliated with the Federal Council of Churches, who formed the backbone of interfaith organizations like the Los Angeles County Committee for Church and Community (LACCC). Guided by the spirit of their one-time leader, Bishop G. Bromley Oxnam, these clerics downplayed denominational distinctions in order to facilitate social policy initiatives for the eradication of bigotry and unemployment. They also dreamed of a united Judeo-Christian faith that could guide the nation toward a new international order of peaceful interdependence. Many African Americans shared this dream. The heart of their community was Central Avenue, running south of the city's downtown core. By the early 1940s this district was bustling with activity because of the southern black migrants that settled there. These citizens, in addition to strengthening churches like the esteemed and socially engaged Second Baptist, affiliated themselves with several secular institutions. Under the direction of Floyd Covington, the Los Angeles Urban League was one of the most important of these, while under Connelly's the CIO was another. Connelly eventually became editor of the *Daily People's World,* the communist organ that ranked second in importance among politically active blacks only to the *California Eagle,* the African American newspaper owned and edited by Charlotta Bass, whose work at Second Baptist and in the community made her an institution in her own right.[10]

No other activists matched the steadfastness Los Angeles' Jews brought to the Social Democratic coalition. During the 1930s, this constituency had grown to 130,000. In the 1940s, it rode a migration surge from the East Coast that continued until the early 1950s, when it numbered 315,000. Decidedly more Democrat in their partisanship than Los Angeles' native Jewish population, the newest Jewish arrivals saw political action as essential for protecting their freedoms. By now the region was a hotbed for anti-Semitism, ranging in intensity from the staid British Israelism, a trans-Atlantic philosophy of Anglo-Saxon superiority that colored the sermons in some Protestant churches, to the confrontational Silver Shirts and Brown Shirts, responsible for bookstores, chapels, and militias that proclaimed loyalty to Hitler. In answer to the threat, Jewish communities built a network of counterintelligence agencies. The most prominent of these was the Community Relations Committee (CRC), which functioned simultaneously as a civic protective group, public relations organization, and surveillance agency.[11]

The Social Democratic front that zealously tackled California's southern problem was, therefore, a multifaceted one that fed off different negative impressions of the South. Some, like Ford, saw white southerners as a challenge to principles of the common good, while others, like Connelly, saw them as the enemy of class revolution. While the white South conjured up the odiousness of Jim Crow for Los Angeles' black community, for other ethnic communities the threat registered as a challenge to civil liberties. Catholic and Protestant ecumenists saw southern religion as an obstacle to interdenominational cooperation. Their common cause, however, brought these liberals together—with Carey McWilliams as their key spokesman. Indeed, in many ways, the journalist-turned-activist provided the connective tissue between each of the coalition's separate parts. As much as he enjoyed satirizing Southern California, and despite his crusty demeanor, McWilliams was also a tall dreamer, deeply committed to the place. In his grand vision, Southern California was blessed with a uniquely multicultural environment in which citizens were witness to an experiment in civic nationalism that embraced all peoples, regardless of faith, color, or class. Should Southern Californians pass this test, surely the rest of the nation would follow suit. "Here," he proclaimed, "America will build its great city of the Pacific, the most fantastic city in the world."[12]

A grand vision indeed, yet McWilliams was not so idealistic as to ignore its immediate implications for party politics. During the Depression, California underwent a monumental shift in political alignment. In the 1930s, with economic dislocation capturing the citizenry's political interests, California Democrats finally achieved a breakthrough in this Republican stronghold. They played pivotal roles in engineering Roosevelt's electoral victories in 1932 and 1936, and gained the state house for themselves in 1938 with Cuthbert Olson's gubernatorial win, the first by a Democrat since the 1890s. Olson's victory was sweet yet short-lived—he lost to Republican Earl Warren in 1942—but California's Social Democrats remained committed to his New Deal vision. Their primary intentions during the last stages of World War II thus remained simple: to ensure that the reformist zeal of the New Deal continued to guide the Democratic Party, and ever more so, if possible, toward the Left. At the state level, they wanted Democrats to regain control of Sacramento. By mid-decade they faced a number of challenges toward these ends, not the least of which came from within their own party. Ardent anticommunist Democrats like Samuel Yorty (and ex-Democrat Jack Tenney) threatened to silence the Democratic Left and these candidates' populist appeal promised to attract the state's new Democrats from the South. In white southern migration, Social Democrats thus saw a potentially unfavorable tipping point for their party and the state.

This was the political scenario liberal progressives faced by war's end, but, by and large, they remained focused on the threat that white southerners posed to their experiment in multicultural nationalism. Social Democrats in fact held hope that solving the sociological dimensions of the southern problem was key to the whole equation; assimilate white southerners into liberal understandings of self and society, and surely party politics would take care of itself. As of 1945, this formula seemed to be working. Rallies promoting tolerance, like the "United We Stand" assemblies featuring celebrity speakers Orson Welles and Edward G. Robinson, were galvanizing the city against the twin evils of racism and fascism. Meanwhile, in blue-collar suburbia activists were carrying out "National Evenings," gatherings for "singing, dancing, and sketches designed to familiarize the audience with the cultural contributions of various sections of our national community." As advertised, these evenings targeted "Negro, Mexican, Jewish, Middle European, Oakies, Arkies, Americans All." Cross-cultural understanding like this received a boost from the LACCC, which, in one five-month stretch, conducted over one hundred sixty meetings to promote social unity. Notable gains by organized labor, the vanguard of Social Democratic activism, were yet more reason to suspect good things ahead. By late 1944 *Fortune* magazine declared that labor's wartime advances had broken through Los Angeles' impregnable citadel of anti-unionism. With peace abroad imminent, Social Democrats celebrated yet another milestone that portended exciting steps toward their overarching goal. On June 26, 1945, fifty-one nations gathered in San Francisco signed the United Nations Charter. Attended by some of Los Angeles' most prominent Social Democrats, including labor leader Philip Connelly and Methodist luminary G. Bromley Oxnam, the momentous occasion provided abundant reason for liberal activists to celebrate.[13]

As energizing as these developments might have been, Social Democrats faced the last days of World War II sensing that political passions were about to boil over. Competing Democratic dreams for Southern California now emerged in full relief. Bolstered by recent gains, Social Democrats entered the postwar years determined to extend the New Deal imperative. Conservative Democrats made it clear that they intended to bring down the Left. And southern evangelical plain folk found themselves drawn directly into the fight. Having spent the late 1930s and early 1940s building homes, churches, and communities aligned with their priorities, these pioneers now saw clearly what others in their political party and society thought of them, and the reality more than unnerved them; it demanded they respond. A series of curious events that began unfolding in the summer of 1945 triggered a collision between these constituencies. As Californians struggled through economic reconversion, southern evangelicals became enamored with the Ham and Eggs organization, a populist holdover from the 1930s. Outdated and in some ways outlandish, the movement nevertheless assumed a significance that transcended its idiosyncrasies by setting the stage for realignment. Social Democrats saw in Ham and Eggs frightening images of a society overrun by unchecked provincialism. Southern evangelical crusaders saw it as a way to offset the modernist ideologies they identified with Social Democrats. Action and reaction hence led to a volatile state. The only consensus that existed between warring factions was one of perspective; as Southern California went in the postwar period, so would go the rest of the nation.

THE RETURN OF HAM AND EGGS

It began with a few words hastily typed. Hunched over his desk one evening, in April 1945, the Pentecostal prophet Jonathan Perkins drafted a letter to Gerald L. K. Smith, the one-time chaplain for Huey Long and now vitriolic anticommunist crusader based in Detroit. Wartime Los Angeles had not been good to Perkins. Once a popular Assemblies of God preacher, he was now working shifts at the factory and scraping by with a few dollars earned by pamphleteering. Banned from his denomination, he wrote to Smith as a disenfranchised cleric and disillusioned citizen, yet nevertheless with clarity of purpose. He told Smith that the time was right to organize evangelicals behind a vision of religious revival, economic reform, and political change. Imagine if America were to embrace again the principles of Jefferson and Jesus and the legacy of William Jennings Bryan and Huey Long?[14]

Perkins wrote Smith on behalf of a renewed Ham and Eggs movement. Formally known as the Retirement Life Payments Association, Ham and Eggs was the most sensational of eighty different old-age welfare schemes that had been proposed in California during the 1930s. Its founder, Robert

Noble, a former divinity student and radio announcer, had cut his teeth running the California office of Huey Long's Share Our Wealth organization. Noble was so devoted to the Louisiana senator, in fact, that he draped himself across Long's grave during the politician's funeral in 1935, a performance captured by the national media. After his mentor's death, Noble looked to carry on the Louisianan's quest to redistribute America's wealth by lobbying Congress for an alternative currency—"scrip money." His idea was not too different from Bryan's Free Silver plan: By putting more money in citizen's hands, government would ease their financial burden, raise their purchasing power, and essentially "reflate" the economy. Noble saw this plan as a cure-all for the Depression. On his radio broadcasts he demanded that the state issue scrip to every unemployed person over fifty. "Twenty-Five Dollars Every Monday Morning" became his motto.[15]

Before Noble could transform his plan into a major player in California politics, he was blindsided by conniving brothers Willis and Lawrence Allen. Willis, a shady businessman, had once been found guilty of mail fraud for distributing a hair-darkening tonic called Grey Gone that purported to turn gray hair brown but actually caused it to fall out. Lawrence was a lawyer and more diplomatic than his brother, but just as thirsty for political influence. Unceremoniously, at a board meeting at Clifton's Cafeteria, Willis and Lawrence seized control of Noble's pension organization. "Against this super brother-act," Carey McWilliams sneered, "Robert Noble was a sand bank against a tidal wave." The Allens then hired a savvy salesman from Shreveport, Louisiana—Roy Owens—as their "engineer-economist," and one-time Upton Sinclair ally Sherman Bainbridge as their spokesman. A respected economist and Democratic politician, Bainbridge brought instant credibility. It was Bainbridge who gave the movement its popular name when, in a casual reference to the difficulties of securing food for the elderly in times of hardship, he told an audience "We must have our ham and eggs!" Within months, Ham and Eggs claimed a statewide membership of 362,000 and a supporting constituency of approximately one million people.[16]

Aggressive marketers, the Allens pursued support from a wide demographic. Building on Noble's plan, they lobbied for a state warrant bank to issue thirty "one-dollar warrants" each week to every unemployed Californian over the age of fifty. The scrip could be redeemed for food, but it would also be considered legal tender for the payment of state taxes. This, combined with a 3 percent gross income tax on all persons and corporations, was the Ham and Eggs solution to problems facing all Americans, regard-less of age. The organization's newspaper, *Ham and Eggs for Californians*, ran cartoons showing what could happen if senior citizens were allowed to retire comfortably on their weekly allowance: Younger men would receive promotions into positions vacated by retirees, allowing them to buy homes for their families, women would be allowed to stay home and raise their kids, and delinquent teens would find their way into the workforce. This proposal troubled many voters, but it resonated with the rank-and-file in Los Angeles' blue-collar suburbs. To them, Ham and Eggs offered a com-monsense response to economic inequalities that promised short-term gov-ernment relief without undermining their independence and pride.[17]

Despite its strong support from California's lower echelons, Ham and Eggs failed to achieve legislative success, but it came close. In the fall 1938 election, the Ham and Eggs ballot initiative lost by the slightest of mar-gins (defeated by a vote of 1,143,670 to 1,398,999). While the respectable showing allowed Ham and Eggers to force a special election in 1939, it also crystallized opposition. Business leaders argued that Ham and Eggs' plan would further destabilize the economy by replacing a struggling but proven currency with a worthless one. Others questioned the proposed reorgani-zation of state finances that would see extraordinary power bestowed on the administrator of the warrants and tax-revenue systems. They pointed out that if Ham and Eggs passed, this administrator would be Roy Owens. A ninth-grade dropout, Owens lacked formal economic training and, according to critics, worshipped "the colored God" of the black religious leader Father Divine and his female "chocolate angels." The censure that had the most damning effect was the link between Ham and Eggs and the Left. William Schneiderman, executive secretary of the Communist Party of California, lent credibility to this charge when he said that all progres-sive-minded people needed to support the Allens' measure "as a means to defeat the reactionary 'economy' block and re-inforce the people's man-date for social security and recovery measures, the fight for which must be pressed by the New Deal." The Allens also made broad overtures to indus-trial labor, leaving them vulnerable to further scrutiny from the corporate middle class. The criticism mounted in the weeks leading up to the special election in November 1939. Following a campaign whose intensity rivaled or exceeded that of Sinclair's End Poverty in California campaign of 1934, a record 82 percent of registered voters turned out and soundly defeated Ham and Eggs, 1,933,557 to 993,204.[18]

In 1945, the Allens resurrected Ham and Eggs. Anxious to take advantage of the discontent created by postwar economic reorganization, the brothers started a new referendum initiative for the fall 1946 election. Hoping for a better outcome, they made two adjustments to their 1930s formula, both targeted at one of California's fastest-growing constituencies: blue-collar southern evangelicals.

Ham and Eggs, the Allens decided in the first place, needed religion. They knew that success would depend on their ability to court lower-class Christians just arrived from the South. Institutionally, this meant reaching out to the congregants of the hundreds of churches that encircled Los Angeles' defense industries. The path to these voters came through their preachers, and the preacher who could access this world like few others was Jonathan Perkins. Having canvassed for some of the state's most popular political movements, including Ham and Eggs' rival organization in the 1930s, the Townsend Plan, Perkins was well-connected to the region's politicized pastors. His ability to bridge the ideological gap between popular evangelicalism and the right-wing fringe helped too. In 1945 Perkins published a booklet titled *The Modern Canaanites or the Enemies of Jesus Christ*. Widely distributed by British Israelites, this polemic against Jews made Perkins famous to a network of racist right-wingers. Perkins's real impact, though, came from his relationships with tent-making apostles in the city's modest evangelical churches, and it did not take long for him to earn the Allens' trust by brandishing these ties. Shortly after joining Ham and Eggs, Perkins assembled the California Pastors' Committee to fight Nazi-Communism, comprised mainly of Pentecostal and Baptist ministers but also of celebrity clerics like Bob Shuler. Estimated at one thousand members but likely numbering far fewer, this council of clerics immediately began mobilizing their flocks behind Ham and Eggs.[19]

The Allens also succeeded in one other critical repackaging of postwar Ham and Eggs: They turned it into an anticommunist organization. Stung in the 1930s by their links to the Left, and cognizant that anticommunist sentiments animated their new constituency, the Allens presented the new and improved Ham and Eggs as a patriotic, authentically American initiative based on democratic principles. They wanted to assure their evangelical followers that lobbying for economic reform was not the same as advocating collectivism. With Perkins having written his appeal on their behalf, the Allens entered into an agreement with Gerald L. K. Smith whereby he would tour California for Ham and Eggs but also be allowed to promote his own Christian anticommunist organization. The deal was enticing for Smith, who saw Los Angeles as a new base for political operation. After the death of his boss Huey Long, Smith had moved to Michigan with the intention of picking up his mentor's fallen scepter and becoming the people's next champion. The move produced mixed results. Despite the strength of his anticommunist organization, the Committee for One Million (later the Christian Nationalist Crusade), which in 1943 claimed one million members and media access to almost forty million listeners, Smith failed in his quest for a Republican nomination for the Senate. The result left him embittered toward "Wall Street Republicans and their Jewish friends." Shortly thereafter, mounting financial and legal pressures and opposition from local officials had Smith looking west for a change of pace. Their deal with Smith was equally beneficial for the Allens. By mid-fall Smith was responsible for doubling the number of subscriptions to the Ham and Eggs newsletter and forcing the organization to look for bigger auditoriums. Throughout the campaign the Allens would remain "tickled pink" with Smith's ability to generate publicity, even of the most frequent, negative kind. They would also learn the heavy price that came with this devil's bargain.[20]

HUEY LONG'S LAST STAND

The Allens' plan was nothing less than the resurrection of Huey Long's "Share Our Wealth" campaign to "make every man a king." By appealing simultaneously to the economic interests and conservative religious values of working-class Christians, they believed they could carve out a third way between the industrial unionism and progressive liberalism that animated the Left, and the strident antistatism that energized the Right. Ham and Eggs, in other words, attempted to meet plain-folk evangelicals in the middle. Proud in their self-sufficiency, these citizens welcomed government and, to some extent, unions' checks on corporate capitalism but only if it empowered them in the marketplace. They welcomed state efforts to level class distinctions through equalization plans and wanted the federal government to function as a safety net in times of need, but they preferred that it stay out of their lives once times got better. Whatever its contradictions, "Share Our Wealth" was a mantra that still made sense to this crowd, and the Allens wanted to tap that familiar and comforting logic.

From May 1945 through June 1946, Ham and Eggs advanced this

agenda through local rallies for rank-and-file workers as well as at special crusades hosted by Smith designed to attract middle-class Californians with anticommunist priorities. Although the large crusades would get the headlines, it was the local rallies that offered Ham and Eggers the most substantive hope. In community halls throughout the state, neighbors gathered to sing, speak, and listen to a message of empowerment based on workers' rights and religious commitment. It was a fleeting moment, not to be repeated again in the postwar period, in which common laborers called forth in unison the virtues of Christ and the CIO.

Perkins took charge of Ham and Eggs' ground-level attack and used his pulpit and pamphlets to turn the movement into a full-fledged evangelistic campaign. At a downtown Los Angeles meeting in fall 1945, with the "rattle and clatter from passing streetcars outside on Hill Street," Perkins invoked the unencumbered life he and many of his listeners had experienced back in Oklahoma and claimed Ham and Eggs would restore it. He also advertised his booklet *The Preacher and the State*, which attacked preachers who, in his mind, had abandoned their Christian defense of the poor and joined the "unions of the rich" (the Chamber of Commerce) to protect the rights of property. Though he knew some evangelicals were torn about promoting social justice rather than individual salvation, Perkins reminded the crowd that they should not ignore "plain scripture on economic matters." What they had to do, Perkins proclaimed, was stretch their political awareness beyond the narrow confines of charity and involve themselves in affairs of the state. "Ham 'n' Eggs' plan [is] outlined in the Bible. If the ministers can't see this, or won't," he thundered, "get some new ministers! We must wake up the preachers and the politicians!"[21]

Perkins' effort to blend working-class imperatives and evangelical ardor grew more important throughout the fall of 1945 and into spring of 1946. At one meeting in March, for example, a platform of preachers listened to Leslie G. Taylor, executive secretary of the CIO's shipyard union in San Pedro, discuss Ham and Eggs' "economic education" of the common worker; on another day Taylor and his compatriots were treated to a sermon by a Methodist preacher and a selection of gospel favorites sung by Rev. James Warren Lowman, a regular soloist at Ham and Eggs meetings. Lowman's rendition of "The Stranger of Galilee" was preceded by the heartrending testimony of Laguerre Drouet, a former Water and Power employee of twenty years, American Federation of Labor (AFL) member, and World Wars I and II veteran, who had converted to Ham and Eggs after reading Perkins's *The Preacher and the State*, which had revealed to him "God's Law" and that "Labor deserves a break." Organizational changes reflected Perkins's influence as well. With increasing frequency, Ham and Eggs meetings were scheduled on Sunday afternoons so that people could proceed in their finest dress directly from church to meeting halls, where they were treated to orations that resembled homilies more than speeches. Perkins's efforts delighted the Allens. Speaking before supporters, Willis Allen boasted, "The ministers opposed Ham and Eggs in the last campaign, but I am sure that they won't in this campaign, because of what Jonathan Perkins [is telling] them."[22]

While Perkins's religious stumping ran smoothly, Smith's anticommunist crusade proved far more volatile. It began well, on May 27, 1945, when the Allens introduced Smith to an audience of five hundred Ham and Eggers. Four nights later, before an invitation-only crowd of two thousand gathered in Los Angeles' Embassy Auditorium, they heralded him as Ham and Eggs' great hope. Smith was joined on stage at this larger rally by a greeters' panel that included local radio commentator G. Allison Phelps; Claude A. Watson of the Prohibition Party; F. C. Woodworth, superintendent of the Southern California District Council of the Assemblies of God; and Bob Shuler, who opened the meeting with prayer. To Smith's glee, upon his request for audience members to indicate if they were ministers, over three hundred people raised their hands. Perkins had promised a "parade of Fundamentalist preachers" behind Ham and Eggs, and early returns suggested his bravado was not an empty gesture.[23]

Smith's appearance in Southern California sparked great excitement among the region's evangelical citizens. For the next six months the Smith-led rallies, designed to support Perkins's local gatherings, became the movement's focal point and made for great public spectacle. At Los Angeles' Polytechnic High School Auditorium on November 3, 1945, three thousand supporters arrived for an evening of revivalist preaching, old-time hymn singing, and political barnstorming. Willis Allen led the audience in the Pledge of Allegiance and "The Battle Hymn of the Republic" and announced that Ham and Eggs had reached 495,000 supporters committed to the redistribution of wealth "among the people regardless of color, class or creed." Allen then introduced Smith "as representative of 3,000,000 'thinking people . . . and 21 patriotic groups." To the thrill of the crowd, Smith leaped to the podium and into a diatribe against "the mangy Reds!" With both hands clasping the microphone and a venomous snarl on his face, Smith descended into a seemingly uncontrollable (but in fact choreographed) rant, eliciting shouts of approval from the audience and finishing with the promise that the "stinkin Reds can't run me out of this town!" As if turning off a light switch, he regained his senses and announced that it was time for prayer.[24]

After supplication by the pastor of Trinity Baptist Church, Smith resumed his sermon by navigating the same anthology of maxims that had fueled his politics since the 1930s. He began by listing his friends and enemies: Philip Connelly and the CIO (foe), Jack Tenney (friend), Orson Welles and Hollywood Jews (foe), Henry Ford (friend), schoolteachers who love Stalin more than Lincoln (foe), fascists who picket public gatherings (foe). In the closing minutes of his speech, Smith turned somber and lamented the hardships that had befallen average Americans because of the New Deal Left. He invited his audience to think about what their fight against an overbearing state meant for their communities and their status as free individuals. Lest they forget the grand purpose of their struggles, Smith then invoked the spirit of his mentor, Huey Long, reciting the eulogy he had composed ten years earlier to honor the slain Louisiana statesman. "'The lives of great men do not end with the grave. They just begin. This place marks not the resting place of Huey P. Long, it marks only the burial ground for his body. His spirit shall never rest as long as hungry bodies cry for food, as long as lean human frames stand naked, as long as homeless wretches haunt this land of plenty.'" Fifteen minutes later, Smith brought the valedictory to a close with typical hyperbolic panache: "'His [Long's] unlimited talents invariably aroused the jealousies of those inferiors who posed as his equals. He was the Stradivarius, whose notes rose in competition with jealous drums, envious tomtoms. His was the unfinished symphony.'" Sensing the poignancy of the moment, Smith closed the meeting with a recitation of a Longfellow poem and prayer. The meeting adjourned, Perkins and his brethren shuffled out of the dank auditorium into the crisp, Southern California night.[25]

MOBILIZING FOR DEMOCRACY

Smith's arrival on the West Coast shocked Social Democrats. In the wake of the initial Smith–Ham and Eggs meetings in May 1945, they expressed panic that the red-baiter might make a permanent move to Los Angeles, perhaps to succeed the late Aimee Semple McPherson at her imposing metropolitan church, Angelus Temple. Knowledge of Smith's activities in Detroit buttressed these fears. In the wake of Detroit's race riot of 1943, which resulted in thirty-four deaths and tremendous damage to this "arsenal of democracy," Michigan's own network of Social Democratic agencies had pinpointed white southern plain folk and preachers—especially high-profile ones like Smith and J. Frank Norris—as the cause. Other comprehensive studies concluded that over one thousand "little church communities" of white southerners had been set up in houses, basements, and abandoned stores, led by between 2,500 and 3,500 southern "Baptist" itinerant preachers eager to southernize Detroit. White southern migration had remade Detroit into a "Bible Belt," one observer noted, "not as illiterate but just as devout as the 'Bible Belt across the deep South.'" All of these reports overestimated the cause-effect relationship between southern transplants and the riots; Detroit was a caldron of racial tension because of several unrelated factors. Just the same, the perception that Smith and a band of southern clerics represented trouble quickly transferred west to Los Angeles and immediately escalated with the emergence of Ham and Eggs. Aware of his hometown's readiness to serve as a hothouse for Smith's ideology, Carey McWilliams warned: "Because we live in a community that has spawned some curious cults and weird movements . . . we are inclined to dismiss these recent occurrences as merely another manifestation of erratic conduct induced by a climate that . . . makes people grow lax and hysterical. We make a serious mistake, however, to dismiss these recent events as crackpotism."[26]

Once the initial furor died down, Social Democrats began planning their defense. Following an emergency meeting of the LACCC, called just days after the public unveiling of the Smith–Ham and Eggs alliance, religious leaders contacted the Assemblies of God headquarters in Missouri to find out about Perkins's pastors' committee and were initially relieved by the reply from General Secretary J. Roswell Flower. In the first of two letters, Flower discussed Perkins's "unedifying" activities and his "perverted conscience in all such matters." According to Flower, Perkins had "played a trick" on the district office in Pasadena by stealing a mailing list which he then circulated under the auspices of the California Pastors' Committee to fight Nazi-Communism. A follow-up letter from Flower was more troubling. Yes, Perkins and Smith had measurable followings among Assemblies of God pastors, Flower admitted, but efforts were being made to curtail the influence of such agitators. "Assemblies of God ministers as

a whole are not bigoted," Flower concluded, and "we deplore the extrava-
gances which are found in the Pentecostal movement, but, by the grace
of God, we are endeavoring to avoid these extravagance[s] . . . and we
believe that the Lord has blessed us in the holding up of a high standard
of holiness and Christian living." Flower's pledge to rid his denomination
of renegades might have been sincere, but he knew California Pentecostals were heavily involved in the Ham and Eggs movement; even his own
district superintendent, F. C. Woodworth, was a supporter. Indeed, Woodworth's involvement with Smith and Perkins, along with the active support
of other established ministers, suggested that a significantly larger portion
of plain folk and preachers supported the crusade than originally assumed,
and not just because they had been hoodwinked. While many of these
people seemed conflicted about the sharper racist and anti-Semitic notes
in Smith's rhetoric, all found his ideological tenets to be reasonable.[27]

With gathering speed triggered by this discovery, Social Democrats
increased surveillance, sending spies sponsored by the Community Relations Committee to Ham and Eggs meetings. Working as individuals or in
pairs, CRC operatives infiltrated Perkins's local gatherings, and in threes,
fours, or larger groups they attended Smith's massive rallies, then submitted typed reports. No detail went unnoticed; they documented the
smells of the meeting hall, the sounds of the singing, and the speeches
and emotional response in the crowd. In their specifics, CRC findings
were invaluable, for they brought to life a religious world that still seemed
so foreign and in many ways incomprehensible to Social Democrats. This
data also helped them create a counterstrategy and a countermovement
called Mobilization for Democracy (MFD).

Led by McWilliams, Orson Welles, and State Attorney General Robert Kenny, MFD devised several countermeasures for the fall of 1945.
Its activists first tried to secure an injunction from Los Angeles officials
prohibiting Ham and Eggs' use of school auditoriums like the one at Polytechnic High. MFD introduced the motion at a school board meeting on
October 14. With 500 representatives of 250 civic organizations present
and McWilliams, Eddie Cantor, and Socialist Workers Party leader Myra
Tanner Weiss delivering speeches on its behalf, MFD implored school
officials to outlaw the Ham and Eggs meeting scheduled to take place
two nights later. The basis of MFD's argument was that Smith threatened
social order in encouraging a "form of violence anathema to free speech."
The American Civil Liberties Union (ACLU) saw things differently, how-

ever, and defended Smith on the grounds that MFD's petition itself was the "savage blow at free speech." The defense won the debate and school board members voted to allow Ham and Eggs the use of Polytechnic auditorium, stating, in the process, that they were not a censoring body.[28]

Irate over this decision, MFD activists reverted to simpler, more devastating tactics. First they sparked a recall of Meade McClanahan, a city councilman who frequented Ham and Eggs rallies. McClanahan's Thirteenth District—the battle zone—was a working-class community of bungalows and apartments (including the one Perkins inhabited) that also included pockets of affluent liberals and radical artists. MFD mounted a smear campaign against McClanahan, putting up posters with the politician's name below photographs of Hitler, calling him a "peanut politician," "Negro-hater," "Jew-hater," "labor-hater" and the dupe of businessmen and "backward people." McClanahan's defenders met the barrage by canvassing local churches, while a Committee of 500 (comprised mostly of pastors and women) fought the recall street by street. Despite these efforts, the MFD handed McClanahan a humiliating defeat that left him financially bankrupt and personally despondent. Writing to Smith in the wake of the recall election, a glum McClanahan admitted, "It is a very hard blow to me and my family. . . . I have been recalled and my reputation for having linked myself with you is so reprehensible in the eyes of so many that I feel practically down and out." Even as the recall played out, MFD activists adopted a second strategy of picketing Smith's rallies. At the infamous October 16, 1945, meeting, for example, fifteen thousand banner-waving citizens circled Polytechnic's auditorium. As MFD literature would later proclaim, the protestors delighted in unity:

> Hundreds of servicemen and Legionnaires were in the line, together with masses of AFL and CIO unionists, Jewish, Negro, Mexican people, women, students, civic leaders and citizens from all walks of life. Thousands of signs and banners were carried. Loud speaker trucks were used for slogans, announcements and short talks. The picketing lasted for three hours. It was Los Angeles in action against Gerald Smith.

In the wake of the rally, Ham and Eggers complained to city officials and Mayor Fletcher Bowron promised to control the picketers. On November 3 protestors again appeared at Polytechnic but were met by police. While Smith waxed eloquent on Huey Long's legacy inside the auditorium, police outside arrested seventy-nine of the most belligerent demonstrators. In frustration, MFD marched to the Olympic Auditorium, where they held a spirited mass meeting of their own.[29]

To the dismay of city officials, the confrontations involving Ham and Eggs escalated in the coming months, galvanizing an alliance of right-wing opponents. Although not necessarily in agreement with the Ham and Eggs agenda or supportive of Smith, conservative Democrats and allies gathered from Republican groups, middle-class evangelical churches, and business associations had contempt for a common adversary. Writing to Bowron about his own involvement with Ham and Eggs, Shuler spoke for his cohort when he suggested that Smith, though reprehensible as an individual, represented a much larger struggle against evil forces that threatened the country: communism, secularism, and moral degeneracy. Such a cause was worth fighting regardless of who stood next to you in the trenches. But there was more to this unity than a shared enemy. These groups had grown increasingly wary that communist radicals in government, mainline Protestantism, organized labor, and Hollywood were creating a new political establishment that wanted to extend the power of the New Deal state to extreme ends.[30]

As tensions mounted with MFD, Ham and Eggers thus found themselves the beneficiaries of support from a more expansive right wing, especially those who had once been invested in California's New Deal Democratic coalition. Both Samuel Yorty and Jack Tenney supported Ham and Eggers out of solidarity and political opportunism, but Tenney did so with particular pomp, appearing at Ham and Eggs meetings to offer the heartrending story of his personal conversion to the Republican Right. Shuler's involvement with Ham and Eggs became crucial now too. Still a registered Democrat but independent in his political activity, he quite literally stood at the collision point between Ham and Eggs and MFD. On the night of Smith's October 16 meeting at Polytechnic, Shuler had taken a beating that left him bleeding and raging mad. Following the ruckus, Shuler drafted a letter to Bowron describing in great detail MFD's aggressive tactics. When attempting to enter the auditorium, Shuler wrote,

> I was set upon by this mob, with policemen looking on, was kicked, struck over the head with a stick and twice pushed to my knees. I was cursed, called a son of a bitch by a Jewish girl, though I had never spoken a word and did not say a word. I saw an old lady, trying to enter

the building, soundly beaten by two young women. Finally the old lady turned and left, crying as she went. . . . There was no picket line in front of that High School building. It was a mob. It was a mob in action.

Shuler compared his experience to a lynching: "I know a mob. I stood by the side of the Sheriff of Lamar County, Texas, until a mob that burned two Negroes trampled us down and went over us. This mob [MFD] was just as malicious and mischievous . . . as was that mob." Shuler was turning the southern problem on its head: Dixie was rising in California because belligerent union leaders and communist agitators were willing to risk violence in order to defend at any cost a permanent and intrusive New Deal state.[31]

If Shuler had kept his comments private, opposition to MFD might not have gelled so quickly. But throughout the Ham and Eggs campaign Shuler voiced his frustrations from his pulpit and on the editorial pages of the *Methodist Challenge*, by now one of the more widely read periodicals on the West Coast, both by politically conscious evangelicals and religiously curious political conservatives. His editorial of October 1945, titled "That Mass Meeting," was typical for the way it sought distance from Ham and Eggs while championing its cause. "I do not belong to any movement with which Gerald Smith is associated," Shuler began, "But between the crowd that gathered at the Olympic Auditorium, with their cries of 'Kill Smith, Kill Smith, Kill Smith,' and the orderly audience that sat in the Shrine Auditorium and heard Smith on the same night, there can be no choice for any good, sound Christian American."[32]

Accosted by the Left, bombarded by the Right, Ham and Eggers soon felt embattled. By now they were convinced that "political agitators" on the Left were muscling them out of their God-given rights of political expression. One woman wrote to Smith: "I know I am sounding very radical, but golly, it's been proven, over and over and over again, that by being fair, and mild and meek, one loses against the rabble rousers. They use strong tactics, yet so subtle, that the ordinary man becomes confused in his mind." But while disgusted with the Left, Ham and Eggers were equally disillusioned with Tenney and Shuler's Right. These citizens were in agreement with Tenney and Shuler about the dangers of communism, secularism, union bureaucracies, and a New Deal political machine, but they were not willing to give laissez-faire capitalism a free pass or completely jettison New Deal programs that had benefited them. With the 1946 election approaching, they faced a conundrum. Should they lean Left with those who sympathized with their economic plight but vilified their religion, or should they lean Right for the sake of a united Christian, conservative front?[33]

For the Allens, prospects did not look good in the spring of 1946. The MFD's counteraction had begun to corrode their movement's public support. As spring wore on and Ham and Eggs seemed unlikely to secure the necessary signatures to get on the fall ballot, the Allens knew they had to commit to one or the other side. Though battered by political circumstances, many Ham and Eggers were still convinced that they could hold the middle. Perkins remained their loudest advocate, but he too was growing leery of the Right's disregard for Ham and Eggs' Christian-laborer identity. In spring of 1946 Perkins wrote to Smith, "I fear that some of your recent statements concerning strikes are unfortunate, and that they sound Anti-Labor," but "in your heart I know you to be a friend of Labor. I intend to oppose Communism as strongly as ever, but I also intend—God willing—to defend the right of Labor . . ." In Smith's absence, Perkins stated his position more forcefully. "I don't want Communism, but I don't want the rich standing with their feet on the necks of the poor anymore, either. We are being foolish to defend the rich against Communism. We have been fighting to protect the rich and not ourselves."[34]

Unfortunately for Perkins, the Allens had tired of both of them. As spring turned to summer, Willis Allen wrote Smith to tell him that their alliance was now too risky for maintaining relations with AFL and CIO brass: "As you know, many leaders of both A.F. of L. and C.I.O. are strongly opposed to you. It is essential that we have their friendship and support if we are to win and we have found it necessary to assure both these organizations that we are not expecting to have you out here for our campaign." Knowing Smith planned to return to Los Angeles later that summer, Allen finished with a plea that he "not come to California now because it would not help your cause any and certainly would in all probability prevent us from gaining our position on the ballot." In a stunning reversal, the Allens then agreed to back an MFD gubernatorial candidate, Robert Kenny, in the upcoming Democratic primary. Kenny pledged a constitutional amendment that would "provide an adequate system of pensions and work opportunity," thereby gaining the support of the purported 492,000 Ham and Egg members, and in return Lawrence Allen was promised the office of state attorney general should Kenny become governor in November.[35]

For Ham and Eggers, the Allens' shift made no sense at all. At a meeting in mid-May, Lawrence Allen tried to justify the new tactics, saying they would optimize the Ham and Eggs political position for the fall election. Already agitated, the overflow crowd became even more upset when it was revealed that Perkins had resigned in protest. Perkins explained that he was not willing to "be swallowed up by Kenney [sic], the Pal of the Commies." Evidently neither was Ham and Eggs' blue-collar, evangelical majority. With Perkins gone, these Christian workers abandoned the cause. Appropriately laced with the apocalyptic imagery of Revelation, the last two sermons they heard on behalf of Ham and Eggs were delivered by Texas preacher J. A. Lovell to half-full auditoriums in late May and early June. One was titled "Goodbye Capitalism" and the other, "Goodbye Communism," but they might as well have been titled "Goodbye Ham and Eggs," for the movement's fate was sealed in the June 4 Democratic primary when Republican incumbent Governor Earl Warren cross-filed his candidacy and outpolled Kenny in the attorney general's own party. Ham and Eggs once again found itself on the outside looking in.[36]

So ended the uneasy alliance of revivalist religion and economic radicalism. In the end, Ham and Eggers were forced to choose between Christ and the CIO. Meant to bridge these interests, Ham and Eggs effectively served as a wedge that drove them apart. Larger political forces in a way overrode this organization's best intentions. By inviting Smith to join their crusade, the Allens embroiled it in fierce ideological warfare. Then, by turning left, they outraged evangelical citizens who had joined expecting Ham and Eggs to take up Huey Long's fight for rank-and-file ideals of home, church, community, and guild. Southern plain folk now saw their leaders, cowed by an assertive band of Social Democrats, asking hardworking citizens to renounce their rights as white, Bible-believing Americans in return for labor hegemony and a permanent welfare state. This realization caused them to revisit long-held assumptions about their place in the Democratic Party and, more generally, American politics.

OPERATION DIXIE

With Ham and Eggs and its pre–World War II political ideals disintegrating, Southern California's local plain folk and preachers found themselves without a clear vision or voice. They did not know how they would fit in the postwar political world. Even as Ham and Eggs collapsed, the conundrum grew more complicated as battles with radical labor on the shop floor and in the neighborhood reached a climax. By early spring of 1946, protests against corporate cutbacks and downsizing around the country culminated in nationwide work stoppages in the largest auto, steel, and electronics industries. America's workforce, emboldened by union gains during the war, was desperate for immediate financial relief and determined to fight for increased control over its means of production. Rank-and-file evangelical citizens in California grew nervous with organized labor on the march. What disturbed them was that financial security no longer seemed like the sole concern or even the base proposition of these union drives. Cultural order, not class solidarity, now seemed to rest in the balance.[37]

The CIO's Operation Dixie drove this point home. In 1946, with hopes of capitalizing on wartime gains, CIO political strategists undertook a quest to organize the South's lowest-paid employees. From the beginning their endeavors met stiff resistance from residents who correctly sensed that the CIO had an ulterior motive. By penetrating the ranks of southern industry and proposing interracial solidarity among black and white workers, CIO activists also wanted to challenge Jim Crow. Their goal was to initiate a "Second Reconstruction"—an all-out assault on systems of racial oppression and economic inequality. They knew this would be unpopular, but they were unprepared for the viciousness of the reaction. Business leaders portrayed CIO actions as communist ploys. Incensed white supremacists employed even harsher rhetoric: Should the CIO's organizing drive succeed, they said, blacks and whites would not only share the same unions but also become lovers and co-conspirators in the creation of a mongrel society. In the face of such opposition, Operation Dixie ultimately foundered by 1950, leaving the South a bastion of free market capitalism and, for a few years more at least, a Jim Crow stronghold.[38]

In its initial stages between 1946 and 1948, however, the early, hopeful success of Operation Dixie was exactly what white southern evangelicals in California feared most. Some of their apprehension was attached to political initiatives that the CIO undertook locally on behalf of fair employment practices. In 1946, Social Democrats aligned with the CIO-PAC managed to get on the ballot Proposition 11, a statewide Fair Employment Practices Commission (FEPC) bill meant to ensure fairness in hiring, firing, and promotions in industry, and essentially destroy patterns of racial bias. Though they failed to see it passed, Social Democrats could claim success for FEPC-style reforms. The pro-labor *California Eagle*, for instance, announced the employment of black GIs at the General Motors plant in South Gate as a significant break in "the Jim Crow policy of hiring in Los Angeles" and a sign of bigotry's loosening grip on Los Angeles. Viewing Southern California as ground zero in the CIO's national campaign, southern evangelicals thus anxiously read their church papers for news of developments in the South and connected them to their own experiences on the West Coast. Operation Dixie was not necessarily disturbing on economic grounds; Baptists or Pentecostals who attended church together often worked together in the same factories, and the sense of loyalty they brought to their congregations often spilled over into a sense of responsibility for their place of employment. Church membership did not automatically negate union membership or devotion to the protection of workers' rights. It was the total political package radical labor leaders envisioned that made southern evangelicals suspicious. As many had witnessed firsthand in Ham and Eggs, those in command of the CIO brought with them a host of issues that offended conservative Christian sensibilities on multiple levels.[39]

The fear of losing white racial privilege was certainly one critical concern for southern evangelicals, but in their rhetoric, at least, it was trumped by a fear of losing religious privilege. Operation Dixie was, above all else in their minds, an attack on the South's Protestant core. Their anxieties quickly spiraled outward from unease with circumstances in the South to distress over the plight of the nation. Just as the CIO's southern drive heated up, Southern Baptists, for instance, read in their denominational organs how the Federal Council of Churches was promoting unionization below the Mason-Dixon line. Liberal Protestants affiliated with the FCC were indeed heavily invested in the southern labor campaigns, working with CIO organizers to reach workers through rallies, seminars, and even colorful comic books with titles like *The Bible and the Working Man*, which proved that "unions were Christian." Though unwilling to critique conservative clerical involvement in the labor wars, white southern evangelicals openly resented the fact that liberal religious leaders provided so much energy for Operation Dixie. In their eyes, ecumenical authorities working within the Social Democratic alliance were using their religious activism to prop up a political agenda, and flaunting their political agenda to acquire religious advantages. Gone was any semblance of church-state separation; liberal mainline Protestantism now seemed unshakable in its intent to use government power to affect social change.[40]

Of even greater concern was the fact that Catholics were heavily invested in the crusade. California's southern evangelicals learned that northern Catholics were working hard to convert southern laborers. Southern evangelical leaders emphasized that they were not opposed in theory to Catholics proselytizing their home region. "We want them to have full religious freedom and rights all over the world," one diplomatic Baptist pointed out. The problem, however, was that Catholics could not be expected to reciprocate. How, other, less diplomatic critics asked, could a religion "just as totalitarian as Nazism in Germany, or Fascism in Italy, or Communism in Russia" be expected to allow democracy to flourish? Southern fears of Catholic incursion into the labor pool thus spun easily into anxiety about Rome's rise in national affairs. Signs of capitulation seemed everywhere, including the White House. Shortly after the war President Truman agreed with Pope Pius XII to station a United States "representative" at the Vatican, selecting Myron C. Taylor for the role. Convinced the move was made to legitimate the power of the Catholic Church, evangelicals lobbied for Taylor's resignation as "ambassador" to the Vatican and claimed victory in 1950 when Truman asked Taylor to step down. Yet this was just a minor victory, California's southern evangelicals proclaimed, in an ongoing defense against the expansion of Catholic power.[41]

Catholic internationalism usually reminded southern evangelicals of a more imposing liberal juggernaut: the United Nations (UN). It would take time for them to develop a comprehensive critique of the UN, but first impressions were overwhelmingly unfavorable. Watching closely as liberal luminaries like G. Bromley Oxnam assumed a seat at the table at the UN-'s founding conference in San Francisco, evangelical pundits published reports exposing the UN as a godless society set on destroying America's Christian foundations. That the UN purportedly changed plans to open its first session in prayer because of Russian dissent was galling enough, one observer wrote, but the fact that liberal religious leaders like Oxnam allowed this to happen *on American soil* was absolutely unacceptable. Surely, he added, they did so out of solidarity with their communist friends in California labor, union men like Philip Connelly and Harry Bridges who were there to witness the gathering. Reading such negative assessments, southern evangelicals internalized a number of criticisms of the UN, for instance that it inhibited American foreign policy and weakened American national culture. Amid the labor wars, though, the accusation that rang truest for them was that the UN was the logical end to the Social Democratic agenda: It started with workers' rights and ended with a new political program for humanity. The UN's Universal Declaration of Human Rights, drafted in 1948 and presided over by champions of the New Deal, made southern evangelicals certain that the industrial unionism of the CIO visionaries was only an initial step toward world domination. Union politics might have been local politics, but southern evangelicals knew it had universal implications.[42]

Even still, in postwar California local politics is where union politics played out with clearest intent. Whereas fears of losing control of their workplace panicked evangelicals into thoughts of the world's end, fears of losing their neighborhoods elicited a more focused and ferocious response. An issue of grave concern earlier in the decade, housing resurfaced as a civic crisis in the late 1940s as war veterans returned to Los Angeles. In 1948 Governor Earl Warren estimated that his state needed an extra 900,000 new homes to house the estimated 850,000 GIs who had settled here after the war. A housing shortage was one source of the problem, but the more vexing one was that even when homes were available, white Angelenos insisted they get to decide who occupied them. While white property owners systematically excluded nonwhites from renting their apartments, they also used restrictive covenants to prevent them from buying property next door. As late as 1946, eighty percent of Los Angeles' residential property fell under such codes. In the immediate postwar years, struggles to end this system of apartheid turned quiet communities into clamorous ones. Violent battles occurred in places like Pasadena, Glendale, and Eagle Rock, but they were especially bad to the south of the city, where the housing shortage produced the most hurried construction of affordable homes; this was a region whose social composition was still in flux and lack of regulation allowed residents, real estate agents, financiers, and developers to set its future course. Americans of all racial and ethnic origin wanted to plant their families there. Conflict was inevitable.[43]

With uprisings like Ham and Eggs quelled and workplace reforms under way, Social Democrats turned their attention to this next contested sphere. In early 1947, Mobilization for Democracy and another leading civil rights organization, the Civil Rights Congress, amalgamated under Robert Kenny's chairmanship, "launched a campaign for 5,000 new members and organization affiliations" and marshaled them to combat race restrictions in hot zones like Compton. Eager to display its new, coordinated strength, MFD set several strategies in motion, one being to notify "all CIO local unions . . . in the Compton, South Gate, Lynwood areas, that their membership should be warned not to sign any restrictive covenants, whether sponsored by the Veterans War Memorial Corporation or the Compton Chamber of Commerce." MFD activists, energized by the Ham and Eggs struggle, made formidable gains, but they faced equally determined opposition from the locals, many of whom had likely been Ham and Eggers.[44]

The battle that ensued between Social Democrats and homeowners was every bit as dramatic and southern in flavor. White southerners were not the only residents upset. County officials like John Anson Ford were inundated with letters from white citizens of all kinds who feared black encroachment. By allowing blacks to move into her neighborhood, one anxious woman explained, her community would see a reduction in its tax base and the exiting of a "higher class of people." But in the stream of angry letters there were plenty of southern-inflected tirades. W. F. Hoffman's was one of the most straightforward: "I am sure that you just do not know the nigger. You have always lived in your own world of high personal pride and honor and have only looked at him with the wrong end of the telescope in your eye." Ford replied:

> You as a Southerner, know the Negro situation in a way that I, a Northerner, cannot know it. . . . [But] many good Southerners while keenly aware of the deep problems of the Negro situation, are determined to improve the relations between the two races. . . . I am of the opinion that a Southerner rather than the Northerner can find and are finding the answers to this most difficult of problems.

Correspondence between civic leaders and white residents certainly exposed southern segregationist sympathies, but it was the return to Los Angeles of Gerald L. K. Smith that lit the fuse. In a way, Smith never left; through his paper—*The Cross and the Flag*—and other writings that he bundled together and mailed to churches and service clubs throughout Los Angeles, Smith's opinions about housing politics remained relevant. But his investment in the controversy increased once he began a lecture tour to drum up support for his own political machine, the Christian Nationalist Crusade. With a growing sense of dread, spies working for the Community Relations Committee reported that meetings like the one held in Convention Hall on December 8, 1946, portended Smith's rising popularity. On this evening, before a stately audience devoid of "rabble-rousing" elements, Smith railed against "the refugees taking up all the housing that rightfully belongs to 'our boys who fought to protect us.'"[45]

As their battle against Smith intensified, Social Democrats began documenting Ku Klux Klan activities. The key to defeating the restrictive covenant, left-wing activists asserted, was to defeat the Klan. The Council for Civic Unity (CCU) held screenings of a documentary called *The Burning Cross* and distributed circulars titled "UNI-FACTS," which at one point in 1946 purported eighteen different Klan-related incidents in a ninety-day period, including cross burnings on the University of Southern California's campus, where "KKK" was also "daubed on the Trojan statue and at seven places on the administration building." The same newsletter noted a raid by Robert Kenny's office on a Klan meeting place in Los Angeles that "netted a 10-foot cross, studded with light bulbs, thousands of pamphlets, and several dozen hooded white robes." Meanwhile, the MFD published reports of Klan operations in its newsletter and discussed it on the radio. Invariably these warnings blamed racial violence in part on indifferent law enforcement and government officials.[46]

Smith's agitation on the far Right and MFD's activities on the Left drew moderates into the mix. Responding to the MFD on a series of evening radio addresses in the fall of 1946 titled "It Is Happening Here," Los Angeles Mayor Fletcher Bowron countered critics by saying that police had investigated the Klan incidents and found them to be pranks. Drawing on an article published in *Reader's Digest* by George Benson, Bowron then warned his listeners that MFD was a communist organization "undertaking a campaign—to throw fear into the hearts of many persons." The day after his radio broadcast, in a letter to DeWitt Wallace, editor of *Reader's Digest*, Bowron slammed the MFD for "frightening Negroes with the Ku Klux Klan bogey and making Communists out of them." In his estimation, the MFD was a rogue organization whose "emotional appeals . . . would outdo . . . Aimee Semple McPherson in her palmiest days." Bowron ended his note by suggesting Wallace publish a story about Southern California as a lesson for the nation. "I believe there is much material here in Los Angeles for an article that would convey timely warning to the American people of what is going on in our country in the name of democracy."[47]

As Bowron fought the MFD on the radio, a quieter campaign by Social Democrats achieved the most significant legal victory of their postwar crusade. In 1946 white homeowners in the upscale Sugar Hill neighbor-hood of Los Angeles tried to prevent several wealthy African Americans from moving into the community. Among the shunned was actress Hattie McDaniel, who had recently won an Academy Award (the first ever for an African American) for her role as Mammy in *Gone with the Wind*. In a case that quickly made its way to the California Supreme Court, the white residents charged that their black neighbors had broken Sugar Hill's racial covenants. The African American residents filed a robust counter-action. A brilliant young lawyer and advocate, Loren Miller, who was, for all intents and purposes, a black Carey McWilliams, led them. Dur-ing the 1930s Miller had joined Langston Hughes on a trip to the Soviet Union to observe its economic programs. Upon his return to Los Angeles, clearly inspired by this experience, Miller spent the rest of the 1930s and early 1940s as a leading constituent of the Communist Party, an editorial-ist with Charlotta Bass's newspaper, the *California Eagle*, and a dynamic public spokesman for civil and human rights.[48]

Fiery and charismatic in person, Miller was spellbinding in the court-room. Working under the auspices of the National Association for the Advancement of Colored People (NAACP), Miller represented the Sugar Hill defendants and, by pointing out technical flaws in the covenant sys-tem and rendering ludicrous the idea that white racial purity could be a prerequisite for residence in any community, won the historic case. McWilliams wrote that Miller's heart-stopping performance before the California Supreme Court drew an audience of the "brightest social lights in the Negro community." Like the Sleepy Lagoon appeal McWilliams had litigated a few years earlier, the Sugar Hill case electrified Southern California's Social Democrats and gave Miller extra incentive to take the fight to the federal level. In 1947 he and fellow activists in the NAACP argued before the Supreme Court that restrictive covenants were socio-logically damaging to blacks and that states worked against the Constitu-tion when sanctioning these discriminatory agreements. In May of 1948, the Supreme Court handed down its historic decision in *Shelley v. Krae-mer* that effectively abolished restrictive covenants in the United States.[49]

When the decision was reported in Los Angeles, African American citizens and their Social Democratic allies were overjoyed. "California Negroes Can Now Live Anywhere!" cried one headline in the *Los Angeles Sentinel*. Next to a picture of Hattie McDaniel's palatial home, another proclaimed, "Homes Like These No Longer 'Out of Bounds.'" Unlike the failed 1946 FEPC campaign, the Sugar Hill and *Shelley* cases suggested that Social Democrats were winning the labor wars. Three years after McWilliams and his interracial coalition of leftist and liberal activists had entered the fight, these constituents felt that the southernization of their society had been rolled back. Surely they concurred with the *Los Angeles Sentinel* when, in October 1948, it announced, "Jim Crow Is Dying" in Southern California. And they likely agreed with another newspaper, which wrote glowingly that Southern California "could be used as a fine model for future improvement in race relations in many sections of the United States." In the coming few years it would become obvious that the Social Democratic sense of accomplishment was premature. The South—a new South—still had much to say about the direction of Southern California politics.[50]

SOUTHERN EVANGELICALS WEATHERED THE labor wars feeling entangled in a gnarled web of ideologies, interests, rhetoric, and reaction. Even the supremely confident Bob Shuler became demoralized. Throughout the Ham and Eggs affair, Shuler's opinions in the lengthy editorial section of the *Methodist Challenge* grew more pointed and acerbic, his voice more shrill. In April 1946, when Ham and Eggs first seemed headed toward collapse, Shuler lashed out at MFD, labeling it a terrorist organization "fronting for the Reds." In July of the same year he rejoiced at the outcome of the June primaries in which Kenny went down to ignominious defeat. "Mr. Robert W. Kenney [*sic*], whose brave fight on Gerald L. K. Smith won for him the unanimous Communist support for Governor of California, is now a wiser and sadder man," Shuler wrote with great satisfaction. "Mr. Kenney's high card was his fight on the Ku Klux Klan," but "it didn't fire" because "it was a dub, a blank"; there was no Klan, just radical left-wingers who wished there to be one for their own "political capital." What the primary results really showed, Shuler concluded, was that voters had "grown weary with the C.I.O. Political Action Committee" and had gone to the polls ready to declare "their independence of such iniquitous leadership." Unfortunately for Kenny and the Social Democratic Left, the angry preacher added, "You can't fool all of the people all of the time."[51]

But Shuler floundered when trying to offer his readers a future direction. In fall 1946 Shuler penned a short commentary aptly titled "Befuddlement."

As a dyed-in-the-wool southern Democrat who longed for clear-cut options, Shuler lamented his party's loss of coherence. In previous periods of disorder, he had cast his vote for (and run on) Independent and even Republican tickets. But what he observed in the immediate aftermath of World War II stood out as an exception. At the national level, the party of his youth was fractured, with Democrats of all kinds "yelling at the top of their voices, saying different things at the same time." None knew how to answer the labor question; none could predict whether their party would adhere to the Social Democratic vision of the New Deal or pursue a path toward a limited state; none seemed to know which path a majority of American citizens preferred. In Southern California, the future for southern Democrats seemed even bleaker. Realizing this, Shuler seemed ready to offer at least one piece of helpful advice. California's southern evangelicals deserved to know when they had passed a point of diminishing returns, he wrote, the point at which their party no longer seemed worth fighting for. Shuler suggested that this moment had finally arrived.[52]

5

NEW ALLIES

Dr. George S. Benson, the President of Harding College, has been doing a most effective work throughout the country and over the air on behalf of our American way of life. Because he is literally a crusader and because, too, his appeal has been to the common man, I am unhesitatingly giving him my support.[1]

—J. HOWARD PEW, 1947

WHERE BOB SHULER EMPHASIZED "BEFUDDLEMENT," GEORGE Benson stressed opportunity. Benson was on the road promoting his vision of Christian capitalism when the Ham and Eggs affair erupted. In a form letter to supporters in 1946, he proudly laid out his operation: a weekly column, which now appeared in 3,500 newspapers around the country, monthly bulletins to 25,000 "carefully selected addresses, including many labor leaders," a dramatized radio program "done by professional talent in New York" heard weekly on 56 stations in 31 different states, a weekly comment in more than 20 labor journals, and a lecture schedule that had Benson talking to "labor groups, civic clubs, women, colleges, and high schools." In each context he hoped to "re-sell the American public on the value of Constitutional Government and Freedom of Individual Opportunity." "In a Republic where national matters are decided by popular vote, it is imperative that the public be impartially informed," Benson proclaimed.[2]

His drive impressed benefactors, especially J. Howard Pew. Sun Oil Company's chief executive declined to give money when Benson first approached him in the early 1940s, but now he began mailing Benson checks. He also continued to recommend his friend to fellow corporate executives as someone who could relate to people from all walks of life. In a letter to the president of Gillette Safety Razor Company in Boston, Pew wrote that Benson was doing the "best job of anybody" at selling free enterprise "because he appeals to the great middle class of people." "Representing as he does a very small college, and having no ax to grind other than that of the welfare of the American people, he is free of the taint of propaganda." In a letter to the chairman of a sugar refining company in San Francisco, Pew reiterated that Benson was a crusader who did well with the "common man." Pew's endorsements thrust Benson into a new realm of success and helped spark a right-wing revolt. During the last years of the decade, Benson tapped the affluence in Pew's realm of high finance to expand Harding College's extensive Christian free enterprise curriculum. Benson's allies were pleased with Harding's success, but what really thrilled them was the way this educator envisioned a united conservative movement that could begin rolling back the New Deal. If there was anything to be gained from the labor wars, corporate conservatives like Pew surmised, it would be the awakening of the American people to the desperate plight of capitalism, and if there was anyone who could draw the American people to this painful recognition, Benson seemed to be the man.[3]

BENSON'S ACTIVITIES WERE PART of a bold political venture that conservative businessmen and intellectuals began carrying out in the late 1940s and early 1950s to combat what they thought was an entrenchment of a permanent New Deal, social welfare state. A few victories against organized labor in the legislative arena invigorated this budding coalition, but their accomplishments were short-lived. Pressured by the Right, President Harry Truman's Democratic Party purged itself of left-wing influences and shifted to the center, away from the most ambitious Social Democratic impulses. Meanwhile, the national GOP shifted to the middle by promoting an agenda that welcomed a corporate-labor partnership and state involvement in the economy. Dwight Eisenhower's 1952 electoral win confirmed this stand and set the tone for a decade of "modern Republicanism." In response to the centrist turn, conservatives stepped up their mission to build new grassroots associations and lobbies, hoping to push their president and party toward the right.

Southern California served as the lab for this endeavor, its evangelical entrepreneurialism a catalyzing force. Along with Benson, John Brown and George Pepperdine emerged as important liaisons between religious and nonreligious conservatives, elite Republicans and disenfranchised plain-folk Democrats. Recognizing a valuable teaching moment amid the labor wars, these men began dismissing Huey Long's "demagogic" populism and Gerald L. K. Smith's malevolence as ugly relics of the past. Confident these excesses could be drained from southern evangelicalism, they used their communications and educational systems to cultivate cosmopolitan sensibilities in their faith communities and connect them to the machinations of modern conservatism. It was time, they declared, that southern evangelicals shed their outsider status.

OUTLINES OF A MOVEMENT

In the late forties, as Pew assumed his letter campaign for Benson, "conservatism" was neither a coherent political philosophy nor a recognized political label. Yet, as the 1950s neared, this ideology and movement began to acquire a vague outline, thanks to several developments, past and present.

It was during World War II that "conservatism" showed signs of convergence in the parallel worlds of finance and academia. Still wounded by the Depression and the New Deal's perceived attacks on corporate capitalism, businessmen affiliated with organizations like the Chamber of Commerce, Liberty League, and National Association of Manufacturers spent the war years reorganizing and rethinking their political strategies so as to popularize their free enterprise beliefs. One breakthrough came with the 1943 founding of the American Enterprise Association (later American Enterprise Institute), which united former NAM and Liberty League experts, yet strove to distance itself from some of the inflexible, elitist laissez-faire policies these groups had propagated in the 1930s. The AEA functioned as a think tank in Washington, D.C., researching and analyzing policy and publishing pamphlets by a handful of anti–New Deal, pro–free market scholars on subjects ranging from antitrust issues and farm price supports to social welfare and Social Security. Through its communications, the AEA connected corporate conservatism to intellectual conservatism, which itself was just beginning to emerge. In 1943 Ayn Rand published her novel *The Fountainhead*, and Albert Jay Nock his autobiography, *Memoirs of a Superfluous Man*; both represented the eccentric but cultivated side of a sophisticated critique, which posited that old-fashioned American principles of free markets, limited government, private property, and self-reliance—in short, classical liberalism—had been squelched by the New Deal. In 1944 this intellectual revolt gathered steam with the founding of *Human Events*, a small-circulation newsletter, the publication of Ludwig von Mises' antistatist treatises *Omnipotent Government* and *Bureaucracy*, and most famously the release of Friedrich von Hayek's *The Road to Serfdom*. Against the backdrop of Nazism in Germany and social welfarism in Britain, Hayek argued that state planning led to totalitarianism. He urged Western societies to resume the journey on the "abandoned road" of classical liberalism. Published first in Britain, Hayek's book caused a sensation in the United States in the fall of 1944, making him a favorite on the lecture circuit and eventually opening up an academic post for him at the University of Chicago.[4]

The labor wars were the true breakthrough moment for the conservative movement. They not only rallied the Right but raised the specter of communism for a broader middle-class citizenry. Teamed principally with right-wing Republicans, but assisted by southern Democrats, the emerging conservative coalition exploited this mounting fear and this opportunity to secure a major victory for the GOP in the 1946 congressional elections, then score a key legislative win in 1947. In June of that year, over President Truman's veto, Congress passed the Taft-Hartley Act. Seen as a repeal of the pro-labor Wagner Act of 1937, this measure prohibited sympathy strikes and secondary boycotts, required all union officers to sign anticommunist loyalty oaths, and, most importantly, permitted states to pass right-to-work laws that made union membership only a voluntary condition for employment. These tenets struck a substantive blow to labor, but more importantly a devastating hit on its perceived power. Organized labor's wartime momentum now seemed stalled.[5]

In actuality, the Taft-Hartley Act was not the final conquest business conservatives had hoped for, but it was a launch for further political action just the same. The passage of Taft-Hartley came in large part because of a new mood within liberalism, which after 1947 pressed for further moderation of the New Deal vision. In stark contrast to the economic restructuring called for by Social Democrats and the CIO, liberals within the Democratic Party set different goals. Influenced by John Maynard

Keynes, they instituted an economic plan begun in the late 1930s, which asked government to stimulate growth by investing in the public sector and "priming the pump" of private consumption. They also demanded compromise in the workplace. Union officials purged their constituencies of communists after the Taft-Hartley Act, and by the end of the decade a depoliticized CIO joined the AFL in calling for collective bargaining power as the supreme goal. Gone were the dreams of an egalitarian society. Business, too, made sacrifices, but they were hardly as burdensome as a radical CIO would have demanded. Collective bargaining and Keynesian economics meant that unions and an active state would be equal partners with business in cold war economic life. In 1948, Truman defeated Republican Thomas Dewey by presenting a platform friendly to business yet still respectful of labor's and government's expanded role. In 1952, Dwight Eisenhower frustrated conservatives with a similarly centrist platform that acknowledged the modern necessities of an active, welfare state.[6]

Though unsatisfied with what they viewed as tepid political steps, business and intellectual conservatives saw in them further reason and hope for political insurgency. While the short spurt of right-wing legislation allowed them to expand their base, the entrenchment of a new liberal order convinced them that much work yet needed to be done.

Southern California's business conservatives were primed for the next step. Propped up by powerful chapters of the Chamber of Commerce and NAM in Los Angeles, business interests had held their own against labor's advances in the early 1940s. Then, political developments on the Left after the war bolstered the Right's fortunes. Even in the midst of their campaigns for fair employment and housing practices, Social Democrats lost ground in California's Democratic Party. In 1949, a purge of communists in California's CIO, including veterans like Slim Connelly, fractured the union and essentially disenfranchised the broader Social Democratic movement. In a last desperate push, left-wing allies rallied in 1948 behind the Progressive Party, led nationally by Henry Wallace, before settling back into a marginal role in the Democratic ranks.[7]

Meanwhile, conservatives surged forward with capable movement leaders like Leonard Read and James Fifield. In 1938, Read became manager of the Los Angeles Chamber of Commerce, at that time the largest local chapter in the world. He immediately set out to combat the radicalism he saw exemplified in Ham and Eggs. Only a "profound educational reorientation would suffice to quell the forever babbling cauldron of erroneous doctrine," he believed. Through various campaigns, including one called Pamphleteers, Inc., which reproduced and mailed the oldest and latest works of classical liberalism to a select group of supporters, Read pursued his mission. In 1945, Read resigned and moved to New York, hoping to take his cause national. A year later, with the help of a few high-powered corporate executives and intellectual conservatives, he established the Foundation for Economic Education (FEE), in Irvington-on-Hudson, with the goal of reeducating Americans in classical liberalism. "A new generation, one which has never experienced economic liberty, is taking over," FEE's founding documents warned. "The job of economic education must be undertaken now while those who appreciate the value of liberty are still in a position to support it." By 1952 FEE's "integrated program of production, promotion, and distribution" of free enterprise thought had made treatises by Adam Smith and John Locke available to 28,712 people through a mailing list, pamphlets, study groups, radio programs, and lectures.[8]

James Fifield was an equally gifted progenitor of the libertarian renaissance. When he moved to Los Angeles in 1935, to take over leadership of the financially strapped First Congregational Church, he brought with him Spiritual Mobilization (SM), a "non-profit, non-sectarian, non-theological" organization he established that same year in Chicago to "arouse the ministers of all denominations in America to check the trends toward pagan statism." Spiritual Mobilization looked to shore up faith in capitalism among ministers and encourage business leaders to keep faith at the forefront of their activism. A talented businessman in his own right, Fifield marketed this message with great effect. From its headquarters in the Freedom Center Building on Wilshire Boulevard, SM put out a magazine entitled *Faith and Freedom*, a radio program called *The Freedom Story*, and "Pause for Reflection," a newspaper column. By the late 1940s, "more than 16,000 ministers of all denominations" were "enrolled" in Spiritual Mobilization and standing "uncompromisingly for Freedom under God." Meanwhile, in 1949, with his five-thousand-member church thriving and its debt dissolved, Fifield established the Freedom Club, a monthly lecture series. At First Congregational, guests gathered for dinner and talks by many of the country's leading conservatives on current politics. This unique forum quickly became a popular one for local residents and a career-affirming event for the nation's right-wing crusaders.[9]

EVANGELICAL CONNECTIONS

At the same time that business and intellectual conservatives began constructing a national movement, evangelicals were coalescing in new religious organizations that shared a similar agenda. The most important arose the same year as the American Enterprise Association. In 1943, at the behest of J. Elwin Wright and Harold Ockenga, leading New England churchmen, delegates from around the country gathered in Chicago for the founding of the National Association of Evangelicals (NAE). Ockenga had set the tone for this meeting one year earlier when, in a keynote address to the National Conference for United Action among Evangelicals, he lamented the fact that evangelicals had "suffered nothing but a series of defeats for decades" because the "terrible octopus of liberalism," the "poison of materialism," and "floods of iniquity" that enveloped America. Addressing the new NAE in 1943, Ockenga spoke with the same seriousness but more optimism: "This nation is passing through a crisis which is enmeshing western civilization." The NAE "is the only hopeful sign on the horizon of Christian history today. If we who are gathered here meet our responsibility . . . it may well be that the oblique rays of the sun are not the rusty red of its setting but the golden rays of its rising for a new era."[10]

The NAE, at its base, functioned as an interdenominational association for Protestants worried about liberal theological trends, but it was also a clearinghouse for activism against the "terrible octopus of liberalism." Unwilling, like business and intellectual conservatives, to stand by while New Deal liberalism extended its power over church and community, the NAE rallied to stem the tide. Its mouthpiece, *United Evangelical Action*, amplified evangelicals' political anxieties and resolve for change. This periodical offered advice on current events, monitored government policy, and disseminated complaints about Congress's acquiescence to liberal interests. The NAE's field office in Washington, D.C., supplied this information, while also filing protests that ran the political gamut. In its 1949 annual statement it reported that legislative trends were pointing to collectivism:

There are bills which could be used to control families. If they are passed, these federal medicine bills, it appears that it will not be long before you will hear of "baby crop quotas." There are bills classified

under the high-sounding phrase, "Fair Employment Practice Commission." F.E.P.C. bills . . . would open the way for large numbers of
bureaucrats, "investigators," to pry into one's personal business. It is
class legislation of the worst kind, sailing under the false banner of
civil rights. . . . If this bill passes you can anticipate the arrival of that
day when the government will tell you with whom you must work, with
whom your children must attend school, whom you must hire. The
police-state is near at hand if these bills pass.

In this same report, NAE director R. L. Decker declared that in order to
fight conspiring foes, the NAE needed to "sponsor a nationwide, evangelical 'Secret Service,'" comprised of "trusted, loyal, evangelical people in
every city and region of America who is [sic] in a place of any importance
or influence, in public life or educational or business circles."[11]

Daring in its call for evangelical counterintelligence, Decker's organization also pursued tangible goals in communications and industry. During the early 1940s, radio networks offered free airtime to ministers of
the Protestant, Catholic, and Jewish faiths. Assuming that mainline ministers affiliated with the Federal Council of Churches were the most representative voice of American Protestantism, network managers let them
provide the programming. Irate that the FCC exercised such power, and
that conservative programming suffered while liberal offerings thrived,
evangelical leaders formed the National Religious Broadcasters (NRB) to
lobby for evangelical ministers who wanted equal access to the country's
airwaves. The NAE also created the Commission on Industrial Chaplain-
cies, which sought to provide the workplace with an "applied Christianity"
that could help solve "employees' personal work problems, and at the same
time improve labor-management relations." R. G. LeTourneau, the heavy-
equipment manufacturer who relocated to the South during the late
1930s, provided the model. Highly successful during the war at building
American military might (70 percent of all heavy earthmoving equipment
used by the Allies was built in his plants), LeTourneau was also effective
at crafting an industrial chaplaincy program that encouraged his workers to participate in daily chapels and technical and theological training seminars. Employees, in turn, had at their disposal several services,
such as counseling, hospital visitation, and wedding and funeral support.
LeTourneau's desire—and by extension the NAE's—was to solve postwar
economic challenges by reasserting traditional Protestant values. "Christi-

anity is so sane, so practical, so workable, that its application brings about solutions to the unrest and turmoil that appear everywhere in our industrial society," he would say. "That is why Industrial Chaplaincy is 'Christianity with its sleeves rolled up.'"[12]

From the moment of NAE's birth, Southern California evangelicals had their "sleeves rolled up," ready to help this organization. They not only recruited the largest number and size of churches into the NAE but also saw its highest-profile institutions join this march for orthodoxy. Radio preacher and businessman extraordinaire Charles Fuller was notable in this regard. Besides attracting capacity crowds at Long Beach's Municipal Auditorium for live broadcasts of the "Old Fashioned Revival Hour," Fuller also parlayed his wealth and influence into the founding of Fuller Theological Seminary in Pasadena. Under the presidency of Harold Ockenga, and with leading evangelical theologians Carl Henry and Wilbur Smith anchoring its faculty, this school soon became the intellectual base for the "new evangelicalism."[13]

A second core institution was Church of the Open Door (COD). No other single congregation better characterized the aspirations of the NAE and Southern California's evangelical establishment. Founded in 1915 as a supporting ministry of the Bible Institute of Los Angeles, COD's impetus came from Lyman Stewart and Reuben Torrey. Stewart, a transplanted oil baron from Pennsylvania and owner of the Union Oil Company, provided the money, world-renowned evangelist Torrey the intellectual glue. The COD ran impressive publishing ventures and welcomed a steady stream of famous preachers through its doors, but its exalted status was best expressed by stunning architecture. Built in the Italian style, replete with carved pillars, archways, and a rooftop garden, COD was flanked by thirteen-story dormitory towers that housed BIOLA students. The building's crown jewel was its three-tiered auditorium, furnished with four thousand theater-style seats, an eight-story-high skylight that illuminated the entire ceiling, and the city's grandest pipe organ. The "largest set of chimes on the Pacific Coast" rang out from above the north tower, and COD's classic façade boasted two giant neon signs rising almost thirty feet above the towers that proclaimed "JESUS SAVES," which, on clear nights, could be seen for miles.[14]

This church's demographics and theological prescriptions were classically evangelical, too. Drawn from earlier westward migrations from the Midwest, characteristically white-collar in class, and Presbyterian, Congregational, or Brethren in denominational background, COD congregants personified Victorian Protestantism from the late nineteenth century. These were heirs to classical Anglo-American evangelicalism who drew inspiration from D. L. Moody and Billy Sunday and a sense of urgency from premillennialist theology. Premillennialists saw and interpreted the world through the lens of biblical prophecy as headed toward an inevitable, cataclysmic end. In contrast to the more liberal postmillennialists, who believed end times would be preceded by a period of societal perfection, premillennialists expected Armageddon would occur after an extended period of societal decay and decline. This view of the end times supported COD's other core precepts of revivalist religion. Rather than waste time on building large, cumbersome governmental and institutional structures that might ease society's problems—but likely fail and then be destroyed in the apocalypse—premillennialist evangelicals were to focus their attention on missions and evangelism, and any endeavor that gave priority to spiritual revival and personal salvation.[15]

COD's congregants displayed political preferences that grew out of their demographic profile, eschatological fears, and association with the NAE. In the 1930s, their end-times beliefs, blended with their midwestern strand of conservative thought, caused them to rail against the *isms* perceived to be at the center of the New Deal—socialism and internationalism. These were considered the ultimate examples of humanity's false hope for societal improvement, and the end for Christian America. COD members saw in Roosevelt the forerunner of the Antichrist from Revelation. The president, in their minds, had already taken initial steps toward socialism, leaving the door open for secular tyranny, serfdom, and the utter ruin of the human race. After World War II, COD's members gradually adjusted their principles in accordance with the shifting global order. In the late 1940s they exchanged their isolationist views for an interventionist approach to foreign policy, so as to endorse an aggressive anticommunist crusade by a strong, American nation-state. All the while they retained their pro-business stand on domestic issues and, as illustrated by the sermons that emanated from their pulpit, stepped up a defense of Christian individualism and free enterprise capitalism. Certainly few within its pews were as wealthy as COD's founder, but most church members believed that free market capitalism was God's preferred system for his people.[16]

In both the style and substance of their faith, California's conservative evangelicals thus harbored a worldview that was similar to that of business and intellectual conservatives. Though perhaps for slightly different reasons, the philosophical underpinnings of individualism, voluntarism, capitalism, and a limited state rested at the base of their political conscience. Besides shared loyalties to the GOP, and core precepts of its right wing, there was remarkable overlap in leadership between camps. Union Oil executives, for instance, sometimes worshipped at COD, in their free time they sat on boards at the Chamber of Commerce and James Fifield's Freedom Club, and subscribed to national organizations like Leonard Read's Foundation for Economic Freedom and, closely related, J. Howard Pew's Christian Freedom Foundation. A rich benefactor in his own right, Charles Fuller already had ample influence within Southern California's business community when he reached out for assistance in building his evangelical seminary. In the early 1950s Fuller Seminary also solicited and received help from Pew, who, in part because of respect for Ockenga, channeled funds during the 1950s to the NAE. In turn, NAE officials included him in its "inner circle"—the "Secret Service" Decker once envisioned.[17]

As of the late 1940s, however, Southern California's business and religious conservatives did not yet extend far into southern evangelical circles. For California's conservative establishment—like its liberal one—southern plain folk and preachers posed a problem. This was true even for California's native evangelicals, who viewed southern evangelicals nervously, as if they were distant cousins who deserved attention but could easily cause embarrassment if they were allowed too close. Despite a shared faith, unfamiliarity and distrust kept these two constituencies apart. The Church of the Open Door was a case in point. During the prewar period, COD's congregational culture discouraged southerners from attending en masse, both for theological and political reasons. Although it was becoming more popular in the South, most southern evangelicals did not yet feel embattled enough to embrace the kind of premillennialist theology that was preached at COD. This was true of COD's politics as well. Upon their arrival in California, southern evangelicals still saw Roosevelt as a savior of sorts and the Democratic Party as a vehicle for positive change. COD members, on the other hand, were staunch Republicans who preferred a demure politics, not the raw, fighting kind found in the western South. Huey Long–style barnstorming had no place in their pulpit or pews.[18]

Not surprisingly, rank-and-file southern evangelicals had even less reason to connect with Southern California's corporate conservatives. Few of them had time during World War II to read the works of Hayek and Rand; besides, the free market had not been friendly to them as of late. Business conservatives were equally wary of southern evangelicals and unsettled by the excesses of their radical economic thought and intemperate leaders. The way southern evangelicals railed against big business as easily as big government disconcerted them, as did the overtly racist, anti-Semitic rhetoric that seemed to accompany these rants. Southern evangelical populists, in short, were not yet natural allies for the West Coast's conservative elite.

CONSTRUCTING COSMOPOLITANS

Entrepreneurs like George Benson, John Brown, and George Pepperdine saw the potential of such an alliance, however. In their estimation, southern evangelicals held similar core values that placed them on the right side of the political divide, and their preachers and churches remained untarnished by (and already mobilized against) liberal trends. True, lingering notions of cultural superiority and class difference would not die easily. Just the same, these three men believed that through education, rank-and-file southerners would become indispensable partners in the fight against the liberal state. To this end they spent the late 1940s and early 1950s expanding their communications and educational systems in hopes of encouraging southerners to participate in broader cultural encounters, temper their racial attitudes (and especially language), and think and act in accordance with postwar cosmopolitan trends.

Of course, their cosmopolitanism was very different from the Social Democratic ideal. However much they encouraged encounter and exchange, these evangelical leaders expected it to happen in a controlled environment, with encounter taking precedent over exchange. At no point did they believe greater openness to other ideas, peoples, and modern forms of social and political organization should dilute the evangelical sense of identity or purpose. Unlike liberal cosmopolitans, they were not interested in absorbing new truths from encounters as much as they were in using new encounters to win people over to their truth. Theirs was a functional view: To reach out into the modern world was to learn how better to convert people to the Christian message. Moreover, as much as they were willing to absorb the progressive spirit of cultural pluralism, evangelical entrepreneurs did not want this spirit to lead to the dissolution of Protestant certitudes or the dismantling of the Protestant establishment. Social Democrats and liberals more generally, it seemed, were too determined to relegate religion to the private sphere (in hopes of rendering all faiths equal in the public sphere) and use the courts and federal government to enforce this new arrangement. Evangelicals believed that this eagerness to level the playing field allowed for backdoor concessions to powerful, ill-intentioned religious entities, like the Catholic Church, and a secularization of American society in a way never intended by the founding fathers. Still, even within their constricted purview, Benson, Brown, and Pepperdine heartily endorsed the notion of a culturally aware and socially engaged evangelicalism in which fellow parishioners learned to appreciate different peoples and ideas and think and act as urbane citizens—in short, as cosmopolitans.[19]

John Brown especially looked to media for help spreading this ideal. In the early 1940s the Arkansan had inaugurated his California Enterprise in order to generate higher financial yields for his educational plant. Purchased as investments in 1937, Brown's School for Girls and Military Academy were, by the late 1940s, generating healthy profits. These academies nicely assisted Brown's financial plan, but it was the 1948 purchase of Southern California radio station KGER that captured his imagination. Besides running his own radio station in Arkansas, and maintaining a half-hour radio program on Beverly Hills station KMPC in California, Brown had become heavily invested in the National Religious Broadcasters. Thanks to his and this agency's lobbying, by 1949 over 1,600 evangelical radio programs aired each week around the country. Wanting to enjoy a share of this success in the nation's fastest-growing market, Brown bought KGER and immediately replaced its country music with gospel music and cigarette advertisements with invitations to local revivals.[20]

The new KGER made an immediate contribution to the religious culture of postwar Southern California. Appealing to "people who carry the pocket books and who have the homes that build the nation," KGER became the self-designated "Station of the American Home." As a conduit of the new evangelical spirit, the station offered ministries geared to a range of conservative Protestant sensibilities. Brown's own program, *God's Half Hour*, was a staple, but many other offerings soon rivaled it in popularity, including *The Mizpah Half Hour*, produced by Long Beach First Foursquare Church, *The Radio Revival*, from the United Fundamentalist Church, *The Latter Rain Revival Hour*, offered by Immanuel Gospel Temple, and *Church of the Old Time Religion*, provided by the Bethel Church of Christ. As ecumenical as KGER's offerings were, they could also be highly specialized. Listeners wanting lessons on witnessing could tune in to *The Radio Soul Clinic*; those wanting to hear women preach could count on Olga Graves's *Gospel Friends Broadcast*; those seeking miracles could tune in to Oral Roberts's *Healing Waters*; those worried about their children's spiritual state had options like *Redemption Ranch* or *Radio Kids Bible Club*. And KGER's programming also included shows that targeted non-English-speaking Christians. Fourteen churches affiliated with The Voice of Latin-American Council of Christian Churches of Southern California, for instance, produced a weekly Spanish broadcast "meant to reach souls in outlying areas with the Gospel of Jesus Christ." It featured a choir of young people "faithful and zealous in their aim to spread the 'Good News' of salvation."[21]

Brown's vision for an integrated media ministry was perhaps best represented by two of KGER's most popular programs: *The Chosen People*, hosted by American Board of Missions to the Jews, and *Message to Israel*. Both programs were designed to connect Jews and evangelicals at an exciting moment. When Brown purchased KGER, American society was coming to terms with the anti-Semitism that had flared up during the 1930s and 1940s. By the late 1940s, evangelicals like Brown were grappling with the fact that they had contributed to anti-Semitism's high tide. On occasion, they had allowed virulent preachers to promote unflinchingly racist condemnations of Jews; more frequently, they had traded in popular anti-Jewish stereotypes. Evangelicals' conflicted theological handling of Judaism had rendered them incapable of dampening any degree of anti-Jewish hostilities. While stressing Jewish chosenness, on one hand, they also taught that Jews faced special judgment for rejecting Christ as the Messiah and explained Jews' persecution in these retributive terms. Prior to World War II, evangelicals were at once Jews' closest friends and coldest enemies.[22]

After World War II, evangelicals at once wrestled with the dawning recognition of what had transpired in Nazi extermination camps and grew excited about what they considered the Jews' much-improved fortunes in the Middle East. Those, like Brown, who adhered to premillennialism believed that Jews needed control of their homeland before Christ's return could occur. Only after the Hebrew prophets' plea for a New Israel was fulfilled would a sequence of events leading to this glorious end unfold. The founding of Israel thus offered abundant reasons for evangelicals to join Jews in celebration. Speaking on Los Angeles radio about the day the Jewish National Council proclaimed Israel a nation—May 14, 1948—one bible professor called it "the greatest piece of prophetic news that we have had in the twentieth century." Others proclaimed Israeli statehood the "most significant event since Jesus Christ was born" and a sign that "Jesus could come at any moment." With the world's end now seemingly closer, evangelicals set out to evangelize Jews before Armageddon. Proselytizing "Hebrews" was already an essential activity in evangelicalism prior to World War II, but it intensified considerably after 1948. With rising urgency after the war, for instance, COD's Jewish Department, headed by Daniel Rose, a prominent citizen and Jewish convert to Christianity, carried out an aggressive witnessing campaign. Rose's department oversaw activities that included "Jewish Witness Class," "Jewish Young People's Meetings," "Bible and Literature Distribution," and "Intercessory Prayer Groups." Rose's impact on COD was physical as well. It was he who purchased the inviting neon-red JESUS SAVES signs that adorned the church's exterior.[23]

Brown used KGER to further this evangelical appeal to Jewish Americans. To be sure, his philo-Semitism was benevolent but patronizing, and not without its own subtle anti-Semitic strain. He and others within his religious orb still viewed Jews as a peculiar people set apart for their heritage, awaiting special judgment from God. And while they heaped attention on developments in Israel, they would do so principally to learn what these trends said about their own future as faithful Christian servants awaiting their Messiah's return. Nevertheless, Brown made an effort to rid evangelicalism of the most odious xenophobia. Using KGER as his megaphone, he called on fellow citizens to embrace the Jews as allies and Jewish culture as authentic and special, and to reject those, like Gerald L. K. Smith and Jonathan Perkins, who trafficked in anti-Semitism.[24]

Like Brown, George Pepperdine wanted to instill cosmopolitan sensibilities in transplanted southern evangelicalism, and he considered higher education essential to this progression. In the late 1940s Pepperdine's college hit its stride. Bolstered by the GI Bill, 1949 school enrollment neared two thousand, with seven hundred registered veterans looking to invest federal funds in their futures. Though Pepperdine's finances and the school's enrollment would both decline by the end of the decade, in 1950

Pepperdine's campus reverberated with the sounds of the good times. With an expanding student body came the need for new buildings, and with that the constant drone of construction. The extracurricular happenings were more vibrant still. Relying on their school paper *The Graphic* as a guide, coeds learned what to wear when attending beach parties, class banquets, and parades regularly scheduled on campus. Some collegians honed their skills in the arts, particularly classical music, opera, and drama, all strengths of the school. In 1951 Pepperdine's Community Symphony Orchestra presented Brahms's *Requiem*, a grand performance featuring the school's combined choruses, augmented by the choirs of James Fifield's First Congregational Church. "Spring Sings," operas, and especially musicals became mainstays on the college schedule. So did victories in forensics and debate. Based on a theology that stressed inductive reasoning, Church of Christ culture was a natural breeding ground for great debaters. Pepperdine College translated this into a competitive advantage. During the 1946–1947 academic year, its debating team swept opponents from the University of Southern California, College of the Pacific, and three different branches of the University of California system. The squad of nine was led by five women, whose success set an example for other coeds in coming years.[25]

Under the direction of Hugh Tiner, who succeeded Batsell Baxter as president in 1939, the college also became a formidable force in intercollegiate athletics. Although small, Pepperdine College managed to hold its own in several high-profile sports. Since 1939, when the Waves first burst on to the national scene with a record-setting victory in the two-mile relay at the famous Drake Relays (a race called by stadium announcer Ronald Reagan), Pepperdine's runners often stole the limelight, capturing All-American honors and participating on the United States Olympic team. Basketball and football vied for similar attention. Like the University of Notre Dame under Knute Rockne's legendary coaching in the 1920s, Pepperdine College boasted its own Four Horsemen backfield in the late 1940s; they led the Waves to an undefeated season and to the Will Rogers Bowl in Oklahoma City. Although never able to compete with classic NCAA football powers, Pepperdine earned a reputation during the late 1940s as a dominant team among small liberal arts colleges.[26]

The 1950s also brought a shift in the school's racial arrangement and, to some degree, attitude. Pepperdine College had long reflected the dominant racial biases in the Head, Heart, and Hand pedagogy, which envisioned Christian vocational training as a means of uplift for the South's poorest white people. This began changing in the late 1940s and early 1950s when the school welcomed a higher percentage of black students into its community and black athletes onto its sports teams. Though modest, Pepperdine College's demographic changes (like those of John Brown University, which also began enrolling African Americans in the 1940s) demonstrated a racial progressiveness that would not be contemplated in many institutions in the Deep South for at least another decade. Pepperdine also sought to engage Southern California's emerging multiculturalism. In 1950, it hosted a campus-community forum that featured its seventy-four foreign students on stage, some decked out in traditional garb, all seated in front of a row of flags representing their native countries. According to a school pronouncement, at that time no other California college student body had a higher percentage of internationals. A statement about white Protestantism's heightened sense of superiority and mission to the world as well as its embrace of a global sensibility, the event nevertheless left a powerful impression: Southern evangelicalism could no longer be dismissed easily as a provincial religion for a parochial people.[27]

CONSTRUCTING CONSERVATIVES

Besides turning their constituents into cosmopolitans, Brown, Pepperdine, and Benson also wanted to turn them into thinking conservatives. Southern plain folk, disenchanted with their political status, seemed ready for instruction in the new political thought emerging on Southern California's Republican Right. Evangelical entrepreneurs believed that through full exposure to their pedagogy, these citizens would indeed become co-activists in the revolt against the liberal leviathan.

Brown pursued this union through a rigorous packaging of Christian media, missions, and education. Besides turning KGER into the Station of the American Home, he also shaped it into the station of Christian Americanism, giving certified conservatives space to discuss their ideas and apply them to a global context. More subtly, KGER's broadcasts also systematically endorsed the work Christian businessmen were carrying out in the quest for a capitalist order. Like his close friend R. G. LeTourneau, Brown saw Southern California as a regional base from which this worldwide campaign could be launched. During the 1940s, LeTourneau had begun establishing missionary bases in Peru, carved out of dense forests by his heavy equipment, and offering aviation training at his institute, which prepared students to fly missionaries and supplies into South America. Wycliffe Bible Translators, a large missionary agency based in Southern California, was one of LeTourneau Institute's most important recruiters. Brown used his radio empire to publicize LeTourneau's efforts and immerse his listeners in the pro-business, pro-expansion imperatives that the evangelical industrialist championed to combat communism and save the lost. At the same time, Brown's schools followed LeTourneau's lead in preparing young people for work with agencies like Wycliffe, service in the military, and careers in the corporate sector. With so many ventures, and so much confidence, it was obvious that both men believed that by making southern evangelicalism modern they would also engineer a nation and world for Christ.[28]

The political culture George Pepperdine cultivated at his college reflected this same grand vision of evangelical Christianity and free enterprise capitalism, if on a localized scale. In the immediate postwar years, the *Graphic* carried countless advertisements from companies that supported Pepperdine's work. Reading the school paper almost became a lesson in corporate sponsorship, and by extension free market prerogatives. Even the extracurricular events covered in the *Graphic* came couched in politics. Debating was a case in point. International developments that Pepperdine College debaters tackled in competition were also taken up for discussion in the college's World Affairs Lecture Series, which saw esteemed Republican and Democratic politicians speak on key political issues. Some level of bipartisan flexibility was allowed on campus during the late 1940s and early 1950s, but when it came to curriculum, the school's founder was adamant that it be consistent with the priorities of his Republican allies. Like Benson and Brown, Pepperdine worried about economic crisis in the postwar years, and grew troubled by the appeal of populist panaceas. Not that he was insensitive. He liked to recall that he, too, once adhered to the "screwy ideas" of William Jennings Bryan and Free Silver Populism, but that he had come to realize how they were "decidedly socialistic in nature." Already strong in its business administration program, Pepperdine College, at its founder's urgings, now became an intellectual hub for serious Christian libertarian thought. One of the many spokesmen George Pepperdine welcomed to his grounds was fellow Kansan Howard Kershner, J. Howard Pew's associate, who led the Christian Freedom Foundation and edited its magazine, *Christian Economics*. By 1954 Pepperdine was buying hundreds of copies of *Christian Economics* and Kershner's book *God, Gold, and Government* for students, and inviting him to speak on campus.[29]

Among his peers, George Benson stood out for his outreach work. Having established a solid fiscal foundation for Harding College in the early 1940s, Benson set out in the late 1940s to disseminate his message more widely in "large industrial territories." Benson's elite business advisors, with whom he met often at places like New York's Metropolitan Club, agreed that his work needed to be expanded and vowed to help him "overcome obstacles in securing contributions from people who do not know Harding College." Armed with a list of contacts, Benson hit the road. Between 1946 and 1949 he traveled the country, meeting with industrial executives and giving talks about the dangers of expanded government. The Beech Aircraft Company gave him a small plane, and Benson kept up his torrid pace of two hundred speeches a year.[30]

Benson's exhilarating itinerary was as expansive thematically as it was geographically. On one hand, for instance, he began a crusade against federal aid for education. When appearing before the House Committee on Education and Labor in 1945, Benson argued that Washington needed to stay out of the workings of local school districts. Schools, in turn, needed to set their "house in order, rather than ask for federal aid to keep a disorderly house supplied with unnecessary funds." Painful as it might be in the short term, he continued, they would grow stronger as a result of their forced self-reliance and, at the same time, limit government's propensity and ability to tax. One of the "greatest fallacies in regard to Federal aid," he said, was that it did "not cost the states anything"; in truth, every dollar came with a hefty price. "It should be remembered," he warned, that "'aid' will always be weighted with a group of bureaucrats and political hangers-on, to be paid by the same states that are getting the aid. So in the name of economy and common sense let us keep local responsibility and operate as economically as possible." Three years after first introducing these charges, Benson appeared on the American Broadcasting Company network to repeat them. In a 1948 radio speech, he cautioned that educational assistance represented yet another wedge for government control. "Should we start federal aid to our public schools now," he pleaded, Americans "would see virtual federal control within a decade, to be followed within one more decade by nationalization of industrial production, transportation, utilities, and agriculture."[31]

It was the nationalization of the American economy that worried Benson most. During his first appearance before Congress, in 1941, Benson had spoken against New Deal spending as a naïve schoolmaster who had learned simple lessons about frugality. After World War II, he studied the nuances of Keynesian economics so that he could offer his audiences a substantive critique rather than simply an emotional appeal. He was a sharp apprentice. Through close readings of the latest libertarians, Benson constructed a refined argument against Keynesian liberalism, which he articulated in a long letter to the United States secretary of the treasury, sent in the summer of 1947. Using Britain as a comparison—and Friedrich von Hayek as inspiration—he wrote:

> I believe we are nearer to the point of turning down that same road that England is following than our people realize. We have a tremendous amount of industrial confusion. We have a lot of serious class feeling which is already growing to rather dangerous proportions. We have tended to make individual success unpopular by criticizing the men who have succeeded in developing our own essential industries and producing our own essential services. We are burdened with a heavy debt and there is before us the necessity of settling down to real serious and hard work but we are not in a mood to accept serious minded hard work.

Benson's letter next laid out a four-point recovery plan that read like a Chamber of Commerce brochure: first, "lower taxes particularly in the higher brackets"; second, government expenditures should be "pared down to the bone"; third, "an increase in productivity" was needed; and fourth, there should be "less interference with the law of supply and demand." Each point was followed by extensive analysis that criticized Keynesian liberalism for promoting deficit spending, government regulation, social welfare, and consumption at the cost of heavy inflation, national debt, declining industrial production, and loss of individual initiative. This was a straightforward (and one-dimensional) reading of Keynesianism not so different from corporate executives' condemnations of federal policies during the 1930s. Yet Benson made it digestible and compelling, at least to the uninitiated.[32]

Benson brought this message with him west after the war. Perhaps sensing the political crisis stirred up by Ham and Eggs, he arrived in Los Angeles in 1946. It is unknown if he addressed Ham and Eggers directly, but if he did it is likely he added a few cautions to his morality tale. As critical as he was of Keynesianism, Benson also censured currency schemes offered by organizations in the William Jennings Bryan and Huey Long mold. Here Benson channeled Pew, to whom he often looked for advice. In one of many letters Pew sent to his friend, he compared the current fiscal crisis to the 1890s, when Bryan's Populists, who wanted to "reflate" the economy by using silver coinage, battled gold-standard Republicans. "In the early days," Pews ruminated, "the currency was debauched by stamping out more coin—later by the use of the printing press—and now through a complicated system in which the Government sells bonds to the banks and the banks open up a credit with the Government; but the effect is the same and inflation is the result." He did not stop there.

> When government provides a segment of the people with something for which they have rendered no service, that segment of the people have lost their freedom; for when they become dependent on the Government for their livelihood, the Government can depend on them—they have lost their character and here become fit subjects for a totalitarian state.

Pew's words were the same ones others used to undermine the Ham and Eggs platform. Like Keynesianism, Ham and Eggs sanctioned fanciful restructuring of a reliable money system and made citizens dependent on government handouts. It allowed dictatorial managers to acquire power based on emotion rather than sound thinking and fiscal orthodoxy. Benson agreed: It was imperative Californians now be guided by a tested and trustworthy political blueprint, not by nostalgic platitudes.[33]

Whether Ham and Eggers heard him or not, it is evident Benson's protests against Keynesian economics and radical panaceas fell on enough friendly ears in Southern California for Harding's illustrious president to be introduced to many of the region's wealthy benefactors and conservative leaders. On a 1946 swing through Los Angeles, Benson held his first freedom forum, a training session in free market capitalism for local citizens. He was encouraged by the response and held similar seminars in 1947 and 1948. Although he was adamant that his was a nonpartisan platform, it was California's most powerful right-wing Republicans who asked him to return. In 1948, Don Belding, president of a Los Angeles-based advertising agency, proposed that Benson launch a "nationwide seminar to attract business, industrial and professional leaders to discuss the basic internal problems of America" and "plan an educational campaign to reach the public." In essence, Belding wanted Benson to establish a permanent freedom forum, held annually at Harding College. The goal was to provide information "about the merits of Christian morality, constitutional government, and the free-enterprise system," and secondly offer workshops for conferees in the basics of comparative government and economics. The assumption was that these trainees would then disseminate this same information to employees, church members, neighbors, and fellow citizens in their own communities. With the California Institute of Technology's Nobel Prize–winning physicist Dr. Robert Millikan as its keynote speaker, Benson's first forum was an elaborate affair that drew 160 well-dressed, urban-dwelling executives and managers to rural Searcy, Arkansas. Forum participants were housed in the modest homes of faculty and townspeople, which added a sense of authenticity and charm to the event. During the next fifteen years an estimated 3,600 corporate leaders representing 1,000 companies and associations would join church leaders, educators, and politicians in making this same trek to northeastern Arkansas.[34]

Besides mining Southern California's financial resources, Benson also took advantage of its entertainment industry. Throughout the 1940s he consulted Walt Disney about creating educational cartoons. In 1947, Harding's president secured a million-dollar donation from the Sloan Foundation (negotiated privately with Alfred P. Sloan), then teamed up with former Disney executive John Sutherland to produce ten animated cartoons in a series dubbed *Adventures in Economics*. The films, distributed by MGM through its five thousand theaters nationwide, starred "Dr. Utopia" and other not so subtly named heroes and villains of capitalism. Heavy-handed but good-humored in their polemics, *Adventures in Economics* broke viewership records and, more importantly in Benson's mind, pricked the public conscience. By 1950 they had been seen by twenty-five million Americans. In 1952 the *Nation* best captured what Benson had managed to accomplish:

> Drop into a movie house anywhere, or into a women's club meeting or a Main Street lecture hall, or pick up a small-town newspaper, and you are likely to be introduced to hoary economic theories adapted to modern use by the sage of Harding College at Searcy (population 4,000), Arkansas.

The liberal journal ruefully admitted that Benson's "obscure college" now exerted a "greater influence on the economic thinking of the American people than most of our great universities," in order to warn its readers that a political uprising might be brewing.[35]

JEFFERSON AND JESUS TURN RIGHT

As eager as these evangelical entrepreneurs were to engineer a broad conservative coalition, they knew this transformation would take time. The political philosophy of Jefferson and Jesus did not, in other words, forge an instant bond between southern plain folk and the burgeoning conservative movement or find an instant home in the state's Republican Party. It would take another decade for southern plain folk to turn decisively Right and Republican in their political allegiances.

Still, something had changed dramatically for rank-and-file southern evangelicals in the 1940s. They were scarred by their personal run-ins with Social Democrats and disillusioned by the way the New Deal coalition bowed to the progressive agenda. Although many would hold on to their Democratic registrations, perhaps to remind them of their roots, they entered the 1950s as independents more determined than ever to vote with their conscience. This, after all, is how they had always approached the ballot box. In California, the end of cross-filing privileges and assertion of party control in the late 1950s would force them to choose sides, yet right now the flexibility of California's political system suited a people in transition. In this context small-*d* Democrats started to become little-*r* Republicans.

Jean Vandruff and Marie King followed this path. After quitting his assembly-line job at Douglas Aircraft in 1942 to enlist, Vandruff found himself copiloting a bomber over the Pacific Ocean. He returned from the Pacific theater a hero. While on one of its missions over Saigon, Vandruff's crew had been engaged by nine Japanese Zero fighter planes. They destroyed five enemy aircraft, but Vandruff's plane sustained heavy damage and stayed airborne just long enough for its crew to parachute to the ocean below. Vandruff was plucked from enemy waters by an American submarine patrolling the area, then seven days later whisked back to the Philippines for recovery. Appropriately enough, on July 4, 1945, the proud American returned "home" to California in search of a new career. Vandruff wanted to find a profession in which he could dictate the pace and terms of his production. While working at Douglas, Vandruff had witnessed union shop politics and decided that someday he would be his own man: assembly lines, membership dues, and bosses were not for him. And so the twenty-three-year-old Oklahoman set off in a different direction. In the fall of 1945 he enrolled at the University of Southern California to study engineering and architecture, and began pursuing other financial investments. Able to earn a small nest egg by selling an innovation of his—a radio speaker made to enhance the quality of sound in automobiles—Vandruff combined his profits with monies saved from military service and his veteran's benefit package to buy him and his parents—who moved to California in 1942—a new, three-bedroom home in Downey, a white-collar community in southeastern Los Angeles County. In 1949 the Vandruffs packed belongings in their South Gate apartment and bid good-bye to the working class.

After moving from South Gate to Downey, Jean also invested himself in the fate of his neighborhood and country. The labor wars during the 1940s frightened Vandruff, as did the intensity with which Social Democrats—"Communists and Socialists," in his mind—seemed to take over the Democratic Party by the early 1950s. In 1952, along with his parents and his brother Shannon, Jean took a bold step by leading the local chapter of Democrats for Eisenhower and casting their votes for the Republican Party. Family members still living in the western South scoffed at the decision and called them traitors, but the Vandruffs saw themselves as realists; they were dealing with political circumstances in Southern California that no one back home could imagine. And so a decade after counting on Franklin D. Roosevelt to save them from Depression-era poverty, the Vandruffs turned their backs on a political party they believed had turned on them.[36]

The beginnings of Marie King's rightward journey were similar to Vandruff's. Immediately after arriving in Los Angeles in 1944, King found work in the legal offices of MGM. Every day, she rode the streetcar from the apartment she shared with her sister in Hollywood to MGM's immense campus on National Boulevard, where she wrote contracts and supervised a filing crew. This routine, and the reasonable pay that came with it, were cut short in 1945 and 1946 when Herbert K. Sorrell, president of the Conference of Studio Unions (CSU), called for a studio-wide strike and demanded that industry executives agree to collective bargaining. The strike, which lasted 238 days and involved 15,000 workers, halted production at MGM, 20th Century Fox, Universal Studios, and Warner Brothers. This phase of protest ultimately ended with violent standoffs between protestors and police on the grounds of Warner Brothers. In September 1946, CSU officials began another round of agitation, calling for picket lines around the studios and encouraging striking employees to prevent replacement workers from entering the grounds. King found herself in the middle of the controversy. She had not wanted to be part of a union, but because of industry rules she was required to join the CIO-led CSU. Rather than cave to union pressures, she decided to use her position as a legal secretary to document union abuses. At first she focused on Sorrell, who, like much of CSU's leadership, had ties to the Communist Party. Conscious of this and aware of Sorrell's other "immoral, unjust, and un-American" activities, King voted against his boldest strike measures. In 1946, she went a step further by recording maltreatment against strike-breakers. In a final act of defiance, she typed and secured signatures on harassment reports dictated to her by fellow workers, handed them over to MGM executives for their use against the unions, and in October 1946 resigned and rode her last streetcar home.

During the next few years King would toil in a number of law firms before finding herself in 1950 working for James Fifield at the offices of Spiritual Mobilization. Always earnest in her political ideals and now looking to Fifield as a mentor, she attended Freedom Club meetings and invested herself in several patriotic and women's groups. Like Vandruff, King bolted to the GOP in 1952 to help Eisenhower's camp run its local campaign. With her marriage in 1956 to Walter Koenig, who shared her passion for activism, Marie began a new life in Pasadena, politically intense and fully engaged. "Hupey" Long would have been pleased.[37]

IN 1949 MARIE KING ATTENDED evangelistic meetings in a revival tent erected at the corner of Washington and Hill streets in Los Angeles, held by a young upstart named Billy Graham. King likely heard about this relatively unknown pulpiteer via KGER. It was John Brown's radio station that first broadcast word of Graham's arrival and marketed the evangelist's crusade throughout the fall of 1949 through over 2.5 million radio sets in the Los Angeles basin.[38]

Graham came west to speak on America's impending apocalypse, a calamity he felt certain would come by way of communist operatives and their secularist schemes. Besides the fact that he arrived in a moment of growing international instability set off by the cold war, his timing could not have been any better for Southern Californians seeking reprieve from the volatile politics of the late 1940s. After a period of political turmoil racked by violence over race, work, religion, and community, Graham seemed the perfect fix. Here was someone who could deliver a familiar message of repentance and reconciliation without becoming too judgmental or overly sentimental. Folksy yet polished, hard-driving yet gracious, Graham was a plain-folk preacher with broad appeal and a bright future.

Indeed, for southern evangelicals, Graham represented the beginning of a new phase on the West Coast. Overcome for a time by the clamor of the 1940s, and now united by political circumstances, southern plain folk, preachers, and entrepreneurs were ready and able to continue their errand for Christian Americanism together. They had settled in their new state and made it their home. Now Graham and his cohort would turn it into their city on a hill.

III

SOUTHERN
SOLUTIONS

Western culture and its fruits had its foundation in the Bible, the Word of God. . . . Communism, on the other hand, has decided against God, against Christ, against the Bible, and against all religion. Communism is not only an economic interpretation of life—Communism is a religion that is inspired, directed, and motivated by the Devil himself who has declared war against Almighty God. . . . The Fifth Columnists, called Communists, are more rampant in Los Angeles than any other city in America. . . . In this moment I can see the judgment hand of God over Los Angeles. I can see judgment about to fall.

When God gets ready to shake America, he might not take the Ph.D. and the D.D. and the Th.D. God may choose a country boy! God may choose a man no one knows, a little nobody to shake America for Jesus Christ in this day. A hillbilly, a country boy! who will sound forth in a mighty voice to America, "Thus saith the Lord!"

—BILLY GRAHAM
LOS ANGELES, 1949

6

PLAIN-FOLK
PREACHING
MAINSTREAMED

*My friend, don't laugh at the country preacher. He has a message
from God. Many of the sophisticates and intellectuals in Amos'
day were wrong. They can be wrong in our day as well. God still
says, "Come now, and let us reason together. . . ." But don't be
deceived.*

God is not soft. God is not sentimental.[1]

—J. VERNON MCGEE

IN SEPTEMBER 1949, IN A MAKESHIFT CATHEDRAL IN DOWNTOWN
Los Angeles, a gangly, unproven, thirty-three-year-old Billy Graham
delivered an ultimatum: Repent or watch the City of Angels crumble
before the judgment of God. Graham arrived in Southern California just
two days after President Truman had announced that the Soviet Union
had detonated an atomic bomb. Certain that the Soviets had their war-
heads trained on Los Angeles, Graham preached out of honest fear that
anything less than complete repentance would result in America's ruin.
As she sat in the crowd, Marie King was not the only one feeling guilt for
her nation's sins, or the only one enamored with the young preacher. Graham seemed to have this effect on everyone.[2]

He certainly affected Stuart Hamblen. Prodigal son of J. H. Hamblen,
the venerable Texas preacher and founder of the Evangelical Methodist
Church, Hamblen was a legend, known on the West Coast as a cham-

pion rodeo rider, singer, and the voice of the *Cowboy Church of the Air*, a popular country music program. Grudgingly appearing at a Bible study organized by the Hollywood First Presbyterian Church, the imposing star was surprised at how easily he struck up a conversation with Graham, the guest of honor. Graham, for his part, attributed the chords of friendship to shared southern sensibilities; a relationship soon blossomed. Promised airtime on his new friend's radio program, Graham saw to it that his revival, designated the Christ for Greater Los Angeles Campaign, received plenty of public notice. Los Angeles' favorite singing cowboy, meanwhile, found himself overcome by guilt, kneeling with his new confidant to pray the sinner's prayer. His conversion shook the city. Hamblen quit smoking and drinking the products advertised on his popular show and told his audience to do the same (a move that cost him his job), then, at the behest of fellow entertainer John Wayne, wrote a hit song about his experience called "It Is No Secret What God Can Do." Their curiosities piqued by the conversion of one of the city's brightest stars, Angelenos now packed Graham's tent, forcing organizers to expand the temporary auditorium, extend the event another five weeks, and press for more advertising. By now, though, the word was out. Locals chatted about the revival in barbershops and buses, on streetcars and shop-room floors, and a hungry press corps spread the word of Graham's monumental success. Soon *Time* and *Newsweek* joined the rush to "puff Graham" by profiling the evangelist, and when other celebrity converts like Louis Zamperini and Mickey Cohen came forward, "the headlines screamed again." Though buoyed by the new fame, Graham's robust message remained the same: Heed the perils of communism and the benefits of Christ.[3]

THE 1949 CHRIST FOR GREATER Los Angeles Campaign signaled that southern evangelicalism would lead California's postwar awakening. This was Bob Shuler's assessment, at least. A chief organizer of Graham's crusade, he wrote in the *Pentecostal Evangel* that with the exception of a few Presbyterians and a scattering of Congregational, Northern Baptist, and Bible churches, Los Angeles' "ecclesiastical leaders and their following remained aloof, some of them scoffing, some condemning." Had it been left up to the establishment, in other words, Graham would have failed. But because of the consistent efforts of "the Assembly of God, the Church of the Foursquare Gospel, the Church of God, the Pentecostals, the Southern Baptists" and fundamentalist Baptist churches, his efforts were triumphant. Then there was Graham himself, a preacher cut from a time-honored mold. "He preaches the errors of sin and the horrors of hell," Shuler explained, yet "holds up the mercy of the Lord in every sermon." "His altar calls are free from design or trap. He is above all a pleader. He pleads with sinners and they come." Graham was a country preacher who refused to pander to the sensitivities of the modern self, Shuler concluded, but what made his arrival truly momentous was its timely appeal. In an age of frenzied uncertainty, citizens yearned for commonsense solutions to complex political problems. In Shuler's mind, Graham's evangelistic rally proved that good answers came from southern saddlebag saints and their no-frills, no-nonsense American gospel.[4]

Graham's sensational impact indeed testified to the advent of a new generation of southern preachers in postwar Southern California. Aided by a folksy charm, but lacking the harder-edged prejudices that tainted their predecessors, these clerics delivered an appealing homespun gospel. Southern California's evangelical community changed as a result, as did the region's inchoate conservative movement. These new ministers were diplomats who closed cultural chasms between southern and non-southern evangelicals by championing a shared theology of evangelism and end-times expectation while also bridging gaps between religious and secular conservatives through the construction of a broad association of anticommunist activism. Meanwhile, they represented a more profound change for transplanted southern evangelicals themselves. Their charisma and collective resolve shining through at a propitious time, these clerics helped their people shed the stigma of an outsider past and replace it with a confidence that came with acceptance among peers.

PURGE

Graham may have been an overnight sensation, but the mainstreaming of plain-folk preachers in Southern California was a product of new criteria for leadership within southern evangelicalism. Roused by a new wave of expansion, but fearful of losing control of their ministers as they had earlier, southern denominational leaders now purged their ranks of undisciplined clerics and demanded compliance from those ministering on the West Coast.

Interchurch consolidation helped Baptists carry out this mandate.

Sparked by the subversive work of Robert Lackey and his fellow Land-markists in the early 1940s, the Southern Baptist Convention officially broke all remaining, long-standing territorial arrangements with the Northern Baptist Convention in 1950. At the same time that this break-through justified the work Southern Baptist ministers had been doing on the West Coast since the Depression, it also meant that SBC head-quarters in Nashville demanded their full cooperation in orderly, national expansion. The days of nonconformist clerics and loutish district heads like Lackey, in other words, were over. Conceding this point, perhaps, Lackey left his post, making way for genteel Baptist diplomats to take charge. Meanwhile, many of California's southern-based, independent Baptists realigned in the new Baptist Bible Fellowship (BBF). This alli-ance broke off from J. Frank Norris's network of churches, which had reached north and west from Texas in the late 1930s. The BBF, headquar-tered in Springfield, Missouri, quickly evolved into a powerful institution, particularly in midwestern industrial centers, where white southerners had been gathering for decades. Drawing the most attention were flag-ship churches shepherded by well-known preachers. Pastored by Dallas Billington, a Kentuckian who once worked the line at Goodyear, Akron Baptist Temple set the standard when it opened its new, million-dollar facilities in 1949 to a crowd of twenty-five thousand and a press corps that included *Collier's* and *Life* magazines. Determined to match their colleagues, BBF pastors in California spent the early cold war years laying the foundations for their own empires.[5]

Pentecostal leaders matched their Baptist counterparts in strengthen-ing connections between the South and Southern California. Their work paid immediate dividends in pastoral leadership. While still forced to contend with an occasional disenfranchised prophet or unemployed tent maker, authorities in the Assemblies of God grew increasingly confident that the quality of pastors making their way west was matching the quan-tity; that pulpits could be staffed with seminarians instead of salesmen. During the Ham and Eggs affair, Assemblies of God general secretary J. Roswell Flower had lamented the way his clerics became embroiled in controversy. In the late 1940s and early 1950s, he pledged to keep his pastors from supporting questionable causes. "We trust that our breth-ren will profit from this experience," Flower told his Southern Califor-nia district superintendent, F. C. Woodworth, whose own participation in Ham and Eggs had been embarrassing. The positive outcome, Flower graciously added, was that these circumstances forced his preachers to become aware of the dangers of careless political associations. Together, Flower and Woodworth set out to protect their churches from demagogues. Besides undertaking broader surveillance of local church life, they instituted reading tests and formal reviews as part of leadership certification. They also encouraged their charges to invest themselves in the new evangelicalism represented by the National Association of Evangelicals, in which Flower was a key leader. As in Baptist circles, maverick Assemblies of God pastors would no longer roam free on the West's religious frontier.[6]

Not surprisingly, some of the veteran preachers who had looked to California as an escape from ecclesiastical control disliked Flower's initiatives. "While I believe in strong organization, I do believe in democracy and the right of the smallest to voice his opinion," Southern Californian W. E. Long stated in opposition to Flower's mandatory "Fellowship Certificate" renewals. For his part, Flower emphasized he was working in the local church's best interest and was "sorry that so many of our brethren on the West Coast misinterpret the intent and purpose of the clause." The intent of the amendment, Flower reiterated, was to shore up the local church by rooting out dictatorial pastors. "Of course, strong minded pastors who are determined to rule their churches with an iron hand will not take kindly to such an interpretation." In essence, Flower faced a familiar challenge in southern church circles: How does one marshal independent-minded Christians behind a controlled, cooperative master plan?[7]

Most disgruntled prophets, however, converted to Flower's vision, and the most important perhaps was Jonathan Perkins. Initially the former Ham and Egger joined the chorus of opposition to centralization. In 1949, he wrote Flower with a litany of complaints, presented with flashes of characteristic hyperbole. "There was a time when all Assemblies were free to engage or call any pastor or evangelist they desired, but you have done away with self-government, and now the local church is groaning beneath the weight of Council bondage." "You have been responsible for taking many Assemblies into your movement with the assurance they were going into a Fellowship, but you mislead them into a religious Dictatorship instead." "You have sold out Acts 2:4 to the National Association of Evangelicals with regard to Pentecostal testimony on one hand, and you have gone by leaps and [bounds] into the direction of Roman Popery on the other." But then Perkins underwent a catharsis of sorts that began with self-reflections on race. In 1950 he wrote about his personal contact with David Weissman, an editor with the Anti-Defamation League, in which he expressed guilt about the bigotry that stained his convictions. Certain, now, that he had "thrown away a brilliant pulpit career to mix politics with Religion," Perkins grieved the loss of a healthy witness because of his reckless anti-Semitism. Of his meeting, Perkins would recount:

> He asked me for one of my chief criticisms of the Jews, and I replied that Jews were entirely sensitive to criticism, and they should get over their touchy spirit. Suddenly the tears started rolling down his cheeks, and he said "Perkins that kind of statement is alright for your side of the fence, but you have not had your people burned alive" and instantly I saw the Jewish people in a new light. As I talked with David Weisman I decided that I would never be unfair to another Jew as long as I lived.

In his twilight years the prophet would seek solace in his family and church—a Methodist cathedral on Wilshire Boulevard—and redemption of sorts as a reinstated Assemblies of God speaker and volunteer official on Los Angeles mayor Tom Bradley's Committee on the Aging.[8]

Perkins's change of heart came at the same time denominational officials, aspiring to the new evangelical cosmopolitanism, were imploring their people to sever all ties with anti-Semitic spokesmen like Gerald L. K. Smith. Tellingly, even the outspoken J. Frank Norris contributed to this endeavor. At the end of the 1940s, Norris renounced the politics of Smith—his onetime friend—as unacceptable for any God-fearing, truth-abiding Baptist. This break grew in part out of expediency. Purged from the Baptist association he had created, and wanting affirmation for a career now ending, Norris saw little benefit in maintaining ties with someone whom respected religious leaders considered a fraud. Yet as an earnest premillennialist, excited about events in Palestine, he also was disturbed by Smith's escalating rhetoric, which now posited that "Jesus Christ was not a Jew" and that white Anglo-Protestants were God's chosen people. These ideas were dangerous, Norris charged, for they were once "the chief stock in trade of Hitler and Goebbels and Company." They were also counterproductive. Smith has "made a great fight against Communism," Norris wrote, "but he will lose the effectiveness of his fight when he is doing the Hitler-act of fighting the Jews under his attack on Communism. The Jews of Palestine are not Communists, they are

Nationalists, and no Nationalist is a Communist." Norris was speaking for the emerging evangelicalism that now passed him by, one that was no longer willing to let old alliances jeopardize their quest for progress.[9]

He also acted in accordance with the new evangelical spirit of engagement. In an unprecedented ecumenical gesture, Norris met Zionist leaders in Palestine and shared fears of world communism in a special session with Pope Pius XII at the Vatican. At home, meanwhile, he reached out to powerful politicians and helped rally his state behind Dwight Eisenhower in 1952. "There is a moral issue more than a political issue involved in this campaign," he told the president. "It is a religious crusade of Free America." Eisenhower's thank-you note, dated August 4, 1952, was likely one of the last letters Norris read. On August 20 the preacher died of a heart attack.[10]

COLD WARRIORS

While the purges within southern evangelicalism allowed church officials to mainstream its pastors, the threat of communism encouraged a new generation of southern pastors to mainstream their message. In the months surrounding Graham's Los Angeles appearance, signs of a strengthening communist campaign grew rapidly in number and frequency, and with news of each development, perceptions of this threat rose to frenetic levels. A few ambitious, independent southern ministers joined a new class of political pundits in presenting themselves to Southern Californians as American democracy's advance guard and their message as the antidote to this culture of crisis.

The unrest in Asia helped fuel this anxiety. Political conditions had been deteriorating there since 1946, when Chiang Kai-shek and his Nationalist forces attacked Mao Tse-tung, who had aspirations for a united, communist China. Counting on American help, Chiang moved aggressively against Mao and in the process overextended his power. The Truman administration, preoccupied with Europe and the Middle East, had little to offer Chiang. By late 1949, the momentum had shifted entirely as Mao's army gained complete control of China and forced Chiang into exile on the island of Formosa. A few months later, North Korea invaded South Korea, thrusting the United States into direct confrontation with communism. Truman dispatched American troops into South Korea, cloaked them in UN authority, and readied for war. Under

General Douglas MacArthur, UN forces engaged in a seesaw battle with North Koreans and the Chinese until reaching an impasse. MacArthur planned to break it with "a naval blockade of China's coast, a massive air bombardment of its industry, and the 'unleashing' of Chiang [Kai-shek] for a mainland invasion." Anything less, he said, "would betray the brave soldiers who were fighting and dying in a senseless stalemate." While Truman deliberated, MacArthur criticized the delay. Truman responded by relieving the general of his command. Much to the disappointment of many Americans, the war went on without its hero, and ended many months later in the stalemate he had wanted to avoid.[11]

Just as communism was looking invincible across the Pacific Ocean, 1950 brought the threat home. In 1948, ex-Communist Whittaker Chambers testified that Alger Hiss, a New Deal–era State Department official, had been a communist comrade in the 1930s. Hiss declared his innocence, but was convicted of perjury on January 22, 1950, which brought closure to a case that had riveted Americans for months. Truman called Hiss's case a "red herring," but this made circumstances worse. Days later, on February 9, 1950, Republican Joseph McCarthy delivered his famous speech in West Virginia, during which he claimed to have a list with the names of 205 communists working in the State Department. Though the list had been manufactured, the pronouncement galvanized the news media, and set McCarthy off onto a four-year campaign to rid the federal government and America's most important cultural institutions of communist spies.[12]

This series of jolts sent American politics into rancorous revolt and did serious damage to Californian's political psyche. A gateway to Asia, California in particular felt the weight of Chinese communism's triumph. This emotional burden was evident when, in April 1951, General MacArthur returned home to the United States from Korea. After fifteen years and two wars in Asia, he disembarked before a reverent crowd in San Francisco, a symbol of quixotic valor. Shortly after his arrival, Los Angeles City Council adjourned in "sorrowful contemplation of the political assassination" of this man. Just a few months earlier, in 1950, this same passion had moved California senator William Knowland to stand in Congress and demand that the "story of a five-year-old Chinese Communist atrocity against a U.S. Army captain" be included in the official record. Knowland described how John Birch "was shot through the leg and then murdered . . . his body tossed in a railroad ditch." It was Knowland's intention to chastise the United States government for the failure of its foreign policy in Asia, while at the same time turning the Baptist missionary into a national hero. J. Frank Norris had venerated John Birch as a saint during World War II, but Knowland now read him into history as the "first casualty in the Third World War between Communists and the ever-shrinking Free World."[13]

Meanwhile, California's own "McCarthys," state senator Jack Tenney and Congressman Richard Nixon, hounded homegrown leftists. In June 1949, Tenney released his government committee's *Fifth Report*, a seven-hundred-page taxonomy of California's alleged communists. Not surprisingly, Social Democrat Carey McWilliams topped the list. McWilliams responded with a blistering article in the *Nation* (one of his last editorials as a Californian before moving east to edit this publication) that excoriated Tenney for destroying innocent lives. Like Tenney, but with more polish, Nixon also brought national attention to anticommunist activities in Southern California. Soon after his electoral victory over Jerry Voorhis in 1946, Nixon earned a seat on the House Un-American Activities Committee (HUAC) and began investigating Hollywood. A few anticommunists associated with the Motion Picture Alliance for the Preservation of American Ideals (MPAPA) like Ronald Reagan named people they thought warranted investigation, which led ultimately to prosecution of the "Hollywood Ten." As HUAC's public face, Nixon rode the acclaim to another stunning election win, this time for Senate. Nixon's adversary was the darling of Los Angeles' Democratic establishment: Helen Gahagan Douglas. In 1945 she had been voted into Congress by Social Democrats for championing the dissolution of HUAC. In 1949 she used the pages of the *Congressional Record* to blast Tenney's *Fifth Report*. Badges of honor within her stronghold of Westside Los Angeles, these actions made her vulnerable in Nixon's base. Douglas was "pink right down to her underwear," Nixon charged; to try to prove the point he distributed a "pink sheet" that listed the Democrat's voting record and ran under slogans like "Don't Vote the Red Ticket, vote the Red, White, and Blue Ticket" and "Be an American, Be for Nixon." The barrage worked. In November 1950 the 37-year-old from Whittier became California's newest Senator.[14]

The pervasive sense of crisis implicit in Nixon's victory turned Southern California into a hub of anticommunist activity. Several high-profile conservative spokesmen now traveled west to battle the Red Menace on America's most vulnerable soil. Not all of these pundits were dynamic speakers; a great many were bookish analysts. Two studious types included

Whittaker Chambers and James Burnham. Following the Hiss hearings, Chambers published *Witness*, his 1952 bestseller. Recounting his own flirtation with communism during the 1930s, Chambers explained that this political system forced an inescapable choice between "irreconcilable faiths": God or Man, spiritual freedom or enslavement. In communism, Americans faced a foe whose revolutionary ideas had already crept into their government through New Deal liberalism. According to Chambers, the revolution had "been inching its ice cap over the nation for two decades." A professor at New York University, Burnham had also made the stark turn away from 1930s communism. In books published during Truman's presidency, he lashed out at Washington's containment policy, which assumed that communism would collapse if merely prevented from expanding. Though liberals within Truman's party saw containment as an aggressive stance, Burnham viewed it as a defensive posture. In his mind, the United States needed to roll communism back rather than wait for it to fall on its own. This struck a nerve with those Americans disillusioned by the Korean War.[15]

Anticommunism's leading pundits were General Albert C. Wedemeyer and Clarence Manion. Wedemeyer, who had been a top commanding officer with MacArthur in China, criticized the federal government's lack of support for American interests in Asia. With the self-confidence of a military strategist, he balanced libertarian and traditionalist ideals in his lectures and editorials and demonstrated how an anticommunist message had potential for intellectual convergence on the political Right. Meanwhile, Clarence Manion, dean of the law school at the University of Notre Dame in the 1940s, made a name for himself by organizing Democrats for Eisenhower in 1952. Eisenhower awarded Manion the chairmanship of the Commission on Inter-Governmental Relations. Manion lost Eisenhower's trust as quickly as he gained it, however, when he supported the 1954 Bricker Amendment, a series of proposed (and failed) constitutional amendments that sought to restrict executive power in dealings with foreign powers, and protect national sovereignty against the expanding authority of the UN. Eisenhower vigorously opposed the Bricker Amendment and dismissed Manion, who returned to Indiana, where he established the Manion Forum. Along with a newsletter, his agency produced a radio program on which Manion and guests parsed international political happenings with an anticommunist slant. By the early 1960s the program was broadcast on over 250 radio stations and 15 television stations in 42 states.[16]

Through expanding media channels established by intellectual and corporate conservatives in the early 1940s, the words of Burnham and Chambers, Wedemeyer and Manion, made their way into the homes of Southern California's right-wing public. In 1950 *The Freeman*, run by Leonard Read's Foundation for Economic Education, became heavily invested in anticommunism after it absorbed *Plain Talk*, a principal organ for pro-Chinese nationalist lobbyists. Only the *American Mercury* was more ardently anticommunist in the 1950s. At the same time, through radio, seminars, and public gatherings, the new cold warriors connected academics to activists, ideas to emotion, and in the process created a vibrant political culture. In Los Angeles James Fifield's Freedom Club, at First Congregational Church, had monthly talks by the likes of Manion and Wedemeyer, who also served on the Freedom Club's advisory committee. Through its monthly newsletter, the Freedom Club sent out transcriptions of anticommunist speeches and a Reading List on Communism, Socialism, and Liberty for its seventeen Freedom Club branches in Beverly Hills and Van Nuys, Bell Gardens and San Diego, and communities in between.[17]

Fifield also helped promote another species of political pundit—the Christian anticommunist crusader. Two firebrands in particular began working California with great success. Born in Arkansas, Billy James Hargis escaped poverty through Bible school education and ordination in the Disciples of Christ. In 1947, while pastoring a church in Sallisaw, Oklahoma, Hargis organized the Christian Crusade, the first Christian anticommunist organization of its kind. Under its auspices Hargis ran an Annual Anti-Communist Leadership School, a daily broadcast, and a publishing and lecture ministry producing right-wing films, speeches, and leaflets. He saw in Southern California the resources necessary to make this elaborate campaign work and, by the early 1950s, scheduled meetings there on a frequent basis. By linking Tulsa and Los Angeles, Hargis became one of America's foremost Christian anticommunists, second only to Carl McIntire. Like Hargis, McIntire was shaped by Oklahoma's religious culture. Raised by missionaries to the Choctaw Nation, McIntire took his frontier sensibilities with him to Princeton Theological Seminary, where he became embroiled in the fundamentalist-modernist controversy that split Presbyterians in the 1930s. Founder of the American Council of Christian Churches (ACCC), a fundamentalist counterweight to the more irenic NAE, McIntire joined the anticommunist campaign flourishing in the West. By the mid-1950s McIntire's magazine, *Christian Beacon*, and his radio program, *The Twentieth Century Reformation*, were staples for anticommunist activists in California, and his Highland College in Pasadena was one of their vital training sites.[18]

Two other important Christian anticommunists were Fred Schwarz and Major Edgar Bundy, evangelicalism's own "Manion" and "Wedemeyer." An Australian Baptist with Jewish lineage, Schwarz traveled internationally with a sponsorship from McIntire, and then came to Los Angeles in 1950. In 1952 he began appearing at Fifield's Freedom Club, billed as an authority on communism. Schwarz eventually established a Christian anticommunist research center in Long Beach, California, the Christian Anti-Communism Crusade, and distinguished himself as a scholar who could out-think the reds. If Schwarz was the professor, Bundy was the general. A career air force officer and intelligence agent, Bundy had been stationed in China's western provinces during the Communist revolt of the early 1940s. He returned to the United States wanting to warn the nation of what he had seen. While testifying before the Senate Appropriations Committee in 1950, he advised that funds for Europe be diverted to the hotter military zones of Asia, specifically China; were China to fall to Communism, Japan, India, Burma, and the Philippines would soon follow. And, most assuredly, South Korea would submit to North Korea. When China did fall, and South Korea submitted, Bundy was "hailed as a political clairvoyant." His testimony caught the attention of Congress and also the interest of the Church League of America, a Christian anticommunist institute run by author and advertising executive George Washington Robnett, in Wheaton, Illinois. Under Robnett's direction, the Church League emerged as the premier information-gathering site for the anticommunist Right. By the mid-1950s Bundy was in charge of this organization and disseminating its data. Though welcomed nationwide, Bundy's operation garnered particular respect among transplanted southern evangelicals in California. Although born in New England, Bundy grew up in Florida, was educated at Oglethorpe University in Atlanta, and took ordination in the Southern Baptist Convention in Alabama. Bundy's southern evangelicalism made him particularly comfortable in Southern California. With both Robnett and his in-laws in the state (they had moved from the South to Los Angeles), Bundy made it a point to visit and speak there often.[19]

COUNTRY PREACHERS WHO CAME TO TOWN

As much as independent ministers like Hargis and McIntire, Bundy and Schwarz made headway in the 1950s with their blistering Christian anticommunism, the day belonged to country preachers like Graham, southern clerics who preferred just to nudge people with their truth. Amid the threat of nuclear annihilation, when Californians were learning how to "duck and cover" and construct their own bomb shelters, these southern saints were able to gently connect their followers to a familiar past and hopeful future, even while assailing the feared fifth columnists.

Who were these new celebrity preachers? Some came from famous preacher families. At the time of Graham's revival in 1949, Bob Shuler was nearing the end of his pastorate. It pleased him to see a new crop of young men like Graham emerge. None received a louder endorsement, however, than his own boys, Bob Jr., Jack, and Phil. Nurtured under their father's ministry and trained by his friends at Bob Jones College, the Shuler sons were now pursuing a pastoral career. It was Jack Shuler, in fact, who had headlined the Christ for Greater Los Angeles Campaign the year before Graham's big entrance and who would, throughout the 1950s, rival Graham as America's supreme evangelist. An earnest anticommunist conservative, Jack Shuler nevertheless shunned his father's biting discourse and deliberately avoided strident politicking, choosing instead to preach a less fiery gospel. It was not decisive or immediate, but even as he heralded Graham's coming and his sons' successes, Bob Shuler too was being set aside as a remnant of the old southern evangelicalism.[20]

Only a few members of the new generation could boast lineages like the Shuler boys; the rest arrived by virtue of their own ambition. Theologically conservative and culturally innovative, these younger clerics rounded off the sharp edges of their fathers' doctrine, made it more inclusive and inviting, and adapted the Texas theology of the previous generation to the rising middle class. They were every bit as tough, however. Products of southern poverty and California's postwar boom, these steely, self-made men personified rugged, bootstrap individualism. In keeping with their autobiographies, they preached sermons with subtle but obvious political meaning in an effort to equip citizens with black-and-white answers to a world seemingly draped in communist red. The master of this was J. Vernon McGee, cold war California's proudest plain-folk preacher.

Able to boast at his retirement a repertoire of over a thousand sermons covering every verse in the bible, McGee's favorite was the one he preached on Amos, "The Country Preacher Who Came to Town." Amos, McGee would tell his audience, was "a fruit-picker and a herdsman . . . a country boy" who answered God's call by leaving his "whistle stop" hometown of Tekoa on the shores of the Dead Sea to go prophesize on the "boulevards of Bethel," the golden capital of the Northern Kingdom of Israel. Met there by an intimidating crowd of liberal cosmopolitans, Pharisees and Sadducees who scorned him, Amos refused to "mince words" or "pull his punches." McGee told his listeners that Amos in fact relished the opportunity to expose the sin of his detractors and warn them of the forthcoming day when their false peace would be destroyed by Assyrian sword. Many were the lessons to be gained by this parable, McGee would preach, but none greater than this: never underestimate the country preacher, for he is the messenger of God.[21]

It almost goes without saying that the story of Amos was roughly his own. Born in Hillsboro, Texas, in 1904, McGee was the product of an austere, Scot-Irish plantation household whose roots extended back to North Carolina. McGee's father had rejected the comforts of home for adventures in the western South, but by his late teens he found himself sharecropping and addicted to alcohol. McGee's mother grew up in a middle-class German Protestant clan from Nashville and was unaccustomed to the challenges of the frontier, but she nevertheless taught her children upright Christian living. It was her own religious commitments, McGee remembers, that allowed his mother to get through the tragedies that beset the family in the 1920s. After yet another failed cotton crop in western Texas, McGee's father moved his family to the town of Springer, Oklahoma, where he found work at a local cotton gin. McGee went to school, chopped cotton for a dollar a day, and, for the first time in his life, enjoyed a routine, even hunting possum on occasion. But his father died while repairing the gin and McGee, forced into manhood at age fourteen, moved with his mother to live with relatives back in Nashville. Two years later, while worshipping at Second Presbyterian Church, he renewed the pledge to serve God that he had made when his father died.[22]

Thanks to the largesse of two widows who saw unusual potential in the young man, McGee made good on this pledge by attending preparatory school, college, and finally Columbia Theological Seminary, in Georgia, and Dallas Theological Seminary, in Texas. McGee thrived in the formal academic setting, but it was local religious folk who taught him the most. One of his fondest memories of his seminary years was being called to speak at a small Baptist church in the "cotton mill section of Sherman, Texas." It was there that he met a woman everyone in the church called "Grandma," an elderly lady in failing health who could barely read or write. The legend among townsfolk was that Grandma had once traversed the Texas plains in a covered wagon with her husband, fighting off Indians with her rifle. Grandma proved equally adept with scripture. At the congregation's request, McGee made a visit to help her with daily devotions and, out of fear of overwhelming her with his knowledge, decided to dumb down his exegesis of John 14. After a few minutes of bored courteousness, Grandma spoke up: "'young man, had you ever noticed this?'" As McGee sat up surprised, he later recalled,

> she made comments to bring out some things in that passage which I had never heard before. In fact, there was no professor in school who had ever mentioned what she mentioned about that passage of Scripture. Before we got through the chapter, she was telling *me* and I was listening.

Humbled, even embarrassed, the young seminarian left Sherman that day convinced that the essence of Christian faith lay outside the academies and cathedrals of the cosmopolitan center.[23]

Even still, McGee's ambition led him to America's own modern-day "Bethel": Los Angeles. After ministering full-time in Cleburne, Texas, McGee and his wife, Ruth Jordan, accepted an invitation in the early 1940s to assume leadership of Lincoln Avenue Presbyterian Church, in Pasadena, California. His family and young congregation grew quickly, and McGee flourished as a youthful presence and vibrant personality within Los Angeles' evangelical subculture. By the late 1940s, McGee had established connections to Fuller Seminary, just a few blocks from his church, and the school's esteemed professors made frequent appearances at his church, especially fellow southerner Wilbur Smith. McGee's biggest leap, however, came after officials from the Church of the Open Door offered him the position of senior pastor following the resignation of the famed Louis Talbot. McGee accepted the call and, in January 1949, became COD's fifth pastor.[24]

When McGee, in his soft Texas drawl, introduced himself from COD's pulpit as "a plowboy from Cleburne, Texas" he effectively gave notice to his parishioners that their institution was about to be southernized. Laid-back in his demeanor, yet unbending in his convictions, McGee truly personified the new, Southern California version of Texas theology. Behind the façade of a relaxed pastor was a strong-willed visionary who expected things done his way. At the first meeting of COD's elders' committee, held just four weeks after his installation, McGee arranged to have himself named chairman of the board, a move unprecedented in the church's history. In similar fashion, the micromanaging pastor doled out a long list of requests and duties for his associates at the first executive board meeting, quite unlike Talbot's hands-off approach. McGee's task-oriented vision may have been narrow, but his goals for the church were farsighted. McGee assumed COD's pastorate with one central goal in mind: to raise the church's profile. Soon after assuming the pulpit, he pursued his own daily radio program, one that would allow him to reach the Southland and at the same time provide publicity for COD, so he turned to his good friend John Brown at KGER and made history. McGee began his first broadcast with the same warm words of welcome that he would repeat daily for the next two decades: "It is high noon in downtown Los Angeles and high time for the High Noon Bible Broadcast." In no time, COD's membership began a steady climb, rising from 3,300 in 1949 to 4,400 in 1965.[25]

Meanwhile, McGee quickly became KGER's superstar. Stardom came by way of his resonant and illustrative oratory. Remembered as "catchingly different" for its nasally timbre and Texas twang, his voice transported the willing listener back to a simpler time. In fact, his radio show traded heavily on nostalgia. Writing of her devotion to McGee, one woman noted:

> Your program is my daily Bible reading. . . . My husband also listens and some of our friends are daily listeners of your program. In fact we feel like you are an old friend of ours since you once lived here in Texas near our home.

For his part, McGee embellished the horse-sense quality of his sermons, especially those delivered to a live audience. An early convert to visual aids while preaching, McGee loved nothing more than to pull out his "electric blackboard" (overhead projector) and "stereopticon" (slide projector) to help him illustrate passages from the New Testament. Pictures of a boy fishing on the banks of a river or hunting possum in the woods (just as he had done as a boy, he would remind his audience) were not infrequent "homely additions" to his Sunday sermons or weeknight Bible studies.[26]

Besides his unique cadence and catchy props, McGee also "preached in simplistic terms" and "brought a complex theology right down to earth where [all] could grasp exactly what the Scriptures were teaching." Although a student of the elegant pulpit presence of great evangelical orators, it was the lesson learned back in Sherman, Texas, that left a deeper impression on McGee: The simplest reading of scripture was always the profoundest. McGee worked hard to teach this to young pastors. Writing to one such understudy, he revealed the key to good homiletics:

> Make it simple. . . . Remember this when you are preparing a sermon and you think it is finished, go over it and simplify it, then you go over it again and make it more simple, then you go over it a third time and make it so simple that you're ashamed of it. Then you will be ready to preach it! And when you preach that kind of a simple sermon your main elder will come to you after the service and say, "My, preacher, you were sure wading deep this morning!"

McGee systematized this philosophy. In 1950 he launched a program that became his signature contribution to postwar evangelicalism. Initially designed to give structure to COD's midweek meeting, McGee's *Thru the Bible* covered one short, scriptural passage each day, which, over the course of five years, amounted to the entire Bible. The concept was an instant success. Three years later McGee's program had already garnered two thousand registered participants. Over the next two decades it would evolve into a publishing empire and a broadcasting phenomenon with daily programs heard on over seven hundred radio stations and in over twenty-five languages worldwide.[27]

McGee's ministries presented a different conception of evangelicalism from the one COD had long been accustomed to. Resolutely orthodox, McGee nevertheless had less patience for the cerebral refinements of classical evangelicalism that COD's former pastors entertained. Not that he shunned them. As with an increasing number of southern preachers climbing their profession's ranks in the late 1940s and early 1950s, McGee was, for instance, a premillennialist, comfortable with COD's traditional emphasis on biblical prophecy. Prior to World War II, most clerics in the predominantly Protestant South had not seen a reason to identify with this pessimistic, countercultural, crisis theology. Amid the turmoil of the postwar years, however, this thought system began to make better sense. Yet even as they adopted this outlook they altered it. Once a complex doctrine that encouraged intellectualizing, McGee and his cohort helped turn it into an impetus for local activism, cultural engagement, and American global intervention. Changing world circumstances certainly precipitated this turn, but McGee's southern pragmatism nevertheless lent COD's apocalyptic thinking a new, tangible feel. Even while expounding on elaborate eschatological truths, he sacrificed the philosophical for the ethical, the abstract for the personal dimension, and the treatise for the parable. Like a true southern preacher, he preferred to draw the story and its redemptive qualities out from his text rather than overwhelm his listener with doctrinal complexities. "When the plain sense of Scripture makes common sense, seek no other sense" was McGee's maxim, preached often to his congregants, in part to ensure that their shared "blessed hope" of Christ's sudden and unexpected return led to real change in their lives and communities.[28]

McGee also imposed on COD his preference for the style of evangelical expression found in Dallas and Nashville. Wanting to surround himself with those familiar with his brand of religion, he hired assistant pastors from the western South and carefully nurtured ties with fellow southern preachers. Starting in 1949, McGee began annual speaking tours (work-related trips he considered "vacations") through the South, often stopping at Dallas Theological Seminary, as well as places like Oklahoma City, Amarillo, Houston, and Memphis. The most anticipated of visits "back east" were those that took him to John Brown University in Siloam Springs, Arkansas. Beyond their alliance at KGER, McGee and Brown shared plow-to-pulpit autobiographies and the innate ability to shape a modern gospel grounded in a simple past that appealed to devotees who had traveled from the Depression-era South to cold war California. When they listened to McGee at church or on Brown's radio waves, it was as if they had never left home.[29]

FROM PULPIT TO POLITICAL STUMP

With the southernization of their doctrine and congregational culture, COD congregants would find their church's politics had changed as well after McGee assumed control. Beginning in the early 1950s, McGee used the COD pulpit to speak out against his ideological foes. Unlike the heavy rhetorical artillery of some Christian anticommunists, however, McGee relied on low-caliber weapons—his sermons and stereopticon—to make his point.

Not that McGee ever saw his ministry in overtly political terms. He liked to emphasize that, in contrast to other churches (liberal and conservative alike), which invested themselves in government affairs, COD was only interested in saving individual souls. To a degree he was right. Most weeks, McGee's microphone rang out with heartfelt calls to Christ's cross and a life of spiritual sacrifice. Political commentary appeared only occasionally, and his followers often had to read between the lines to grasp his point. Moreover, McGee's few direct references to affairs of the state were usually part of a sweeping anticommunist discourse that targeted the red menace in holistic terms. For McGee, anticommunism was existential, not political.[30]

But McGee's claim was also misleading. On most occasions the Texas transplant's anticommunism came couched in conspicuously political assumptions. Echoing the likes of J. Edgar Hoover, whom he lauded, McGee believed that communism was "religion's mortal foe" and a tool used by Satan to eradicate Christian democratic values. Working from this totalizing worldview, he was always willing to entertain even the most fantastic theories of internal subversion and conquest by fifth columnists, including those advanced by Joseph McCarthy. One of his favorite sermons, for instance, titled "Origin of Communism," offered a history lesson laden with conspiratorial charges that began in the late twelfth century and continued through Jean-Jacques Rousseau and Adam Weisshaupt, ending with wild condemnations of Karl Marx, Friedrich Engels, and Vladimir Lenin, and praise for Martin Dies. This historical foray into radical philosophy was "scheduled to provoke serious minded Christians to recognize the menace." He always concluded such sermons with a simple summary—communism was rooted in lawlessness, anarchy, and Satanism—and followed with words of comfort: "It is dark in the world just now—never too dark for [a] child of God."[31]

McGee used such occasions also to make another point: The people best equipped to fight communism were those with the least patience for mental games—commoners unencumbered by the complexities of humanist ideas, plain folk schooled by life rather than by the Ivy League. In this vein, his anticommunist lectures always assumed a distinctively southern, populist tone, and in most cases they relied on visual aids for extra effect. "Will Russia Destroy the U.S.?" and "A Nation at the Crossroads," two of McGee's more popular anticommunist homilies, for instance, were delivered with the help of the pastor's stereopticon. "I wish I could take you to your home town tonight [but the] best I can do is take you to mine," he began, while leading his congregation on an elaborate slide show tour of Oklahoma and Texas. Beginning with images of his childhood home, McGee moved slowly through a repertoire of thirty images, talking all the while about the values each image portrayed and their potential power in helping ward off communism. Reserved for the end was a picture of the Dallas skyline. McGee let this image glow longer than all the others to drive home the idea that the moral centeredness of Dallas made it "truly one of [the] great cities of America." With the slide finally dimming, McGee invited his congregation to sing the "Battle Hymn of the Republic." Personalized stories, pictures, sounds, and a trace of vulnerability gave McGee special access to his parishioners' hearts. This was the genius of the new country preacher.[32]

His savvy shined through in other contexts as well. While discussing communism, McGee also commented directly on related political trends. Regularly, he launched into invectives against "Collectivism," Catholicism, "Socialism," "Secularism," and "Liberalism," always reserving special criticism for the latter. In his mind, this expansive movement represented the truest threat to the godly ideal of autonomous individuals bonded in local community by shared religious convictions and the commitment to liberty. McGee wove a powerful discourse of grassroots opposition against this Goliath that started with theology and ended with politics, and in between connected relevant commentary on race, citizenship, pluralism, and international cooperation.

McGee's threefold critique of liberalism began on theological grounds. COD's pastor believed that the open fellowship promoted by liberal religious leaders led to a false unity. By nature, he argued, Protestantism drew its energy from distinctive doctrines and the contest for truth. To downplay this marketplace style for the sake of cooperation was to invite the watering down of religious faith, the emasculation of religious practice, and ultimately the appearance of false teachings in the church. Ecumenical unions also made citizens and local congregations subservient to artificial associations, rendering powerless those most invested in the maintenance of orthodoxy. Having submitted to ecumenism, McGee emphasized, true believers could expect their traditions to sink into the modern morass of ambiguity and ambivalence.

Resisting liberalism was, secondly, an eschatological issue for McGee. Liberal Protestants who championed a social gospel and postmillennial doctrine that suggested the world could get better with time offered false hope. No agency was more heretical on this count than the National Council of Churches (NCC), heir to the Federal Council of Churches. In choosing to privilege collective, social activism over individual conscience and belief, the NCC advanced the commonest heresy in history: that humans could attain perfection. "I say it kindly but none the less dogmatically," McGee preached, but "it is one of the inanities of the human intellect and a foible and fable of man's imagination that any method contrary to God's method will succeed." Like Nimrod, who yearned to reach the heavens with the tower of Babel, built by the hands of man, ecumenists wrongly assumed that a higher state of being could be realized on their terms. As much as this misplaced confidence dethroned the Babylonian king, McGee reminded his audience, it could easily destroy America.[33]

McGee, finally, argued that liberalism was misguided in its promotion of peace. Nowhere in scripture was peace the ultimate goal of the church; the fight for truth and freedom always had outweighed the pursuit of "peace at any cost." In fact, widespread talk about peace among nations signified only the brief quiet before the apocalyptic storm. Christ was the sole "Prince of Peace," he insisted, and any individual or group that looked to fill this role in his absence was blaspheming. This was not to say that international harmony should be discouraged, McGee was quick to add, but simply that it was a task too great for human beings: "Man may have his theory for promulgating world peace," the preacher warned, "but only God's plan will work." Here the fight against liberalism touched the realm of policy, for as McGee reminded his parishioners, out of this distorted philosophy had emerged America's own tower of Babel: the UN. "There is in the United States an organization that I am confident can and will become the instrument in setting up the stage for [the] fulfillment of prophecy," he proclaimed. "This organization is located in New York City [and] may have a large part in man's final act of the sordid drama of sin." Evangelical preachers routinely condemned the UN in the early 1950s as a harbinger of one-world government spoken of in the Book of Revelation, but it was McGee's delivery that revealed his ability to whittle this foreboding and knotty concept down to simplest application. One of his most powerful homilies took his audience on a visual tour of the new UN headquarters in New York. McGee himself had taken the pictures while on a "privately-conducted, behind-the-scenes tour," and he interspersed his snapshots of the General Assembly and the array of national flags with contrasting images of doom (Times Square, Wall Street, Adlai Stevenson) and bucolic delight (tidy farms, majestic waterfalls). It was an ominous aesthetic; McGee wanted his congregants to emerge convinced that the UN was beating a political path for the Antichrist.[34]

McGee also hoped his audience exited his slide show with a sense of accountability for the present. The UN threatened personal freedoms here and now, he thundered, but look what U.S. investment in this multi-national organization also meant for the character of their nation. Relying on a mental picture this time, McGee described the "chaos" he had witnessed during lunch with delegates at the UN. It was the cacophony "of all sorts of languages and dialects" and the "utter godlessness of the place" that convinced him that the UN's multiculturalism would be the undo-ing of true Americanism. Fears of pluralism and secularization combined with eschatological obsession with internationalism thus turned McGee's visuals into an urgent plea for action. The UN was a portent of the apoca-lypse, he argued, a political machine that demanded coordinated resis-tance on the part of all Bible-believers.[35]

A pastor by calling, McGee was therefore a pundit in practice, whether he fully acknowledged it or not. With a sweeping, colorful critique of liberal ecumenism, he succeeded at drawing up a political blueprint for his followers, one that dovetailed with the grand designs of conservative insurgents. Granted, not everything he outlined was revolutionary. That communism represented Christianity's antithesis was a familiar trope in evangelical circles long before McGee took hold of it. Yet he managed to connect it better than most to the new anticommunist ideology that was taking shape and providing a critical link between intellectual, corpo-rate, libertarian, and traditionalist conservatives. Much like Chambers's, McGee's ideological taxonomy painted New Deal liberalism as commu-nism in an embryonic state; the difference between them was simply a matter of degree. And much like Burnham, Manion, and Wedemeyer, McGee critiqued the liberal foreign policy personified by Stevenson, the Democratic diplomat whose image he singled out, as soft and servile to other nations. These linkages were deliberate, on McGee's part; prior to each of his sermons he read extensively in the anticommunist literature of his day, eager to pluck out sermon illustrations and even entire texts that he attached to his sermon notes for use in the pulpit. In this way, his parishioners did not have to frequent James Fifield's Freedom Clubs or a local conservative bookstore to learn about the latest anticommunist analysis by conservatism's leading thinkers; McGee brought this analysis to them.[36]

McGee's anticommunism also prodded his parishioners into Manion's orbit of Catholic conservatism. The shift was somewhat ironic. Like many evangelicals at the time, McGee was staunchly anti-Catholic and had sermons in his repertoire that asked leading, rhetorical questions such as "Is Romanism as Great a Menace as Communism to America?" Yet he noted that distinctions needed to be made between Catholics as religious-minded individuals and the Catholic Church as a corrupt, totalitarian entity. McGee conceded that there were "many fine and patriotic Catholics" who believed in the supreme virtue of religious and political freedom but still worshipped in an oppressive religious system. He had grudging respect for Catholic anticommunists in Eastern Europe, and for the ideas of Russell Kirk and William F. Buckley found in the *National Review, Manion Forum, American Mercury, Reader's Digest, National Review,* and *Christian Economics,* which he also studied in preparation for his sermons. McGee appreciated these writers' understanding of human fallibility and their deep concern for the loss of custom and community, tradition and moral centeredness. Like them, McGee felt that political problems necessitated spiritual solutions.[37]

In keeping with his wide reading in these periodicals, McGee also shared his fellow conservatives' prescriptions for race and citizenship. Like most on the Right at the time, McGee viewed racism as a tragic by-product of the human condition that could be erased only gradually through change in citizens' hearts and minds. Even if there was now reason to support desegregation, he still felt that social readjustments needed to take place gradually. Otherwise, the social vacuum left behind would be filled by communism. His firsthand account of the "chaos" and "utter godlessness" at the UN resonated with this discourse, as well as with the language of his religious cohort, which stemmed from the logic of black-white separation. A product of the South, McGee thought it was best if blacks and whites worshipped in separate spheres. Even in the West Coast cosmopolitan context, McGee's segregationist sympathies did not die; COD continued to be a predominantly white bastion well into the 1960s, though more by cultural expectation than formal decree. And while he lauded the efforts of individuals to eradicate racism, he did little to promote them. His belief in the pervasiveness of human sin and his deep skepticism of the ability of human agencies to eliminate the scourges of racism, poverty, and sickness—"these crippling curses of humanity"—worked against a progressive, activist stand on the matter.[38]

Although COD's country preacher and others like him would not completely reassess their racial prejudices until the 1960s, even in the 1950s they took an initial step by soundly rejecting the language of white superiority used earlier by southern preachers like Bob Shuler. Well into the 1950s Shuler continued to propagate a rigid Jim Crow racial order in the name of anticommunism. He believed the emerging civil rights movement witnessed in Operation Dixie in fact to be communism's slickest ploy. "I was born and reared in Virginia" and "served as pastor in Tennessee and Texas," so "[I] know the Negro problem first hand," he insisted, in a 1951 article titled "Negroes, Ahead of Schedule":

> I have vigorously defended the Negroes and maintained their right to enjoy any privilege enjoyed by any other American. No man can rightfully accuse me of racial prejudice or of being unfriendly to the Negro people. But I have seen and do see the perils that attend the swift rise to prominence and power of the Negroes, a people separated from the jungle barbarism and slavery by less than two centuries.

In a string of articles meant to defend his beloved South, Shuler revealed an equally malodorous outlook. On one hand he boasted of a South that was reforming its social order, while on the other he worried about these processes going too far too quickly because of communist agitators. He admitted as much in a 1953 piece in which he railed against black-white intermarriage and insisted that southern states be allowed to handle the "Negro question" on their own terms. In Shuler's mind, the dismantling of Jim Crow was akin to the UN's attempts to override American sovereignty: both were communist-inspired ruses to poison pure Anglo-Saxon blood and destroy the traditional American values for which his people stood.[39]

Tellingly, McGee chose to distance himself from "Fighting Bob" Shuler and his old Virginia and Texas ways. Instead, he personified the New Evangelicalism, the New South, and the New Southern California. He did so simply by avoiding substantive talk about racism and civil rights

altogether. This approach was popular within the new evangelical establishment in the 1950s, and openly advocated by leaders like Billy Graham's father-in-law, L. Nelson Bell. A respected missionary and leader
within the southern Presbyterian Church—McGee's former denomination—Bell wrote that it was "wasteful to 'divert our emphasis' from the
project of winning souls to Christ by going after particular groups." It was
also un-Christian and unhealthy: "when we have hate in our hearts for
any people, it does something to us rather than to them." Like Graham,
who would soon take a more assertive stand on civil rights by desegregating his southern evangelistic crusades, Bell knew that evangelicals
needed to put aside the racial baggage of their past in order to more effectively counter the ascendant liberal empire.[40]

By virtue of his silence, it seemed McGee agreed, though because of
his location he was never pressed to engage the issue in quite the same
way. Unlike Bell and Graham, who would find themselves in the middle
of the civil rights battles soon to unfold in the South, McGee would spend
the 1950s relatively removed from the fray. After the heated labor wars of
the 1940s, which brought race to the center of grassroots political combat
and an end to de jure segregation in their community, Southern Californians would flock to the suburbs in the 1950s, distancing themselves
from the recent racial hostilities. Thus McGee would proceed untested
on these issues until the early 1960s, when he and other evangelicals living in Southern California would finally confront their lingering, exclu-
sionary assumptions and practices. Until then, he would focus on what he
believed to be his fundamental task: winning souls to Christ and protecting them from the Satanic red menace.

BESIDES RAISING AWARENESS OF communism and its ideological hand-
maidens, McGee counseled his parishioners on how to turn their nation
around for God. Upon his arrival in the late 1940s, he began imparting
new anticommunist, conservative doctrine simply by telling the story of
his own life. Then, gradually, through the early 1950s, he charted a bolder
political course of action for his followers. Agitated by an "intrusive" state,
McGee became convinced that "only an immediate and continuous uprising of conservative thought [could] halt our nation's plunge into socialism"—this, and the final destruction of Franklin Roosevelt's legacy. Like
other southern plain-folk preachers, McGee had welcomed the New Deal

as a temporary correction to the excesses and failings of capitalism, but now it was obvious, in his mind, that New Deal liberalism was actually a halfway house to communism. In one telling sermon that called for a "New Age, not a New Deal," McGee elaborated on a catalogue of political failings: from the abandonment of Christian economics to the continuation of the Fair Deal, from rampant moral degeneracy to the disappearance of traditional education. Animated by the very same impulse that commanded communism, each of these developments, McGee ventured, could be traced to the New Deal. What did this require of his listeners? Severing this system's ugly tentacles of influence in their churches, schools, businesses, and government. But how to begin? By looking first for inspiration in the western South, the cradle of Christian democracy.[41]

Many other southern clerics of McGee's age asked their parishioners the same questions and provided the same answers. By doing so they provided an inestimable service to the new conservative movement. While realigning Southern California evangelicalism on a southern axis, McGee and his fellow southern preachers also turned their ministries into meeting points for expanding strands of conservatism. Able to deliver an irenic gospel of anticommunism that was folksy yet not flippant, and deeply informed by wide reading in new conservative literature, these men solidified the groundwork for a broader coalition among right-wing thinkers, pundits, and activists. Of course, as much as they performed this diplomatic role well within broader religious and political circles, within their own transplanted southern evangelical subculture these clerics still had plenty of work to do before rank-and-file members felt completely at home in a Southern California conservative coalition. Having trained their parishioners to recognize every portentous shade of communism, southern plain-folk preachers now set out to teach them how to be comfortable in the sunshine of suburban wealth.

7

THE NEW GOSPEL
OF WEALTH

WE BELIEVE: In the Book, the Blood, and the Blessed Hope;
In a strong Bible teaching-Bible preaching emphasis; That soul-
winning evangelism and training in discipleship are the primary
responsibilities of the church; In providing for the total and bal-
anced education of our children as a vital part of the church pro-
gram; In basic, old-fashioned Americanism and the free enterprise
system; In an uncompromising stand against Modernism, Social-
ism, Communism and every form of "One Worldism![1]

—Bob Wells

ALTHOUGH HE DID NOT ATTEND THE CHURCH OF THE OPEN Door, Jean Vandruff often tuned in to J. Vernon McGee on KGER likely while driving Southern California's busy thoroughfares, scoping out land for new development or shuttling between construction sites. Vandruff, like so many of his neighbors, was a man on the go. In his freeway existence there was no time for lunch, much less midweek sermons. McGee's *Thru the Bible* program was ideal, in this sense, because it offered scripture in digestible doses. These brief forays into the Bible, accompanied by familiar tunes and McGee's Texas drawl, did much good for this southerner's soul.

In the mid-1950s, while saddled with a relentless schedule, Vandruff surely needed such moments of reconnection with a settled past. Exhilarated by his early success as an entrepreneur, he decided to combine his interests in architecture and business and start a home building company with his brother Shannon. Together these two ambitious Oklahomans acquired a handful of vacant lots in Downey, incorporated Cinderella Homes, and began building affordable tract homes that maintained the style and quality of the custom-made California rancher. The Vandruff brothers were proud to advertise family-oriented open-floor plans that allowed a housewife to be in constant touch with her husband and children, even while she worked in the kitchen. Jean's layouts reflected his values as much as his creativity; communication between husband and wife was critical, he believed, so by removing walls he was in fact improving marriages. His exterior designs were deliberate too. Built wide and low to the ground, with clipped ceilings, long roof overhangs, big, wide windows with custom shutters and oversized planters, the Vandruff house had a fairy-tale feel perfect for any suburban magicland. Function, form, family, and fantasy thus comprised the Vandruffs' philosophy and, in the new suburbs of Los Angeles and Orange counties, this formula was an instant hit. By 1954 they were building six houses at a time in Downey and scurrying to find more land. In 1955, they secured 40 acres on the west side of Anaheim and a guaranteed loan for the construction of 168 houses. When the houses went on the market they were sold out in three days. Another thousand people added their names to a waiting list for Cinderella Home's second development. Within a year, seven hundred houses were under contract with the Vandruffs, whose multi-million-dollar operation was now the largest of its kind in Orange County.[2]

Jean, meanwhile, began pursuing personal interests with the same verve that had made him a successful businessman. Eleanor Kouri was a native Oklahoman who had recently arrived in California after working at Ford in Detroit. Determined to woo her, Jean would drive his new companion to the Coconut Grove in Beverly Hills' Ambassador Hotel in his Cadillac Coupe deVille. Prior to her move west, Eleanor had been voted Ford's Beauty Queen and had been a professional singer in Oklahoma, so the glamour of Freddie Martin's orchestra at Beverly Hills' premier dining club, surrounded by Hollywood's best-looking people, impressed her. But as a dedicated Christian who shied away from alcohol and other nightclub activities, Eleanor was more attracted to the prospect of a family with Jean, and on June 27, 1952—five weeks after meeting—the two were married. In 1958, the couple relocated to Orange County, claimed a Cinderella home, and began living the life worthy of their suburban paradise.[3]

JEAN VANDRUFF'S RISE WAS remarkably swift amid California's economic boom, but thousands of other southern evangelicals also translated early cold war gains into affluence, taking control of the loosely clustered communities that now annexed the Southland's last open space. Decentralized, racially uniform, defense-centered, pro-business family sanctuaries, these communities suited their religious and political sensibilities perfectly. During the mid-1950s they built hundreds of new churches, interdenominational organizations, and media enterprises, all of which testified to their command of suburbia. Such economic empowerment bred intellectual change. The monumental leap from Depression-era poverty to middle-class respectability left them convinced of capitalism's Christian virtues. Some among them had already drawn such conclusions earlier in the 1940s, but most had been cautious, echoing inherited populist revulsions toward Wall Street that had once fueled Huey Longism and Ham and Eggs. Such protests, however, had never been condemnations of capitalism as much as complaints about the way greedy captains of industry adulterated it. In early cold war California, where personal wealth seemed to bubble up from the rich suburban soil itself, the democratic promises of pristine capitalism appeared restored, and such caution was hard to find anywhere in a pew.

Evangelical preachers and entrepreneurs took this moment to trumpet a new gospel of wealth that identified threats to pristine capitalism in big government. A blend of libertarian ideas and new Christian teachings on wealth, this gospel encouraged parishioners to internalize the personal ethics of stewardship and proper money management. It also urged them to protest a political order whose bureaucratic tendencies and Keynesian initiatives undermined these godly principles. In both contexts, southern evangelicalism's conversion to the new gospel of wealth was politically momentous. Its expanding ministries became forums for economic thought while its flourishing churches morphed into informal action committees ready to advance the interests of a conservative movement now breaking through at the state level. On a national stage, all of these developments heralded a striking transformation: Southern evangelicalism was no longer the poor person's religion.

COLD WAR AWAKENINGS

Of course, southern migrants like Jean Vandruff never thought of themselves as poor in pocket or spirit, so when reflecting on their postwar economic rise, they tended to highlight continuity over change. In their

minds, their success after World War II flowed from the very same qualities that got them through the Depression—namely, the dignity of hard
work and discipline. But as much as self-made men like Vandruff attributed their postwar affluence to individual initiative, unprecedented government spending in the defense sector deserved much of the credit, too.

California's postwar boom arrived with stunning rapidity and unparalleled effect in the early 1950s. Growth in automobile, petroleum, rubber, and food processing industries provided some momentum, but it was
the sharp rise in military expenditure brought on by the cold war that
thrust Southern California's economy into a frenetic state of expansion.
In the decade between 1952 and 1962, Pentagon spending would etch
itself into every facet of Southern California's economy, with 38 percent
of its manufacturing directly tied to a defense sector subsidized by four
billion dollars' worth of government contracts. At the midpoint in this
surge, in 1959, 321,600 Southern Californians worked in defense-related
industries, either in aircraft and missile manufacturing or in spin-off sectors like aerospace electronics. In San Diego County, three out of every
four manufacturing employees worked in the aerospace industry, while in
the larger Los Angeles–Long Beach area, the number was one in four. By
1964, cold war production centers like Los Angeles County and Orange
County had more balanced economies, yet even then 41.5 percent of their
total manufacturing employment—numbering 354,700 employees—was
defense-related.[4]

The defense industry's extraordinary hold on Southern California society was mapped onto the landscape as well. Thriving aerospace companies like Douglas and Northrop, North American Aviation and Lockheed,
erected office buildings, plants, bunkers, and testing grounds. Built away
from the city center to maximize available space, these sprawling campuses formed a crescent around Los Angeles like ramparts ringing a fortress. One of the campuses that contributed to this visual was Autonetics,
North American Aviation's electronics division, whose headquarters in
Anaheim's undeveloped northwest corner consisted of 27 buildings and
a 260-acre parking lot. Hard at work within its security fences, twenty-
five thousand Autonetics employees, generating a two-hundred-million-
dollar annual payroll, assembled radar units, guidance controls, and
other advanced electronic or electromechanical systems for submarines,
missiles, and fighter aircraft. At the very end of his presidency, Dwight
Eisenhower would warn Americans about the encroaching, totalizing

influences of the military-industrial complex. But even as early as his second inauguration, in 1957, the military-industrial complex was not simply
encroaching on Southern California; it was imprinted on its soul.[5]

New suburbs clustered around the Southland's defense complexes bore
witness to this fact. Because of government initiatives like the Federal
Housing Administration and Federal-Aid Highway Act, which guaranteed
long-term mortgages and funded freeway construction, lax or fluid zoning
requirements, and entrepreneurial initiative that ran loose in the postwar boom, these communities assumed a form not before seen in North
America. Defined by some as postsuburban and others as exurban, they
mirrored the decentralized features of the new postindustrial economy
that supported them. These were not bedroom communities for commuters, but rather self-contained villages meant to fulfill their inhabitants'
every need—work, worship, education, and play. Their relationship to the
defense sector made them subservient to its interests. There were schools
that prepared youngsters for this knowledge-based economy, civic centers
and shopping malls that provided families with essential and luxury services, and entertainment districts that offered leisurely escape. Around
Long Beach, neighborhoods that had been carved out of dairy farms gave
allegiance to Douglas; Lockheed ruled the communities raised out of
the San Fernando Valley's ranch land. These were Southern California's
ultramodern versions of the company towns that proliferated in the steel
belt, their semiconductors and jet propulsion labs the antitheses to the
belching smokestacks of Cleveland and Pittsburgh.[6]

Hundreds of thousands of Americans were drawn to California's
boom. By the mid-1950s, an average of one thousand people were moving into the state every day, with 70 percent of these settling first in the
expanding residential tracts that bordered Los Angeles and San Diego
and now sprouted haphazardly in Orange County. These sojourners were
generally younger (under the age of thirty-four), more educated, and more
highly skilled than those who had traveled west ten years earlier, but they
were just as southern. In the 1950 census, Texas officially supplanted Illinois as the state that made the largest contribution to California's population growth, with Oklahoma and Missouri joining these two states to
round out the top four. To demographers monitoring statewide population growth, this marked an end to a century-long migration saga that
had seen either a northeastern or midwestern state claim the leading role.
But for those Southern Californians accustomed to incoming southerners

since the Depression, the latest statistics indicated just another phase in the southernization of their society.[7]

If defense money built the exurbs, bonds of class, race, and religion held them together. The united quest for "patios, pools, and a pleasant way of life" now drove Californians to the housing tracts where class distinctions were less pronounced. Economic diversity still existed, but, thanks to rising incomes and the possibility of home and car ownership, it was now muted. Some cold war suburbs housed well-paid laborers, small-time businessmen, and midlevel managers in three-bedroom ranchers. Others accommodated young professionals in sprawling four-bedroom versions of the same-styled abode. Whereas a Ford or Chevrolet was likely parked in the driveway of the former, sometimes it was a Lincoln or Cadillac in the latter. Still, in both cases the car and house confirmed their owner's abilities to participate in the marketplace. Consumption proved to be the great equalizer.[8]

This American dream, at whatever level, was attainable for many Southern Californians, but only for those who were white. For black, Latino, and other minority Californians, the cold war boom proved tragically illusory. Granted, the suburban dreams that drove whites to new neighborhoods did allow blacks and Latinos some room to exercise greater control over the communities they left behind. Yet these were small consolations. In the housing market, de facto segregation prevented blacks from relocating outside the city's central corridor. Although the abolishment of restrictive covenants in 1948 brought a swift end to de jure segregation, it did not eradicate racial exclusion. During the 1950s white homeowners found other ways to guarantee the racial homogeneity of their neighborhoods, often relying on the selective practices of land developers and real estate agents, who ultimately dictated patterns of settlement, and exerting peer pressure on their fellow homeowners through neighborhood and civic associations. Financial agencies and mortgage lenders whose funding practices rewarded low-risk clients (white middle-class) in low-risk locations (new suburbs) helped whites lock down their suburban enclaves. Civil rights activists like Loren Miller, who had played such a pivotal role in abolishing restrictive covenants, rightly recognized that dismantling de facto segregation would prove far more vexing. Despite his best efforts to reverse racist residential patterns, by the end of the 1950s Southern California's suburban communities would be the most segregated in the entire United States.[9]

For blacks in South Central Los Angeles and, similarly, Latinos in East Los Angeles, physical distance from these all-white suburbs exacerbated the other part of their problem: finding employment. Already limited by their lack of acquired skills and experience within aircraft manufacturing, minorities found it even more difficult to break into the new aerospace industry. For most, the prohibitive costs of commuting denied them a place in California's most vibrant economic sector. Settled in exclusive neighborhoods that bordered exclusive industries, white suburbanites thus lived in a homogeneous reality. Los Angeles' urban crisis in the 1960s would awaken some to the precariousness of this social order, but amid the serenity of their suburbs in the 1950s, white Californians spent little time pondering the racial complexities of an employment and housing system that, to them, seemed innately just and good.[10]

Yet a third pillar of cold war culture—religion—worked alongside class and race to structure the California suburbs. Life in this 1950s setting seemed to revolve around public displays of devotion. Billy Graham set the tone at the beginning of the decade by praying on the White House lawn after meeting with President Truman. Caught on film, Graham's display sent a message to the public that faith was now welcomed in Washington. Even though the evangelist received criticism for his actions, including from Truman himself, who labeled him a publicity seeker, Graham's message stuck. Three years later, at his inauguration, Dwight Eisenhower opened his presidency by offering "a little private prayer" for his administration. And to the Pledge of Allegiance he added the words "one nation under God," a phrase that reflected American society's new emotional attachment to the Judeo-Christian tradition. In Southern California's cold war suburbs, however, the phrase became an edict and an ethic, not simply a sentiment.[11]

SUBURBAN SAINTS

As individuals who had embraced the politics of national defense during World War II, southern evangelicals looked to the cold war boom as confirmation of who they were not only as laborers but also as citizens. And now as consumers, awarded purchasing power and a new station in neighborhoods built to their tastes, these patriots shed their sense of embattlement for one of entitlement. Having arrived—physically as well as metaphorically—in middle-class suburbia, they set about making sure that their churches' fortunes grew in sync with the advancements that had redefined their personal lives.

The cold war boom was most evident at the congregational level, where southern evangelical churches received sudden injections of energy. Young and economically stable, the second generation of southern migrants joined the upwardly mobile class of first-wave southern transplants to lead their religious communities into a new era of expansion. By the early 1950s Clifford and Marie Allen, for instance, saw their church's membership book brimming with new names, its pews filled with dentists, engineers, plumbers, and mechanics. In October 1953, after seeing its membership nearly triple in less than two years, Southern Missionary Baptist purchased five acres on a major Santa Ana artery, changed its name to Bristol Street Baptist, and began construction on a quarter-million-dollar campus with an educational complex and an auditorium seating 1,500.[12]

The type of rebirth Bristol Street Baptist experienced was a common occurrence. Whether large or small, richer or poorer, Southern California's Churches of Christ, as well as its Pentecostal, Baptist, Nazarene, Foursquare, and independent churches, found their buildings overwhelmed with new members and neighborhoods rich with potential converts. As one moved outward from Los Angeles' manufacturing hub toward the quieter communities sprouting in its hinterland, southern evangelical growth grew more astounding. By the early 1950s, working-class suburbs like Bell Gardens, once distinguishable for their ratty, self-built houses, oil-slicked gravel roads, open cesspools, overgrown yards, and small livestock, now exhibited traits of the middle-class subdivision—tract homes connected to city sewage systems, street lamps lining asphalt boulevards, and plenty of trimmed crabgrass where domestic pets could play. Evangelical congregations reveled in such progress and eagerly reported advancements in the local press. In 1957, the Bell Gardens Assemblies of God church, for example, dedicated a new five-hundred-seat auditorium, a modern structure paid in full at its completion. Just a few blocks away, Southern Baptists announced their own impressive achievements. First Baptist Bell Gardens now boasted an attendance of 450, an ambitious building program, and a church-plant network of 7 churches, with combined enlistment of 3,000. Less than two decades after its run-in with local authorities over the misappropriation of land, First Baptist was hailed by community leaders as a pillar of social stability and by its denomination as a model of soul-winning success.[13]

In new suburbs like Northridge and Gardena, Bellflower and Lake-wood, southern religious folk swept their neighborhoods with street wit-nessing and tent revivalism, in much the same way their predecessors had ten years earlier. Throughout the 1950s, bold and outspoken cler-ics routinely preached on street corners and built canvas cathedrals on plots of undeveloped land. Those encouraging tent revivalism were often the neediest churches—Pentecostal congregations, for instance, whose unceasing evangelism drove their membership through the roof and out the doors of their existing church buildings. While tent revivals brought flashes of rapturous joy, evangelicals were most pleased by steady church expansion. Whether it was the Church of the Nazarene or Church of Christ in Long Beach, or the Assemblies of God in Norwalk and Lake-wood, every denomination could claim unprecedented statistical achieve-ments. Few congregations, however, matched the singular efficiency of Calvary Baptist in Bellflower. Founded in 1935 as the First Fundamental Church of Bellflower, this congregation erected its first meetinghouse in a dairy field on the town's edge. In 1949 it constructed a larger audito-rium in order to retain the middle-class families that now filled the pews. There would be constant new construction during the following decade. By the early 1960s, when a former professional country musician from Alabama named H. Frank Collins became its pastor and gave the church national presence, Calvary was already an imposing force as the epicenter for fundamentalism in southeastern Los Angeles County.[14]

Churches in Bell Gardens and Bellflower would quickly be over-whelmed by growth in yet a third terrain, where southern evangelicalism's potential was just beginning to be imagined. Imagination was indeed welcomed in this place, rightly suggesting that such potential was great. Across Los Angeles County's southern border sprawled Orange County, where home builders like Jean Vandruff, prosperous business enterprises like North American Aviation, and entertainment gurus like Walt Disney sought to revamp ranch land and citrus groves into a bourgeois utopia. By the mid-1950s development was already well under way, particularly in the county's northwest corner. Once isolated, towns like Santa Ana, which Marie Allen first encountered in the early 1940s, expanded almost overnight into conjoined suburbs. Here the virtues of patriotism, entre-preneurialism, localism, and family values assumed conspicuous form in such fantastic creations as Disneyland and Knott's Berry Farm, Walter Knott's brainchild, and such wild innovations as drive-thru restaurants and drive-in churches. Here, southern evangelicalism would help take California's cold war awakening to the next stage.

Pentecostal leaders were among the first to clue in. Having struggled for much of the 1940s to bring order to their constituency, Assemblies of God administrators now marveled at the statistical triumphs of their church. By 1955 Southern California Assemblies of God churches dominated the national body in missionary support, church construction, and several other measurements of financial well-being. And when denominational leaders declared a campaign for "1,000 New Assemblies Churches in 1955," Southern California Pentecostals far outpaced every other district in the country. "In 1955 more housing units went up in Orange County, California, than in all but eleven of the forty-eight states," the *Pentecostal Evangel* proclaimed:

> Remarkable gains have been made by the Assemblies in this area, for in its report on this county, *Christian Life* says, "Fastest spreading group, without doubt, is the Assemblies of God." In 1940 we had three churches in Orange County. In 1949 we had eighteen. Now we have forty-two!

Church scribes were even more amazed by visual signs of progress. Once relegated to shacks on unkempt streets in Los Angeles' blue-collar suburbs, Pentecostal congregations now commanded prime meeting space on Orange County's palm-tree-lined boulevards. In cold war suburbia southern evangelicalism was the faith of the future.[15]

Southern churchmen and churchwomen took command of this future by crafting a religious system perfectly suited to their new suburban home. Change in the pulpit helped. The seminarians that now came to the West Coast were willing to adapt to the mores and demands of their new neighborhoods. These pastors saw proliferation, not concentration, of their efforts as a key to success. Earlier, the large, central church had been considered the ultimate goal; the church that drew members by virtue of its imposing size was typically considered the most effective one. In Los Angeles, two such institutions were Bob Shuler's Trinity Methodist and J. Vernon McGee's Church of the Open Door. Located within blocks of each other in the city's center, both counted on their location to provide instant and lasting credibility. After World War II, however, centrality became a burden; in a landscape fractured by freeways, the downtown church became antiquated.

Trinity failed to adapt and thus fell quickly. By 1948 it could still claim four thousand members, but that was down from roughly five thousand a decade earlier. Bob Shuler's autocratic leadership and controversial politics around this time might have contributed to the trend, but most of Trinity's members remained loyal to their church because of, not despite, their pastor's activism. In fact, when Shuler announced his retirement in 1953, he "released" his former parishioners to worship elsewhere. This may have been a final act of self-importance, but he also realized that his followers were "scattering all over the city, joining evangelical churches in the hope of finding a message and program that for many years characterized the activities of Trinity." After 1953, the church would exist only as a shell of its former self. With Shuler's pronouncement, written from his home in Los Angeles' east suburb of El Monte, the region's bastion of Southern Methodism officially succumbed to sprawl.[16]

Were it not for McGee's innovations, Church of the Open Door would have experienced a similar fate. Like Trinity, COD was a central congregation that relied on its physical presence for authority. Its rococo façade and neon towers gave it a slightly stronger visual presence than Trinity, but even thirty-foot JESUS SAVES signs were hardly readable when glimpsed at fifty miles per hour from the new downtown freeways. McGee recognized the threat of suburbanization and acted quickly. The first move was subtle. McGee revamped COD's weekly congregational prayer meeting by moving it to Thursday evenings (making it less likely to conflict with other churches' midweek services) and taking time to field the audience's questions about current events and cultural issues, ranging from capital punishment to child rearing, eternal security to social welfare. Within three years the weekly prayer meeting was the largest of its kind in the country, with an average of 2,500 people driving in from as far as fifty miles away. The second move was more radical. During the second executive board meeting of his tenure, McGee announced a new campaign of "sectional meetings" in the homes of church members. Within the year, Bible study "cell groups" were active in most of Los Angeles County's residential communities. COD's pastors, meanwhile, were canvassing at an astounding rate. In six months, one pastor alone covered 7,000 miles and visited over 1,100 homes.[17]

McGee's strategies brightened COD's prospects but had unintended consequences. Other congregations soon adopted McGee's more horizontal structure of power, dispensing with top-down ecclesiastical models. This did not negate the appeal of the large church or an august senior pastor. But, like COD, these entities now operated more as pivots in expansive orbs of suburban ministry. Within this diffuse, democratized setting, ministers gained authority by the strength of their personality and the marketability of their skills. Clerical authority, in other words, was no longer an assumed or assigned right but a provisional dispensation awarded by people in the pews. McGee's model also delegated a striking amount of power to the laity. Laymen and laywomen had always exercised extensive power in southern evangelicalism, yet the unique demands of California's postsuburban landscape enhanced their managerial authority in the church even more. Their economic advancement meant they had the time, means, and incentive to assume such heavy responsibilities.

What emerged from this convergence of contingencies proved to be one of the most important tools of modern evangelism: the parachurch organization. Interdenominational in their appeal and tied together by interpersonal connections, these organizations operated completely outside of ecclesiastical control in hopes of evangelizing people who might otherwise ignore organized religion. Roused by the revival that seemed to sweep throughout the country in the 1950s, parachurch ministries began to reconstitute America's religious establishment. By the middle of this decade they touched every sector of California society. Veterans of war and prisoners of the state, senior citizens and high school students, suburban housewives and Hollywood celebrities, rich businessmen and struggling workers: All had access to businesslike, efficient parachurch organizations that operated under market principles with military-like precision. Conservative Christians of all kind supported these enterprises, but southern evangelical initiative—already so in tune with postwar economics—truly powered this grand experiment in religious restructuring.[18]

One particularly successful parachurch ministry, Campus Crusade for Christ, embodied this mode of inventiveness. Bill Bright, founder of Campus Crusade, moved from Coweta, Oklahoma, to Los Angeles in 1944. A slightly built, energetic, smooth-talking young man, Bright learned to direct his drive toward evangelistic activities under the counsel of Henrietta Mears—who, next to pastor Louis Evans Sr., was Hollywood First Presbyterian's most prominent leader. Mears urged Bright to join a partic-

ular Bible study comprised of highly ambitious and successful young people, some of whom were actors, others students and young professionals.
Besides placing him in contact with California evangelicalism's next generation of leaders—including Billy Graham, whose propitious introduction to Stuart Hamblen prior to his 1949 crusade would occur at Mears's
Bible study—Bright's involvement confirmed his commitment to Christian service. A tireless evangelical, Bright was also an entrepreneur with
great ambition. In 1951 he started a candy company, Bright's California
Confections, whose products were soon sold in high-end stores like Nei-
man Marcus in Dallas and B. Altman in New York. He also applied his
business acumen to ministry. Partnering with his wife, Vonette Bright, a
recent graduate of Texas Women's University, Bill ventured to the University of California, Los Angeles (UCLA), and began evangelizing the student body. Recognizing the need to reach the "future's decision-makers,"
the Brights assembled a student team under the banner of the Campus
Crusade for Christ to help organize religious gatherings at sorority houses
and fraternities, and within a few months they had 250 personal commitments to Christ. Among the converts were the student body president and
top athletes like UCLA quarterback Donn Moomaw. Bright's experiment
in evangelism at UCLA rapidly morphed into a national movement.[19]

Whereas Bill Bright sought to evangelize the next generation, Demos
Shakarian created a parachurch organization to save his own. Born
in 1913, Shakarian came from an Armenian family that had moved to
Los Angeles in 1905. Already exposed to Armenian Pentecostalism, the
Shakarians helped jump-start its American equivalent during the Azusa
Street revival of 1906 and thereafter became respected leaders within the
local Pentecostal community. Throughout the 1940s, on the strength of
the family's thriving dairy business, Demos and his wife, Rose, sponsored
tent meetings in communities across the region. These became electrify-
ing events often led by major evangelists like Charles Price. A onetime
disciple of Aimee Semple McPherson and William Jennings Bryan, Price's
eloquent "full gospel" preaching, in which no New Testament teaching
was ignored—healing and speaking in tongues included—was already
respected throughout the Southland. Not long after the war, Shakarian
invited one hundred area businessmen to a chicken dinner at Knott's
Berry Farm in Orange County to raise money for a revival at the twenty-
thousand-seat Hollywood Bowl. After the last cups of coffee and plates of
boysenberry pie were consumed, Shakarian asked those in attendance to

testify to God's work in their daily lives. One after another, men in attendance began to stand and confess the challenges they faced as Christian businessmen and their desire to see the gospel penetrate this cutthroat world. In the fall of 1951, Shakarian asked Oral Roberts to help start a permanent association he would call the Full Gospel Business Men's Fellowship International (FGBMFI). Days later, a handful of men met on the second floor of Clifton's Cafeteria with Shakarian and Roberts. After the concluding prayer, someone started singing "Onward Christian soldiers, marching as to war" and others quickly joined hands and joined in "with the cross of Jesus going on before." Shakarian later wrote that the "Sunday school-like simplicity of it had an odd kind of power. On and on we marched and sang." Within a month FGBMFI had signed articles of incorporation, chosen a board of directors, and begun gathering businessmen of all denominations behind a vision of workplace evangelism, discipleship, and spiritual discipline.[20]

Evangelicals like Bright and Shakarian were driven by the quest to save souls in their suburbs, but they also found new ways to link this vital task to their enlivened culture of abundance. Throughout the 1950s they built an alternative media system of television, film, and music that drew know-how from Los Angeles' entertainment industry and used it to promote the sacred goals of effective evangelism and Christian fellowship. Pure enjoyment factored in too.

With John Brown's and KGER's help, radio ministries remained the center of suburban evangelical culture, but television and film made swift inroads. Television proved too expensive for most preachers at this early juncture, but a number of America's most popular religious leaders took their chances and soon increased already enormous followings. In Burbank, where most television was produced, pioneering televangelist Oral Roberts used the medium to showcase the natural flamboyance of his charismatic gospel. What radio could only convey in a single sensation, television allowed him to deliver in multiple dimensions: the sound, emotion, and physicality of a real-life Pentecostal tent revival. All that was missing was the smell of a sawdust floor. Billy Graham surpassed Roberts's use of modern media by embracing the silver screen. In 1950, just months after the groundbreaking Los Angeles crusade, Graham's team purchased a documentary film company and turned it into World Wide Pictures (WWP). Based in Burbank, WWP christened its ministry by producing the feature film *Mr. Texas*, premiering it at Graham's Hollywood Bowl Crusade in 1951. Shortly thereafter, in 1953, WWP released *Oiltown, U.S.A.*, the story of a wealthy oil baron who realizes the futility of earthly quests for money and power and, challenged by Graham's gospel, turns to God. The movie struck a chord with the nation's evangelicals, particularly those living in oil patches like Texas and Southern California, but Graham's collaboration with Hollywood—and all the sinners therein—also exposed him to criticism from some who feared Protestantism's surrender to secular society. In Graham's mind, however, harnessing faith to entertainment was simply an updated way of reaching a culture in need of Christ.[21]

Commercial music aroused the same mix of fear and excitement. Although the strictest fundamentalists decried any type of music that could not be found in a hymnal, most made room in their lives for the popular songs of their native South. Prior to World War II, southern musicians had carved out a vibrant subculture in Southern California, using local radio stations to promote hillbilly, bluegrass, and country-western music and develop a distinctive "California Sound." After the war, the California Sound turned sacred. While driving the freeways linking Los Angeles' and San Diego's suburbs, one could tune to radio stations like KGER and expect to hear old recordings of "Keep on the Sunny Side" and "Can the Circle Be Unbroken" by the Carter family, or the Oak Ridge Boys (then the Oak Ridge Quartet) harmonize on "I'll Lose My Blues in Heaven." For the average southern transplant, however, there was no substitute for hearing music live. Having relocated from Nashville to Orange County to build his dental practice, Robert Byrd, for instance, loved going to local jamborees with his wife, Mary. They were Southern Baptist—worshipping alongside Marie Allen at Bristol Street Baptist Church—but on these occasions, when they joined their Pentecostal brethren to sing along with the Statler Brothers, denominational distinctions did not matter.[22]

Still a young man, Robert Byrd also enjoyed the music of another Tennessean whose recordings were popular among southern evangelical youth. Parents were less enthusiastic, but even the strictest father found it difficult to criticize Pat Boone. Raised on the outskirts of Nashville, Boone's popularity blossomed along with cold war suburbia. White middle-class suburbanites were looking for safe, contemporary music, and the charismatic, clean-cut Boone delivered. With his smooth, melodic covers of African American rhythm and blues hits like Fats Domino's "Ain't That a Shame" and Little Richard's "Tutti Frutti" Boone established himself as pop music's Crown Prince, with Elvis its King. For southern evangelicals, Boone's appeal went deeper than his hit music and white buck shoes. Raised in a devout Church of Christ family that could claim Daniel Boone as a forebear, Boone wore his all-American heritage proudly on his sleeve. As a young man, he studied theology at David Lipscomb College in Nashville, then preached in local Church of Christ congregations while studying at North Texas State University. After moving to New York to work on Arthur Godfrey's talent show, Boone completed his degree at Columbia University and raised four daughters with his wife, Shirley. By the late 1950s, Boone's professional career had exploded; his fans now saw the twenty-five-year-old in Hollywood films, working as Chevrolet's advertising spokesman, and writing advice books for adolescents. For California's Christian parents, Boone was a young man who embodied the principles they sought to instill in their kids; California's Christian teens, however, saw a pop icon with a glamorous life not so foreign from their own.[23]

LESS GOVERNMENT, MORE MONEY, MORE MINISTRY

Even as southern evangelicals discovered a Christian culture of abundance, they also recognized its destructive potential. With affluence, after all, came the possibility for excess, and with excess came the propensity for sin. As these citizens grew more invested in their ministries and absorbed in their popular culture, they began to ask fundamental questions: How is wealth to be managed and toward what end? In their search they turned inward to right living for answers, but they soon learned that the ultimate solution existed beyond them in the realm of right governance.

In a way, the question of what to do with more money was one many Americans asked in the affluent 1950s, but it also revealed a consciousness unique to the evangelical mind. From Jack Kerouac's beatniks to Hawaii's surfers, Sloan Wilson's "Man in the Gray Flannel Suit" to William Whyte's "Organization Man," Norman Vincent Peale's positive thinking to Betty Friedan's "problem that has no name," American culture in the 1950s flashed with tension about the meaning of life in an age of material prosperity. Congregating in the plush pews of their new churches or well-appointed living rooms, southern evangelicals confronted the paradoxes of wealth. But even as they faced these universal issues, they did so within a keenly evangelical framework, one that found the rules for proper financial management in scripture. Theirs was not, in other words, an intellectual engagement meant to scrutinize the structural underpinnings of capitalism or, conversely, simply put one's mind at ease with the system. It was, rather, an exercise in devotion, of learning how to interpret financial reward in the context of spiritual blessing and maximize money for advancement of Christ's kingdom on earth. By drawing on old Christian principles of stewardship in innovative ways, southern evangelicals thus composed a new gospel of wealth.

As it was conveyed to the average evangelical suburbanite, the gospel of wealth preached blessedness and taught restraint. The first step was to accept the spiritual blessings that came with abundance. Growing up in the Depression South, southern evangelicals had been taught that wealth could bring either "curse or blessing," but in reality few had opportunity to test the theory. Within Church of Christ and Pentecostal circles especially, where poverty was the assumed station in life, prosperity was barely imaginable and so was viewed as a likely pathway to hell. To prove that poor people had the direct line to God, preachers and parishioners cited scripture's tragic account of the rich young ruler and its injunction that it is harder for a wealthy man to see heaven than for a camel to pass through the eye of a needle. Yet when surrounded by the conspicuous comforts of suburbia, these same evangelicals found such maxims unnerving and untenable. Could wealth be also a blessing, perhaps even a sign of divine approval? They learned, of course, that it could—that the Bible had as much good to say about rich people as poor ones and as much instruction to give about the potential of money as the pitfalls of materialism. Job, Solomon, King David: These were exemplary figures who wrestled with (and sometimes stumbled over) the implications of wealth but in no way shunned or decried it. Wealth was good, provided it was put to the right use.[24]

The new gospel of wealth's first tenet rested on its second tenet, that the blessing of money could be realized only in the context of Christian character. Taught in I Corinthians 10:26 that "The Earth is the Lord's and all that is therein," suburban evangelicals discovered that good money management was part of Christian devotion. In the process of questing after an honorable wage, the committed Christian also internalized lessons in faith, spiritual discipline, and family. Reversing this logic, suburban evangelicals began to equate spiritual well-being with the health of their finances. As they learned in Matthew 25's parable of the talents, the amount of money a person earned was far less important than what he did with it. The most dedicated Christian, therefore, was the one who had his house in order—the one who paid debts, saved for the future, and found godly ways to enjoy the excess fruits of their labor. Proper money management also meant Christian giving through tithes, offerings, and charity. In the nineteenth century, stewardship had been a solemn code among rich gentlemen who, in a patrician's ritual of duty and power, sought to contribute their wealth to the extension of God's work. In post–World War II Southern California, the command for stewardship grew more sophisticated and multifaceted with the democratization of wealth. The directive to make and give money permeated all aspects of religious life in the California context, but in a way that proved infectious rather than burdensome. Absent, in other words, was the gravity that accompanied stewardship decades earlier; California evangelicals gave freely and enthusiastically. Watching with excitement as revival engulfed their neighborhoods, they reached deeper into their pockets convinced that every penny they gave drew their communities closer to God.[25]

Not surprisingly, then, their district newsletters and denominational newspapers pulsated with stories on property gains, financial statistics, and investment plans. Pentecostals outdid everyone with their exuberance. Monthly installments of the Assemblies of God's district newsletter, the *Informant*, not only conveyed an advanced understanding of the gospel of wealth but also served as a makeshift classified ads page. Skimming through the hastily typed document, church members could see the latest statistics for giving, read about the ongoing construction of churches overwhelmed by new members, learn of the latest property appraisals, and gain a valuable lead on "Pontiacs at Near Wholesale Price" offered by "Rev. Don Turpin, sales-manager for the Pontiac Agency in Ontario." California Pentecostals had always used their press to solicit buyers and sellers for basic goods, as well as evangelistic necessities like banjos and tents. But by the mid-1950s their tone had changed. Big-ticket items were now the commodities of choice, reports of market gains now welcomed alongside news about unceasing revival.[26]

Wrapped in the familiar teachings of stewardship, the gospel of wealth reoriented cold war Southern California's evangelical culture in new ways. Once-hesitant capitalists now celebrated the range of opportunities free market thinking offered them. Structured to meet the unique demands for ministry created by California's postsuburban society, parachurch organizations, for instance, not only taught the new gospel of wealth as the Christian's best path to individual fulfillment but also sanctified in their outreach a new, corporate formula, which at its essence meant: more money, more ministry. This unspoken mantra encouraged them to work hand in hand with California's corporate culture, now less centered on production and more on service, consumption, and a global market. With little hesitation, parachurch ministries looked to supplement (and even supplant) the productive center of the old economy—the denomination—with a consumer-friendly approach attuned to the new, service-based economy. Whereas the denomination wanted to control the market of faith, the parachurch organization looked to exploit it with the confidence that its mechanisms (rather than central planning) would produce a wide range of "religious goods and services" to meet everyone's needs. By stepping out in this way, parachurch organizations sacrificed the security that came with centralized control, but for the entrepreneurs running them, the benefits of independence far outweighed the risks. As long as they were allowed to operate freely, these entrepreneurs felt that Christianity would come to dominate just like American business.[27]

Demos Shakarian and Bill Bright led the way by effectively blending the priorities of evangelism within the new corporate structure. As the Full Gospel Business Men's Fellowship International movement gained steam in Southern California, Shakarian began forming chapters across the country. Drawing especially from within the Assemblies of God, FGBMFI benefited from the denomination's rapid growth, but its independence also allowed it to look elsewhere for supporters. Within a few years laymen from other denominations were welcomed into the fold, among them managers, surgeons, building contractors, attorneys, and corporate executives. Bound by a spirit of interdenominational fellowship and international evangelism, these men sponsored large conventions and founded a magazine, *Full Gospel Business Men's Voice*. In each of these forums Shakarian taught new recruits the FGBMFI philosophy that "God 'prospers' people who are committed to him." When it came to the business of evangelism, Bill Bright was every bit Shakarian's equal. Within California's competitive religious marketplace, one had to target a specific clientele if one expected one's ministry to thrive. Bright targeted a clientele with unlimited growth potential. By the late 1950s California's college campuses were bursting with young people open to new knowledge, and Bright soon perfected marketing techniques to draw in these inquisitive minds. Following Billy Graham's lead, he incorporated film and music, but one of his most successful strategies was also the simplest. Wanting to organize staff training, Bright wrote the *Four Spiritual Laws*, which condensed God's plan for salvation to four truths: "God loves you," "Man is sinful and separated from God," "Jesus Christ is God's only provision for man's sin," "We must individually receive Jesus Christ as Savior and Lord." Campus Crusade packaged the formula into a stand-alone, wallet-sized booklet that its workers could easily pitch to the curious consumer. All of these strategies worked splendidly—so well, in fact, that by 1959 the organization was active at forty colleges around the country and in Asia. At the same time, Bright came to recognize another truth: that "more money, more ministry" was a cyclical argument. As his ministry expanded, so too did the financial apparatus supporting it, with district and regional managers overseeing the flood of donations sent by people from around the world. Determined to win the next generation for Christ, Campus Crusade now functioned as a multinational corporation.[28]

Small-town-turned-suburban evangelicals began to adopt not only the confidence of corporate capitalism but its political expectations. The gospel of wealth became a blueprint for political economy framed by the philosophy of free enterprise, which southern evangelicals almost universally considered a Christian and American system of thought. Intuitively, they sensed that the lessons from the Bible that governed their microeconomic behavior should also determine their macroeconomic dynamics. Practically, they knew that evangelism was wedded to a political order that privileged voluntarism over state welfare as the best answer to society's problems. To their formula for outreach, in which more money was sought for more ministry, southern evangelicals thus added a third element: less government.

In the process, they jettisoned, or at the very least softened, their pre–World War II inhibitions with capitalism and joined other conservatives in aggressively promoting free enterprise. To be sure, this was only a small step to make. Already by the late 1940s southern transplants embroiled in the labor wars had chosen to support free market principles over industrial unionism. Even before that, southern plain folk had always seen themselves as defenders of pristine capitalism and Jeffersonian economics, which privileged individual entrepreneurship, personalized market and commodity relations, and owner-controlled property. Still, their reorientation during the 1950s was no less significant. Whereas earlier they had been at odds with corporate power, their new dogma saw government as capitalism's greatest threat. The shift forced southern evangelicals to gloss over some of the inherent tensions within their new creed. For example, although wary of Keynesian inflationary policies that allowed government to take on debt to prime economic growth, they welcomed government's heavy investment in the defense sector. They were apprehensive about unchecked corporate power, but their new gospel of wealth, in fact, encouraged fewer regulations. Southern evangelicals could (and did) downplay such strains by arguing that a powerful military was necessary to protect and advance democracy, and that big business was the engine in America's war on global communism. This was a standard apologia for those populist conservatives heavily invested in the fight against Keynesianism, but it nevertheless revealed the degree to which southern evangelicals had been transformed by their recent social experiences.

What was truly striking about southern evangelicals' new discourse was not that it was vulnerable to contradiction but that it made them zealous converts to the cult of free enterprise, which by the late 1950s operated as the fulcrum for California's budding conservative movement. During the labor wars of the late 1940s and the local anticommunist campaigns that followed, conservatives of all stripes had bonded out of fear of a common enemy. Beginning in the mid-1950s, however, shared impulses cohered into more substantive demands for the future of American political economy, especially in the region's newest suburbs, where citizens began constructing a network of free enterprise organizations. Middle-class housewives now gathered regularly to read and discuss libertarian tracts they had acquired via mail or at one of the Southland's right-wing bookstores. College-aged men and women read classic treatises by Friedrich von Hayek and Russell Kirk, or recent hits like Ayn Rand's *Atlas Shrugged*. Male breadwinners counted on *Human Events*, *The Freeman*, and *National Review* to help them understand Washington's latest fiscal policies. And in Orange County, free enterprise economics grew into a pastime for the entire family to enjoy. In the county's "hub of happiness," tourists visited Walt Disney's Tomorrowland, where they were whisked through a future promising the perfect union between technology and economic freedom. Families visiting Knott's Berry Farm, in nearby Buena Park, could see the pioneering spirit of the old West came alive at a ghost town, take a patriotic tour that recreated the lives of the founding fathers, or stop in at the Freedom Center to collect free enterprise pamphlets for people back home.[29]

As much as they immersed themselves in this invigorating free market culture, it was through familiar channels that southern evangelicals gained their ideological footing. George Benson's National Education Program became indispensable in this regard. As of 1957, the NEP's award-winning cartoon series *Adventures in Economics* had been viewed by an estimated thirty-five million people, including "industrial employees, schools, colleges, civic clubs and other community groups, [and] armed service personnel" privileged with exclusive showings. Complementing the message of this series was the American Adventure Film Series, which tracked economic development from the failed communal experiment of Plymouth Colony to the profit system's triumph in the twentieth century, and flannel-board kits, of which "What Women Can Do" was one of the most popular. By the late 1950s over 750,000 of Los Angeles' high school students trained in civic programs had received instruction from NEP material. In Orange County, meanwhile, local citizens counted on Benson's column "Looking Ahead," published weekly in the *Register*, to be a watchdog against liberalism. Each of these media forms taught these eager Christians how to converse with fellow conservative activists in a shared logic of free enterprise.[30]

Though influential, free market advocates like Benson did not usurp the pastor in the average parishioner's economic instruction. Despite the democratization of evangelical ministry, the preacher still enjoyed the last word on political economy. As ever, J. Vernon McGee epitomized this power. On his daily radio program, in his weekly Bible studies, and through COD's cell groups, he conveyed a straightforward message about money. When practiced in accordance with Christian morality and the primacy of local community, free market capitalism was, quite simply in McGee's mind, the most "Christian" of any economic system ever introduced in history. Liberal, Keynesian economic policy, he said bluntly, deprived people of their sense of self, purpose, and power. Stated another way, by preventing individuals from making choices in the market, Keynesian economics also stripped their authority over choices in the realm of faith. When applied to the church, the effects of liberal economics were no less disastrous. By downplaying the role of the autonomous individual in society, Keynesian policies dulled the work ethic and limited the range of opportunities for voluntary, private welfare agencies, essentially undermining Christ's commission to serve others. Individuals and communities could not freely give of themselves for purposes of Christian

witness or charity, McGee reminded his listeners, unless they had something to give. For the Christian believer, spiritual and economic freedoms
were completely dependent on each other.[31]

McGee's message about the state was equally pointed. Keynesian economic and social policies were not only infiltrating Americans' personal
lives but robbing citizens of the fullness of citizenship promised by Thomas
Jefferson and the Constitution. Americans' growing complacency was facilitating the rise of government power. The prevailing sentiment, McGee told
listeners, was that "government has the key to the door of prosperity . . .
and has the solution to our problems. . . . Government is the haven of rest
toward which men are directing their frail weather beaten arks of life from
the raging storm." But liberal economics were burdening government with
debt, weakening the fabric of local institutions, rendering society vulnerable to the totalitarian impulse of communism, and thus working directly
against God's design for the United States. How could America continue to
exist as a beacon of light to the world when it failed to adhere to its cherished principles of freedom, self-initiative, and discipline? How would the
purest form of democracy nurtured in the local communities of America be
exported if these ideals and these communities were no longer allowed to
flourish? There was no definitive answer, McGee reminded his suburban
audience, only the promise that a grave future would soon be upon them if
the gospel of wealth did not inspire political resolve.[32]

REPUBLICAN REVOLT

Heeding McGee's call, Jean Vandruff and his southern compatriots became "suburban warriors" for the conservative cause. A longtime
believer in the primacy of the individual and efficacy of capitalism, Vandruff's success in Orange Country's unregulated frontier convinced him
that he needed to defend his new gospel of wealth through evangelical
activism. While his brother Shannon signed up with Demos Shakarian's
FGBMFI, Jean found his outlet in Central Baptist Church, located a few
blocks from his Anaheim home. In its pews he sat next to churchgoers
from all parts of the Southland, but mostly southerners who had been
part of Baptist churches prior to coming to Anaheim. Some worked in private business, but others were engineers, operatives, or managers at local
defense industries like North American Aviation, just beginning to enjoy
the secure life in the suburbs.[33]

Central's preaching made Vandruff feel at home as well. At the moment he joined Central, it had already welcomed major evangelical leaders to speak from its pulpit, and in the next few years it would invite many more, be they shining stars of the Los Angeles scene like Wilbur Smith or upstarts from San Diego like Tim LaHaye. Marketing itself as a "church with convictions," Central was an important stop for staunch conservatives like Bob Shuler, who visited and was introduced to the church in 1959 as "one of the most outstanding Christian leaders of the past generation." Shuler, in fact, seemed ready to christen it the next Trinity Methodist, especially after his son and daughter-in-law, Phil and Maria Shuler, joined the congregation. And as part of the offshoot of J. Frank Norris's denomination—the Baptist Bible Fellowship—Central was the first stop on the West Coast circuit for the BBF's trendsetters. Even in its infancy the congregation hosted a "who's who" ranging from mavericks like Harvey Springer to senior statesmen like Bob Jones.[34]

The man recruiting these speakers, and the preacher who Vandruff heard from Central's pulpits on most Sundays, was Bob Wells. Born in Alabama during the interwar years, Wells had entered ministry in the early 1940s as pastor of the Galilean Baptist Church of Dallas and editor of John R. Rice's *The Sword of the Lord*. He also founded Dallas Bible College. Although successful in Texas, Wells felt called to travel as an evangelist throughout the late 1940s and early 1950s, speaking to large crowds in midsized cities like Grand Rapids, Michigan; Toledo, Ohio; and Lynchburg, Virginia. He first encountered Anaheim during a West Coast swing in the mid-1950s. Impressed with the religious energy and entrepreneurial verve of the place, he decided to leave the revival circuit and construct his own southern Baptist tabernacle, West Coast–style.[35]

Wells's maxim was "Evangelism and Patriotism." The first began bearing fruit in 1956, when a handful of Orange Countians pitched Wells's torn circus tent on the corner of Gilbert and Crescent streets in western Anaheim. Wells's nightly gatherings, fueled by evangelical star power and full-page advertisements, quickly became a spectacle worthy of front-page headlines. Scripted in bold, one of many printed invitations appearing in Santa Ana's *Register* listed Central's celebrity recruits:

Some of the greatest names in the entertainment field will add glamore [*sic*] to the intercity evangelistic crusade which opens Sunday. . . . Tim Spencer, founder and for many years a member of the "Sons of the

Pioneers" . . . Redd Harper, star of many western motion pictures . . .
Mrs. Stuart Hamblen, wife of the former cowboy star whose career has
been devoted to Christian work since his conversion during the Billy
Graham revival of 1949 . . . Arnie Hartman, said to be the world's most
accomplished accordionist . . . screen star Lee Childs, organist Les
Barnett and others.

Following the conclusion of the campaign in mid-September, Wells and
his family, joined by three other families, founded Central Baptist and
secured a fifteen-acre orange grove in an area yet to be zoned for development. By spring of 1957 neighbors recognized Wells's church as the "most
rapidly growing church in Orange County." In competition with other
California congregations, Wells and company took on labor-intensive telephone and door-to-door canvassing programs. During a battle with Grace
Baptist Church of Riverside, Central "broke all records" by contacting a
thousand homes and won the contest in dominant fashion. Jean Vandruff
thrived in this climate of perpetual evangelism and even won prizes for
his proselytizing.[36]

If evangelism brought Vandruff to Central, politics would help keep
him there. Bob Wells expected his charges to remain vigilant in the political realm, and he was determined to do his best to assist them. In the fall
of 1958, when Central's political rise was just beginning, weekly Sunday
bulletins provided pastoral advice on a couple of key ballot initiatives in
the upcoming election. One concern was Proposition 16, which sought to
impose a tax on private schools. Wells's editorial in the October 12 church
bulletin was simply titled "No, No, a Thousand Times, No!" He explained
that Proposition 16 was another wedge for liberalism because it would
place "punitive taxes on Christian and other nonprofit day schools, [and
open] the door to eventual taxation of all Church property—churches,
Sunday School units, fellowship halls, colleges, seminaries, hospitals,
orphanages, homes for the aged, camps and conference centers."[37]

Although Proposition 16 seemingly hit closer to home, it was a second concern—Proposition 18, a right-to-work ballot initiative—that
truly set Wells on edge. By commanding his congregants to vote yes on
the measure, he thrust them into the middle of a stirring revolt within
the Republican Party triggered by a new round of labor wars, mounting frustration with Dwight Eisenhower, and the rise of Edmund (Pat)
Brown's Democratic Party. The Kohler strike in Wisconsin became a

flashpoint. In the early 1950s Kohler workers voted to join the United Auto Workers (UAW) union, setting company owner Herbert Kohler at odds with Walter Reuther, the UAW leader. Begun in April 1954, the strike lasted until the 1960s. Because of the length and ferocity of this confrontation, and the newsworthy men at the middle of the mêlée, the Kohler strike became a rallying cry for conservatives. Their anger found an outlet in a Senate Select Committee chaired by Senator John McClellan of Arkansas. The McClellan Committee was established to curtail corruption within the labor movement, but at the insistence of one of its members—Barry Goldwater—the committee branched out to investigate UAW's handling of the Kohler strike. In a three-day session, Goldwater went on the attack against Reuther, but the labor leader emerged victorious. Few congressmen believed that Reuther and the UAW were guilty of malfeasance; they simply represented one side in an ugly fight between two antagonistic interests. Goldwater might have lost his ballyhooed showdown with Reuther, but he emerged a hero to businessmen. By taking on labor's leading light, he guaranteed himself a future on the national stage. During the congressional elections of 1958, he helped corporate leaders champion right-to-work referenda that appeared on several state ballots, like Proposition 18 in California. These initiatives sought to outlaw mandatory union membership in the workforce and limit government regulation in the workplace, but conservatives also saw them as a way to push Eisenhower's GOP to the right.[38]

By 1958 conservatives' list of complaints with Eisenhower was long. Domestically, they complained that his administration had begun to encroach on constitutional liberties and states' rights. Edgar Bundy, acting as president of the Abraham Lincoln National Republican Club, charged that "the so-called Republican leadership is giving the country a bigger New Deal program and people cannot recognize it because it is being dished out under the guise of Republicanism!" Eisenhower's foreign policy agitated Bundy's allies even more. In magazines like *American Mercury* and *National Review* and on radio programs like Clarence Manion's, citizens learned about Eisenhower's failure to address Soviet suppression of Hungary's democratic revolution in 1956, communist uprisings in third world countries, and the slick tactics of new Soviet premier Nikita Khrushchev, all of which confirmed their sense that middle-of-the-road Republicanism could not handle the pressures of global communism. A number of conservative political action groups formed in 1958 with intent to destabilize Eisenhower's Republican establishment. One soon trumped the others in reputation. On a December day, eleven corporate executives traveled to Indianapolis to hear fellow businessman Robert Welch lay out a case for action against communist infiltration. Noting that there had been an "800% expansion of Communist membership in the last 20 years," which threatened to devalue the dollar and lead to "economic collapse and political and social chaos," Welch proposed a counteroffensive unit that would "fight dirty." A North Carolinian, raised a Protestant with roots in southern Baptist fundamentalism, he naturally gravitated to stories of the martyr John Birch. In 1954 he had even written a biography of his hero, *The Life of John Birch*. Welch thus suggested the new organization be called the John Birch Society (JBS).[39]

The founding of the JBS illustrated a nationwide effort by the Right to pressure the Republican center during Eisenhower's last years in the White House, yet it was at the state level that conservatives first began achieving electoral change. William Knowland's 1958 gubernatorial campaign became the trial run. Beloved by the right wing for his hard-line anticommunist, pro-capitalist politics, Knowland brought significant clout to the California campaign and had little difficulty attracting donations from business leaders nationwide. Knowland repaid his peers' respect by making Proposition 18 his signature issue. Free enterprise preachers like James Fifield helped present the right-to-work initiative as a referendum on whether "freedom" or "tyranny" would reign. Voting no on 18, he bellowed, was tantamount to renouncing "the idea of democracy" and proving "ourselves unworthy of the founding fathers" and God's law of freedom. Others thought differently. Opposed to Proposition 18's harsh anti-labor tone, moderate Republicans remained reticent. Democrats, meanwhile, reveled in the GOP's turmoil. Throughout the 1950s they had laid the groundwork for an assault on the Republican establishment in Sacramento. In 1953, they formed the California Democratic Council (CDC) to offset the grassroots work of the California Republican Assembly (CRA), and to reunify Social Democrats behind the leadership of State Attorney General Pat Brown. Brown campaigned in 1958 on a platform of "Responsible Liberalism." If elected, he promised, he would increase welfare benefits, improve the health care system, and expand government investment in transportation and education. Backed by an emboldened labor movement, Brown routed Knowland at the polls and defeated Proposition 18. For the first time since 1878, the Democrats controlled the state senate, assembly, and governor's chair.[40]

The 1958 election was an obvious setback for California's GOP, but not for its right wing. As much as it upset moderate Republicans, fresh leadership and organizational drive fostered optimism on the Republican Right. Several new agencies pledged to carry on Knowland's crusade, including the JBS and the California Free Enterprise Association (CFEA) established by Walter Knott to continue the "Yes on 18" fight. The CFEA soon surpassed Fifield's Spiritual Mobilization as the region's premier free enterprise association. This transition came as Fifield's organization—like his downtown Los Angeles church—faced decline. Although he would continue at First Congregational until 1967, he retired from SM in 1959, and Reverend Edward W. Greenfield, who had been tasked with revitalizing SM in Fifield's wake, took his skills—and likely SM's national mailing lists—to Knott's Berry Farm, where he was hired to help run the CFEA. There, Greenfield would also pastor the white steeple church Knott built in honor of the Southern Methodist church he had attended as a child on Southern California's frontier.[41]

THE 1958 ELECTION WAS a boon for Central Baptist, now located just blocks from Walter Knott's amusement park. Throughout the campaign, Bob Wells had set aside time during Sunday services to answer questions such as "Is Right to Work Legislation Good or Bad?" In his sermons, meanwhile, he criticized Eisenhower's moderate policies, praised Barry Goldwater and William Knowland, and spoke in a cataclysmic tone about Pat Brown's ascent. As people like Jean Vandruff and his peers faced a critical juncture in their understandings of capitalism, community, and citizenship, Wells's forthright politics appealed in their simplicity and power. Central offered spiritual nourishment, advice on Christian living, and practical instruction for voting and activism. In the next few years California's ideological battles would become more intense, its elections more seriously contested. During this transformative period, California conservatives would begin to see Bob Wells and Central as a key ally in their assault against liberal Democrats and moderate Republicans.[42]

Central began acquiring its reputation in the Knowland campaign, but it would begin to flourish as a marshaling zone for suburban activism in subsequent contests over education. Frustrated with the lack of alternatives to the "liberal" public educational system, southern evangelicals began constructing their own schools. Like many other churches, Central opened a K–12 institute in 1958 to teach Southern California's youth the three Rs in a climate friendly to a forth R—religion. Christian colleges did the same for higher education, but also became think tanks where conservatives from different ideological backgrounds could congregate to map out a new direction for their community and country. Pepperdine College assumed this burden in the early 1960s, for the good of its familiar traditions and for the benefit of its new wealthy friends.

8

DECLARATION OF
INDEPENDENCE

On January 11, 1960, the Board of Trustees of Pepperdine College
reaffirmed its strong advocacy of the private competitive economic
system. . . . Believing in the fundamentals of personal initiative,
decentralization of government, personal integrity, and in oppo-
sition to the growing trends toward collectivism, the Board of
Trustees on that date rejected the concept of government loans for
financing dormitory construction, and at the same time instructed
college officials to make no application for government aid, choos-
ing rather to depend upon private financing to meet the needs of
an expanding enrollment at Pepperdine College.[1]

—M. NORVEL YOUNG

S HORTLY AFTER CENTRAL BAPTIST CONGREGANTS WENT TO THE
polls in Anaheim, on November 21, 1958, Pepperdine College welcomed eight hundred alum, esteemed guests, and the press to South Central Los Angeles for the inauguration of its new president, Norvel Young,
and to announce a new era in American Christian higher education. At
least 175 of them were dignitaries, representing educational institutions
from around the country, schools ranging in stature from the august Harvard University to unproven Magic Valley Christian College. The most
important guests were seated on stage, waiting their turn at the dais. Paul
Smith, president of Whittier College and the keynote speaker, waited the
longest but had the most to say. He spoke at length about the importance
of harnessing republican virtues to a patriotic, forward-looking, nation-

strengthening educational program. Delivered just months after the Soviet Union had launched *Sputnik*, the speech had implications for all educators, but Smith's words had special traction for Pepperdine College administrators as they took this moment to revisit their school's founding purpose.

Norvel Young stood next and, in his characteristically understated manner, "pledge[d] the College administration to these objectives. First, the pursuit of academic excellence. . . . Second, the cultivation of Christian values." The new president then added specifics: the "building of a dedicated, unusually qualified faculty," "tripling of Pepperdine's endowment," "raising of admission standards," and the "bolstering of areas of understanding with Alumni, patrons, and business and community leaders." Though recited like educational boilerplate, Young's generic-sounding speech was, to each constituency in attendance, a timely political statement. For business leaders, Young's speech was a promise to make his campus a free enterprise zone, a place to sustain Senator John McClellan and Senator Barry Goldwater's right-to-work politics. Conservative parents heard guarantees that Pepperdine College would immerse young people in the uncompromised fundamentals of classical libertarian and constitutional thought and provide their children with a first-rate academic experience. And to faculty and church supporters, Young's general reference to the "cultivation of Christian values" actually conveyed the specific message that this school would be saved from its "secular, liberal drift." With this business-minded educator and Church of Christ preacher from Lubbock, Texas, at the helm, things promised to be different. Pepperdine College was about to return to its roots.[2]

YOUNG'S STRATEGY WOULD PROVE more transformative for Pepperdine College than anyone could have imagined that afternoon in South Central Los Angeles. The preacher and his wife, Helen, returned to California after a fifteen-year southern hiatus determined to reclaim their alma mater's heritage. Pepperdine College had struggled during the 1950s to maintain a distinctive identity and survive economic crisis. Under its founder's mandate, it had remained financially independent, committed to George Pepperdine's philosophy of autonomy but wholly dependent on his success in the business world. In the postwar years Pepperdine's investments failed, leaving his college vulnerable. Operating in the red and incurring an unworkable level of debt, Pepperdine College approached the 1957 academic year bankrupt and ready to close its doors. Unable to tap the same funding offered public universities in this period of government largesse, Young solicited help from wealthy Republican leaders. These donors allowed him to reassert his school's independence and the precepts first articulated by its founder twenty years earlier. In exchange, Young turned his school into an organizational center for the conservative movement. Right-wing politics was this small school's salvation.

This school's political marriage to the Republican Right was indicative of southern evangelicalism's growing, ground-level support for the nascent conservative movement. During the anticommunist, free enterprise politicking of the 1950s, southern evangelical transplants had helped protest the machinations of a liberal state. They faced the 1960s with yet other concerns on their mind: secular liberalism's infiltration of their public schools and the need to build their own private ones. This quest within evangelicalism came at a perfect time for a broader base of conservatives. In addition to providing their children with a safe educational experience beyond the authority of the state, conservatives looked upon the new evangelical educational institutions as a natural meeting ground for parents, patrons, and activists. In the process of building these schools together, these allies continued to consolidate an identifiable political movement, one that entered the 1960s ready to coalesce around a maturing ideology and a new cohort of captivating politicians.

THE POLITICS OF PEDAGOGY

The phenomenon in which Norvel Young found himself immersed was national in scope. At the heart of the matter were anxieties about the way America's schools were preparing children for life in the cold war era. What skills and values did they need to thrive as individuals and at the same time strengthen their country? Who would be in charge of transmitting these skills and values: parents and the community or educational professionals and government? How would success be measured? As a cultural trendsetter, Southern California was the site of the fiercest struggle over these fundamental concerns. The battle began over teaching philosophies in primary and secondary public schools before widening to encompass the principles and economics of private education at all levels.

California's southern evangelicals became grassroots leaders in both facets of the fight.

It started with the hire of a new school superintendent in Pasadena, the comfortable middle-class community bordering Los Angeles to the northeast. A progressive thinker, Willard Goslin came to the City of Roses in 1948 as an accomplished educator who at the time presided over the American Association of School Administrators. Pasadena's citizens were impressed, at least initially, but by the winter of 1949, a group of conservative women began to complain that Goslin was deemphasizing reading, writing, and arithmetic—the three Rs—in the curriculum and, worse yet, asking for tax hikes to increase governmental aid to education. "Progressive Education Means Progressive Taxation!" cried the council. "Vote NO on the School Tax Increase" echoed the Property Owner's Division of the Realty Board. This minority ultimately defeated Goslin's proposed school tax increase measure and succeeded in deposing the superintendent. The incident might have passed without notice if not for *Time* magazine's former news bureau chief David Hulburd, who provided a behind-the-scenes account of the episode in a book called *This Happened in Pasadena*. Published in 1951, Hulburd's critical portrayal showed that the anti-Goslin contingent was drawing a line in the sand for the entire nation. "What . . . happened in Pasadena could easily happen in other cities where modern educational systems [come] under attack," Hulburd warned. Known as a testing ground for progressive educational methods, Southern California now earned national stigma as the place where backlash against such liberal thinking was about to erupt.[3]

The outbursts happened incrementally and with varying intensity throughout California's Southland during the 1950s, but they reverberated loudly and consistently in the region's new cold war suburbs where recent arrivals to the middle class identified education as the key to their children's status in the new economy. Here, critics had two basic complaints: first, that public education was too progressive in method, and, second, that it was too soft on communism. Beginning in the late 1940s, educators like Goslin began promoting "life-adjustment" curricula, emphasizing socialization as much as academic training. Based on principles first articulated by educational philosopher John Dewey earlier in the century, life-adjustment techniques sought to uplift individuals (hence society) by training them to become responsible workers, homemakers, and citizens. This pedagogy encouraged schools to focus on the practical and social application, rather than the acquisition, of knowledge. For California's educators struggling to meet the diversifying needs of the state's exploding student population, such flexible emphases on acculturation and pluralism obviously held much appeal. New extracurricular additions like school guidance counselors were seen as critical advancements, as were general efforts to bring public education in line with modern sociological and psychological standards. Teachers and psychologists, counselors and clinicians now teamed up to promote healthy, holistic development of America's most impressionable minds.[4]

To many parents, new emphases on the "whole student" meant that teachers were shirking their responsibility to impart "real knowledge." In their minds, this damaged young people. With traditional subjects like mathematics, spelling, and writing no longer the bedrock of classroom training, America's youth were being taught how to share with each other but not how to compete, how to feel comfortable in social settings but not how to become confident independent thinkers. Critics saw this as a therapeutic turn in education and they despised it. They were convinced that supplanting the three Rs with "parlor games" would lead to a loss of American economic and political acumen. Resurrecting charges that had been leveled earlier in the century against Dewey, conservative parents also believed that they, not professional educators, were best equipped to cultivate the civic consciousness of their children. If exposed to the whims and fancies of the "experts," their children would come to embody all of the same effete traits exhibited by liberal administrators. And if this were to occur, American self-reliance and individual initiative would devolve into dependency and affirmation. With their spirit quenched, Americans would cease to be authentic in any meaningful way.[5]

Of course those who harbored such fears about educational experimentation had a much larger threat in mind: communism. Stories of China's brainwashing techniques had surfaced during the Korean War, and Hollywood movies at the time played up communist mind manipulation. Convinced that the reds had developed sophisticated psychological weapons, conservative parents worried that subversives would undermine the nation by controlling their children. Any parent who relinquished their authority to state educators, the critics brayed, paved the way for the destruction of Western civilization. Other trends encouraged parents to think this way. For instance, they decried new teacher-training group sessions designed to promote cooperation and consensus in the classroom. Administrators like Goslin used small-group discussions to create a sense of camaraderie among staff members and collective investment in the larger project. Critics grew suspicious of this and also of the new "group dynamics" strategies being employed in Parent-Teacher Association (PTA) meetings. Instead of forums for open exchange, they charged, the PTA meeting had become another lab for social scientists to manipulate the minds of citizens.[6]

Within this climate of suspicion, no other constituency grew more active than middle-class women. Historian Michelle Nickerson explains that, in Southern California, middle-class women at the center of grassroots campaigns against progressive education helped drive the conservative movement. Afforded time during the day because of their comfortable standing, many housewives and mothers conducted research on educational trends, scrutinized school administrators, attended PTA meetings, ran for seats on the school board, and established their own countersubversive agencies. Affiliated with the right-wing organization Pro-America, it was two housewife activists, in fact—Louise Hawkes Padelford and Frances Bartlett—who led the charge against Goslin. Meeting in their living rooms, they amassed complaints about watered-down curricula and communist insurrection and connected them to a wider protest against state infringement on the private sphere.[7]

Goslin's ouster validated Padelford and Bartlett's efforts, yet even as the Pasadena controversy died down, the much-publicized local revolt against the United Nations Educational, Scientific and Cultural Organization (UNESCO) drew housewives out of their quiet cul-de-sacs into the zenith of their political influence. The Southern California Council for UNESCO initiated a door-to-door campaign to promote UNESCO's multitiered agenda for international understanding. Supported by over six hundred civic organizations, the Southern California Council for UNESCO boasted a remarkably sweeping enterprise, which its Chairman proudly described to the press:

Utilizing the abundant facilities of press, motion pictures, radio, and television in this region, . . . the council expects . . . to furnish speakers, program suggestions, literature and promotion materials about UNESCO, community forums, and publicity for local projects. In addition, it will give instruction on . . . helping of foreign school children, and the methods of "adopting" stricken European communities.

Convinced that UNESCO was another wedge for progressive pedagogy and leftist politicos, women launched a counteroffensive. They coordinated an alliance of organizations that included the Women's Republican Study Group, a Catholic women's group in the San Fernando Valley called the American Public Relations Forum, and several other libertarian and religious associations. With gathering momentum, anti-UNESCO advocates finally forced Los Angeles County officials to reconsider their support of the UN's global educational initiative. During a string of raucous school board meetings late in 1951, administrators decided to ban materials produced by UNESCO. With a key victory won, Southern California's "mothers of conservatism" branched out into other realms of educational politics.[8]

FIGHTING FOR THE "FOURTH R"

Southern evangelicals worked alongside the Padelfords and Bartletts of the Republican Right in the fight against progressive pedagogy. They invested themselves in this first wave of educational politics largely because of their understanding of spiritual conversion, in which the individual had the rational ability to "choose" salvation. Christian parents shuddered at the prospect of communists brainwashing their children before they were able to make decisions for Christ. But they also believed in a Bible-based system of character development that demanded that parents, pastors, and Sunday-school teachers, not educators, shape a child's value system. When they looked at their schools' life-adjustment pedagogy, they saw more than the usurpation of parental authority; this was blatant reversal of a divinely sanctioned chain of command. As activists, meanwhile, southern evangelicals brought unusual energy and experience to the crusade for traditional education, having fought school boards and PTAs over textbooks and evolution in the South since the 1920s. Any initiative that reduced the Protestant investment in public education or retracted privileges allotted Christian private education thus galvanized this electorate in a special way. During the 1950s, these crusaders faced a string of ballot referendums that directed their mounting dissent into a more comprehensive grassroots retaliation against liberal educational trends, one that even Willard Goslin and David Hulburd—or Padelford and Bartlett—could not have imagined possible.

Early in the cold war, evangelicals had been wholly committed to public education. Provided the schools upheld the three Rs and Protestant values, evangelical parents believed public education could serve as a basis for Christian democracy; this, after all, is what public education had been designed for in the first place. Gradually they lost faith in this project. Their doubts surfaced in 1948, when the federal government outlawed "released time," which allowed students time away from class for instruction in their faith tradition. Evangelicals in California were incensed by this measure, but not as much as by what came next at the state level. During the 1950s, American Civil Liberties Union advocates began scrutinizing legislation and cultural institutions—schools and churches especially—that seemed in breach of church-state separation. In 1956, ACLU activists instigated legal measures to undo a 1952 ballot measure (Proposition 5) that required schools and churches to pledge an anticommunist loyalty oath in order to maintain tax-exempt status. This led to a fierce contest between conservative Protestants and their liberal counterparts in which conservatives ultimately prevailed. Despite their victory, evangelicals began to doubt that they could defend their nation's bedrock Protestant values, especially against the ACLU's powerful allies like Attorney General Pat Brown. At the same time the ACLU was challenging Proposition 5, Brown, a devout Catholic and liberal Democrat, prohibited prayer and Bible reading in public schools, even when performed for strictly "religious purposes." Local pastors like Bob Shuler formed the California Christian Citizens Association to oppose Brown's effort to "secularize" the schools, but the opposition was too disorganized to mount a successful challenge. Brown's maneuver struck a bitter and permanent blow at evangelicals' ideals for public education and made him their sworn enemy.[9]

More importantly, it marked a turning point. As Brown's and the ACLU's pluralist agenda seemed to overtake the public school system in the late 1950s, a growing number of evangelicals reluctantly concluded that they needed an alternative system of private education. In an ironic twist, they looked to Brown's religion for ideas. Shuler channeled the evangelical position:

Not only are Roman Catholics . . . guarding against the atheism and Communism of UNESCO with their parochial schools but thousands of Protestant or so-called "Christian" schools are being undertaken for the same purpose. That may be the solution, but it is a most difficult and unfair solution. Protestant Christianity gave rise to the public schools in America [and] has faithfully defended and sustained them.

It is therefore a terrible tragedy we face, as we see our public school education coming under the control of paganism, atheism and Communism, all three of which are . . . enthroned in the United Nations.

Shuler's lament contained the signs of a fading reality (Christianity's presence in public education) and seeds of political potential (evangelicals' respect for conservative Catholics), but mostly it reflected disillusionment with the present situation. However disenchanted they might have been, these citizens nevertheless began their preparations, first by shoring up a legislative defense of private education.[10]

Their earliest touchstone tests included Proposition 3, a 1952 initiative that extended tax-exempt status to religious schools, and Proposition 16, sponsored by the ACLU in 1958 as an attempt to revoke this earlier ruling. Evangelicals had secured the victory in 1952, thereby protecting their cherished financial freedom, but the fight in 1958 was more intense. Against a coalition of liberal activists, they held rallies and distributed fiery protest literature. Protestants United Against Taxing Schools, their key organization, cautiously welcomed Catholics as allies but, in the main, advertised the effort to vote down Proposition 16 as a fight to "defend [the] Protestant tradition." Leading the charge were Rolf McPherson (Sister Aimee's son, and President of the Church of the Foursquare Gospel) and Bob Wells. Under Wells's watchful eye, Central Baptist's weekly bulletins provided detailed instructions on how his parishioners should engage in the campaign against the ballot initiative. These efforts produced the desired effect. In November of 1958, Proposition 16 failed, affirming Christian private schools' right to continue business as usual, at least for the time being.[11]

This political lobbying was merely one component of an evangelical educational system and advocacy network that began to flourish in Southern California during the late 1950s. Though still far behind the Catholic parochial system, Protestant schools grew rapidly in the early cold war period, enrolling 19 percent of the nation's private school students in the late 1940s (compared to 12 percent in 1938). Recognizing this trend, in 1947 the National Association of Evangelicals formed an affiliate board to oversee the Christian school movement. The interdenominational National Association of Christian Schools (NACS) henceforth became the premier council of its kind. Its stated goals were to "assist in organizing and establishing new schools," to "strengthen existing schools" through the provision of curricula and teacher training, and, finally, to "provide a voice for the cause of Christian education" by way of political advocacy and a magazine, the *Christian Teacher*. NACS's numbers grew steadily during the 1950s. In 1952 its directory claimed 146 institutions nationwide, 38 total in California, 32 of which were based in its Southland. In 1965 its directory contained 228 schools, with 61 located in California and a vast majority of these in the state's southernmost counties, most affiliated with Baptist, Nazarene, or Assemblies of God churches.[12]

NACS director Mark Fakkema, who also edited the *Christian Teacher*, helped guide this growth by keeping NAE supporters abreast of the latest developments in national educational policy. Already in the early 1950s his headlines were inflammatory: "The Modern Revolutionary War," "John Dewey Is Dead," and "Tools to Combat Subversive Tendencies" were typically militaristic. In a 1951 piece, "The Present Educational Battle," Fakkema reminded his readers that theirs was a protest against poor educational quality as much as the absence of God in public schools; teaching the fourth R, after all, was impossible without the other three. More forcefully than most evangelical educators, Fakkema also managed to fuse this complaint to a damning critique of an overbearing state:

> The battle of this generation is not against child indoctrination. All real education of children implies indoctrination of some sort. This all-important question is: who shall indoctrinate—the parents or the subversively slanted educational "planners"? This is the battle at the educational front today. The parent-controlled school system clearly occupies the Scriptural position.

Although meant to galvanize Christian parents in every state, Fakkema's "battle" was really with California's courts and politicians. One-fourth of his organization's membership operated in California (accounting for over eighteen thousand students by 1961), and it would be there that his efforts were concentrated. In January 1958, Fakkema published a report on Proposition 16. Seeing Pat Brown's initiatives as evidence of public education's final failure, Fakkema also wrote to awaken American evangelicals to the threat Proposition 16 posed for their pocketbooks and their children. "To be forewarned is to be forearmed in this political battle"; the time for independence from the public school system was now.[13]

Bob Wells's Central Baptist answered the call. In 1958, Central established its own school, which recognized the "Bible and Christian philosophy of life as the pervasive core of all knowledge and experience." Wells's school started with a K–9 program; then, in 1963, he founded Orange County's first Christian high school, Heritage High. Supported by Walter Knott, Heritage Schools, as Central's educational system was designated, was a direct response to what Wells considered the academic and moral decline in the California public school system. Against the "pagan sin capital of the world," where "the pressures of Hollywood, attractions of the beach, and the casual way of life" had caused the "erosion of character and dependability" among Southern California's teens, Wells's team of administrators proclaimed that Heritage would stand as a bastion of traditional Christian liberal arts training. Here, under the guidance of teachers trained at the South's leading Christian colleges, Knott's grandchildren along with several hundred other kids would learn from a curriculum that melded liberal arts with biblical training and full immersion in a program of "Christian Americanism."[14]

Designed as a retreat from public education, Heritage was not meant to be a refuge from the world. Its mission was to train youth to be dedicated patriots. Every component of the institution's "total education" reflected this ideal. At Heritage, students would face challenging and highly competitive standards based on traditional measures. "Tragic as it may seem," school administrators pointed out,

> [public] schools no longer WANT to turn out INDIVIDUALS. Instead, they seem intent on molding children into socialist "Group-concept" patterns [and] a "peaches and cream" world in which everyone passes and no one fails. . . . A "never-never land" in which the bright students are held back, so that slower students won't be embarrassed, feel discouraged or "left-behind."

Although a strict dress code suggested that at least a few signs of collectivism persisted in Heritage's halls, in principle the school was designed to sharpen notions of personal freedom and responsibility. Special attention was given to screening teachers to ensure that they were willing and able to teach rugged individualism as America's supreme value. School officials took the hiring process seriously. Included in the employee's application and yearly review process was an intimidating list of questions on faith and patriotism that required extended, thoughtful, essay-length answers, the idea being that no pink progressive ever step foot in this new stronghold of red, white, and blue.[15]

Comprised of selected parents, teachers, and administrators, Heritage's board of education also devoted hours of energy crafting curricula and screening textbooks promoted by California's public educators, especially those covering American history. Such intense scrutiny was necessary, according to Heritage's superintendent, because these tomes were "written with a political interpretation of the facts of history, including the elimination of God and Christianity." After one especially long, laborious evaluation session that produced mounds of data, Heritage's scrutinizers found that one popular textbook contained "only 26 words [devoted] to Gen. Douglas MacArthur" and treated "Benedict Arnold . . . as not really a traitor." Another textbook interpreted the "events of World War I and the Korean War so as to further the ideals of big government control." All of this pointed to the "socialistic bent" in Southern California public education and compelled Heritage officials to consider alternative classroom materials published by George Benson's National Education Program and the Foundation for American Christian Education (FACE), for which two of Wells's educational associates, Rosalie Slater and Verna Hall, had created their own pilot program. Soon to become a staple for Christian educators as far east as Tennessee, Slater and Hall's pedagogy emphasized the fundamentals of free enterprise and the ideals of the founders. They paid special attention to patriots like Patrick Henry, whose battle cry for individual freedom and decentralized government—"give me liberty or give me death"—symbolized their curriculum. At each level of instruction, students worked toward the completion of a major project. In the earlier grades this meant the writing of an essay on the Constitution and its meaning for the American citizen. Sixth grader Shirley Matthews won top prize by writing, "I am an individual. Since I am an individual I have responsibilities. There are many responsibilities I have but I think the most important one is having self-control and self-government." By twelfth grade, students wrote speeches and reenacted the Constitutional Convention. The best of these projects were presented before a large audience at Knott's Berry Farm's Independence Hall.[16]

At Heritage students also learned how to act as individuals. Under the direction of Heritage's drama department, students put on elaborate school plays that revisited the ideals of early American life and related them to the realities of California's cold war suburbs. Instructor Carol Monroe crafted musicals and dramas like *Walkin' Through the Land* and *God of Our Fathers*, which folded the themes of frontier democracy and colonial republicanism into a patriotic message. Every word spoken in the performance was weighted with ideology, as well as clear notions of gender and nationhood. *Walkin' Through the Land*, for example, included an extended soliloquy on Republican womanhood by "Female Speaker 2" that put femaleness in its "proper" place:

> Thanks to God, I am a woman. Let me be absolutely and essentially, and uniquely woman. I am inescapable woman in my soul. That necessity [is] in my freedom: as the tigress glories in her stripes, as the lark glories in her son, as the river glories in the banks that alone gives her freedom to be the river, so I, my life lies where I live—in my family. Both my parents and the future man and children that will be my true home, in my country (not in mere society), in my work, (for those I love, and not as a busy body trying to reform the world) and in making myself beautiful and gracious and wise for those I love.

Such spoken assumptions about the submissive wife would become more prevalent in Heritage's artistic offerings in the late 1960s, but earlier in the decade moral mothers like "Female Speaker 2" often shared the stage with brave, assertive frontierswomen. The two images were never presented at odds. Heritage women were instructed to be devout mothers but also courageous countersubversives, citizens who used their suburban quiet time to counteract the ways of communism in the community. Given responsibility for designing better textbooks—exemplified by model mothers like Slater and Hall—or attending school board meetings to keep educators like Willard Goslin in check, Heritage women were commissioned for engagement in politics that impinged on the home and threatened the underpinnings of society.[17]

If Heritage's female students were taught how to be America's moral guardians, its male students were raised to be its valiant protectors. Virtually every aspect of Heritage's curricular and extracurricular routines reminded people of the school's ties to national defense. Heritage's seven-man football team proudly donned jerseys adorned with the Patriot's *P*, and its school float, staffed by male students wearing Union, Confederate, and World War II army fatigues together raising the flag of Iwo Jima, appeared in Orange County parades decked with United States flag bunting. In *God of Our Fathers*, another Carol Monroe musical, young men offered tribute to their country's greatest speeches, beginning with

Abraham Lincoln's Gettysburg Address, moving through General Robert E. Lee's inspirational words, and ending with a fighting charge from General Douglas MacArthur. The combination of songs and soliloquies that appeared in *God of Our Fathers* were typical of most other Heritage musicals for the way they interspersed tunes that represented the pomp of the imperial North and the grit of the courageous South. Led toward a crescendo in the last act, audience members were encouraged to join in the singing of the "Star Spangled Banner," "Dixie," "Battle Hymn of the Republic," and "Over There."[18]

Audience participation of this sort was frequent at Heritage, and the school soon became an epicenter of political activity in the community and promoted its Parent Teacher Fellowship (PTF) as an alternative to the local PTA. During the early 1960s, Bob Wells and his political friends would speak regularly at PTF meetings about anticommunism strategies. These talks were often supplemented by "surveillance reports" provided by Heritage's pastors and parents on Anaheim school board discussions of the teaching of evolution and sex education, the latest curricular and extracurricular developments at local colleges, and even new trends in legislation at city and county offices. Much more than a school, Heritage was, from the moment of its inception, a new home base for conservatism.[19]

RESTORING FAITH

The same would soon be said about Pepperdine College. Upon his return to Southern California, Norvel Young confronted a tempest in postsecondary education every bit as tense as the one that rattled primary and secondary schools. The core issues were the same: California evangelicals were convinced that their state colleges were becoming havens for secular liberalism. Like others recently ascended to California's middle class, evangelicals recognized that their children's academic credentials would determine their future in the new knowledge-based economy. As their teens got older, evangelical parents thus faced the frightening prospect that sons and daughters seeking degrees in engineering and nursing, business and science, would have to enter California's vast postsecondary infrastructure, a state-run factory system, in their opinion, that drained students' sense of spiritual and personal worth.

Evangelical parents did not worry alone. In 1952, William F. Buckley Jr.'s provocative *God and Man at Yale* in fact had helped trigger a minor revolt against the educational system of the Eisenhower era. In 1953, Frank Chodorov founded the Intercollegiate Society of Individualists (ISI), with Buckley as president. Like Leonard Read's Foundation for Economic Education, ISI supplied a national constituency with libertarian and traditional conservative literature, but also served as a clearinghouse for alternative educational materials for private colleges—Catholic, Protestant, libertarian, and otherwise—scattered across the country. By frequenting right-wing bookstores and subscribing to an assortment of periodicals, Southern California evangelicals stayed apprised of these broader critiques of higher education. But mostly they framed their own answers to the problem. One strategy they employed was campus evangelism of the kind Bill Bright introduced at UCLA. By the end of the 1950s, Campus Crusade for Christ and a number of other parachurch organizations, including Navigators and Intervarsity Christian Fellowship, had mastered one-on-one and cell-group evangelistic techniques to reach college students. Their ultimate goal was the same: to instill in youth a deeply rooted sense of faith from which they could draw emotional strength when defending their beliefs on their college campuses. University training did not, evangelicals believed, have to bring about retreat in the spiritual realm.[20]

Despite these efforts, other evangelical parents and ministers pushed more aggressively for religious private education. This, however, proved much more complicated at the postsecondary level. Building an elementary school or a high school on church property was one thing, but raising a college from the ground up or expanding an already established one into a viable institution of higher learning was a daunting task, one few evangelical communities could even contemplate. Conditions in the 1950s made it all the more so. Just as demand in Christian higher education began to increase in the 1950s, the financial resources available to Christian colleges began to decline. Whereas Eisenhower's generous cold war distribution of federal education funds bolstered state institutions, private schools floundered in the 1950s. In 1951, half of the nation's nine hundred private schools were operating in the red, which their administrators blamed on higher costs due to inflation. Not all was bad for these educators. Private colleges, including evangelical ones, benefited indirectly from federal programs like the GI Bill and had some access to other subsidies for construction and maintenance of school plants and fellowship programs, but in ways this only made matters worse. As Pepperdine

College experienced in the early 1950s, the departing wave of GI students left behind expanded infrastructures, raised expectations for growth, and a surfeit of debt.[21]

Complex epistemological and economic problems thus framed Young's inauguration as Pepperdine's president, yet because of his personal experiences, he was confident they were surmountable. A trailblazing idealist, Young was temperamentally equipped for the task of rebuilding a floundering college. He had already proved he could be an effective institution builder in Texas. Since leaving Southern California as newlyweds during World War II, Norvel and Helen Young had become the Church of Christ's dynamic first couple. After finishing doctoral work at George Peabody College, Norvel accepted leadership of Broadway Church, in Lubbock, Texas. Under the Youngs' guidance, Broadway grew to become a model congregation, with nearly two thousand members and a sparkling neo-Romanesque-style building setting denominational trends. As their church grew, Norvel and Helen moved to unify their denomination. Having already helped start the *20th Century Christian* in the late 1930s, Norvel now helped form 20th Century Christian Bookstore and Publishing, which quickly became the Church of Christ's most important clearinghouse. Helen, meanwhile, established her own reputation in letters by writing and helping edit the quarterly *Power for Today*, a booklet that became the preferred devotional guide in the average Church of Christ home. Together, they traveled to churches throughout West Texas, extending their ministry. The people were always excited to see the Youngs, daughter Emily would later recall. They looked forward most to Norvel's preaching. "Whenever daddy would offer the invitation at the end of the service . . . he would walk down the middle of the aisle with his arms extended wide and his hands wide open. He would invite the people to come to Jesus." This passion for the Youngs was on full display when, after thirteen years of diligent labor, Broadway Church hosted a giant picnic in their honor and presented them with a new yellow Buick station wagon. Reporting on Broadway's celebration, *Time* magazine captured the scale of what the Youngs had become when it described them as "the nearest thing to a binding force for the 1.2 million members and 15,000 fully autonomous churches that comprised the Church of Christ movement."[22]

Shortly after this celebratory picnic, Helen and Norvel Young answered George Pepperdine's plea for administrative help and moved to Los Angeles. They immediately realized that rebuilding their alma mater would be more difficult than first imagined. The school's faith appeared to be crumbling, and its institutional framework worked against any easy solution. Although Pepperdine wanted to avoid a specific denominational affiliation, he had nevertheless intended the school to complement the Church of Christ's mission to youth, education, evangelism, and citizenship. This intrinsic ambiguity festered and over time swelled into confusion: Was Pepperdine College to be a religious institution that made room for secular training or a secular academy that allowed space for spiritual development? By the early 1950s, many Church of Christ people believed that Pepperdine had chosen to be the latter and in fact had begun an irreversible slide into secularity.[23]

There were legitimate grounds for their concern. Hoping to steer the institution away from its "sectarian tendencies" toward a more cosmopolitan, academic respectability, President Hugh Tiner—a former superintendent of Los Angeles County schools—had loosened chapel requirements so that students no longer had to attend daily. Raised in Texas Church of Christ culture and still devoted to his religious ancestry, Tiner nevertheless saw himself as an innovative educator. After World War II, this impulse led him to endorse UNESCO. A leading delegate to the UNESCO conference in San Francisco in 1947, it was Tiner who chaired the Southern California Council for UNESCO and whose proclamations in 1948 had sparked such swift reaction from conservative parents. At the same time that he promoted new trends in public education, Tiner's supreme quest was to make his school a leading private liberal arts institution. Helping him was Dean E. V. Pullias. An accomplished academic in his own right, Pullias brought credibility to the school and a vision for private education modeled on the more progressive University of Southern California just a few miles away. For him, Pepperdine's secularization was not such a bad thing.[24]

Failing in health, and troubled by the polarized reaction his school was causing in church circles, George Pepperdine looked upon Norvel Young to return Pepperdine College to its religious roots. The first year was full of campus turmoil. Immediately upon Young's arrival, Pullias resigned and accepted a teaching position at the University of Southern California. Then, in the spring of 1958, nearly half of Pepperdine's faculty, including the associate dean of students and business manager, resigned in protest. Even the librarian joined them. The local press fed the firestorm by running negative headlines like "Teachers Quit Pepperdine" and "Mass Exodus Impends at Pepperdine." Convinced Pepperdine College was headed toward heavy-handed Church of Christ control, the dissenters purposefully hamstrung Young's administration by resigning at the very end of the spring semester, leaving only a few months to restaff for the fall semester.[25]

Once past the damage-control phase of his presidency, Young began constructing a long-term solution to his school's flagging identity. Though hardly a sectarian of the kind Pullias had feared, Young embraced the theological traditions of his community. Initially he thought of paring Pepperdine back into a Bible college to erase incongruities in the school's mandate, but he soon grew confident that he could achieve a workable balance between the precepts of the church and the priorities of the academy. During the summer of 1958, Young hired a crop of young professors trained principally in southern Christian universities and aggressively recruited "Christian students and students who wanted to prepare for the ministry." This new strategy had a trickle-down effect on campus culture. Two years into Young's presidency, students were required to attend chapel every day; pleasingly, to him, they seemed to do so out of conviction rather than obligation. And at 10:30 nightly, men living in Baxter Hall and women residing in Marilyn Hall gathered "to sing hymns, join in prayer, and read from the Bible," a devotional routine the *Graphic* heralded as part of Pepperdine's new, "more well-rounded education."[26]

But Young's most important move was his reinstitution of the Pepperdine Bible Lectureship. Instituted in 1943 as a way to gather congregants on campus to hear the Church of Christ's most respected preachers, Pepperdine's annual lecture series had dwindled as fractures among church, school, and community worsened. Just prior to Young's arrival, the series was disbanded altogether. In a community like the Church of Christ, which resisted formal denominational organization, the Bible lectures were an important way to affirm collective identity, especially in California, where Church of Christ members were geographically isolated. Young's move to reinstate the lectures was welcomed by students and local church folk alike. By 1960, the weeklong event had outgrown the campus auditorium and had to be held in the much larger Shrine Auditorium. In 1962, Pepperdine's Bible Lectureship, now held in the Los Angeles Sports Arena, drew over ten thousand Church of Christ folk from around Southern California and the South. On March 22, after listening to Ira North, of Madison Church of Christ, in Nashville, preach on "Christ or Materialism," and singing hymns in harmony, unassisted by instrumentation, the audience heard George Pepperdine speak his last public words. While reclining on an ambulance gurney, a weakened Pepperdine clutched the microphone and, with great pride in his voice, repeated what he had said privately to Young just a few months earlier. There, while talking at the president's home and looking over the lush, green lawns, pale blue buildings and palm-tree-lined promenade cutting through campus, he said, "If I died today, I would die a happy man." He passed away four months later.[27]

What Pepperdine no doubt recognized as a frail seventy-six-year-old man, looking out over his hushed audience in the spring of 1962, was that Young had succeeded at bringing his school back into communion with the faith of his childhood. Unfortunately for Young, his school now labored under a more fundamental problem: finances. At the school's founding, George Pepperdine had guaranteed his school would operate free of financial ties to church and state; Pepperdine's wealth, generated from his auto supply company and channeled through the George Pepperdine Foundation, was to be the sole funding stream for the school. But the solid investments the Foundation had made throughout the 1940s in aircraft manufacturing, chemicals, and real estate were now increasingly stretched thin by diversification and mismanagement. As Pepperdine's failures mounted, additional capital was required, leading to greater losses and a burden of debt that could no longer be maintained by the Pepperdine Foundation. The indignity of lawsuits followed, leaving Pepperdine in a cycle of insult and embarrassment. What pained Pepperdine most was that "the assets which he placed in the Foundation for the purpose of building a large endowment for the college, had been swept away." In 1956, the school was operating with an annual deficit of close to a million dollars, and when the Youngs arrived in 1957, the school faced insolvency. Young needed a ready-made solution.[28]

RESTORING FINANCES

Above all else, though, Young wanted a financial strategy that would increase his school's profile without undermining its philosophical commitments. At first he turned to Church of Christ people for help. "Like a barnstorming politician," his secretary later recalled, "Young would spread his word to all who would listen, sometimes to several groups in a day, revived only by a quick nap in the back of the Buick and an unwavering belief in the mission of Pepperdine College." Through all of this, Young sought a modest goal: to raise the fund-raising total beyond the meager twenty-five thousand dollars that came in to the school each year from local congregations. Young made progress, but the gains were far too modest for his school to realize any dramatic turnaround; he needed a better plan.[29]

Young did not have to look long or hard for one: His former mentor, George Benson, had already perfected the solution. Whereas most private colleges like Pepperdine had struggled during the 1950s, Benson's Harding College was thriving. Early during Pepperdine College's faculty troubles, Benson had advised Young on hiring and even suggested some of Harding's staff. Then, in the fall of 1958, with the core of Pepperdine's new faculty in place, Benson helped Young reach out to city officials and conservative donors. He told Young to write a direct petition to the city of Los Angeles and its business community emphasizing George Pepperdine's voluntary commitment to civic life and valuable service to the community. Benson suggested that Young propose a new arrangement: in exchange for help raising five hundred thousand dollars over the following three years, Pepperdine College would step up its training in "American private enterprise economy" and "Christian character and leadership and citizenship." Young followed through, and by November of 1958 he was reporting widespread enthusiasm for the campaign. In a December letter to Young, Benson expressed "congratulations with the way the business people of Los Angeles are responding to this effort to raise money for Pepperdine."[30]

As the fund-raising campaign gathered steam, Young, with Benson's help, looked for ways to demonstrate Pepperdine's commitment to "citizenship training." First, Young made Pepperdine the West Coast distribution center for Benson's National Education Program material. Prior to this, NEP pamphlets, films, and curricula were filtered to California conservatives through freedom bookstores and Walter Knott's California Free Enterprise Association. Pepperdine now assumed the dominant role within the California network, enhancing the school's public recognition. Second, Young established the Pepperdine freedom forum, an annual seminar based on the Harding College model. This was not an unprecedented move. By the late 1950s, freedom forums had in fact become a popular mechanism for fund-raising in Christian colleges across the western South. None employed it more effectively than John Brown University, which, in the late 1950s, began holding an annual American Heritage Seminar, ostensibly to "perpetuate the . . . free enterprise system, and to inculcate Christian principles into the American way of life and business" but also to clean up some of the financial shortcomings that plagued John Brown's empire at the time of his death in 1957. With his father's death and the loss of senior patrons like Jesse H. Jones, who had died the year before his father, John Brown Jr. began rebuilding his school's fiscal infrastructure, and the freedom forum format helped immensely in generating interest and money. JBU's seminars were headlined by many of the same spokespeople who routinely appeared at Harding, but also by John Brown Sr.'s dearest friends, ranging from local broadcaster Paul Harvey and evangelical industrialist R. G. LeTourneau to Californians Walter Knott and J. Vernon McGee.[31]

Young's decision to implement the freedom forum concept might have been influenced by other southern schools' success, but it was clearly driven by Benson's own fruitful work in California. Since the late 1940s Benson had held freedom forums throughout Southern California on an invitation-only basis. By the late 1950s it had become apparent that this type of lecture series could easily become an annual event. In the summer of 1959, after a year of preparation, Young oversaw Pepperdine's first freedom forum. Held over three days in June, the conference brought two hundred businessmen and civic leaders to campus to listen to lectures and participate in discussion groups meant for three purposes:

> To refresh the conferees with the fundamental facts about our American system and the forces now seeking its destruction; to create, discuss, and demonstrate educational materials and techniques which will effect a clearer understanding of our American heritage; and to stimulate influential thought-leaders who attend the Forum so that they may return to their respective organizations and communities better prepared to carry the Forum's citizenship education to their fellows.

Headlining the event were keynote speakers no doubt familiar to the southerners within the crowd: Dr. Willard J. Graff, Springfield, Missouri, school superintendent, and Benson, whose sermon on "Faith in God, Constitutional Government, and Our Private Enterprise Economy" set the tone. The highlight, however, was a special luncheon for 750 people at the Biltmore Hotel, headlined by Arkansas Senator John L. McClellan, who was advertised as the "hard-fisted chairman of the Senate Rackets Investigation Committee," recognized "for his leadership in exposing malfeasance, extravagance, and mismanagement in government, and more recently, for his forthright investigation of improper activities in the labor-management field."[32]

Within a week, Young was receiving letters of congratulations from Los Angeles' elite, including those with media clout, like Edward Gilbert, of the Los Angeles Times, who gushed, "Never, in all the years I have been attending meetings, conferences, seminars or what ever you choose to call them, have I been so inspired as I was by Pepperdine College's Freedom Forum." Young no doubt appreciated the praise, but the money was more convincing. In August, he wrote Benson, "still feeling the good effects of the Freedom Forum," and in September, after the final tally was completed, he informed Benson that the donations had pushed Pepperdine into the black for the first time since 1951.[33]

With the help of William Teague, Benson's former vice president for development, who now joined Pepperdine's staff, Young began leading Pepperdine toward loftier goals. He began building trust with local businessmen who had reacted with enthusiasm to Pepperdine's first freedom forum, including some of Southern California's most recognizable names: Richard Ralph, owner of the Ralph's supermarket chain; Bryant Essick, president of Essick Manufacturing Company; Jack Horton, president of the California Edison Company; and Walter Knott, all of whom were given seats on Pepperdine's President's Board, a council of executives set up to advise the freedom forum and the school's citizenship program. Young looked out of state as well. Dallas's well-known financier Clint Murchison Jr., for instance, acted as chair of finances. And although "conservative" and "Republican" would soon become necessary qualifications for membership on Pepperdine's executive boards, early in Young's presidency Democrats with centrist views still received invitations to join, especially if they were Pepperdine alum. Two of Pepperdine's most heralded graduates—and two of Young's closest supporters—were Gordon and Kenneth Hahn, who used their popularity within Los Angeles County politics to enhance their alma mater's profile.[34]

In its initial push to attract donors, Pepperdine thus gained access to several well-heeled conservative executives, but none were more important to Young than Henry Salvatori. Widely known as Los Angeles' most powerful Republican, Salvatori was also an internationally acclaimed geophysicist who had published several pioneering studies on methods and techniques. His Western Geophysical Company and the Grant Oil Tool Company, manufacturer of oil drill production and pipeline equipment, were immensely profitable. At the moment he met Young, just prior to the first freedom forum, Salvatori's net worth was listed at $5 million, with an annual income of $1 million. His portfolio would grow substantially over time and with it his patronage of Pepperdine, but in the late 1950s Salvatori's real worth to Young was as a liaison to other donors. With his help, Young and Teague were introduced to Frank Seaver, president of Hydril, an international oil tool firm. At a meeting between the three men, Teague and Young asked Seaver if he would consider donating $1,000 to support Pepperdine's citizenship program. Instead, Young would later recall, Seaver wrote out a check for $7,500 and, "with a grin, handed it to me saying, 'Do you think this will help?'" The transaction not only put Pepperdine's project over the top but also opened the door to another donor, Richard Scaife, newspaper publishing magnate and overseer of the Mellon fortune in Pittsburgh, who invested in Pepperdine's program and pledged petrogrants from the family business, Gulf Oil.[35]

Now a corporate executive in his own right, Young sharpened his business skills, yet at the same time he fell back naturally on his pastoral instincts. Whether he knew it or not, this helped recruit another major donor: Charles "Tex" Thornton. Young had known Thornton through mutual friends in Lubbock, when the latter was at Texas Tech University. After college, Thornton moved to Washington, D.C., and worked his way into the United States Interior Department and then the War Department. Immediately following World War II, he teamed with "whiz kids" Robert McNamara and Arjay Miller to rebuild the Ford Motor Company. Thornton moved to Southern California in the early 1950s, where he completely reorganized Hughes Aircraft Company, raising its revenue to $200 million. Thornton then borrowed $1.5 million and bought Litton Industries, a small microwave tube company, and transformed it into a billion-dollar conglomerate responsible for the production of seemingly everything, from aircraft guidance systems to McGuffey Readers. When the corporate titan and school president met again in California, they did so under radically different circumstances but not, as Young would emphasize, on different terms. Shared priorities in family and free enterprise—

commonalities struck earlier in their relationship—still provided the glue to their friendship, though finances now strengthened the bond.[36]

Young's pastoral connections are also what helped cement his school's ties to Hollywood, Pepperdine's second most important financial resource in its turnaround years. Pepperdine College had always liked to publicize its connections to Hollywood, but at its nadir its fixation on Tinseltown assumed an urgent quality. Young recognized that by reestablishing ties to Hollywood, Pepperdine would get media attention and thus more funds. The Youngs nurtured this relationship by inviting to their eighteen-room presidential mansion Los Angeles' most famous conservative celebrities. A stunning centerpiece to the thirty-four-acre plot of land that Pepperdine purchased in 1937, the house played host to dozens of Hollywood greats.[37]

The Youngs' favorite Hollywood guest—Pat Boone—was their most frequent. In June 1959, Boone recorded his last *Pat Boone Chevy Showroom* with Shirley and his four daughters at his side. Boone "rolled the four little Boonelets out in a box with a shipping label marked 'To Disneyland' . . . sang 'May the good Lord bless and keep you,'" then waved good-bye to his New York studio audience and headed west to California. By the fall of 1959, the Boone family was settled in Los Angeles, where the Church of Christ community helped ease their transition into the West Coast lifestyle. As a boy in Tennessee, Pat had been part of Helen's Bible class at the David Lipscomb church. Not long after the Youngs moved to Lubbock, Norvel returned to Nashville to baptize thirteen-year-old Pat, an event Boone would recall to Norvel fifty years later in biblical allegory: "You became, in that precious moment, my 'John the Baptist,' and my life was changed forever." In ways he could not have imagined at the time, the moment changed Norvel's life as well, for Boone became heavily invested in Pepperdine's recovery after his arrival in Los Angeles. Individually, he lent his talent and celebrity status to the promotion of several Pepperdine media events, and frequently visited the campus to speak or sing at chapel services and lead the school's annual youth forum. Behind the scenes, meanwhile, he expanded communication between Young and Hollywood conservatives, all of which would prove vital for the school's future.[38]

By January of 1960, this future looked much brighter than it did three years earlier. As a consummate pastor-diplomat, Young had assured Pepperdine at least another decade. All facets of his economic recovery plan had paid off, and the school's identity was tied firmly to its religious and political roots. Young celebrated Pepperdine's fiscal freedom by crafting the school's own official Declaration of Independence (see this chapter's epigraph). Written to parrot the founding fathers, the document affirmed the school's rejection of federal control and funding. Young's declaration also thanked the school's many new donors: "We, of course, are indebted to the 97 men and women who invested in this program in amounts of $100 to $50,000. They came from all walks of life and represented every area of friends of the college. Their confidence in the future of Pepperdine is most inspiring." Printed in papers throughout the country, the pronouncement served as an effective marketing ploy and proudly proclaimed Pepperdine's new link to the Republican Right.[39]

As Young's gratefulness showed, evangelical educational institutions had a lot to be thankful for in this political marriage of conviction and convenience, yet the relationship benefited both parties. As far as Pepperdine's patrons were concerned, the school was a symbol of their success. In pedagogical terms, Pepperdine's embrace of an alternative approach set a pace for other private schools to follow. Former Hollywood screenwriter and radical-turned-conservative columnist Morrie Ryskind spoke of this exciting development when he lauded the new Pepperdine as "an oasis of non-conformity in an academic desert of monolithic liberalism." In political terms, Pepperdine's institutional makeover meant that conservatives now had access to a new command center where patricians and populists, businessmen and intellectuals, students, teachers, and parents could rally behind a shared agenda for political change. Through a sustained and rigorous give-and-take of ideas and moral support on the Christian campus, conservatives could grow closer in their prescriptions for a world they knew needed fixing.[40]

BY THE TIME PEPPERDINE hosted its third freedom forum, in early April of 1961, the event had become a must for local citizens and candidates aspiring to political leadership. An estimated 1,500 executives, businessmen, educators and a "small but enthusiastic group of college students" paid a registration fee of $100 to participate in three days of seminars, public lectures, and workshops. As the *Graphic* later reported, the forum saw a wealth of important issues discussed, such as "the outlawing of the Communist Party, U.S.A., the seating of Red China in the U.N., the Kennedy Peace Corps and its desirability, the merits of the John Birch

Society, and the doing away with personal income tax." The finer points of these issues elicited heated debate, even among the forum's slate of headline speakers, which included George W. Robnett, the Church League of America's retired founder and now a Pasadena resident; Wayne Poucher, director of the *Lifeline* radio program; Paul Terry, editor of the *San Diego Union-Tribune*; Robert Peterson, superintendent of schools for Santa Ana; and Anaheim industrialist William Aldrich. While most agreed that the Communist Party should be outlawed, Red China refused, the Peace Corps disbanded, and the John Birch Society commended, some encouraged greater flexibility. On one critical point, all in attendance wholeheartedly agreed: that a firmer educational commitment to free enterprise and anticommunism was desperately needed if America wanted its next generation to live the dream for which its current generation had sacrificed so much.[41]

Three full days of such lively, invigorating exchange culminated in a sit-down televised luncheon at the lavish Biltmore Hotel with Senator Barry Goldwater. Already a superstar in the eyes of Southern California conservatives for his work in the right-to-work campaign and his book *The Conscience of a Conservative*, released a year earlier, in April 1960, Goldwater's appearance on Pepperdine's behalf was a major coup for Young and Teague. Enthusiastic and engaging, the Arizona senator delivered a rousing sermon that illustrated his firm but measured conservative conscience. On the China issue, he charged, there could be no compromise: China did not deserve a seat in the UN. With regard to the Peace Corps, Goldwater bucked the majority opinion by highlighting its potential value, provided it was run properly. On the other matters, Goldwater advised strength in the response to communism but also caution when curtailing the freedoms of political expression on Left or Right.[42]

This crowd welcomed the senator's political commentary, yet his earnest emotional appeal drew the greatest response from the audience. Goldwater was in fine form delivering his doctrine of cowboy conservatism. He concluded his comments with a nod to his hero, America's ultimate cowboy president, Theodore Roosevelt. In 1917, Goldwater said, Roosevelt had delivered a stern warning to the American people: "Prosperity at any price, peace at any price, and safety first instead of duty first are the things that will destroy the United States." America needed this message, Goldwater said, because an age of prosperity, peace, and

security had made it soft once again. Fiscal responsibility, national solidarity, strong defense, and a courageous citizenry—these were the priorities Roosevelt called forth from his people, and these were the principles
for which Goldwater now wanted his audience to fight. Unlike Roosevelt,
however, who delivered his message shortly before his own death, Goldwater promised to be there to lead.[43]

9

SENTINELS OF
FREEDOM

*The delicate balance that ideally exists between freedom and
order has long since tipped against freedom practically everywhere
on earth. . . . [F]or the American Conservative, there is no difficulty in identifying the day's overriding political challenge: it is to
preserve and extend freedom. As he surveys the various attitudes
and institutions and laws that currently prevail in America, many
questions will occur to him, but the Conservative's first concern
will always be: Are we maximizing freedom?*[1]

—BARRY GOLDWATER,
THE CONSCIENCE OF A CONSERVATIVE

FOUR MONTHS AFTER BARRY GOLDWATER TOPPED THE GUEST LIST
at Pepperdine's freedom forum, Los Angeles flocked to the Sports
Arena for a five-day citizens' training program, organized by Fred Schwarz,
called the Southern California School of Anti-Communism. Its climax came
on Wednesday, August 30, 1961, when sixteen thousand teens and their parents packed the building for "youth night." After the "Star-Spangled Banner,"
a popular hymn, and the Pledge of Allegiance, a series of famous guests
spoke. The first was Marion Miller, a mother and suburban housewife-
turned-celebrity who appealed for more anticommunist education in public schools. Miller had just published her acclaimed autobiography, *I Was a
Spy*, which described how, for five years, she infiltrated Los Angeles' Left as
an informant for the Federal Bureau of Investigation (FBI). Ronald Reagan
was next. Like Miller, he warned that teens were now communists' principal

target in the same way Hollywood had been a decade earlier: Communists "will appeal to your rebellious nature. They will make you feel your patriotism is hollow. Then they will fill up the vacuum with their philosophy." Roy Rogers, Dale Evans, and John Wayne followed with similar cautions.

But the night belonged to the celebrity who appeared last. After singing a few songs, Pat Boone spoke about his family and his country as he usually did, but his impromptu speech came to a surprising conclusion. "I don't want to live in a Communist United States," he told the crowd. "I would rather see my four girls shot and die as little girls who have faith in God than leave them to die some years later as godless, faithless, soulless Communists." A hush fell over the audience, followed by a wild ovation. Although he had not thought hard about this statement beforehand, Boone did not hesitate once the idea crossed his mind. His surprise at the power of this admission caused tears to well in his eyes, which only added to the emotion that overtook the crowd. Though Shirley Boone was none too happy about it, Pat's spontaneous pronouncement proved to be the highlight of the night, and one of the most exhilarating moments of the entire week.[2]

FIFTEEN "SPIES" FROM THE Community Relations Committee, the Jewish civil rights agency, were present that evening. Having documented local right-wing activities since the 1940s, they were not surprised by the popularity of Schwarz's seminar, but their sixteen-page final report pointed to something new. This rally had an air of confidence and collective verve not witnessed before on Southern California's political Right. Audience members were

> well dressed, middle class people, who had come from all parts of Southern California. The average age of the adults seemed to be in the middle thirties. . . . In addition, a great number of children were brought—some for every session. This fact plus the prior publicity gave the whole School an air of a Tent Evangelical Meeting. [P]eople seemed to be in a holiday mood, wearing their Sunday best and almost all speeches were sermonic rather than instructive.

One CRC spy noted discomfort with the "nascent anti-semitism of many in the audience," and a few others complained about the "Messiah-feeling that the audience showed for Schwarz." A handful of observers were convinced that the Southern California School of Anti-Communism had an "atmosphere of a neo-Fascist political meeting," but most did not feel that it posed so serious a threat. In the main, the event impressed CRC activists and made them wonder what political challenges "the liberal side" would face next. Yes, they agreed, the School of Anti-Communism was a "destructive, noisy, red-baiting campaign," but it was also the product of an organized people now ready to affect political change.[3]

CRC agents were right. Schwarz's seminar resounded with political conviction and expectation because it represented the culmination of a decade of grassroots mobilization against New Deal liberalism and the beginnings of a new phase of action. The citizens in the Los Angeles Sports Arena were united; over the next three years they would mount a coordinated revolt, thanks in large part to the work of transplanted southern evangelicals, who believed that liberal initiatives undertaken by Democratic governments in Washington and Sacramento threatened their ideals. In rapid succession, these activists would generate several reform movements and ballot initiatives and carry their momentum into Barry Goldwater's landmark 1964 presidential campaign. Schwarz's School of Anti-Communism had the feeling of a tent revival because for so many of its participants it was a religious as much as a political happening. Matching Schwarz's Baptist zeal with their own evangelistic fervor, these citizens believed their society was edging toward collapse. Like Schwarz, they were convinced America's deliverance could only come through Christ's second return. In the meantime, though, they looked to Goldwater conservatism as a short-term fix.

THE CONSERVATIVE CONSCIENCE

The political action now undertaken by Schwarz's allies was different from anything they had engaged in before. Since the late 1940s, Southern California conservatives had been building an expansive network of free enterprise and anticommunist organizations and busily rallying suburbanites behind ground-level initiatives for neighborhood reform. It was not until William Knowland's failed 1958 campaign for governor against Pat Brown, however, that this process of mobilization evolved into a full-blown pursuit of partisan and electoral power. The "Rollin' for Knowland" campaign may have missed its mark at the polls and fractured California's Republican Party, but it invigorated conservatives, leaving them wanting more. With Brown solidly entrenched in Sacramento, Knowland's supporters turned their attention to national politics and Barry Goldwater for a way to build on their momentum.

Clarence Manion, the pundit who had played such a vital role in sparking the right-wing movement, helped set conservatives' sights on the man for the next moment. Manion first heard Goldwater speak in South Carolina in 1959, after which he encouraged the politician to write a book. Despite some reluctance at first, Goldwater consented, and, with the "guiding hand" of ghostwriter L. Brent Bozell, brother-in-law of William F. Buckley Jr., he published *The Conscience of a Conservative* in April 1960. Manion kept after Goldwater, urging him to run for office that year. Though he wanted only to pressure Richard Nixon, Dwight Eisenhower's assumed heir, Goldwater agreed to a preliminary campaign. "Preliminary," however, was not in the lexicon of those galvanized by the Senator's invigorated conservatism. By July sixty-three South Carolina delegates had already pledged themselves to him. South Carolina Senator Strom Thurmond called Goldwater "a man of great intellect, wisdom, judgment, industry, integrity, sincerity and courage." "Knowing the Southern people as I do," he proclaimed, "it is my opinion that if he should be selected as the nominee of either major political party, he would carry the South; and if elected, he would make a great President."[4]

By summer, over four hundred Goldwater for President committees were operational throughout the country; sixty-five of these worked the suburban communities of California, principally in its southern counties. In late June, for example, Mrs. Jo Poland founded a chapter in San Diego and within days a "nucleus of fifty men and women" were canvassing door-to-door with copies of *Conscience of a Conservative* and manning a booth at the county fair "to enlist every other resident who desires . . . a return to Conservative, pro-Constitution principles in our federal government." Activists like Poland suffered a devastating blow just prior to the election when behind closed doors Nixon and liberal Republican Nelson Rockefeller negotiated a moderate party platform. Calling this pact the "Munich of the Republican Party," Goldwater fumed at having his constituency brushed aside by the East Coast elite. He answered with a gracious but decisive speech, delivered to the 1960 Republican National Convention, urging conservatives to support Nixon but to take back their party in time for 1964. California conservatives needed little prompting, for their hearts already belonged to Barry.[5]

Southern church folk certainly found much to love about Senator Goldwater. Although he was not one of them theologically—his Jewish background and nominal Episcopalian faith discomforted some, but not enough to discredit him or his philosophy—he had the right disposition. Like their preachers, whom they preferred seasoned by nature and life experience, they viewed the tanned, angular Senator as a man of the western South. In his rigid gaze and stoic, sometimes- stormy demeanor, this maverick proved that their frontier still existed. And Goldwater's unapologetic approach seemed refreshing too. The "rough-hewn citizen-statesman" of his promotional material who put aside "personal ambition and partisan advantage to battle for the public good" resonated with them, and though they knew this image was exaggerated it certainly rang much truer than the caricatures promulgated by his opponents. Amid the suspicion that seemed to plague American politics in the early 1960s, Goldwater iconoclasm was not only reassuring to southern evangelicals, but also more constructive.[6]

His political philosophy enchanted them, too, particularly as it was outlined in *Conscience of a Conservative*. A short, 123-page booklet, blunt and accessible, *Conscience of a Conservative* read like the literature they obtained from their church bookstores. With point-blank precision it substantiated their long-held belief that a social welfare system was skulking its way into power and suppressing the spirit of individualism. Washington, Goldwater warned them, now represented a "vast national authority out of touch with the people, and out of their control," and headed towards absolutism. What truly impressed southern evangelicals, though, was what Goldwater had to say about sectors of society for which they felt particularly responsible: local community, national defense, and education.[7]

Central to Goldwater's philosophy, of course, was the primacy of autonomous communities obeying the higher laws of free labor, private property, and moral responsibility: the foundation of Goldwater's ideal society and his vision of personal fulfillment. "It has been the fashion in recent years to disparage 'property rights'—to associate them with greed and materialism," he lamented, yet "this attack on property rights is actually . . . another instance of the modern failure to take into account the *whole* man." Government initiatives that siphoned tax money from property owners to support welfare assistance programs galled Goldwater. The cycle of dependency this created was, in his estimation, psychologically damaging: It transformed "the individual from a dignified, industrious, self-reliant *spiritual* being into a dependent animal creature without his

knowing it." Instead, local communities and their core institutions—
"churches, private hospitals, religious service organizations, community
charities"—needed to reassert their moral obligation to their individual
members. Government needed to step aside and let people learn how to
take care of themselves.[8]

Southern evangelicals also admired the way Goldwater threaded notions
of self-reliance into his foreign policy and educational standards. In *Conscience of a Conservative*'s longest chapter, "The Soviet Menace," Goldwater argued for jettisoning Eisenhower's containment doctrine in favor of
a hard-line strategy that amplified the superior economic, technological,
military, and nuclear arsenal of the United States. The senator believed
that such displays of power, though potentially catastrophic, would ultimately force communism to stand down and let America determine its
own fate. This brinksmanship frightened the majority of Americans—his
opponents would label him a trigger-happy extremist—but since their
arrival on the West Coast, southern evangelicals had fought in two foreign
wars, supported missionaries in cold war hot zones, and staffed Southern
California's defense plants; Goldwater's inclinations comfortably matched
their own. His views on education were no different. In his book's most
succinct chapter, Goldwater repeated verbatim the complaints George
Benson had raised before Congress in the late 1930s, when he charged
that federal intervention in education was unconstitutional and unnecessary. At the same time, Goldwater reiterated the doubts conservative
parents harbored about the quality of public education. Because of John
Dewey (whom he mentioned by name), American public education had
lost its way. "In our anxiety to 'improve' the world and insure 'progress,'" he
wrote, "we have permitted our schools to become laboratories for . . . the
predilections of the professional educators." As a result, teachers no longer
inculcated young people with the values, knowledge, and courage needed
to excel as individuals. Goldwater finished this thought with another popular evangelical refrain: "If we would improve education in America—and
advance the fortunes of freedom—we will not rush to the federal treasury
with requests for money. We will focus attention on our local community,
and make sure that our schools, private and public, are performing the job
the Nation has the right to expect of them."[9]

California's southern evangelicals also appreciated what Goldwater
had to say (or chose not to say) about race. In his book's most controversial section, he defended states' rights over civil rights and flatly rejected

Brown v. Board of Education. "Despite the recent holding of the Supreme Court," he explained, "I am firmly convinced—not only that integrated schools are not required—but that the Constitution does not permit any interference whatsoever by the federal government in the field of education." Simplistic and misguided in its treatment of structural inequalities in the South, Goldwater's proclamation nevertheless reflected his frontier idealism and a refusal to bend his western libertarianism on even this most troubling issue. In his opinion, race reform could only come locally through changed hearts and minds. For pragmatic white citizens in Georgia and Alabama, Mississippi and South Carolina, who sought to justify their defiance of government-imposed race reform, this stance was immensely appealing, and it would be one reason why his southern strategy would win him the Deep South.[10]

Goldwater's states' rights strategy certainly won over California's southern evangelicals, but for reasons beyond raw racial politics. Having fought and lost California's first civil rights battle in the 1940s, they were not interested in another round of resistance. And after a decade of living in a suburban culture legally free of Jim Crow, they felt that their race problem had been solved. After the 1964 presidential election, during the Watts riots of 1965, they would be forced to confront, finally, the gaps and falsities in this worldview. But in the early 1960s their conservative conscience was shaped less by the jarring politics of race than through sustained, catalyzing encounters with communism, capitalism, and new patterns of community development.

GOLDWATER'S EVANGELICAL FRONT

In the lead-up to the 1964 campaign, California evangelicals enlisted their churches, schools, associations, and ministries on Goldwater's behalf. They did so consciously and deliberately, with a sense that they were about to make history. After two decades of fighting the Left, they were not averse, in fact, to using the enemy's language to describe their politics in the enemy's Marxist discourse of an "evangelical front" and "hegemony of hope." Though they had begun assimilating into California's broader evangelical community, by this point, southern pastors and parishioners stood out for their exceptional contributions. From the corporate to grassroots levels, they preached the Goldwater gospel. If such a thing as an evangelical front existed, than they were its vanguard.[11]

The annual freedom forums of the early 1960s testified to this. In theory, these conventions were designed to be bipartisan affairs, in which Democrats and Republicans could discuss capitalism, democracy, anti-communism, and national defense. Southern evangelical colleges may have advertised them as such, but what transpired was undifferentiated politicking for the Goldwater doctrine. Harding College led the way. Between the mid-1950s and mid-1960s, anyone who had any clout in Goldwater's Right spoke in Searcy, Arkansas; Leonard Read, Clarence Manion, Albert Wedemeyer, and Fred Schwarz were just a few of the popular conservative pundits invited to share their expertise with attendees drawn from corporations, industries, schools, and churches. Pepperdine College, meanwhile, matched Harding at every turn. In annual installments that grew exponentially in size and reputation after Goldwater's appearance, the school hosted many of these same people, while also welcoming intellectual stars like Russell Kirk and Friedrich von Hayek.[12]

Freedom forums lent structure to Goldwater's evangelical front, but anticommunist crusades gave it emotion. Ten years earlier, more politically cautious plain-folk preachers like J. Vernon McGee had enjoyed a prominence in Southern California that barnstorming anticommunist crusaders like Billy James Hargis, Carl McIntire, Edgar Bundy, and Fred Schwarz could only dream of. But by the early 1960s the roles were reversed. Hungary's failed anti-Soviet revolution in 1956, China's ascendancy, clashes between communist and nationalist interests in Africa and Latin America, and Fidel Castro's peasant revolution of 1959 made evangelicals more receptive to the hard-line solutions that Hargis, McIntire, Bundy, and Schwarz could deliver.

Of this group, Schwarz and Hargis had the largest national presence. The Southern California School of Anti-Communism in late August 1961 marked the pinnacle of Schwarz's career. That same season, he spoke before the Texas legislature, held meetings at Los Angeles' Biltmore Hotel, and organized a string of suburban rallies throughout California's Southland. He closed his whirlwind year (one in which his organization's revenues rocketed from $367,000 to $1.2 million) by headlining a one-night rally in the Hollywood Bowl, featured by *Life* magazine and funded by Patrick Frawley, owner of Technicolor, Inc. and the Schick Safety Razor Company. Hargis was not as popular as Schwarz in the media mainstream, but he surpassed him in his abilities to muster grassroots support. Throughout the early 1960s he made regular tours of Southern California, visiting donors and churches that helped boost his Christian Crusade's fund-raising beyond any other right-wing anticommunist organizations of its kind.[13]

McIntire and Bundy canvassed California with equal enthusiasm. In 1962, McIntire made a number of trips to Southern California, holding a Faith-Freedom Rally in the San Fernando Valley on one occasion, and on another attending a San Diego function coordinated by the energetic rookie pastor of Scott Memorial Baptist Church, Tim LaHaye. LaHaye assumed his role with gusto, drawing as much energy from the event as he supplied. "The conservative people of the city rallied in an amazing manner," he told a colleague. Fifteen hundred locals showed up to hear McIntire speak in a local public school auditorium (opponents had protested them using the venue) but his message was interrupted by a bomb scare that LaHaye attributed to "left wingers." "They tried to eliminate people from the building by scare before we took the offering, hoping that they could ruin us. Praise the LORD, this was impossible, because GOD was on our side." Many of the same people from the same churches and organizations that LaHaye mobilized returned to hear Edgar Bundy, the "J. Edgar Hoover" of Christian counterintelligence. Bundy kept an expansive database on subversive organizations, sold and rented anticommunist films, and published books like *Collectivism in the Churches*, an encyclopedic manual that became evangelicalism's definitive guide on the subject. He also organized Counter Subversive Seminars, sponsored by church, corporate, and civic bodies, in which participants studied Bundy's textbook, *A Manual for Survival*, which cautioned readers:

> do no try to fight alone. Join and actively support reputable organizations. . . . If no local group is available to join, then locate a few experts with former FBI, Army, Navy or other intelligence experience and form a small study and action group; get anti-Communists to speak at the local clubs and luncheons; and never allow anyone in your hearing to slur the FBI, the House Committee on Un-American Activities, the Senate Internal Security Subcommittee, the Church League of America, the American Council of Christian Churches or any other organization which you know to be fighting subversion.[14]

Bundy's work indeed helped define yet another dimension of the evangelical front: countersurveillance. During the early 1960s church folk participated in a "spy system" that mirrored the apparatus maintained by left-wing activists. The similarities were not coincidental. Since the early 1950s at least, California conservatives had become aware of CRC informants monitoring their meetings; sometimes they even opened proceedings by greeting the spies among them. Right-wing activists soon began spy work of their own, taking as their inspiration women like Marion Miller, one of the star speakers at the 1961 Southern California School of Anti-Communism. Evangelical women and men followed Miller's example, though within a more rigid system of counterintelligence structured by their preachers and by periodicals. Countless pastors-turned-pundits served as cogs in this rapacious knowledge-making machine. None was more important than G. Archer Weniger, pastor of Foothill Boulevard Baptist Church, in Oakland, California. By the late 1950s, Weniger's congregation of eight hundred was considered a key outpost for conservatives, particularly those with southern allegiances. While maintaining ties to conservative Baptists in the Midwest, his principal loyalties tied him to the southern axis, represented by the Baptist Bible Fellowship and Bob Jones University (formerly College), where he sat on the board of trustees. His paper the *Blu-Print* earned a devoted following among fundamentalist Protestants in California; one reader said the *Blu-Print* was to current conservatives what Bob Shuler's *Methodist Challenge* had been for an earlier generation.[15]

Like Shuler, Weniger not only commented on political happenings, he shaped them. His fondness for "keeping the water hot," as he liked to say, began when he observed college students protesting the House Un-American Activities Committee hearings in San Francisco in May 1960. News agencies broadcast to the nation images of defiant youth being dragged down the steps of city hall and handcuffed for insubordination. In subsequent days these very same images were spliced together by HUAC officials into *Operation Abolition*, a documentary they hoped would show American citizens the devastating hold that communism had on young people. Writing in *Blu-Print*, Weniger charged that students not only disparaged the nation but also desecrated its religious heritage with their "treasonable delight [in] singing 'Mine Eyes Have Seen the Glory of the Coming of the Lord'" at the height of their picketing. Weniger's firsthand account spread through his and other periodicals. Businessmen and housewives, police chiefs and pastors, government officials, church groups and free enterprise associations in California, Texas, and across the South inundated the pastor with requests for reprints of his story. Many of them intended to distribute Weniger's account during local showings of *Opera-*

tion Abolition. One businessman in San Antonio wrote Weniger with the news that his firm had already shown the film to "some 14,000 people in approximately 170 civic, church, military, etc. groups." The pastor's reputation would soon be on the rise, he added, once his literature started finding its way into the hands of so many anxious patriots.[16]

The HUAC hearings turned Weniger into an important conduit for political data and news. While fellow pastors like Tim LaHaye (a Bob Jones alum) conveyed insider perspectives from rallies in their towns, local men and women writing on behalf of agencies like the California Intelligence Bureau of Los Angeles and the Literature Procurement Committee passed along their reports from school board and city hall meetings, Sunday school and church services. Weniger then editorialized and disseminated them in print. Meanwhile, he transmitted whatever details he thought important to religious and political leaders, as well as Republican Party executives. One such leader was Raymond Richmond, a key Goldwater organizer, who greatly appreciated Weniger's work. "The *Blu-Print* . . . is one of the most valuable and interesting vehicles that crosses my desk," he noted. In gratitude Richmond forwarded Weniger's material (with a nudge for financial assistance) to his friends, including two oilmen in Texas and California.

> Rest assured they will read it. They may not read the Scripture as often as they should (and who does) but they avidly devour every line that comes to them upholding the conservative (and therefore fundamentalist) point of view. It is my purpose over a period of time to convince these extremely wealthy men that your wing of the Baptist Church is a front line fighting force for just about everything they believe in.

This bottom-up flow of information was reciprocated with top-down praise. Weniger thanked his *Blu-Print* constituents by telling them how high-powered people were using grassroots vigor for concrete political action. In their living rooms, country clubs, churches, and study groups, alert readers digested Weniger's encouraging words, then went out in search of their next lead.[17]

REARMING THE NATION

In the three years leading up to the 1964 presidential election, in response to what they considered an assault on Christian American values by the liberal administrations of Presidents John F. Kennedy and Lyndon Johnson and Governor Pat Brown, Weniger's warriors carried out a blitz of their own. Two clusters of issues in particular caught their attention: strong national defense and neighborhood autonomy. Responding to these threats helped California's southern evangelicals solidify interregional political ties with the South, ratchet up an already militant political discourse, and ultimately prepare the way for the Goldwater campaign.

To be sure, southern evangelicals' efforts did not unfold in isolation; as illustrated in Weniger's and LaHaye's operations, they often functioned as pivots for broader political operations carried out by other groups, from the transparent California Republican Assembly and United Republicans of California (UROC) to the highly secretive John Birch Society. Asked to join the JBS, Weniger, for instance, declined on the grounds that it was not theologically conservative enough, but this did not stop him from attending JBS functions, working with JBS officials, and keeping lines of communication open with JBS informants. Likewise, Tim LaHaye declined to join, but he worked closely with JBS cells in San Diego, often speaking at their training seminars and preaching a similar party line. LaHaye's hesitation ultimately hurt the JBS. As LaHaye's church became politically powerful, JBS members increasingly abandoned their own cell groups to take part in Scott Memorial's more elaborate ministries. Convinced that LaHaye was "neutralizing" their foot soldiers, JBS authorities confronted him, demanding he stay clear of their work, and even published pamphlets warning their members to avoid his "Rapture Cult." These JBS leaders were mistaken, though. LaHaye, Weniger and their evangelical allies were not interested in neutralizing the JBS or any of the other organizations. The strength of their personalities simply demanded that they lead, not follow, the right-wing insurgency.[18]

These clerics came to the fore in 1961 to protest the proclamations for peace made by President Kennedy before the United Nations. In the fall of that year, shortly after Schwarz's School of Anti-Communism, Kennedy challenged the Soviet Union "not to an arms race, but to a peace race, to advance together step by step, stage by stage, until general and complete disarmament has been achieved." Reading reports of this development, evangelicals imagined a worst-case scenario: If disarmament became policy, national independence would be forfeited, leaving America's self-defense in the hands of the UN.[19]

This is the message General Edwin Walker and veteran senator Strom

Thurmond brought to Southern California in the months surrounding Kennedy's negotiations. In the spring of 1961, the Department of Defense had admonished Walker, commander of the Twenty-fourth Infantry Division in West Germany, for foisting on his troops lectures, seminars, a reading list, and a voting guide that he packaged in a "Pro Blue" curriculum on the perils of communism. Shortly after it was instituted, a newspaper for GIs accused Walker of recruiting his soldiers for the John Birch Society. The newspaper was slightly incorrect. Walker's reading list included Robert Welch's *The Life of John Birch*, but in fact his program depended far less on JBS doctrine than on instructional materials supplied by Bundy, Hargis, and Harding College. These nuances aside, the negative publicity surrounding Walker's case forced the Defense Department to take action. After a three-month inquiry, it dismissed charges that Walker had disseminated JBS material but concurred that he had stepped beyond "long-standing customs of the military service and beyond the prerogatives of a senior military commander." Officials hoped that by going easy on the general the affair would end; he was not punished for his actions, just reassigned. Walker resigned on principle, however, so that he could be "free from the power of little men who, in the name of my country, punish loyal service." Neither the general nor the media would let this matter rest.[20]

And neither would Thurmond. Using his seat on the Senate Armed Services Committee, Thurmond fought back vigorously against fellow senator J. William Fulbright, who had written to Kennedy following the Walker episode that something needed to be done to curtail right-wing educational activities in the military and to combat "extreme rightists" associated with Harding College. Like Kennedy, Fulbright believed that a "peace race" was the United States' only option in the cold war, and that brazen military officials threatened this ideal. His note to the president led to a directive restricting military personnel from taking part in right-wing seminars. Incensed by this action, Thurmond publicly criticized the Fulbright memo as "a dastardly attempt to intimidate the commanders of United States armed forces" and "a serious blow to the security of the United States." Backed by Goldwater and other Republicans, Thurmond called for Senate hearings on military "muzzling" and in early fall 1961 had his wish granted. This set the stage for a political spectacle. Billed by many as the most exciting senatorial event since the labor racketeering investigation, the hearings pitted Thurmond against Defense Secretary Robert McNamara. For McNamara, the Senate investigation into the Defense Department's apparent soft stand on communism evoked Joseph McCarthy's red-baiting a decade earlier. For Thurmond, the hearings conjured up memories of a humiliated General MacArthur deposed by the same liberal Democrats who had "muzzled" Walker. This would be a referendum on the nation's commitment to strong military leadership and national defense.[21]

Even before the hearings began, politicians with stakes in the contest scheduled speaking engagements in Southern California, knowing that this was the key battleground for public opinion. On the evening of November 18, while three thousand right-wing activists picketed outside, inside the Hollywood Palladium Kennedy delivered a speech to Los Angeles that pulled no punches:

> In the most critical periods of our Nation's history, there have always been those on the fringes of our society who have sought to escape their own responsibility by finding a simple solution, an appealing slogan or a convenient scapegoat. And under the strains and frustrations imposed by constant tension and harassment, the discordant voices of extremism are heard once again in the land. Men who are unwilling to face up to the dangers from without are convinced that the real danger comes from within. They look suspiciously at their neighbors and their leader. They call for a "man on horseback" because they do not trust the people. They find treason in our churches, in our highest court, in our treatment of water. They equate the Democratic Party with the welfare state, the welfare state with socialism, socialism with communism. They object quite rightly to politics intruding on the military— but they are anxious for the military to engage in politics.

While visiting Los Angeles on November 29, Thurmond responded with indictments of his own. At an appearance before two thousand people in Santa Monica, he railed against the "pussyfooting diplomats" who had destroyed Walker's career. Walker had to share some of the blame, he admitted, but the crux of the matter was that liberal internationalists had compromised America's national defense. Texas Republican senator and soon-to-be Senate Armed Services Committeeman John Tower likely touched on such themes just four days after Thurmond appeared in Santa Monica in a "guest sermon" delivered from Bob Shuler's old pulpit at downtown Los Angeles' Trinity Methodist Church. Tower, the son and grandson of Methodist preachers, offered his homily in honor of the church's fortieth annual Texas Day.[22]

The hearings began in January and ended in June 1962. One after the other, the committee called military officials to answer questions regarding the freedom of political expression in the armed services. Was anticommunist doctrine allowed in the ranks, or was it suppressed by liberal censorship? Thurmond pushed hard for evidence of the latter. Time and again committee members reined him in out of fear he was crossing the threshold from judicial questioning into interrogation. After months of this debate, the committee finally released its findings in October, just as the Cuban Missile Crisis was boiling over. Thurmond's allies suspected that the government had timed the release to bury the whole affair. The report itself disappointed them too, for while acknowledging the Pentagon's inept censoring of military officials, it found no evidence that the Department of Defense had "muzzled" its staff.[23]

By now national media had turned to Cuba, but in Southern California there was a panic that the referendum on national defense had tilted in favor of liberal Democrats. From 1962 through 1963, General Walker helped feed this anxiety. In January 1962, he was invited by James Fifield to speak at a large rally where he "received a wild ovation from a throng of 12,894 in the Sports Arena." No doubt bolstered by this friendly reception, he ran in the Texas gubernatorial primary and then was arrested in Oxford, Mississippi, for "inciting rebellion" as federal marshals tried to desegregate the University of Mississippi. By early 1963, the former general was back in the limelight, traveling through California and the rest of the country with Billy James Hargis on a speaking tour called Operation Midnight Ride, named in honor of Paul Revere. Nightly, both men appeared in front of a large screen on which a picture of Christ was superimposed on a map of the United States.[24]

While Hargis and Walker fanned the right-wing firestorm about the military on the national level, throughout 1962 and 1963, evangelicals worked locally to further the cause. Under Pastor Bob Wells's guidance, Central Baptist Church reserved its Sunday evenings for current events talks and, in the summer months, "crisis crusades," held outdoors in the church's parking lot. Christian anticommunists like McIntire, Hargis, and Walker often headlined these festival-like affairs. Wells returned the favor by canceling midweek services so his congregants could attend Operation

Midnight Ride. Edgar Bundy was Central's most frequent guest. On several occasions he attended a weekend crisis crusade to deliver its keynote address, then stayed for the remainder of the week to tutor Central's members in his surveillance techniques. Considering what transpired in the coming months, Bundy's words of advice must have left their mark.[25]

As talk of arms reductions grew, Wells became more agitated. "It is important that we not be deceived about all of this talk about peace and safety," he wrote; the Bible was clear in its warning that "when they say 'peace and safety' we may expect sudden destruction to come upon us." Wells's message was that disarmament meant the loss of America's sovereignty, dignity, and Christianity. In the following months his parishioners, including some JBS members, took it upon themselves to shore up military resolve. Their actions began in 1963 and culminated in early 1965, when they clashed with officials at North American Aviation. At issue were highly sensitive materials the company produced for the air force. Written in conjunction with a contract proposal, the documents, entitled "Factors Operative in a Post-Arms Control Situation," described "a series of hypothetical world events" that might occur should the White House enact a disarmament policy. Included in the fifty-four pages were predictions of apocalyptic doom that included "the explosion of a nuclear device this year by Indonesia, overthrow next year of the Cuban government and complete world disarmament by 1976." In actuality, these predictions were just a few of many possible scenarios outlined carefully to "give the Air Force as wide a range of factors as possible that conceivably could develop in the event any one of a number of current arms control proposals would be adopted."[26]

Wells and his congregants did not see these scenarios as hypothetical. Central's unnamed spies, able to gain access to this information because of their standing as senior engineers at North American, relayed the documents to their pastor so that the public could be alerted. Interpreting the documents in much the same way he approached scripture—literally— Wells announced that he had evidence that liberal politicians planned to "sell our Republic out to the UN." This was the message he delivered to an especially large crisis crusade, which Central widely advertised:

These documents spell out what steps are to be taken to guarantee General and Complete Disarmament for the entire world . . . placing all military power into the hands of one central power. . . . The results of a number of present conflicts between nations are spelled out. Closer co-operation with Russia is charted. We are told when Red China will be admitted to the U.N. This is an amazing revelation and the date when this will happen is also indicated. . . .With the help of our overhead projector, these charts will be displayed on the screen for everyone to see. . . . Bring your Bible along and see for yourself. Be sure to come early and bring a friend!

Wells's audience responded favorably to his blend of evangelistic and politi-cal pleas: Subsequent church newsletters reported, "The message was well received by an enthusiastic crowd and there were a large number of con-versions and several additions to the church. People are stirred up over the issue and the word is going everywhere throughout the country." Word indeed spread. Wells urged his flock to write Santa Ana Rep. James Utt (R-California), Sen. James Eastland (D-Mississippi), and Senators Thur-mond and Tower, voicing support for a strong military, and to assist the Americans for National Security (AFNS), a lobby group intending to sue the federal government's Arms Control and Disarmament Agency for mis-use of public funds. He then embarked on a speaking tour in an attempt "to awaken people." Assistants accompanied him with photocopied charts and maps for display purposes, and hundreds of printed copies of North American's documents ready to be distributed upon request.[27]

NEIGHBORHOOD WATCH

The sensationalism that accompanied Wells's crisis crusades trivialized them in the eyes of some skeptics, but disarmament was not something he or his constituents took lightly. Fundamental to their political philoso-phy, strong national defense was also their livelihood, so to challenge the need for a strong military presence was to undermine the very existence of their communities. The same held true in their worries about Ameri-ca's "moral disarmament." As controversy over national defense heated up, they became equally alarmed about a second cluster of issues surround-ing the sanctity of education and property.

It might not have been a complete surprise to California evangelicals when the United States Supreme Court officially banned school prayer— the matter had already surfaced on a state level—but the 1962 ruling was as devastating for them as it was for evangelicals nationwide. When

Billy James Hargis received the news, he privately told his family that "this was really the beginning of the end for America, that the country had turned its back on God, and that any country that did that couldn't stand." Preachers throughout the nation decried the decision and, with their congressional allies, set plans in motion to reverse them.[28]

New York Congressman Frank Becker suggested a constitutional amendment to keep prayer and the Bible in school. Under its proposed terms, the Becker Amendment would "make prayer and Bible reading constitutional, 'if participation therein is on a voluntary basis, in any governmental or public institution, or place.'" As this amendment effort gained steam between 1963 and early 1964, California's religious conservatives wrote their congressmen protest letters expressing "the will of the majority," as well as notes of encouragement to those, like Goldwater, who backed the Becker Amendment. At Church of the Open Door, J. Vernon McGee delivered sermons lambasting the Supreme Court's actions and calling on America to sign a "Declaration of Dependence" on God. California Pentecostals learned from their national organ that "Your Letter Is a Ballot": "Instead of complaining about corrupt politics . . . Christians should do something to correct the situation." This same journal decried the "Supreme Blunder" of the prayer rulings and encouraged readers to speak out against them in school meetings. Californians subscribing to National Association of Evangelicals literature found a tempered but no less passionate response. The NAE admitted that the Supreme Court was in line with a strict reading of the First Amendment, but it also expressed "'grave concern' over the trend toward secularism . . . inherent in this decision" and told its members to "encourage local school officials to continue 'voluntary, non sectarian religious observances.'"[29]

Bombarded by this advice, citizens took action. In April 1963, two Southern California Republican assemblymen decided to use the Supreme Court decision as a legislative wedge. Robert Badham of Costa Mesa and E. Richard Barnes, a former navy chaplain and Southern Baptist pastor from San Diego, introduced a bill in the state legislature "prohibiting the teaching of any theory opposed to recognized sectarian doctrine," including (and especially) the theory of evolution. When asked to explain their measure Badham described it as "fair play legislation":

I have been shocked to learn . . . of the incessant pressure by atheistic and agnostic groups, including the Communist party, to drive from

the public school all reference to God and respect for religious principles. . . . My bill simply provides that if it is illegal to present religion in
the schools, it must be equally illegal to present anti-religious doctrine.

The anti-evolution legislation never got off the ground, but Badham was
voicing the same puzzlement many evangelicals now felt. Was there reason
why, "at a time when we are protecting atheists and agnostics from prayers
which may be offensive to them . . . we cannot protect those with religious
faith from irreligious teachings which are equally offensive"? Eight months
later, in the La Mesa School District of San Diego, an organization called
Parents for Prayer carried out what was believed to be the first recall election of its kind in the nation. In January 1964, three school board members came under fire for supporting a strict policy that disallowed "prayers, or
other religious exercise used as part of the school program." Frustrated that
the board would not allow "voluntary, non sectarian religious observances"
in the manner advocated by the NAE, Parents for Prayer used politics to
replace its leading members with three citizens—a physician, a school-
teacher, and a Baptist minister—who saw things their way.[30]

Spread out around California's Southland but triangulated by Goldwater's evangelical front, these episodes cohered into collective action.
Preacher-pundits like Weniger learned of local happenings and then disseminated this information through fundamentalist channels. National
leaders, in turn, kept abreast of the situation on the West Coast, rallied
their supporters there to continue the fight, and planned campaigns to
assist their efforts. No politician thrived more in this system than Strom
Thurmond. Thurmond was an ally of major fundamentalist organizations
like the ACCC and the BBF and offered considerable support to Bob
Jones University, on whose board he sat with Weniger. In the summer
of 1963 the senator headlined a conference called For God and Country,
held at Carl McIntire's convention hotel in Cape May, New Jersey. Not
long after this gathering on the East Coast, Thurmond returned for a visit
with friends on the West Coast.[31]

He had many to see. By 1963 the statesman had a tremendous following of Californians who applauded his strong stand on national defense
and other matters close to their heart. The letters he received from two
Los Angeles women were typical: "thank you dear Senator for your courage and true American spirit"; "please remember you have the prayers
of the people who appreciate that you are trying to wake up America to

what it is losing." Others asked for his assistance. An administrator at Sacred Heart Parish's high school in Lancaster, just north of Los Angeles, thanked Thurmond for his "efforts in support of our beloved Republic" before requesting one hundred copies of his newsletter. A similar appeal came from two groups in San Diego: the Associates for Americanism and the Counter Subversive Committee of the American Legion. A Long Beach resident enclosed a dollar with a plea for material on "centralized government" that he could distribute to his "study groups." Letters from Pepperdine people were included in Thurmond's correspondence, including an excited one written at the height of the disarmament controversy by Trent Devenney, the school's student body president. Devenney was a Thurmond devotee who wanted to spread the senator's message:

> Since I talked to you in August, we have gotten two student newspapers started here in California. One is in Bakersfield and the other is in Los Angeles. The circulation of both together is between ten and twelve thousand. Besides the students, there are a lot of adults that would like to do some active work to support you. There is a large network of patriots in California . . . who would like to stage some sort of demonstration. . . . Maybe you could suggest the most advantageous time, and also tell us if you approve of this type of support (i.e. a peaceful demonstration).[32]

The type of commitment Devenney pledged Thurmond became even more pronounced among Californians in early 1964. At the urging of supporters, Thurmond toured the region speaking on behalf of Project Prayer for Constitutional Amendment Action, an initiative to back the Becker Amendment. A national organization, Project Prayer nevertheless had a strong Southern California feel, with several of its most active spokesmen serving in leadership. Actors Ronald Reagan and John Wayne, financiers John Tuttle and Cy Rubel, and Christian advocates Pat Boone and Harold Fickett, pastor of First Baptist Van Nuys, were all part of this campaign. Like the disarmament protests, Project Prayer proved a unifying experience for conservatives. Thurmond was everywhere, speaking in campus auditoriums and civic halls, appearing on television and the radio, and dining with benefactors like D. B. Lewis, president of Lewis Food Company, and participants in First Congregational Church's Freedom Club.[33]

The passion Thurmond provoked ultimately came up short—fierce debate among religious and political leaders undermined the Becker Amendment in May 1964—but it transitioned into an even more sweeping and aggressive legislative attempt to protect the moral, economic, and racial character of their communities. Proposition 14 was the 1964 ballot initiative that sought to reverse the 1963 Rumford Fair Housing Act, which prohibited housing discrimination on the basis of race. Led by the California Real Estate Association (CREA) and its umbrella lobby, the Committee for Home Protection (CHP), critics charged that the Rumford Act undermined private property and conceded too much regulatory power to the state. During the spring of 1964 these dissenters—many of whom had participated in the Project Prayer campaign—sparked a movement that forced a fall referendum on the issue over whether the Rumford Act should be abolished (as Proposition 14 argued) or protected under the law (as anti–Proposition 14 forces argued).[34]

The subtext for Proposition 14 was a wide-ranging concern with government encroachment on what southern evangelicals considered to be their sacred space. Since the 1930s, they had taken full advantage of lax zoning on Los Angeles' periphery. First in Los Angeles County's blue-collar suburbs and then in the new defense subdivisions that sprouted in the San Fernando Valley and Orange County, they had positioned their churches in optimum locations that best served "collective witness." In the early 1960s the city caught up to them, as did the reality of life in a regulated environment. Southern evangelicals responded with predictable trepidation. At stake, in the first place, was their freedom to evangelize by pitching revival tents on vacant residential lots and preaching on street corners. Angry that city officials were shutting these activities down, the *California Southern Baptist* complained, "If our Baptist forefathers had lived in California, most of them would probably have spent a good bit of time in jail. . . . If we can be told where to preach and where we cannot preach, it is only a short step to being told *what* we can preach." Even worse, church construction was now limited. L. E. Halvorson, the superintendent of the Southern California District of the Assemblies of God, announced the end of an era in the *Pentecostal Evangel* in 1960. "We are deeply grateful to God for the 99 new Assemblies of God churches started in our District during the past five years," but, he said, "God apparently stirred up His children to work hastily before open doors of opportunity were closed through zoning restrictions, building requirements, and rigid regulations." Halvorson was correct; his church's freedom of space was diminishing. In

1959 the Supreme Court "upheld the right of a municipality to prohibit the erection of a church building in a residential area by enforcement of zoning ordinance." The days of congregations embedding themselves in neighborhoods, it appeared, were over. In Orange County, meanwhile, development plans for Irvine, a new city in the southern section of their county, allotted space for churches only on the four corners of major streets. In the minds of evangelicals like Jean Vandruff, this meant that conservative churches would suffer doubly by not being able to build in residential areas or compete with mainline churches for a few prime spots.[35]

At stake in the second place was the collapse of suburban empires southern evangelicals had just begun to see peak. In the early 1960s Southern California Assemblies of God churches outpaced their counterparts around the nation in growth and financial giving; six of the ten most generous (and likely wealthiest) congregations resided in Southern California. Southern Baptists were also doing well in the Southland. In the months before the vote on Proposition 14, the Southern Baptist General Convention of California celebrated its twenty-fifth anniversary, announcing that there were now roughly 201,905 SBC members worshipping in 838 churches, with the largest percentage clumped in and around Los Angeles and San Diego. These churches were responsible for 171 new "mission churches," 872 pastors (plus an additional 602 music ministers, evangelists, and unassigned pastors), 177,753 Sunday-school enrollees, and church property worth $81,456,252. As proud as SBC members were of these numbers, they were even more excited about the untapped potential of still-developing suburbs, where the next wave of growth was yet to crest. Young people from across the South were now commissioned as "summer workers" to conduct vacation Bible schools and door-to-door canvassing in Orange County and the San Fernando Valley, and forty SBC laymen from Amarillo arrived eager to carry out "one of the most intensive visitation and witnessing campaigns in the history of California Baptists." Their sponsor was Marie and Clifford Allen's Bristol Street Baptist, whose 1,200 members celebrated the church's silver anniversary in the early 1960s by dedicating yet another new building (a fourth) on its eight acres of prime real estate in Santa Ana.[36]

Jean Vandruff's church trumped even the Allens' in ambition. Convinced that "nothing short of an all-out conquest for people" was acceptable in the early 1960s, Central Baptist held "spiritual boot camps" at which congregants learned the latest outreach techniques. Encouraged to "study your prospect," "study your surroundings," and most importantly "visit with a smile," individual trainees visited as many as five hundred houses in a month. Central brought in fresh recruits from Bob Jones University each summer through Operation Outreach. During one summer alone, this group knocked on fifty thousand doors within a thirty-square-mile radius of the church. Less than ten years after a handful of its people first assembled in an orange grove, Central's enrollment skyrocketed; with close to four thousand members and an average attendance that frequently exceeded that number, a Sunday school of two thousand students, and annual tithing of close to half a million dollars, Central could claim fairly that it was now the largest BBF congregation in California and the second largest independent Baptist church (next to First Baptist Van Nuys) west of the Rocky Mountains.[37]

In an overt way, southern evangelicals linked their future as church builders to the referendum on the Rumford Act. Proposition 14 was ostensibly about private property, but these religious conservatives also sensed that those who supported the Rumford Act had something more nefarious in mind: government control of all space—private, public, and sacred. The fact that each of these spatial grids was heavily racialized, drawn along white and nonwhite lines, did not figure prominently in their language, but it was a critical factor. Their religious empires were white religious empires, walled from the multicultural city by the middle-class ideology of property rights. Faced with the possibility of losing control of their homogeneous communities, southern evangelicals began working for Proposition 14 in spring 1964, at the very same time the Goldwater moment finally arrived. By now their political emotions were at a boil. Having spent the last three years involved in campaigns that sought to defend the principles rooted in their errand and articulated in *Conscience of a Conservative*, they were ready for the fight.

"In Your Heart You Know He's Right"

"In Your Heart You Know He's Right" was the motto Goldwater's handlers chose to galvanize people in 1964, and though opponents ridiculed it, the slogan proved effective in channeling a "born again" religious zeal into their political movement. More importantly for Goldwater's team, it became a winning formula, at least during the summer months, when their campaign and the Proposition 14 crusade went into high gear.

Goldwater's first major hurdle was the Republican primaries. Since the late 1950s, evangelicals in California had been enthusiastic about the possibility of a Goldwater ticket. By the mid-1960s, the Arizona senator's handlers were taking notice. Having gained credibility through radio programs, newsletters, speaking appearances at freedom forums and anticommunist rallies, and the Becker Amendment, Clarence Manion and other Goldwater advisors easily convinced electoral precincts to incorporate churches in their local publicity and registration drives. Parachurch ministries like Campus Crusade for Christ, which had the ear of young Christian conservatives on California's college campuses, also now gained the notice and approval of Goldwater's campaign managers.[38]

In truth, evangelicals hardly needed to be told what to do. In the weeks leading up to the June 2 California primary, both Goldwater and his opponent, Nelson Rockefeller, stepped up the urgency of their campaigns. Evangelicals responded accordingly. Writers and publishers like Weniger and preachers like Wells and LaHaye hammered home the idea that voting Goldwater was a Christian requisite. By late May members of Central Baptist and Scott Memorial Church already seemed convinced and went out into the streets to spread the word. Many brought the official "Californians for Goldwater" pamphlet, which summarized Goldwater's politics in two pages, and devoted a third to his personal traits; Goldwater was "An Outstanding Man; A Real Man; A Different Man; A Courageous Man; A Fighting Man; A Party Man; A Dynamic Man; An All-American Man." Precincts handed out "Footsoldier Program Instructions" telling workers not to be too aggressive when knocking on neighbors' doors, but many were already well versed in such witnessing strategies.[39]

Regardless of their prior experience in door-to-door fieldwork, these activists treated their proselytizing as if there was much more than an election on the line. In Pasadena, Marie Koenig (formerly King), now a busy mother, committed significant portions of her week to clipping articles from newspapers and making a case for Goldwater—both privately, in conversations with family, friends, and neighbors, and publicly, at the Lutheran (Missouri Synod) Church to which she and her husband now belonged. As she had been for Huey Long in Louisiana, Koenig was completely devoted to her politician. Helen Young's heritage, too, was now refracted through her activism. Like her mother, who had coordinated political campaigns in Oklahoma City, Young was compelled to make her political convictions count. By virtue of her status as President Norvel Young's spouse and one of Pepperdine College's ambassadors to the conservative elite, she attended the same Republican women's meetings that Koenig attended. Because she shouldered heavier religious responsibilities, she did not match Koenig's political drive, but she was every bit as dedicated to their collective cause.[40]

Meanwhile, the institution Helen Young represented broke out in Goldwater fever. Students began producing anticommunist films for distribution in local industries and schools, as well as a radio program featuring "top American business and political leaders, along with the popular Pat Boone." Endorsed by Boone's allies in Hollywood, Pepperdine sold these ventures to the public as part of its curricular agenda to "parry the angry sweep of the hammer and sickle." Under the leadership of Trent Devenney and subsequent student-body presidents, Republicans came to dominate the campus both culturally and politically. Whether in public forums or the pages of the *Graphic*, political debate grew fierce, yet only between moderates and right-wingers, and over issues like whether "extremism" was a virtue or vice. Pepperdine's students were, without question, for Goldwater, and in the run-up to the election they climbed into key posts on the California College Federation of Young Republicans (Devenney became its president) and helped bring the region's Republican youth on board the Goldwater express.[41]

But even Pepperdine's well-choreographed Goldwater campaign hardly matched Central Baptist's. Here, after Sunday and weekday services, congregants enjoyed access to a Goldwater table set up on the front lawn (just far enough from the church so as not to violate tax laws) and church vehicles for travel to local political rallies. On May 30, just before the California primary, congregants amassed in Central's parking lot to meet buses to take them on the short journey to Knott's Berry Farm. James Redden, Central's new music pastor, had never seen anything like it before. A Tennessean by birth, Redden was a conservative by conviction, but he found the sight of vehicles festooned in Goldwater paraphernalia a bit surreal. As he watched through his office window, the stream of sedans fell dutifully in line behind the school buses. Once at the amusement park they joined thirty thousand other Goldwaterites in a raucous program featuring cameos by John Wayne and Ronald Reagan, songs by a group of right-wing folksingers, and a speech—his last before the primary—from the cowboy conservative himself. One *Wall Street Journal* reporter, after observing rallies such as Walter Knott's, could not hide his East Coast bewilderment. "Mr. Goldwater . . . is proving to be a powerful crowd pleaser. The evangelistic fervor of his rallies, at times embellished with choir singing and prayers, lifts most audiences to high emotional pitch."[42]

This high emotional pitch carried conservatives through the primaries to the Republican Convention in San Francisco. Rockefeller's "Stop Goldwater" campaign never caught fire. Even though Rockefeller was victorious in 46 of the 58 California counties on June 2, he lost to the Arizona senator by 58,000 votes. With the exception of Santa Barbara, Goldwater won every Southern California county, and in Los Angeles and Orange counties he won big, with a combined 207,000 votes. The victory propelled him to the GOP convention in mid-July as the party's presumptive choice. Billy James Hargis heralded Goldwater's nomination as "one of God's blessings to Christian Conservatives." It was obvious, Hargis stated, "God has been working on the side of Christian Conservatives the last eight months."[43]

And the confidence spilled over to the Proposition 14 campaign, which Hargis's evangelical allies now took to the next level. Their value to the crusade was twofold. First, in order to defeat the Rumford Act's fair housing legislation, the Committee for Home Protection and its allies underscored the "sacredness" of private property. Blending fears of communism and racial integration with biblical exegesis, conservative clerics in the CHP camp argued that the Rumford Act was a rejection of both New Testament teachings and Old Testament law. By allowing government dictatorial power over private property, they asserted, fair housing laws opened the door to restrictions in other spheres. Pro-Rumford people were not only on a slippery slope to communism but also in violation of the Ten Commandments: "Thou shalt not covet thy neighbor's house . . . nor anything that is thy neighbor's," and "Thou shalt not steal." Evangelicals also provided organizational support to Proposition 14's "yes" side by supplying print media, pulpit authority, and spirited activists. At the behest of CHP, pastors printed a booklet containing a six-point rejection of the Rumford Act, which held that by undercutting property rights, fair housing negated the ability of human beings to realize their natural rights in voluntary association with one another. McIntire's association of pastors and the Southern California Committee of Christian Laymen commissioned their parishioners to deliver this pamphlet and its message door-to-door, block-by-block in every suburb.[44]

The printed materials distributed by conservative preachers succeeded in stirring up emotional debate inside as much as outside evangelical cir-

cles. The prospects of increased government regulation of space represented a multifaceted threat to churchgoers, not the least of which was
diminished congregational autonomy. But a blend of racial and economic
anxieties figured into the apprehension as well. Southern Baptists' church
papers roiled with disagreement about the racial implications of suburban privilege, and during the yearlong campaign for Proposition 14 the
arguments grew more animated. In the early fall of 1964, one writer's
doubts about both Proposition 14 and the Rumford Act matched those
of many SBC citizens: "California voters are faced with an unfortunate
dilemma on the November ballot. . . . There is no question . . . certain
racial groups have been victimized by racial discrimination on the part of
property owners." The problem was that the Rumford Act was "poor legislation," taking away one set of freedoms in order to promote another. In
the weeks that followed this editorial, men and women from around the
state weighed in on the subject. What became apparent was that the only
consensus was on the timid contention that Southern Baptists were just
average people trying to do the right thing.[45]

Nevertheless, these "average people" grew more supportive of Proposition 14 as the no side became more vocal. During the summer and
fall, labor advocates, mainline Protestant leaders, and a number of civic
and human rights groups working under the title Californians Against
Proposition 14 (CAP 14) began holding town hall meetings to present
the merits of fair housing. Their purpose, CAP 14 officials told volunteer
workers, was "to educate the non-committed, the rational people who may
not understand," not to debate and try to "save . . . right wingers from
paranoia." When this failed, the no campaign began matching opponents
blow for blow. Governor Brown approved a frontal attack that painted the
CHP alliance as a shill for the John Birch Society, White Citizens' Council, Nazi Party, and Mississippi-style racism. The slogan "Don't Legalize
Hate," framed next to a sketch of Abraham Lincoln and John F. Kennedy,
became a familiar ensemble on CAP 14's billboards and brochures. This
strategy backfired, however, because Proposition 14 advocates, including
those with ties to McIntire, had worked hard to minimize overtly racist, anti–civil rights rhetoric in their campaign. They recognized that support for Proposition 14 would be hard to come by if the measure could
be linked to the politics of George Wallace or other outspoken southern
segregationists. Besides that, Brown's comments alienated voters in the
middle who resented his broad, racially loaded accusations.[46]

Rather than appealing to Californians' sense of logic or fear, CAP 14 leaders chose a third tactic: an appeal to conscience. A vote against Proposition 14 and for the Rumford Act was not a vote to alter the system, they now argued. Rumford policy would not upset the current makeup of communities or give minorities special privileges, and it would not breach private property. As admitted in CAP 14 promotional literature, fair housing legislation would in fact likely do little to "change racial housing patterns." What it would do is prove that Californians were well intentioned and genuinely interested in breaking down racial barriers through dialogue and understanding. In order to facilitate this process, CAP 14 leaders encouraged their rank-and-file workers to share testimonies of faith. White and black preachers joined this movement, but laymen like David Collins, a self-identified Christian realtor, seemed to have the greatest effect. While speaking before the Anaheim Board of Realtors and writing for local newspapers, Collins testified as to why he opposed Proposition 14:

> I cannot support any program that will deprive my brother, regardless of his faith or color, of his God-given right to enjoy the fruits of this land in equal measure. . . . Are we to be forced to distinguish between a Christian and a realtor? I believe we must be both. Can we, in good conscience, turn our backs on a group of fellow human beings who ask only that <u>we</u> accept them as the Lord accepts them?

Armed with this moral sensitivity, CAP 14 activists approached the ballot box confident that their message would hold sway. Like Goldwater conservatives, they seemed sure that their politics had the best chance when judged in the precincts of voters' hearts.[47]

FREEDOM'S FERMENT

Both CAP 14 and the Goldwater campaign suffered emotional defeats in the 1964 election. The political lesson Goldwaterites learned, however, was the most bitter. The sense of momentum at Goldwater's nomination in July, supported by the gains of the previous three years, had inspired grassroots activism, but the emotionally charged quest for freedom crumbled under the pressures of a national campaign. Goldwaterism simply peaked too soon.

At the Republican National Convention, held in mid-July at the Cow Palace, in San Francisco, Goldwater uttered a famous line that would seal his fate: "Extremism in the defense of liberty is no vice, and moderation in the pursuit of justice is no virtue." A vague catchall, easily interpreted in many different ways, Goldwater intended the statement to show voters that he did not accept compromise. It also offered his opponents an easy target. Fellow Arizonan Stephen Shadegg cringed at the way it "ripped open old wounds and erected barriers" instead of promoting conciliation in the GOP and in the nation. Even Dean Burch, the pragmatic chairman of the Republican National Committee, had to admit that the speech "gave the people who were determined to beat Goldwater over the head, a handle to beat him with." Lyndon Johnson's Democrats happily pounded at the Republican candidate, beginning with his refusal to sign the Civil Rights Act and, correspondingly, his entire southern strategy. In a climate of incredible racial upheaval, any presidential candidate would have been hard-pressed to win on a states' rights platform, yet this is exactly what Goldwater attempted. Goldwater spent little time differentiating himself from staunch segregationists like George Wallace, on the assumption that the differences were self-evident. Yet many southern conservatives clung to Goldwater's doctrine as a way to save their dying order. Goldwater's stand on states' rights may have been ideologically pure in his mind, but in application it resembled Wallace's racism. Liberal Democrats made sure to stress this point.[48]

Their most damning criticism of the Republican leader, however, grew out of his Cow Palace speech and subsequent missteps that allowed Democratic campaigners to paint him as an extremist. Since the mid-1950s a number of intellectuals had postulated a new, radical trajectory in national politics, one they designated as "pseudo-conservative." According to scholars like Richard Hofstadter and Daniel Bell, the line of political activities that ran from McCarthyism to Goldwaterism represented a desperate attempt by a discontented class of Americans to salvage their station in a changing modern society. The new conservatism was, in their estimation, like the Populism of old—an irrational expression of status anxiety, social dislocation, and paranoia. Expanding on this notion, Democratic strategists treated Goldwater "not as an equal who has credentials to be President," as one White House aide suggested, "but as a *radical*, a preposterous candidate who would ruin this country and our future." They exposed Goldwater's ties to the "radical right" and harped on his public endorsements (some delivered flippantly) of a strong nuclear arsenal and unilateral foreign policy, which had come to seem dangerous in light of the Cuban Missile Crisis, and counterproductive amid diplomatic efforts to stabilize the cold war. They lampooned his campaign slogan, suggesting he was itching to drop the bomb: "In your heart you know he might." Then, in September, during "Monday Night at the Movies," the Johnson campaign aired a commercial that portrayed a young girl in a field, picking the petals off a daisy while a monotone voice in the background counted down from ten in anticipation of a nuclear holocaust. While the last image of an atom bomb's detonation filled the screen, Johnson's voice clarified its meaning: "These are the stakes: to make a world in which all of God's children can live, or to go into the darkness. We must either love each other, or we must die." The apocalyptic message caused such furor that the "daisy" commercial was never aired again, but it had done sufficient damage to the Republican side.[49]

Each jab Democrats dealt Goldwater hurt evangelicals acutely. As with most conservatives, they felt that Goldwater was victimized by a double standard in the press. There was truth to the claim—members of the national media did speak from an eastern regional prejudice and in certain instances they felt it their duty to "unmask" Goldwater, even if it meant dabbling in exaggeration. And Goldwater's frequent speaking gaffes made it easy for reporters to seize on his candor. Evangelical pundits, however, saw a larger conspiracy at work. Edgar Bundy, for instance, devoted every page of a November 1964 issue of his newsletter to exposing the skewed press coverage of the fall campaign. The negative journalism put forth by liberal religious periodicals infuriated him most. "The *Christian Century* . . . has been publishing full page smears against Mr. Goldwater since the conclusion of the Republican National Convention," he charged, and it has "received large gifts from tax-exempt foundations for carrying on this smear campaign." In a subsequent statement he revealed some of the ironies in his accusation.

The Church League of America, which has never participated in any political campaign and which has never opposed or supported any legislation, denounces this immoral, un-Christian, and un-American campaign against a presidential candidate, and especially calls for a nationwide exposure of those tax-exempt religious organizations which are violating federal laws.

Bundy was right in that the *Christian Century* had published scurrilous pieces on Goldwater, including one that compared his candidacy to the rise of Nazism in the 1930s. But Bundy's own claims to apolitical innocence were false. Like Carl McIntire and Fred Schwarz, he had retained his religious organization's own tax-exempt privileges by avoiding an outright endorsement of Goldwater. But it required very little effort to read between the lines to see that his enthusiasm for Goldwater was every bit as fervent as the *Christian Century*'s campaign against him.[50]

As Democrats gained the upper hand in the fall of 1964, even Goldwater seemed ready to concede defeat. His team pressed on, however, and perhaps in an effort to rejuvenate—or at least salvage—the campaign, looked for help from the South and Southern California. In mid-September Strom Thurmond announced that he was switching his party affiliation to Republican, articulating what many of his fellow white southerners were feeling but had not yet fully processed. The "Democratic Party has abandoned the people," and it is now "the party of minority groups, power-hungry union leaders, political bosses, and businessmen looking for government contracts and favors." If it remained in power, "freedom as we know it in this country is doomed." Soon after this televised proclamation, Thurmond returned to the West Coast to help the Goldwater team mount one final charge in friendly territory. The same legion of conservative supporters that had greeted his earlier California tours cheered him and his hard-driving message once again.[51]

While Thurmond peddled Goldwater's hard-line positions on foreign policy, other California Republicans began selling the nurturing side of Goldwater conservatism. In the weeks leading up to the November 3 election, Goldwater appeared in a number of nationwide telecasts that included his formal address on "Morality and Government," which charted the decline of the American family and the Judeo-Christian order. John Wayne was recruited to add drama to this morality tale. Late in the campaign Wayne, at the behest of the California Goldwater for President Committee, narrated a thirty-minute film about Goldwater's life. Rather than foreground his stature as a rugged frontiersman, the movie highlighted Goldwater's role as a father who entered politics to protect his children's future. Politics was about individual freedom, but according to the tribute, it was also about the right to worship freely, pray in schools, secure a first-rate education, and live in safe communities. "Politics," Goldwater explained, as images of suburbia flashed in the background, was "young people getting married and forming families, buying homes."[52]

This very same maxim, delivered in desperation by a candidate now with little chance for victory, is what carried the day for Proposition 14. Perhaps sensing an end to the Goldwater phenomenon, in the fall of 1964 Southern California conservatives stepped up their campaign to pass Proposition 14. Even national commentators saw the intensity of this political battle. An editorialist in the *Saturday Evening Post* predicted that "the outcome of the fight could have as much nationwide significance as the parallel battle between President Johnson and Senator Goldwater." As the struggle unfolded, CAP 14 gained the rising support of liberal Protestant, Catholic, and Jewish organizations, but they were at a disadvantage. Proposition 14 advocates benefited from direct organizational ties to the Goldwater campaign (even though Goldwater tried to downplay them) and a financial capability that far surpassed anything CAP 14 could muster. By accentuating the moral dimensions of their campaign, and appealing to voters' hearts, CAP 14 gave its opponents an ideological edge as well. Hesitating to defend the Rumford Act as a way to correct deep-seated structural inequalities, CAP 14 was left flailing in the murky rhetorical waters of open-mindedness and human decency.[53]

The yes side did the opposite by acting decisively. The activists who worked under the banner of the CHP claimed Proposition 14 was crafted in the spirit of pluralism, egalitarianism, and even color blindness. They argued that both white and black suffered when government enacted laws that impinged on their private freedom. It was the Rumford Act that was discriminatory and anachronistic, and Proposition 14 that marked progress towards racial equality. This argument brushed over the complexities of racial discrimination and the ingrained prejudices of market logic, but as a campaign slogan it worked marvelously. A "Goldwater 64" brochure said it all: "The right of a property owner to manage his property as he sees fit is a civil right, a human right, a moral right—however one chooses to express it."[54]

THE DAY AFTER the polls closed, voters, activists, politicians, and pundits were left to sort through some mystifying results. The national result proved to most Americans that Goldwater conservatism was a minor blip outside the liberal consensus. President Johnson won his mandate by an astounding 43 million to 27 million votes (61 percent to 39 percent of votes cast). While Goldwater won Arizona and five southern states, he failed to carry any others; even California went to Johnson, though Goldwater won solidly in San Diego and Orange counties and tallied respectable results in neighboring counties. Pat Brown and California's Democratic Party, on the other hand, suffered a devastating setback. When the final ballots were counted, Proposition 14 passed by a stunning two-to-one ratio, with 4,526,460 Californians voting in favor and 2,395,747 against. Proposition 14's decisive victory meant the end of the Rumford Act, but it signaled something bigger as well. Having woefully misjudged the California voter on this issue, Brown and his coalition were never able to recover. Some of the governor's advisors were shattered by the result. Believing that "people in the goodness of their hearts would vote no on 14" and that fair housing was a "clear moral issue," they could not understand why a majority of Californians felt differently. Looking back on the decision and the shock that accompanied it, Lu Haas, a Brown press assistant, would recall that "Liberalism died in '64, if you want to pick a date."[55]

But Haas knew this only in hindsight. In the months that followed the 1964 election, liberal Democratic hegemony in California and the nation at large seemed intact. Much of the editorializing painted a bleak future for the Right; November 3, 1964, in their estimation, was the date conservatism died. One columnist in the *New York Times* confidently claimed that Goldwater had "not only lost the presidential election yesterday but the conservative cause as well. He has wrecked his party for a long time to come and is not even likely to control the wreckage." *Time* magazine added that the "conservative cause whose championship Goldwater assumed suffered a crippling setback. . . . The humiliation of their defeat was so complete that they will not have another shot at party domination for some time to come." An NBC commentator happily bid adieu to Goldwater's legion of "classic Republicans, segregationists, Johnson-phobes, desperate conservatives, and radical nuts . . . the coalition of discontent." Commentators were even more anxious to say good-bye to the evangelical front that had provided the Goldwater movement so much support. Over the next few years journalists and scholars turned their attention to the period of political ferment they had just witnessed in American evangelicalism, and wrote about it as a final, fruitless attempt to thwart modernity. Writing in 1967, William G. McLoughlin, one of the leading historians of religion at the time, disparaged the religious "fringe" groups and neo-evangelical radicals who had

positioned themselves "lock, stock, and barrel with Senator Barry Goldwater," and equally dismissed the notion that they represented a sea change
in American Protestantism. Instead, McLoughlin posited that this "third-
force" in American "Christendom" had already reached its "high-tide." "The
new evangelicals" may have shown themselves to be the "spiritual hard-core
of the radical right," and "demonstrated that the United States now has a
permanent, powerful, and respectable ultra-right in its political spectrum,"
but they had not shown that they could be anything but a reactive voice
crying out from the margins.[56]

Even as McLoughlin's essay was released, evangelicals and their conservative allies were beginning to prove him wrong. Certainly if they
had been privy to the entire scope of Goldwater's movement and evangelical support, McLoughlin and fellow critics may not have been so
eager to write it off. By assuming that Goldwaterism was an irrational
reaction against modernity, they underestimated the extent to which it
was actually centered by a historic and developing tradition of thought,
and grounded in profound social, economic, and political grievances and
interests. And by assuming that Goldwaterism was simply another outlet
for the same conspiratorial obsessions witnessed in McCarthyism, they
overlooked the exaggerated culture of suspicion and surveillance that
enveloped Southern California's entire political spectrum in the early
1960s. Goldwater activists operated with the same substantiated fears as
their left-wing counterparts at this time, that there were indeed citizen-
spies among them.

Moreover, critics failed to account for the differences among Goldwaterites. True, amid the political fury of the 1964 election, nuances were
difficult to identify, but in actuality, key distinctions existed, even within
California's evolving southern evangelical community. As much as vocif-
erous Christian warriors like Hargis, McIntire, Weniger, and Wells, took
the lead in marshaling this advance guard for Goldwater and Proposition 14, they were supported by a multitude of activists with a range of
emotions and priorities that did not always match their fundamentalism.
Goldwater's sentinels of freedom may have been swept up together in the
heightened political tension of the day, but most of them were also reflec-
tive people and savvy political actors who recognized that emotional cries
for freedom could only take them so far. Immediately following the 1964
election this silent majority began sorting out a new future for their faith
and their politics.

IV

SOUTHERN
STRATEGIES

As a result of our victory, we started something in this State. We are being watched . . . watched by those all across this land who once again dare to believe that our concept of responsible, people-oriented government can work as the founding fathers meant it to work. If we prove that here, we can, as I have said before, start a prairie fire that can sweep across this country. But to start that fire, we must nurture the flame here at home or it will flicker and die and those who come after us will find only the ashes of lost hopes and dead dreams.

—RONALD REAGAN, SPEECH TO
CALIFORNIA REPUBLICAN ASSEMBLY, 1967

I believe we can start a glow and a fire here on the West Coast that can sweep this nation.

—BILLY GRAHAM,
SPEECH TO CALIFORNIA LEGISLATURE, 1971

10

CREATIVE SOCIETY

"The Great Society" . . . is "great" alright: great in cost, great in inefficiency, great in taxes, great in waste, great in its swollen bureaucracy. And by those measures it is "greater" every day! I propose a far better solution. So that it may be easily remembered and also accurately described, I have called it, "The Creative Society." The "Creative Society" idea is that there is present, within the incredibly rich human resources of California, the dynamic solution to every old or new problem we face. The task of a state government committed to this concept is to creatively discover, enlist, and mobilize those human resources.[1]

—RONALD REAGAN, 1966

IN THE WAKE OF BARRY GOLDWATER'S DEFEAT, SOUTHERN California conservatives needed a new champion. Ronald Reagan soon emerged as their man. But how could this former actor and his supporters repackage Goldwater politics in a way that would win over a wider public? The breakthrough occurred on the evening of Monday, November 30, 1965, while Reverend William Steuart (W. S.) McBirnie was driving home from a meeting at Ronald Reagan's home in Pacific Palisades with Henry Salvatori and a few high-powered members of Reagan's inner circle—his "Kitchen Cabinet." The commute back to Glendale was long, so McBirnie had plenty of time to think. Upon his return home, he crafted a lengthy letter and mailed it to 1669 Onofre Drive, Pacific Palisades. When Reagan opened the envelope he found the key to his future.

The challenges facing Reagan if he chose to run in the 1966 California state election were many, McBirnie wrote, but none would be insurmountable if he found a politics he could call his own. "Almost every successful candidate of any historic importance in modern times has offered a positive program, packaged in some kind of slogan or neat description: New Deal, Fair Deal, New Frontier, Great Society, New Order, etc." McBirnie claimed to have found just the right one for his friend: "Creative Society." As a campaign motto, Creative Society evoked the right blend of frustration with current politics and hope for reform. But McBirnie envisioned a much higher ceiling. The philosophy of a Creative Society would show all Americans that there existed in California "the human resources, to solve any problem—without the growth of bureaucracy." Each troubled sector of society, he asserted, "could be overhauled by new thoughts" and "a new atmosphere of freedom to deal with old, tough problems." And gone for good would be the "tired old stereotypes of Right Wing vs. Left Wing." While liberals would embrace the "compassionate, progressive answers" provided in this plan, "conservatives would rejoice in greater self government and wider participation by more people on the local level."

McBirnie closed with one final burst of grandiose thinking. "It really could have *national* repercussions if it can be made to work in California. It is a mile above the so-called 'Great Society.'" Confident in his friendship with Reagan, he seemed unconcerned about the hyperbole that flashed through his letter; McBirnie did not need to worry, because Reagan was a man who thought just as grandly about starting a conservative "prairie fire" in California. The politician liked his preacher-friend's plan and decided to make it his own.[2]

RONALD REAGAN WAS ALSO a practical thinker. He recognized the challenges that awaited conservatives after 1964. Goldwater's campaign had exposed the Republican Right's flaws, making it apparent just how far it was from electoral success. The Arizona senator had been unable to shake the extremist label and he had hurt himself by refusing to soften his stand on states' rights. In the months following the 1964 debacle, Reagan emerged with answers. Together, the politician and his advisors demanded that conservatives clean up their act and start thinking about ways to gain the political center.

The relationship between McBirnie and Reagan epitomized the collaborative role evangelicalism would play in conservatism's future. Following the emotional letdown of 1964, evangelicals began reevaluating their single-minded politics. What transpired during the mid-1960s was a sorting process that led to clearer demarcations between those who would espouse Reagan's responsible conservatism and those who would advocate a radical conservatism—between "new evangelicals" who sought the political middle and "fundamentalists" who relished independence. The differences registered on a sliding scale, yet the realignment within evangelicalism was important to Reagan's emerging synthesis. Within the fundamentalist camp, activists who were willing to play by Reagan's rules provided the Republican Right with populist energy. Within the "new evangelical" camp, Reagan identified allies among patrons and power brokers who believed that for the sake of Christian witness and political respectability evangelicalism needed to tame its ideological imperatives and help construct a creative, color-blind conservatism.

Amid this political ferment, transplanted southern evangelicals began wrestling with their own set of difficult issues: Were they still southern? Whose South, whose faith, and whose politics did they represent? Which of these Souths did they need to jettison? Decisive answers to these questions would come in the late 1960s with the rise of a new generation. Yet even as they contemplated the upheaval of the mid-1960s and Reagan's ascent, southern plain folk, preachers, and entrepreneurs began reshaping their errand. The result was a true Southern California creation that they could take to the rest of the nation.

CONSERVATISM'S GREAT WHITE HOPE

Despite predictions of its demise after Goldwater's defeat, conservatism did not suddenly go away. One reason was because it remained firmly entrenched in Southern California, which was just entering a new phase of national prominence. Carey McWilliams, now editor of the *Nation*, was not alone in marveling at the transformation that had overtaken his home. In the early 1940s he believed that Southern California was an "island on the land," set apart from the country. Two decades later he saw in Southern California "the America to come."[3]

This declaration, offered by a leading liberal, cheered the country's conservatives who banked their survival on more California magic, and specifically on Reagan, whose leadership credentials were certified October 27, 1964, when he spoke one last time before the federal election on Goldwater's behalf. In front of a television audience, Reagan delivered an oration compared by some to William Jennings Bryan's momentous "Cross of Gold" speech of 1896. Like Bryan's famous address, Reagan's "A Time for Choosing" pulsated with an unmistakable populist beat: "This is the issue of this election, whether we believe in our capacity for self-government or whether we abandon the American Revolution and confess that a little intellectual elite in a far-distant capital can plan our lives for us better than we can plan them ourselves." From this early statement to its final plea for "peace through strength," Reagan's address hit on every point raised by Goldwater in *Conscience of a Conservative*, but smoothly, without a sharp edge.[4]

For conservatives coming to terms with Goldwater's downfall, Reagan's television appearance was a bright ray of light. In the eighteen months between the fall of 1964 and the California state primaries in late spring 1966, Reagan felt the weight of increasing expectations, as admirers from around the country urged him to run for governor. Politicians, businessmen, clerics, and housewives bombarded him with encouragement. An elderly woman on a "very small income" spoke for many rank-and-file citizens when she handwrote a note and enclosed five dollars "to help a little—if only to buy stamps." "I certainly hope and pray that Mr. Reagan is nominated and elected. We sure need a change. I'm very much afraid—if the American people don't wake up soon, there will be no more U.S.A. as we have known it." This same month, in June 1965, an oilman from Texas sent a similar letter, only on typed company letterhead.

> PLEASE PLEASE PLEASE make up your mind to enter the Governors race in California. If we can get you elected Governor for two terms and then get you nominated for the presidency . . . we would have a chance of getting the United States back to where it was about twenty years ago. . . . It is going to take men like you to get into POLITICS if we are ever going to . . . restore the Country back to the PEOPLE instead of to the BEAUCRATS we have operating and running the Country.

Letters originating farther east joined those streaming west from Texas. A group of Democratic women in Louisiana, calling themselves the Louisiana Republican Political Action Council, recorded a campaign song called "Ronald Reagan Can Do the Job," and sent it to their new hero. Higher up the political ladder, Strom Thurmond wrote regularly and, at the beginning of 1966, after Reagan had officially declared his candidacy, offered him help. "As you know, I am also running this year, but in the past couple of years I have made a good many friends in Southern California and I will be happy to help you in any way I can."[5]

Scattered through Reagan's correspondence during this transitional time were letters from evangelicals hoping to attach their own political aspirations to him. Reagan seemed ideal to them, in part because he claimed a compelling spiritual narrative, one that was far easier to grasp than Goldwater's Jewish heritage and Episcopalian faith. Reagan confirmed his religious commitments in the tumult surrounding the 1966 election with a born-again experience. By February 1967 word of his spiritual conversion was spreading quickly through the press, and Reagan willingly encouraged it. In an interview with a newspaper, he admitted his recent epiphany before adding, "I can't conceive of anyone trying to meet the problems we face today without help from God. . . . I have spent more time in prayer these past few weeks than I have in any previous period I can recall." In subsequent exchanges with Christians, Reagan used language drawn from the evangelical lexicon. Writing to a pastor after becoming governor, he testified to the moment he "accepted the Lord as my personal savior," and of his plans to conduct his office according to Jesus's teachings. Reagan met other standards of association as well. Besides befriending high-profile Christians like Pat Boone, Reagan regularly attended the Bel Air Presbyterian Church, respected in conservative circles for its orthodoxy and its dynamic minister. Bel Air's spiritual leader was Donn Moomaw, who in the early 1950s was one of the first students at UCLA to convert under the ministry of Campus Crusade for Christ. Ten years later, the onetime star quarterback was a respected pastor and poster boy for this youth ministry, the man celebrated by evangelicals for leading Reagan to Christ.[6]

Reagan also testified to a political conversion narrative that connected with California evangelicals, especially the southerners among them. In his Goldwater campaign speech and public addresses that followed, Reagan made it clear that the New Deal zeitgeist in which he had come of political age had been bankrupted by the Democratic Party and its postwar turn to big unions and big government. Constantly, in reference to his 1940s work as president of Hollywood's Screen Actors Guild and as a friendly witness for Richard Nixon and the House Un-American Activities Committee, he relayed tales of personal frustration with labor bosses who abandoned Franklin D. Roosevelt's ideals. Reagan's ability to speak critically of unions while distancing himself from strident anti-labor rhetoric was a boon for his relationship with southern evangelicals who shared the same scars he carried from the 1940s labor wars. Of course, the capstone of Reagan's political conversion was his 1962 switch to the Republican Party. Here again, his experience resonated with southern transplants. Throughout the previous decade, these citizens had adapted their traditional beliefs to the exigencies of modern conservatism without completely severing ties to the party of their youth. But by the early 1960s the time had come for them to get serious about their partisan commitments.[7]

Democratic Governor Pat Brown thrust this reality upon them. Brown won the 1958 gubernatorial race on a platform of "Responsible Liberalism," which resuscitated the Social Democratic agenda of the 1940s. Once elected, he passed in rapid-fire succession forty-three (out of a proposed forty-four) reform measures that increased Social Security and welfare benefits, revised the health care system, and doled out state funds to transportation and education. By the end of his first term Brown's team was dreaming grandly of a coalition that could rival Roosevelt's with its imaginative ideology and party discipline. In 1959, Brown made a bold move toward a permanent Democratic majority by abolishing cross-filing, which, since its inception in the Progressive era, had allowed candidates to run in both party's primaries. This system benefited better-funded, incumbent candidates—typically, Republican ones—so Brown eagerly dismantled it and made party registration (an area in which Democrats held the upper hand) more important. Philosophically and practically, Brown thus forced southern evangelicals into choosing sides. Like Reagan, many of them had remained *little-r* Republicans since the early 1950s, still registering as Democrat but voting Republican, all the while thinking as Independents. In response to Brown's New Deal liberalism, they reconsidered their affiliation. Throughout the rest of the 1960s they would weigh equally Democratic and Republican options in presidential, gubernatorial, and congressional elections and often vote differently at national, state, and local levels. Moreover, they would rely heavily on another product of progressivism—the ballot initiative—to express their political views outside party lines. But Brown's actions represented a tipping point for them. Voting on principle for "the man, not the party" now came with heavier costs. In Reagan they found the burden lightened, for in their eyes he honorably served both principle and party.[8]

Reagan's salvation stories won him the support of Goldwater evangel-

People streaming out of Billy Graham's "Canvass Cathedral" in downtown Los Angeles, 1949. The eight-week revival vaulted Graham onto a national stage as the country's rising star evangelist.

Billy Graham's preaching platform straddles second base in Anaheim's brand-new "Big A" stadium, 1969. The ten-day revival broke records for the Graham evangelistic team and underscored the dramatic transformation that had turned Bible Belt evangelicalism into a Sunbelt phenomenon in just two decades.

Created in the 1930s as an industrial, blue-collar suburb with a distinctive rural feel, Bell Gardens always had a split personality, even into the 1950s, when this photo was taken.

"Fighting" Bob Shuler served twenty days in prison in 1930 for using his religious radio program to champion his controversial politics. As is evident in this photo, he did not seem to mind the inconvenience or media attention that came with his detention.

Like the churches southern migrants built in the late 1930s and early 1940s, Pepperdine College was comfortably embedded in its neighborhood. George Pepperdine wanted his students to have access to the city but also shelter from its vices on a campus surrounded by (and attuned to) suburban values.

The founding members of Pepperdine College's Alpha Gamma, a women's honor organization, here pictured in the spring of 1938. A young Helen Mattox, recently relocated from Oklahoma, stands in the first row, second from right.

Carey McWilliams, reclining here in 1941, was instrumental in bringing the "southern problem" to light for California progressives. His impatience with southern evangelicalism lacked the biting edge of H. L. Mencken's, but not the intensity.

Chester Estep, a nonstriker opposing union action at Warner Bros., finds himself in the middle of bloody violence during Hollywood's "labor wars" immediately following World War II. Finding herself embroiled in the controversy, Marie King used her position in the legal offices at MGM to document violence against nonstriking workers like Estep and report on other union activities to MGM executives, all in hopes of curtailing communist influence in Hollywood and Los Angeles.

With McWilliams's help, Mobilization for Democracy organized large public protests outside meetings held by Ham and Eggs and Gerald L. K. Smith. These protestors are part of the fifteen thousand that surrounded the Polytechnic High School on October 16, 1945.

The Church of the Open Door, here pictured in the early 1950s, was a grand, classical monument to the conservative Protestant establishment that had gained cultural power in Southern California during the early twentieth century.

With over four thousand theater-style seats, an eight-story skylight covering the entire ceiling, and the city's grandest pipe organ, the Church of the Open Door's interior was every bit as spectacular as its exterior. The resplendent church auditorium also served as a stunning venue for the Bible Institute of Los Angeles' graduation ceremonies, here photographed just prior to World War II.

Two generations of southern preachers pose for a photograph in Los Angeles during the late 1940s. A green Billy Graham stands between the Reverend Bob Shuler (*right*) and a younger, unidentified associate.

J. Vernon McGee preaching from the pulpit at the Church of the Open Door.

A sign outside a revival tent in the middle of an undeveloped Los Angeles sub-
urban neighborhood announces the arrival of southern evangelist Doug Winn.
The revival, held sometime in the early 1950s, was sponsored by John Brown's
KGER radio station, along with several churches and parachurch ministries.

These eight students were judged the best in
the Heritage Schools' patriotic costume contest. More importantly for Pastor Bob Wells,
they were considered prime examples of
Central Baptist Church's theological,
pedagogical, and political vision.

Twenty-five years earlier, Helen Mattox had
been photographed outside this same building as a young transfer student from Harding
College, in Arkansas. Here, in the 1960s, she
is pictured with her husband and Pepperdine's
president, M. Norvel Young, displaying the
refinement and confidence of a leader in her
church, school, and community.

In August of 1961, sixteen thousand young people and their parents packed Los Angeles' Sports Arena for "youth night" at Fred Schwarz's Southern California School of Anti-Communism. Pat Boone, pictured here onstage next to Ronald and Nancy Reagan and other famous anticommunist crusaders, delivered the evening's signature line when he declared he would rather have his four daughters shot than subject them to communist rule.

Senator Barry Goldwater arrived at Pepperdine College's third freedom forum in 1961 with great fanfare as the politician with the "conservative conscience" ready to lead a right-wing revolution. Here he playfully points to the Pepperdine flag as Norvel Young and another dinner guest look on. An elderly George Pepperdine is peering over Young's shoulder.

Pepperdine College students declaring their support for Republican candidate Barry Goldwater in 1964.

Family values and cowboy conservatism blended together at a Republican rally in Dodger Stadium, held just as the Goldwater movement was beginning to gather steam for the 1964 election.

Billy Graham found a friend and natural ally in Ronald Reagan, here pictured with Nancy Reagan during the 1969 Anaheim crusade.

In the wake of the Watts riots, Billy Graham and other evangelical leaders in Southern California began building a "color-blind conservatism" and interracial coalition. Reverend E. V. Hill, looking up at the famed evangelist, was always eager to have Graham occupy his pulpit at Mount Zion Missionary Baptist Church in South Central Los Angeles.

144

Ruth Graham preferred to avoid the spotlight, but during her husband's 1969 meetings in Anaheim she broke the pattern by speaking to eleven thousand women gathered for the largest sit-down meal held west of the Mississippi River.

Evangelical youth, like this young man, joined housewives in providing crucial grassroots support for Billy Graham's 1969 Anaheim crusade.

William Banowsky confronts student protestors in front of Pepperdine College's administration building. The demonstration was emblematic of growing racial tensions on the South Central campus following the tragic shooting of Larry Kimmons by a school security guard.

Pepperdine's young vice president makes a point during a postdebate press conference while Bishop James Pike prepares a response. The well-publicized debate at the University of California, Santa Barbara, in early 1969 was a boon to Banowsky's career and Pepperdine College's future. Bishop Pike would die later this same year.

Held three years after Woodstock, "Godstock"—Campus Crusade for Christ's Explo '72 in Dallas—confronted the same challenges of rain and mud. It also sparked a similar youthful zeal for an idealistic vision of America's future.

Richard Nixon addressing the South's silent majority at Billy Graham's Knoxville, Tennessee, crusade in 1970. Just to the right, E. V. Hill applauds along with other white and black preachers (most positioned outside this frame).

Pat Boone did his best to lead undecided Republican delegates into Ronald Reagan's camp. Unfortunately for him and many of his California evangelical brethren, these efforts came up short, and Gerald Ford locked up the Republican nomination.

By 1977, when this photo was taken, Arthur Blessitt was no longer the Southern Baptist rebel who wanted to save Hollywood's Sunset Strip; he was a veritable institution, known internationally for his traveling evangelistic work and welcomed like an apostle to the nation's largest religious gatherings.

"Democracy is in the streets," young radicals had declared in the 1960s. By the late 1970s, as battles over gay rights, abortion, the ERA, and property taxes heated up, "democracy" was evident on Southern California's largest boulevards. Large, dramatic demonstrations against the Briggs initiative, like this one held in Los Angeles, were a common occurrence during the Proposition 6 campaign of 1978.

Around this same time, E. V. Hill led his own march through South Central Los Angeles in support of social justice and Christian morality. Dressed in overalls and a straw hat, and equipped with a megaphone, Hill was truly "of the people." Later, in early 1980, he would help lead other evangelicals in the largest of all Christian marches, this one through the streets of Washington, D.C.

Pepperdine's campus—the "Malibu Miracle"—at dusk, looking east toward Los Angeles.

icals, but as much as he impressed upon them the legacy of his decision making, he also asked that they make a resolution. Enthusiasm of
the kind witnessed during Goldwater's run was not enough, he insisted;
what was needed was discipline of the kind that had held Brown's Democratic Party intact and in power. In this vein, Reagan started working to
shift conservatism to the center, where electoral gains could be made.
He started by expunging zealots from Republican ranks. On September
24, 1965, he denounced the John Birch Society, setting off a bout of hard
feelings. Since its founding in 1958, the JBS had played a pivotal role
in marshaling members behind conservative candidates, particularly in
Southern California, the JBS stronghold, where an estimated 30 percent
of the nation's one hundred thousand members lived. Reagan's actions
were unforgivable in the eyes of John Birchers, many of whom wrote to
say they were "terribly disappointed" in his "vicious attack." "We don't go
along with the excuse that you have to smear this wonderful organization
in order to be elected," one particularly upset JBS couple wrote. "Life is
too short to turn your back on all you believe in for the selfish purpose of
trying to win a few years of political power here on this earth." "Don't kid
yourself, Mr. Regan [sic], by isolating The John Birch Society you are also
isolating many Birch sympathizers who would make up the bulk of your
hardest workers and financial supporters here in California." Aware of
this, Reagan cushioned his denunciations by insisting that he knew many
"fine upstanding citizens" in the JBS and would be "most proud to have
their support." But his point was made: His conservatism would not be
Goldwater's. Nor would he stand for the internal squabbling that racked
the GOP during Goldwater's run. Shortly after his Birch statement, Reagan introduced conservatives to his Eleventh Commandment, which read
simply, "I will not speak critically of any Republican and . . . will wholeheartedly support whoever is the nominee of the Party."[9]

Better party discipline put Reagan on surer footing as he looked ahead
to the primaries, but long-term success still required a positive message.
If Reagan wanted to squelch conservatism's "anti-" culture, he needed
to stress a "pro-" platform. Into the mix stepped McBirnie, the preacher
from Glendale who brought a rare ability to bridge high and low politics.
The pastor had already demonstrated this talent during the Proposition
14 campaign, when he emerged as a fierce defender of private property,
but the true display of his developing political acumen came in the fall
of 1965. Just as Reagan was expelling the JBS, McBirnie delivered a

speech to the California Republican Assembly, which begged Republicans to focus on their real enemy, Brown's Democrats. CRA officials were impressed, noting that Reagan's own campaign managers "could not have performed any better than the Reverend had." Weeks later, McBirnie came through again by putting into words what Reagan had been trying to articulate: the Creative Society. In January 1966, now committed to this vision, Reagan formerly announced his candidacy for Republican leadership. He would run, he declared, on a forward-looking conservative agenda drained of the fundamentalist poisons of the past and in command of the political center. The centrist vision was appealing to the Republican rank and file, and Reagan stormed the California primary in June, winning 77 percent of their vote.[10]

Thanks to McBirnie's ingenuity and Reagan's intuition, conservatives who had pleaded for "Ronnie to run" now saw their wishes about to be fulfilled. After rumblings in 1958 and a burst of hope in 1964, their electoral victory—their revolution—seemed inevitable. Most of Reagan's devotees did not dwell on the fact that their leader was moving closer to the political middle, or that a collapsing Democratic coalition was handing them this opportunity. All that mattered was that they were about to win, finally.

Their victory in the fall of 1966 was not guaranteed, of course, but two momentous political disruptions gave Republicans confidence, and both brought the political center to Reagan. Campus unrest was the first. Since their demonstration at the HUAC meetings in San Francisco in 1960, Berkeley students had become a liability to Democrats, who needed to control radicalism to preserve the party unity on which Brown's governance depended. Compliance is not what the Free Speech Movement (FSM) had in mind, however, when it began a wave of campus protests in the fall of 1964 against administrators' decision to outlaw on-campus recruitment for civil rights organizations. Their crowning achievement came on December 2, when one thousand FSM-led students occupied Sproul Hall, the university's nerve center. An agitated Governor Brown forced students out. Just as they did four years earlier at the HUAC protests, television cameras captured images of policemen dragging limp students down flights of stairs to paddy wagons waiting below. This time the images spoke volumes of a Democratic alliance coming undone.[11]

As much as student unrest was beginning to tear apart Democratic ranks, it was events in South Central Los Angeles the following summer that laid the immediate groundwork for a Republican resurgence. In August 1965, only days after Lyndon Johnson signed the Voting Rights Act, the Watts section of Los Angeles erupted in violence after a white highway patrolman arrested a young black motorist. Within days of the incident, Watts was ablaze; rioters plundered stores and set them on fire while local residents desperately tried to secure their families and homes. At the conclusion of the crisis, 34 people were dead, hundreds had been injured, and $35 million in damage had been done. The political carnage was colossal as well, especially for California's Democratic Coalition. Brown's administration remained hopeful that Great Society programs could ameliorate the dire conditions in Watts, but this bright outlook no longer seemed feasible either to left-wing or right-leaning Democrats. In the wake of Watts, activists in the California Democratic Council, the grassroots organization founded in 1953 to revitalize the Democratic Left, began distancing themselves from Brown out of frustration with a soft-pedal, centrist liberalism that failed, in their mind, to address structural inequalities. Doubted by Social Democrats, Brown next found himself battered by conservative Democrats who gravitated toward his chief rival, Los Angeles Mayor Samuel Yorty, and his law-and-order political agenda.[12]

Despite these setbacks, Brown overcame Yorty in the Democratic primaries and pressed on for a third term by defending the embattled liberal middle. He did so by painting Reagan as the "extremists' candidate." In August of 1966, Democrats released a twenty-nine-page report, which outlined Reagan's reliance on "Fright-Wing" money from the East and South, his "Brain Trust" of Walter Knott and Henry Salvatori, his position as a "Front Man" for Welch's JBS, and his unhealthy accord with religious extremists like Patrick Frawley and Fred Schwarz. Many dismissed these sweeping indictments as smear tactics. Still, Brown refused to stray from this strategy. In September he sent Reagan a telegram rehashing these charges and asking him to repudiate them or else "the Democratic Party will continue to produce documented evidence day by day of your deep involvement with the radical right." This led nowhere, but in October Brown finally found a way to pin Reagan down—McBirnie. Through back channels, McBirnie's Creative Society letter found its way into Brown's hands, who leaked it to the press hoping to prove the Republican candidate's ties to right-wing religious extremists and highlight his inability to think on his own.[13]

McBirnie's biography also made its way into print, and the details were salacious. During the 1950s McBirnie had enjoyed two careers, one as a salesman and the second as a Southern Baptist minister in San Antonio. His ministerial career crashed in 1959, when he confessed an adulterous affair with Wilma Jean Durham, one of his parishioners. With his ministerial license revoked, McBirnie moved west. The salesman-seminarian's smooth delivery quickly made him a star on Southern California's anti-communist lecture circuit, and his polished looks and intellect a natural fit for the upper-middle-class enclave of Glendale, where he settled. By 1963 McBirnie was pastor of the city's United Community Church and a talk show host on his own program, *The Voice of Americanism*. Eager to exploit McBirnie's flaws, Brown's Democrats encouraged media scrutiny. Tom Brokaw contributed with his own exposé on KNBC-TV's evening news, in which he described McBirnie and Durham's secret rendezvous in Laredo, Mexico, and the street fight that ensued when Durham's husband tried to confront McBirnie with a loaded pistol. Brokaw's segment had an unmistakable warning: Frontier lawlessness had come to Los Angeles and was running Reagan's campaign.[14]

Despite such coverage, Brown's charges did not stick. McBirnie effectively denied being the architect of Creative Society, insisting that its core ideas were Reagan's alone. Reagan backed this claim by stating that McBirnie (whose "inestimable help" he was "proud to have") simply encapsulated the philosophy he had held to for fifteen years. The more disturbing fact, he emphasized, was that Democrats had stolen McBirnie's letter from Republican headquarters. What right did they have to talk about the GOP's lawlessness? This rebuttal seemed to satisfy the majority of Californians. Able to deflect criticism without appearing defensive, Reagan also had an appealing agenda and a party united behind its doctrine. Conversely, by harping on extremism in Reagan's camp, Brown opened the door to criticism of his own; as far as California voters were concerned, it was the Democratic Party that was now rife with extremists from Berkeley, Watts, and the CDC. Such a divided party could hardly be expected to bring unity to a fractured society. As the election arrived, members of Brown's crumbling coalition gave Reagan extra momentum. Yorty's California Moderate Democrats lent their support to Reagan, as did Mexican-American Democrats for Reagan and Labor for Reagan. Reagan also drew encouragement from Jerrell Babb, who spoke for the Texas State Society of Southern California. "Ronald Reagan is a very capable and able statesman who speaks the language . . . that former Texans like to hear,"

Babb explained, while adding that the "one-half million Texans living in Los Angeles County" would help Reagan's cause. Reagan did not need to hear Babb to know from whence he spoke. During his campaign stops in the Texas and Oklahoma enclaves of Los Angeles County—suburbs like Norwalk, where people worked on the Apollo Project at the North American Aviation plant during weekdays and worshipped at their Baptist and Pentecostal churches on Sunday—Reagan heard Babb's endorsement repeated a hundredfold. On November 8, 1966, he saw it manifested in an electoral victory by a margin of one million votes.[15]

FORGING A RESPONSIBLE EVANGELICAL RIGHT

Reagan's win marked a historic turn in California politics and certainly a cause for conservatives around the country to celebrate. Yet it was also sobering. Years of passionate pursuit of power had enlivened the Right, but what happened now that it was in hand? How did one manage it? At his inaugural, Reagan suggested that these questions were very much on his mind. "We have come to a crossroad—a time of decision—and the path we follow turns away from any idea that government and those who serve it are omnipotent. Along this path government will lead but not rule, listen but not lecture. It is the path of a Creative Society." Reagan did intend to rule, however. Toward this end he began reconstituting a responsible Republican Right that could sustain its influence. This required a responsible evangelical Right, which in turn necessitated a reining in of transplanted southern evangelicals. To hold their confidence and continue tapping their considerable resources, the governor enshrouded the ceremonial side of his politics in an aura of heartfelt, homespun Protestantism. One-on-one to southern evangelicals, meanwhile, he promised an agenda that would get socialism and secularism out of the community, and God back in. From this point forward, however, he wanted to proceed cautiously, always courting the patricians and power brokers among them but controlling the populist preachers and activists like McBirnie, whose zeal was a liability.[16]

Southern evangelicalism's elites were Reagan's natural allies and so proved easy to handle. Disappointed by the outcome of the Goldwater crusade, Christian capitalists who funded Pepperdine College, sat on executive boards, and supported the local Chamber of Commerce quickly fell in line behind Reagan's vision for a centrist conservatism.

They recognized that decades of movement building would flounder if conservatives were not able to craft a pragmatic approach. The coalition-friendly outlook of these patrons also enlivened power brokers who mediated between evangelicalism's corporate elite and its rank and file. The Church of Christ educators who ran Pepperdine performed critical ambassadorial roles at the state level, as did Pat Boone. Billy Graham did such work on a national scale. Although not as close with Reagan as another California statesman—Richard Nixon—Graham enjoyed a relationship with the governor that had an equally long history. The two men first met at a fund-raising event in Dallas in 1953. While seated next to Graham, Reagan debated with W. A. Criswell, pastor of Dallas's First Baptist (Graham's home church at the time), about whether the movie industry was "of the Devil." By the end of the argument Reagan had convinced his detractor that Hollywood was also producing wholesome films. "Ron had not only changed a man's mind," Graham would recall, "but he had done it with charm, conviction, and humor—traits I would see repeatedly as I got to know him." Reagan appreciated the same traits in Graham, and for that reason cherished any opportunity to meet with him. His appearance at Graham's California revivals was one expression of this camaraderie, while the evangelist's appearance before the California legislature in 1971 was another. Graham's ties to philanthropists at Criswell's church and contacts with the National Association of Evangelicals surely gave Reagan extra reason to take pleasure in this friendship. Both supplied clout (and funding possibilities) with a powerful religious constituency.[17]

Reagan welcomed counsel from evangelical statesman like Boone and Graham, but he was determined to keep harder-driving religious activists—those who had helped cast a darker light on Goldwater—at a healthy distance. Their work in the trenches was invaluable, and Reagan would never lose sight of this, but a clearer partitioning of power was in order. Most evangelical citizens welcomed Reagan's measures. Goldwater conservatism had been close to gospel truth for many of them, and when it failed, these constituents were left with tough questions: Had they become too caught up in the excitement of Goldwater's movement? What was the Christian's proper role in politics? There were many subtleties of thought on these matters, yet most agreed about one thing: the no-holds-barred campaign of 1964 had given fundamentalists like Billy James Hargis and Carl McIntire far too much leeway, and allowed them to pervert politics with intemperate religion and pervert Christianity with self-serving politics.[18]

This was the prevailing opinion that emerged in Southern California's evangelical community during the mid-1960s, and it led to a permanent split. Prior to 1960, a relatively uniform excitement with church growth and the presence of a powerful Left opposition had helped brush over some of the internal tensions that were beginning to divide evangelicals elsewhere along fundamentalist-moderate lines. Billy Graham's much-publicized evangelistic meetings in New York City in 1957, for instance, had led McIntire's allies to denounce the evangelist's inclusive style. The schism was precipitated by Graham's willingness to work with the Protestant Council of the City of New York, an agency that included churches affiliated with the National Council of Churches. By linking himself to the NCC, fundamentalists charged, Graham was linking himself to apostasy. Through McIntire's West Coast connections, these accusations registered with Southern California evangelicals, but they did not resonate fully until Graham's Los Angeles revival, six years later, in 1963. Welcomed to the City of Angeles by his fellow Southern Baptists and hailed by most evangelicals as a tremendous boost to their Christian witness, Graham was nevertheless boycotted by hard-liners for recruiting liberal churches and allegedly preaching a watered-down gospel.[19]

The 1964 election accentuated this emerging divide in Southern California evangelicalism and forced southern pastors and parishioners to pick sides. J. Vernon McGee chose Graham and as a result became a lightning rod of controversy. After he played a leading role in the 1963 Los Angeles crusade, fundamentalists like Archer Weniger, who sided with McIntire, wrote McGee off as a traitor to the tribe. In the fallout from this controversy, McGee helped reify new divisions within evangelicalism by publicly delineating a few new categories of conservatives. First, there were the "fighting fundamentalists"—the McIntires and Wenigers. "They spend their time telling every other Christian group what is wrong with them. . . . They are without sin, for they cast the first and last stone at others." Then there were the "reforming fundamentalists," men (though he did not name names) like McBirnie: "They have the flag in one hand and a Bible in the other. They wave the flag more than they teach the Bible. They believe that if certain reforms are made in the country, a revival will come. This group is to be commended for their zeal, but it is zeal without knowledge." McGee's third category comprised the "old-fashioned" evangelicals in Billy Graham's camp who accepted the fundamentals of the faith and focused on saving people with them, while also redeeming the culture around them. "I belong to this group," McGee concluded.[20]

Though meant to explain theological divisions, McGee's typology essentially outlined the new political demarcations in Southern California evangelicalism. Those identifying with the "old-fashioned" majority sanctioned the responsible conservatism endorsed by Graham and Reagan. They believed that evangelicals—like conservatives generally—needed to trim the excess within their community, abide by Reagan's Eleventh Commandment, and focus on constructive solutions to America's political needs. Moreover, they contended that politics had "to be used gingerly," as an accessory to—not the focus of—the church's influence. Evangelicalism could only alter the political realm if it reached individuals with the gospel first—and after that, if it played by the rules of democratic engagement and political decency.[21]

The "fighting fundamentalists" held on to the independent spirit they had loved about Goldwater. They were ideologues first and party members second, and never willing to compromise that point. Whereas the new evangelicals in Graham's camp saw their task as one of delicately engaging politics and culture, hard-core fundamentalists saw theirs as one of soundly denouncing politics and culture. Within California conservatism, Weniger best represented this anti-establishment stance. When writing in the 1970s to a potential *Blu-Print* subscriber, he outlined the position his allies first assumed in the wake of the Goldwater purge.

> This is . . . a militant Fundamentalist paper, which takes the Separatist position from all forms of apostasy, unbelief, heresy and inclusiveness. We deal strictly in controversial material, which some people are not constructed to take. We have no interest in convincing our enemies, but simply confirming our friends. . . . We would like to know precisely how you found out about this paper, why you want it, and if you take the same position we do. If these questions offend you, then you'll be offended by the Blu-Print.

Weniger's harsh response reflected, on one hand, the paranoia of having his magazine used by the opposition and, on the other, the satisfaction of being sequestered with a small cadre of zealots duty bound to protect the purity of the church and conservative principles.[22]

A much larger group of "reforming fundamentalists," many of them former allies of Weniger's, began taking a slightly different tack. They, too, had been scarred by the Goldwater defeat, yet they were not content to propagate Weniger's implacable politics or separate themselves completely from McGee and Reagan's center. Henceforth this loose body of activists—drawn principally from Baptist, but also Pentecostal and other church circles—would assist Reagan's Right in extrapartisan ways, mainly through single-issue campaigns at the precinct level. These activists would construct a web of citizens' action groups operating outside formal party and church lines. Using lessons from the Goldwater campaign, and drawing on their media expertise in radio, direct mail, and canvassing, these organizations would emerge alongside other interest groups as the Republican Right's most potent weapons of advocacy.

W. S. McBirnie's resourcefulness during Reagan's first term suggested just how powerful reforming fundamentalists would become. By the time Reagan inaugurated his administration, McBirnie was operating in the shadows again, cordoned off from GOP headquarters. Seemingly satisfied with this arrangement, the pastor erected a volunteer organization of activists, which, under the auspices of Voice of Americanism (VOA), began publishing and mass-distributing hundreds of thousands of pocket-sized books on every imaginable subject. Meanwhile, McBirnie supplemented VOA with his California Graduate School of Theology and the Center for American Research and Education. The latter specialized in seminars conducted by the nation's leading conservative thinkers. Excited by this institute's potential, McBirnie boasted that it would soon become for the Right what the Center for the Study of Democratic Institutions at the University of California, Santa Barbara (UCSB), was to the Left. He was just as excited about his seminary, built to prepare "pastors to be both professionally competent and perceptive about the dangers confronting their churches and their country." Overseeing McBirnie's ventures were the same pastors that served at his United Community Church (UCC). McBirnie's assistants were Don Sills and Robert Grant, the former a Baptist trained in BBF circles, the latter a Wheaton College graduate like Billy Graham. This team turned UCC's campus into a hub of political piety. As a hint of what they planned for the coming years, they assembled several guides for the 1968 election. One was called *The Bible and National Affairs*, which provided readers with biblical "proof texts" for 230 different political issues. A second was *Dr. McBirnie's Election Guide*, which appraised "all the major candidates, issues and implications" at the presidential and congressional levels. "We are packing into it all the information gained from our personal interviews and correspondence with candidates," McBirnie proudly stated. "We are now in a very crucial hour, and all we do is done for the good of America, the glory of God, and the saving of our precious freedoms." McBirnie lauded nonpartisanship and credited a few Independent candidates for serving these divine aims, but he also made it clear that, as a party, only the GOP fully embodied them.[23]

FORGING A COLOR-BLIND GOSPEL

The construction of a responsible Right also depended upon conservatives' willingness to deal with race. After seeing Goldwater's struggles with his states' rights platform, it became clear to GOP strategists that they needed to craft a "color-blind" doctrine. Whereas in his first test with extremism southern evangelicals had caused some of Reagan's headaches, in this second test they provided him with invaluable support.

This color-blind doctrine was tied together by a weave of political calculations and genuine sentiments for change. Attached to a broader strategy by the GOP to win the South and the nation's Silent Majority, the race-neutral ideology offered a softer social plank without entertaining the race-baiting of throwback candidates like George Wallace. Reagan and other Republican proponents of color-blind conservatism, in sum, asserted that the heaviest work of race reform had already been completed by federal civil rights legislation, leaving the last remnants of racial discrimination to be cleaned up by citizens through interpersonal exchange and the workings of a meritocratic capitalist system free of government control. The final steps toward a postracial era, they believed, could be taken without further reparative action through the courts and legislation or social programs; in fact, race would become irrelevant only when liberals managing these spheres stopped foisting it onto the public consciousness.[24]

Liberal Democrats, of course, attacked this line of reasoning. To them, color blindness was indeed an improvement over the blatant bigotries of an earlier era, but by decreeing racism dead, it absolved white suburbanites of lingering guilt, when in fact prejudice remained entrenched in profoundly skewed economic structures and rationale. The end of racist talk and attitudes, Reagan's detractors thundered, did not presage the end of racially exclusive suburban landscapes. In many ways, it allowed racial signifiers to become lodged in subtler yet more powerfully negative economic descriptors—like "blight," "crime," and "welfare"—where they were harder to pry out. Democratic leaders like Jesse Unruh acted out this frustration when charging that Reagan was a "more attractive" George Wallace whose political program for race reform did not have any teeth, let alone substantive reasoning behind it. Yet like Pat Brown's earlier condemnations, Unruh's charges never stuck. The governor's affable personality and disarming tone enabled him to paint color blindness only as healthy progress.[25]

Reagan's creative conservatism thus advertised a society liberated equally from Jim Crow reactionaries, who emphasized race to salvage a dying order, and civil rights advocates, who emphasized it to solicit government reforms. His administration stayed close to this theme. As governor, Reagan commissioned a 1968 report on human relations, "the first in a series of creative studies on some of the greater issues of our day and our state." "We know that our . . . community is disrupted by strife," Reagan emphasized. "Government has been attacking the evils of discrimination for years. But the false promises of too many politicians have smashed the hopes of too many of our people." In order to close the "expectation gap," Reagan promised to bypass a cumbersome bureaucracy and apply a new spirit of interpersonal relations. Toward this end he toured the state to meet with leaders of ethnic and racial groups, appointed the "first Negro to head a major state department" and "75 Negroes, Mexican-Americans, Orientals and other minority members . . . to boards, commissions and executive positions," and advanced bills "dealing with the problems of low-income citizens." He also created the California Job Training and Placement Council for the inner city. Each of Reagan's undertakings reflected his belief in three "forces" for solving the problem of human relations—"the great and growing middle class," the "dynamic and productive enterprise system," and "creative government." Another Republican report, filed later in his governorship, boasted that Reagan's emphasis on cooperative engagement by the private and public sectors had allowed him to make the GOP the party of "color-blindness." By trying to "build on points of similarity rather than on points of difference," the GOP represented the party of racial progress.[26]

From the outset of his 1966 campaign, California's southern evangelicals believed that Reagan did indeed represent a positive, postracial social order. Initially they found the concept of a color-blind society somewhat difficult to grasp, however. For over a decade, a majority of them had lived relatively isolated lives in suburbia, set apart from the metropolitan complex and its simmering racial tensions by the subtle workings of political economy. Notions of a normative, white Christian Americanism certainly motivated the political campaigns they undertook in the 1950s and early 1960s to protect their suburban utopias, but this was not a motivation to which most of them ascribed explicit racial meaning. It was not until Watts that southern evangelicals were forced to confront their perceived racial innocence. The range of their responses made clear that the new postracial conservatism Republican leaders envisioned would not be realized so easily.

George Wallace exploited this uncertainty when he toured the region in 1968 for his third-party candidacy. While making his way through Los Angeles County, speaking at some of the same shopping malls Reagan had visited during his 1966 gubernatorial campaign, the Alabaman filtered anxieties about neighborhood preservation and taxation into a rhetoric saturated with racist innuendos. Wallace channeled this influence through church circles. Alvin Mayall, a Baptist pastor from Bakersfield, and William K. Shearer, director of the Proposition 14 campaign with ties to right-wing preachers, helped orchestrate Wallace's California campaign, while BBF pastors also lent crucial support. Reagan remained his first choice, but Bob Wells voiced support for Wallace in his Anaheim church, illustrating the latter's appeal to some hard-shell evangelicals. During the mid-1960s, the fast-growing Central Baptist Church shifted further to the right, becoming a bastion of anti–Billy Graham fundamentalism. Correspondingly, it also assumed a hard-line stand on race. In the month after Watts, Wells, for example, delivered a sermon titled "L.A. Riots—Who is to Blame?" The sermon excoriated civil rights leaders for calling the racial problem a "white problem." "Are we who are white to sit back and let the negro make such false accusations? Are we to remain quiet in view of such character assassination?" Wells asked. In a subsequent sermon he admitted that the "Sins of the White Man" had contributed to racial discord, but this concession was nowhere to be found in the pages of the *Voice of Truth and Freedom*, one of several new media ventures Central started in the mid-1960s. In its pages, editor Larry Asman's racial conservatism eclipsed even Wells's own. One of Asman's most pointed editorials after the Watts riots was titled "An Interview with

Abraham Lincoln." This four-page dialogue with America's "spotless apostle of human liberty" was meant to demonstrate the relevancy of Lincoln's racial thought. Social Democrats may have claimed the emancipator as one of their own, but Asman wanted people to remember that Lincoln was also the proponent of free land, free labor, and racial exclusion. Using quotes lifted from the president's speeches, Asman argued that segregation was constitutional and reflected a natural order sanctified by God and the nation's founding fathers.[27]

Public proclamations like these led outsiders to assume that Central's pews were full of racist rage. Writing in the fall of 1966, one *Newsweek* reporter wrote:

Many Orange Countians are natural conservatives: former Southerners, skilled workmen, technicians in the new industries earning well above the average family income. And there is a large backlash population for whom one of Orange County's major attractions is its small (12,000) Negro minority. Moreover, the most outspoken local church—the fundamentalist Central Baptist Church of Anaheim—is on the right-wing team, with . . . Rev. Bob Wells . . . experienced . . . at imparting a segregationist flavor to a sermon.

Wells likely dismissed such articles as proof of a slanted media, but for rank-and-file church members, these broad strokes painted over a more ambivalent racial consciousness. Many likely applauded Wells for taking a firm stand against civil rights leaders who, in their minds, seemed influenced by communist thinking. And chances are that no congregants were disturbed by the racial homogeneity of their churches, since this was the national norm in American Protestantism. But some of Wells's parishioners, like Jean and Eleanor Vandruff, were also independent thinkers. While attending the church for its strong preaching and educational programming, they were also open to wider-ranging viewpoints. Eleanor even defied her pastor by supporting Billy Graham's ministry and its centrist stand on faith, culture, and politics.[28]

Like Central, Southern Baptist churches also spent the post-Watts period sifting their racial politics. SBC district leaders used their church paper to categorically denounce Wallace's style and reassure outsiders that racism was "not an issue [with] California Southern Baptists." California's SBC churches, they said, were "welcoming people of all races" and demonstrating "complete readiness to receive into their number any person without regard to race or national origin." Despite these confident (and overstated) declarations of inclusiveness, Southern Baptists faced the post-Watts years wrestling with their racial views. Consensus was no sure thing. The top echelon of SBC leadership in California followed the lead of the SBC's national social agency, the Christian Life Commission, by issuing pro–civil rights decrees at annual meetings and, through the pages of the *California Southern Baptist*, outright condemning segregation as an "offense to the gospel" and "a sin against God" and calling on SBC institutions to integrate. California Southern Baptists also took notice of the turnabout on race by W. A. Criswell, who, by virtue of his presidency of the SBC and his pastorate at the denomination's largest church, served as a bellwether for change. At the onset of civil rights backlash in the 1950s, Criswell had stood before South Carolina legislators to blast the *Brown v. Board of Education* ruling and the "bunch of infidels" who had concocted it. Twelve years later he owned up to his "colossal mistake" and admitted that his segregationist rant was the product of an unintelligent reading of scripture and a callousness to pervasive inequalities. Citizens who read the *California Southern Baptist* and respected Criswell seemed ready to make this same about-face in their own personal and communal lives on the West Coast.[29]

Yet racial politics was often more complicated at the grassroots level, where darkening financial trends helped exacerbate tensions. In Los Angeles' blue-collar suburbs particularly, where SBC churches had first been built, there was a sense that once-vibrant communities were unraveling because of combined economic and racial factors. During the rush to build new homes and churches during the late 1950s, Southern Baptists had failed to anticipate the flip side of their free enterprise heaven: inflation. After 1965, amid rising racial hostilities, dramatic increases in property values raised mortgage and taxation stresses, creating income gaps, which citizens and their churches found difficult to bear. In 1968 California's Southern Baptist treasurers reported that 672 of the 847 churches in their fold were mired in debt totaling $35,472,262 statewide. One-third of SBC churches in California shouldered debt that was more than three times their annual receipts. Residents who attended these churches faced household challenges of their own and a real estate market made tenuous by social upheaval. Growing crime rates, together with these personal and congregational anxieties, made the raw politicking against minorities and liberal elites by anti-tax, anti-establishment candidates like Wallace and Samuel Yorty appealing to some of SBC's rank and file.[30]

By and large, Southern California's Southern Baptists did not, however, find solace in the platitudes of preachers or politicians who harkened back to Jim Crow. Rather, they followed the lead of Billy Graham, who, like Reagan, endorsed a color-blind conservatism that stemmed from his trust in individualism and doubts about the efficacy of government programs. His confidence in this philosophy remained unwavering, even after touring Watts in August 1965. During his visit to South Central Los Angeles, Graham walked and talked with local pastors in order to gain a deeper sense of the problems facing their parishioners. At one point he was decked out in a bulletproof vest and allowed to see the damage to South Central from the bird's-eye view of a helicopter. The experience left the usually temperate evangelist angry at the total disregard for authority, worried about "sinister forces" at work in the nation, and convinced that a "great racial revolution" was just begun. In much the same way Reagan could tease out the racially inflected message of law-and-order politics without ever speaking in its harshest tones, Graham used the Watts encounter to express his displeasure with a radicalized civil rights movement and a welfare state that had helped create these circumstances. Torn by competing emotions, Graham nevertheless insisted that "God is color-blind" and that racial injustice was at root a personal sin best solved by spiritual regeneration.[31]

This message made perfect sense to California Southern Baptists, who always saw evangelistic pleas to the heart as the best antidote for any social ill, and between 1965 and 1968 they began putting it into practice. During this period they desegregated their pews, built interracial "mission churches," and held Race Relations Sundays to connect with their black brethren in the National Baptist Convention (NBC), the century-old black Baptist denomination that mirrored the SBC in cultural influence across the South. On these special occasions white SBC clerics and black pastors affiliated with the NBC exchanged pulpits, while congregants together heard sermons on the evils of discrimination. "Through such efforts," coordinator Jack O'Neal explained, "our social ills [can] be remedied because spiritual relations will have become operative." White churches, like First Southern in Pasadena, followed O'Neal's lead by

accepting the entire memberships of nonwhite mission churches and bap-
tizing them into full fellowship. SBC delegates attending state conventions now pledged support for interracial programs, while at home they
received through their church paper a continuous flow of updates on
national progressions in racial exchange.[32]

All of these initiatives gave white Southern Baptists a sense of progress that betrayed inherent shortsightedness in their thinking. Although
not wanting to sound off against Billy Graham's color-blind doctrine with
the same cynicism leveled from the radical Left, a few prominent voices
within the black evangelical community were willing to expose weak-
nesses in this ideology. Even Tom Skinner, a black evangelist who once
traveled with Graham's team, cautioned white evangelicals against thinking too optimistically about their race reforms. "We are facing an explosive situation in this country," he would say, "and my black brothers are
not kidding when they say that if they don't get justice America will burn."
Watts was merely a symptom of much deeper problems in American society and a forewarning of more serious problems yet to come if evangelical
citizens did not help champion a more aggressive, social-justice solution
to the urban crisis. Race Relations Sundays and pulpit exchanges between
white and black churches were a healthy start, he agreed. And he did not
undermine Graham's teaching that personal denunciation of racism was
the basis upon which race reform could take place. But at the same time,
he had little patience for the way Graham and O'Neal's perspective—
shaped in suburban outposts or by intermittent glimpses of urban carnage
from above—glanced over an endemic crisis. Racism was a sin, Skinner
agreed, but one that was not easily purged by prayer, personal interaction,
right thinking, or a rosy outlook.[33]

Regardless of the sobering advice, white Southern Baptists were revivi-
fied by their efforts to heal racial wounds, so much so that they glowingly
measured their own work against the federal government. In April 1968
the *California Southern Baptist* declared, in an editorial on the Kerner
Commission's investigation of civil disorder, that it was time for white
evangelicals to own up to their role in the violence that had rocked their
cities, and to promote and practice race renewal. "Our churches can help
in the current racial dilemma. . . . We can supply the one thing most
needed—the one thing that government programs cannot supply at any
cost. We can supply the ingredients of love, compassion and understanding." Such was the essence of the color-blind gospel. To its critics, these

words may have sounded simplistic and even patronizing, but to those who uttered them they were heartfelt and empowering, and not just for white people.[34]

FORGING INTERRACIAL TIES

In important ways, the chimera of racial innocence forged in 1950s suburbia gave California's southern evangelicals something to hang their hopes on. The crisis of Watts, in their eyes, was sudden and violent, but also short, suggesting to them that they could emerge from the discord as rapidly as they entered it. And in their minds they were, after all, not Mississippian or Alabaman, trapped still in Jim Crow's grasp, but Texan or Oklahoman and now also Southern Californian, people eager to construct forward-looking solutions. Already leading examples of church growth, Christian patriotism, and community values, they took it upon themselves now to become a national inspiration for interracial harmony. As difficult a time as it was, in the months surrounding Watts, Southern California's southern evangelicals were confident that by purging racist thoughts they could shatter barriers of racial privilege and make their lifestyle available to everyone who worked hard enough to attain it. This meritocratic gospel received a boost from unprecedented Pentecostal happenings in Los Angeles' middle-class defense communities.

In 1960, seventy members of St. Mark's Episcopal Parish, a church of 2,600 in Van Nuys, claimed to have received "the baptism of the Holy Spirit," a supernatural encounter the likes of which they said replicated events described in the Book of Acts affecting Christ's followers during "Pentecost": "Suddenly a sound like the blowing of a violent wind came from heaven and filled the whole house where they were sitting. All of them were filled with the Holy Spirit and began to speak in other tongues as the Spirit enabled them." This outpouring of New Testament fervor would not have been so surprising had it taken place in an Assemblies of God church, but the fact that it purportedly occurred in a predominantly liberal denomination generated extra attention. *Time* magazine noted, with some playfulness, "glossolalia [speaking in tongues] seems to be on its way back in the U.S. churches—not only in the uninhibited Pentecostal sects, but even among Episcopalians, who have been called 'God's frozen people.'" Episcopalian authorities were not amused. Although St. Mark's rector Dennis Bennett encouraged glossolalia and other charismatic activities like divine healing, California Bishop James Pike, who saw the practices as theologically improper and culturally immodest, demanded they cease. Despite Pike's censure, St. Mark's continued to serve as a breeding ground for what became known as Neo-Pentecostalism, or the charismatic movement. Its facilitation of the Blessed Trinity Society and the magazine *Trinity* in fact placed it at the center of a revival that rapidly spread throughout the entire Anglo-Protestant world.[35]

Though international in scope virtually at its birth, Neo-Pentecostalism flourished first as a local phenomenon in Southern California. Like Jean Stone, the wife of a Lockheed executive and founder of the Trinity Society at St. Mark's, those who provided lay leadership in this movement came from the region's middle- and upper-middle-classes. Often they were business people with prior involvement in parachurch organizations like Demos Shakarian's Full Gospel Business Men's Fellowship International, one of the most important progenitors of the 1960s charismatic revival. Surprising observers, this contemporary religious awakening began to infiltrate other well-established churches, including Donn Moomaw and Ronald Reagan's Bel Air Presbyterian Church, and its counterpart, Hollywood First Presbyterian. In 1964 the Hollywood congregation claimed to have six hundred "speakers in tongues."[36]

One of the most important converts to Neo-Pentecostalism was Pat Boone, who was counseled into a charismatic experience by his wife, Shirley, and George Otis, general manager of Lear Jet Corporation and a middle-aged millionaire. After converting to Neo-Pentecostal teachings, Otis started High Adventure Ministries in Van Nuys and began sharing his "testimony to the power of God and the adventure of jet-age Christian life," which Boone found compelling. Following their own spiritual awakening, Boone and his family turned their home into a makeshift church. Friends and fellow celebrities were welcomed there to learn about the Bible's supernatural teachings and their application in the modern world; if the opportunity arose, they were baptized in the family pool. These activities excited the Boones but did not sit well with the Church of Christ, still their denominational home, which saw the charismatic gospel as out of line with its core theology. In 1969, church elders "dis-fellowshipped" them, leaving more than a few people angry. "By such disciplinary action," one preacher vented, "the denomination may have anathemized [sic] one of conservative Christianity's most widespread thrusts in Hollywood history." Crushed by this decision, the Boones transferred to Church on the

Way, an assembly of the International Foursquare Gospel, and continued proselytizing for their new faith.[37]

Besides their entrepreneurialism and embrace of experiential faith, lay leaders in the Neo-Pentecostal movement were also actively conservative in their theology and politics. As Boone liked to say when disarming doubters, charismatic Christians were "literal not liberal." They believed that the supernatural gifts of tongues, prophecy, and healing Jesus bestowed on the first Christians were still available to contemporary Christians as a witness to Christ's presence in modern times. Radical for the way it at once spurned denominationalism and went against Protestant convention (which said that New Testament manifestations of the Holy Spirit had ceased) Neo-Pentecostalism was nevertheless quintessentially orthodox. It affirmed the authority of the individual and the local community and promoted an innovative, intense dissemination of this gospel. It also assisted the repackaging of GOP politics. The people who joined the Blessed Trinity Society were Republican. And they were political advocates who believed that personal and social morality were inextricably linked—that the outpouring of the Holy Spirit on one's personal life compelled the individual to hasten its outpouring in every realm of society. But for a difference of opinion on a relatively minor theological point, charismatics were "reforming fundamentalists" in every other regard. In fact, when explaining his typology of California evangelicalism, J. Vernon McGee reserved a final category for "charismatic fundamentalists." "They too have a Bible in one hand," he explained rather impatiently of their outlook, "but experience in the other. You need a miracle or an experience, and if you missed out on one or the other, you simply missed out. There are some rather ridiculous 'experiences' happening these days." However "ridiculous" some evangelicals thought the charismatic experience to be, there was no denying that the Neo-Pentecostal movement was a gathering cultural and political force that promised to shape the Republican Right.[38]

As it emerged in the late 1960s, Neo-Pentecostalism extracted much of its energy from pastors with southern roots. This should not have been too surprising. It was in Los Angeles earlier in the century, after all, that the Azusa Street revivals, interracial gatherings led by southern preachers, prompted the first wave of Pentecostalism. One pastor who did much to promote this second wave of Pentecostalism was Ralph Wilkerson. Wilkerson came to Southern California from small-town Oklahoma. In the early 1960s the Assemblies of God preacher started the Christian Center Church in his own home in Anaheim. Shortly thereafter, Christian Center moved into a conventional structure and began growing at an unconventional pace because of its receptiveness to the charismatic revival. Wilkerson was invested in the Neo-Pentecostal movement from the beginning, but in 1966 he assumed a more critical role with the disbanding of the Blessed Trinity Society and the end of Jean Stone's leadership. The Oklahoman was a perceptive publicist and he seized this opportunity to turn his church into the new St. Mark's and the next worldwide organizational center for Neo-Pentecostalism. In 1967 Wilkerson's congregation began hosting annual charismatic clinics; eight hundred participants attended the first installment. Then, in 1969, Wilkerson again took advantage of another institution's struggles to help his own church prosper. Directly across the street from Disneyland stood the Melodyland Theater. The 3,200-seat circular auditorium, which opened in 1963, had hosted some of America's famous performers, from Jack Benny to Ray Charles, Sonny and Cher to the Grateful Dead. A clash of cultures with family-friendly Disneyland contributed to the riskier Melodyland's demise, and in 1969 its owners placed the property on auction. Wilkerson purchased the building, kept the name Melodyland, and began constructing a religious home for a responsible, color-blind, Republican Right.[39]

He did not set out to build a political operation of the kind functioning at Bob Wells's church just a few blocks away, but the size of his congregation and the cultural exchange that went on inside its plush auditorium had a political impact. Unlike Wells, whose Baptist mind judged scripture and the world in rigid terms, Wilkerson's Pentecostal mentality transcended strict categories. As such, it was better suited to the race-neutral conservatism of Reagan's era. Melodyland's pastor took the words of Neo-Pentecostal theologian Michael Harper seriously, in calling Holy Spirit–led Christians to be "concerned about justice, public morality, and the plight of the under-nourished" as well as committed to "destroying racial barriers, and reconciling deeply entrenched prejudices." Working under this mandate, Melodyland invited black and Mexican American leaders to participate in its charismatic seminars, created social programs for drug addicts, and invested heavily in various urban ministries. All the while, during regular Sunday services a racially mixed crowd drawn from lower- and middle-class backgrounds was led in worship by black musicians like Andraé Crouch and guest pastors from Los Angeles' black churches, like Fredrick

Price. The songs and sermons these artists delivered came wrapped in a theology that stressed each individual's access to the supernatural workings of the Holy Spirit, an extraordinary release from sin through personal salvation, the miraculous blessings of healing and redemption, and the promise of health and wealth to any who faithfully trusted God, regardless of skin color or class. Wilkerson's answer to Watts was Billy Graham's, only with more daring utopian aspirations and an added bit of flare.[40]

CONSERVATISM'S GREAT BLACK HOPE

One of Melodyland's frequent guests was a black preacher with charismatic sympathies, Reverend Edward V. (E. V.) Hill, of Mount Zion Missionary Baptist in Watts. Hill personified the color-blind gospel that white, middle-class suburban evangelicals spoke of, though he came to it from a very different, difficult life of Jim Crow segregation, racial discrimination, poverty, and urban violence.

The young Baptist minister was born in Columbus, Texas, in 1933, and raised in Sweet Home, thirty miles southwest of San Antonio. Left alone with four children, Hill's mother barely survived on $12.50 a week, and often was forced to rely on "leftovers from the white people's table"—her employer's kitchen scraps. "It was always a happy day when someone in that family was sick and didn't want to eat their steak," E. V. Hill would later recall. "Mother would take that steak . . . those leftover rolls and put them in a sack . . . chop it all up together and make hash." But those days were rare, and while still a young child Hill began to suffer from malnutrition. Aaron and Ella Langdon, an elderly black couple from the area, noticed his sorry condition and suggested to his mother that they raise him in the country, "where there was plenty." The plenty turned out to be a two-room log cabin and an abundance of "wild rabbit, squirrel, hickory nuts, and wild berries," a near-paradise for the young Hill. Despite the Langdons' limited resources, they treated the boy as their own son. Hill loved nothing more as a child than to sit with "Poppa," listening to the radio or reading his favorite stories. At the age of eleven, Poppa passed away, leaving his surrogate son and Momma to live on meager supplies but also, E. V. always noted, a surfeit of self-help.

In those days there was no check on the first and fifteenth, there were no social workers, and the only charities we ever got were apples, oranges, jelly, sugar, and cheese. But no checks. Momma and I had to pick cotton during the summer, and shake peanuts and pull corn. Sometimes we'd kill a hog and put it in the smokehouse, and get some syrup. That's how we lived in those days.

At Momma's urging Hill also learned how to live on faith. The same year Poppa died, Hill experienced the religious conversion Ella Langdon had been praying for. "This great big old God . . . came and entered my heart and saved me. . . . A little old country boy, a little old semi-orphan boy with nothing but a two-room log cabin to live in, insignificant to everybody who saw him."[41]

When Hill was fourteen, Langdon declared to her congregation that he was going to finish high school. At that time, young black men in the community rarely advanced past the tenth grade; work on a white man's farm for two dollars a day was the highest ambition, and the most useful course for family and community. Hill graduated, and Langdon took him to the bus station, gave him five dollars, said she would be praying for him, waved good-bye, and sent him off to Prairie View College. Hill had won a four-year scholarship to the school meant to assist his completion of a Bachelor of Science degree in agriculture. But farming was not his future. Instead, he began working his way into ministry within the National Baptist Convention. In 1955, the same year he married his college sweetheart, he moved to Houston to take over the pulpit at Mount Corinth Missionary Baptist Church. Although only twenty-one, Hill's preaching sparkled with potential, and he demonstrated considerable political acumen. During the late 1950s he served as a member of both the National Association for the Advancement of Colored People and the Negro Chamber of Commerce, and was appointed to the executive board of Martin Luther King Jr.'s Southern Christian Leadership Conference (SCLC). He also pursued political office, becoming the first black candidate to win a primary in the race for Houston's City Council. For his efforts Hill garnered respect within the local Democratic Party, and was the target of death threats from the Ku Klux Klan.[42]

In 1961 he was hired to be pastor of the struggling, financially strapped Mount Zion Missionary Baptist Church in South Central Los Angeles. Mount Zion had a rich history, dating from the previous century. By the time Hill arrived, however, only a dedicated few of its purported 581 members attended Sunday services; because of escalating tensions in the Watts community, policemen were needed to keep guard while worship took place, encouraging many parishioners simply to stay home. As church lore has it, at this time Mount Zion's "only assets were a small band of people who believed that if they held out, deliverance would come." The confident young preacher from Houston was their deliverer. Hill was a man "of a thousand voices," ranging from a "whisper to a raspy roar," and on any given Sunday he used a dozen of them to convey the gospel. At first his staid congregation did not know what to make of the display; elders kept silencing congregants who responded emotionally to Hill's preaching, until finally Hill himself asked these elders to stop: "How can I get a fire started when every log that starts burning, you drag it out?" The spiritual fire Hill started had material benefits as well. By 1964 the church's financial problems were on their way to resolution, its membership was steadily increasing, and congregants were celebrating completion of their once grand sanctuary's refurbishment.[43]

Around this time, Hill's politics underwent an overhaul. By his own admission, he was a "hellraiser" in Houston politics, a "very liberal Democrat." He was also unequivocal in his support of Martin Luther King Jr.'s civil rights initiatives, so much so that he nominated King for the SCLC's presidency. Shortly after his move to Los Angeles, however, Hill grew wary of Social Democrats and civil rights activists, both of whom he saw beginning to lean too far to the Left. His theology was critical to the switch. While growing up, Hill had internalized a redemptive message devoid of radical implications. Shaped by the Langdons' quiet perseverance, his country church's sense of collective strength, and an unassuming education, Hill's world was not King's world. His inherited outlook stressed personal salvation over political reconstruction and encouraged individuals to rely on bonds of community and diligent hard work. Hill was not oblivious to the social strife that faced him in Houston. "No one hated white people more than I did," he would later explain.

> I was born amidst hatred and discrimination. I saw all of the evils, and I grew up not only hating white people, but I hated them with what I felt was the sanction of the Holy Ghost. And I really can't even remember when I stopped hating white people. All I do know is that I don't anymore. Because I have a great love that has come through a miraculous birth in Christ.

In Houston, for a time, Hill's politics were fully in keeping with the SCLC's ambitious project of race reform. Yet he could not shake the doubts that the civil rights movement was looking for the answers in the wrong places—economics, politics, and government—and slowly drifting from the real solution: personal redemption nurtured in the confines of tightly bound, morally upright families, churches, and communities. By 1965 Hill had shed his commitments to the Democratic Party's liberal program of social reconstruction and had decided to fight economic and racial injustice in the same manner as did Billy Graham: one individual soul at a time.[44]

In making this decision, Hill chose a political path relatively unnoticed by the national media but nonetheless traveled by other black clergymen in the 1960s. He began following it shortly after the Watts riots. In August 1965, Mount Zion found itself at the heart of the chaos in South Central Los Angeles. The largest single fire during the riots burned just four blocks from the church. Hill naturally became a focal point for those seeking explanations for the crisis and suggestions for its long-term resolution. In response to queries from Washington, Hill listed a number of factors leading to the violent outbreak, none of which fit neatly with federal officials' theories of economic dislocation. In the first place, Johnson's Great Society had promised more than it could deliver, leaving South Central blacks with raised, unrealistic expectations about the prospects of aid and great disappointment when it did not materialize. Local people, on the other hand, had come to see rioting as a means of protest, and as a way to rebuild the community; "burn it down and start over" was something Hill said he heard often among his neighbors.[45]

Hill's critique of big government, wrong intentions, misplaced frustration, and social disorder surely struck liberal leaders as odd and out of sorts with their critique of urban violence, but it intrigued more than a few conservatives. One individual who seized on Hill's viewpoint was Mayor Sam Yorty. In the months after the riots, Yorty appointed Hill chairman of the Mayor's Committee on Economic Opportunities and then to the Los Angeles Housing Authority Commission. In the coming years Hill became one of Yorty's most enthusiastic backers. He touted the mayor's no-nonsense law-and-order politics and, citing his integration of city hall and the police and fire departments, promoted Yorty as "Mayor of all of the people." For Yorty, who had come under fire as a backlash politician, Hill was a godsend. Calling Hill one of his "ablest trouble-shooters" and identifying him as someone who had the ear of the people at street level, the mayor appreciated the pastor's contributions to his staff and coveted his leverage.[46]

This hearty endorsement placed Hill in a tenuous spot. From Social Democrats' point of view, Hill's actions were detrimental to the cause of black freedom. Hill first incurred their wrath in 1969, when he supported Yorty over the black moderate Tom Bradley in the mayoral race. For the remaining years of Yorty's administration, ending in 1973, Hill climbed into higher posts on the Housing Authority Commission, the Los Angeles City Fire Department Commission, and eventually the Los Angeles Planning Commission. With each new appointment came a new salvo of criticism from those who hated his politics. Reflecting on his relationship with the mayor just prior to Yorty's last year in office, Hill admitted that he had needed police protection from the local Black Panthers, Black Muslims, and other nationalist groups. He wore these threats with a sense of honor, as signs of his courage, but it was the criticism he received from law-abiding, Democratic loyalists that stung him. He wrote to the mayor,

> I think the Negro community has intentionally tried to discredit you. I
> have found a great deal of satisfaction being a part of your team in spite
> of the many kinds of persecutions that I have had to endure because of
> my faith in you.

As far as some were concerned, Hill was a traitor to his race. Even some black evangelicals like Tom Skinner found Hill's critique of the civil rights movement disgraceful and his "hearts and minds" approach to solving social problems detrimental to black social action. Drastic times required drastic solutions, they believed, and this meant consciously attaching a radical evangelical spirit of social justice to the goals of political reconstruction advocated by the Left.[47]

Charges that he had sold out his people upset Hill because he was no pushover. Mount Zion's pastor in fact had a powerful vision of local political action. While rising in government, Hill also built a thriving church community with social agencies that touched every need of the surrounding area. By earning the trust of government officials, Hill gained access to power and money, which he channeled toward social initiatives he thought more effective than federal programs. His ties to the Ford Foundation and the federal Office of Economic Opportunity (OEO)

were indicative of this approach. The Ford Foundation was invested heavily in the urban renewal programs of the Johnson administration, and it
is in this context that the philanthropic organization funneled $450,000
to the OEO for use in South Central Los Angeles. The OEO's plan was
to fund 1,400 students to complete job training in new skill sets. Under
Hill's direction the program became something different, a place where
young people could be counseled about "a change in hair-do . . . taking a
bath, [and] not being mad at the world." For Hill, community restructuring could not come through economic improvements alone; its residents
needed to internalize the ethics of self-help, self-discipline, and moral fortitude. Most importantly, they needed to be saved. "When I lived in the
segregated South," he would say, "there were a whole lot of privileges that
I did not have. There are some I have not enjoyed now. But I tell you the
greatest privilege to be enjoyed has been mine ever since I was eleven
years old. And that is that I've had the privilege of singing aloud, 'I'm a
child of the King!'"[48]

Out of these convictions, and by way of his political ties, Hill brought
to Mount Zion an authority that rivaled anything witnessed at Melodyland or Central Baptist in Anaheim. By the late 1960s Hill's church saw
street-level action of the most intense, evangelical kind. Supported by a
membership now over one thousand, Mount Zion administered a web of
agencies built in coordination with local government and other benevolent associations, an apartment complex called Mount Zion Towers, and
the Victory Teen Post, a center where young people were "brought off
the streets and given guided recreation, counseling, and tutoring." The
pride of Mount Zion's outreach was the World Christian Training Center. Its central purpose was to train "at least one person out of every
block in South Central Los Angeles" "in the faith of Jesus Christ, how
to share faith, and how to take their block for Christ." During the 1970s
the ministry would recruit over four thousand people, inspiring the SBC
and Campus Crusade for Christ to undertake similar ministries in other
American cities. Already in the late 1960s, however, Hill's work on this
scale was catching white evangelical leaders' attention. It was with Hill,
for instance, that Billy Graham consulted and toured during his visit to
Watts. The two became fast friends, and out of this relationship would
grow a plethora of other alliances with national implications.[49]

Graham and Hill's closeness notwithstanding, it was local Baptists
who developed the strongest ties with Mount Zion. In the middle of the

Watts riots, SBC reformer Jack O'Neal contacted Hill to see what help he could offer, to which Hill responded, "interpretation to the outside world" (he wanted it known that Watts was the work of "the lawless and ungodly" minority), food, clothing, and prayer. SBC members provided this and more. They entered into a formal arrangement with the NBC whereby church groups would help black churches rebuild and evangelize their neighborhoods. These indigenous initiatives soon dovetailed with a national program called US-2. Under the sponsorship of the SBC's Homeland Mission Youth Corps, US-2 commissioned college students to do two years of service in America's cities. It was, for all intents and purposes, the religious equivalent of President Johnson's Volunteers in Service to America (VISTA) program. "The government has planned every kind of activity for the Youth of the City," US-2 literature advertised, "but in all their planning they have forgotten one thing, JESUS CHRIST." In the summer of 1966 the first team of fifteen US-2 workers arrived in Watts, creating an integrated missions team to conduct daily "vacation Bible schools" and witnessing campaigns. Over the next few years, dozens of other students followed the same path, from Oklahoma and Texas to Los Angeles' metropolitan core. They came from all-white churches to worship in all-black congregations and work for a unifying gospel that knew no color. Such, at least, was the message they imparted to the people on the streets of a ravaged community.[50]

THIS IS THE SAME LESSON that Graham, Hill, Boone, and Reagan conveyed to the citizens gathered in suburban Anaheim's Big A stadium for the Southern California Crusade in September of 1969. In a very real sense, Graham's rally was a post-Watts confirmation of postracial conservatism. Though he did not dwell on racial discord when giving his sermons, its political implications were everywhere—in the language he used to describe Southern California's "strip-city" landscape, and in the guests he chose to sit on stage. More than that, Graham's revival was a post-Goldwater confirmation of Reagan's conservatism. Like the governor, Graham championed the vision of a creative society, one in which racial gaps were bridged through changed attitudes, evangelical political activism was made respectable, and Christian virtues of personal initiative and community responsibility were lifted up as the answer to society's troubles.[51]

For transplanted southern evangelicals sitting in the Big A, Graham's appearance also came in the middle of transition in their political lives. During the past few years, they had begun to merge into the political center and had the ear of a key political leader. The ascent to insider status did not accord well with all southern evangelical transplants, especially the fighting fundamentalists. Their South and their Southern California remained Goldwater and Wallace's, but these were dying orders. For the willing majority of southern evangelicals, the time was now to begin melding their errand with a discourse of Southern California Republicanism, marked by principles of an earlier dispensation—free enterprise, anticommunism, and a limited state—but packaged in a new creative, inclusive conservatism. Whereas they had once considered themselves exceptional for being southern, they now began to consider themselves exceptional as Southern Californians.

Reagan himself helped frame their new mission. Wracked by violence and dissent, America was desperately waiting for a constructive answer, Reagan proclaimed, in his first published report on human relations. It was time that

> California take the lead in solving our racial problems and that here we begin in the new agenda which will strengthen our entire society. We must show the world that a free nation can cope with the pressing problems of modern life, and that a free society—with its variety, flexibility, and spontaneity, and its willingness to experiment—can cope with them much more effectively than any other system.

Reagan's document came adorned with colorful pictures of smiling, socializing, active white and nonwhite young people and direct references to evangelical youth organizations like Campus Crusade for Christ. The young patriots in these photos and ministries had neither the time nor the predilection for campus protests and the counterculture, the booklet suggested. They were the type of young people who witnessed for Christ on Watts's streets; they were "Jesus people" who frequented Melodyland and evangelized California's beaches. And they were responsible, young conservatives who studied at Pepperdine College.[52]

11

JESUS PEOPLE

The revolution of hate, drugs, and violence has at least for the moment taken a back seat to a spiritual movement built around the teachings and personality of Jesus. I have observed his strange power at work on college campuses. . . . I have seen joy come to the lives of young men and women who have found something more significant to do than take pot or go to bed. Call it what you will, Jesus has something! It is not possible to find anything more empirical than the exclamation of thousands of students who are saying simply and humbly, "Once I was blind; now I see!"[1]

—William Banowsky

On a quiet evening in the spring of 1969, just as final preparations for Billy Graham's Anaheim revival were being made, a white security guard at Pepperdine College shot and killed a young black man. Larry Kimmons was part of a group of local teens who liked to play basketball at the college gymnasium; school officials usually allowed them the privilege, but on this day the building was occupied, so they asked the athletes to leave. What transpired next remained obscured by the emotions of the event, but the end result was a tussle between Kimmons and Charles Lane. Lane had a loaded shotgun in his hand, which went off, leaving Kimmons dead.[2]

An angry protest followed, setting the quiet campus on edge. In the weeks after Kimmons's death, a group of Pepperdine undergraduates belonging to the Black Student Association chained the doors of the administration building and staged a protest on the building's steps. With the school in lockdown mode, President Norvel Young turned to his closest advisor for help. William (Bill) Banowsky, the school's new vice president, responded by confronting the student protestors and promising them he would have police jail them if they did not cease and desist. The ultimatum diffused a hostile situation but did not solve a deepening problem. During the next few months the campus divided along racial lines, and administrators found it difficult to locate any support either from the school's white church community and donors or from its predominantly black neighbors in South Central. Banowsky received death threats from the Black Panthers, whose local headquarters was only eight blocks away. "Bad things will happen to you and your family," one handwritten note warned, if Pepperdine was not handed over to "black control." Banowsky's and Pepperdine's days, it declared, were numbered.[3]

In one sense, the school's days had been numbered since the Watts riots four years earlier. During the crisis in August of 1965, Pepperdine had been evacuated and its grounds taken over by the National Guard, which used the campus as a staging area for sorties into the riot zone. Once order had been restored, Pepperdine resumed operations, but with nagging doubts about what lay ahead. The campus itself had sustained minimal damage, thanks to the help of local community leaders—white and black—who promised to protect the school. But school confidence was shattered. How would the institution recruit faculty, students, and donors to a place condemned? Young recognized this trouble immediately. Even before the Watts violence had cooled, a prominent board member who lived in Dallas resigned. Young sensed there would be more back-turning from people in Tennessee and Texas who were already "suspicious and ready to believe the worst about California." And he was equally sure that parents in Pasadena and the Pacific Palisades would be even less excited to see their kids study in Los Angeles' inner city. Marking the end to a period of tenuous existence in the city, the Kimmons shooting thus forced a move that Young and his colleagues had been contemplating for four years: the opening of a new campus, far from the menacing streets of South Central—on the safe and enticing shores of Malibu.[4]

IN MAY 1970, JUST MONTHS after Pepperdine College's tragedy, the National Guard shot and killed four students at Kent State University, provoking Bill Banowsky to declare this period "the saddest semester in the history of American higher education." Though searing, the violence witnessed on Kent State's grounds was already a familiar sight in California. There had, in fact, been many "saddest semesters" in California's recent past, representing for the state's governor both a threat and a political opportunity. In the face of the violence, Ronald Reagan reacted with force, as if revolutionaries stirring up Berkeley and tatterdemalions squatting in San Francisco might overwhelm society at any moment. Behind the scenes, he used the crisis to recruit young people invested in his Creative Society and eager to fight back; conservatives, too, he seemed to say, would have their students shock the status quo.[5]

Southern California's evangelicals were primed to help. With the authority of an ever-expanding institutional base backing them up, they announced that it was time for a "moral backlash," one "that will take us back to a new respect for God and for his Word." Using a variety of tactics and underscoring a range of political emphases, they stepped up efforts to shield their youth by expanding their private educational system. Theirs was not just a defensive posture, though. Whereas earlier they feared for their young people's freedom in a society threatened by authoritarianism, in the late 1960s they celebrated their young people's sense of order in a climate of anarchy. More than that, they encouraged their children to bear witness to New Testament teachings and harness their enthusiasm to the conservative revolution. Their offspring performed admirably on both counts, though not always in a way that impressed the elders. During this critical moment, Christian young people transformed the faith of their fathers by adopting cutting-edge, countercultural forms created by the secular forces they sought to offset. Such willful adaptation to hippie ways did not always sit well with the older crowd, but the end result of this rebellion bettered even the stodgiest parent's expectations. By 1972 the creative conservatism evangelical young people helped forge emerged shiny with California exuberance, flush with California confidence, and ready to win the nation.[6]

"The Mess at Berkeley"

As anxious as Watts made them, the crisis in higher education set off louder alarm bells for evangelicals. The sight of long-haired youth clashing with police in Berkeley, conducting love-ins in San Francisco's city parks, and building hippie communities in Big Sur reminded them of how easily their own clean-cut kids could "turn on, tune in, and drop out." This realization came shrouded in cataclysmic political meaning. As evangelicals saw it, the long-standing liberalization of California had young people in a state of outright rebellion. But the same television nightly news that broadcast images of young malcontents also carried pictures of Ronald Reagan staring down disgruntled faculty and condemning the "mess at Berkeley." This was a leader who recognized the severity of the situation and deserved evangelicals' abiding support.[7]

Reagan's relationship with Berkeley and the sprawling system of higher education it symbolized was rocky from the very beginning. While campaigning for the governorship, Reagan spoke as the man who would squelch the academy's "spirit of permissiveness" and return traditional values to the college classroom. The Republican was always careful not to sound reactionary, like George Wallace, who, at the time, liked to issue blanket condemnations of all "pointy-headed intellectuals" and "briefcase totin' bureaucrats." Reagan, like most Californians, took pride in his state's world-class educational system and, practically speaking, did not want voters to think he was callously bashing it for political gain. But there was no doubt that he and left-wing students and liberal faculty had very different ideas about how it should be run. Their face-off began in October 1965, when Reagan censured anti–Vietnam War marchers and chastised authorities for not stopping them. Then, as the campaign heated up in 1966, at the site of Barry Goldwater's "Extremism is no vice" speech, he delivered a fiery sermon about Berkeley that rivaled Goldwater's in political effect. In front of a giant American flag, he told an electrified crowd that the "small minority of beatniks, radicals and filthy speech advocates" had "brought shame to a great University." Reagan blamed campus immorality on a "leadership gap in Sacramento" that had allowed a culture of "appeasement" to take root. It was time for "decisive action to restore the university to its once high standard."[8]

Reagan's dealings with Berkeley grew even more acrimonious after he became governor. Within his administration's first month, it had become obvious that cutbacks in the university budget were necessary. Reagan fired university chancellor Clark Kerr and called for a reduction in spending, which angered teachers, but it was the implementation of a tuition charge for resident students—the first ever—that lit the powder keg. "No tuition" became a rallying cry on campuses across the state. During one march, 7,500 students and professors—most from Berkeley—held signs adorned with caricatures of Reagan as a gangster that said "Tax the Rich" and sustained a steady chant, "We are people," while he tried to address them. Millions of Californians who watched a television replay of the rally saw only a demonstration of bad manners in the crowd and, on stage, a statesman who had more invested in "the people" than those who booed him. Even Jesse Unruh, the Democrat who stood on the protestors' side, admitted that rude antics by "the left-wing" were "really giving Reagan a lot of help." In May 1969, Reagan's clash with Berkeley peaked when students commandeered a patch of university-owned land scheduled for redevelopment and renamed it People's Park. After weeks of occupying the space, planting flowers and laying sod, the squatters found their makeshift paradise fenced off. Students took to the streets to protest, and a deadly riot ensued, involving thousands of demonstrators and the National Guard and resulting in seventeen days of martial law.[9]

By this point campus violence had spread, making Reagan's Berkeley mess multicentered. Across the Bay, at San Francisco State College, students in the Third World Liberation Front clashed with college president Samuel Hayakawa over the Vietnam War and their demands for the creation of an Ethnic Studies program. Meanwhile, farther south, public officials faced an even more perplexing situation. Considered by most to have a laid-back student body with few political hang-ups, the University of California, Santa Barbara, suffered an outburst in February 1970. Inspired by the speech of a popular civil rights attorney, who denounced the fascist tactics of a "capitalist establishment," UCSB undergraduates burned a Bank of America in nearby Isla Vista, a quaint seaside town. The following day Reagan arrived to survey the situation. After calling the demonstrators "cowardly little bums," he declared a state of emergency. In April, two months after the initial attack, during which militants continued to burn corporate establishments, student Kevin Patrick Moran was struck by a stray bullet from police officers while trying to extinguish (not start) a fire at a Taco Bell. No one could determine who killed Moran, but it mattered little. Reagan, at wits' end, offered Moran's father personal condolences, then told reporters, "The bullet was brought about . . . and sent on its way several years ago when a certain element in this society decided they could take the law into their own hands."[10]

At each step in the Reagan-Berkeley standoff, evangelicals applauded the politician's political counterpunches. Shouting the loudest praise were fundamentalists like Archer Weniger and Bob Wells, who proclaimed the governor's tactics justified and, if anything, too lenient. In the *Blu-Print*, Weniger alleged that California's schools were out of control because of radical, communist leaders and self-serving intellectuals who incited the spoiled rich kids. Worse yet, liberal clergymen were helping the intellectual elite. No one was more suspect, in Weniger's eyes, than Bishop James A. Pike. Pike first registered on Weniger's radar after becoming Episcopal Bishop of California in the late 1950s. In 1960 Pike began dropping theological "bombshells" that obliterated orthodox theories of the Trinity and the Virgin birth. Later, as his political stand for civil rights, gay rights, women's rights, and antiwar activism intensified alongside an outspoken personal embrace of the counterculture, Pike became devilish in the evangelical imagination. His status in their eyes as a false prophet for the Left was secured in 1967 when he left the episcopate and became an associate of the Center for the Study of Democratic Institutions at UCSB. Weniger dutifully tracked all of Pike's moves and used them to justify his vicious attack on secular higher education. He may have settled for Reagan's handling of "pointy-headed" types, but Weniger seemed wistful that the less patient, stronger-willed George Wallace could not have a crack at them.[11]

So did Wells. On Sundays Wells sustained a relentless assault on those he identified as culprits behind campus unrest. Few well-known figures in radical student politics were left out of his homiletics, but he kept special tabs on clergymen like Pike. When Pike's name surfaced in sermons, it was most often in the context of the antiwar movement, another topic that got Wells's blood boiling. As a patriot pastor of a church populated by defense workers and military personnel, he spoke with passion about the commitment of America's soldiers in Asia. More so than Weniger's, Wells's ruminations on campus politics were often joined to a larger countercampaign. The action that took place at Central Baptist in 1967 typified his approach. In early spring, Wells's congregational informants monitored California State College, Fullerton, where anti-Vietnam sit-ins were held. Wells published a full report of them in an issue of *Voice of Truth and Freedom*. Letters home from Bill Picking, a graduate of Heritage High School stationed with the U.S. Marines in Vietnam, were packaged with the Fullerton report in an editorial titled "Spirit of Antichrist—the 'Teach-In.'" The two pieces made a perfect foil. "Contrast the patriotism expressed in these heart-touching letters with the sickening disloyalty evidenced at the recent Fullerton 'Teach-In,'" Wells advised. Picking's testimonials were indeed heart-touching in the way they told of his hatred for war, the sin of killing, and the willingness to fight "if my God given rights are in danger." Picking also reported the good news that he had led "18 Marines" to the Christian faith. Wells used these contrasting images of America's youth to electrify his summer crisis crusades. In late August 1967 he closed the series with a sermon unambiguously titled "Hippies, Beatniks, Mini-Skirted Exhibitionists and Other Assorted Nuts and Crackpots!!!" Wells's swashbuckling style once again proved well timed, and thousands of people flocked to hear the sermon. Just as he had done during the disarmament standoff a few years earlier, Wells turned a controversy over national security into a parable for stronger families, stricter morality, and the need for citizens to accept Christ.[12]

DISCIPLINING THE YOUNG

Amid the clamorous politics playing out in Berkeley and Fullerton, evangelicals continued to harbor long-standing anxieties about adolescents, but with a heightened sense of crisis. As in the early 1960s, they still believed that communism had fearsome designs on their children's souls. Now, however, it seemed these designs were more easily transmitted through a subtler "secular humanist" philosophy that privileged the freedom of expression and gratification over moral virtue. The question that divided them was how to suppress this conspiring force. If evangelicals generally agreed with Reagan on his appraisal of the youth problem, they differed on the measures that Christians should take to address it. Were "hippies, beatniks, mini-skirted exhibitionists" to be excoriated or engaged with the gospel? Were evangelical young people to be protected from the "assorted nuts and crackpots" or allowed to test some of their innovative thinking? Separatists like Weniger embraced a fortress mentality and cordoned themselves off from the mainstream. As a result, they had little to offer Reagan's Christian coalition. On the other hand, "reforming fundamentalists" like Wells saw the youth problem as a reason to widen their political activities. Their formula—to build strong institutions in the private sector while lobbying for reform in the public—was not new, but in concert with a strengthening Reagan Right it acquired added power.

Evangelical private education entered a new phase of growth in the late 1960s and early 1970s, across the country but especially in Southern California. Elsewhere in the South, federal rulings forcibly desegregating public schools encouraged some parents to send their children to all-white

Christian institutions, beyond the government's reach. Racial considerations surely figured into the reasoning of Southern California evangelicals as well, but not as much as fears of a second wave of progressive
pedagogy. In the late 1960s they believed that John Dewey's methods had
taken education further afield into secular humanism. Having stripped
individuals of an authentic self (as evangelicals believed had happened in
the 1950s), Dewey's progenitors now seemed set on stripping society of an
authentic, absolute truth in God. In the words of one California educator, the culmination of two decades of liberal maneuvering meant that
"progressive education" had become more than a method—it was "an ideology" of situational ethics that held that "all values are relative to time,
place and condition, all standards variable, and all truths mutable."[13]

Using their private academies as marshaling zones, determined evangelicals sought to undermine this "new morality" in public education.
Wells's congregation proved what they could achieve when properly mobilized. In the late 1960s, Heritage's parent association helped lead the fight
to ban the Sexuality Information and Education Council of the United
States (SIECUS) from continuing an experimental sex education program in Anaheim high schools. Several local parents objected to this program's inclusiveness of homosexuality and "non-traditional" family values.
Wells joined the charge. In spring 1969 he preached hard-hitting sermons
on sex education in public schools, one titled "Is Sex Training Sin Training?" His sermonic calls for action, delivered in the run-up to a school
board election, helped conservative candidates win control of Anaheim's
school board. Those on the wrong side of this onslaught were awed by
their opponents' political machine. "They had such rapid communications," one school counselor later recalled. "There was such an efficient
organization behind this. We were just flabbergasted." Shortly after the
election, Anaheim's emboldened parent-activists forced the resignation of the school superintendent, Paul Cook, allowing the new school
council to ban SIECUS material from city schools. The moral backlash
spread. Veterans of Anaheim's sex education war took their case national
in hopes of advancing coast-to-coast opposition. One of the most aggressive was John Steinbacher, a leader of Anaheim's school board coup, who
wrote *The Child Seducers*, which claimed that sex education was a ploy
by communists to alienate students from their parents and ultimately to
drain them of their patriotism. As Steinbacher traveled the country giving lectures, Wells made sure that his parishioners remained aware of the

author's activities, and diligent in their supervision of Anaheim's public educators.[14]

As large and active as it was, Wells's school was eclipsed at this time by another that shared its name, philosophy, and penchant for politics. In the Goldwater years, Wells's contemporary Tim LaHaye was a lesser light in the world of fundamentalist politics. During the Reagan governorship he became an outright star, having built his San Diego congregation into a vast complex bursting with an active membership of over a thousand. In 1970, Scott Memorial Church added Christian Heritage College to its offerings, with the stated aims to teach young people "within a consistently Biblical philosophy" and to help make the church the "headwater" for education and politics. This outlook made LaHaye and his congregation increasingly popular among conservatives, and soon his location in San Diego's modest North Park neighborhood became inadequate. In the early 1970s Scott Memorial relocated to El Cajon, a fast-growing suburb in the city's northeast corner. It was a community that looked very much like the one Bob Wells had moved to ten years earlier—overwhelmingly white, middle-class, military-supported, and highly protective of its demographics.[15]

By now, LaHaye's political activities also began to outshine Wells's. In 1966 he helped galvanize support for Proposition 16, an anti-obscenity measure initiated by E. Richard Barnes, the minister-turned-congressman from El Cajon, and William Shearer, Barnes's former aid. The Proposition 16 campaign curried favor from several influential ministers and wealthy backers like LaHaye and Patrick Frawley, yet ultimately failed in its fight against the "Smut Capital of the World." LaHaye extended himself to a larger degree on another, related issue: opposing the teaching of evolution. Much of his politics, in fact, grew out of his abhorrence of evolutionary theory. Because of Darwinism, he charged, "destructive systems such as communism, fascism, racism, and animalistic amorality have been conceived and nurtured in an educational milieu emphasizing the evolutionary doctrines of struggle and survival." LaHaye led a new wave of anti-evolution activism by helping spark legislative drives and laying the groundwork for a creationist system of training. In 1970 he recruited Henry Morris to help found his college. Morris was an outwardly gentle, soft-spoken, PhD-holding Texan who set the scientific and evangelical communities afire with fierce critiques of evolutionary theory. In 1961 he coauthored *The Genesis Flood*, which argued that "Noah's flood, rather than eons of erosion, sculpted the earth." At the time he met LaHaye, in 1970, Morris's *Genesis Flood* was already a standard text for evangelicals and the principal lens through which they envisioned a new, creationist science. Understandably, evangelicals throughout Southern California viewed LaHaye's luring of Morris from Virginia Polytechnic Institute to Heritage College as a major coup. LaHaye saw this arrangement as the first step in a massive effort to purge Darwin from society.[16]

In order for LaHaye's endeavors to work, evangelicals felt they needed to "discipline" their educational politics at a higher level. In their opinion, the "values drift" of the late 1960s was so expansive that greater coordination among concerned parents and churches was needed to prevent it from progressing further. In addition to fortifying their schools, therefore, they expanded their ecumenical networks. The California Association of Christian Schools (CACS), the umbrella organization to which both Wells' and LaHaye's institutions belonged, was one of the most ambitious of these. Since its birth in the 1950s as a state arm of Mark Fakkema's National Association of Christian Schools, the CACS had helped fuel the growth of Christian education principally by strengthening member schools. In 1966 the agency extended its services to "personnel outside of our association who are keenly interested in the Christian school movement." The CACS, in other words, was now the most powerful "spokesman-agency" of private education in California, a lobby that legislators would have to take seriously.[17]

Several factors worked in the CACS's favor. Between 1966 and 1972 the organization's membership growth rate was 400 percent. At the start of this steep statistical climb, CACS represented 68 member schools; at the end it represented 246, with a total student population of 35,000. These numbers, and a host of other data—overall membership, number of teachers, annual conference participants—made the CACS by far the largest state association in the NACS. People outside California noticed this West Coast phenomenon. In 1968, radio commentator Paul Harvey, already a favorite guest of Christian colleges like John Brown University, spoke at the CACS President's Dinner. His speech invigorated the eight hundred educators in attendance. "America cannot retain its world-wide leadership by adhering to the 'average,'" he proclaimed. The time had come for the "uncommon man" to lead the country. Young people educated in CACS schools exhibited the uncommon traits he was looking for, a point he made on his national radio broadcast the next day: "Years ago it was argued that students maturing in a 'sheltered environment' would, like hothouse plants, be unprepared for the cold outside world." However, "more and more Americans are realizing that it is in fact the public or state-school student who is over-protected. He is 'sheltered' from religious instruction and exposed to all forms of non-Christian philosophy and behavior." Harvey followed with a detailed report on the CACS, lauding it as the largest and most elite organization of its kind. "Based on Achievement Tests, students of the CACS are academically a year ahead of the national average," he emphasized. Harvey's plug gave CACS officials critical ammunition to rally supporters.[18]

The CACS's most vital support, however, came through the rising reputations of its most enthusiastic local sponsors, including James Dobson. Dobson was a product of the evangelical western South; he was born in Shreveport, Louisiana, during one of his parents' hiatuses from their work as traveling evangelists for the Church of the Nazarene. For most of his early life he lived with relatives in different Oklahoma and Texas towns, while his parents traveled the region preaching the Nazarene gospel. Despite his peripatetic childhood, James embraced the faith of his parents and never strayed from it. After graduating from high school, he left the Rio Grande Valley, where he was living at the time, to attend Pasadena College, a Nazarene school in Southern California. Under the guidance of his favorite college professor, the young southerner became convinced that his career would be about "lashing" modern psychology to his traditional Christian worldview. After graduating from Pasadena College in the late 1950s and completing doctoral work at the University of Southern California, he joined the faculty of Los Angeles' Children's Hospital and the Department of Pediatrics at USC's School of Medicine. Much like Henry Morris, Dobson wanted to balance evangelical precepts with contemporary science, and much like Morris's, Dobson's breakout moment came with the publication of a book. In the late 1960s, he became distressed at what he considered to be the breakdown of family values. His answer was *Dare to Discipline*. Published in 1970, the book was equal parts "parenting guide, political manifesto, mass-culture analysis, and hand-book on the illicit drug counterculture." His introductory denunciation set the tone:

> In a day of widespread drug usage, immorality, civil disobedience, vandalism, and violence, we must not depend on hope and luck to fashion the critical attitudes we value in our children. That unstructured tech-

nique was applied during the childhood of the generation that is now in college, and the outcome has been quite discouraging. Permissiveness has not just been a failure; it's been a disaster!

Dare to Discipline attacked Dr. Benjamin Spock's "child-centered' theory of parenting, which had dominated American home life since the 1950s. Dobson instead promoted tough love, parent-centered practices, and a return to belief in moral absolutes. Backed up, as it was, by impressive PhD credentials, Dobson's commonsense-sounding advice appealed to those who objected intuitively to Spock's philosophy. For CACS officials, *Dare to Discipline* was the perfect tool to recruit parents and patrons to a values-based education.[19]

Where Dobson carried the philosophical mantle for the CACS, a trio of statesmen advanced its political mandate. Max Rafferty and John Schmitz were two important allies. Also a Louisiana-born, Los Angeles-based educator, Rafferty had a history of stumping for conservative educational policies before he became acquainted with the CACS in the late 1960s. As California's superintendent of schools, Rafferty earned a favorable reputation among California conservatives for slamming Berkeley radicals and backing traditional education. Many of these citizens supported Rafferty's run for the U.S. Senate in 1968, which ended in a loss to Democrat Alan Cranston. Schmitz matched Rafferty's anti-Berkeley and pro-CACS lobbying. He became a particular favorite among Orange County's religious conservatives when, amid the SIECUS battle, he successfully worked to enact a law prohibiting mandatory sex education in state schools. His most important initiative on CACS's behalf, however, was parental tax credits. In 1973, after a two-year period of negotiation, a version of Senate Bill No. 2 was signed into law, providing families with children in private schools state income tax credit. As CACS lobbyists who worked with Schmitz announced to the group's members, the "fact that California has pioneered tax credit legislation will add momentum to a federal tax credit bill that is pending before the United States Congress next legislative year."[20]

The CACS's other political protector was the man who signed the bill. During his early governorship, Ronald Reagan developed a relationship with Christian educators that grew inversely to his rapport with public ones. In 1969 Reagan gestured to an alliance with the CACS by attending its annual rally in Anaheim, an event announced as "the largest Christian school gathering in the history of our country." Twelve elegantly dressed young women representing different CACS high schools escorted him through a standing, applauding crowd of eight thousand to the stage. Once seated, Reagan was treated to an arrangement of classical hymns and patriotic songs sung by a two-thousand-voice student choir, which ringed the top tier of seats in the cavernous auditorium. After the final notes of "Savior, Like a Shepherd Lead Us" and "Battle Hymn of the Republic" rang down from the rafters, Reagan gave his formal address. He began by praising Christian parents as "the bulwark of morality that's so essential to the foundations of freedom." "God is not dead on your campuses," he said, and "as a result . . . we will be . . . leaning on you more heavily in the troublesome times to come." As if he was channeling Dobson, Reagan transitioned seamlessly from talk about parenting to politics, from Benjamin Spock to Thomas Aquinas and the recent cultural explosion that had parents looking for answers to the relativism assailing their kids. "Today we are told that . . . all standards are relative to societal considerations of man and society. And man and society are whatever mere mortals choose to make of it. But the obligation is to help young people find truth and purpose. We can no longer afford to starve the spirit and thus kill the soul." At the end of his speech, Reagan surprised CACS supporters by announcing that henceforth the third week of each November would be Private Education Week. CACS officials had been the chief lobbyists for this dispensation and so were thrilled. In thanks, they closed the event by presenting the governor with a Bible that had his name inscribed on the cover. The gift was only fitting, CACS head Eugene Birdsall intoned, for this book was "the foundational textbook of all our schools."[21]

RECRUITING THE YOUNG

Of course, the reason Reagan and his CACS hosts were so gracious to each other had everything to do with disciplining the young in yet a final way, by turning them into earnest and effective ambassadors for California's creative conservatism. Their recruitment of Christian youth acquired urgency between 1968 and 1972, when Congress lowered the voting age to eighteen. Suddenly, both political parties had to figure out how to court eleven million potential new voters. Republicans jumped into action. Anticipating the passage of the Twenty-sixth Amendment, Congressman Donald Riegle reaffirmed young people's importance to the

GOP. We must, he insisted, "put together a program that would give them 'a piece of the action' so to speak. This would not only attract them to our party it would also give the term 'participatory politics' meaning." "After that," he explained, the GOP must "funnel the new voter into something like a 'Republican Youth Party.'" "Let us train superior Republican candidates early so that we control the next fifty years of the Congress." Once the Twenty-sixth Amendment passed in 1971, California's Republican Party made youth recruitment a top priority. Confidence was high among officials that they could capture a majority of these new voters, provided they design a platform of appealing, dynamic, and diverse issues—getting out of Vietnam, environmental problems, improving the job market, and even law and order. Republican leaders believed that most youth were law-abiding citizens who wanted people to live by a strict code of ethics. Championing this code would be their main tactic in the competition for the state's 2.6 million new voters aged 18 to 24 who would participate in the 1972 election.[22]

Even if only vaguely aware of these numbers, Southern California evangelicals sensed a sea change. W. S. McBirnie came away from the 1968 election ready for a fight. "In the next election vast numbers of college students, now under subversive attack, will be of the age to vote," the reverend emphasized in his postelection literature. "They hold the balance of power, and we have only four years to popularize conservatism and expose the evils of the Left in a way that they will accept." It was time for the Republican Right to "move into the youth field with daring imagination and brains," he declared. McBirnie embraced this challenge by expanding his Center for American Research and Education. Already a focal point for intellectuals, it now became a place where students from around the country could take seminars in American conservatism. To complement his city campus, meanwhile, the preacher purchased a retreat center called Forest Springs, located in a rustic setting next to "a flowing stream of pure water . . . breathtaking mountain scenery, [and] thick stands of tall trees," just seventeen miles from Glendale. The spot was ideal for summer camps and conferences—a place where young people could discuss the state of their country's spiritual and political health and, most importantly, in McBirnie's mind, think about ways to cleanse their schools. One way he proposed was through the expansion of his Students Against Violence in Education (SAVE) program, which "started out as an effective 'underground' infiltrating and training team" but, because of escalating campus politics, was about to go "above-ground to present the Pro-Christian, Anti-Communist, God and Country philosophy."[23]

McBirnie also invited Republican politicians to his campuses, with the intent of having them interact with his youth. Always a featured guest, Strom Thurmond, on one occasion in November 1970, delivered an especially impassioned speech to McBirnie's students after receiving an honorary doctorate at the California Graduate School of Theology. Substantively, Thurmond's speech bridged the harder cold war conservatism he had long campaigned for with the softer conservatism of the Reagan governorship. Feeding off an enthusiastic response, he launched into a grander homily on religious and political history.

> For our nation to come through these dangers with safety and the preservation of our liberties, we need not only to remain strong economically and militarily, but—above all—we must be strong spiritually and ever seek the guidance of Almighty God. We must be sure—as Mr. Lincoln so aptly put it years ago—not only that God is on our side, but more importantly, that we are on God's side, individually and as a nation.

The senator's words struck the perfect note in Glendale but fell flat elsewhere. After speaking on McBirnie's campus, Thurmond delivered his same core message at UCLA and at the University of California, Riverside (UCR). In both places, vocal students heckled him and threw vegetables. Defiant, Thurmond shouted back, "Listen to me if you've got any guts," while struggling through his scripted pleas for America to revive "patriotism and traditional . . . values," solve "the orgy of welfare spending," and reject the "alien doctrine of liberalism." For McBirnie, the hostility shown toward Thurmond simply underscored the necessity of a well-coordinated Republican youth movement.[24]

Though hesitant to engage in partisanship, Bill Bright was equally serious about channeling youthful devotion into a conservative, Christian, Republican politics. Like mainstream evangelicalism in general, Bright and his organization, Campus Crusade for Christ, had revised their priorities after 1964, away from politics. Yet the political dimensions of Campus Crusade were never well hidden. In the late 1960s the majority of Campus Crusade's money and energy came from right-wing Republican financial sources and supported Bright's "less government, more money, more ministry" mindset. More importantly, Campus Crusade's "apolitical campaign" represented only a different kind of intervention in politics, one better able to match trends on the Left. In this decade, marked by rising and falling hope, fear, and rage, left-wing politics had already become something much more profound than voting—it was cultural and it was personal. To conduct voting drives in Mississippi or march on Washington with Martin Luther King Jr.—or to burn draft cards and public buildings—was to put one's life on the line for a set of beliefs. It seemed only natural to Bright and his activists that they put their own existential politics on the line.[25]

They did, in spectacular fashion. Campus Crusade began a more aggressive outreach program in 1967 at the exact moment Reagan first began tackling Berkeley. On Monday, January 23, just days after Reagan fired Clark Kerr, left-wing students at Berkeley congregated at Sproul Hall for a protest. Campus Crusade, however, already occupied Sproul Hall's front steps for their own protest, this one against the secular age. Left-wing students had no choice but to join the throng of five thousand in listening to a Christian folk ensemble and a football player from a southern university, who gave his testimony of faith. Then, Campus Crusade speaker Jon Braun sermonized on "God's love as the only solution for the world's problems," in hopes of convincing at least a few student radicals that there was another path to fulfillment. Kerr's firing created fortuitous circumstances for Christian witness, Braun believed, and he and his staff were not about to let this opportunity pass. Following his last petition for listeners to receive Christ, hundreds of Crusade members sifted through the crowd in search of people willing to talk about God.[26]

So began Bright's Berkeley Blitz. In the months that followed this encounter, Campus Crusade activists spread their message of personal salvation and Christian devotion as the antidote to social sin. While members of the student Left and their political cousins in the counter-culture were organizing sit-ins and a Human Be-In, six hundred Crusade activists were using Berkeley's student directory and a phone bank to contact each of the school's twenty-seven thousand students, and sweeping the campus mall with their witnessing booklet, the *Four Spiritual Laws*. This was merely the groundwork for larger rallies that brought evangelicalism's most dynamic speakers, including Billy Graham, to the school to advocate the "right revolution—spiritual revolution" and the devoted Christian life of chastity. "Free sex isn't free at all," Jon Braun repeated to his audiences at Berkeley and on other California campuses during this time. "You've tried everything else, why not try Christ?" Graham asked at many of these same locations.[27]

Throughout the late 1960s and into the early 1970s, Campus Crusade's blitz expanded. Wanting to mirror every move by the Students for a Democratic Society (SDS) and the antiwar movement, Campus Crusade workers disrupted protest rallies by seizing free speech platforms and carrying signs and chanting slogans of their own: "Prince of Peace," "Students Denouncing Sin," "Boycott Hell! Accept Jesus." Although better equipped to match the intellectual preoccupations of the student Left than the cultural experimentation of hippies and yippies, a few Campus Crusade activists also branched out in hopes of reaching this tougher crowd. Led by former Crusade leader Jack Sparks, activists affiliated with the Berkeley-based Christian World Liberation Front (CWLF) affected the general hairstyle and appearance of Abbie Hoffman and Jerry Rubin to spread the teachings of the New Testament. Meanwhile, they commandeered school fountains for impromptu baptismal services and penetrated the ranks of leftist organizations. In the spring of 1970, history repeated itself when members of the CWLF refused to give up the steps of Sproul Hall to antiwar protestors, thus squelching what may otherwise have been another epic display of left-wing resistance. In part out of frustration with their counterparts, the antiwar protestors decided instead to set Berkeley's ROTC building ablaze. This event, and the Christian students' stand against the radicals, may not have stirred much attention in the mainstream media, but California conservatives surely counted it as an important moral victory and a sign that not everything in Berkeley was bad.[28]

EMPOWERING THE YOUNG

For their part, Southern California's evangelical youth felt somewhat pressured into conformity, but the late 1960s and early 1970s also gave them tremendous opportunity. Their elders may have been busy working to keep them in the fold, but they had far too much freedom in the Golden State to accept blindly the faith handed down to them. This was true for all evangelical young people, of course, but it was especially so for those raised in southern evangelical homes, who found some of the traditions of their southern churches constricting, and the liberties afforded by Southern California too overpowering to resist. Inspired to explore a range of new ideas about the world, these cold war babies entered the 1970s as empowered Jesus people eager to create a Christian counterculture.

This second generation of southerners found plenty of inspiration from a legion of young preachers committed to a contemporary Christian worldview. The more daring among them drew energy from an emerging "evangelical Left," which decried evangelicalism's ties to the Republican Right and chastised the community for not taking a stronger stand against poverty, the Vietnam War, racism, and other social injustices. Jim Wallis, founder of *Sojourners*, the principal outlet for this group, offered a critique of society that dovetailed at key points with the secular Left's philosophy. Meanwhile, Tom Skinner joined Wallis in castigating white evangelicals for being part of American society's problem. "We have been duped by a certain kind of Americanism," Skinner proclaimed at youth conferences in California and around the country. It was, he said, at odds with scripture's calls for social justice. "Any person who receives Christ and His power into his life will also become a radical. He can go out into a system in the name of God, directed by godly principles and the Word of God to change the system."[29]

Skinner and Wallis's unconventional, left-wing evangelical theology attracted advanced white and black college and seminary students in Southern California, yet for a larger percentage of southern evangelical youth, a simple recasting of traditional evangelicalism by an emerging cohort of young, magnetic pastors who looked more like their peers than their parents was radical enough. In their quest for cutting-edge, these clerics settled on convention, but it was convention animated by the lingua franca of their age. Whereas California's left-wing, countercultural youth claimed Marx, Mao, Camus, and Timothy Leary as their great revolutionaries these ministers asked young people to claim Jesus as theirs. If they needed to rebel against their middle-class upbringings and find authenticity in a plastic age, these contemporaries suggested that they locate it in the Bible and a life of self-sacrifice, perhaps in global missions or as missionaries in America's inner cities. Evangelical teens and twenty-year-olds were told it was okay to feel disillusioned in their age of relativism, but they could not expect to find peace by joining mass society's rebellion against God. The much more effective—and "radical"— solution was to cut against society's grain by chasing truth through personal encounter with the divine.[30]

Groundbreaking Pentecostal preachers seemed particularly adept at selling this solution. Throughout the 1960s, youth growing up in Southern California's Assemblies of God congregations imbibed the lessons of daring personalities like David Wilkerson, a former minister to drug addicts in New York City, who parlayed his experiences into a national ministry called Teen Challenge and a best-selling book, *The Cross and the Switchblade*. In this autobiographical account, Wilkerson told of his infiltration of the inner city's culture of gang warfare and drugs, showing throughout the power of personal faith in solving race violence and social problems. In New York he counseled drug addicts by way of a "thirty second cure," what he referred to as the baptism of the Holy Spirit, and throughout his career he claimed that this remedy was far more successful than any other government rehabilitation program.[31]

Through Pentecostal networks, Wilkerson's compelling testament to God's power over the ghetto spread west. Teen Challenge became a staple in Assemblies of God circles, drawing thousands of students together annually for massive rallies typically headlined by Wilkerson himself. By 1967 Teen Challenge oversaw drug prevention programs at schools all over California's Southland. "Already 50 student-body assemblies have been conducted this school year," the Assemblies of God announced in February 1968, "17 in the month of January alone." "With nearly 2,000 students in each assembly, [Teen Challenge] is reaching thousands of young people for Christ each week." In May of the same year, the Los Angeles program director reported that he had by then spoken to 70,000 students and had helped coordinate workers for the ministry's halfway house and Girls' Home. In Orange County, Teen Challenge officials offered another look at their endeavors: "Every week dedicated teams are sent to schools, P.T.A. groups, rallies, beaches, street corners, jails, service clubs, youth groups and churches. Scores of hippies and troubled youth are reached for Christ every weekend at the Coffee House in Huntington Beach." Neo-Pentecostals were also inspired. Ralph Wilkerson (no relation to David) regularly invited *Cross and the Switchblade*'s real-life hero to Melodyland, and Pat Boone produced a movie version, in which he starred as David Wilkerson and twenty-one-year-old Erik Estrada played Nicky Cruz, the Puerto Rican gang leader saved out of violence.[32]

Los Angeles' Southern Baptist youth had their own "David Wilkerson," Arthur Blessitt, the son of a cotton farmer, born in Mississippi and raised in northern Louisiana. Just as hundreds of California civil rights workers from Berkeley and UCLA began making their way east to help register black voters in his home region, Blessitt came west to California to redeem young people. By the mid-1960s he was bringing his unorthodox evangelical message and methods to the seediest areas of Los Angeles, all the while telling his Southern Baptist protégés to "revolutionize your neighborhood" by witnessing in "bars, brothels, and pornographic book-stores as well as on buses and airplanes and in schools." Blessitt asked them to be Jesus people, faithful servants of Christ who believed that no social location, even Hollywood's notorious Sunset Strip, was out-side the purview of their Maker. The scraggly-looking minister wore this label proudly while carrying a large wooden cross on Hollywood's streets, setting up a Christian coffeehouse—His Place—and campaigning to eliminate adult entertainment establishments, drug havens, and prostitu-tion rings. For his earnestness—and failure to abide by loitering laws—Blessitt's ministry was temporarily shut down by city officials in 1969, but in an example of true anti-establishmentarianism, he fought "The Man": "All they had was money, guns, influence, intimidation, and jails," he told young evangelicals. "I would have a New Testament in my hand, a cross at my back, and Christ at my side. I couldn't lose." Ably defended by the American Civil Liberties Union, Blessitt beat the charges and continued to hold church on Sunset Strip.[33]

Many young Southern Baptists admired this example of courage. Like Blessitt, Letha Trammell was a southerner who found Los Angeles' streets in need of her attention. Trammell came to Mount Zion Missionary Bap-tist Church in 1966 as part of the Southern Baptist Convention's US-2 program. The recent graduate of Oklahoma Baptist College arrived at Hill's church completely sure of her mission. "I go with the confidence that God is sending me to this area, and therefore I know he will be with me," she told her questioning family. Although they believed in Letha's abilities, her parents opposed her decision to journey west; no good news ever came from Watts, and the notion that a bashful white southern woman could reverse this trend seemed ludicrous and dangerous. But Letha saw things differently. It was up to a new generation of Christians to show the nation a way out of the chaos that now plagued its cities and campuses. For her, Watts was the Lord's call. Trammell's outlook was contagious, even for E. V. Hill, her high-energy boss, who cautiously wel-comed the naïve Oklahoman into his convulsing neighborhood. Back in the Arkansas and Oklahoma towns where she grew up, Trammell had had little contact with nonwhite neighbors and, as she herself admitted, no chance "to discover how I felt about people of other races." Once in Watts, she quickly earned the respect of her black peers with hard work. During her first summer, she and eleven other young missionaries held forty-eight vacation Bible schools for five thousand children. The following summer, after a year of work on Mount Zion's staff, she joined an integrated team of "Japanese, Spanish, Indian, Caucasian, and Negro" students to organize Bible schools throughout Watts's parks and backyards. The sense of fulfillment derived from these crusades left Trammell depressed at the thought of leaving Los Angeles, and in 1968, when she finished her two-year assignment, she decided to stay. By the time she boarded Mount Zion's buses to attend Billy Graham's Anaheim evangelistic rally in the fall of 1969, Trammell was working full-time in Hill's church and living in Watts. Like the thousands of other young people who joined her at the Big A, she was convinced that, through the gospel of personal redemption and Christian witness, California could glimpse the Kingdom of God.[34]

Whereas Trammell steered her devotion into street witnessing, another young Baptist who attended Graham's Anaheim crusade found his outlet for Christian renewal in rock and roll. David Diggs was born in Kentucky to parents with roots in Texas and Arkansas and deep ties to the Southern Baptist Convention. His father was a Southern Baptist chaplain in the United States Air Force and his mother a teacher with a proud family lineage of SBC leadership. When he was six years old, in 1958, his family moved to Southern California, where it eventually settled in Anaheim and at Euclid Southern Baptist Church. By the age of sixteen the aspiring musician had grown tired of his church's "square music" and had decided to explore other options at Calvary Chapel. Calvary had been opened a couple of years earlier by Charles "Chuck" Smith, a pastor ordained in the Church of the Foursquare Gospel, who struck out on his own in the Orange County beach town of Costa Mesa. There he came in contact with young hippies who coveted the sense of communalism that flourished in the counterculture but not the drug habits that came with it. Over the next few years Smith expanded his congregation with contemporary preaching and praise music, held mass baptismal services in the Pacific Ocean, and established the Christian magazine *Maranatha*. Eventually a music company—Maranatha Music—grew out of this enterprise. By 1971, when *Time* and *Look* profiled Calvary to illustrate the Jesus movement, Smith's congregation had just opened a four-thousand-seat building that drew an estimated twenty-five thousand people to its multiple weekend services.

Diggs found his niche at Calvary, playing guitar and producing music in its worship band, but with increasing regularity he also attended Melodyland, another hub of the Jesus movement. Under the influences of Neo-Pentecostalism, this Anaheim church actually surpassed Calvary when it came to exploring new worship styles. Whereas Chuck Smith preferred a toned-down folk style of music, Ralph Wilkerson allowed for a harder-edged rock and roll; whereas Calvary liked its young members to wear their faith with some restraint, as a sign of their newfound Christian discipline, Melodyland told them to check their inhibitions at the door. Racially and economically diverse, Melodyland was also designed to be culturally eclectic and experimental, all of which accorded well with its theological imperatives to break down conventions and reclaim the miraculous dimensions of the New Testament church. Diggs enjoyed Melodyland's diversity and excitement—particularly the chance to listen to accomplished musicians—and drank in its charismatic teachings.[35]

Whether encountered at Calvary or at Melodyland, Diggs found the discourse of his new cohort refreshingly unifying in its rearticulation of ancient biblical teachings. Like Christians in Christ's time, the Jesus people believed they had to reject extant institutions and embrace agape—love for God—as their organizing principle. Ecumenical in its embrace of all evangelicals, the Jesus movement was nonetheless exclusive; only those who made "decisions for Christ" were able to embrace agape and join the community. As Smith's *Maranatha* magazine emphasized, the earthly rewards of this decision were worth the commitment: "Agape love" is "just a beautiful, beautiful kind of a life of just loving, just giving; not making demands, not pressuring for its own way, but just willing to give."[36]

The Jesus people may have embraced the laid-back language of love, but they were also hard-driving; they prepared for the horrors of the Book of Revelation every bit as much as they prayed for the peace taught in the Books of Matthew and First Corinthians. Diggs and his peers, in fact, lived in a state of anticipation of Christ's Second Coming that was intensified by the literature they read. The same magazine that contained Smith's call for "agape love," for instance, also sounded off about war in the Middle East.

PRAISE GOD! God's time-table for the end of the world as we know it is now coming to pass. The Israelis, God's chosen people, are now at war with the Arab nations, fulfilling Bible prophecy. Little Israel, with only three million people, shall defeat the Arab nations of fifty-eight million people; through the power of God! Amen. It might at times appear as though we are pro-Israel and anti-Arab, but such is not the fact. If we are anything, we are pro-Jesus and anti-devil.

"Arabs Defeated, Russia Is Next!" the article announced, before listing the signs Christians should expect before "the Rapture." Longer treatises on the end times filled in the important details. In 1970 Hal Lindsey, a seminarian from Houston who came to Los Angeles to work with Campus Crusade at UCLA, published *The Late Great Planet Earth*, a current events guidebook that allowed Southern California's young evangelicals to measure how close they were to the Second Coming. Their music conveyed an even more heartrending sense that time was running out. In 1972, Larry Norman, the Jesus people's "Bob Dylan," recorded the album and anthem that defined them. *Only Visiting This Planet* included several hits like "Why Should the Devil Have All the Good Music," but none captured the mood better than "I Wish We'd All Been Ready," which featured a mournful chorus about being left behind on earth after Christ raptured his saints. Norman's music, like the songs David Diggs performed in his Christian bands, was meant to draw listeners closer to God, but the goal was also to win souls to Christ. Love, Christian fellowship, communalism, belief in miracles, experiential faith, the expectation of Christ's return: these were merely the outlying pillars of the Jesus movement's faith that circled around the center column of belief in the fundamental importance of evangelism. There was only one way to fulfillment on this planet and life in eternity, Diggs's fellow rebels believed, and it was by way of the Cross.[37]

The parents of these rebels appreciated this message, but they were concerned about its presentation. In much the same way that Letha Trammell's parents had hesitated when she had announced that she was moving to Watts, Diggs's parents disapproved of his experimental Christianity. As true-blue Southern Baptists, his parents were always suspicious of Pentecostal churches. Calvary Chapel and especially Melodyland struck them as Holy Roller institutions. All of their misgivings fell by the wayside, however, once they began attending Melodyland with their son. Caught up in the religious fervor that shook the auditorium on Sundays, David's parents submitted to the Spirit and became Holy Rollers themselves; his mother even spoke in tongues, something neither David nor his father could claim. Other parents and pastors had stronger doubts. Jean and Eleanor Vandruff distrusted Melodyland's charismatic message and style and its pastoral leadership, even though Jean's brother and business partner, Shannon, began attending there. They were more willing, however, to allow their oldest sons to attend dynamic but more conservative churches like Calvary with young people their age.[38]

The Vandruffs' and Diggses' eventual acceptance of the Jesus people indicated one bit of negotiation between young and old evangelicals, but for southerners there was a second, more difficult, step to take. They had to accept the fact that through cultural adaptation their children were becoming Southern Californian. As their children began participating in new youth ministries, gravitating toward the cross-current examples of David Wilkerson and Arthur Blessitt, attending nondenominational churches like Calvary Chapel and Melodyland, and investing their efforts in parachurch organizations like Bill Bright's Campus Crusade for Christ, first-generation southern church folk faced yet another erosion of southern identity. For some people, their church's emerging "Californianess" was disturbing. By the late 1960s, one California Southern Baptist noted, tensions had developed between young ministers and congregants who claimed California as their native state and those who still "salute the 'eyes of Texas,' stomp their feet with 'Boomer Sooner,' or break out in hives at 'That Good Old Baylor Line.'" Similar stress surfaced in other Pentecostal, Baptist, and Church of Christ settings, where the new generation of transplanted southern evangelicals remade their faith communities with California flare.[39]

For all their worries, this style had strayed little from the southern way, and those who recognized this fact found encouragement in new trends. Radical in appearance, the Jesus people, at their core, were orthodox. It was their parents' plain-folk evangelicalism repackaged—an absolute devotion to biblical literalism, prophecy, morality, and collective witness cloaked in social intervention and cultural innovation, all transmitted by new media. And although their elders fretted at times, the politics of the Jesus people was not so different, either. Though more socially engaged in issues of race, poverty, drugs, and war than their elders, Jesus people still upheld the fundamental political tenets of a limited state, free enterprise, anticommunism, a strong military, and core Christian values—creative conservatism incarnate. This augured well for southern evangelical institutions that now fully embraced and identified with the new Southern California ethos, as well as for Ronald Reagan and the Republican Right.

DEBATING *PLAYBOY* AND BISHOP PIKE

No southern evangelical institution better exemplified the embrace of Southern California's new conservative synthesis, or hinted more strongly at its prosperous future with the GOP, than Pepperdine College. During the late 1960s and early 1970s, the school's marriage to California's Republican Right was consummated with the arrival of Bill Banowsky, the new-generation preacher who, as Pepperdine's vice president, employed each of southern evangelicalism's responses to youth politics and folded them into a marketing strategy for institutional growth. Watts and Berkeley, of course, had everything to do with this shifting focus. While the first crisis represented a nadir in the life of Pepperdine, the second marked its apotheosis. Amid California's protracted campus wars, Republican donors grew even more appreciative of Pepperdine's unwavering stand for conservative values. The Berkeley mess, in other words, had created an unprecedented opportunity for Pepperdine. Someone just had to take advantage of it.

Banowsky was up to the challenge, which is why Young hired him. Raised in a strict Texas Church of Christ home and educated at David Lipscomb University, Banowsky was, in Young's phrase, a "five-gaited-horse'—a man of many talents," who combined Christian intellect and morals with Hollywood handsomeness. After hearing Banowsky speak as a college senior to a gathering of Church of Christ educators in 1958, Young invited him to work in his administration. While serving as Pepperdine's dean of students, Banowksy also completed a PhD in communications at USC. Itching for new challenges, he left California in 1963 to take over the pulpit at Broadway Church of Christ in Lubbock, Texas, the congregation Young had vacated five years earlier. In 1967, Young proposed that Banowsky return to Los Angeles to assume the vice presidency of his school. Banowsky agreed and moved to Los Angeles in time for the 1968 school year. As president, Young had worked hard as a diplomat, bringing divergent groups together for dialogue about faith, politics, and, most importantly, Pepperdine College. Banowsky was brought on to be the fiery promoter, the person who would inspire people around him to higher achievement. Only thirty-two, he became an energetic pitchman for Pepperdine's values-centered conservatism.[40]

Just how far he might go was first witnessed in public relations. Banowsky was orthodox in his theology and social values, and passionate about expanding his church's influence in the Protestant world. In fact, his first book—*The Mirror of a Movement*, published in 1965—was written with this purpose in mind. He also wanted to challenge his church's youth to be engaged in the world, and his school to be a center of ecumenical exchange between Church of Christ and non–Church of Christ people. He saw no reason why this typically Southern California formula of traditional thinking, cutting-edge culture, and passionate activism could not emanate from Pepperdine as an answer to society's woes. All of these aspirations and all three of his primary constituencies—students, church folk, and corporate elite—came into focus in the late 1960s as he hatched a plan to bolster his college's profile and budget.[41]

Banowsky's idea was to use one of his fortes—debate and rhetoric—to generate a fresh public image for Pepperdine. Specifically, he would engage leading liberal thinkers in debate, under the glare of lights and cameras, in hopes of exposing their flaws and highlighting his church's and his school's strengths. Banowsky first tested this strategy in Texas, when he debated Anson Mount, *Playboy* magazine's religion editor, on the subject of sex, marriage, and morality. During a two-hour event held at Lubbock's municipal auditorium, 2,400 college students from nearby Texas Tech University watched as Banowsky and Mount grilled each other on the "playboy philosophy." The exchange was lively, if predictable. Mount indicted Protestants for Puritan prudishness and argued that *Playboy*'s position for freer sexual expression and flexible ethical standards was healthy because it allowed innately good human beings both to decide for themselves "matters of right and wrong without dependence on clerical taboos" and to adjust their moral compasses to the present culture. Banowsky countered by arguing that *Playboy* dehumanized women, cheapened the act of sex, and ultimately limited human freedom by making individuals slaves to the flesh. It visited upon society "a new kid of tyranny" based on a cult of pleasure-seeking conformity. Banowksy's hometown arena and family-friendly argument made his case the stronger of the two, as far as audience members were concerned. One Texas Tech student said he had never seen "anything create as great and as lasting an impression on students as the discussion did. Dormitory Bible studies have already been arranged as a result of the debate." Thousands of other young people, meanwhile, followed the proceedings via radio, television, and newspaper. Banowsky followed up on the debate by publishing *It's a 'Playboy' World*, which quickly became a Christian how-to book for dealing with the sixties counterculture and cemented Banowsky's status in the Church of Christ as the rock-star preacher of his generation.[42]

Once settled in California, a few months later, Banowsky decided to take on a more accomplished adversary in a more hostile setting. Banowsky would face the dean of California liberal Protestantism, former Bishop James Pike, on his turf at the University of California, Santa Barbara. Planning for the Banowsky-Pike showdown started months in advance, so as to allow the debaters plenty of time to prepare and their publicists time to drum up attention. Although sponsored by one of UCSB's evangelical student organizations, Pepperdine took the lead in planning the affair. Under Young's direction, the school hired Spencer-Roberts & Associates to promote the event. Behind the scenes, meanwhile, Banowsky collected information on the man he would be confronting. Pepperdine's champion found himself inundated with advice, including from James Bales at Harding College, who "xeroxed some material" on Pike he had gathered from Archer Weniger. Just weeks prior to the debate, Banowsky met personally with Pike to discuss the upcoming event. In a follow-up letter, he thanked him for his "warmth and graciousness," then reiterated the ground rules they had established.

> You will be doing everything to be as liberal as you can be suggesting expressions and circumstances where sex outside of marriage is justifiable, approvable and even preferable. I, by way of contrast, will take the position that the ultimate sexual intimacy should be exclusively limited to the marital relationship. While you are leaning over to be as liberal as you can be, I will lean the other way and be as conservative as my conscience will permit.

Banowsky wanted this event to be as exciting for the audience and predictable for the combatants as possible.[43]

His preparation paid off. On January 3, 1969, the two men met before an overflow crowd of 1,500. Although forced to cut his own honeymoon short to be in Santa Barbara ("How many people do you know who would interrupt a honeymoon just to TALK about sex!" Banowsky quipped during his introduction), Pike was in fine form. Both speakers, in fact, won style points. Garbed in clergyman's regalia—a "dark gabardine suit" accessorized with a lapel button "emblazoned" with the peace symbol—Pike began his comments by saluting the New Left in the room and entering into an off-the-cuff "dialogue" about the necessary freedoms of personal conscience in an age of violence and coercion. Playing the conservative to a tee, Pepperdine's executive—dressed in a "charcoal-gray suit with broadly spaced pinstripes and a blue-and-red-striped tie"—opened his session with prepared comments stating the need for an objective truth and moral order amid cultural chaos. The twenty journalists flown in to Santa Barbara by Spencer-Roberts could not have scripted it any better. As one of them commented after the event, Pike effectively used a "free-flowing style which would have put Bob Hope to shame," while Banowsky looked and gestured "like a Kennedy."[44]

The substantive dimension of the evening's proceedings also proved engagingly divisive. Although Banowsky tried to peg him as a progenitor of the playboy philosophy, Pike made it clear that his "situation ethics" was as much opposed to Hugh Hefner's freewheeling sexuality as it was at odds with Banowsky's inflexible views. Situation ethics was not the absence of law, Pike insisted, but the acknowledgment that, while important, society's moral code always needed to be revisited and, if necessary, reconstituted according to the spirit of the age. Regardless of the subject—sexuality, civil disobedience, or war—you "cannot know the answer to a given ethical question in advance of the context of a situation." And regardless of the societal context, "in certain crucial personal decisions, an individual conscience must take precedence." Banowsky countered by pressing the bishop for concrete examples of how his "New Morality" worked without spinning into subjectivism. Although acknowledging "ethical decisions are never easy to make" and insisting that he "was not a legalist," Banowsky stayed firm in his conviction that "we, nonetheless, live in a world that must be undergirded by moral restraints." This applied especially to sex and marriage, he added, topics that he continued to focus on even as Pike wandered into discussions about war and peace. "Some things are always right and some things always wrong," and sex outside of marriage was always the latter, he charged. Speaking to students directly, perhaps in hopes of touching the same spirit of activism Pike tapped, he added that it was time for "a 'moral revolution' in the biblical tradition."[45]

In the end, Banowsky won the debate while Pike won the audience, and in this regard both succeeded, because Pike had little interest in playing by the rules Banowsky followed. Where Banowsky realized true victory, however, was in public perception. His strong showing reflected well on his school, and in the weeks that followed he was deluged by mail, most coming from Church of Christ people who felt proud. One woman wrote that "to see an attractive, articulate young man take such a position was heartwarming and encouraging. The strength which you can bring to Pepperdine and to the cause of decency is needed and we applaud your willingness to stand up and be counted." Students, ministers, and advocates for family values responded positively, too; one went so far as to call Banowsky "the great, white hope of the church." Pundits and donors also chimed in. The Church of Christ's journals heartily congratulated Banowsky and passed judgment on his opponent. Pike was "the contemporary," one paper wrote. "Detached from traditional authority, he roamed the philosophical range, guerrilla-fashion, coming back only at his pleasure to confront Dr. Banowsky. . . . It's an old, old story, one recounted nearly any time a liberal meets a conservative." The secular media's impression of Banowsky was no less positive. One newspaperman admitted surprise that Banowsky had not been a "one-note arch-fundamentalist lamb being led to the verbal slaughter in college land." "He is IN this complex, changing the world. . . . Which doesn't mean that he is a compromiser on the Gospels and the way he sees Christ." Clearly Banowsky had prepared well, and so had Spencer-Roberts. Besides flying journalists to Santa Barbara, the firm also got CBS to tape the debate for a documentary and the Los Angeles evening news. More than any other medium, perhaps, it was television that introduced Banowsky to the wealthy donors who had the capacity to assist Pepperdine. Although already a powerful Church of Christ layman and Pepperdine supporter, local businessman Archie Luper wrote Banowsky after watching the debate at home. "May I take this opportunity, Bill, to welcome you to Southern California and I would like to state that not only does Pepperdine need you, but more important—Jesus needs you here in California." Luper's letter—like many others that would follow—came with a check.[46]

THE MIRACLE AT MALIBU

Debating Bishop Pike had worked brilliantly for Banowsky. But as much as this breakthrough had opened doors for Pepperdine, allowing it to market itself as a uniquely stable and moral institution—a refreshing alternative to Berkeley—Banowsky's school still needed to distance itself from Watts and fill the "prestige gap." A new campus in Malibu was to be the physical manifestation of that ambition. Through his extensive ties, Norvel Young was put in contact with members of the Adamson family, long-time ranchers in the area, which offered to sell him 138 (eventually 485) acres of their mountainous land in Malibu. Young asked Richard Scaife to help him secure the property and start the costly enterprise of developing it. The patron came through with a half-million dollars. Meanwhile, Banowsky took the lead in convincing the Pepperdine community why a move to Malibu would be beneficial. "The only chance our kind of college will have for greatness—and perhaps even for survival—in the next quarter century must come from its distinctiveness." In a lengthy report to the board of trustees, Banowsky wrote that the Malibu land was immune to urban change, had strong ties to Los Angeles, and would help recruitment of faculty and donors. And then there was the natural beauty. "A college built at Malibu will forever have an edge in distinctiveness on the weight of location alone!"[47]

With the board's approval, and the vocal endorsements of Henry Salvatori and Walter Knott, Banowsky, appointed director of the Malibu property, aimed for maximum "prestige" by hiring renowned architect William Pereira. Pereira laid out a master plan of soft-white, red-tile-roofed Spanish Mediterranean–style buildings nestled on the slopes of the Santa Monica Mountains and glittering "like diamonds" over the sea. How to pay for this glitter became Banowsky and Young's real challenge. In fall 1969, Salvatori helped the school contact conservative donors around the country. One of the most important was B. D. Phillips Charitable Trust of Pennsylvania, which committed $1,550,000, this raising Pepperdine's pledge total to $8 million. Salvatori, Young, and Banowsky then doubled that total with an enormously successful black-tie fundraiser they called the Birth of a College dinner and hosted at two Beverly Hills hotels, in February 1970. Over three thousand guests heard Banowsky tout Pepperdine's Malibu miracle and Ronald Reagan, keynote speaker for the evening, bemoan Berkeley's mess. Before the gala came to a close, Young bestowed an honorary doctorate of laws on Reagan, saying, "You have exhibited exemplary leadership . . . and served with distinction as governor." Scaife assisted Young in the ceremony and seconded these sentiments when calling the governor "one of the outstanding leaders of our time." It was only Reagan's second honorary doctorate; his first had come from Eureka College, the small, private school—not so unlike Pepperdine—from which he had graduated. Young and Scaife's gesture thus left him appreciative and even vulnerable to an upbeat prediction for the new decade now upon them. Thanks to institutions like Pepperdine, and the people who made it work so beautifully, he announced, America will surely recapture the "spirit of the '70s—the 1770's" in the 1970s.[48]

The next eighteen months flashed by for Pepperdine administrators. On May 23, 1970, ground was broken on the Malibu property. Many of the esteemed guests who had attended the Birth of a College dinner now traded their gowns and tuxedos for more comfortable attire to trudge among the sagebrush on the rocky soil high above the Malibu shore. Banowsky capped the morning ceremony with a speech whose words would become etched in Pepperdine's annals. "What we hope to create here, in these hills, is a spirit of place. A place where minds will be opened, where lives will be changed, where lasting friendships will be formed." "From this day forward let it be known that, in this place, 'We look not at the things that are seen, but at the things that are unseen; for the things that are seen are temporal, but the things that are unseen are eternal.'" During the next year, as hurried construction progressed, Pepperdine College became Pepperdine University, and a short time later Banowsky was named president of the new institution, with Young becoming chancellor. In March of 1971 Pepperdine gained occupancy of the historic Adamson-Rindge Beach House, a mansion with panoramic views of the ocean, located between Malibu Pier and Malibu Creek, which would house its chancellor. Now, instead of being fenced off from South Central's treacherous streets, Norvel and Helen Young—its new occupants—entertained in a glamorous setting, looking south into the sun over golden, cresting waves.[49]

Finally, in 1972, Pepperdine University was split into two campuses. The one George Pepperdine built thirty-five years earlier entered a phase of uncertainty. The once idyllic suburban community that butted up against school grounds was now plagued with the highest crime rate in the city. The demographics of the school were different, too. When Pepperdine opened in 1937 it was a white institution; now, 25 percent of the student body was black, one of the highest percentages for any integrated college in the country. The question facing this original Pepperdine was how to adjust, when part of the college was evacuating for a new, upper-class paradise. As the opening of the Malibu campus neared, Banowsky insisted that the Los Angeles branch would remain open, specializing "in training teachers for inner-city education, in training social workers, and middle-management business executives." In response to those who wondered how their campus would survive when all the money flowed elsewhere, Banowsky assured them that "Malibu is the salvation of the Los Angeles campus." The law of trickle-down economics would have a positive effect for the entire Pepperdine family, he said, since funds raised because of the Malibu setting would also be funneled to South Central. A more difficult question had to do with race: How would he keep whites on Los Angeles' campus and have blacks attend Malibu's? Banowsky's tongue-in-cheek answer—"We'll use scholarships and even helicopters if necessary"—was meant to underscore Pepperdine's commitment to an integrated college culture, but it also exposed the limits of color-blind conservatism, which still readily acquiesced to an economic logic of racial distance and separation.[50]

The other Pepperdine built by a community of wealthy donors in Malibu, meanwhile, entered an ambitious era. School officials designated the Malibu campus Pepperdine's liberal arts college, an interdisciplinary institution built around a "unity of knowledge" and geared to the education of the whole person—mind, body and spirit. "Instead of the traditional, highly-organized and fragmented liberal arts departments," school promotional material read, "learning will be grouped into four major subject areas to provide an opportunity for the cross-pollination of ideas": the humanities, the social sciences, natural sciences, and communications. Students would not be exposed to the large lecture hall settings that some blamed for the anomie felt by youth at state schools; rather they would learn through small, seminar-style classes, individual mentorship, and hands-on fieldwork. For such a conservative institution, the pedagogy curiously smacked of progressive thinking, but in Banowsky's mind it was quite simply an extension of George Pepperdine's Head, Heart, and Hand model for his school. There were other signs that Pepperdine's pedagogy would stay constant with the founding vision. A centerpiece of the school's liberal arts program was the Center for American Studies, geared to instill in young people a commitment to the U. S. Constitution and its prescriptions for republican governance. Of all the groundbreaking ceremonies that punctuated Pepperdine's schedule at this time, none was more publicized and important than the dedication of the building that housed the center, a structure funded by philanthropist Jerene Appleby Harnish. On April 9, 1972, Harnish and the new institute were honored in a ceremony at which San Francisco State College's former president, and now California Senator Samuel Hayakawa, delivered the main address. Other political leaders and donors made their own visits to

Malibu during the following months to inaugurate other shimmering new edifices, which bore names like Huntsinger, Phillips, Payson, Pendleton, Firestone, and Seaver. Just a few months later, eight hundred students moved in and began classes on their "dream campus." They came with the highest academic credentials of any student body ever enrolled at the school. And as one in this cohort explained, they also came "with a real sense of excitement . . . that we were creating new traditions. There was a positive pioneer spirit."[51]

BANOWSKY'S DEBATE WITH PIKE was not his last public clash with a left-winger. In 1970, Herbert Marcuse, a professor at the University of California, San Diego (UCSD), and the intellectual father of the New Left, complained about a scheduled campus lecture by Christian anti-communist speaker Fred Schwarz. Banowsky leaped to Schwarz's defense in a *Los Angeles Times* op-ed titled "An Unwitting Score for Tolerance." "Marxist philosopher Herbert Marcuse has been credited with spelling out the revolutionary rationale that guides the New Left," Banowsky started; "now, quite unintentionally, he may have scored a point for the other side." By opposing Schwarz's speaking engagement, he explained, Marcuse committed the same act of violence against free speech that the professor had been subjected to by voices on the Right. Marcuse replied in a *Los Angeles Times* editorial of his own. "I did not deny Dr. Fred Schwarz' right to be heard on the campus; I denied his qualification to appear as lecturer in an accredited course." In an essay that followed, Marcuse leveled charges against the "conservative establishment"—the "tyranny of the majority" as he called it. "It is the Establishment which practices intolerance and enforces conformity on a global scale, and which systematically creates and perpetuates its own majority, thereby destroying the very basis of liberalism." "The liberal tradition has been betrayed—not by me . . . but by the power of the one-dimensional society and those who control it, and under whose control the media, and the general pressure for conformity, have all but monopolized the formation of publican opinion." Marcuse and Banowsky clearly disagreed on who exactly the establishment and outliers were in their society, but Pepperdine's executive probably did not mind being linked to the former. If there was such a thing as a conservative establishment, Banowsky wanted his school and his southern evangelical faith to stand at the center of it.[52]

12

MORAL MAJORITY

*Our founding documents did not say that this will be a country of
many religions; they said that this would be a Christian nation.
I'd like to have a president who would remind this nation that it
was founded to be a Christian nation. I would like to see a Congress that would open up in the name of Jesus! I'd like to see a
people who would call on Jesus to solve their problems.*[1]

—E. V. HILL

I N THE SUMMER OF 1972, A MULTITUDE OF EVANGELICAL YOUTH
flocked to Dallas, Texas, for an event heralded as Explo '72. The Great
Jesus Rally, or Godstock, as it was also known, was a weeklong festival
organized by Campus Crusade for Christ. During the congress, held in
mid-June, young "delegates" from around the world soaked up an old-time
gospel message and danced rapturously to the beat of Christian rock and
roll. On the last day alone, 150,000 people jammed an abandoned freeway site to take part in a nine-hour music concert headlined by "Righteous Rocker" Larry Norman and Johnny Cash, a recent convert to the
Christian faith.

Eighty thousand teens and twenty-year-olds, meanwhile, filled the
seats of the Cotton Bowl for nightly services like the one held on June
14, a warm, humid Wednesday. Before the service began, the participants
started a football-style chant—one side of the stadium shouted, "Praise
the Lord"; the other answered, "Amen." Singing and testimonials followed. The most affecting testimony came from "Phil," a senior at the
University of Tennessee. Only two years ago, he admitted, he had been
a nihilist conspiring to bomb buildings. At one point he even contem-

plated assassinating George Wallace. But now, he exclaimed, his life was infused with meaning because of his faith in God and his optimism that American society could be redeemed. Phil's words set the scene for the evening's keynote speaker, Reverend E. V. Hill. Campus Crusade head Bill Bright introduced Hill as a man "very dear to him." Those listening to a broadcast of the message on Billy Graham's *Hour of Decision* learned that Hill, "a black man from Watts," was chairman of the forthcoming South Central Los Angeles Crusade, sponsored by Graham's evangelistic association. Hill began by asking his listeners: "Who are we, who are we not?" He stated, "We are not of one town, of one race, or one denomination." But as one body united by a shared gospel, "We're going to take this world for Jesus Christ." Racial strife, war, poverty, pollution: Each one of these global problems, he asserted, can be solved if people stop looking to government for assistance and concentrate on saving people's souls. Continuing in his participatory style, Hill pushed hard toward his final rhetorical question: Could changing individual hearts lead to universal reform? "Yes," he shouted, "just look at the masses in Dallas tonight!" Then, in a last flourish of emotion that drove his raspy voice to a bellow, Hill roused his people with a proclamation that clanged with conviction.

> For I declare tonight, as one who has his past in the struggle for justice, as one who has attempted to better the conditions of men, I am finally convinced that a better world will come with better people. And better people can only come through the power of God. And the power of God deposits in every heart who believes the love of God. And the love of God is so rich and so sweet it flows to the highest mountain and to the lowest valley. The love of God penetrates hard hearts! Oh, how I love Jesus!

As his last confession rang out, Hill's listeners leaped to their feet to declare their love for Jesus and their own dreams for a broken humanity. Once the furor died down, hundreds answered the altar call and quietly committed themselves to a life of Christian service.[2]

EXPLO '72 WAS ORCHESTRATED by and for conservative Republicans as they prepared for the elections that fall. No one was blind to the maneuver; many marveled at it. A survey conducted by the *Dallas Morning*

News found that Explo's delegates favored Richard Nixon by a margin of 5 to 1. During the week, these youth took every opportunity to let their opinions be known, by saluting five thousand attending military personnel, for instance, and cheering a telegram from Nixon, which repeated Hill's mantra that "the way to change the world for the better is to change ourselves for the better" through "deep and abiding commitment to spiritual values." None of these public displays of political religiosity escaped notice. Chicago-based evangelical journals like *Moody Monthly* and *Christianity Today* weighed in with awe at the Texas-size revival, while *Life* magazine and the *New York Times* editorialized the happenings in Dallas as a portrait of Nixon's Middle America. Sacred and secular media alike published wide-angle photographs of a sea of well-behaved young people rocking to the beat, with index fingers pointed heavenward in salute of Jesus, "the one way" to salvation. Proud southern son and accomplished journalist John Egerton, meanwhile, provided a view of the action from the heart of it all. With more than a hint of cynical resignation, he concluded that this religious gathering was a sign of the "southernization of America" and the "Americanization of Dixie." "The modern, acquisitive, urban, industrial, post-segregationist, on-the-make South . . . is coming back to the Mother Country, coming back with a bounce in its step, like a salesman on the route, eager to please, eager on making it. There ain't no revolution." In Egerton's mind, the rise of Nixon's evangelical South foretold the nation's decline.[3]

Regardless of their point of reference, journalists covering Explo '72 failed to see the missing link: The Dallas Jesus festival was the product of an ascendant Southern California as much as it was the creation of a new, assertive South. And where they saw the "southernization of America" on a north-south trajectory, they should have looked for it on an east-west axis. During the previous generations, transplanted Oklahomans and Texans like Bill Bright and E. V. Hill had "southernized" Southern California evangelicalism, creating an awesome political force. As a way to compete in a cultural marketplace saturated with faiths of all kind, adjust to new arrangements of urban space, capture and hold the hearts of their young, and vie for control of a fiercely contested political sphere, they had turned Southern California evangelicalism into the vanguard of American evangelicalism. By the early 1970s, this emboldened religiosity had drawn on its entrepreneurial sense to help forge a creative, centrist, youthful, color-blind conservatism and fasten it to Ronald Reagan's Republican Right.

Explo '72 and Nixon's 1972 presidential campaign were, in a very real sense, attempts to take this California synthesis national.

Thanks to the aid of Southern California evangelicals, Nixon's strategy would work, at least for the moment. During the 1972 election campaign, these citizens helped entrench Nixon in Washington. Meanwhile, they solidified their power base with Reagan in Sacramento and adopted the confidence of a political establishment. In the long term, of course, Nixon would prove a great disappointment, and Reagan's governorship would end, leaving evangelical conservatives wondering if their revolution had already run its course.

NIXON'S SUNBELT STRATEGY

The political strategy Nixon and his evangelical allies implemented in 1972 rested on a dawning recognition that America's post–World War II political landscape had undergone a fundamental shift. Since World War II, the South had gradually been reconstituted by its boosters and reimagined by pundits as the Sunbelt, a region loosely defined by its distinctive economics, metropolitan spaces, community life, and culture. Postindustrial in its dependence on service industries, high-tech manufacturing, and information and defense sectors, this region was also posturban in its layouts, with communities stretching out from city edges rather than concentrating in the core. A distinctive climate of political thought settled over this sprawling terrain. Residents of this corporate dreamland internalized the pro-growth, antiregulatory assurances of free market capitalism and sought to limit the reach of the federal state in sectors that did not serve these interests. The myth and ethic of self-help and independence matched the surroundings, as did the culture of localism and community protectionism that grew up alongside it. By the early 1970s, partisan change was catching up to these larger trends and Nixon's GOP realized it. After decades of dormancy, the one-party Democratic South was fragmenting and becoming a competitive two-party place.

Nixon's Republicans were certainly not the only ones to recognize this shift. An endless array of appraisals described the transfer of influence to the South that ran the full gamut of popular and political culture. Whether encountered in the rebel sounds of Lynyrd Skynyrd and the Charlie Daniels Band or the gentler tones of Opryland, the groomed environs of Disneyworld or the rowdy climes of stock car racing and college football, Dixie seemed to be rising, quite audaciously as far as many commentators were concerned. Indeed, most writers were as leery of this trend as John Egerton; some, like Kirkpatrick Sale, were downright fearful. In his book *Power Shift*, published at the same time as Egerton's, Sale spoke critically of the way a new class of regional boosters had pried "the balance of power in America away from the Northeast and toward the Southern Rim." Here, along the "broad band of America that stretches from Southern California through the Southwest and Texas, into the Deep South" a

> power base took shape, built upon the unsurpassed population migrations that began to draw millions and millions of people from the older and colder sections of the Northeast [and] upon an authentic economic revolution that created the giant new postwar industries of defense, aerospace, technology, electronics, agribusiness, and oil-and-gas extraction. . . .

Sale, along with other prognosticators, saw clearly that this "Southern Rim" had achieved supremacy by the early 1970s and would dictate American politics for the "foreseeable future."[4]

Nixon and his advisors approached the 1972 election wanting to lock up this southern rim for the GOP, yet they were at odds over how to do it; in a time of remarkable fluctuation, it proved difficult to judge which South they needed to court—the residual Old or the rising New. In 1968 Nixon had focused on the New by appealing to a "Middle America." Conspicuously absent in his campaigning was an overt, George Wallace–style appeal to racial attitudes reminiscent of the Old South. Nixon's reliance on Strom Thurmond, who campaigned for him, and his racially tinged "law and order" critique of social reform meant that the legacy of Jim Crow—however far removed he claimed it to be—was never completely out of the picture. But there was no doubt that Nixon's "calculated inattention" to the race question made him the moderate's choice. Nixon's centrist conservative strategy gained him the presidency, but without the overwhelming support he would have liked from voters who still seemed drawn to Wallace's hard line.[5]

The 1970s midterm elections offered Nixon a chance to flirt with the Old South, and he did, by adopting some of the advice offered by Kevin Phillips in his 1969 book *The Emerging Republican Majority*, which

famously identified the rising Sunbelt (a term he coined) and its conservative political culture as a boon for the GOP. Phillips argued that to ensure
its southern destiny the GOP needed a political package that was fiscally
and socially conservative enough to win the confidence of the new mon-
eyed suburbanite, but also racially conservative enough to attract Wallace's
voters. Certain circumstances made Phillips's strategy enticing. In 1970,
the Internal Revenue Service (IRS) pledged to rescind the tax-exempt status of private schools not abiding by *Brown v. Board*. Meanwhile, new
legal injunctions ordered the desegregation of schools through a busing
program. Predictably, these initiatives produced a backlash among some
white southerners. Wanting to exploit these racial anxieties without doing
damage to the president's rectitude, Nixon's team had him talk tough on
race but "stay out of the affair" and let the "Courts take care of it and take
the fall." Republican state-level candidates, meanwhile, talked *and* acted
tough in hopes of turning slim leads into solid advantages. In the end, this
southern strategy proved costly. By shifting to a harder Right, the GOP
left the right-of-center open, giving moderate Democrats the opportunity
to reclaim lost ground. Republicans would deal with this misstep for the
rest of the decade by battling against a new crop of Democratic politicians
like Florida's Governor Reubin Askew and Georgia's Jimmy Carter.[6]

Nixon, however, had the opportunity to regain lost momentum in
1972, and he seized it by reacquainting himself with the New South.
Even during the rush of interest in Phillips's strategy, Nixon's southern
advisor Harry Dent had warned Republicans to "disavow Phillips' book as
party policy." He told Republicans to emphasize "that this administration
has no Southern Strategy but rather a national strategy which, for the first
time in modern times, *includes* the South, rather than *excludes* the South
from full and equal participation in national affairs." During the 1972
campaign Nixon's team once again saw things Dent's way. With Wallace
out of the picture, ending the threat from the right, and George McGov-
ern forcing Democrats left, Nixon freely pursued the middle by retooling
his centrist semantics. Speaking in Atlanta on the eve of the election, he
followed the exact course Dent had laid out for him. "Now, it has been
suggested that . . . I have a so-called Southern strategy. It is not a Southern strategy; it is an American strategy." He continued:

> There is, in this part of the country, a deep religious faith . . . a great
> respect for moral values. There is a great devotion to what we call

character. But let me say that in that religious faith and in that devotion to moral values and in that respect for character, while it exists in the South, it exists throughout this nation. [You] can call them old-fashioned, but the day America loses its moral values, its dedication to idealism and religion, this will cease to be a great country. We are not going to let that happen.

Nixon's decision, therefore, was essentially to replay his 1968 campaign. He would set his sights on "middle-income, middle-aged, middle-educated" voters with an agenda of lower taxes and economic growth. And he would defend "the 'old values' of patriotism, hard work, morality and respect for law and order." A demonstrative faith in God and free enterprise and a celebration of postliberal and postracial progress, Nixon believed, was the formula that would win him the Sunbelt's silent majority.[7]

NIXON'S SILENT MAJORITY

Although never explicitly stated as such, Nixon's 1972 Sunbelt strategy was a quintessentially Southern California strategy. Considering that their region became "Sunbelt" first, at a pace of development that the South would not match until the early 1970s, Southern Californians certainly had something to teach their southern brethren. This was readily apparent in the realm of evangelical politics, where Christian activists had played such a crucial role in crafting the creative conservatism that Nixon now sought to implement.[8]

Nixon drew on the Southern California evangelical know-how in several ways, especially through his use of Christian ceremonial politics and friendship with Billy Graham. Nixon's camaraderie with Graham was, of course, long-standing and legendary. It had been struck in the 1950s, when the two first started corresponding about anticommunist politics. With atypical brazenness, Graham championed Nixon for president during the 1960 federal election and again in 1962 when he ran for the California governorship against Democratic incumbent Pat Brown. Graham's importance to Nixon grew exponentially in 1968 when he helped convey to Americans and especially southerners the need to abandon the dying, Democratic coalition and avoid the excesses of Wallace's American Independent Party. Throughout the early 1970s, Graham served as Nixon's right-hand man: he once told the presidential candidate, "Anything you can think of you want me to do . . . and I'll do it." There was no greater illustration of this relationship than Youth Day at Graham's evangelistic crusade in Knoxville, Tennessee, in the spring of 1970. Before an over-flow crowd of one hundred thousand in the University of Tennessee's Neyland Stadium, Graham made the unprecedented gesture of invit-ing Nixon to share his stage. Now publicly linked, both men paid trib-ute to America's silent majority and the Christian young people before them who stood as its ambassadors. "In this day of student unrest on the campus, here on one of the largest universities in America," Graham exclaimed, "tens of thousands have been demonstrating their faith in the God of our fathers. All Americans may not agree with the decisions a President makes—but he is our President," leader of "the blacks as well as the whites." Nixon followed with the same message. The "solid major-ity" of young people who greeted him in the stadium, he announced, were the country's future.[9]

Thanks to Graham's ties and their own mature network of ministries, Southern California evangelicals played a crucial role in Nixon's cere-monial politics from the very beginning. The same sentiments heard in Knoxville in April 1970, for example, echoed from the steps of the Lin-coln Memorial, in Washington, D.C., on July 4, when Graham leaned on his California allies to help lead Honor America Day, an interfaith affir-mation of Nixon's America. Despite being harassed by left-wing radicals in the crowd, Pat Boone, clad in red, white, and blue, got the central mes-sage across. "Patriotism has become a bad word," he bemoaned, but "our country is not bad." "We've had some problems, but we're beginning to come together under God." Graham concluded Boone's thought by saying that it was time to wave the flag proudly again. "Instead of an iron cur-tain we have a picture window," he explained, through which people see all of America's flaws—its poverty, racism, pollution. We have to "check our stitches," and with the bicentennial only six years away, it was vital that the nation start doing so now. The evangelist pointed to Southern California's Jesus people—the "one way youth" he had seen evangelizing Los Angeles' streets and worshipping on Orange County's beaches, with index fingers raised in praise of Jesus—as prime examples of how to mend social ties.[10]

Two years later, he encouraged Bill Bright to bring "one way youth" to Dallas for Explo '72. At Graham's urgings, Nixon's advisors sought a relationship with Bright in hopes of using Campus Crusade to mobilize Christian collegians for the GOP, much like they had been mobilized for Barry Goldwater. The Nixon White House was already hard at work nurturing relationships with other evangelical youth organizations, including John Brown University, whose student choir, Sound Generation, was invited to sing patriotic songs at the spring 1970 Annual Presidential Prayer Breakfast in Washington, D.C., and at the Republican National Leadership Convention later that same year. Nixon and his advisors celebrated the work John Brown's students were doing to disseminate the GOP's message, yet in Campus Crusade they identified a higher political calling. And so Bright was asked specially to dine with the Nixon team and discuss the larger goals of the national Republican youth movement. Writing after one of these dinners, Nixon aide and ordained Southern Baptist minister Wallace Henley reminded Bright of the potential in his movement for sacred and secular ends. "The myriad ministries of Campus Crusade show a compassionately pragmatic concern to really implement the Great Commission," Henley stated excitedly. "It seems to me there is much room to develop a media strategy, and perhaps Campus Crusade is the vehicle for this offensive, too. By media strategy, I mean doing things like syndicated news columns, developing evangelical-oriented radio and television spots, undertaking a specific effort to land some of the big names on Christian talk shows. The possibilities are numerous."[11]

If Bright was Nixon's favorite California youth director, E. V. Hill was his most valuable California preacher. Few major ceremonial gatherings were held in honor of Nixon's silent majority without him. It was Hill who emceed the Honor America Day, for instance, and began proceedings by announcing that he was a survivor of Watts who wanted to encourage all races to pay homage to a nation founded on Christian principles. Seven years ago this summer, he exclaimed, Martin Luther King Jr. stood on this same spot and spoke about his dream for America; after years of chaos, it was time for Americans to dream again. Hill was there in Knoxville, too, seated on Nixon's left, and he would accompany Graham on numerous trips through the South, proclaiming, as he did a short time later in Georgia, his ideals for racial healing. "I have come here tonight to join the hands and hearts of the folks who are . . . involved in the number one problem that men of all colors have . . . their relationship with God." "I know personally that there can be no proper relationship with one's brother without a proper relationship with one's God," he added, before emphasizing that "hundreds of thousands" of Californians were praying for Atlantans. Few could testify to salvation across the Sunbelt like E. V. Hill.[12]

And few helped Nixon more in courting black religious constituents to the GOP. Knowing they held slim chances of winning the African American electorate, Nixon's advisors felt that they needed to woo at least a portion of the black vote to guarantee victory. Their Sunbelt strategy of 1972 included a concerted effort to court middle-class blacks who lived in the South; here, Harry Dent noted optimistically, blacks were more conservative, friendly to free market capitalism, and "had already passed through most of the desegregation crises and were more integrated than their northern friends." Unable successfully to recruit black celebrities and athletes, Nixon's advisors instead chose preachers as their middlemen. In December 1971, Henley stated the strategy succinctly. "At some point within the next two months, it might be extremely worthwhile to invite some of the Nation's major black religious leaders to the White House for a red-carpet, highly visible briefing," followed by a secretive, "non-visible session."

> The goal, of course, would be to get them committed to work for RN . . . for the following reasons: 1. The black religious leaders influence thousands of people, and we must get them in our camp before the opposition gets them. 2. Anything we do with blacks will be cut up as nothing [more] than political courting if we wait eight or nine months before the election before reaching out. 3. We need to get their ideas on getting the black vote.

This tactic did not lead to a groundswell of support among black clerics, but when it was coupled with letter writing and speaking engagements designed to share information with ministers in the Southern Baptist Convention and National Baptist Convention about "the Nixon Administration's work with minorities," some seeds of support were sown. For Hill, White House visits and encounters with the president had the desired effect. Prior to the election, the pastor formally endorsed Nixon's candidacy, making him the leading voice for a fledgling but symbolically significant "Black Silent Majority."[13]

Nixon's team recruited southern white preachers as well, with greater rewards. Besides speaking at Southern Baptist churches and schools,

Henley and Dent invited ministers to the White House's Prayer Breakfast and sent letters asking them to nudge their parishioners into the Republican camp. For many of these pastors, the act of visiting Washington precipitated excited responses. After returning home from a White House get-together in October 1972, one clergyman, who headed the Evangelism Division for Southern Baptists in Texas, told Henley that "it was a thrill just to get to be in your presence and to have fellowship with the other men. . . . My brother, you did not have to invite me, because you know I am voting for Mr. Nixon anyway. . . . However, I really do thank you for the wonderful privilege that you gave me to be in Washington yesterday." Henley received countless notes of this kind, including some from executives of the Southern Baptist General Convention of California. Henley told these men that he read the *California Southern Baptist* regularly and that the Nixon White House welcomed and deserved their spiritual support. "We have an active prayer cell here in the White House," he added, "and be assured that your prayers will be reciprocated."[14]

Behind all the ceremonies and correspondence, Southern California preachers also did the grittier work of campaign organizing. In 1970, just as he was making a name for himself through public debates, Bill Banowsky mapped out his own political aspirations and even hired Spencer-Roberts to help set a twelve-year course, including a run for the state legislature or statehouse in 1974 and for the U.S. Congress or the White House sometime thereafter. In the meantime, he began working his way into Republican leadership positions. Chairmanship of Nixon's 1972 reelection campaign in Los Angeles was part of that effort. Like Graham and Bright, Banowsky and his Pepperdine colleague James Wilburn, another Church of Christ preacher who worked on Nixon's national Committee to Re-Elect the President, provided inestimable support as liaisons between the religious and secular grass roots and the party brass.[15]

They also helped bring in the money from the Sunbelt's corporate sponsors. Nixon's campaigns represented a threshold of sorts between the financial operations of Barry Goldwater's cold war Right and the emerging Sunbelt Right. J. Howard Pew, who had been part of the conservative movement from the beginning, offered assistance to his political friends one last time. In spring of 1970, he lent leadership and considerable funds to Honor America Day and dined on Nixon's yacht, *Sequoia*, while cruising the Potomac River with the younger generation of right-wing backers, among them Richard Scaife and Henry Salvatori. A year later he passed away, leaving behind an exhaustive list of organizations indebted to his largesse. During Nixon's run in 1972, the Scaifes and Salvatoris of the conservative world picked up the torch. They were joined by patrons like Clint Murchison Jr., Pepperdine's finance board chairman and school trustee, whose sponsorship of Graham's evangelism, Campus Crusade for Christ, and Explo '72 helped complete the circle of sacred trust that proved vital to Nixon's election win in 1972. After this victory was secured, Murchison and his brethren took time to relish the emerging Sunbelt establishment they had created. It was in this frame of mind that Graham wrote Banowsky, in mid-November 1972, to congratulate him on "the great victory you helped shape for President Nixon" and to invite him to strengthen ties with E. V. Hill, now a mutual friend. "In my judgment he is the most charismatic of all black speakers in the United States," Graham offered. "He and other black leaders like him may be the key to the racial problems facing the country." Clearly satisfied with their work for Nixon, neither Graham nor Banowsky was content to rest.[16]

REAGAN'S MORAL MAJORITY

After the election, Banowsky spoke gravely about the task ahead: "This is not the time to sit back. . . . The growth of the Republican Party in California will directly affect the course of America in the years of the immediate future." Evangelicals shared Banowsky's conviction that this was a critical period in the life of the conservative movement, as well as his confidence that they could do something great for the nation. In contrast to the 1960s, when they still battled for legitimacy, Southern California evangelicals now began to think and act as if they were insiders, political actors with access to the apogee of power.[17]

Their self-assurance stemmed from several factors, but one of the most important was their continued allegiance to Ronald Reagan, whose leadership impressed them far more than Richard Nixon's. The president may have garnered their votes, but Southern California evangelicals never trusted him the way they did Reagan; they were Nixon's "silent majority" in a truer sense of the word, buoyed by his political success but never boisterous about it. Their halfhearted relationship with Nixon had a long history, stemming from his days as vice president, when he seemed to ingratiate himself to silk-stocking Republicans like Nelson Rockefeller, but their questioning of him intensified with each vacillating decision he seemed to make as president. On one hand, he denounced Democrats for their "welfare mess," forced busing, and big government. Yet, on the other, he proposed a guaranteed income for the poor, encouraged the Equal Employment Opportunity Commission (EEOC) to advance affirmative action programs, and expanded government initiatives in health care, family planning services, and environmental protection. His doubters had an equally difficult time making sense of his foreign policy. While Nixon talked about getting out of Vietnam, he instead entered into long negotiations; and though he represented himself as a cold war protector of American national interests, he appeared eager to follow John F. Kennedy's path into disarmament treaties with the Soviets. By 1971 Nixon was on shaky ground with his party's conservative base, and his advisors knew it. Patrick Buchanan summed up these feelings when he wrote H. R. Haldeman and John Ehrlichman that the president was "no longer a credible custodian of the conservative political tradition of the GOP," leaving the "Republican True Believers without a vocal champion." Buchanan's memo suggested a changed course to bring conservatives back into the fold, and by the 1972 election much salvaging had taken place, including in Southern California. Although some evangelicals there voiced support for John Schmitz, their chief advocate for private education who ran as the American Independent Party's presidential candidate, they remained solidly in the Nixon camp.[18]

Yet by and large, they stayed loyal out of a lack of alternatives. Central Baptist's Bob Wells represented this wavering mindset. During the 1968 presidential race, he offered a sermon titled "Be Sure to Vote Right in the Election," which contained positive words for Nixon. Soon, however, Wells's sermons changed in tone; by the early 1970s, their titles alone were damning: "Did Nixon Help or Hinder" castigated the president for his policies, while "The Red China Fiasco—Nixon's Covenant with Death and Agreement with Hell" utterly denounced him. As far as Wells was concerned, Nixon had become a typical Washington insider who privileged power over ideals. He was someone you voted for out of calculation, not passion. In stark contrast to Nixon, Reagan inspired Southern California evangelicals, more so in the early 1970s than ever before. Once again, Wells's sermons spoke volumes. Just before the 1966 state election, he had delivered a homily titled "If Reagan Wins What Then?" It was meant to caution his congregants against putting too much faith in one politician. "I have wondered many times during the past couple of years," Wells admitted, "if God did not permit the conservatives to suffer a smashing defeat in the 1964 election because too many people had their eyes solely on a man and had taken their eyes off God." But then Wells went on to underscore Reagan's importance as a man who could stir the emotions. "Let me pose the unpleasant possibility that if by chance Ronald Reagan should not win—do you know what would happen? There are a lot of people who are just going to sit down and cry. Some of them are going to be so disgusted and disappointed that they will conclude that life isn't worth living." Reagan's win bolstered Wells's trust for the politician and his parishioners' faith in the political system. And when Reagan began his second term, Wells heralded him not only as an inspiration but also as a master politician. He openly hoped that Reagan and his movement might soon have a chance at national leadership.[19]

In anticipation of this alluring, hypothetical future, Southern Californians began assisting a new wave of coalition building on the Republican Right in the early 1970s. Conservatives of all stripes from around the country contributed to this endeavor. Existing groups like the American Enterprise Institute and the American Conservative Union were reinvigorated by liberalism's pronounced troubles and recent Republican successes and ready, in Denison Kitchel's words, to create a "'climate of thought' whose effect would be to move the whole national spectrum toward the right." These organizations were joined by a plethora of new powerhouses motivated by the same goal. The most notable were advocacy agencies like the John M. Olin, Adolph Coors, and Scaife Family foundations. The Heritage Foundation, created in 1973, was also vital. Under Edwin Feulner and Paul Weyrich's guidance, the Heritage Foundation dedicated its efforts to fighting antibusiness and anti-Christian sentiments in order to widen the wedge for conservatism. Southern California businessmen heavily populated the Heritage Foundation's board of trustees, and when this organization made its first pronounced statement in 1974 by supporting a public school boycott in West Virginia, it worked in tandem with Bob Dornan, an aspiring politician from Los Angeles. Some of the Heritage Foundation's key strategists, moreover, applied lessons from Southern California's grass roots. Richard Viguerie, for instance, had assisted Max Rafferty's 1968 campaign for the Senate. During the Republican primary, the Texan's direct-mail firm mailed four million letters to households rallying support for the underdog candidate. Rafferty won the primary and lost the election, but Viguerie's tactics were resoundingly successful and launched him onto a national stage alongside Weyrich, Feulner, Morton Blackwell, and Howard Phillips as one of the young Turks of conservatism.[20]

Southern California evangelicals were especially critical to this next revolutionary stage, with Pepperdine leading the way with refreshed political resolve. The freedom forums that once catered to Goldwater's libertarianism now offered a new class of presenters, from Republican stalwart Bob Dole to sociologist and emerging neoconservative Daniel Bell. Pepperdine's broadening conservative conscience was also evidenced in the Great Issues Series. This annual program addressed social concerns peculiar to Pepperdine's old campus in Los Angeles, but it also raised issues touching on the environment, urban development, and globalization. Banowsky oversaw his school's political maturation as an extension of his own. In the months following the Nixon campaign, he appeared on William F. Buckley's *Firing Line*, hosted his own television program, and wrote a regular column in the *Los Angeles Herald Examiner*, where he raised trenchant critiques of the energy crisis, women's rights, busing, suburbanization, and other pressing matters. By applying a centrist conservative perspective to each—the need to legislate conservation, for example, or expand women's rights without undercutting traditional values—Banowsky constructed a wide ideological umbrella. This vaulted him into a new level of influence. At the governor's urging, he was chosen as a Republican national committeeman, a nonsalaried post that required him to help draft party platforms and mobilize the GOP base. A stream of other appointments to corporate and civic boards followed, leading a conservative newsletter, the *Right Report*, to predict that he would soon be one of the "top political officers in California." "Articulate, attractive and conservative," it elaborated, "Banowsky at 36 could be the fresh new face many GOP leaders are looking for.. . . " In a July 1974 issue of *Time* magazine, Banowsky was ranked in the top fifty of a "who's who" of the nation's young political stars. Clearly, Pepperdine's boss, like the wider conservative movement he represented, was on pace with a lofty plan.[21]

They were not marked, like Banowsky, for future success in the GOP's upper echelon, but other evangelical preachers contributed to the forging of a right-wing majority in the early 1970s. In keeping with a broader ideological shift on the Republican Right that came with political ascendancy, they no longer saw themselves as insurgents fighting against a tyrannical liberal establishment but as protectors of constitutional principles, republican virtues, and traditional values. Through their ministries, political action committees (PACs), and research institutes, they strived for dominion over their culture and sought to make their political majority a moral one, their American republic Christian.[22]

The foundation for these endeavors—strong, autonomous churches—had been laid decades earlier. Now it became clear just how culturally imposing these churches could be. During the early 1960s, in the context of Goldwater's rise and fall, analysts had commented on evangelical churches' impressive authority, yet few predicted these institutions' continued growth. This changed in the early 1970s, when census data and a number of sociological studies declared evangelical churches the surging force in American religion. Statistical trends for California were particularly striking. With 320,000 adherents statewide, the SBC was now the second largest Protestant denomination in the state. In San Bernardino and Riverside counties, Southern Baptists were the largest Protestant group; in Orange and San Diego counties, they were close. Census numbers revealed a similarly steady, sharp ascent for other conservative evangelical entities in these locales, and none of these reports even accounted for the emergence of booming independent churches. According to Dean Kelley, a liberal Protestant scholar and the author of *Why Conservative Churches are Growing* (1972), these church bodies were flourishing because they demanded theological strictness and complete commitment from their members, which offered cohesion in an otherwise chaotic world. Peter Wagner, an evangelical scholar in Southern California, repeated Kelley's findings, only with a prescriptive intent; he urged his church brethren to continue identifying new markets and niches, diversifying styles of worship, and pursuing bottom-line gains in membership, building programs, and community outreach. In sum, he encouraged them to continue following a blueprint for growth first laid out in the 1950s by visionaries like J. Vernon McGee.[23]

One did not need to read Kelley and Wagner in the early 1970s to realize that evangelicalism's McGee-style strategy had paid off. A visitor to Anaheim, perhaps traveling with family to Disneyland, now needed to drive only a few blocks on any given Sunday to find a large, thriving church. Those with fundamentalist proclivities could plot a course west to four-thousand-member Central Baptist. The traveler with teenaged kids might choose to attend one of Chuck Smith's Calvary Chapels, either in Costa Mesa or Santa Ana, which cumulatively welcomed twenty-five thousand people weekly. Pentecostals had the opportunity to stay close to Disneyland and attend Melodyland Christian Center, Ralph Wilkerson's twelve-thousand-member church-in-the-round, located just across the street; or, they could make their way to the Orange County Worship Center—nearby, in Santa Ana. Churchgoers with other denominational ties could venture north to Fullerton and First Evangelical Free Church, now led by Texas transplant Charles Swindoll, while those with Southern Baptist loyalties could make their way either to the two-thousand-member Westminster or Bristol Street Baptist. Anaheim's panoply of Protestant parishes was replicated throughout California's Southland, meaning visitors elsewhere enjoyed similar options.[24]

Another evangelical entity with illustrative, sprawling influence was Christian media. John Brown's radio station, Billy Graham's movie company, Oral Roberts's television program, Larry Norman's Christian rock and roll: Since the 1950s, these creations of California's cold war boom allowed church leaders to reach a fragmented society. During the early 1970s, Southern California became American evangelicalism's entertainment hub. Its radio and television programming continued to reach the nation's Protestant homes, while Graham's movies reached ever-larger audiences with blockbuster hits. Consumers could now purchase the books on which many of Graham's movies were based—as well as specialty Bibles and bumper stickers, T-shirts and tracts, and Christian contemporary music—at one of many religious bookstores like the Amazing Grace Christian Superstore. Purveyors of this Christian paraphernalia enjoyed the added privilege of gathering annually at Anaheim's space-age-looking Convention Center to market their wares and hear about the next avant-garde product.[25]

At Melodyland, just two blocks away, large crowds, multimedia, and plenty of glitz were combined into perhaps the best example of evangelicalism's new power: the "electric church." Weekly, in the glare of theatrical lighting and television cameras, its stylish pastor preached seventy-minute sermons that paused only for applause, prayer, and healing ceremonies, all designed for dramatic effect. "I think church should have some entertainment to it," Ralph Wilkerson stated simply. "It shouldn't be boring. People aren't boring. God certainly isn't boring." Ennui was impossible to find in Wilkerson's church. After perfectly staged worship services ended, congregants browsed the church store for records, books, and souvenirs. During the week, they attended Bible study groups, prayer breakfasts, and women's groups, and took classes at the Melodyland School of Theology (MST). A few Melodyland members also attended seminars at their church's Ecumenical Research Academy, the world's leading Neo-Pentecostal institution for advanced study in charismatic theology, Christian healing and medicine, and church renewal. There six hundred students received instruction from the academy's respected faculty, most of whom, like MST's president J. Rodman Williams, held PhDs from Ivy League universities and the nation's top seminaries. Nothing stirred Wilkerson's parishioners' enthusiasm, however, as much as the annual Charismatic Clinic, when Neo-Pentecostalism's dynamic male and female, white, African American, Mexican American, and international preachers descended on Anaheim for a week of full-gospel worship. These were the times, the church proclaimed, when Melodyland was truly "in motion" for God.[26]

Melodyland's momentum helped Southern California evangelicals set yet another benchmark in Christian media during the early 1970s. In 1973, with Wilkerson's assistance, Paul and Jan Crouch created a Christian television network. Born to Pentecostal missionaries and raised in Missouri, Paul Crouch had moved to California in the early 1960s to manage the Assemblies of God's broadcast facility in Burbank. For the next decade he and his wife, Jan, the daughter of a Pentecostal preacher from Atlanta, dreamed about starting a station like Pat Robertson's Virginia-based Christian Broadcasting Network. After their pastor prophesied that their new ministry would come to pass, they leased a failed television channel, rented studio space in an Orange County warehouse district, borrowed cameras and equipment from Melodyland, and started the Trinity Broadcasting Network (TBN). Things were difficult at first; money was short, and technical troubles were frequent, but by 1975 TBN was raising interest across California and, with it, financial support. The two years that followed brought one milestone after another. In 1975, Demos Shakarian helped the Crouches break ground on a new headquarters, and the following year TBN moved into a sparkling campus in Orange County. Following more prophetic advice from his pastor, Paul Crouch decided to take TBN global. After installing a campus satellite (named the Holy Beamer), Crouch went to Israel to anoint his new technology. On May 1, 1977, from the Mount of Olives, with Jerusalem's mayor by his side, Crouch initiated religious broadcasting's first live satellite telecast. Fourteen days later, back in California, TBN became the nation's first twenty-four-hour Christian station.[27]

Melodyland and TBN's spectacle announced a new dawn for evangelicalism's technological age, but it also assisted its larger political project. During the crucial post-1972 election period, evangelicals' flourishing enterprises and broadening interests helped them gain a footing in Sacramento. Lobbying became a parallel task for them and, for some of their ministers, a second career. A seasoned cleric who followed this course was W. B. Timberlake. The lawyer-turned-pastor had worked with U.S. Coast Guard Intelligence during World War II, investigated communist infiltration for the Civil Services Commission in the 1950s, and, in the early 1960s, served as president of the Southern Baptist General Convention of California. Just as Nixon's Sunbelt strategy was taking shape, Timberlake became a liaison in Sacramento, channeling news on legislation to the Southern Baptist community while conveying this constituency's wishes back to legislators. Empowered by this work, he eventually resigned from the pastorate and become a full-time lobbyist as head of the Committee on Moral Concerns. Timberlake's efforts dovetailed with those of younger lobbyists, who built similarly formidable organizations, including the California Christians Active Politically (CCAP). This organization's head was Pat Matrisciana, a former member of Campus Crusade for Christ and Berkeley's Christian World Liberation Front. The religious leaders who advised the relatively young Christian radical had reputations that preceded them. Pat Boone chaired CCAP's executive committee, and he was joined by several of his allies, including Tim LaHaye, George Otis, prophesy author Hal Lindsey, Frank White of Knott's Berry Farm, state assemblyman Bob Burke, businessman Bill Voit, and broadcaster-author Margaret Hardesty. CCAP's focus was straightforward: "to help get Christians elected to office." Candidates running for office had to be "qualified Christians," which limited CCAP's pool of favored politicians. Those who earned the label, though, had their names splashed across CCAP's promotional literature, disseminated widely through church circles.[28]

Many of these same leaders worked simultaneously to shore up evangelicalism's moral majority in their own research centers. At the same time that Timberlake and Matrisciana established a presence in Sacramento, in San Diego Tim LaHaye's Institute for Creation Research (ICR) became the premier site for Christian study of human origins and the epicenter of the evangelical quest to mainstream creationism. Meanwhile, at Pasadena's Fuller Seminary, researchers analyzed church growth and the globalization of evangelicalism. Nearby in Glendale, at W. S. McBirnie's California Graduate School of Theology, these same phenomena were studied with a more obvious political intention: to investigate money management techniques, the global economy, and foreign policy. A bit farther to the east, in Pomona, James Dobson's work as a Christian psychologist blossomed into Focus on the Family, soon to be the supreme advocate for right-wing family values. Twenty miles south, in Anaheim, radio personality Walter Martin, the "Bible Answer Man," built his Christian Research Institute, which embraced "more than 26 specialized fields of research knowledge" and distilled information about "contemporary trends, both secular and theological" into practical application for the public. A few blocks away, in Buena Park, Martin's pastor, Ralph Wilkerson, helped guide the Institute of Applied Christianity, established jointly with the Christian Freedom Foundation at Knott's Berry Farm to provide seminars on "conservatism in economics, government, and religion." By mid-decade, evangelicals had constructed countless other think tanks that allowed a community of experts to offer alternative Christian commentary on pretty much any subject from church accounting to worship music, Arab oil embargoes to the World Bank.[29]

ALL IN THE FAMILY

Southern California evangelicals had succeeded at constructing a parallel moral universe all for themselves, yet this never distracted them from a political compulsion to make their society moral. This imperative grew more urgent as local contests over family values erupted into hostile statewide battles. Out of an ever-present, trenchant fear that their republic could disintegrate, evangelicals focused more heavily on social issues and, in the process, encouraged an alliance of former foes—Protestants with Catholics, reforming fundamentalists with charismatics. During the early 1970s these groups became one political family, together manning the nation's front line in the struggle for home and hearth.

The catalyst for political unity was the liberalization of abortion law. In 1967, Democratic state senator Tony Beilenson proposed the Therapeutic Abortion Act, which sought to amend California law to "allow abortions in cases of rape or incest, when a doctor deemed that the birth was likely to impair the physical or mental health of the mother, or when there was 'substantial risk' that the child would be born deformed." Beilenson's was not the only measure of its kind—Colorado's Republican-majority legislature had already approved a similar amendment—but its appearance in California set off a political time bomb. The fight that ensued over Beilenson's initiative was heated, to say the least. While Catholic cardinal Francis McIntyre and some of his prelates claimed the bill advocated "legalized murder," Beilenson argued that his initiative would "restore a degree of freedom of choice and of conscience to many thousands of women." Torn between his conscience (which sided with McIntyre's) and political calculations (which saw Beilenson's point), Reagan prevaricated and in the process exacerbated tensions. The governor wished that Colorado, not California, would be the laboratory for abortion law, but, cognizant that many of his Republican colleagues favored the bill, he signed it into law.[30]

Evangelicals were caught off guard by Reagan's decision and unable to marshal the same level of resistance they saw (and admired) among Catholics. Spurred on by their priests, who recognized that liberalization of abortion in California would have national repercussions, Catholic parishioners sent thousands of protest letters to their state representatives and helped organize the Right to Life League and Mothers Outraged at the Murder of Innocents. It was in this moment that Southern California evangelicals began abandoning their anti-Catholicism. In truth, this attitude had been softening for quite some time. Since the 1950s, evangelicals had often distinguished between Catholics and the Catholic Church and applauded the work rank-and-file parishioners were doing for anticommunism and traditional education. The Catholic-evangelical rapprochement was further aided by Neo-Pentecostalism's emergence, which created a theological context for unity. By stressing the pre-Reformation catholicity of Christian believers, this movement encouraged Protestants to commune with Catholic brethren in an ecumenical, experiential faith. By heightening the quest for holiness as the ultimate calling, it compelled individuals across church lines to purify their hearts and minds and make their bodies clean vessels for Christ. Many Catholics responded favorably to Neo-Pentecostal overtures. By 1970 there were "pentecostal prayer groups" on Catholic college campuses and communities in every corner of the country. In 1973, twenty thousand charismatic Catholics attended a week-long "renewal conference" at the University of Notre Dame; in 1974, twenty-five thousand attended the same event; and in 1975, an international conference held in Rome drew ten thousand pilgrims from fifty countries to hear "Pope [Paul] VI express his warm appreciation" for a movement that now counted at least three hundred thousand American Catholics.[31]

Following the Beilenson bill, evangelicals and their Catholic brethren started teaming up in crusades for moral reform. Among the first was the 1972 anti-obscenity campaign, which, under the banner of Proposition 18, tried to do what Proposition 16 in 1966 had attempted: enable citizens to police pornography. Wanting stronger countermeasures against the pornography industry and convinced that the federal government would be of no assistance, activists launched an advocacy group in 1971 called Hollywood Community Against Pornography. Some joined this organization to fight the spread of venereal disease, while others did so to protect property values. Regardless, churchmen and churchwomen provided the driving force. Pastors circulated petitions in their pews demanding that officials step up legal action against the area's sex establishments, and congregants spread the word on the street. "What is needed," explained Pat Boone, who headed the organization, was a "grass roots spiritual militancy." It was time for citizens to "stand up and be counted" and "take advantage of court processes."[32]

Boone and his fellow reformers took this mandate with them into the Proposition 18 crusade the following year. Serving as the state chairman of the Committee for YES for Proposition 18, the Christian entertainer used his connections to help fill his organization's grassroots army. In the months leading up to the election, the committee garnered endorsements from the State Chamber of Commerce, the California District Attorneys Association, and the Los Angeles County Commission on Obscenity and Pornography. The governor's office followed suit. Reagan announced his support "as a parent" deeply concerned about the "tragic pollution of our sociological climate by the commercial interests who are flooding us with pornography." He assured the public that this was a "reasonable, well-drafted measure, designed to give law enforcement the weapons it badly needs to help communities protect themselves against smut." Despite its high-energy coordinator and door-to-door suburban crusaders, Proposition 18 failed. Boone attributed the loss to a "massively financed campaign of smears . . . [by] commercial interests who gain so much from pornography," Reagan suggested that Hollywood liberals had misled voters to believe that Proposition 18 meant censorship. In truth, even some of Reagan's closest conservative friends in Hollywood saw the initiative as an attack on free speech and voted no.[33]

Proposition 18's proponents gained the larger victory, though. In 1973, Marvin Miller, owner of a mail-order business who had been convicted in Orange County Superior Court for distributing obscene literature, had his case come before the Supreme Court. Chief Justice Warren Burger's majority opinion in *Miller v. California* affirmed that obscenity was not protected under the First Amendment. It also extended state power to prosecute vendors of sexually graphic products and expanded citizens' rights to impose "community standards" when deciding what media met the criteria of "obscene." Burger's unexpectedly favorable ruling launched Southern California evangelicals and Catholics into a new phase of activism. According to one Catholic circular, "News for Good Neighbors," Burger had "told the communities they can enforce their pornography laws and pass new ones to protect themselves from the rising 'tide of commercialized obscenity.'" To illustrate what God-fearing citizens could now accomplish with the Court's blessing, the Catholic newsletter cited the example of Larry Lorenz, a Baptist pastor who recruited "his flock" to picket an adult theater. His "little band of Christians" stood tall as they were "kicked, spit upon, and cursed" by the theater owner's "counter-pickets." The violence continued until voters replaced their councilmen with "men who were willing to vote for decency." "The smut movies stopped the next day," the Catholic paper proclaimed, and the brave Baptist's movement quickly spread.[34]

By the time the Supreme Court had ruled on *Miller v. California*, Catholics and evangelicals inspired by Lorenz were already attending to other national issues: the Equal Rights Amendment (ERA) and *Roe v. Wade*. Neither instantly galvanized California's religious right wing like the anti-obscenity initiative, but they did set in motion grassroots campaigns that would grow quickly over time. Passed in Congress with relatively little opposition in spring of 1972 and ratified by state legislators soon thereafter, the ERA was a moot point for California conservatives before they could even react. From the outset, they would be forced to fight against this measure in states other than their own. These same citizens greeted the *Roe v. Wade* decision with more immediate alarm. Already in 1970, grassroots organizations like the California Republican Assembly were pledging support for a "Right to Life" platform advanced by religious conservatives. By 1973 right-to-life sentiments spread through California's churches as well, including Southern Baptist ones. Despite the SBC's official position at the time, which allowed for abortion in cases of rape, incest, and other hardship, a reader of the *California Southern Baptist* expressed the sentiment in the pews that "abortion almost always involves a total disregard for the rights of the unborn" and is "utterly sinful."[35]

Well-orchestrated anti-ERA and right-to-life campaigns would not crest in California until later in the decade, but local evangelicals and Catholics began coalescing during Governor Reagan's second term. One of the earliest conduits for their anger was Christian Family Renewal, founded by Catholic newspaper editor Murray Norris. Norris's dedication to politics arose when his boss asked him to write against his conscience and Proposition 18, the anti-obscenity initiative. "Because of this and the publisher's refusal to stand against abortion," he recounted for supporters, "we parted company." The maneuver left the newspaperman of twenty-five years scrambling.

> I was faced with the choice of moving . . . or doing something else. I sat down and made a list of the things that I thought should be done about the moral evils that were attacking my family and the other families throughout this nation. I told God that if He would support my wife, my 13 children and me, I would do everything I could about that list.

A former college professor with a law degree, Norris was a talented and prolific advocate. In addition to producing newsletters and booklets, he also authored pro-life comic strips geared to teenagers. Two of his first and most popular were titled *Victim*, which dealt with pornographic addictions, and *Who Killed Junior*, a graphic, twenty-four-page text meant to discourage young women from having abortions. Published in 1973, shortly after *Roe v. Wade*, this was the first mass-produced anti-abortion tract of its kind. The success of these publishing ventures forced Norris to recruit an executive committee and a staff of volunteers. His chief officers were a former FBI agent and a local businesswoman, while his advisors included a Catholic politician—Robert Dornan—a handful of Catholic and Protestant pastors, a councilwoman, and prominent Neo-Pentecostal friends George Otis and Pat Boone.[36]

Under Norris's guidance, Christian Family Renewal laid the groundwork for an assault on the ERA and *Roe v. Wade*. With a sense of fury, his writings explained why these two federal impositions threatened the traditional home. None of them traded in nuance. In one of his newsletters he included an addendum titled a "Family Bill of Rights," which stridently and somewhat contradictorily defended the nuclear family against every government incursion—education, taxes, and social welfare—while also demanding that politicians make protection of the traditional family their primary concern. In another, he included the "Creed" published by "Women for Home and Family," an Anaheim-based Protestant organization. "We are convinced that women should unite, forget doctrinal differences, and proclaim their rightful place in the home and family, under the Lordship of Jesus Christ, through love, the Word and deeds," it declared. Norris also began holding marriage workshops around the state, taught by guest "faculty" like antipornography crusader Larry Lorenz and other Lutheran, Pentecostal, and Catholic reformers. As popular as these seminars were, however, they did not measure up to Norris's success as a journalist. By the mid-1970s Norris was reporting that Christian Family Renewal had distributed 3 million copies of *Who Killed Junior*, and thousands of other booklets, and that it was responsible to "155,000 individuals and groups" who counted on the newsletter "for advice, direction and tools to win victories over the moral evils such as abortion, pornography, Satanism, homosexuality and amoral sex education."[37]

If Murray's organization linked Catholics and evangelicals, others united Neo-Pentecostals and Baptist fundamentalists. Believing that "signs and wonders" like speaking in tongues had ceased in Christ's time, the latter had always been uniformly suspicious of the former, but, during the rise of Neo-Pentecostalism, Baptists began dividing over the issue. For separatist, fighting fundamentalists like Archer Weniger and Bob Jones, there was little question that the charismatic movement was apostate. Replying to a Southern California woman's query about Neo-Pentecostals, Jones spoke bluntly:

> They are involved with Roman Catholic priests in . . . every kind of unscriptural infidelity and religious adultery. I tell you this charismatic movement is of the Devil. . . . When you defend it, you are defending something that God forbids. I find the same kind of tongues movement prevalent among certain fanatical Arabs, Moslems, and Buddhists; and missionaries in the depths of Africa find it among the pagan rites of jungle sacrifice.

By the time Jones wrote this letter, in the mid-1970s, however, the majority opinion among less rigid, reforming fundamentalists was that Neo-

Pentecostals were of the same faith. Once-ardent critics like Tim LaHaye and W. S. McBirnie in fact began empathizing with this side of the evangelical family and strengthening bonds through shared teachings on prophecy and culture. LaHaye and McBirnie's inclusiveness earned them Weniger and Jones's wrath, but such censure carried minimal weight. Baptist fundamentalists may have dictated evangelical politics in the Goldwater years, when their exacting belief in truth and liberty accorded well with the ideologue's vision, but in the emerging, holistic, ecumenical Reagan Right, when body politics took precedence, charismatics enjoyed the upper hand.[38]

This new communion of Baptists and Pentecostals was coordinated at the grassroots level through evangelicalism's new culture industries. During the Proposition 18 campaign, leaders from these faith traditions, for instance, strengthened ties in the National Alliance for Family Life, which used Southern California as an operational base. Baptists and Neo-Pentecostals locked arms in these multifaceted agencies, yet they also connected in more intimate settings. At Melodyland's research centers, interfaith conversations about modern counseling methods led naturally into interfaith talk about family politics. Meanwhile, LaHaye helped popularize Murray Norris's concept of the traveling seminar. He and his wife, Beverly, started Family Life Seminars to "enrich good marriages, salvage bad ones, prepare young people for marriage and lead people to Jesus Christ." Instantly, they generated a tremendous response for their celebration of sex in monogamy and for their willingness to bring the bedroom to bear on politics. Their seminars tweaked raw anxieties, shared by Baptists and Pentecostals, that contemporary political culture was undermining the sacredness of marriage.[39]

The second, more impressive way charismatic and reforming fundamentalists achieved unity at the grassroots level was through housewife activism. Pastors may have encouraged grassroots mobilization in the escalating culture wars, but local evangelical women spearheaded it. Beverly LaHaye, Vonette Bright, Shirley Boone, Virginia Otis, and other wives of high-profile leaders used their platforms to inspire "their sisters in Christ." Beverly LaHaye spent the early 1970s becoming evangelicalism's own Phyllis Schlafly. Like her Catholic counterpart, LaHaye argued that it was only through a rejection of modern feminism and the legislation that supported it, coupled with a return to biblically ordained roles of the supportive wife and mother, that American women's "plight" would be solved. Though less vocal than LaHaye, Bright used her influence for the cause and even queried the possibility of starting a women's political movement in Southern California. She never saw this plan realized, but by the mid-1970s she was heavily invested in Campus Crusade's "feminars"—conferences for female staff—in which she urged Christian women to fight the "not very feminine" feminist movement. Along with LaHaye and Bright, Virginia Otis and Shirley Boone carried out large, public campaigns that declared that biological differences between men and women demanded distinctive roles in society. In accordance with the divinely sanctioned "complementary" duties assigned to them, women needed to submit to male headship in the home and, outside the domestic fold, exercise authority as moral guardians of the Christian republic.[40]

As important as these four individuals would become to a mature Christian women's movement, the driving impulse came from those who attended their rallies. It came from rank-and-file Protestant and Catholic suburban housewives who had already been active together in local school board battles, anticommunist surveillance, and Goldwater canvassing, or had seen their mothers take part in each of these tasks. It came from women long active in church schools like Central Baptist's, where monitoring textbooks, writing and directing patriotic plays, and chaperoning young people to the nation's heritage shrines had always been seen as their vital contribution. By the early 1970s many of these women listened intently to LaHaye and Schlafly and agreed that the ERA would force women into male domains (the workplace and the military, for example) and their children out of home care, and that *Roe v. Wade* tragically sacrificed the rights of the unborn for misconceived rights of women.

They also counted on guidance from women whom they sat next to in church or who wrote for their denominational papers. For Southern Baptist women, Betty J. Coble matched this humbler profile. The transplanted Arkansan was no LaHaye or Schlafly, but she taught hundreds of women in Sunday school at her Southern California church and wrote for the thousands who read the *California Southern Baptist*. In 1973, she started a column called "Who Says?" In it, she spoke with passion about the need for evangelical women to protect their family's foundation. "The Bible presents an organization that is fantastic," she declared in her first editorial. "God in His wisdom has made every part of this universe with perfect order and He has not left woman out. He instructed man to be the leader; woman to complete, complement, and follow." Coble then added a standard analogy for Southern California evangelical conservatives. "Logic reasons that any business can not survive with two heads." As evident in any well-run corporation, she summarized, a top-down executive structure was beneficial for everyone. This corporate model gave women "the provision of love, guidance that is with her own interest in mind, and someone with whom she may completely share herself. There is no way a monotary [sic] value can be placed on this." Family values and fiscal responsibility designed for maximum returns, all delineated in a rationale of republican virtue and sacred order: This was the Sunbelt doctrine that Baptist and Neo-Pentecostal, evangelical and Catholic wives and their husbands now sanctioned together.[41]

APPROACHING THE APOCALYPSE

For all their diligence in pursuing dominion over their society, Southern California evangelicals approached America's bicentennial with fear of impending ruin. At the very moment their movement seemed to reach the pinnacle of power, they saw it tested by two events of 1974—one unexpected, the other anticipated. Both confirmed their prior assumptions about their political captains and challenged them to take their political philosophy to the nation with more deliberate speed.

The first blow to evangelical conservatives was Watergate. In August 1974, after months of growing controversy, President Nixon resigned in order to avoid the more humiliating fate of impeachment. Ironically, his resignation followed a series of events that began the very same week as Explo '72. On June 17, 1972, the night "one way youth" danced to the rhythms of Christian rock music in downtown Dallas, five men associated with the Committee to Re-Elect the President (CREEP) broke in to Democratic National Committee headquarters at the Watergate complex in Washington, D.C. An investigation of the break-in ensued, and in July 1973, Nixon ordered that Watergate special prosecutor Archibald Cox be fired after he sued to obtain taped conversations from the White House that Cox believed would implicate Nixon. The "Saturday Night Massacre"—October 23, 1973, when Cox and others involved in the investigation were dismissed—hinted of greater malfeasance in Nixon's administration and led to an impeachment investigation by the House of Representatives and a Supreme Court order for the White House to turn over its recordings. The tapes were the "smoking gun" that Cox and congressional leaders had anticipated, and revealed Nixon's attempts to cover up the Watergate break-in. In an effort to save face, the president resigned. On August 9, 1974, he was gone, leaving Vice President Gerald Ford in charge.[42]

Nixon's exit left conservatives demoralized. Whatever their impressions were of Nixon prior to Watergate, they wavered now between two emotions: utter disgust and complete disillusionment. One of conservatism's "young Turks," Howard Phillips, summed up these feelings when he stated that "Under Richard Nixon, our ideological opportunity has been squandered, our loyalties have been unreciprocated, and our party's reputation for integrity has been virtually destroyed." Evangelicals were equally distressed. Billy Graham had not imagined that anything so offensive would emerge from the Watergate investigation. The evangelist was quick to dismiss charges against Nixon early on, but once he learned of the White House tapes and the vulgarities that peppered the president's language, he was revolted. Feeling betrayed, Graham backpedaled from political ties but pledged to help the fallen president as a friend. In Southern California, evangelicals shared the revulsion. They condemned the sin while trying not to condemn the sinner, but for many this was too fine a distinction, especially since they had suspected Nixon from the very beginning. Those closer to Nixon were the most outspoken. Following the midterm elections of 1974, which saw the GOP punished at the polls, Banowsky spoke harshly of his former boss. "We must make it clear that we are just as shocked and sick at the abuse of power as any other Americans," he explained. Nixon's actions represented not only a crime against good government but a crime against America's "free institutions." Nixon as well as the Republican Party, Banowsky thundered, needed to acknowledge their guilt and seek restoration in the court of public opinion.[43]

The second blow to conservatives in 1974, of course, was the end of their two-term partnership with Ronald Reagan. Reagan closed his governorship at the height of popularity, thanks in part to the Watergate scandal. Throughout the two-year ordeal, Reagan defended Nixon, demonstrating a loyalty maintained by few other Republicans. Counterintuitively, his allegiance to the president in fact solidified his image in the eyes of many Americans as a man of integrity. So while other Republican leaders' stock plummeted amid the presidential scandal, Reagan's rose sharply. Immediately after Nixon's resignation, when approval for and registration in the Republican Party was plummeting, a poll found that three out of five Californians believed their governor had done a good or excellent job in office, a rare accomplishment in a state with such polarized politics.[44]

Their governor's rising popularity only heightened Southern California evangelicals' growing sense of loss, but for the moment, at least, celebration was in order. In the spring of 1974, Reagan and his allies seemed eager to reward each other for years of work. Reagan endorsed a national evangelical campaign to declare April 30 "a day of humiliation, fasting, and prayer in California." In his words, this was to be "a moment for citizens of this state . . . to humble ourselves before God, to acknowledge our dependence upon Him, to ask forgiveness for our sins, and to give thanks for His great love for us as personified by His son, Jesus Christ, who is our Saviour [sic] and Lord." Drawing their heaviest support from local chapters of Campus Crusade for Christ, Melodyland, and five hundred other "pivotal churches," organizers of the statewide initiative "saturated" their communities with pleas for people to pray. "We believe the life of our nation is at stake," their literature read. "The destinies of millions of Americans are in the balance. GOD STANDS READY. YOUR PRAYERS—WITH THE PRAYERS OF MILLIONS OF OTHERS—CAN CHANGE OUR NATION'S HISTORY." In the summer, Banowsky helped evangelical conservatives' Republican brethren return Reagan's favor by chairing an appreciation gala for the governor. The dinner was designed to "show appreciation to a friend who answered the most demanding of all callings, giving eight years to provide impeccably honest leadership for California." It was also meant to bring together those who shared a common desire to "perpetuate his [Reagan's] brand of leadership in the California Legislature in the future." On both counts, the tribute dinner was a rousing success. The friends whom Reagan had counted on throughout his governorship filled the Century Plaza Hotel's ballroom, and money needed to keep the politician's movement alive boosted the GOP's campaign budget.[45]

A few months after the celebrations ended, Banowsky and his fellow conservatives finally faced the harsh post-Nixon, post-Reagan reality. The lingering stain of Watergate, the proliferation of interest group and ethnic identity politics, and the country's deteriorating economic conditions all served to reinforce the perception of a seriously divided America in steep decline. The country's once-powerful northern rim, from Minnesota to Massachusetts shouldered much of this burden. While deindustrialization was draining northern urban centers of their factories and jobs and turning the entire region into the Rustbelt, spiraling debt was driving once-thriving metropolises like New York to bankruptcy. The situation was no better for the United States on an international scale. In an age of energy shortages and shifting markets, American companies were finding it difficult to compete with more efficient producers in Japan and Germany; Toyota and Volkswagen stole market shares from Detroit automakers, while oil-producing nations in the Middle East inflated gas prices. The Vietnam War finally came to an end in 1975, but this underscored the fact that U.S. military might was as much of a fantasy now as its economic prowess. The only thriving sector of society seemed to be Hollywood, which captured Americans' disillusionment in some of the best movies ever made.[46]

Conservatives, despite their gains, certainly felt circumscribed. Because of Watergate, an emboldened Democratic Party was able to solidify control of Congress. Moderate Republicans, meanwhile, leveraged Nixon's follies to shift the GOP back to the center, a transition symbolized by President Ford's choice of Nelson Rockefeller as his vice president. Forced to the margins again, conservatives began fighting with each other over their future. Ideological purists like Richard Viguerie contemplated a third party, but gave up when Reagan—their chosen leader—refused to defect. Class divisions surfaced, too. In a *Los Angeles Times* editorial published in December 1974, William F. Buckley Jr. wrote that the conservative movement's only hope was for sophisticates such as himself to teach populists the "rudimentary" "arithmetic" of political economy and to recruit a leader to convince them that the "pointy-headed intellectuals" George Wallace types railed against were not villains and that "taxing the rich" was no proper solution to society's problems. Always ready to editorialize, Banowsky defended the populists. "I like Bill Buckley a lot," Banowsky readily admitted, but "in my judgment, what really keeps such a coalition from occurring is not, as Mr. Buckley alludes, the stupidity of the ordinary people, but rather the elitism of the patricians."[47]

For some evangelical conservatives, there was even worse squabbling inside their own faith communities. Banowsky's life became a case in point. As much as he wanted to defend the populists against Buckley, he now faced his own difficulties with them. During the mid-1970s Banowsky came under fire from ideologues within the Church of Christ, men like one-time student president Trent Devenney and corporate sponsor Archie Luper, who had lauded Banowsky after his debate with Bishop Pike. Fearful that Pepperdine was becoming too moderate theologically and politically, these critics mustered a case that centered on finances. They charged that Chancellor Norvel Young and Banowsky had received bonuses from a secret fund set up by university trustees. Although a separate account had been established to fund Young and Banowsky's retirement plans, no illegal activities had transpired, and the accusations ceased, but not before damage was done to Banowsky's reputation. The aspiring politician took another hit just a few months later, in the spring of 1975, when the Reagan tribute dinner that he had overseen the previous year came under scrutiny. Banowsky's planning committee had failed to file an official report acknowledging that monies raised at the event would finance Republican candidates. This blunder put Banowsky's name in headlines of local newspapers. By mid-1975 the toll on Banowsky was evident. Battered by the right flank, which wanted him to be less of a party man and more of a purist, and disillusioned by criticism from church insiders who thought Pepperdine was too secular, Banowsky resigned as National Committee member and retreated from the political dream he had drafted in 1970.[48]

It was easy, therefore, for Banowsky and his fellow evangelical conservatives to be discouraged about America and its political future—their political future—by 1976. When Billy Graham stood before the throngs of people gathered in Washington, D.C., for Honor America Day celebrations on July 4, 1970, he had warned America about "checking its stitches" before the bicentennial. Six years later the evangelist had watched his nation, disgraced and limping, slip deeper into trouble. And the evangelical conservatism he and Banowsky had helped shape was, like the Republican Party, fractured and uninspired. When 1976 arrived, Banowsky, Graham, and their evangelical brethren were not, to say the least, in a festive mood. Understandably, perhaps, a few stated that the signs of the times pointed to Christ's impending return; other evangelicals gave up and quietly prepared for the rapture.

There were, however, a few silver linings in these clouds of apocalyptic doom. The final years of Reagan's governorship had, for instance, allowed evangelicals in Southern California to lay a strong political foundation. After the mid-1970s tribulation, they would rely on these roots to regain the lost momentum of Sunbelt conservatism. Moreover, the interfaith political action committees, research institutes, and advocacy groups they had consolidated after Nixon's reelection boded well for a more sweeping, Sunbelt counteroffensive following the 1976 election. They also placed evangelicals in an optimum position to respond to changing rules and attitudes at the national level. After Watergate, Congress passed legislation meant to democratize political processes in Washington. Particularly important was a 1974 bill that limited individual contributions to political campaigns, thereby decreasing the power of large corporate and union donors and reducing the chance for corruption. Delivered by a Democratic majority, the edict was in fact a boon to struggling right-wing Republicans because it played to their strengths in grassroots mobilization. In an ironic twist, perhaps, America's post-Nixon malaise benefited the Right in another way by legitimizing its conceptions of politics and personhood. That big government was untrustworthy and leaders fallible were fundamental truths that conservatives had been preaching for decades. Now, in light of Nixon, they were difficult to deny.[49]

Evangelicals in Southern California enjoyed other important advantages because of their experiences during the early 1970s. Most significantly, they possessed a compelling message of national renewal and the sophisticated mechanisms in place to deliver it. With a particular brand of ceremonial politics honed in the 1972 election, evangelicals proclaimed their faith as the solution to the Watergate fallout. In the months leading into the nation's bicentennial year, E. V. Hill appeared at yet more Billy Graham crusades to restate his pleas for reclamation of Christian America's founding principles. Like Graham, Hill preached that Watergate was a moral failing representative of a much more profound amoral decadence in America, and that judgment was coming unless America repented. This same effective message was dispensed through a campaign begun by Bill Bright: Here's Life, America. During the final days of Nixon's administration, Bright had been busy. In 1974 he and Arizona congressman John Conlan organized Third Century Publishers to politicize evangelicals in every congressional district. With the help of several businessmen, they started mass-producing books like *One Nation Under God*, written by Rus Walton, a director of the American Conservative Union. Bright also founded the Christian Embassy to evangelize members of Congress. In fall of 1975, he began an evangelistic drive so bold that it made even some of his most ardent supporters nervous. "The next 16 months," he explained to his staff, "will very likely determine the destiny of our nation." "We have fourteen months before the November 1976 elections to turn the tide," or else "we will experience another thousand years of dark ages." Bright's base goal was to share Christianity with at least twenty-five million people. Toward this end, Campus Crusade carried out a "citywide saturation campaign" based on E. V. Hill's model of urban evangelism. Block-by-block witnessing was Bright's solution to America' bicentennial struggles, and though it would fall far short of its statistical goal, it effectively announced Sunbelt evangelicalism's revitalization and fresh investment in the nation's political future. Within months, Here's Life, America was operational in 200 cities, including New York City, whose local efforts were supported by 801 churches, Mobil, and Coca-Cola.[50]

Their homegrown "electric church" also primed Southern California evangelicals for an advanced role in Sunbelt conservatism's revitalization. As witnessed in Trinity Broadcasting Network's mission, by mid-decade the evangelical political doctrine came wrapped in a glitzy package of color-blind, interfaith, family-centered, free market conservatism that radiated from the television screen in infectious ways. At a moment when American society was fracturing along ethnic, racial, regional, and economic lines, TBN reassured evangelicals that their country's melting pot was still functioning fine. When tuning in for the *Praise the Lord* program, viewers encountered black pastors E. V. Hill and Frederick Price and white preachers Hal Lindsey and W. S. McBirnie, Christian crooners like Pat Boone and black musicians like Andraé Crouch, evangelists with Italian and Irish names and revivalists with Spanish- and German-sounding ones. Those tuning in also gained access to a gospel of health and wealth. Even in its early days of financial struggle, TBN dealt its viewers a unified message, straight from Southern California's shimmering suburbs, that all was well with capitalism. Of course, as even some of its preachers admitted at the time—especially Hill and Price, who lived in Los Angeles' less splendid core—not all was well with America's economy. Hill was not blind to the "bread-and-butter" issues of employment, housing, and crime that still plagued his community, nor did he hide his dissatisfaction with this state of affairs. And Price was fully cognizant of the racial inequities that continued to set his parishioners apart from white evangelical ones and forced him to drive forty miles to TBN's suburban campus. But Hill, Price, and the Christian brethren who joined them on TBN's set did not dwell on these realities or mention them other than as evidence of

America's moral failing. In quintessential Sunbelt booster fashion, they preferred to face the apocalypse by stressing the blessed hope of America's illustrious future and Christ's glorious return.[51]

SOUTHERN CALIFORNIA EVANGELICALISM'S MEDIA apparatus was also designed to synchronize political action along the southern rim. At the Christian Book Association's annual conference, held in Anaheim's Convention Center during the fall of 1975, Congressman John Conlan followed a performance by Johnny Cash with a blueprint for this active conviction. "To build a truly just and peaceful society," he explained, "man's law must be in concert with Gods' laws, and the powers of civil government must be restricted by those inalienable rights endowed by Him." This, Conlan emphasized, was what the Revolution was about:

> The God-inspired men who founded this nation rejected the idea of earthly sovereigns and centralized government. They said, "Keep government small and decentralized so that men and women might have the opportunity to rise to the full measure of their potential before their heavenly Father with the talents they have been given in the midst of the variety of natural resources He has provided. And within that environment they might have the freedom to know their Savior in a personal way."

But make no mistake, he cautioned, "the atheistic element is attacking." "When government can take 43 percent of the fruits of your labor and decide how to distribute it, government can control the academic, the intellectual, the social, the moral—and yes—even the religious climate of the community." The state was now society's savior, Conlan declared, and because of it, citizens were becoming slaves to a system.

The congressman then moved on to practical applications. Secular humanists want Christians to stay quiet and out of the political process, he said. "Go ahead with your sermons and song-fests but don't try to apply your Christian principles to contemporary problems," they say; "don't forget 'separation of church and state,'" they say. "Well," Conlan announced, church-state separation "does not mean that God should be divorced from public affairs . . . that Christians are to shun the affairs of civil government . . . that Christians cannot be involved in the realm of public ideas or the application of moral principles to domestic and international issues." Jesus called his followers to go into the world to preach the gospel, and this means going into each sector of society and turning it back to God. How were evangelical citizens to interpret and embody this in their day? By volunteering for grassroots, door-to-door campaigns to get Christians elected to state government and appointed to local councils that control "zoning and can decide whether a church may be built, or whether home Bible classes may be held on a regular basis in areas zoned 'residential.'" It meant praying, mobilizing, and voting on behalf of Christian republican virtues. "I know we are looking for the Lord to come again," Conlan admitted, but "we are also told to occupy until He comes." Here his Sunbelt screed turned into a Sunbelt anthem. In 1976, evangelicals would begin remaking the nation from the bottom up. The apocalypse might still come, Conlan announced, but if it did, he wanted Christ to find his servants feverishly at work trying to save their society. "If that is your determination, as it is mine, then we are going to keep the Gospel moving. And, we are going to give this nation a new birth of freedom under God as it begins its third century."[52]

13

BORN AGAIN

Religious America is awakening, perhaps just in time for our country's sake. If we believe God has blessed America with liberty, then we have not just a right to vote but a duty to vote. We have not just the freedom to work in campaigns and run for office and comment on public affairs. We have a responsibility to do so. . . . If you do not speak your mind and cast your ballot, then who will speak and work for the ideals we cherish? Who will vote to protect the American family and respect its interests in the formulation of public policy?

I know you can't endorse me because this is a non-partisan crowd, but I . . . want you to know that I endorse you and what you are doing.[1]

—RONALD REAGAN,
DALLAS, 1980

ONE WEEK BEFORE AMERICANS VOTED IN THE 1976 PRESIDENTIAL election, Bill Bright organized the National Prayer Congress in Dallas, Texas. Thirty-two prominent evangelicals gave warmly received speeches on different facets of prayer, but two Texans with California ties stood out. Fifteen years earlier E. V. Hill and W. A. Criswell could not have shared a stage; the former segregationist from Dallas and black radical from Houston held very different views of the world. Yet in 1976, their presence attested to the new South and a new Sunbelt evangelical alliance.

Much as he had at Explo '72 four years earlier, Hill gave an impassioned message of reconciliation to Prayer Congress delegates. "I'm a Texan. . . . I breathe comfortably in Texas," he announced, before recounting his struggles with poverty in Sweet Home and the prayers of his adoptive mother as he worked through school. These familiar signposts in Hill's sermon allowed him to impart a moral lesson and turn it into a political plea. There was no social welfare in his hometown, just a lot of neighborly love; no government handouts, just an abundance of faith in human potential. Since adolescence, Hill said, he had learned that prayer was the means by which one came to appreciate this reality. Prayer brings comfort, a sense of direction, and above all proof of a present and active God. In light of the nation's current crises, he concluded, it seemed about time for the lessons of his youth to be replicated, and for citizens to begin praying again.

Criswell took a different tack, relying on his signature fire-and-brimstone style. "If you want to see what America is twenty years [from now]" because it no longer prays, he charged, look at New York City, one of the "filthiest places on the planet," "the place of rendezvousing for the pimp and procurer and the prostitute and the drug pusher and the pornographic peddler." It is the place of pure godlessness, he intimated, yet tragically, America's window onto its soul. Criswell contrasted this hell to a place of godliness he once knew intimately, Texas' dusty plains, "Texahoma" along the Red River. There he had grown up amid scarcity worsened by windstorms that swept away the topsoil. "I have seen the sky, the heavens turn into brass and the earth into iron," he recalled, "I have heard the cattle lowing, thirsting for water." The preacher then talked about his father, a broken man who had struggled to survive on the land, then as a barber in town, before moving west to Fresno, California. With great pride, he said, his father had followed his preaching career from a distance. When Criswell succeeded the famed George W. Truett at First Baptist in 1944 and customers in his Fresno shop openly questioned the wisdom of a poor "Okie" in this revered pulpit, Criswell senior silenced them with the uncharacteristic boast that his boy was "going to be the greatest."

Criswell chose to focus on his father's humility, however, when concluding this speech. Through plague and pestilence, the poor Texan had remained dedicated to God; he prayed for relief from hard times but endured whatever the weather brought him, and rejoiced when divine blessing seemed to shine on his household. Criswell offered one final illustration of this when he described a boyhood encounter with a summer storm that stirred up the dust but also his father's spirits.

I was standing in the back door of our farmhouse by the side of my father and he was shouting at the top of his voice. . . . And looking up into his face I said, "daddy, what you shouting for?" And my father replied, "son the rain, the rain—God hath sent us the rain"; it meant food for our hungry mouths; it meant clothing for our naked backs. God hath sent us the rain.

How stark the difference, Criswell declared with a quivering voice, between this man's faith and the prevailing winds of greed and immorality that now blew over the barren soil of American society. It was time for Christians to pray for rain—for revival, for reformation, for a reconstituted nation. "Oh for the floods on the thirsting lands."[2]

LIKE COUNTLESS OTHER SERMONS delivered during America's bicentennial year, Hill's and Criswell's were layered with transparent political meaning. Their calls for religious awakening were spoken in the standard language of American revivalism, yet as commentaries on society they represented something unprecedented. Fundamentally, they prescribed a new Sunbelt agenda of free market capitalism and decentralized government, patriotism and family values. But thanks to the oratory of skilled preachers, who used the occasion to reminisce on their own odysseys, these prescriptions were also delivered with great sentimentality in poignant tales of a fabled past and enchanted future. In their sacred discourse, these clerics turned shared plain-folk legacies into superlatives of regional privilege; in their political discourse, they turned them into leverage for power. And by referencing the plight of a Rustbelt north, where wayward cities like New York sunk into depravity, they underscored the urgency of their message. Combined, their religious politicking announced that self-made southerners and a rags-to-riches South had finally earned the right to lead the nation.

Between 1976 and 1980, as the United States' crisis of confidence came to a head, E. V. Hill, W. A. Criswell, and their fellow evangelicals consolidated their resources into a united front. With each trip between Dallas and Los Angeles, sojourners like Hill and Criswell traveled pathways laid decades earlier. Now, these crossroads of individual and institutional making were finally consolidated for permanent political ends as residents of the South's swelling metroplexes redoubled their support for fiscal and social conservatism and efforts to turn local campaigns into national ones. As much as suburban saints in Dallas, Atlanta, and Miami contributed to this surge, this was the time for Southern Californians to shine. Having ascended as a moral majority in their state earlier in the 1970s, they had invaluable experience to share with the conservative coalition regrouping itself for the 1980 election. They also had a politician ready to fill the leadership vacuum, a man who could become the standard-bearer for a Sunbelt risen.

"THE YEAR OF THE EVANGELICAL"

The prayer forum that took place in Dallas in October 1976 was part of a national phenomenon that the press labeled a "third great awakening" of American evangelicalism. During the same week as this meeting in Dallas, Newsweek's front cover in fact blared "Born Again!" and declared 1976 "The Year of the Evangelical." Clearly, members of the media were waking up to the reality of a religious resurgence, and, in harmony with journalists like John Egerton, they singled out the reconstructed southern "Bible Belt" as the seedbed of revival. Two symptoms of evangelicalism's bicentennial boom caught their attention: a confident, glitzy, religious popular culture and a presidential candidate who attended church on Sundays.[3]

Newsweek based its analysis of the national religious climate on census data and first impressions of alternative religious media. According to a mid-decade Gallup poll, fifty million Americans now indicated they had had an evangelical, born-again conversion experience. This statistic was striking enough for what it said about evangelicalism's influence, but it was the visuals of a born-again popular culture that underscored its remarkable reach. Conservative Protestants, pundits found, now patronized their own coffeehouses, concerts, television programs, and even supper clubs, where they dined to edifying music performed by Christian artists, some, like Johnny Cash and Kris Kristofferson, who were famous in the mainstream. Through books and record albums purchased at Christian bookstores, evangelicals also enjoyed access to the personal reflections of countless other celebrities, star athletes like Terry Bradshaw and music icons B. J. Thomas and Bob Dylan, and even black radical Eldridge Cleaver, all of whom claimed fresh devotion to the Christian gospel. Few generated more interest than convicted Nixon aide Charles Colson, whose 1976 autobiography of spiritual regeneration, Born Again, was more than a purge of his former life in the White House; it was a perfectly timed treatise on America's turn to God.[4]

At the same time that Colson's testimony of personal faith hit bookstore shelves, pollsters were evaluating another barometer of evangelicalism's ascendancy: end-times belief. They found that a majority of Americans believed in Christ's impending reappearance, with many subscribing to premillennialism, whose assumptions about earth's cataclysmic end seemed to become more popular with each new cycle of war in the Middle East. Wanting to help Israel survive until prophecy could be fulfilled, and keen on converting its people before Armageddon, many Christians flocked to the Jewish nation with a sense that they were bearing witness to the last days. Even while they toured the Holy Land in record numbers, they began studying it with renewed seriousness in the United States. By the mid-1970s Hal Lindsey was a household name, his end-times essay, *The Late Great Planet Earth*, an international bestseller. In 1978 he released a movie version. "After seeing this graphic account of political unrest around the world, the ever present danger of nuclear holocaust . . . cruel scythe of famine, outbreak of new diseases, genetic experimentation, depleted energy supplies," promoters promised, viewers will ask, "'How much longer do we really have?'" In another sign of evangelicalism's changing fortunes, Orson Welles—once a staunch critic of evangelicals—thought enough of the project to narrate it and in essence reprise his role from an apocalyptic story—*The War of the Worlds*—that had made him famous four decades earlier.[5]

As much as it seemed like all of America had been swept up in bornagain, end-times mania, several critics questioned the trend. Militant fundamentalists were appalled by what they saw as the adulteration of the conversion experience. "These are strange and confusing days indeed!" one Los Angeles Baptist pastor wrote sarcastically, with reference to Charles Colson's discovery of Christ. "In a day of unparalleled religious, political and moral degeneracy, all of a sudden it seems that almost everyone is . . . an EVANGELICAL." Meanwhile, highbrow evangelicals questioned Hal Lindsey's lowbrow genre. "Doomsday" had become "chic," one editorialist wrote, in *Christianity Today*. Lindsey's mangling of scripture on the silver screen not only lacked integrity, in this reviewer's estimation, it also promoted "Doomsdayism" at the sacrifice of trust in God's mercy, all simply for ratings and box-office receipts. Critics uninterested altogether in evangelicalism targeted the born-again, end-times phenomenon from a cynical perspective. "These are good times for rebirth," said one writer; "sinners are reborn humbly, politicians proud and loudly." Still, all of these criticisms simply accentuated evangelicalism's new status as a glittering, global venture.[6]

And those who dismissed evangelicalism's ascent also had to come to terms with the fact that America was about to go to the polls to elect a president whose beliefs mirrored Colson's and bore sympathies for Lindsey's. Battling, born-again presidential candidates openly expressed their faith in 1976 in order to relate to voters. If awkwardly, Republican incumbent Gerald Ford courted Protestants by testifying to his Episcopalian theology. While on the campaign trail he spoke at the annual meetings of both the National Association of Evangelicals and the Southern Baptist Convention. Editorialists in *Christianity Today* lauded these efforts, but far more journalists were drawn to Ford's competitor, Jimmy Carter, the public figure who more than any other personified evangelicalism's exploding popularity. In the months leading up to the fall election, the press published over a hundred articles analyzing the faith of this devout Southern Baptist from Georgia. Carter sent reporters scurrying to his hometown and journalists to the library to find out more about the born-again concept. "We have checked on the religious meaning of Carter's profound experience," news anchor John Chancellor announced with some clumsiness during a telecast. "It is described by other Baptists as a common experience, not something out of the ordinary."[7]

Declared normal by the media, Carter played up the folksy qualities of his faith, but he also worked hard to show that his religion was no marketing ploy. At the Democratic National Convention, on the night of his acceptance speech, he stressed his humble, Christian roots as the foundation upon which he and the Democratic Party would help heal the nation. Then he took to the campaign trail, talking about his devotional life, his daily practice of praying twenty-five times, for instance, and his nightly ritual of reading portions of scripture in Spanish. Meanwhile he trumpeted family values and promised a White House Conference on the American Family to help restore the public-private partnership in preservation of this sacred institution. Carter's earnestness worked—almost too well, in fact. Just weeks before the election, *Playboy* magazine published an interview with the candidate in which he admitted that he had "committed adultery in my heart many times" by looking on "a lot of women with lust." For those who had warmed to Carter because of his faith, this confession was difficult to process. Some clergymen reacted swiftly to the interview because it appeared in a magazine that was considered anathema to their worldview. W. A. Criswell was "highly offended" by Carter's behavior and used it as reason to endorse the GOP. Carter's own pastor said that he wished his parishioner had used "different words" to describe his failings, but said that otherwise it represented a genuine confession fully in keeping with New Testament teachings.[8]

Carter's gaffe, however, was not damaging enough to erode the support he had generated among evangelicals, especially Southern Baptists living in the South, who generally followed Reverend Bailey Smith's lead instead of Criswell's. Earlier during the campaign, while standing before fifteen thousand SBC delegates at their annual convention, Smith had charged that his country needed "a born-again man in the White House" whose "initials are the same as our Lord's." Hoping that one of their own would bring God to America and America to God, Southern Baptist citizens gave Carter their votes. Carter also earned 40 percent of votes cast nationwide by evangelicals, the best Democratic presidential showing with this constituency in over a decade. Regardless of whom they voted for, evangelicals celebrated the Democrat's win as a symbolic victory. Surprised at their community's swift climb into the political mainstream, officials of the NAE jokingly admitted, "We did not expect to have our proverbial lights so abruptly exposed from under their bushels."[9]

CALIFORNIA CONSERVATISM REBORN

In the months surrounding the 1976 election, Southern California evangelicals wanted their "proverbial lights" to shine brighter than ever. Since 1974, they had grown troubled by conservatism's marginalization and a sense that their movement was coming undone. Yet for all their angst, evangelical conservatives and their allies in the Golden State approached the 1976 election sensing a comeback. It was the candidacy of a politician who believed in Christ and his impending return that rekindled their optimism, a man whose initials bore no resemblance to Ford's, Carter's, or their Lord's.

Certainly the born-again, end-times phenomenon also fed Southern California evangelicals' hope that they were on the cusp of something better. When *Newsweek* declared "The Year of the Evangelical," it in fact ratified Southern California evangelicalism as the nation's major religious force. Much of the alternative media that journalists studied was a product of the West Coast. In an illustrative way, American evangelicalism's prevailing sensibilities were best summed up by a Christian carnival held at this time called Jesus, California Style. The fair's organizers spared no expense in constructing a panorama of evangelical panache. Headline acts by Bible Answer Man Walter Martin, Leon Patillo, a former band member of Santana, and Mike Warnke—America's leading Christian comedian—kept people glued to the showground's main stage. When fairgoers finally broke away to walk the midway, they were tempted with sideshows designed for entertainment and edification: twenty different musical groups, art shows, biblical plays and dramatizations, camel rides, Christian handcrafts, and seminars on science, health, family relationships, finances, ethics, and nutrition. As much as Southern Californians taught Americans how to spice up their faith, they also helped turn their expectant gaze towards Israel. Southern California's homegrown Neo-Pentecostal movement prompted much of the excitement. At the Trinity Broadcasting Network, prophecy experts like Hal Lindsey pondered the troubled Middle East and looked for signs of supernatural intervention. Lay leaders like Pat Boone and George Otis, meanwhile, traveled frequently to Israel and even established ties with Minister of Tourism Moshe Kol and Prime Minister Yitzhak Rabin. In 1976, with permission from Kol and Rabin, Boone and Otis, along with Cathoic activist Murray Norris, organized a large "goodwill 'Spirit of 76' Holy Land conference and tour" so Americans could extend "the assurance of Christian love and support for the country of Israel in her time of uncertainty and peril." Otis explained to the press, "We must begin bridging the colossal gap of a 2000-year mis-understanding."[10]

Christians around the country thus found much to imbibe in Southern California's religious enthusiasm, yet this fervor had a more politically significant outlet as well, one that few commentators appreciated in 1976. With their sights set on the South, journalists missed evangelicalism's political rebirth on California's southern coast. One key exception was California expatriate Carey McWilliams. Who are the evangelicals, he asked readers of the Nation rhetorically? They live in "'the missile crescent'" stretching from "Florida . . . to Southern California." They "are by no means exclusively white; thousands of Blacks, Chicanos, Orientals, Indians and White ethnics are also members." Together, he explained, these "God-fearing, up-and-coming types" constitute a "movement not a church," centered in "jerry-built" suburbs constructed on "cheap land" with the aid of "tax inducements, lower wage scales, less union activity . . . [and] a high level of defense spending." The evangelicalism now taking the country by storm, McWilliams summarized, was a producer and product of the Sunbelt economic juggernaut. This much of McWilliams's analysis relied on the offerings of others, but he said more on the subject. With an icy prose that hinted at his deep disregard for this subculture, McWilliams characterized Sunbelt evangelicalism as a safety zone for migrants who had flocked to the metropolis. "The new evangelicals . . . are unlike the fundamentalists of the 1920s," he acknowledged. They embrace new technologies even as they shun evolutionary science, which is more than could be said for the people H. L. Mencken encountered at the Scopes trial. Yet this made evangelicals a more daunting influence, because they now manipulated rather than rejected modernity. The evidence of this was everywhere in Southern California, he emphasized, where Christian ministries parlayed their proximity to high-tech firms and new money into cultural authority. This was the force behind the "God factor" in 1976 politics, McWilliams concluded, and though it was tied to Jimmy Carter, it had a direct line to another "twice born" politician with a higher ceiling of success: Ronald Reagan.[11]

McWilliams read Southern California evangelicals' political preferences perfectly. It was the possibility of Reagan's run to the White House this year that enlivened them far more than the prospect of Ford's or Carter's. They were spurred on by the knowledge of Reagan's born-again experience and devotion to biblical prophecy, the details of which resurfaced because of Otis and Boone's public remembrance of an encounter six years earlier. In October 1970, Reagan had hosted Otis, Pat and Shirley Boone, and pastor Harald Bredesen at his home in Sacramento. Herbert Ellingwood, the governor's legal affairs secretary and a leader in the Full Gospel Business Men's Fellowship International, arranged the meeting. During the visit, Reagan recounted a conversation he had had with Billy Graham about West German Chancellor Konrad Adenauer's premillennialist beliefs. Reagan was impressed by Adenauer's convictions and led his guests into a lengthy discourse about current events in Israel. Before leaving the mansion, the group held hands to pray. After a few seconds of awkward silence, Otis broke out in a prophetic utterance no one standing in the Reagans' foyer had expected. Otis would later recall that the "Holy Spirit came upon me and I knew it."

> There was this pulsing in my arm. And my hand—the one holding Governor Reagan's hand—was shaking. I didn't know what to do. I just didn't want this thing to be happening. I can remember that even as I

was speaking, I was working, you know, tensing my muscles and concentrating, and doing everything I could to stop that shaking.

Otis's words grew animated as well and led to a divination from the Holy
Spirit about Reagan's future: "If you walk uprightly before Me, you will
reside at 1600 Pennsylvania Avenue." Sheepishly, Otis ended the prayer,
leaving the governor speechless and the guests anxious to say good-bye.[12]

The memories of this gathering compelled Otis and Boone to help
Reagan vie for leadership of the GOP in 1976. Like other conservatives,
Otis and Boone saw Reagan as a much-needed corrective to Gerald Ford.
In the same way that Nixon had infuriated them with his middle-of-the
road maneuvers, Ford earned conservatives' censure for his. By 1976 he
had negotiated an arms treaty with the Soviets, dined with China's officials, contemplated a reworking of the Panama Canal treaty, raised taxes,
and staffed his cabinet with moderates. Making the situation worse for
conservatives is that Ford did not take them seriously. His estimation of
Reagan was equally low. Ford moved toward the 1976 Republican Party
National Convention assuming that his challenger was "a phony," his misguided movement no real challenge at all.[13]

It did not take long after Reagan's entry into the Republican race for
Ford to realize that he had miscalculated. The Republican primaries in
1976 were fiercely combative. In each state, local party apparatchiks fulfilled their assigned roles by lending the president their support, yet invariably they faced off against Reagan's grassroots supporters who refused to
concede Ford's candidacy. Reagan and Ford, meanwhile, exchanged sharp
verbal blows. While Ford attacked Reagan's plan to reduce taxes and government, Reagan responded by undermining Ford's dealings with Panama's left-wing regime. Reagan's assertions put him in an advantageous
position in Texas and California, where he won convincingly, despite
Ford's effort to paint him as an unemployed actor. "There are no retakes
in the Oval Office," Ford told Texans. Reagan supporters in Lubbock and
Longview paid no heed, while those on the West Coast answered the gibe
with taunts of their own. Playing on caricatures of the president as an oaf-
ish man who had taken too many blows on the football gridiron, California conservatives flew a large banner that read: "Reagan's ahead because
Ford bumped his." Clearly the GOP's Eleventh Commandment, which
Reagan had codified in the 1960s to forbid Republicans from speaking ill
of their own, was now a "dead letter."[14]

Otis and Boone joined the fray in an effort to sway voters toward the man they felt was ordained. Otis worked behind the scenes. During the primaries, just as the mainstream press began describing Carter's faith, Otis interviewed Reagan for his radio program, in order to publicize the politician's Christian commitments. Happy for the opportunity, Reagan described his abiding trust in the Bible as a guide to spiritual health and end-times prophecy. More authentic-sounding than Ford's, and at the very least equal to Carter's in forthrightness, Reagan's testimony struck what Otis believed to be an ideal tone. Excited, Otis and allies within the Los Angeles County Citizens for Reagan disseminated the testimonial over the airwaves and into local papers. Whereas Otis's work for Reagan amounted to consciousness raising, Boone's dealt with the brass tacks of campaigning. Chosen a California delegate for the Republican National Convention in Kansas City, Boone relished his role. Reagan's aides were thrilled to have him there; Ford's found him a nuisance. Heading into the convention with a delegate count too close to call, Reagan's and Ford's teams worked furiously to recruit uncommitted delegates. The most coveted was Mississippi's delegation, headed by Clarke Reed. Boone became Reagan's front man in the attempt to woo these southerners his way, and the strategy almost worked. One of the Mississippians was a black preacher who had lionized Reagan during the politician's visit to his state months earlier. Boone used him as an entry into Reed's constituency and then began spreading his Tennessee charm. Watching the maneuver unfold, Harry Dent, who now worked as a southern strategist for Ford, admitted that the Boone effect was golden. "My goodness," he warned his companions, "if they can take the preacher from under us, who is immune from the Boone-Reagan charisma?"[15]

Ultimately, California charm was not enough, and Reed's delegates went Ford's way, making it impossible for Reagan to overcome Ford's numbers. Despite their candidate's loss, Boone and his fellow conservatives left Missouri emotionally recharged because of two lesser victories. With a final flurry of activity, Reagan's supporters succeeded at forcing a number of key planks into the GOP platform, which called for the restoration of school prayer, a strong foreign policy, and "the right to life for unborn children." A second sign of life on the Right was manifested in the response to Reagan's powerful concession speech. Invoking General Douglas MacArthur for effect, Reagan challenged Republicans to con-

tinue their fight for freedom. "We must go forth from here, united, determined that what a great general said a few years ago is true, 'There's no
substitute for victory.'" Reagan's oration left the arena's occupants spell-
bound and his supporters openly weeping. A delegate expressed what
many of his allies were feeling at the time when he called it the "most
bittersweet moment of my life." By the end of the convention it seemed
obvious, in one reporter's mind, that "Ford won the nomination, but Reagan won their hearts."[16]

Southern California evangelicals took Reagan's loss hard and approached
the election with little enthusiasm. The Republican and Democratic candidates did nothing to elicit a different response from them. Ford and Carter
aimed for the center in their political campaigning and left voters confused
as to the difference between them. Even Carter's religion failed to stir up
much passion among Southern California evangelicals. Like their brethren
elsewhere, they embraced Carter's candidacy as a sign of their faith's new
status in public life; some likely voted for him because of his testimony.
But whether they marked their ballots for him or not, the prevailing sense
among Southern California evangelicals was that Carter's personal convictions were no match for the political machine he represented.[17]

Quite tellingly, even California Southern Baptists doubted Carter.
They lauded him for being an upstanding Christian and honorably representing their denomination, but from the beginning they seemed more
intrigued with Reagan's spiritual biography. The *California Southern Baptist* helped pique this curiosity by publishing Otis's Reagan interview and
reminiscing about the former governor's illustrious career. Their hesitancy
with Carter, however, cut deeper than their enthrallment with Reagan;
Southern Baptist or not, Carter, it seemed, was not entirely forthcoming
with his liberal Democratic political program or up-front with his Social
Democratic political associations. In a frank, ominous tone that hinted
at the heated politics about to explode in California, editor Elmer Gray
warned readers that Carter was becoming "strange bedfellows" with the
gay community. "One of the queerest things that happened in the campaign before the California primary was the endorsement by homosexuals of Jimmy Carter," he explained. "Obviously homosexuals are political
opportunists and care nothing for traditional ideas of honor and gratitude." Something within Carter's coalition did not bode well for Christians; Southern Baptist or not, to vote for the man, Gray implied, was to

vote for a political party that was using Christianity to cover an agenda that went contrary to biblical teachings.[18]

Gray's ambivalence seemed to represent the majority opinion among Southern California conservatives. After a close election that saw Ford squeak by Carter in California but Carter win a tight national race, they focused again on winning grassroots battles, with hopes of another run at the bigger prize in 1980. Convinced at first that Reagan was God's man for the hour, they now reasoned that his hour had not yet come. Few entertained the thought of its not coming at all.

SUNBELT RISING

By 1978 Southern California evangelicals were certain that Reagan's moment had finally arrived. At this juncture, many evangelicals living in the South still saw Carter and a rejuvenated Democratic Party as a solution. Southern California evangelicals, on the other hand, were solidly Republican and doubtful of Carter from the beginning. In the late 1970s they began selling their brethren on the point that Carter was unworthy of Christians' support. His indecisive foreign policy gave them ammunition. Though he appointed staunch cold warrior Zbigniew Brzezinski as his national security advisor, he also chose the anti–Vietnam War liberal Cyrus Vance to be his secretary of state. Disturbingly, to his critics, Carter seemed predisposed to Vance's guidance. He used policy to advance human rights goals, continued arms reduction talks with the Soviets, and signed a treaty granting legal control of the Panama Canal to the Panamanian government. Moreover, Carter did not seem able to solve conditions at home. Although tamed for a short time, stagflation reappeared during his presidency, leaving the country's economy more vulnerable than ever. His handling of cultural politics fared no better. Though he had campaigned for family values, he now supported women's and gay rights and the Equal Rights Amendment (ERA), delayed the White House conference on the family he had pledged, and generally seemed unconcerned about the abortion issue.[19]

In 1978, Southern California's evangelicals began turning their criticisms into concrete political action. Although Carter's presidency loomed large in their thinking, it was local developments that helped them reconsolidate a regional movement. Their catalysts were two state ballot initiatives: Proposition 13, a proposal to freeze property taxes, and Proposition

6, which sought to ban gays from employment in public schools. Both litmus tests drew coast-to-coast attention; both helped Sunbelt conservatives draw close again in partisan accord.

Conceived by Howard Jarvis, once a leader in the group Businessmen for Goldwater, Proposition 13 was a homeowners' quest to halt skyrocketing property tax hikes. Since 1970, these citizens had seen their incomes rise 50 percent; at the same time, their income, sales, and property taxes had risen over 150 percent. California's homeowners felt pinched, and Proposition 13 seemed like a way to ease the pain. But the initiative also offered conservatives a chance to curtail what they considered excessive welfare spending by the state government and force Governor Jerry Brown and Democratic legislatures to funnel the state's four-billion-dollar surplus into tax relief. There was an element of history repeating itself in all of this as well. The organizations that supported Brown—unions, civil servants, and civil rights lobbyists—reminded conservatives of the combatants they faced during Proposition 14's property rights battle in 1964, when Pat Brown, Jerry's father, ran the state. As they had done then, conservatives responded in 1978 by mobilizing behind a ratcheted-up rhetoric of political dissent.[20]

Whereas Proposition 14 had been about protecting sacred property, conservatives saw Proposition 13 in broader terms as an attempt to rearticulate the logic of free enterprise in the context of a national anti-Keynesian revolt. Preachers like Bill Banowsky and W. S. McBirnie assisted the cause. Banowsky did so as both a school administrator and an editorialist. In the role of the former, he created yet another forum for free market thought at Pepperdine, one that grew out of necessity as much as political foresight. In the previous few years, Pepperdine had faced a budget crunch stemming from school expansion. Since 1967, Pepperdine's total assets had grown from $7.8 million to $68 million, its enrollment from 1,247 to 8,983, but with the assets came a pressing need for cash flow. The crisis crested in the fall of 1975 at a moment when the school should have been basking in the glow of national attention. On September 20, President Gerald Ford spoke before eighteen thousand people to inaugurate the Firestone Fieldhouse. The week before his Malibu visit he had survived an assassination attempt; Pepperdine now bore the costs of heavier security. The school's finances grew worse in the succeeding months. During the spring of 1976, Pepperdine officials announced that in order to make payroll they would have to phase out programs at the Los Angeles campus and freeze tenure appointments and wages in the entire university. Faculty disapproved and organized a one-day strike. One white professor spoke succinctly about the situation when he said, "I'm a Goldwater Republican. . . . For me to even consider joining a strike or collective bargaining is an indication that this is the last act of desperation of a basically abused faculty." Meanwhile, black faculty and students on the Los Angeles campus suggested that the dire financial conditions also revealed the racial prejudices dividing the two Pepperdines. "Malibu attracts such an elite group," Leon Watkins complained; "we are not in the same vision—they don't see what I see." What Watkins saw was a university fragmenting along political, class, and racial lines.[21]

Determined to save his school, Banowsky conceived of the Pepperdine University Associates. This was to be an elite group of donors who pledged at least $1,000 annually. In honor of their contributions, each donor would be designated a University Associate and invited to attend an annual dinner to "hear a speaker of international stature." Banowsky's plan worked; 428 donors stepped forward, representing both the old and the new in the Pepperdine family. Those who had been with Pepperdine for a while included Henry Salvatori, Charles Thornton, Walter Knott, Clint Murchison Jr., Richard Scaife, and Ronald Reagan. New contributors like John Olin, Joseph Coors, and William Ahmanson joined these veteran members. In a parallel move, Pepperdine expanded the school's board of regents so that it would be open to the university's new "major stockholders." On the evening of February 9, 1977, these luminaries assembled at Los Angeles' Beverly Wilshire Hotel for the Founding Four Hundred dinner. The evening's festivities were grand, with guests decked out in tuxedos and evening gowns enjoying a multicourse meal served on fine china under sparkling crystal chandeliers. Leonard Firestone, former United States ambassador to Belgium, chaired the dinner and helped introduce the keynote speaker, Milton Friedman. The University of Chicago professor and freshly minted Nobel laureate came to Pepperdine's fete with a golden reputation as a mastermind behind the anti-Keynesian revolt. "We are very far . . . along the road to losing our freedom," he told the crowd, with a nod to Friedrich von Hayek. "There is no possibility of a future society," he continued, unless capitalism is allowed to flourish. Friedman suggested that Washington's handling of business was not so different from Yugoslavia's, but then he ended with wry optimism. Thanks to state mismanagement, Americans were finally grasping the need to revolt against New Deal fiscal policy. "I welcome government waste," he declared, because "waste . . . brings home the fact that more government is not the proper way to solve our problems."[22]

The dinner saved the school, but the fete meant more to a resurging Sunbelt conservatism. In no small way, it had helped restore the coalition that had elected Nixon. Each economic sector of the Sunbelt's "power base"—defense, aerospace, technology, electronics, agribusiness, oil and gas extraction—was represented in Pepperdine's select council, yet the unifying effect extended beyond dollars and cents. In addition to the freedom forums and Great Issues Series it continued to run, Pepperdine's annual dinners now provided extra reason for conservatives to think collectively. Illustrative of this coming together was the second annual Founders dinner, in 1978. On this occasion William F. Buckley Jr. himself seemed eager to mend ties by headlining the banquet and taking on John Kenneth Galbraith in a televised debate dubbed "Socialism v. Capitalism." Once chastised by Banowsky for his stuffy elitism, Buckley arrived at Pepperdine's gala advertised again as a friend.[23]

By allowing Friedman and Buckley a platform from which to proclaim the free market doctrine, Banowsky also gave further impetus to the Proposition 13 tax revolt, brewing at this exact moment. Pepperdine's chief executive connected the two in editorials he wrote for the *Los Angeles Herald Examiner*. "There is a fresh wind blowing across the hills of America," he declared. For forty years government had relied on spending to stimulate the economy when what was needed was a sedative to stop inflation. What had emerged from this pattern, he explained, was the "notion that if medicine will make a sick economy well, continuing the medicine will produce a state of economic euphoria." Neither chemistry nor the economy works that way, Banowsky emphasized. Rather, what was needed was hard medicine—a reduction both in spending and in taxes, just as Proposition 13 prescribed. The two necessities were interlocking, in his mind, since high taxes were a reflection of high spending, which in turn reflected a bulging bureaucracy. Banowsky declared that it was time for citizens to discipline their government.[24]

W. S. McBirnie galvanized the rank and file with this same proclamation. Having already produced literature deconstructing Jimmy Carter's every political move, his printing press now cranked out pro–Proposition 13 pamphlets that embedded criticism of the White House in a broader critique of political economy. McBirnie touted Proposition 13 as a solution to many economic woes. On one hand, it would free up cash for private investment; on the other, it would force the unemployed to become constructive members of society. "Welfare doesn't solve problems," he declared, "it only produces millions of freeloaders who need a strong kick to get back into the working population. The trick is to motivate—or, if necessary, force—them to work." Government would not suffer under the bill, McBirnie reassured his followers, now bombarded with anti–Proposition 13 arguments, it would just have to learn how to:

1. Cut wasteful expenses. 2. Stop reckless year-end buying . . . to justify bigger budgets. 3. Eliminate . . . salaries far in excess of private employment. 4. Bring public pension plans into line with those offered by private employers. 5. Bar illegal aliens from getting welfare, medical and dental care costing millions of dollars annually. . . . 6. Eliminate grandiose government plans for massive forced busing of school children. 7. Abolish public appropriations for quasi-public special interest groups.

In point-by-point form, McBirnie drew a line in the political sand between taxpayers and tax recipients. In effect, it was also a line that separated white suburbanites from an urban, interracial class of citizens, whose work and wages were more dependent on the public sector that Proposition 13 sought to cut.[25]

With McBirnie's help, California's suburban homeowners won the standoff. On June 6, 1978, Proposition 13 passed by a 65-to-35-percent margin. This meant that property would be taxed at a flat 2 percent rate of its actual value, and that no subsequent tax increases could be implemented without a two-thirds majority vote. The bottom line for government was a six-billion-dollar loss in property taxes designated for public works and services. Democrats had warned that Jarvis's bill would create a crisis—budget cuts, unemployment, lost educational programs— and now they faced this reality. Where it created a crisis for Jerry Brown, Proposition 13 created a defining moment for Southern California's conservatives. As McBirnie proudly announced, this was "one of the greatest grassroots rebellions since the Boston Tea Party." "Californians 'fired the shot' heard around the nation when they showed up in record numbers to demand a firm STOP to big-spending government bureaucrats."[26]

The measure took on added importance for Southern California evangelicals. By replaying the battles of the early cold war era, when they first fought government's infringements on their gospel of wealth, Jarvis's measure reminded them that economic freedom was a requisite for religious liberty and hence a vital pursuit. Proposition 13 reconnected Southern California evangelicals with a pre–cold war era as well. This initiative's logic was buttressed by a "supply-side" theory of economics, articulated by Proposition 13 advocate and USC economist Arthur Laffer, which placed priority on tax cuts as the truest stimulant for economic growth. Ideologically, this scheme harkened back to a frontier ideal of pristine capitalism, where unadulterated marketplace competition—not state planning—made America work. Southern California evangelicals became certain again during the Proposition 13 contest that this was the economic system God had intended for his people.[27]

It was their pursuit of a "pristine" social order that led these same citizens into their second ballot war of 1978. Evangelicals had anticipated it for two years. In 1975, California passed Assembly Bill (AB) 489, which decriminalized sodomy. The legislation sent evangelicals into a panic. Just months after AB 489 was passed, Orange County Southern Baptists agreed on several resolutions casting judgment on their statehouse. They condemned gun control and called on legislators to defend creationism, but one pronouncement stood out. "Whereas recent [legislation] has been passed [legalizing] homosexuality," it read, and "Whereas homosexuals are now trying to demand the right to obtain jobs previously forbidden to them; Whereas God's word says homosexuality is a sin (Romans 1) and a sin that God particularly hates":

> Be it resolved that we oppose all attempts to legalize homosexuality and urge the repeal of the present law. Be it further resolved that while we hate the sin of homosexuality we show [our] love to the homosexual by sharing with him the only answer to his problem, the Gospel of Jesus Christ. We believe Jesus died for the homosexual also.

Pastors in an emerging right-wing advocacy group called Family Lobby, meanwhile, announced a campaign to include a Public Decency initiative on the 1976 ballot. If passed, this measure would restore older decency laws and, according to lobbyists, guarantee protection of the young. Under AB 489, they emphasized, schools were not allowed to fire teachers because of sexual orientation. This was serious, they insisted, because there was already evidence that homosexual teachers were spending "classroom time promoting their sexual lifestyle." Despite flooding Christian bookstores and newspapers with stories of homosexual subversion, supporters of the "Public Decency" initiative did not secure enough funds and signatures for a spot on the ballot.[28]

Evangelical lobbyists did, however, generate enough fear to move sentiments forward. In late fall 1976, W. B. Timberlake, of the Committee on Moral Concerns, suggested a new course of action. AB 489, he noted, had "caused a great deal of moral outrage and unprecedented interest in the governmental processes" and thousands of letters insisting Governor Brown not sign the bill into law. Now that it had been signed into law, he stated, it was time to redirect the rage. Timblerlake suggested that Christians begin by petitioning against gay pride celebrations. He offered a recent demonstration in Atlanta, where pastors presented sixteen thousand letters to the mayor protesting the city's Gay Pride Day, as a model to follow. Because of its large gay community (estimated at 10 percent of the county's population), Timberlake and fellow activists saw San Diego as pivotal in the fight. Tensions soon flared there when the Gay Liberation Front, endorsed by the city's Human Relations Committee, decided to make an annual gay pride parade one of the nation's largest. The initiative was, in part, an act of solidarity with the Metropolitan Church, a gay congregation that local residents wanted relocated because of its proximity to a school. Metropolitan Church refused to move. As its resolve grew, so did the gay community's, and with each progression came a reaction from evangelicals who grew agitated by their city's apparent open-door policy on sexual freedom.[29]

It was the son of a Pentecostal preacher from Oklahoma, now a state assemblyman from Orange County, who turned conservatives' concerns to the polling booth. His inspiration came from another Sunbelt city. On June 6, 1977, John Briggs flew to Miami to observe the Dade County referendum on gay rights. In January the Dade County Commission had passed an ordinance outlawing discrimination against gays in housing, public accommodations, and employment. Gay activists hailed the ruling as a major victory, one that they hoped would start a national trend; evangelical conservatives immediately set out to reverse it by successfully demanding a referendum. Former Miss Oklahoma and the spokeswoman for Florida Citrus Commission Anita Bryant took up the cause and, in league with Save Our Children, Inc., succeeded at rallying conservatives against what they called the "sin and immorality law." Pastors from around the country lent their support by profiling Bryant on their television programs and staging a pre-referendum rally in the Miami Convention Center. All of this impressed Briggs, who attended a press conference the following day, when a beaming Bryant announced her organization's victory at the polls (the gay ordinance was repealed). "Tonight, the laws of God and the cultural values of man have been vindicated. The people of Dade County—the normal majority—have said, 'Enough, enough, enough.'"[30]

Briggs returned home determined to make California the location for a major plebiscite. Just days after San Francisco City Councilman Harvey Milk led a march to protest Bryant's victory, Briggs stood on the steps of San Francisco's city hall to announce a campaign to remove gay teachers from California's schools. His statement led to Proposition 6, the most anticipated contest in the 1978 election. "Homosexuality is the hottest issue in this country since Reconstruction," Briggs would boast and in a sense he was right. Politically, the Briggs initiative represented the first time that an entire state would vote on gay rights. It also pitted against each other two growing constituencies that saw sexual politics in Manichean terms. As Randy Shilts, a gay journalist covering Milk's career, noted, few groups "were as evenly suited to battle each other."

> Both gays and evangelicals shared a profound experience that shaped their politicking; they had both been born again. For evangelical Christians, it was a theological experience, finding God in a sinful world. For gays, it was a social experience called "coming out," expressing one's gay sexuality and identity in a generally hostile heterosexual world. Both camps . . . saw themselves in an ultimate struggle.

Briggs and Milk fueled the epic clash by holding public debates throughout the state. While the San Francisco councilman was cheered in the North, crowds in the South jeered him. In both environments Briggs thrived. "We cannot exist without the family, without the church and without the nation," he charged. "And if the initiative is defeated," that is going to confirm "the prediction of General MacArthur, who stated that no civilization has ever . . . survived when it falls into a period of general economic decline and moral decay." He added, "This free love and gay liberation is a greater danger than communism."[31]

Briggs's sensationalizing wore thin even with the most ardent religious conservatives in California, but the seriousness of his cause superseded the embarrassment his bravado elicited. Throughout the state, these activists rallied behind Proposition 6 with the same born-again, end-times zeal witnessed on their opponents' side. In Pomona, one member of Central Baptist Church helped fold fliers for the California Defend Our Children Committee, the political arm of Briggs's ballot initiative. "This isn't politics, it's the Lord's work," she insisted. Other activists who endorsed Timberlake's Committee on Moral Concerns and canvassed their neighborhoods for the Pro-Family Coalition passed out literature from Murray Norris's Christian Family Renewal, including comic books that utterly condemned homosexuality. In San Diego, LaHaye preached for Proposition 6 from his pulpit and in televised debates. In an effort to coordinate all of their demonstrations, meanwhile, these pastors and activists joined the American Christian Cause, headed by Reverend Robert Grant, W. S. McBirnie's former assistant pastor and a graduate of the California Graduate School of Theology.[32]

Despite their diligence, Proposition 6 failed at the polls, leaving its supporters wondering whether Briggs's dire predictions would now come to pass. In the days leading up to the election, Briggs's majority support dwindled as his biting rhetoric registered as a reckless witch hunt and Milk reminded Californians that people's livelihoods were riding on their vote. The Democratic Party also helped Briggs's initiative go down to defeat, but another reason for its demise came from within Republican circles. Along with centrist conservatives who grew embarrassed by Briggs's actions, Ronald Reagan denounced Proposition 6 and suggested that those who shared his beliefs do the same. "Whatever else it is, homosexuality is not a contagious disease like measles," Reagan contended rather tentatively.[33]

Evangelical conservatives did not believe all was lost, though. Whether they supported Briggs or leaned Reagan's way, Propositions 6 and 13 had allowed them to join their activism with their brethren's in Atlanta and Miami. The ballot wars of 1978 also helped them crystallize Sunbelt evangelicalism's opposition to Carter. For pastors like LaHaye, who had fought for these measures, the decisive end to any lingering enchantment with Carter came while meeting personally with him at a prayer breakfast. When they asked why "he as a Christian and a pro-family man" favored liberal legislations of the kind that benefited gays and feminists, Carter argued that these measures benefited the family. At that moment, they realized that something radical had to be done before more damage was done. "I stood there and I prayed this prayer," LaHaye recalled: "'God, we have got to get this man out of the White House and get someone in here who will be aggressive about bringing back traditional moral values.'"[34]

SUNBELT RISEN

Once the 1978 ballot battles were over, rank-and-file evangelicals segued back into the cultural political battles begun earlier in the decade. Debates over abortion and the Equal Rights Amendment had never gone away, but for a short time fiscal and foreign policy matters and gay rights referenda had overshadowed them. In the last months of the decade they erupted again.

The momentum started in the pews, drawing veteran and novice Christian activists alike into a new round of campaigning. David Diggs personified the new crusaders. Diggs, as with other former Jesus people, became more politically active as abortion became more contested. Still a musician, now working for Pat Boone, he began supporting pro-life campaigns and, along with his wife, managing a crisis pregnancy center. Raised in a Southern Baptist, Democratic home to parents from Texas and Arkansas, he was far from his ancestors' affiliations but still, in his mind, tied to his religious and political heritage. Citizen-activists like Diggs directed their zeal into interfaith organizations that built on the grassroots energy of the early 1970s. Christian women's groups that had once urged housewives to become accountable for their neighborhoods, for instance, now morphed into imposing, national organizations like Beverly LaHaye's Concerned Women for America (CWA), founded in 1978. Philosophically, CWA pulled together parallel strands of conservative sexual politics and wound them into one coherent ideology of female "submission"—to male leadership, motherhood, patriotism, and country. Practically, CWA gave California women the chance to affect the national debate over the ERA. Within eighteen months of incorporation in January 1979, CWA was using $10 annual fees from its 105,000 members to finance a newsletter and radio programming that targeted states where the ERA had not yet been ratified. By now LaHaye's mailing list was larger than Phyllis Schlafly's and her influence felt well beyond the feminist debate. In LaHaye's own words, hers was an effort to combat every perceived threat to the family.[35]

What Beverly LaHaye did for housewife activists, Tim LaHaye and Robert Grant did for pastors. In 1979, LaHaye used Proposition 6 as a springboard for a new political action group, Californians for Biblical Morality. The seven hundred self-proclaimed "prophets of God" who joined this organization originated petitions and held public rallies in which Christians were asked, "How can we be more vocal in urging elected officials to make laws and decisions based on traditional biblical morality?" Counted among the "prophets," Grant nevertheless wanted to provide more than questions for church people. During the Proposition 6 campaign, the Internal Revenue Service had warned Grant's American Christian Cause not to overstep its tax-exempt status, so Grant started Christian Voice, an entity legally removed from the church. Grant's organization began mailing "moral report cards" to thousands of churches in order to assist their decision making in upcoming elections. Similar to the voting guides his boss, W. S. McBirnie, had offered in the 1960s, Grant's designated candidates and issues as "Christian" and "un-Christian." Grant also wanted to shape politics from within the system and established a non-tax-exempt political action committee called the Christian Voice Moral Government Fund. Under Gary Jarmin's leadership, Moral Government rose to the top of the fund-raising pyramid; by 1980 it was the eighth largest fund-raiser among all political action committees.[36]

Even as they expanded their own organizations nationally, the LaHayes and Grant joined reforming fundamentalists from around the Sunbelt in solidifying a "Religious Right." Richard Viguerie and his allies—Morton Blackwell, Paul Weyrich, Ed McAteer, and Howard Phillips—had become aware of evangelicals' mounting political anxieties through interaction in the Heritage Foundation and Bill Bright's Christian Embassy and Third Century. In 1978 they took steps to fuse this dissent in three national organizations. Initially they approached Grant to see if Christian Voice would become the flagship. Protective of his independence, Grant declined the invitation, but he did not seem to mind his recruiters using Christian Voice as a model for two sister organizations. One was the Religious Roundtable, founded in 1979 by McAteer. A devout Southern Baptist businessman and a leader in the Christian Freedom Foundation, McAteer used his broad connections to enlist the Sunbelt's most powerful pastors, including James Robison, the fiery Baptist from Dallas who became the Religious Roundtable's spokesman.[37]

This same year, Blackwell approached Lynchburg, Virginia, pastor Jerry Falwell about starting a third political agency. Falwell's own politicking during the previous year warmed him to this proposal. In 1978 Falwell traveled to California, where, working alongside pastors affiliated with LaHaye, Grant, McBirnie, and the California Graduate School of Theology (on whose board he sat), he helped fight for Proposition 13 and Proposition 6. In between sojourns he established the *Journal-Champion*, a Christian periodical with a political bent. "We must not be limited" in our political awareness, the minister explained with respect to the *Journal-Champion*'s focus, especially "at a time when . . . governmental processes . . . affect the vitality and very existence of our churches and Christian schools." Throughout 1978, Falwell kept readers abreast of California's ballot wars. Briggs's plebiscite garnered his attention, but no more so than Jarvis's. Echoing McBirnie's proclamations, he warned that it was time for politicians to "roll forward the clock in progress toward individual initiative and individual freedom and family responsibility in our society." "If we want to control inflation, we should set our spiritual house in order." In 1979, Falwell took this message of moral and monetary conservatism with him into the meeting with Blackwell, after which he decided to form Moral Majority. Because of Falwell's high profile and newspaper— renamed *Moral Majority Report*—Moral Majority soon became the face of the Religious Right, yet alongside Grant's Christian Voice and McAteer's Religious Roundtable it functioned as just one part of a political trinity based in three strategic sites along the southern rim: Los Angeles, Dallas, and Lynchburg.[38]

This triad of organizations represented a vast system of pastoral politics whose lifeblood came from entrepreneurialism. Like the clergymen under whom some of them worshipped, ardent corporate boosters approached 1980 eager to dismantle finally and completely the liberal state. Rising corporate taxes, increasing federal deficits, and expanding regulation greatly dismayed these business leaders, as did their sense that citizens had become psychologically dependent on government. William E. Simon told them how to fight these trends. In his 1978 memoir, *A Time for Truth*, Nixon's former treasury secretary argued that business needed to construct a "counterintelligentsia" to destroy society's "dominant socialist-statist-collectivist orthodoxy." A select group of businessmen spent the last years of the 1970s building this counterintelligentsia. The Business

Roundtable, formed in 1972 for chief executives of Fortune 500 companies, offset negative stereotypes of business by taking out ads in *Reader's Digest* and designing education programs. The less exclusive Chamber of Commerce, meanwhile, increased circulation of its newspaper, *Nation's Business*, sponsored television shows, and employed any media that could sell the market to the masses. Both associations, moreover, attacked the problem of inadequate representation on Capitol Hill by forming political action committees. They worked efficiently. Outclassed by organized labor PACs in 1974, by 1976 corporate PACs outnumbered their counterparts two to one and, by the early 1980s, four to one. Through these conduits, small business leaders joined chief executives to petition for deregulation. And in concert with various taxpayer advocacy groups, they advanced initiatives like Proposition 13, which further closed the gap between Main Street and Wall Street.[39]

Sunbelt evangelical interests coursed through this counterinsurgency, with Southern Californians lending key support. Behind a good deal of the corporate push, for instance, was Justin Dart, the chairman of a Los Angeles pharmaceutical business and an esteemed member of Pepperdine's Founding Four Hundred. Shortly after Dart heard Milton Friedman at Pepperdine's fortieth-anniversary gala, he started traveling the country teaching executives how to establish PACs. His passion won him the unofficial title of "Johnny Appleseed" of the corporate movement. Evangelical power brokers sowed seeds of corporate revolt in other ways by framing Dart's strategy in sacred terms. The time had come for "those who love God" to elect leaders who were "pledged to reduce the size of government, eliminate federal deficits, free our productive capacity, ensure sound currency," one leader cried out. Parachurch lay leaders Bill Bright and Demos Shakarian continued to recruit the Sunbelt's merchants and financiers into their ministries then thrust their organizations' religious influences into pro-capitalist politics. Even ostensibly narrow Religious Right organizations served in this capacity. Named after the Business Roundtable, Religious Roundtable was set up to be a "forum for exchange on . . . Biblical responsibility in government." Ed McAteer's holistic vision was evident in his executive council, on which pastors, businessmen, and politicians shared equal authority. Christian Voice's recruitment was even more far-reaching, with pastor-lobbyist Richard Zone and author-advocate Hal Lindsey complementing twenty-eight congressmen to make it "the nation's largest Christian conservative lobby." "We're <u>tired</u>

of seeing the federal government trample all over our time-honored and sacred Christian values," Robert Grant stated, when outlining Christian Voice's intentions. "We're <u>tired</u> of seeing our nation's wealth squandered on crazy, vote-buying welfare schemes, and of seeing our very sustenance being destroyed by inflation and wasteful big-government spending. We want to return to the old values of hard-work, thrift, and obedience to the laws of God. In other words, WE WANT OUR COUNTRY BACK!"[40]

From Southern California eastward, the Sunbelt "power shift" Kirkpatrick Sale had spoken of years earlier was thus fully reengaged. When surveying the political landscape, some, like Richard Viguerie, were so bold as to say that a New Right had finally escaped the shadows and was ready to lead America. After spending the mid-1970s expanding their institutes, journals, and communication systems and doing so while cordoned off from the halls of power, Viguerie believed that the time had arrived for his cohort to become the Republican Party's "insiders," his coalition the Washington crowd.[41]

WASHINGTON FOR JEFFERSON AND JESUS

Southern California evangelicals naturally drank in the excitement these changing fortunes provided them, yet their perspective was slightly different from Viguerie's. They were, in fact, just as ready to return to an Old Right as they were to usher in a new one. For these evangelical conservatives, the final stride toward the 1980 election was about reconnecting with something rooted and familiar: the principles that had enlivened them for decades, a level of political influence they once enjoyed, and a relationship with a politician who preached their gospel of Jefferson and Jesus, California-style.[42]

With memories of Ronald Reagan's 1976 defeat still lingering, Southern California evangelicals now pledged to generate the momentum for him to win. Reagan's dedication made their task easier. In 1976 he had exasperated supporters by not committing decisively to the Republican leadership contest, but in 1980 he exhibited a welcome certitude. Time away from politics gave him resolve. After his loss to Gerald Ford, Reagan had stayed in the public eye by writing editorials, hosting a radio show in Los Angeles, and speaking around the country. Initially he avoided criticizing Carter in these venues, choosing to comment only on general trends; he seemed eager to sequester himself from heavy politics and, instead, relax on his new ranch. By 1978, however, he was rested enough to think about another run for the presidency. By now his agenda was more spirited, too. He chastised the president for his handling of the Panama Canal affair. Then, after a new treaty put the matter to rest, he turned his attention to Carter's other vulnerabilities. Meanwhile, he directed his curiosities to right-wing insurgencies cropping up around the country, championed supply-side economics and a pro-life platform, and gradually laid the foundation for his national plan. By the fall of 1979, Reagan's political maneuverings had positioned him for GOP leadership, and on November 13, in New York City, before a crowd of northeasterners whose trust he hoped to earn, he announced his candidacy.[43]

Reagan's declaration thrilled Southern California evangelical conservatives. Throughout the Republican primaries in the spring of 1980, they campaigned for their candidate. Robert Grant's Christian Voice established Christians for Reagan, which carried out a direct mail campaign. The thousands of form letters it sent out asked Christian citizens if they were sufficiently informed.

Do you know Teddy Kennedy's stand on taxpayer-paid abortions or Jimmy Carter's position on "gay rights" or George Bush's view on prayer in our public schools? Have you compared these candidates' positions with that of Ronald Reagan? My dear fellow Christian and fellow voter, you owe this analysis to yourself and your family, but mostly to your Lord.

Besides advancing Reagan as the only moral candidate, Christians for Reagan also tore down the president. "Mr. Carter has given us soft-spoken words about his personal beliefs and backed away from every opportunity to truly stand up for these beliefs in the political arena. Mr. Carter is afraid of offending Gloria Stienem [sic] . . . but not afraid of turning his back on his God!" Richard Zone asked citizens to mobilize their communities and donate money. Any contributions, he promised, would be invested in the distribution of Reagan's spiritual biography to the forty-five million citizens who tuned in to Christian radio and television. Zone also intended to mail copies of George Otis's 1976 Reagan interview to five million homes. On the cover of the printed testimony was a picture of Otis and Reagan clasping hands in prayer.[44]

At the same time that Grant started issuing precinct-level advice for the primaries, other clergymen began painting the 1980 election in epic terms. Tim LaHaye's *Battle for the Mind*, published in April, warned believers to fight the forces of "secular humanism" before it was too late; privately, he deemed the book his best attempt to make Carter a one-term president. LaHaye provided a sweeping indictment of "secular humanism"—"man's attempt to solve his problems independently of God." Because of this philosophy's fiercest proponents—the "American Civil Liberties Union (A.C.L.U.), National Organization of Women (N.O.W.), Unions, Hollywood Movies, Porno Magazines, Supreme Court, Government Bureaucrats, Public Education, College Universities, the Ford Foundation"—society was succumbing to the pressure. LaHaye grounded this crisis in a long political history refracted through his own life story. Interspersed in his analysis were his accounts of what he had been through on the West Coast. During World War II, he wrote, he had manned the guns of a B-29 aircraft, alongside a Catholic, a Mormon, and a Southern Baptist, all of whom returned home anticipating a fight with communism but soon confronted a more nefarious foe: liberalism. After becoming pastor, he grew attuned to this destructive force. Then, during Barry Goldwater's campaign, he began to act. He built a college and a think tank, battled city hall over zoning restrictions, and fought gay rights. In the process he grew to admire Reagan and to despise Carter as the shrewdest of all secular humanists.[45]

LaHaye and other pastors begged evangelicals to win back the nation, and they responded by recalibrating their ceremonial politics, always their forte. The same month that LaHaye's book was released, a group of pastors coordinated a Washington for Jesus rally. The vision behind Washington for Jesus came from a Sunbelt view of the world; its chief organizers—Demos Shakarian, Pat Robertson, John Gimenez, Bishop J. O. Patterson, and Bill Bright—represented the "missile crescent's" white, white ethnic, black, and Latino Pentecostals and Baptists that Carey McWilliams had described as "God-fearing, up-and-coming types." One hundred sponsors endorsed the event, at least eighty-five Sunbelt-based, roughly thirty from California. Their names and associations testified to forty years of evangelicalism's evolution along the Bible Belt: Pentecostal stalwarts Rolf McPherson of the Foursquare Church and Thomas Zimmerman of the Assemblies of God, for instance, as well as Neo-Pentecostals Pat Boone

and Jack Hayford, televangelists Jim Bakker and Paul Crouch, Jesus people Arthur Blessitt and Chuck Smith, Southern Baptist luminaries James
Kennedy and Charles Stanley, black evangelicals E. V. Hill and Bishop
Jesse Winley, presidents of parachurch ministries and chairmen of missionary agencies, corporate executives, celebrities, and a handful of Catholic priests. Wanting to bring one million people to the Washington Mall to
pray on April 29, this council also intended to make a political statement
by establishing offices in each of the nation's 380 congressional districts,
"interceding" Congress for moral legislation, and marching on the city's
streets. "Washington for Jesus will be a unique experience," organizers proclaimed, commemorating April 29, 1607, when Puritan settlers dedicated
the nation to God by erecting a cross on Virginia's coast. And "for once,"
they added with reference to a more recent history, "the city of D.C. will
not be the site of any unruly march or protest. It will be blessed with a
once in a lifetime celebration of the Lordship of Jesus Christ."[46]

The planners planned and the people came. Months before the
momentous gathering, churches around the country began prayer campaigns and sustained them for weeks. Days prior to the rally, four thousand women attended the Christian Women's Leadership conference
in Washington's Constitution Hall, where black evangelist Sarah Jordan Powell taught them how to be "Proverbs 31" women ("She looketh
well to the ways of her household, and eateth not the bread of idleness.
Her children arise up and call her blessed"). On the evening before
the main event, pastors packed the same auditorium to hear James
Robison speak on the sins of the nation, while thirty thousand youth
filled RFK Stadium to hear Arthur Blessitt show how to absolve them.
Finally, on the rainy morning of April 29, before an unprecedented
amassing of Christian journalists and telecasters, pilgrims descended
on the nation's hallowed ground. They marched under colorful ban-
ners (Hawaii for Jesus; Cops for Christ) and dour ones (America Must
Repent or Perish); and they streamed by the Capitol in a manner that
caused some to recall the Book of Joel: "Straight forward they march,
/ never breaking rank. . . . No weapon can stop them." Once seated
in an unbroken strand between the Washington Monument and the
Capitol, these citizens listened as E. V. Hill opened in prayer: "We
come here today not seeking power from the government, but we're
asking that thy Holy Spirit, which is the power, will fall upon us afresh
and anew." Much later, Hill's prayer would be immortalized as having

been uttered the instant the sunshine broke through the clouds, but in that momentary warmth the audience only wanted to celebrate the next song, speaker, and sermon that rang out from the stage. Some resonated with heavyheartedness, while others reverberated with hope. Collectively, they beseeched the nation for a return to New Testament teachings and America's founding principles. As Pat Boone said, with some levity, this was America's "Sermon on the Mall."[47]

In the months that followed, those who rallied in Washington, D.C., turned their focus toward the presidential race. Reagan turned his gaze on them. Thanks in part to grassroots organizations like Robert Grant's, Reagan emerged from the primaries as the GOP's standard-bearer. Early on, some conservatives in the western South were torn between Reagan and John Connally, the polished and charming Texan. But Connally's polish led to his downfall; his expensive suits and conspicuous ties to the silk-stocking crowd made him an all-too-easy target for the populist base. George Bush faced the same criticisms but stayed in the race long enough to become Reagan's running mate. So by mid-July, when delegates traveled to Detroit for the Republican National Convention, Reagan's leadership was guaranteed. The day after giving an acceptance speech that underscored the importance of old-time values—"family, work, neighborhood, peace and freedom"—Reagan, his party rejuvenated, left Michigan with a mandate, a running mate, and a lead in the polls.[48]

His next task was to lock up the loyalties of his most important constituents: corporate and evangelical conservatives. The first constituency was still slightly divided. Wall Street executives questioned Reagan's unproven supply-side economics, Main Street businessmen his level of devotion to this doctrine, but both were open-minded enough to entertain his overtures. After a closed-door summit in New York, several financiers left with less hesitancy about Reagan's supply-side thinking and inspired by his commitment to the free market faith. Assisted by his executive advisory council, chaired by William Simon and comprised of several former Kitchen Cabinet members—including Justin Dart—Reagan's courting of corporate kingmakers continued into the fall. At the same time, he curried the favor of small-time capitalists with whom he had always felt comfortable. With the help of Amway and other corporate agencies that were tapped into the grass roots, Reagan disseminated the Jeffersonian dimensions of his economic philosophy. By November, his strategy had paid dividends in an interlocking system of exchange that saw his political truths pass fluidly between corporate headquarters and shop-room floors, executives and employees, Fortune 500 giants and mom-and-pop corner stores.[49]

By now, his courtship with evangelical conservatives had borne fruit, too. Former Congressman John Conlan knew what Reagan had to do to lock up this "Christian vote market": share his faith. Reagan's first chance came at a meeting sponsored by the National Religious Broadcasters in August 1979, when he was asked pointedly: "If you died and you were standing before God at heaven's gate, what reason would you give for him to let you into heaven?" Citing John 3:16, Reagan said simply (and rightly, in his inquisitors' view) that he "wouldn't give God any reason for letting me in. I'd just ask for His mercy, because of what Jesus Christ did for me at Calvary." Faced with the same query weeks later, John Connally responded far less effectively: "Well, my mother was a Methodist, my pappy was a Methodist, my grandmother was a Methodist . . . and I'd tell Him that if He was letting those other guys in, He ought to let me in too." Reagan improved his rapport with evangelicals over the next twelve months by interacting with Falwell's Moral Majority and grassroots organizations like Citizens for Reagan, voicing approval of Washington for Jesus, and then, in August of 1980, appearing at a national meeting of the Religious Roundtable in Dallas.[50]

Reagan's rendezvous in Texas was his coup de grace. The visit was James Robison's idea, "something God put on my heart," he explained. With McAteer's blessing, Robison asked several political candidates to attend a National Affairs Briefing. Too absorbed in the Iran hostage crisis, and likely feeling too embattled, Carter declined the invitation, but Reagan promptly said yes. The two-day event drew thousands of pastors and parishioners and four hundred journalists to Dallas' new Reunion Arena for a referendum on the country's political struggles. Before a sea of American flags and a steady chorus of "hallelujahs" and "praise the Lords," key spokespeople took their turn at alerting Americans to the threats of the "ERA, abortion, homosexuality, and America's deteriorating military might." Phyllis Schlafly and the LaHayes were there, as were politicians Jesse Helms and Philip Crane, senior educator George Benson, Amway cofounder Richard DeVos, and Dallas Cowboys coach Tom Landry. W. A. Criswell and E. V. Hill attended, too. "We need to return to the God of our pilgrim fathers, to the faith of our praying mothers, to the God who can save us," Criswell cried out in yet another tribute to his nation's (and his own family's) past, one similar to the tribute he had offered in his Prayer Congress sermon four years earlier.[51]

The rally's last words were reserved for Robison and Reagan. Having scheduled his sermon as the set-up for Reagan's, Robison stoked the crowd as only he could. Days before, at a local meeting, he had warned that only 30 percent of "God-professing people" voted, compared to 95 percent of labor unions, "ninety eight percent of the liquor industry interests," and all the "radicals" and "gays." Robison repeated his rebuke in Reunion Arena, before singling out his enemies again. "Not voting is a sin against Almighty God! I'm sick and tired of hearing about all the radicals and the perverts and the leftists and the Communists coming out of the closet! It's time for God's people to come out of the closet!" Reagan sat on stage during Robison's fiery sermon, and his visible delight in the preacher's theatrics further endeared him to the audience. Finally, it was the politician's turn. In his introduction, scripted with Robison's help, he delivered the meeting's signature line: "You can't endorse me, but I endorse you." Then, in a speech that was interrupted by "amen" and applause more than twenty times, Reagan pledged to "keep government out of the school and the neighborhood; and above all—the home." Attendees had anticipated this message, but not the aside that came next. Wanting to keep things simple, Reagan raised a hypothetical, asserting that if he were shipwrecked with only one book he hoped it would be the Bible. "All the complex questions facing us at home and abroad," he added, "have their answer in that single book."[52]

The response to Reagan's performance was extraordinarily positive. His concluding parable sent the crowd into a boisterous standing ovation. Afterward, delegates insisted that the briefing had remained bipartisan, but no one could resist singing Reagan's praises. A lifelong Democrat and onetime Carter supporter, with considerable leadership experience in politics and his church, Arch Decker spoke for many when he proclaimed himself a reconstituted voter who now saw Reagan Republicanism as the answer. "I believe he is more a moral, Christ-centered individual," Decker said when comparing Reagan to Carter, the "charlatan." Herbert Ellingwood, Reagan's former legal affairs secretary, echoed Decker's sentiments in a personal note. He also congratulated Reagan for preparing evangelical hearts for action with a message of small government and strong national defense, fiscal responsibility and family values, core tenets rooted in populism's yesteryear.[53]

Reagan took this message of Jefferson and Jesus with him on the road. His Southern California friends joined him, physically in some cases but, more importantly, in spirit. Political action groups like Citizens for Reagan stepped up their efforts to disseminate their candidate's biography and beliefs in the East, while national committees like the Reagan Victory Fund, chaired by Robert Dornan, came west to call on Southern California Christians for help. "I wish it were possible to list all the California members on our stationery, brochures and newspaper ads," Dornan wrote to West Coast boosters, "but we'll have to limit it to those who reply quickly and who send a generous contribution." Southern California evangelicals also joined their brethren around the nation in holding one of many regional "Pro-Family Conferences" as an alternative to the "White House Conference on Families," which Carter finally brought to fruition. Seven thousand evangelicals attended the Long Beach rally. The conference's success helped spark other initiatives, such as an attempt to lobby Congress for repeal of the Supreme Court rulings on school prayer. All of these religious undertakings injected energy into Reagan's campaign.[54]

Spurred on, Reagan spent the last weeks of the race seeking to do what Nixon had done in 1972: lock up the Sunbelt. Carter tried to stop him by conjuring up the memory of another Republican's southern strategy, one that had proved less successful. Just like Barry Goldwater's opponents, Carter struck out against Reagan by connecting him to bigotry and extremism. While campaigning in Georgia, he lambasted Reagan for a speech given in Mississippi, in which the Californian championed states' rights and promised to restore "local governments the power that properly belongs to them." "This is a message that creates a cloud on the political horizon. Hatred has no place in this country," Carter charged. Reagan's terminology had once stigmatized Goldwater as the segregationist's candidate. Yet unlike Goldwater's words, Reagan's were not easily decoded as racism, something Carter's camp subsequently realized. Long committed to a color-blind conservatism, Reagan's politics were not racially benign but neither were they easily parsed in racist terms. And thanks in part to his interracial evangelical coalition and its members' focus on the politics of money and morality, Reagan's states' rights discourse registered in the way he wanted it to: as a postracial, populist plea for a free society bounded only by the limits of entrepreneurial imagination, communal responsibility, and devotion to God and country. Recognizing this, Carter scaled back his accusations about race but not about extremism. During a televised debate in late October, he did his best to portray Reagan as Goldwater incarnate—a maverick who would be too generous in his use of the military and draconian in his cuts to Medicare. "There you go again," the Republican replied, as if to chastise Carter for telling tall tales. Reagan followed up on this line with a closing question for the audience that pinned Carter's presidency down for good: "Are you better off than you were four years ago?"[55]

Reagan spent the last few days of the campaign walking with a lighter step in stops along the country's southern rim. In each locale, evangelical plain folk, preachers, and entrepreneurs were there to boost his confidence. Just as they had in 1976, George Otis and Pat Boone once again assumed leading roles, with Otis continuing to spread Reagan's testimony and Boone assuming the grittier work of campaigning. In one telling moment, late in the contest, Boone and Reagan shared the stage at the county fairgrounds in Shreveport, Louisiana. "I've been out job hunting," Reagan said to the crowd after it finally stopped whistling approval. Rather than talk at length about his candidacy, Reagan chose to tell a few jokes about Hollywood and pay tribute to Louisiana's fine citizens, leaving the serious task to Boone. After reclaiming the microphone, Boone exalted his friend's accomplishments in California and dreamed big about what he could do as president. Reagan's folksiness and Boone's barnstorming worked beautifully for the setting. Such displays had worked magic in this place for generations—this was, after all, Huey Long country. From the epicenter of the western South, Reagan traveled a well-trodden trail back to San Diego for his final campaign celebration. There a crowd not so different from the one in Shreveport greeted him, eager to hear just one more political sermon and sing one last patriotic hymn.[56]

BOONE WAS THE FIRST EVANGELICAL to congratulate Reagan on his landslide victory. Once the polls closed, he telephoned Reagan, who was reclining at home in Los Angeles. Surprised his friend was not out celebrating, the startled Boone asked whether he could be one of the first to address him as "Mr. President." Reagan liked the sound of that, as well as the remembrance that came next. "Mr. President, do you remember that prayer circle at the mansion, back when you were governor?" Boone asked. As the entertainer would later recollect, Reagan answered, "I sure do. I've thought about it many times in the last few months." Reagan's acknowledgment and his own role in a prophecy fulfilled left Boone "bathed in goose bumps."[57]

Boone's fellow evangelicals were just as thrilled by what had happened that evening, and their excitement only grew as the reality of a Republican president settled in. Reagan honored their passion and their political work on inauguration day. He did so in an extravagant display of triumph that conservatives felt befitting of the new Sunbelt dispensation. And in an even bolder gesture to the new era, the president-elect circumvented tradition by holding his swearing-in ceremony on the West rather than East Front of the Capitol, facing the Pacific instead of the Atlantic. From this vantage point he spoke to his frontier and his people in a language they knew so well. Donn Moomaw, Reagan's pastor at Bel Air Presbyterian Church and the former UCLA quarterback who helped Bill Bright popularize Campus Crusade for Christ, spoke in this dialect when opening the ceremonies in prayer. Then, after paying tribute, as he had throughout the campaign, to his first hero—Franklin D. Roosevelt—Reagan announced the end to the "federal establishment" that had grown out of his champion's political vision. "In the present crisis, government is not the solution to the problem," Reagan put forward with an earnestness and down-home quality that matched Roosevelt's best speech. It was time to make Washington "work with us, not over us; to stand by our side, not ride on our back."[58]

The nation's evangelicals appreciated this, yet it was a much simpler sign that told them they had done right to support this man. As he swore to uphold the awesome responsibilities of his new office, Reagan quoted a verse from 2 Chronicles: "If my people, which are called by my name, shall humble themselves, and pray, and seek my face, and turn from their wicked ways; then I will hear from heaven, and will forgive their sin and will heal their land." Obscure to some, this verse was familiar to Sunbelt evangelicals: it was the verse Jerry Falwell cited while traveling the country speaking on Reagan's behalf, that Washington for Jesus organizers singled out to summarize their event, pastors like W. A. Criswell paraphrased to fuel their jeremiads, and countless Christian citizens heard repeated in their pulpits, pews, and home Bible study. The fact that Reagan had seen fit to quote it was, in their minds, a sign that their country was now in good hands. In Criswell's parlance, it was an assurance that God's people's prayers for rain—for revival, for reformation, for a reconstituted nation—had been answered.[59]

EPILOGUE

WILDERNESS
AGAIN

E VEN AS RONALD REAGAN INAUGURATED HIS PRESIDENCY BY
turning the nation's gaze west, toward a new political frontier, many
of his evangelical supporters in Southern California longingly looked to
the east and an illustrious past. The months surrounding the 1980 election were a time for people who came of age during California's cold war
boom to reflect on two tumultuous generations of change. This was the
moment for southern plain folk, preachers, and entrepreneurs to remember their errand.

The act of remembering varied with each parish and parishioner,
of course, but one emotion was constant: pride. Throughout 1980, the
California Southern Baptist ran a series called Shapers of the California
Southern Baptist Heritage to honor the state conference's fortieth anniversary. Trailblazing pioneers who traveled west in the late 1930s and
early 1940s received the heaviest attention. One of the first to be profiled
was Robert Lackey, the Landmarkist prophet who forced national denominational leaders in Nashville to accept Californians into the Southern
Baptist Convention fold. "R. W. Lackey was no angel," the church paper
acknowledged, "but he was a saint, in the biblical-Baptist sense," who "set
a frantic pace" of evangelism for his church. One of the last to be profiled
was Ola Brister, a pastor's wife who migrated to Long Beach in 1942.
While her tent-making husband tried to refurbish an old store building
into a church, Ola tried to make an adjoining room inhabitable, despite
the lack of running water, heat, and refrigerator. Local prejudices did not
help. On one occasion, when asking for "longhorn cheese" on her daily
trip to the market, she was confronted by a local grocer who told her to

go back to Texas, where she belonged. After shouldering a few additional epithets and a warning that the "law will run you out of that dump over there," Ola Brister replied in a way that surely pleased her faithful friends. "We don't belong in Texas." She said, "We left nothing there," but "the Lord is with us." At that she bounded off, "not discouraged, but happy" that she was able to stake a claim in California for God.[1]

Other evangelical groups were more boisterous in their commemoration. Whether it be W. S. McBirnie's National Pastor's Congress on Church Growth, which ushered in the tenth year of his ministry, a charismatic conference hosted by Melodyland on its fifteenth anniversary, the twenty-fifth-year commemoration of Campus Crusade for Christ, or birthdays honored at countless other churches, Southern California was, in the months surrounding 1980, a beehive of commemorative activity. Two of Orange County's most memorable celebrations were held at the Anaheim Convention Center. To announce its twenty-fifth year and the completion of its new headquarters, the Full Gospel Business Men's Fellowship International drew an estimated twenty-five thousand people to a weeklong series of seminars and rallies. One evening's highlight was Egyptian senator Fikery Maomabate's message on Jewish-Arab relations, followed by a session of prayer for the "Middle East situation" led by Demos Shakarian. Central Baptist occupied the same complex to celebrate its twentieth anniversary. Before rolling television cameras and an auditorium filled with fans of his *Old Time Gospel Hour*, guest speaker Jerry Falwell delivered a sermon that honored Bob Wells and his congregants for decades of service to God and country.[2]

Similar sentiments were heard elsewhere, beyond Orange County's borders. In South Central Los Angeles, Mount Zion Missionary Baptist Church took time in spring of 1980 to salute its pastor at the beginning of his twentieth year of service. A few months before, E. V. Hill had been profiled in *Time* magazine, appropriately in its last issue of the 1970s, evangelicalism's decade. In answer to its questioning title—"American Preaching: A Dying Art?"—*Time* offered proof from Hill's pulpit that it was not. "There is hardly a gifted teacher, TV actor or stand-up comic in America who can surpass the show that Hill puts on every Sunday before 1,400 enthralled parishioners in the black ghetto of Los Angeles," it said. "It is clear that he is down there, an everyman on the street." Hill's parishioners were proud of his political work, too, and they would become prouder yet in succeeding years. At the time of his tribute, Hill was pro-

viding counsel to candidates and supplying his church with voting guides.
After Reagan's victory, Hill would serve on a number of federal advisory
councils, counseling federal officials in much the same way he had once
advised Los Angeles mayor Samuel Yorty.[3]

Pepperdine University welcomed the 1980s and its second decade in
Malibu with ample display of its own success. In January of 1980 Pepperdine's Malibu campus opened its School of Law. It and the School
of Business and Management, the Center for American Private Enterprise, and eventually the School of Public Policy would stand as flag-
ship institutions. With the help of their esteemed faculty—conservative
luminaries like Arthur Laffer, James Q. Wilson, and Kenneth Starr, who
would find a home in Malibu during the coming years—these institutions would guarantee Pepperdine's reputation as a safe haven for conservative thought and Republican activism. At a 1981 school dinner
honoring his father, Justin Dart, Michael Dart spoke on behalf of this
entire constituency when he praised Pepperdine for being one of "the few
universities which is willing to stand up for free enterprise," "academic
freedom," "free people," and "free education." Nestled in the valley below
the ridge on which these centers rested, Pepperdine's liberal arts college
carried out its own advancement before the public's eye. In 1980, it led
the nation in fund-raising among peer institutions. In 1983 *U.S. News &
World Report* recognized the school as one of the top three "comprehensive universities" west of the Mississippi River. The media's fascination
with the shimmering Malibu campus, meanwhile, continued, as its sports
fields and sun-drenched student body became the backdrop for ABC's
Battle of the Network Stars and the 1984 Los Angeles Olympics water polo
championships. Despite all of the attention, Pepperdine also maintained
a quieter emphasis on its Christian-values curriculum, Church of Christ
ties, and Annual Bible Lectureship. By the 1980s thousands of people,
piloting cars and motor homes adorned with California and Texas plates,
could be seen streaming onto campus for one week of worship under the
roof of the Firestone Fieldhouse. Collectively, these images were ample
proof that the Malibu Miracle had become a monument to a conservative
movement forty years in the making.[4]

Hidden behind all of these jubilant displays, however, were signs that
Sunbelt evangelicalism was already embarking on its next progression as
a rising political entity. For decades evangelicals in Southern California
had helped lay the groundwork for the new regional nexus Kirkpatrick

Sale had outlined in *Power Shift*. In 1980 this process had culminated in Reagan's historic presidential win. Yet even as conservatives along the Sunbelt welcomed "morning in America," Southern California evangelicals were approaching the twilight of their moment. This region's conservative Protestantism would continue to change with the times, and stay one step ahead of national trends; its ever-expanding, diversifying community of followers would always display an unrivaled capacity to carve out new paradigms for collective witness and cultural engagement. And because of the perpetuity of this state's culture wars, evidenced in a new cycle of ballot battles every two years, evangelicals there would remain politicized, always eager to push back hard against liberalism on behalf of the nation's conservatives. But as a concentrated force, Southern California evangelicalism would never be the same as it was in its glittering 1970s manifestation.

This diffusion of power would be slow and subtle, but already in the early 1980s it seemed somewhat irreversible. By now there was ample reason to believe, in the first place, that Southern California evangelicalism had let its unbridled boosterism go too far. W. S. McBirnie's and Ralph Wilkerson's careers illustrated this. In the early 1980s, McBirnie's seminary continued to train pastors, and his Voice of Americanism still produced a mound of patriotic material. Growing alongside these ministries was United Community Church, which garnered headlines for its new building. Designed by McBirnie himself, partly as a tribute to his forty years of ministry, it featured a "church-amphitheater" built in a Romanesque style that sat 1,400 people in plush pews circling a stage below. Fifty feet above the stage was a fifteen-foot cross of brass and beveled glass, which directed worshippers' eyes upward toward fifty-two stained glass windows. The money that built this shiny edifice, however, came through shady means, and by the late 1980s the fraudulence was made public. Critics within evangelical circles had begun questioning McBirnie's legitimacy in the 1970s, mostly because of his second divorce and third marriage, but the accusations mounted a decade later as investigative journalists found that the preacher was mishandling money loaned him by elderly followers. These findings ruined McBirnie, just as similar ones would cloud Wilkerson's ministry. In the late 1970s Melodyland was bringing in nearly $4 million in annual revenue, yet it faced $450,000 in overdue bills and $5 million in debt, much of it because of heavy investment in the Melodyland School of Theology, some of it troublingly unaccounted for. Making matters worse was that Wilkerson's authority was too heavy-handed for many of those on MST's faculty. In protest, they abandoned a once-thriving school of six hundred students and formed a competing seminary in Newport Beach. Wilkerson and Melodyland would weather this storm but not before serious, permanent damage was done to the reputations of both.[5]

McBirnie and Wilkerson's endeavors may have been extreme, but the Sunbelt dream that built their empires also nurtured a no less disorienting impatience that presaged another shifting political reality for Southern California evangelicals. At this juncture, in yet another cycle of expansion, they looked for new opportunities farther afield; the suburban periphery once again beckoned, while the city core became something to condemn. Pepperdine's flight from the city was particularly dramatic, in this regard. In 1981, after a decade of struggling to maintain an inner-city presence, the university permanently locked the doors on its South Central classrooms. Resentful that the school was abandoning them, some of Pepperdine's urban students lashed out, but the plans to cease operations went forward. In July 1981, a group of Pepperdine alums, joined by Helen Pepperdine, George Pepperdine's widow, gathered to say tearful good-byes to the forty-year-old campus. This same year, Pepperdine sold the property to Frederick Price, who, like E. V. Hill, had spent the last decade becoming a popular and powerful black preacher. Influenced by Oral Roberts's teachings and trained at Neo-Pentecostal pastor Kenneth Hagin's seminary in Tulsa, Price applied his charismatic theology at his Crenshaw Christian Center in Inglewood. In 1981 he moved this church to Pepperdine's old campus, opened his Faithdome, and took his ministry national.[6]

Pepperdine's move out of the city was one that other institutions felt necessary during the 1980s. Those once-imposing urban congregations that had remained in Los Angeles—Church of the Open Door, for example—now found it impossible to resist suburbia's pull. In the late 1980s COD uprooted from its downtown location and moved to a mountainside campus in Glendora, an idyllic property once occupied by John Brown's preparatory schools. Los Angeles was not the only city feeling white evangelicalism's centrifugal shift. In the communities of northern Orange County—suburbs-turned-cities like Anaheim and Santa Ana— evangelicals began reassessing their churches' futures. Southern Baptists were caught in the middle of this process. In 1980, during its yearlong remembrance of its California heritage, the *California Southern Baptist* in fact paused to assess the denomination's future. Besides honoring the work of old congregations like Bristol Street Baptist Church in Santa Ana, the paper also highlighted the fresh potential of southern Orange County, where planners were drawing up grids for upper-middle-class suburbs like Laguna Hills. On land owned by the Philip Morris Company, at least nine communities, six of them gated, would eventually house more than one million people. With a clear vision of twenty-year growth in this prosperous region, Southern Baptist leaders decided to beat the rush.[7]

Their young visionary was Rick Warren, the proud inheritor of a California Southern Baptist culture he now thought in need of revitalization. Having grown up in a California Southern Baptist church, attended California Baptist College, and served as young assistant pastor at First Baptist Church in Norwalk, Warren was true to his state, but he was also enamored with the Texas theology of W. A. Criswell. Not surprisingly, then, he made his way to Texas for postgraduate training. In 1979, after completing studies at Southwestern Baptist Theological Seminary, he and his wife accepted a call from Crescent Baptist Church in Anaheim to head a mission church with the goal of devising a new regional model for Southern Baptist expansion. The Warrens chose Laguna Hills for their pilot program and, in early 1980, started a home Bible study, began door-to-door canvassing, then shifted gears into a mailing campaign targeting fifteen thousand homes. With a handful of married couples, they founded Saddleback Valley Community Church.

By summer 1980, the *California Southern Baptist* was announcing a new phase in the Warrens' plan. With a keen sense of Laguna Hills' future layout, Rick Warren approached Philip Morris's chief commercial planner to ask about building Southern Baptist churches in the area; the planner admitted that his company had not allocated enough space for churches and asked the young Southern Baptist for advice. In a carefully prepared presentation, Warren suggested that more was needed than churches; considering the fact that Proposition 13 (the Jarvis Bill) had bankrupted the district's school district, a private Christian school was probably in order, and possibly a civic center. He emphasized the great resources Southern Baptists would bring to this part of Orange County. With thirteen million members nationally, almost half a million statewide, Warren was able to promise instant viability, and with the financial backing of the South's largest SBC churches, he was able to guarantee fiscal solidity. Saddleback Valley Community Church, he noted, would rely on the combined sponsorship of a church in Memphis and another in Houston. Philip Morris bought the plan and endorsed Warren's efforts. As the future best-selling author and presidential advisor would claim to his Baptist brethren in 1980, the new Orange County was God's for the taking. "If one makes a big challenge, one gets a big response," he proclaimed. "When I talk about a twelve-year Christian school, a family life center, multipurpose ministries—well people get excited and it's not just business as usual!"[8]

As much as the new Orange County enlivened young Baptists, it reminded elderly Baptists that old Orange County was on the decline, and that Sunbelt churches operated on borrowed time. As congregants at Bob Wells's Central Baptist celebrated their church's twentieth and twenty-fifth anniversaries in 1976 and 1981, many knew it was already past its prime. In the late 1960s, Central had entered the ranks of the Baptist Bible Fellowship's super-churches. Central's pastor and its four thousand members had proven that J. Frank Norris's brand of Baptist religion could thrive on the West Coast. For a number of reasons, Central entered the 1980s in a very different state. Other churches, like First Evangelical Free in Fullerton, began siphoning away Central's membership and vitality. Central Baptist in Huntington Beach did the same. Wells's congregation had started this "mission church" in 1964 to introduce Orange County's newer housing tracts to his fundamentalism. Fifteen years later, the Huntington congregation was thriving on its five-acre campus because of a fresh take on this gospel. Surrounded by newer neighborhoods with younger households, it also became a mobilization site for Orange County's Right, led by local Republican stalwarts and infrequent church attendees Doris Allen and Dana Rohrabacher. Meanwhile, the Anaheim congregation flagged under an outdated outlook. A cold warrior, Wells found it difficult to adjust to the more therapeutic and technological requisites of "Jesus, California style." Where Wells wanted to continue preaching against the communists, Catholics, and Soviets—those menacing foes that had once driven his spies to search out subversive influences—his congregants wanted guidance on other, family-focused issues as well, delivered in contemporary packages and livelier congregational atmospheres. Neither Wells nor his church was a relic at the ministry's twenty-fifth anniversary in 1981, but Southern California's relentless tide of church growth, which they had once ridden to prominence, had turned against them.[9]

If Central Baptist's waning congregational culture illustrated the weakening of evangelical conservatism in Southern California's original defense suburbs, it also emblemized the way Southern California evangelicalism as a whole was losing its leading-edge status in the Sunbelt Right. Quite simply, evangelicals in other regions of the Sunbelt had caught up to Southern Californians in the manufacturing of a vibrant Republican agenda. It would be hard to find a more appropriate symbol of this power shift than Jerry Falwell, whose appearances at Central Baptist's anniversary celebrations signified the changing of the guard. The middle-aged minister from Lynchburg, Virginia, always arrived in Southern California amid a buzz of anticipation, because it was a homecoming of sorts. During the early 1970s, he had developed close ties to Southern California. A favorite on the BBF's speaking circuit, he appeared often at conferences and youth camps in the Golden State, strengthening bonds with BBF preachers like Tim LaHaye and W. S. McBirnie. In 1973, Falwell became co-pastor of the Berean Baptist Church in Orange County after it merged with his Thomas Road Baptist Church. He commuted between these pulpits, in much the same way his denomination's progenitor, J. Frank Norris, had done decades earlier between Fort Worth and Detroit. By the mid-1970s, Falwell was extending his California networks to include Neo-Pentecostals. On more than one occasion he joined their goodwill junkets to the Middle East. Probably the most exhilarating trip came in 1978, when he and Ralph Wilkerson were granted sessions with Israeli Prime Minister Menachem Begin and Egyptian President Anwar Sadat. Besides talking with Sadat about his country's ties to Israel (and serving as Sadat's messenger to Begin), Falwell also got permission for a future revival in Cairo, which he and Wilkerson planned to team-lead.[10]

Falwell's California connections ran deeper than his sojourns there indicated. While still a young man, he had been shaped by the example of Bob Wells. As a traveling evangelist, shortly before he founded Central Baptist, Wells had visited Lynchburg, where he came in contact with Falwell. Under Wells's guidance, the young man recommitted his life to God and the ministry. In the 1970s Falwell presumably learned from Wells again. On his visits to Orange County, he saw a Baptist stronghold built during California's Sunbelt awakening in the 1950s. He could apply its rise-and-fall lessons to his own Baptist stronghold, built by the Sunbelt's next surge. At the time Falwell spoke at Central Baptist's anniversary celebrations, Lynchburg, in fact, was transitioning from an old, "hidebound, stratified, segregated" mill town into a diversified financial center for high-tech firms and corporate headquarters. As journalist Frances FitzGerald observed in 1981, this was not a city so much as it was a "collection of suburbs . . . spread out over fifty miles . . . with no real center." A place of self-contained neighborhoods and overfilled churches, Lynchburg in 1981 was what Anaheim had been in 1956, minus Disneyland's unremitting glare. Much like Wells in the 1950s, Falwell now calibrated his politics to a changing landscape. Early in their relationship, he had decried Wells's work for the Republican Right. When Wells was imploring his church to vote Goldwater and Reagan, Falwell was advising his to stay out of politics. "Our only purpose on this earth is to know Christ and make Him known," he said in 1965. By 1980, Falwell's message had changed. "This idea of 'religion and politics don't mix,'" he stated, "was invented by the devil to keep Christians from running their own country."[11]

With Falwell's help, the South would henceforth become the vanguard for the "Religious Right" he helped shape. Southern California evangelicals would do their part to make this a coast-to-coast operation, of course. Under the guidance of Tim LaHaye, for instance, the Sunbelt's evangelical pastors and entrepreneurs would found one of the most impressive (and secretive) political lobbies of the Reagan era, the Council for National Policy (CNP). This organization would serve as an umbrella agency uniting four hundred church, business, and political leaders (84 percent of whom would hail from south of the Mason-Dixon line and west of the Mississippi) behind conservative fiscal and family prerogatives. Virtually every major evangelical leader would find a designated spot in this political phalanx: LaHaye, Bill Bright, James Dobson, and Henry Morris alongside Ed McAteer, Richard Viguerie, Joseph Coors, Nelson Bunker Hunt, and two dozen politicians. Yet at the same time, Southern Californians like LaHaye could offer only limited political potential for the future. During the 1980s and 1990s the type of religious political organizations LaHaye established in the wake of 1978's Proposition 6 saw their political influence dulled by a rising Democratic coalition and the demographic changes that facilitated it, as well as by more general societal trends toward the liberal side. Religious Right activists certainly proved efficient in taking over control of the GOP—by 1993, conservative Christians controlled thirty-eight of fifty-eight Republican central committees—and an ongoing sequence of ballot referenda on issues like gay rights, private education, and immigration kept this constituency galvanized. Yet this authority over the party apparatus had limited effects. Conditions that once benefited them—weakened party authority and an issue-driven, candidate-centered political system—began working against Religious Right activists in the 1980s and 1990s as they found it more difficult to agree on ideology, control the issues, or find suitable candidates to represent them. Isolated victories would come at the polls, but sustained success would be unattainable. Meanwhile, as the suburbs of Atlanta and Dallas, Memphis and Charlotte grew up and became even more saturated with Republican partisanship at the precinct level, Falwell's Religious Right found a more productive home base.[12]

Many Southern California evangelicals found the South's new suburbs promising as well and played a direct role in populating (and politicizing) them. Indeed, as much as evangelicalism's repositioning within Southern California dulled some of its power, a fourth force of change—more migration—blunted it altogether. This time, the migration was outward-bound. During the 1980s and 1990s, Southern California's political economy underwent dramatic restructuring as a once spectacularly strong defense sector began to lose government contracts, its fight against inflation, and, generally, its luster. A declining tax base (exacerbated by Proposition 13) coupled with rising costs further tore up local neighborhoods. Orange County—once the epitome of California's cold war boom—went bankrupt, marking a very real end to decades of unimpeded prosperity. Cold war defense suburbs that ringed Los Angeles County suffered similar burdens of adjustment, as did the evangelical communities that had banked their livelihoods on this economy. In reply, countless evangelical citizens and their institutions picked up and went east. Some, like James Dobson and his organization, Focus on the Family, were enticed by boosters and cheaper living to a newer defense community tucked away in the Mountain West: Colorado Springs. More often they simply returned to the place from whence they came: the western South. In a dramatic reversal, California began losing southern migrants in the 1980s, Oklahoma and Texas reclaiming them. Retirees, job seekers, and the homesick now steered their automobiles east on Interstate 10. Writing about this rising trend in 1983 that was remaking the Texas "oil patch," social scientist William Stevens declared that the "great surge of post–World War II westing migration" had "bounced off the West Coast and ricocheted back to Texas." He added that "both money and people" were making the trip.[13]

This reverse migration was also primed to "Californiaize" Texas political culture and Republicanize Texas politics, pundits noted. To be sure, they overstated the case for the former, since Texas political culture was always protective of its character. And by the 1980s, Texas and the entire western South boasted a political and cultural authority that the rest of the nation now envied. This was the new epicenter of the new political economy, a home for NASA, Texaco, and Wal-Mart, emblems of the Sun-belt's high-tech, resource-based, service economies and financial clout. In the late 1930s, Houston politician and philanthropist Jesse H. Jones had given an impassioned speech to students at John Brown University in tiny Siloam Springs, Arkansas, imploring them to take control of their region by applying a frontier mentality to its development. It was time, he said, for the western South to become strong and independent of northern industrialists' grasp. Thanks to the work of educator-entrepreneurs like John Brown, George Benson, and R. G. LeTourneau, two generations of Christians had internalized this message and, with the aid of federal funds and venture capital, helped turn the western South into the colonizer rather than the colony.

Still, there were some curious signs that California was having an effect on Texas oil patches—that southern evangelicalism had "bounced back" in the early 1980s. In 1984, in Midland, America's ultimate oil patch, a young oilman prayed with an eccentric evangelist from Louisiana who had gotten his start in Hollywood. While leading a revival in town, Arthur Blessitt—fresh off of another international tour with his twelve-foot cross—met privately with George W. Bush at a local Holiday Inn. The two men talked and prayed about Bush's personal salvation. This, coupled with Billy Graham's counsel the following year, would be the beginning of Bush's journey into evangelicalism and, in a way, the beginning of his road to Washington.[14]

George's Bush's conversion notwithstanding, Californians' role in the Republicanization of Texas politics in the early 1980s was more obvious. One individual who had a hand in this process was Bill Banowsky, the man who helped manufacture Pepperdine's Malibu Miracle. After abandoning his political aspirations in the mid-1970s to focus on his school's crises, Banowsky had stepped up his search for other professional opportunities. In 1978, the right one presented itself in the University of Oklahoma's vacant presidency. Accepting this post just seemed right, Banowsky explained to Richard Scaife: "What appeals to me about it is that this is the major institution of higher learning in the nation's most conservative section. . . . From this position I will have a tremendous base to speak out on the issues and have an important national impact for the things in which we believe." To a friend in Tennessee he explained his decision in personal terms.

> My mother was born in Oklahoma and my Grandad Slater settled in the Indian Territory . . . and preached in every little country town. I am leaving the tinsel and tumble of California and going to my roots in the most crucial academic job in that whole state. The conservative and religious values of Oklahoma give me a perfect opportunity to be an influence for Christ from a powerful post. I am dedicated to being "in the world but not of the world." I intend to really let my light shine.

Banowsky did well in Norman: He raised the school's endowment, expanded the university's infrastructure, and all the while assisted the state Republican Party. Still, in the early 1980s he grew restless again and anxious to make one last move, this one back to Texas. By the mid-1980s he was president of the Dallas-based Gaylord Broadcasting Company, ensconced in Texas's Church of Christ community, and itching for a political role greater than his already important post as the GOP's state finance chairman. Writing in 1985 to George Strake, chairman of the Texas GOP, Banowsky announced his arrival in the Lone Star State. "George, I am a fifth generation Texan from Fort Worth and, after being gone for thirty years, I am thrilled to be back home. It is especially exciting to be a part of the 'Republicanization' of the great state of Texas."[15]

The Sunbelt sojourn Banowsky welcomed most was the one that took him back home. The same was true of many of California's southern transplants. Yet most of them would spend the 1980s and 1990s still living in the Golden State, still looking to the South as a place of origin rather than of destination. And their political future would be different as a result. This was Jean Vandruff's narrative. The Oklahoman's biography began folding into California conservatism's life story from the moment he left Hominy. During the 1950s he had ridden California's cold war boom to financial success, family stability, church involvement, and a conservative political conscience. Following Barry Goldwater's defeat in 1964, Ronald Reagan's inspiring leadership had reenergized Vandruff, but by the mid-1970s he had grown skeptical about politics and, at the same time, worried that Central Baptist had seen its best years. Reagan's election in 1980, and his investment in Jerry Falwell's Moral Majority, gave Vandruff fresh hope about the direction of the country, and he marveled at how his home state of Oklahoma now leaned toward the Republican Right. Vandruff's extended family in Oklahoma had once ridiculed him for voting Republican; now they saw his choice as sound reasoning. Even as his relatives entered a new political era, however, Vandruff sensed an ending of sorts to his. By the 1990s, he was anxious again about his Anaheim community's moral fabric and political future, and likely about its physical and economic layout, which he had had a direct hand in constructing. Once confident in the evangelical conservative errand, Vandruff now wondered whether it could match the dark, mounting forces of liberalism in a California society that refused to stand still. In a way, Vandruff's life had come full circle; he was entering the wilderness again, only this time without assurances that salvation would follow.[16]

ACKNOWLEDGMENTS

In a way, this book sent me on my own errand into the wilderness. At times I felt like it was a fool's errand with no salvation in sight. The incentive to press on came from the many friends, family members, mentors, archivists, colleagues, and fellow researchers who, at different points along the way, encouraged and facilitated my journey. I want to begin by thanking those who had a direct hand in this book's publication. Frances FitzGerald, Mark Carnes, Ene Sirvet, Hasia Diner, and Susan Ware, with the Society of American Historians, were instrumental in connecting this book with a top-flight press. At W. W. Norton, Nancy Palmquist and Don Rifkin did amazing, meticulous work preparing this manuscript for publication, while Anna Oler and Eleen Cheung oversaw the production and jacket design with skill and professionalism. Janet Byrne helped with a thorough round of copyediting. Tom Mayer deserves much of the praise for his scrupulous editing and patience in ushering a novice through the process of book writing. It was an honor to work with him.

Long before Norton got involved, this manuscript first took shape as a dissertation at the University of Notre Dame. Generous funding from the following agencies assisted this first wave of writing: the Social Science and Humanities Research Council of Canada, the Louisville Institute for the Study of American Religion (led by Jim Lewis), the Department of History and the Graduate School at the University of Notre Dame, the Historical Society of Southern California, the Huntington Library in San Marino, California, and the Southern Baptist Historical Library and Archives in Nashville, Tennessee. Money aside, by far it was the relationships at the University of Notre Dame that made completion of the dissertation possible. There I found a vibrant community of people who shared my interests in the study of religion and society, making it the perfect place to learn how to be a historian. George Marsden ably supervised the dissertation, but I am even more appreciative of the gracious advice he's offered these last few years, as the dissertation has undergone revisions to become the book. I received similarly invaluable guidance from three other individuals who helped shepherd the dissertation along, all three of whom remain great inspirations: Gail Bederman, John McGreevy, and Walter Nugent.

Indiana hospitality is legendary, and I've experienced it firsthand while beginning my career. A postdoctoral fellowship from the Lilly Fellows Program in Humanities and the Arts at Valparaiso University enabled me to finish the dissertation and contemplate the next stage. In this transitional year, I relied on the mentoring of Mark Schwehn and Mel Piehl, two men for whom I have inestimable respect, and the camaraderie of Bud Berg, Alan Bloom, Joe Creech, Sara Danger, Margaret Franson, Mary Henold, Kari Kloos, John Steven Paul, Chuck Schaefer, Colleen Seguin, Mary Streufert, Heath White, and Brent Whitefield to help me think long term. At Purdue University, where I have worked for the past five years, I have drawn support from all of my colleagues in the history department. For early help with adjustment to the profession, I'd like to thank my immediate cohort, Stacy Holden, Mike Ryan, and Juan Wang. For taking the time to comment on or simply chat about my written work (or the process of writing), I'd especially like to thank Neil Bynum, Susan Curtis, Charles Cutter, Jim Farr, Nancy Gabin, Will Gray, Pat Hearden, Frank Lambert, John Larson, Bob May, Mike Morrison, Yvonne Pitts, Jon Teaford, Whitney Walton, and especially Randy Roberts, with whom I have enjoyed several extensive (and usually impromptu) "counsel sessions." Jennifer Foray and Caroline Janney deserve special thanks for carefully editing sections of the manuscript. I am grateful to Doug Hurt for his leadership in the department, as well as Rebecca Gwin, Fay Chan, Nicole Federer, and Tamara Johnson for their help with the logistics of research, travel, and teaching. Patrick Brennan and Andrew Wirtz were godsends for their technological wizardry. Larry Mykytiuk provided inestimable help with securing a Purdue Library Scholars Grant, which allowed me to conduct research at Pepperdine University. This funding, along with a Purdue Faculty Summer Fellowship, facilitated much of the research that occurred while I reworked the manuscript. I also want to single out several graduate students who offered incisive and helpful comments on portions of the manuscript: Arthur Banton, Rick Bradley, Mauricio Castro, Mark Furnish, Jimmy Gleason, Timothy Lombardo, Erica Morin, Jamal Ratchford, David Rosenfield, and Andrew Smith. Yet another Indiana-based program—the Young Scholars in American Religion program, sponsored by the Center for the Study of Religion and American Culture at IUPUI—gave me the chance to spend considerable time with some of the brightest minds (and best people) in the field of American religious history. Paul Harvey and Amanda Porterfield, talented scholars and fearless leaders, directed a cohort comprising Ed Blum, Kate Carte Engel, Spencer Fluhman, Rebecca Goetz, Charles Irons, Katie Lofton, Randall Stephens, Matthew Avery Sutton, and Tisa Wenger. Phillip Goff and Rebecca Vasko made my participation in this tremendous program possible; thank you! All of the seminar's participants commented on my book, but the tireless Paul, Ed, and Matt carefully scrutinized chapters and told me how to make them better.

Other scholars have done the same for me in other settings. A postdoctoral fellowship from the Center for the Study of Religion at Princeton University gave me a year away from teaching to think. I want to thank Robert Wuthnow and Leigh Schmidt for facilitating my visit, and David Michelson, Anita Kline, and Barbara Bermel for helping coordinate it. In both seminar and informal settings I gained fresh insight into the study of religion, but Leigh, Matthew Hedstrom, and Lauren Winter especially showed me how to apply it to my own project. Through the Clements Center for Southwest Studies at Southern Methodist University I was introduced to Jeff Roche and the "Political Legacies" project. As a result, an early version of my work on J. Vernon McGee and Bob Wells appeared in Jeff Roche, ed., *The Political Culture of the New West* (University of Kansas Press, 2008). This encounter led to another. During the past two years I have had the privilege of co-editing with Michelle Nickerson a Clements-sponsored volume titled *Sunbelt Rising: The Politics of Space, Place, and Region* (University of Pennsylvania Press, 2011). Working with Michelle—a historian who shares my interest in California conservatism—has been enriching, as have the workshops that have accompanied this project, through which I have gleaned from the phenomenal work of several phenomenal "Sunbelt" scholars: Carl Abbott, Shana Bernstein, Nathan Connelly, Joseph Crespino, Darren Grem, James Guth, Daniel HoSang, Volker Janssen, Laresh Jaysanker, Lyman (Bud) Kellstedt, Matthew Lassiter, Sylvia Manzano, Andrew Needham, and Elizabeth Shermer. More than they know, these scholars' contributions to *Sunbelt Rising* helped fine-tune my thinking on *From Bible Belt to Sunbelt*. I would like to thank David Weber, Ben Johnson, Sherry Smith, and Andrea Boardman for making this engagement possible, as well as Bill Deverell, Carolyn Powell, and Susi Krasnoo at the Huntington Library, where part of the *Sunbelt Rising* volume took shape. I did not get to meet the other contributors to Mark Noll and Luke Harlow, eds. *Religion and American Politics: From the Colonial Period to the Present* (Oxford University Press, 2007), but it was a privilege being part of this esteemed group and sharing some of my book's big-picture, still-developing ideas for this publication. At key points along the way, Mark Noll, Grant Wacker, Harry Stout, and Richard Hughes, veteran religious historians whose work I admire, provided me with the extra encouragement to see my book through to the end. I am also grateful to several other scholars for invaluable help. Matt Lassiter, Joe Crespino, and Ann Ziker provided extensive comments on substantial portions of the manuscript. Whether intentionally or unintentionally, in formal or informal settings, others added their own suggestions that I took to heart. Ryan Anderson, Carl Bon Tempo, James Bratt, Bill Bulman, Joel Carpenter, Donald Critchlow, Bill Deverell, David Di Sabatino, Mark Edwards, Michael Engh, Larry Eskridge, Glenda Gilmore, Robert Goldberg, Tim Gloege, Nicholas Guyatt, John Haas, Mike Hamilton, Barry Hankins, John Herron, Matthew Frye Jacobson, Ben Johnson, Will Katerberg, Kristin Kobes DuMez, Joseph (Kip) Kosek, Kevin Kruse, Bob Lockhart, Nancy MacLean, William Martin, Karen Merrill, Steven Miller, Leonard Moore, Bethany Moreton, Becky Nicolaides, Kendrick Oliver, Rick Ostrander, Richard Payne, Kim Phillips-Fein, Andrew Preston, Axel Schäfer, Amy Scott, Aaron Sheehan-Dean, Michael Steiner, David Swartz, Frank Szasz, Scott Tang, John Turner, Michael Warner, Mark Wild, Daniel Williams, and David Wrobel contributed to the framing and reframing of this book (or simply kept me sane and on pace).

Of course, there would not have been anything to "frame and reframe" had I not been able to gain access to this book's central subjects, through interviews and archival sources. Jean Vandruff, my first interviewee, set the wheels in motion, so I am particularly appreciative of his willingness to share his life story—and I am saddened that his wife, Eleanor, who, between coffee and snacks, sat with us and joined the conversation, has just passed away. All of my other interviewees—a few, like Eleanor and Marie Koenig, who have passed away since we last talked—provided a foundation for this book, and I am humbled by their openness and hopeful that I did justice to their biographies. I am also indebted to those who gave me access to processed and unprocessed material (and photographs) in archives, church records, and personal collections—the core texts upon which this book rests. Deserving special thanks, in this regard, are: Stephen Scholle and Heather VanKoughnett with the Billy Graham Evangelistic Association and especially Bob Shuster, Keith Call, and Paul Ericksen at the Billy Graham Center Archives and Museum; Kristie French at California State University, Long Beach; Tony Gardner at California State University, Northridge; Alan Burns at Clemson University; Alan Jutzi at the Huntington Library; Dale Hardy at LeTourneau University; Janet St. Pierre and Pat Boone at Pat Boone's office; James Smythe, Ethan Henderson, Lynne Jacobsen, and especially Melissa Nykanen at Pepperdine University; Bill Sumners at the Southern Baptist Historical Library and Archives, Kathryn Stallard at Southwestern University; Denise McCormick at Thru the Bible Radio; Robert Montoya and Carol Nishijima at UCLA.

I want—and need—to pay special tribute to the pastors and their assistants who allowed me to peruse materials stashed away in their filing cabinets. I had the privilege of visiting a number of California churches, but none were more vital to my project than Victory Baptist Church in Anaheim, Church of the Open Door (COD) in Glendora, and Mount Zion Missionary Baptist Church in Los Angeles. Judy Cocoris gave me all the time I needed to sift through the boxes of bulletins, newsletters, and minutes housed in one of John Brown's former preparatory school's dorms, now COD's campus. A longtime assistant to E. V. Hill, Letha Logan opened up about her own experiences in Watts during the 1960s and, with Pastor E. V. Hill Jr.'s blessing, directed me through the primary materials documenting her former pastor's remarkable life and career. Finally, and perhaps most importantly, I owe a debt of gratitude to Pastor Tony Birge, who, since my very first day in California, welcomed me into his church to digest the records of Victory Baptist, formerly Central Baptist. Tony was always inquisitive about his congregation's history and eager to understand it in light of larger social and political change, and so he often joined me on my ventures up to the church attic to rummage through all of its fascinating "stuff." These forays were usually followed by chats about what we found. Under his leadership, Victory Baptist has remade Central Baptist into a fresh, vibrant, and diverse congregation that seeks once again to evangelize the northern part of Orange County, a place very different now from the one Bob Wells set foot in during the late 1950s. Tony Birge and the others I list here are in no way responsible for my interpretations of Southern California evangelical politics—these are strictly my own—but I trust they will appreciate the story I tell.

If all of the aforementioned people gave me the chance to carry out my errand, friends and family constantly reassured me that it was not necessarily—or entirely—a foolish one. Through the years I've counted on Roberto Alvarez, Cory Anderson, Bryan Bademan, Glenn and Heidi Cook, Kory Cooper, Michael DeGruccio, Jonathan Den Hartog, Lee and Ilona Francois, Robert Glavind, Brian Kelly, Thomas and Ruby Kidd, Peter Lichtenstein, Spencer Lucas, Gary Massey, Tom McLean, Wayne and Corinna Orobko, Patrick Mason, Jeff Randhawa, Kris Skjervold, Jim Vanderkam, Len Vanderzee, and Kevin and Dawn Vaughn to remind me how enriching life can be beyond the shop. Bill and Lisa Svelmoe and George and Lucie Marsden have done this steadily for the last ten years, during our regular visits to South Bend and while together venturing beyond into the wilds of Michigan and British Columbia. While hunting down sources in the wilds of Southern California and the South I enjoyed (and greatly appreciated) my stays with the Jankowskis, Kidds, Ostranders, and Vaughns; thank you for making my research travel manageable and fun. The most long-suffering of hosts were Cheryl and Mike Crisp, who provided me with three months of accommodation in Fullerton, and Cheryl Koos, Doug Yule, and Ian and Jackson, who opened their Pasadena/Altadena home to me on several occasions, enabling me to do several rounds of follow-up research and, more importantly, get grounded again. Staying grounded is a message two other people imparted to me years ago, both of whom I continue to regard as mentors, exemplary scholars, and friends: thank you, Marguerite Van Die and Michael Fellman.

As special as they are, these friends had the option of tuning out my nattering about the book; my family did not. Through every dramatic turn they've been there, able to offer perspective. For this unconditional gift I thank Tetyana and Michael Klassen, Greg and Janelle Dochuk, and especially my parents. My wonderful in-laws, Ron and Rene Cochrane, spared me the dreaded "when is it going to be done" question and instead offered a shelter from work and a supportive environment in which to relax and just live; thank you for your love and support. Through dinners, movies, telephone conversations, and other fun excursions, Martha Dochuk offered the same welcomed distractions, love, and support, though she never shied away from the occasional "when is it going to be done" query; I wouldn't have wanted it any other way. George Dochuk saw the earlier phase of this book come to pass, and he was the first (and likely only) person to read through the bound dissertation; he did so lovingly, as a proud father, and critically, as a brilliant teacher. Sadly, Dad will not read the bound book, which, for several reasons, hurts deeply, because he is on every page. With a bit of plain folk, preacher, and entrepreneur in him, Dad—a product of small-town Alberta, Canada's Texas—encouraged me to dig deep into the lives of ordinary people as they wrestled with the profoundest social, cultural, spiritual, and political forces of change thrust upon them, forces with which he himself wrestled. On almost an annual basis Dad packed us in the car and drove us from Edmonton to Southern California for summer vacation. Perhaps it's in these southern sojourns that this book was born.

Writing a book is truly a communal effort, but it is also a selfish act, a product of personal introspection and isolation. Only one person in my life fully appreciates this. Debra has been there through it all, patiently shouldering day-to-day responsibilities while I tried to crank out another page and suffering through bouts of my quietness and distraction while I mentally searched for that next transitional phrase or a better verb. Along the way we've enjoyed many book-related adventures together—brainstorming while hiking and kayaking in Vancouver, researching Reagan in the Simi Valley and San Diego (usually before beach time), writing by day in New Jersey and enjoying evenings in New York and Philly, editing the manuscript in Delaware, then searching out the area's best crab cakes, and attending a good (but usually bad) Notre Dame football game every so often as a healthy (but usually unhealthy) diversion from Bible belt obsessions. But Debra sacrificed way too much to see this book published, and I will never be able to repay her. The best thing I can do is promise never to utter another word about J. Vernon McGee and Bob Wells . . . and say simply, "I love you" with all my heart!

NOTES

Abbreviations in Notes

Manuscript Collections

Anaheim Public Library, Anaheim, California
 ALHC   Anaheim Local History Collection

Bancroft Library, University of California, Berkeley, California
 CWP   Carey McWilliams Papers
 SDC   Sara Diamond Collection

Bentley Library, University of Michigan, Ann Arbor, Michigan
 CMSC   Carl McIntire Sermon Collection
 GLKS   Gerald L. K. Smith Collection
 METP   Marcius Erwin Taber Papers

Billy Graham Center Archives, Wheaton College, Wheaton, Illinois
 BGEA   Billy Graham Evangelistic Association Records
 CCP   Charles Colson Papers
 HJT   Herbert John Taylor Papers
 HLP   Harold Lindsell Papers
 LNB   L. Nelson Bell Papers
 NRB   National Religious Broadcasters
 WPI   Interviews of William Pannell
 TSP   Tom Skinner Papers

Brackett Library, Harding University, Searcy, Arkansas
 HUSC   Harding University Special Collections

Calvary Baptist Church, Bellflower, California
    CBC   Calvary Baptist Church Historical Material

Center for American History, University of Texas, Austin, Texas
    JHJP   Jesse H. Jones Papers
    SSBGP   Stephen Shadegg/Barry Goldwater Papers

Central Baptist Church, Huntington Beach, California
    CBCHB   Central Baptist, Huntington Beach, Historical Material

Chicago Historical Society
    CMP   Clarence Manion Papers

Church of the Open Door, Glendora, California
    COD   Church of the Open Door Archival Material

Doheny Library, Archival Research Center, University of Southern California, Los
Angeles, California
    HC   Hearst Collection
    SCRHC   Regional History Collection

First Baptist Church, Long Beach, California
    FBCLB   First Baptist Church, Long Beach Historical Material

First Baptist Church Tustin/Irvine, Tustin, California
    BSBC   Bristol Street Baptist Church Historical Material

First Church of the Nazarene, Long Beach, California
    FCNLB   First Church of the Nazarene Historical Material

Flower Pentecostal Heritage Center, Springfield, Missouri
    AGR   Assemblies of God Records
    JEPB   Jonathan Perkins Biographical File

Fuller Theological Seminary, Pasadena, California
    CHP   Charles Fuller Papers
    DDP   David DuPlessis Papers
    WSC   Wilbur Smith Correspondence

Hagley Museum and Library, Wilmington, Delaware
    JHP   J. Howard Pew Papers
    PFC   Pew Family Collection

Hoover Institution, Stanford University, Palo Alto, California
    WJP   Walter Judd Papers
    DKP   Denison Kitchel Papers

EPP	Edith Phillips Papers
RRC	Radical Right Collection
ACWP	Albert C. Wedemeyer Papers

Houston Metropolitan Research Center, Houston, Texas
| HMSF | Houston Metropolitan History Standing Files |

The Huntington Library, San Marino, California
FBP	Fletcher Bowron Papers
JAF	John Anson Ford Papers
KHP	Kenneth Hahn Papers
LMP	Loren Miller Papers
MKC	Marie Koenig Collection

John Brown University Archives, Siloam Springs, Arkansas
| JBC | John Brown Collection |

John Tower Library, Southwestern University, Georgetown, Texas
| JTP | John Tower Papers |

J.S. Mack Library, Bob Jones University, Greenville, South Carolina
| AWP | G. Archer Weniger Papers |

Knight Library, Special Collections and Archives, University of Oregon, Eugene, Oregon
JIP	James C. Ingebretsen Papers
GRP	George W. Robnett Papers
HEK	Howard E. Kershner Papers
TAP	Tom Anderson Papers
WCMP	W.C. Mullendore Papers

Kroch Library, Special Collections and Archives, Cornell University
| CWP | Clifton White Papers |

Los Angeles City Records, Los Angeles, California
| SYP | Mayor Samuel Yorty Papers |

Margaret Estes Library, LeTourneau University, Longview, Texas
| RGLP | R. G. LeTourneau Papers |

Mount Zion Missionary Baptist Church, Los Angeles, California
| MZM | Mount Zion Missionary Historical Material |

National Archives and Records Administration, College Park, Maryland
| NPM | Nixon Presidential Materials |

Norwalk Public Library, Norwalk, California
    NLHC   Norwalk Local History Collection

Oviatt Library, Special Collections and Archives, California State University–
Northridge, Northridge, California
    LACRC   Jewish Federation–Council of Los Angeles Community Relations
                    Committee Collection
    LACFL   Los Angeles County Federation of Labor Collection
    LAULR   Los Angeles Urban League Records
    WLMC   Rev. Wendell L. Miller Collection

Pat Boone Headquarters, Beverly Hills, California
    PBPF   Pat Boone Personal Files

Payson Library, Special Collections and University Archives, Pepperdine University
    EVP   E. V. Pullias Papers
    NYP   M. Norvel Young Papers
    WBP   William Banowsky Papers
    PUR   Pepperdine University Records

Pollak Library, Special Collections, California State University–Fullerton, Fullerton,
California
    FC   Freedom Center Collection
    CSUF-OHC   Oral History Collection

Ronald Reagan Presidential Library, Simi Valley, California
    RRG   Ronald Reagan Governor's Papers
    EMP   Edwin Meese Papers
    MHP   Max Hugel Papers

San Diego Historical Society, San Diego, California
    SDHRCP   San Diego Human Rights Commission Papers
    SDPRC   San Diego Public Records Collection

San Diego Public Library, San Diego, California
    SDLHSF   San Diego Local History Standing Files

Southern Baptist Historical Library and Archives, Nashville, Tennessee
    JFNC   J. Frank Norris Papers
    SBCR   Southern Baptist Convention Records

Southern California Library for Social Studies and Research, Los Angeles, California
    GLKRF   Gerald L. K. Smith Reference File
    PLACRC   Papers of the Los Angeles Civil Rights Congress

Strom Thurmond Center, Clemson University, Clemson, South Carolina
    HDP   Harry Dent Papers
    STP   Strom Thurmond Papers

Thru the Bible Network Headquarters, Pasadena, California
    TTB   Thru the Bible Historical Material

University Library, Special Collections and Archives, California State University–Long Beach, Long Beach, California
    DHP   Dorothy Healey Papers

Vanguard University Library, Vanguard University, Costa Mesa, California
    PC   Pentecostal Collection

Victory Baptist Church, Anaheim, California
    CBA   Central Baptist Church Archival Material

Walter Reuther Archives of Labor and Urban Affairs, Wayne State University, Detroit, Michigan
    CRCM   Civil Rights Congress of Michigan Collection
    MDCC   Metropolitan Detroit Council of Churches Collection

Wheaton College University Archives, Billy Graham Center, Wheaton, Illinois
    NAE   National Association of Evangelicals Collection
    NACS   National Association of Christian Schools Records

Young Research Library, Special Collections and Archives, University of California, Los Angeles, Los Angeles, California
    ACLUP   American Civil Liberties Union Papers
    CRA   California Republican Assembly Records
    CWC   Carey McWilliams Collection
    KMC   Knox Mellon Collection
    UCLA-OHC   Oral History Collection
    TPC   Townsend Plan Collection
    ULSCP   Urban League of Southern California Papers

Periodicals

AB	*Anaheim Bulletin*
AS	*Anaheim Star*
BBT	*Baptist Bible Tribune* (Baptist Bible Fellowship)
BHH	*Baptist History and Heritage* (Southern Baptist)
BP	*The Blu-Print* (Guy Archer Weniger)
CBNL	*Central Baptist News Letter* (Central Baptist Church, Anaheim)
CC	*Christian Century*
CCH	*Christian Chronicle* (Church of Christ)

CE   *California Eagle*
CN   *Church Notes* (Central Baptist Church, Anaheim)
CS   *Christian Standard* (Church of Christ)
CSB   *California Southern Baptist*
CSM   *Christian Science Monitor*
CT   *Christianity Today*
DMN   *Dallas Morning News*
EO   *Evening Outlook*
FEANV   *Fundamental Evangelistic Association News & Views*
FGBMV   *Full Gospel Business Men's Voice*
FN   *Fullerton News*
GNP   *Glendale News Press*
IPR   *Independent Press-Telegram*
JC   *Journal-Champion* (Jerry Falwell/Moral Majority)
KT   *The King's Trumpet* (Southern California Assemblies of God)
LADN   *Los Angeles Daily News*
LAE   *Los Angeles Examiner*
LAH   *Los Angeles Herald*
LAHE   *Los Angeles Herald Examiner*
LAMDN   *Los Angeles Mirror and Daily News*
LAS   *Los Angeles Sentinel*
LAT   *Los Angeles Times*
LBIPT   *Long Beach Independent Press-Telegram*
MC   *The Methodist Challenge* (Bob Shuler)
MM   *Moody Monthly*
NR   *National Review*
NYT   *New York Times*
OT   *Oakland Tribune*
PAV   *Pepperdine Alumni Voice*
PE   *The Pentecostal Evangel* (Assemblies of God)
PN   *Pepperdine News*
PW   *People's World*
RD   *Reader's Digest*
RNS   *Religious News Service*
SB   *Sacramento Bee*
SBHM   *Southern Baptist Home Missions*
SEP   *Saturday Evening Post*
SFC   *San Francisco Chronicle*
SST   *Sunday School Times*
TF   *The Fundamentalist* (J. Frank Norris)
TG   *The Graphic* (Pepperdine College/University)
TI   *The Informant* (Southern California Assemblies of God)
TN   *The Nation*
TR   *The Register* (*Santa Ana Register*, 1911–1952; *Register*, 1952–1985; *Orange County Register* 1985–Present)
TNR   *The New Republic*

USNWR   *U.S. News & World Report*
VTF   *Voice of Truth and Freedom* (Central Baptist Church, Anaheim)
WP   *Washington Post*
WS   *Washington Star*
WSJ   *Wall Street Journal*

Interviews by Author

Adrian, Dr. John H., March 12, 2002, Anaheim, California
Allen, Marie, April 5, 2002, Garden Grove, California
Banowsky, William, May 2, 2006, Malibu, California
Barnes, Ruby, March 14, 2002, Tustin, California
Barnes, Derral, March 14, 2002, Tustin, California
Boone, Pat, September 1, 2006, Beverly Hills, California
Bundy, Edgar, March 20, 2007, Wheaton, Illinois
Byrd, Robert, April 6, 2002, Garden Grove, California
Byrd, Mary, April 6, 2002, Garden Grove, California
Diggs, David, July 12, 2006, Beverly Hills, California
George, William, April 1, 2003, Siloam Springs, Arkansas
Grisett, Lorin, March 21, 2002, Santa Ana, California
Knutson, Robert, February 7, 2002, Anaheim, California
Koenig, Marie, November 13, 2002, Pasadena, California
Logan, Letha, July 10, 2007, Los Angeles, California
Miller, Margaret, March 18, 2002, Long Beach, California
Noia, Larry, November 16, 2002, Fountain Valley, California
Redden, James, March 18, 2002, Anaheim, California
Scott, Senator Jack, July 10, 2007, Pasadena, California
St. Pierre, Janet, July 9, 2007, Los Angeles, California
Vandruff, Eleanor, March 17, 2002, Westminster, California
Vandruff, Jean, March 17, 2002, Westminster, California
Wallace, Jim, March 11, 2002, Anaheim, California
Wallace, JoAnn, March 11, 2002, Anaheim, California
Wilburn, James, May 2, 2006, Malibu, California
Young, Helen, May 2, 2006, Malibu, California

Introduction: "At Home with the Angels"

1. "Anaheim Crusade: At Home with the Angels," *CT*, October 24, 1969, 40–41. Visual documentation of Graham's Anaheim sermons in Collection 113, BGEA; also *Southern California Crusade Bulletin*, September 1969, Folder 39, Box 16, Collection 12, BGEA.
2. "Anaheim Crusade," 45.
3. "Graham Breaks Attendance Record," September 28, 1969, press release, and "Crusade Closes Before Largest Audience," October 5, 1969, press release, Folder 46, Box 16, Collection 12, BGEA; "Mrs. Billy Graham: Lunching with 11,000," *CT*, October, 24, 1969.

4. "August 1, 1969, News Release," Folder 46, Box 16, Collection 12, BGEA.

5. James N. Gregory, "The Southern Diaspora and the Urban Dispossessed: Demonstrating the Census Public Use Microdata Samples," *Journal of American History* 82 (June 1995), 112; U.S. Bureau of the Census, *Historical Statistics of the United States: Colonial Times to 1957* (Washington, D.C., 1961), 45–47; *Historical Statistics of the United States: Continuation to 1962 and Revisions* (Washington, D.C., 1965), 9–10. The population of Arkansas in 1970 was 1,923,295; Little Rock and Oklahoma City reported populations of 381,123 and 718,737, respectively. These two figures combined fall short of matching the estimated 1.2 million white southerners living in California's southernmost counties.

6. Marie Allen, Marie Koenig, Jean Vandruff, and Eleanor Vandruff, interviews by author.

7. Douglas W. Johnson, Paul R. Picard, and Bernard Quinn, *Churches and Church Membership in the United States, 1971* (Washington, D.C.: Glenmary Research Center, 1974), table 2. Martin B. Bradley, Norman M. Green Jr., Dale E. Jones, Mac Lynn, and Lou McNeil, *Churches and Church Membership in the United States, 1990* (Atlanta: Glenmary Research Center, 1992), 13–14.

8. On Texas theology: Paul Harvey, *Redeeming the South: Religious Cultures and Racial Identities Among Southern Baptists, 1865–1925* (Chapel Hill: University of North Carolina Press, 1997), 151; on southern and non-southern evangelicalism: John Shelton Reed, *The Enduring South: Subculture Persistence in Mass Society* (Chapel Hill: University of North Carolina Press, 1972), 57. "Uncentered" and "unbounded" are drawn from Carl Abbott, "Southwestern Cityscapes: Approaches to an American Urban Environment," in Raymond Mohl, Robert Fisher, Carl Abbott, Roger W. Lotchin, Robert B. Fairbanks, and Zane I. Miller, *Essays on Sunbelt Cities and Recent Urban America* (College Station, TX: Texas A&M University Press, 1990), 65.

9. Clifford Geertz, *The Interpretation of Cultures: Selected Essays* (New York: Basic Books, 1973), 90. On "Steinbeckian pathos": Gregory, "The Southern Diaspora and the Urban Dispossessed," 116.

10. On "plain-folk Americanism": James Gregory, *American Exodus: The Dust Bowl Migration and Okie Culture in California* (New York: Oxford University Press, 1989), 142.

11. On white southern religion and the dismantling of the New Deal and Democratic South see especially Joseph Crespino, *In Search of Another Country: Mississippi and the Conservative Counterrevolution* (Princeton, NJ: Princeton University Press, 2007), James Gregory, *The Southern Diaspora: How the Great Migrations of Black and White Southerners Transformed America* (Chapel Hill: University of North Carolina Press, 2005), Steven Miller, *Billy Graham and the Rise of the Republican South* (Philadelphia: University of Pennsylvania Press, 2009), Bethany Moreton, *To Serve God and Wal-Mart: The Making of Christian Free Enterprise* (Cambridge, MA: Harvard University Press, 2009). The literature on conservatism is too extensive to cite here but will surface in the pages that follow. For an overview, see Darren Dochuk, "Revival on the Right: Making Sense of the Conservative Moment in American History," *History Compass: An Online Journal* 4 (July 2006), 975–99, and the bibliographic essay in Kim Phillips-Fein, *Invisible Hands: The Making of the Conservative Movement from the New Deal to Reagan* (New York: W. W. Norton, 2009). For view of religion in current schol-

arship: Jon Butler, "Jack-in-the-Box Faith: The Religion Problem in Modern American History," *Journal of American History* 90 (March 2004), 1357–78.

12. "Moral geography" is loosely drawn from Simon Schama, *The Embarrassment of Riches: An Interpretation of Dutch Culture in the Golden Age* (New York: Vintage, 1997), chap. 1.

1. PLAIN FOLK

1. Jean Vandruff interview. Vandruff has also written much of his autobiography and posted it online, at www.vandruff.com/jean/autobiography. References to the online version hereafter designated "published autobiography."

2. These recollections of Vandruff's youth are drawn from Jean Vandruff interview and published autobiography.

3. Warren Thompson, *Growth and Changes in California's Population* (Los Angeles: The Haynes Foundation, 1955), 152; United States Bureau of the Census, *Historical Statistics of the United States, Colonial Times to 1970* (Washington D.C., 1975), 4; Donald J. Bogue, Henry S. Shryock Jr., and Siegfried A. Hoermann, *Subregional Migration in the United States, 1935–40*, Vol. 1 (Oxford, OH: Scripps Foundation, Miami University, 1957), 11; Center for Planning and Development Research, *Characteristics of Metropolitan Growth in California, Volume 1: Report* (Berkeley: Institute of Urban and Regional Development, University of California, Berkeley, 1965), 26; Gerald D. Nash, *World War II and the West: Reshaping the Economy* (Lincoln, NE: University of Nebraska Press, 1990), 3–4; Arthur C. Verge, *Paradise Transformed: Los Angeles During the Second World War* (Dubuque, IA: Kendall/Hunt Publishing Company, 1993), 6; Ann Markusen, Peter Hall, Scott Campbell, and Sabina Dietrick, *The Rise of the Gunbelt: The Military Remapping of Industrial America* (New York: Oxford University Press, 1991), chap. 5.

4. Perry Miller, *Errand Into the Wilderness* (Cambridge, MA: Belknap Press of Harvard University, 1956).

5. For a more extensive treatment of the western South's peopling patterns, see Darren Dochuk, "From Bible Belt to Sunbelt: Plain Folk Religion, Grassroots Politics, and the Southernization of Southern California, 1939–1969" (PhD diss., University of Notre Dame, 2005); Jean Vandruff interview.

6. See Dochuk, "From Bible Belt to Sunbelt," 57–62, which draws from Walter L. Buenger, *Path to a Modern South: Northeast Texas between Reconstruction and the Great Depression* (Austin, TX: University of Texas Press, 2001), Ben F. Johnson, *Arkansas in Modern America, 1930-1999* (Fayetteville, AK: University of Arkansas Press, 2000), and Temple Kirby, *Rural Worlds Lost: The American South, 1920–1960* (Baton Rouge, LA: Louisiana State University Press, 1987).

7. Walter Knott, "The Enterprises of Walter Knott," interview conducted by Donald J. Schipper, 1965, UCLA-OHC; William King, "El Monte 1851–1941" (master's thesis, Claremont Graduate School, 1966).

8. Dyer Bennett Interview, CSUF-OHC.

9. Quoted in James Ward Lee, Carolyn N. Barnes, Kent A. Bowman, and Laura Crow, eds., *1941: Texas Goes to War* (Denton, TX: University of North Texas Press, 1991), 23;

Sheila Golding Manes, "Depression Pioneers: The Conclusion of an American Odyssey, Oklahoma to California, 1930–1950, a Reinterpretation" (PhD diss., University of California, Los Angeles, 1982), 320, and table 5-15, 366; Roscoe Crawford interview, CSUF-OHC.

10. Raymond D. Gastil, *Cultural Regions of the United States* (Seattle, 1975), 47–91; D.W. Meining, *Imperial Texas: An Interpretive Essay in Cultural Geography* (Austin: University of Texas Press, 1969), 35, 86–89; Bill C. Malone, *Country Music, U.S.A.*, 2nd rev. ed. (Austin, TX: University of Texas Press, 2002), chaps. 3–5.

11. On popular ("herrenvolk") democracy: George M. Fredrickson, *The Black Image in the White Mind: The Debate on Afro-American Character and Destiny* (Middletown, CT: Wesleyan University Press, 1987 [1971]), chap. 3; Lacy K. Ford Jr., *Origins of Southern Radicalism: The South Carolina Upcountry, 1800–1860* (New York: Oxford University Press, 1988); "Ideology of the Old South's Plain Folk," in Samuel C. Hyde Jr., ed., *Plain Folk of the South Revisited* (Baton Rouge, LA: Louisiana State University Press, 1997), 205–27; Hyde, *Plain Folk of the South Revisited*, 15.

12. See Alan Brinkley, *Voices of Protest: Huey Long, Father Coughlin, and the Great Depression* (New York: Vintage, 1983).

13. On nineteenth-century populism's "modern" traits: Charles Postel, *The Populist Vision* (New York: Oxford University Press, 2007); also Ronald Formisano, *For the People: American Populist Movements from the Revolution to the 1850s* (Chapel Hill: University of North Carolina Press, 2008), 11.

14. On distinctions between cotton cultures and racial politics in the Deep South and western South: Kirby, *Rural Worlds Lost*, 32–34; also Neil Foley, *The White Scourge: Mexicans, Blacks, and Poor Whites in Texas Cotton Culture* (Berkeley: University of California Press, 1997), chaps. 3 and 5; Buenger, *Path to a Modern South*, chap. 7; Chandler Davidson, *Race and Class in Texas Politics* (Princeton, NJ: Princeton University Press, 1990); Murray Wickett, *Contested Territory: Whites, Native Americans, and African Americans in Oklahoma, 1865–1907* (Baton Rouge, LA: Louisiana State University Pres, 2000).

15. Michael L. Kurtz, "New South Demagoguery," in Hyde, *Plain Folk of the South Revisited*, 251; V. O. Key Jr., *Southern Politics in State and Nation* (Knoxville, TN: University of Tennessee Press, 1984), 254.

16. Koenig interview.

17. My use of "Jefferson and Jesus" builds on Michael Kazin, *A Godly Hero: The Life of William Jennings Bryan* (New York: Alfred A. Knopf, 2007).

18. Whitney R. Cross, *The Burned-over District: The Social and Intellectual History of Enthusiastic Religion in Western New York, 1800–1850* (New York: Octagon Books, 1981 [c. 1950]); Linda K. Pritchard, "The Burned-Over District Reconsidered: A Portent of Evolving Religious Pluralism in the United States," *Social Science History* 8 (Summer 1984), 243–65; National Council of Churches, 1957, *Churches and Church Membership*, Series C, Nos. 46–52; Stephen Martin Stookey, "The Impact of Landmarkism upon Southern Baptist Western Geographical Expansion" (PhD diss., Southwestern Baptist Theological Seminary, 1994), 57.

19. David Harrell, "The Evolution of Plain-Folk Religion in the South, 1835–1920," in Hill, *Varieties of Southern Religious Experience*, 24–51. This discussion draws from Grant Wacker, *Heaven Below: Early Pentecostals and American Culture* (Cambridge, MA: Har-

vard University Press, 2003), and Randall Stephens, *The Fire Spreads: Holiness and Pentecostalism in the American South* (Cambridge, MA: Harvard University Press, 2008).

20. This discussion draws from William Glass, *Strangers in Zion: Fundamentalism in the South, 1900–1950* (Macon, GA: Mercer University Press, 2001).

21. National Council of the Churches of Christ in the U.S.A., *Churches and Church Membership in the United States* (New York: National Council of Churches, 1956), table 4, "Reported Church Membership as Percent of Total Population by Major Religious Faiths and by Region, Division, and State"; Samuel Hill, "The Shape and Shapes of Popular Southern Piety," in Harrell, *Varieties of Southern Evangelicalism*, 95. On evangelical notions of rebirth: Donald G. Mathews, *Religion in the Old South* (Chicago: University of Chicago Press, 1977), xvi.

22. Wayne Flynt, "One in the Spirit, Many in the Flesh: Southern Evangelicals," in Harrell, *Varieties of Southern Evangelicalism*, 28.

23. Dochuk, "From Bible Belt to Sunbelt," 93.

24. On the political nature of southern evangelicalism: Hill, "The Shape and Shapes of Popular Southern Piety, 99–102; on evangelical "hardball": Grant Wacker, "Uneasy in Zion: Evangelicals in Postmodern Society," in George Marsden, ed., *Evangelicalism and Modern America* (Grand Rapids, MI: William B. Eerdmans, 1984), 26.

25. Wacker, "Uneasy in Zion," 27; Reed, *Enduring South*, 57; O'Connor quoted in Charles Reagan Wilson, *Judgment and Grace in Dixie: Southern Faiths from Faulkner to Elvis* (Athens, GA: University of Georgia Press, 1995), 17.

26. Quoted in Charles Spaulding, "The Development of Organization and Disorganization in the Social Life of a Rapidly Growing Working-Class Suburb within a Metropolitan District" (PhD diss., University of Southern California, 1939), 46–47; John Allard, "Organizing the United Auto Workers in Los Angeles," UCLA-OHC.

27. Robert Harley Jordan, "A Comparative Study of the Organization, Function and Social Contribution of Selected Adult Secular Groups as Found in Bell Gardens in 1937–1938 and in 1946–1947" (master's thesis, University of Southern California, 1948), 1–5; Robert E. Alexander, F.A.I.A. and Associates, "Norwalk Planning Studies Phase II," March 16, 1970, NLHC; R. Kenneth Browell, "Some Social Implications of the National Defense Problem in Los Angeles County" (master's thesis, Claremont College, 1941), 7.

28. Becky M. Nicolaides, *My Blue Heaven: Life and Politics in the Working-Class Suburbs of Los Angeles, 1920–1965* (Chicago: University of Chicago Press, 2002), 2–4; "Exhibits Ready at Maywood: Industrial Display to Mark City's Birthday Will Open Tomorrow," *LAH*, August 16, 1937; "Twenty-five Years as a City Will Be Celebrated Here August 21–27," *LAH*, August 7, 1949; "Maywood Chief Faces Charges," *LAH*, April 19, 1949, all in Maywood File, HC.

29. Robert Fogelson, *Fragmented Metropolis: Los Angeles, 1850–1930* (Cambridge, MA: Harvard University Press, 1967), 16–19, 137–38; Gabriele Gonder Carey, "From Hinterland to Metropolis: Land-Use Planning in Orange County, California, 1925–1950" (PhD diss., University of California, Riverside, 1997), 134–36.

30. Bell Gardens attracted Oklahomans, for instance, while Maywood welcomed Arkansans and Missourians. See "Waterford Church Observes 'Arkansas Day,'" *CSB*, May 11, 1950; Eshref Shevky and Marilyn Williams, *The Social Areas of Los Angeles: Analysis and Typology* (Berkeley: University of California Press, 1949), 48. Norwalk's reasonably

priced subdivisions proved especially alluring to those of Pentecostal and Church of Christ religious persuasion. See *Norwalk, California* (Norwalk: Norwalk Chamber of Commerce, 1963); *Civic and Business Directory, Norwalk, Los Angeles County, California* (1949); Alexander et al., *Norwalk Planning Studies Phase II*, 13, NLHC.

31. *Bristol Street Baptist Church, 35th Anniversary*, 1974; *Bristol Street Baptist Church: Forty Years of Growth*, 1979, and "Enrollment Book," in BSBC. Texans and Oklahomans dominate membership records for the church's first thirteen years: among the 640 enrolled in Bristol Street Baptist (then called Emmanuel Baptist) between 1939 and 1952, approximately 70 percent came from towns along the northern border of Texas and just south of Oklahoma City; Allen interview.

32. Melvin Gerald Shahan interview, CSUF-OHC; Allen interview.

33. On early church meeting places: "From Old Store Buildings to New Church Buildings," *CSB*, February 8, 1951, 2, and "Advancing in Southern California," *PE*, January 16, 1955. Also, *25th Anniversary and Dedication of the Bristol Street Baptist Church*, 1964, 6, BSBC; "Santa Ana Congregation Plans New Building," *CSB*, January 22, 1953; *Groundbreaking: A 40 Year History of Calvary Baptist Church*, 2–3, CBC.

34. *Groundbreaking*, 2–4. The most useful community study for mapping congregations within Los Angeles' working-class suburbs is Clarence Miller, "A Study of Certain Community Forces of South Gate, California, in Their Relation to Character Education," (master's thesis, University of Southern California, 1935). Included in Miller's thesis are detailed maps that show the stark difference in the positioning of mainline Protestant and southern evangelical churches. While the former occupy space on main arteries, the latter are predominantly embedded in the middle of residential streets.

35. "Bell Gardens Fellowship Meeting," *KT*, May 1941, AGR; "Building Plans Are Important," *CSB*, November 28, 1946. J. Clyde Foster, "I Came to California," *CSB*, January 24, 1946.

36. "My Impressions of California," *CSB*, July 24, 1947; J. L. Blankenship, "Southern Baptist Possibilities in California Outlined," *CSB*, July 9, 1942.

37. Ernest L. Friend, "Building Up Our Sunday School," *KT*, June 1, 1941, 8, AGR; Roland Q. Leavell, "The Southland Is Worth Saving," *SBHM*, September 1941, 11.

38. Allen interview.

39. "Notes from Secretary's Desk," *CSB*, July 9, 1942; Ferris Miller to Mayor Fletcher Bowron, June 10, 1940, Folder 21-40, Box 7, FBP.

40. Mrs. Jennie Ray Thompson to Mayor Fletcher Bowron, September 6, 1948, Folder 51-5705, Box 20; Mr. Carl J. Ghormley to Mayor Fletcher Bowron, November 14, 1947, Folder 51-5037, Box 17; James Matthew Alley to Mayor Fletcher Bowron, May 15, 1950, Folder 40-696, Box 11; Ralph Michelson to Mayor Fletcher Bowron, June 4, 1947, Folder 51-4745, Box 16, FBP.

2. Preachers

1. Undated quote, in letter and file sent from Leatha Perkins Dahlgren to Wayne E. Warner, August 2, 1988, JEPB.

2. J. Frank Norris to Mr. H. B. Earhart, February 25, 1939, Folder 550, Box 12, JFNC.

3. Floyd Looney, *History of California Southern Baptists* (Fresno, CA: The Southern Baptist General Convention of California, 1954), 366–67; Spaulding, "The Development of Organization and Disorganization in the Social Life of a Rapidly Growing Working-Class Suburb within a Metropolitan District," 202–3.

4. Erskine Caldwell quoted by Rosemary M. Magee in "Religion—Preacher, White," in Charles Reagan Wilson and William Ferris, eds., *Encyclopedia of Southern Culture* (Chapel Hill: University of North Carolina Press, 1989), 1301.

5. "Converter of Graham Dies in Louisville," miscellaneous newspaper clipping dated November 2, 1961, Graham, Billy—Evangelist Folder, HC; Richard T. Hughes, *Reviving the Ancient Faith: The Story of Churches of Christ in America* (Grand Rapids, MI: William B. Eerdmans, 1996), 160–61; David Edwin Harrell Jr., *The Churches of Christ in the Twentieth Century: Homer Hailey's Personal Journey of Faith* (Tuscaloosa, AL: University of Alabama Press, 2000), 103–4.

6. "Southern Baptist Convention," *TF*, June 10, 1949, 5; "Dr. Norris as He Is Today After 40 Years in Ft. Worth," *TF*, October 1, 1948, 1.

7. On traits of southern preaching: Gregory, *American Exodus*, 144, 146; Joseph W. Creech, "Righteous Indignation: Religion and Populism in North Carolina, 1886–1906" (PhD diss., University of Notre Dame, 2000), 153; Wayne Flynt, "One in the Spirit, Many in the Flesh: Southern Evangelicals," in Harrell, *Varieties of Southern Evangelicalism*, 44; Harvey, *Redeeming the South*, chap. 5.

8. "Out of the Past and Present," *MC*, October 1946, 7–8; Bob Shuler, "That Old Dad of Mine," *MC*, January 1958, 1, 6.

9. Edward Drewry Jervey, *The History of Methodism in Southern California* (Nashville, TN: Parthenon Press, 1960), 32–37; Lawrence L. Larrabee, "Results of Los Angeles Judicial Election," *Journal of the American Judicature Society* 14, no. 5 (February 1931), 148–49; Jimmy Gleason, "The American Judicature Society and the Pre–World War II Campaign for Better Judges," 14, unpublished paper in author's possession. For treatment of Shuler's life, see Mark Sumner Still, "'Fighting Bob' Shuler: Fundamentalist and Reformer" (PhD diss., Claremont Graduate School, 1988).

10. "Need for Pastors," *1942 Annual Report of the General Convention of California Southern Baptists*, 8, SBCR; "The Challenge of the West to Southern Baptists," *SBHM*, August 1948; V. E. Wolber, "A Pastor's Eye View of California," *CSB*, May 1943.

11. A. G. Osterberg to Rev. J. R. Flower, March 30, 1938; F. C. Woodworth to Rev. J. R. Flower, October 9, 1946, and November 29, 1946; Rev. J. R. Flower to F. C. Woodworth, December 4, 1946, Southern California District Executive Files, AGR.

12. "Vision and Faith," 7–10, California Church History A–Z Folder, SBCR.

13. This estimation is derived from a sampling of ordination applications for pastors working in California between the 1920s and 1960s. See Ordination Applications and J. R. Flower to F. C. Woodworth, August 2, 1944, Southern California District Executive Files, AGR.

14. On concerns with pastoral ordination standards and claims to divine inspiration in the Assemblies of God: General Secretary J. Roswell Flower to District Superintendent A. G. Osterberg, April 22, 1938, Southern California District of the Assemblies of God Executive Files, AGR.

15. "Papers from a Notebook of Jonathan Ellsworth Perkins' Early Life," in Leatha Perkins Dahlgren to Wayne E. Warner, August 2, 1988, JEPB.

16. This sketch of Perkins' life draws from Robert Cunningham to Mrs. Leatha Perkins Dahlgren, August 22, 1980, Leatha Perkins Dahlgren to Wayne E. Warner, August 2, 1988, and "75th Anniversary Celebration Bulletin for Central Assembly of God, Tulsa," JEPB; Ralph Lord Roy, *Apostles of Discord: A Study of Organized Bigotry and Disruption on the Fringes of Protestantism* (Boston: Beacon Press, 1953), 114; Joseph Roos, *The Fifth Column*, Report filed January 5, 1945, Folder 1, Box 86, and Report on Jonathan Perkins, July 10, 1945, Folder 1, Box 86, LACRC.

17. LAHE, September 7, 1935; September 10, 1935; September 11, 1935; Jonathan E. Perkins Obituary, in JEPB; letter from J. Roswell Flower, general secretary of the Assemblies of God, dated August 16, 1945, and Report on Jonathan Perkins, July 25, 1945, Folder 1, Box 86, LACRC.

18. Stookey, "The Impact of Landmarkism," 66, 75.

19. Sam A. Harvey, "The Roots of California Southern Baptists" (ThD diss., Golden Gate Baptist Theological Seminary, 1973), 77–81; S. G. Posey, "Southern Baptist Pioneer Work in California," *Quarterly Review* 15 (Third Quarter, 1955), 5–8; Lackey quoted in Elmer L. Gray, *Heirs of Promise: A Chronicle of California Southern Baptists, 1940–1978* (Fresno, CA: Executive Board, The Southern Baptist General Convention of California, 1978), 22–23.

20. "It Is Not a Question of Territory," *CSB*, August 13, 1942, 2; "Northern Baptists Lost 198 Last Year," *CSB*, July 1945, 3; "Lift Up Your Eyes and Look on the Field," *CSB*, December 1945, 10–11; "Editor of Missions Offers Misleading Accusations," *CSB*, February 1945, 1.

21. "Southern Baptist Infiltration into California," *Missions* 35 (November 1944), 499; "Editor of Missions Offers Misleading Accusations," *CSB*, February 1945, 1; Stookey, "The Impact of Landmarkism," 200; W. Earle Smith, "Our Southern Baptist Friends," *The Baptist Advance*, November 1946, 22–23.

22. "Answering God's Call or Burning the Bridges Behind You," *CSB*, July 9, 1942.

23. Gray, *Heirs of Promise*, 24–25.

24. See "The Subtile [sic] Invasion," *CSB*, February 13, 1947; "Texas Editor Warns Against Federated Church Councils," *CSB*, April 1945.

25. "Baptist Principles in This Hour," *CSB*, September 1944; "A Pastor's Eye View"; "California Southern Baptist Opportunity," *CSB*, February 1943.

26. "Baptist Principles in This Hour"; "California Southern Baptist Opportunity"; "The Cry from the Crow's Nest," *CSB*, December 1944.

27. "Thank God for the Baptists," *MC*, January 1946, 4; "Bishop Oxnam and God," *MC*, July 1945, 1; Robert Moats Miller, *Bishop G. Bromley Oxnam: Paladin of Liberal Protestantism* (Nashville, TN: Abingdon Press, 1992), 91; "Methodist Whirlwind," *Time*, March 22, 1963.

28. Bob Shuler, "I Look to My Friends Once Again," *MC*, November 1951, 1; Bob Shuler, "The Evangelical Methodist Movement," *MC*, June 1948, 10–12.

29. Bob Shuler, "The Evangelical Methodist Movement," *MC*, June 1948, 10–12; Bob Shuler, "The Pentecostals," *MC*, November 1948, 8–10.

30. Norris's enthusiasm for western expansion is expressed in letters filed in Folders 808 and 812, Box 18, and in Folders 991 and 992, Box 22, JFNC. Norris's travels in 1941 are documented in "Happy Meeting of J. Edgar Hoover, Head of the Federal Bureau of Investigation," *TF*, August 15, 1941; "Address of Dr. J. Frank Norris Before

Texas Legislature," *TF*, February 28, 1941; "Marching Through Georgia—Great Revival Sponsored by Governor and Senators," *TF*, March 7, 1941; "Georgia Legislature Is Turned into Revival by 'Flying Parson,'" *AJ*, February 27, 1941; "Great Evangelistic Meeting in Los Angeles," *TF*, December 12, 1941.

31. Norris to Mr. H. B. Earhart, February 25, 1939, Folder 12, Box 7, JFNC; "Six Thousand Mile Tour of South Already Under Way," *TF*, May 10, 1946; "Glorious News from Los Angeles," *TF*, May 14, 1943; "Miracle of Fundamental Baptist Work on the Pacific Coast," *TF*, June 18, 1943. The Southern Baptist Convention provided a higher percentage of its clergy for war efforts than any other denomination. See "They Shall Not March Alone," *SBHM*, February 1945; Robert L. Gushwa, *The Best and Worst of Times: The United States Army Chaplaincy, 1920–1945*, Vol. IV (Washington, D.C.: Office of the Chief of Chaplains, Department of the Army, 1977), appendix C.

32. Arnie Smith, "John Birch, the Missionary-Patriot," *BBT*, August 1999, 24.

33. Quoted in ibid., 25.

34. "John Birch Promoted to Three High Honors and Positions of Trust," *TF*, March 26, 1943; John Birch to J. Frank Norris, April 6, 1944, Folder 152, Box 4, JFNC.

35. John Birch to J. Frank Norris, April 6, 1944, Folder 152, Box 4; "Chinese Reds Slew American Army Officer," *LAT*, November 22, 1945; Edwin James, First Lieutenant, to J. Frank Norris, undated, 1949, Folder 151, Box 4, JFNC.

3. Entrepreneurs

1. Batsell Baxter to E. V. Pullias, July 20, 1937, Series 7, Box 2, File 2, EVP.

2. For the sake of clarity, I will refer to George Pepperdine College, the school's official name at its founding, simply as Pepperdine College, the name by which it would popularly (and by the early 1950s, officially) become known.

3. George Pepperdine, *Faith Is My Fortune: A Life Story of George Pepperdine* (Los Angeles: Pepperdine College, n.d.), 183–85; Jerry Rushford, ed., *Crest of a Golden Wave: A 50ᵗʰ Anniversary Pictorial History* (Malibu: Pepperdine University Press, 1987), 1.

4. Context and quotes from Mark T. Dalhouse, *An Island in the Lake of Fire: Bob Jones University, Fundamentalism, and the Separatist Movement* (Athens, GA: University of Georgia Press, 1996), 35, 37, 40, 44.

5. Rick Ostrander, *Head, Heart, and Hand: John Brown University and Modern Evangelical Higher Education* (Fayetteville, AR: University of Arkansas Press, 2003), 39; Virginia L. Brereton, *Training God's Army: The American Bible School, 1880–1940* (Bloomington, IN: Indiana University Press, 1990), 27, 156.

6. R. G. LeTourneau, *Mover of Men and Mountains: The Autobiography of R. G. LeTourneau* (Chicago: Moody Press, 1967), 198, 216, 222, 239; "Vicksburg Dedication Day," *NOW*, October 13, 1944, 1–3.

7. On Roosevelt and the "Nation's No. 1 economic problem": Bruce J. Schulman, *From Cotton Belt to Sunbelt: Federal Policy, Economic Development, and the Transformation of the South, 1938–1980* (Durham, NC: Duke University Press, 1994), 3–7.

8. Ibid., xiii.

9. Jordan A. Schwarz, *The New Dealers: Power Politics in the Age of Roosevelt* (New

York: Alfred A. Knopf, 1993), 59; Walter L. Buenger, "Between Community and Corporation: The Southern Roots of Jesse H. Jones and the Reconstruction Finance Corporation," *The Journal of Southern History* 56 (August 1990), 508–10. The exact terms of LeTourneau and Jones's relationship is unclear, but it is mentioned in John Brown to R. G. LeTourneau, June 26, 1950, John E. Brown Folder, Box J4S, RGLP. Jones's philanthropic support of several private colleges in the western South is amply documented in JHJP. On "corporate populism": Moreton, *To Serve God and Wal-Mart*, 13–16.

10. Ralph C. Kennedy Jr., and Thomas Rothrock, *John Brown of Arkansas* (Siloam Springs, AR: John Brown University Press, 1966), 88, 36; "John Brown of Arkansas," Clipping from *Threefold Advocate*, October 27, 1939, Biographical Articles Folder, Standing Files; John Brown, Sr. to Mrs. John E. Brown, June 9, 1947, Letters/Correspondence, Brown and Mrs. Brown; 1928–1953 Folder, Box 4; "Bob Shuler Met These on the Trail," John Brown Folder, JBC.

11. John Brown to Mrs. Brown, August 23, 1944, Letters/Correspondence; Brown and Mrs. Brown; 1928–1953 Folder, Box 4; John E. Brown, "Attention! Arkansas!" *Christian Fellowship*, December 28, 1937, Articles and Sermons Folder, JBC; Kennedy and Rothrock, *John Brown of Arkansas*, 42; Brown quoted in Ostrander, *Head, Heart, and Hand*, 49.

12. John Brown Sr., "A Statement to the Board of the John Brown Schools," June 23, 1941, John Brown Correspondence Folder; "A Tribute," *John Brown University Bulletin*, July 1951, Bulletin Folder, JBC.

13. "Jesse H. Jones Address," *The Christian Fellowship*, May 17, 1938, 4–6, Jesse Jones Folder, Standing Files, JBC.

14. "Chronology," Standing Files; *John Brown University Bulletin*, April 1937, Bulletin Folder, JBC. On Brown's radio strategy: Ostrander, *Head, Heart, and Hand*, 66–67.

15. "History-Location-Founder," in *Catalog of the Brown Military Academy*, 3, Brown Military Academy Folder, Box 1; "We Buy Another School," *John Brown University Bulletin*, February 1947, Bulletin Folder, JBC; Kennedy and Rothrock, *John Brown of Arkansas*, 105–7.

16. "Dr. Brown Speaks at Chapel Service," *The Cadet*, March 19, 1940, Brown Military Academy Folder, Box 1, JBC.

17. "Interview with George S. Benson," Oral History Office, HUSC; George S. Benson, *Missionary Experiences*, ed. Phil Watson (Delight, AR: Gospel Light Publishing, 1987), 5–7.

18. Benson, *Missionary Experiences*, 6–13.

19. Ibid., 19–20; Hughes, *Reviving the Ancient Faith*, 157.

20. George Benson to J. Howard Pew, December 9, 1943, H Folder, Box 3; "Harding College Division of Popular Education," attached to George Benson to J. Howard Pew, September 2, 1943, H Folder, Box 3, JHP; L. Edward Hicks, *"Sometimes in the Wrong, but Never in Doubt": George S. Benson and the Education of the New Religious Right* (Knoxville, TN: University of Tennessee Press, 1994), 29–30.

21. "The Hard Way," *Time*, May 5, 1941; Hicks, *"Sometimes in the Wrong, but Never in Doubt,"* 32–33, 35.

22. Context and quotes from Hicks, *"Sometimes in the Wrong, but Never in Doubt,"* 31, 35–37.

23. Ibid., 19, 39; Jno. G. Pew to J. Howard Pew, January 22, 1943, George Benson to J. Howard Pew, February 6, 1943, George Benson to J. Howard Pew, February 6, 1943, H Folder, Box 3, JHP.

24. J. Howard Pew to Lewis N. Brown, May 10, 1943, H Folder, Box 3, JHP. On Benson's itinerary: Donald P. Garner, "George S. Benson: Conservative, Anti-Communist, Pro-American Speaker" (PhD diss., Wayne State University, 1963), 133.

25. On Benson as "commoner": C. D. Brown to J. Howard Pew, November 29, 1943, H Folder, Box 3, JHP. Benson quoted in "Harding College: Division of Popular Education," 3, attached to George Benson to J. Howard Pew, September 2, 1943, H Folder, Box 3, George Benson to J. Howard Pew, January 5 and December 3, 1943, H Folder, Box 3, JHP. On Benson's publishing ventures: Cabel Phillips, "Wide Anti-Red Drive Directed from Small Town in Arkansas," NYT, May 18, 1961, 26; Hicks, "Sometimes in the Wrong, but Never in Doubt," 29, 47–48.

26. George Thayer, The Farther Shore of Politics: The American Political Fringe Today (New York: Simon & Schuster, 1967), 275–77.

27. George Benson to Supporting Congregations, November 20, 1928, HUSC; Hicks, "Sometimes in the Wrong, but Never in Doubt," 9–11, 15–16, 20–22.

28. Pepperdine, Faith Is My Fortune, 58–61.

29. Ibid., 93.

30. Context and quotes from ibid., 94–95, 116.

31. Ibid., 96, 147, 134.

32. Ibid., 151. On Pepperdine's charity: "Pepperdine . . . An Unusual College," PAV, Spring 1964, 1; "As the Twig Is Bent: The George Pepperdine Foundation," Apartment Journal, June 1937, in File 2, Box 2, Series 7, EVP; Rushford, Crest of a Golden Wave, 2.

33. Pepperdine, Faith Is My Fortune, 175. On Depression-era educational politics: Elizabeth A. Fones-Wolf, Selling Free Enterprise: The Business Assault on Labor and Liberalism, 1945–60 (Champaign, IL: University of Illinois Press, 1994), 189–92.

34. On Southern California's extensive Bible school network: NACS 1952 Directory, Evangelical Christian School Movement (1952), NACS. George Benson to Dr. J. D. Bales, February 2, 1976, File 386-1, PUR.

35. On Pepperdine's founding philosophy: Howard A. White, "The Mission of Pepperdine University," 2, File 368-1, PUR. Pepperdine, Faith Is My Fortune, 184.

36. George Pepperdine College Bulletin, July 1937, 6, PUR; Pepperdine, Faith Is My Fortune, 178–80.

37. George Pepperdine College Bulletin, July 1937, 8, 11, 20–23, PUR. On Pepperdine's "wholesome atmosphere": Batsell Baxter to E. V. Pullias, July 20, 1937, Series 7, Box 2, File 2, EVP. Rushford, Crest of a Golden Wave, 6. On Pepperdine's theological requisites: E. V. Pullias to Batsell Baxter, April 20, 1937, Series 7, Box 2, File 2, EVP.

38. "George Pepperdine College: Planning with You," Series 7, Box 2, File 2, EVP; George Pepperdine College Bulletin, July 1937, 3, PUR; "Pepperdine Is a School of Workers," TG, November 24, 1937, 3.

39. Dr. M. Norvel Young, Pepperdine University: A Place, A People, A Purpose (New York: Newcomen Society in North America, 1982), 11; Pepperdine, Faith Is My Fortune, n.p.

40. Bill Henegar and Jerry Rushford, Forever Young: The Life and Times of M. Norvel

Young and Helen M. Young (Nashville, TN: 21st Century Christian, 1999), 46–48, 58, 60; Helen Young, interview by author.

41. Young interview; *Forever Young*, 64–65.

4. LABOR WARS

1. Robert Shuler, "Befuddlement," *MC*, November 1946, 14.

2. Carey McWilliams, *Southern California: An Island on the Land*, 9th ed. (New York: Peregrine Smith, 1980), 375–76. On McWilliams and Mencken, and Southern California's "two sides": Peter Richardson, *American Prophet: The Life and Work of Carey McWilliams* (Ann Arbor, MI: University of Michigan Press, 2005), 19–22, 37.

3. Quote and context for Huey Long politics from Michael Kazin, *The Populist Persuasion: An American History* (New York: Basic Books, 1995), 111–12.

4. "World city" is drawn from Scott Kurashige, *The Shifting Grounds of Race: Black and Japanese Americans in the Making of Multiethnic Los Angeles* (Princeton, NJ: Princeton University Press, 2008), 7.

5. McManus quoted in Peter La Chapelle, *Proud to Be an Okie: Cultural Politics, Country Music, and Migration to Southern California* (Berkeley: University of California Press, 2007), 22, 27–28.

6. Carey McWilliams, "Migration and Resettlement of the People," Folder 23, Box 1, ULSCP; "Basic Principles for a Redevelopment Program," Los Angeles County Government; Relations; Civic Relations; Miscellaneous Folder, Box 68, JAF; Father Riker, *CE*, November 5, 1942.

7. "Among the Language Groups," *CSB*, September 14, 1947, 5; Meeting of the Board of Directors, *CSB*, December 1944, 3; "Bob Shuler Met These on the Trail," John Brown Folder, JBC. On Pepperdine and racial politics: William Trombley, "Pepperdine U. Torn by Tragedy, Internal Dissent," *LAT*, April 18, 1976.

8. For a more extensive treatment, see Dochuk, "From Bible Belt to Sunbelt," chap. 4.

9. Gene Tipton, "The Labor Movement in the Los Angeles Area During the Nineteen Forties" (PhD diss., University of California, Los Angeles, 1953), 343–45; Michael Denning, *The Cultural Front: The Laboring of American Culture in the Twentieth Century* (New York: Verso, 1997), 4–6.

10. Dochuk, "From Bible Belt to Sunbelt," chap. 4; Josh Sides, *L.A. City Limits: African American Los Angeles from the Great Depression to the Present* (Berkeley: University of California Press, 2003), 2, 30, 37–38, 63; Douglas Flamming, *Bound for Freedom: Black Los Angeles in Jim Crow America* (Berkeley: University of California Press, 2005), 116.

11. Shana Bernstein, "Building Bridges at Home in a Time of Global Conflict: Interracial Cooperation and the Fight for Civil Rights in Los Angeles, 1933–1954" (PhD diss., Stanford University, 2003), 9, 88–92; Max Vorspan and Lloyd P. Gartner, *History of the Jews of Los Angeles* (San Marino, CA: Huntington Library, 1970), 201; Deborah Dash Moore, *To the Golden Cities: Pursuing the American Jewish Dream in Miami and Los Angeles* (Cambridge, MA: Harvard University Press, 1996), 96, 113–14.

12. On civic nationalism: Gary Gerstle, *American Crucible: Race and Nation in the*

Twentieth Century (Princeton, NJ: Princeton University Press, 2002), 99. McWilliams, *Southern California*, 377.

13. On sociological approach to the southern problem: Gregory, *Southern Diaspora*. On social democratic action: "United We Stand; Speeches delivered at the Philharmonic Auditorium April 24, 1944," Council for Civic Unity Folder, Box 23, LACFL; "Procedural Rules and Administrative Practices of the Los Angeles County Committee on Human Relations, May, 1946," Committee on Human Relations Folder, Box 72, and "Four Months Report of the Executive Secretary, August 16–December 15, 1945," Folder B IV 2c, Box 69, JAF. On union gains: Kevin Starr, *Embattled Dreams: California in War and Peace, 1940–1950* (New York: Oxford University Press, 2003), 140–41, and Nelson Lichtenstein, *Labor's War at Home: The CIO in World War II* (New York: Cambridge University Press, 1982), 56–57. On Social Democrats in San Francisco: "Dan Gilbert," *MC*, October, 1945, 23.

14. Perkins to Smith, April 25, 1945, Rev. Jonathan E. Perkins Folder, Box 16, GLKS.

15. On Noble's plan: Jackson K. Putnam, *Old-Age Politics in California* (Palo Alto, CA: Stanford University Press, 1970), 89–91; Winston and Marian Moore, *Out of the Frying Pan* (Los Angeles, 1939), 33; David H. Bennett, *Demagogues in the Depression* (New Brunswick, NJ: Rutgers University Press, 1969), 247.

16. Tom Zimmerman, "'Ham and Eggs, Everybody!'" *Southern California Quarterly* (Spring 1980), 78–80; Carey McWilliams, "Ham and Eggs," *NR*, October 25, 1939, 331–33. Bainbridge quoted in Putnam, *Old-Age Politics in California*, 93.

17. Cartoons in Ham and Eggs Folder, FC.

18. "Second Survey of Public Opinion Regarding California Retirement Life Payments Act," October 1939, "Resolution Adopted by the Inter-Denominational Ministers Alliance, September 24, 1939," "Hoaxing California, published by Southern California Citizens Against 30-Thursday," and "Address of William Schneiderman," in Ham and Eggs Folder, FC; Moore, *Out of the Frying Pan*, 51, 156; Zimmerman, "'Ham and Eggs, Everybody,'" 79, 86–91; Putnam, *Old-Age Politics in California*, 105.

19. On the Allens' appeal to southerners: "Don't Go Back to Oklahoma," in "Out on a Limb," Ham and Eggs Folder, Box 15, GLKS. On Perkins: Ralph Lord Roy, *Apostles of Discord: A Study of Organized Bigotry and Disruption on the Fringes of Protestantism* (Boston: Beacon Press, 1953), 113–15.

20. On Smith's political activities and language: Glen Jeansonne, *Gerald L. K. Smith: Minister of Hate* (New Haven, CT: Yale University Press, 1988), 24–25. Lawrence Allen to Gerald L. K. Smith, September 15, 1945, Ham and Eggs Folder, Box 15, GLKS. Report on Earl Craig's "Public Affairs Forum," November 6, 1945 and Report on Ham and Eggs Meeting, November 11, 1945, Folder 12, Box 67, LACRC.

21. Report on Ham and Eggs Meeting, December 3, 1945, Folder 12, Box 67, LACRC; Jonathan Perkins, *The Preacher and the State* (Los Angeles, 1946), 7, 12, 40–49, in Rev. Jonathan E. Perkins Folder, Box 19, GLKS.

22. Reports on Ham and Eggs Meetings, January 20, March 3, and March 24, 1946, Folder 11, Box 67, LACRC; Letter from Perkins to Smith, December 26, 1945, Rev. Jonathan E. Perkins Folder, Box 19, GLKS.

23. "Invades Los Angeles Area," Folder 11, Box 10, PLACRC; "Editorial on Gerald L. K. Smith, Ham and Eggs Movement in Los Angeles," *Prophecy Monthly*, August 1945,

11–12; Smith to Dr. Will Durant, July 11, 1945, Ham and Eggs Folder, Box 15, GLKS; Report on Ham and Eggs Meeting, February 17, 1946, Folder 11, Box 67, LACRC.

24. Report on Ham and Eggs Meeting, November 3, 1945, Folder 12, Box 67, LACRC.

25. Ibid.

26. On Smith's potential move to Angelus Temple: *LADN*, May 30, 1945; *CE* June 21, 1945. On the "southernization" of Detroit: "Interview with Rev. Claude Williams," "Conversation with Judge Charles Bowles," and "Survey of Racial and Religious Conflict Forces in Detroit," Survey of Racial and Religious Conflict Forces in Detroit—1943 Folder, Box 71, CRCM. For a balanced assessment of white southern migration's impact on Detroit racial politics: Gregory, *Southern Diaspora*, 298–99, and Thomas Sugrue, *Origins of the Urban Crisis: Race and Inequality in Postwar Detroit* (Princeton, NJ: Princeton University Press, 1996), 212. McWilliams, "The Growing Danger of Native Fascism," in *Los Angeles Against Gerald L. K. Smith: How a City Organized to Combat Native Fascism!* (Los Angeles: Mobilization for Democracy, 1945), GLKRF.

27. Minutes of Committee for Church and Community Cooperation, June 14, 1945, Committee for Church and Community Cooperation Correspondence and Minutes, April–July 1945 Folder, Box 23, LACFL; J. Roswell Flower to LACCC, August 16, 1945 and August 31, 1945, Folder 1, Box 86, LACRC.

28. McWilliams in *Los Angeles Against Gerald L. K. Smith*; Tom Sitton, "Direct Democracy vs. Free Speech: Gerald L. K. Smith and the Recall Election of 1946 in Los Angeles," *Pacific Historical Review* 57 (August 1988), 292.

29. "McClanahan Faces Recall," in *Los Angeles Against Gerald L.K. Smith*; Anonymous letter to Smith, March 19, 1945, "Committee of 500," and Meade McClanahan to Gerald L.K. Smith, March 24, 1946, McClanahan Folder, Box 18, GLKS; *Los Angeles Against Gerald L. K. Smith*; *LAT*, November 4, 1945.

30. Bob Shuler to Mayor Fletcher Bowron, October 18, 1945, Folder 3, Box 44, ACLUP.

31. Report on Ham and Eggs Meeting, May 19, 1946, Folder 11, Box 67, LACRC; Bob Shuler to Fletcher Bowron, October 18, 1945, Folder 3, Box 44, ACLUP.

32. "That Mass Meeting," *MC*, October 1945, 17.

33. Anonymous letter from woman to Gerald L. K. Smith, March 19, 1946, McClanahan Folder, Box 18, GLKS.

34. Jonathan Perkins to Gerald L. K. Smith, February 21, 1946, Rev. Jonathan E. Perkins Folder, Box 19, GLKS; Report on Ham and Eggs Meeting, January 20, 1946, Folder 11, Box 67, LACRC.

35. Willis Allen to Gerald L. K. Smith, March 28, 1946; Press Release from Lawrence Allen, May 10, 1946, Ham and Eggs Folder, Box 18, GLKS.

36. Jonathan Perkins to Gerald L. K. Smith, May 10 and May 14, 1946, Rev. Jonathan E. Perkins Folder, Box 19, GLKS; Report on Ham and Eggs Meeting, May 26, 1946, Folder 11, Box 67, LACRC.

37. George Lipsitz, *Rainbow at Midnight: Labor and Culture in the 1940s* (Champaign, IL: University of Illinois Press, 1994), 99–100; Lichtenstein, *Labor's War at Home* 203–30.

38. Nelson Lichtenstein, "The Eclipse of Social Democracy," in Steve Fraser and Gary Gerstle, eds., *The Rise and Fall of the New Deal Order, 1930–1980* (Princeton, NJ:

Princeton University Press, 1989), 136; Gerstle, *American Crucible*, 248. On "Second Reconstruction": C. Vann Woodward, *The Strange Career of Jim Crow* (New York: Oxford University Press, 1965 [1955]).

39. Kevin M. Schultz, "The FEPC and the Legacy of the Labor-Based Civil Rights Movement of the 1940s," *Labor History* 49 (February 2008), 71; *Freedom Begins at Home* (Workers Party, Los Angeles, 1946), 10, DHP; *CE*, July 11, 1946; Kurashige, *Shifting Grounds of Race*, 207; Sides, *Los Angeles City Limits*, 63, 78–79.

40. "The Subtile [sic] Invasion," *CSB*, February 13, 1947, 1; "Texas Editor Warns Against Federated Church Councils," *CSB*, April 1945, 3; W. R. White, "We Face a Grave Peril," *CSB*, February 1944, 1–2; "Baptist Principles in This Hour," 4. On liberal Protestant efforts in Operation Dixie: Fones-Wolf, *Selling Free Enterprise*, 228–29.

41. "The Catholic Church and America," *CSB*, April 1945, 3. On evangelicals and the Taylor controversy: Dale Hufft, "Baptists and Separation of Church and State," *CSB*, February 23, 1950, 5; Jill Edwards, "The President, the Archbishop and the Envoy: Religion and Diplomacy in the Cold War," *Diplomacy and Statecraft* 6 (July 1995), 490–511.

42. "Dan Gilbert," *MC*, October 1945, 23; Schultz, "The FEPC," 82.

43. Loren Miller to Ruth Goldner, September 30, 1946, Folder 2—Correspondence 1946, Box 6, LMP; "Memo to Executive Committee Re: Eagle Rock Chamber of Commerce," September 11, 1948, Relations; Agencies; Los Angeles County; Committee on Human Relations Folder, Box 72, JAF. On Warren's assessment of postwar conditions: Starr, *Embattled Dreams*, 194.

44. Civil Rights Congress Bulletin, June 4, 1947, and June 10, 1947, CRC Correspondence, 1947 Folder, Box 23, LACFL; "Report of Executive Committee Meeting," August 5, 1948, Relations; Agencies; Los Angeles County; Committee on Human Relations Folder, Box 72, JAF.

45. Marguerite Herrick to Ford, August 14, 1946, John Anson Ford to J. M. Whitley, October 22, 1946, and correspondence between John Anson Ford and Mr. W. F. Hoffman, June 23, 1948, July 27, 1948, Los Angeles County Government; Relations; Race Relations; Negro Folder, Box 76, JAF; Jonathan Perkins to Gerald L. K. Smith, June 12, 1946, Rev. Jonathan E. Perkins Folder, Box 19, GLKS; CRC Report, December 8, 1946, CRC, Jewish Federated Council of Greater Los Angeles Community Relations Committee; Rev. Jonathan E. Perkins Folder, LACRC.

46. "UNI-FACTS from Council for Civic Unity," June 1946, and "Special Circular—The California Council for Civic Unity," Federation for Civic Unity Folder, Box 69, JAF; see also MFD reports between 1947 and 1948 in Box 3b, LACRC.

47. William R. Bidner to Ford, August 26, 1947, and Radio Transcript for Ford Speech on KFVD, August 28, 1947, Communism, Fascism, Nazism Folder, Box 46, JAF; Mayor Fletcher Bowron to Mr. DeWitt Wallace, Editor, *RD*, September 13, 1946, Xtra Copies 1946 Folder, Box 2, FBP.

48. Flamming, *Bound for Freedom*, 302–3; Elizabeth Gilmore, *Defying Dixie: The Radical Roots of Civil Rights, 1919–1950* (New York: W. W. Norton, 2008), 141.

49. Carey McWilliams, "The Evolution of Sugar Hill," *Script*, March, 1949, 24–35. McWilliams quoted in Sides, *L.A. City Limits*, 99–100. The *Shelly* ruling was reinforced by the Supreme Court's *Barrows v. Jackson* decision in 1953, another text case from Southern California. Together, *Shelley* and *Barrows* officially abolished race restrictive covenants in the United States.

50. "California Negroes Can Now Live Anywhere!" *LAS*, May 6, 1948; Sides, *L.A. City Limits*, 100; "Jim Crow Is Dying," *LAS*, October 7, 1948. Southern California as "fine model for future improvement" quoted from *Pittsburgh Courier* in Daniel HoSang, *Racial Propositions: "Genteel Apartheid" in Postwar California* (Berkeley: University of California Press, forthcoming, 2010), manuscript draft, 13–14.

51. "Ku Klux False Alarm" and "California Shows Resentment," *MC*, July 1946, 17.

52. Shuler, "Befuddlement," *MC*, November 1946, 14.

5. NEW ALLIES

1. J. Howard Pew to Mr. L. R. Campiglia, San Francisco, California, January 16, 1947, H Folder 1947, Box 13, JHP.

2. "Purpose and Objectives of the Department of National Popular Education, Harding College—Searcy, Arkansas," H Folder 1946, Box 9, JHP.

3. J. Howard Pew to Mr. J. P. Spang, August 25, 1947, H Folder 1947, Box 13; J. Howard Pew to Mr. L. R. Campiglia, January 16, 1947, H Folder 1947, Box 13, JHP.

4. Donald Critchlow, *Phyllis Schlafly and Grassroots Conservatism: A Woman's Crusade* (Princeton, NJ: Princeton University Press, 2005), 25–26; George Nash, *The Conservative Intellectual Movement in America*, Thirtieth Anniversary Edition (Wilmington, DE: ISI Books, 2008), 1–5, 16–18.

5. Phillips-Fein, *Invisible Hands*, 32.

6. Alan Brinkley, *Liberalism and Its Discontents* (Cambridge, MA: Harvard University Press, 1998), 129; Lichtenstein, *Labor's War at Home*, 240; Phillips-Fein, *Invisible Hands*, 33; Critchlow, *Phyllis Schlafly and Grassroots Conservatism*, 44–45.

7. Kurashige, *Shifting Grounds of Race*, 211.

8. Phillips-Fein, *Invisible Hands*, 28; "The Foundation for Economic Freedom: Outline of Proposed Activities and Reasons," 2–3, 7, 9–12, Foundation for Economic Education Folder, Box 9, JHP.

9. On SM's agenda: Eckard V. Toy Jr., "Spiritual Mobilization: The Failure of an Ultraconservative Ideal in the 1950's," *Pacific Northwest Quarterly* 61 (April 1970), 78. On scope of SM: "Spiritual Mobilization: Fundamental ideals, policies, organization and activities," October 1, 1951, Folder 3, Box 87, "History of Spiritual Mobilization," Folder 3, Box 92, JIP

10. Ockenga quoted in Garth Rosell, *The Surprising Work of God: Harold Ockenga, Billy Graham, and the Rebirth of Evangelicalism* (Grand Rapids, MI: Baker Academic, 2008), 97–98, 101–2.

11. On NAE ecumenical composition: Joel Carpenter, *Revive Us Again: The Reawakening of American Fundamentalism* (New York: Oxford University Press, 1997), 141. "Report of the Director of Information," Original Minutes, 1963–1964, National Association of Evangelicals Minutes, 63–69, 74–88, Box 32, NAE; "Annual Report of the 'Committee on Christian Liberty,'" 3–4, 9, Minutes of the Meeting of the Board of Administration, National Association of Evangelicals, Tuesday, April 19, 1949, Chicago, Illinois, National Association of Evangelicals Master Minutes 1940s–50s, Box 30, NAE.

12. R. G. LeTourneau, "The Industrial Chaplain" and "Novel On-Job Bible Class Big Hit with D-X Workers," *Tulsa Daily World*, August 22, 1952, 1, Industrial Chaplaincy—Background Material, NAE Files, 1960s, Box 38, NAE; LeTourneau, *Mover of Men and Mountains*, 232.

13. "Minutes of the Executive Committee, Chicago, Illinois, September 9, 1947, 6; 12, September 1947–February 1949 Binder, National Association of Evangelicals Master Minutes 1940s–50s, Box 30, NAE; Phillip Goff, "Fighting Like the Devil in the City of Angels: The Rise of Fundamentalist Charles E. Fuller," in Tom Sitton and William Deverell, eds., *Metropolis in the Making: Los Angeles in the 1920s* (Berkeley: University of California Press, 2001), 220–22.

14. On COD's importance to the NAE: "Report of the Executive Director," 9, in Minutes of the Meeting of the Board of Administration, National Association of Evangelicals, Tuesday, April 19, 1949, Chicago, Illinois, National Association of Evangelicals Master Minutes 1940s–50s, Box 30, NAE; Elders Board Minutes for November 8, 1949, Committees Minutes, A–L Box, COD.

15. COD's demographic profile is drawn from "Enrollment Book, 1931–1935," COD. On the socioeconomic characteristics of classical evangelicalism: Carpenter, *Revive Us Again*, 10.

16. Regular COD guest preacher Louis Bauman suggested, for instance, that the blue eagle of the NRA (National Recovery Administration) was the Mark of the Beast spoken of in Revelation. See Paul Boyer, *When Time Shall Be No More: Prophecy Belief in Modern American Culture* (Cambridge, MA: Harvard University Press, 1992), 107. Sermon titles indicate COD's impatience with the New Deal, populism, and the Democratic Party. See Rev. W. E. Pietsch, "Six Years of the New Deal in the Light of Bible Prophecy," COD Bulletin, February 27, 1938; Dr. Cortland Myers preaching on Upton Sinclair, "Utopia: Where did it come from? What is it? Where is it going? What has Christianity and the Bible to say about it?" COD Bulletin, August 12, 1934, Church Bulletins File, COD. On New Deal "-isms": Critchlow, *Phyllis Schlafly and Grassroots Conservatism*, 34–35.

17. George Marsden, *Reforming Fundamentalism: Fuller Seminary and the New Evangelicalism* (Grand Rapids, MI: William B. Eerdmans, 1987), 156–57. On Pew's respect for Ockenga: J. Howard Pew to Howard Kershner, March 8, 1950, Christian Freedom Foundation: Founding Documents Folder, Box 180, JHP. J. Elwin Wright designates Pew as part of the NAE's "inner circle": J. Elwin Wright to J. Howard Pew, February 4, 1958, National Association of Evangelicals Folder, Box 61, JHP.

18. A COD membership list reveals few transfers and new members from the western South in the years prior to World War II. See Church of the Open Door Membership Log Book, 1931–1934, COD.

19. This discussion draws from Michael Lindsay, *Faith in the Halls of Power: How Evangelicals Joined the American Elite* (New York: Oxford University Press, 2007), 218–22.

20. See untitled report, *John Brown University Bulletin*, April 1949; John E. Brown Sr., "What Hath God Wrought!" *John Brown University Bulletin*, November 1951, JBC; Tona Hangen, *Redeeming the Dial: Radio, Religion, and Popular Culture in America* (Chapel Hill: University of North Carolina Press, 2002), 142–50.

21. "Radio KGER Presents," KGER-Brown Radio File, JBC.

22. "Radio KGER Presents," KGER-Brown Radio File, JBC. On evangelicals and Jews: Robert Wuthnow, *The Restructuring of American Religion: Society and Faith Since World War II* (Princeton, NJ: Princeton University Press, 1988), 76–77; Leonard Dinnerstein, *Antisemitism in America* (New York: Oxford University Press, 1994), xii, 104; Timothy Weber, *Living in the Shadow of the Second Coming; American Premillennialism, 1875–1982* (Chicago: University of Chicago Press, 1987), 137–41.

23. Bible professor quoted in Boyer, *When Time Shall Be No More*, 187. On other evangelical opinions of Israel: Carpenter, *Reviving Fundamentalism*, 98. On Rose and COD: Executive Board Minutes for July 5, 1963, Executive Board Minutes, 1950–1960, File, Board Minutes Box, COD.

24. Boyer, *When Time Shall Be No More*, 224.

25. "New Study Covers Decade, Shows Upward Trend," *AV* (January/February 1962), 18; Rushford, *Crest of a Golden Wave*, 10–11, 61–66; "Social Lites," *TG*, November 30, 1945, 6; "Bab's Gab on Fads," *TG*, October 8, 1948, 4; "Opera Performance Has Music for Varied Tastes; Workshop Productions Gaining Fame Among Students, Citizens," *TG*, March 12, 1948, 1.

26. *Crest of a Golden Wave*, 45–47, 62–70, 92–94.

27. On racial politics at Pepperdine: Trombley, "Pepperdine U. Torn by Tragedy, Internal Dissent"; *Crest of a Golden Wave*, 83, 94.

28. Frequently panels were formed to discuss current events around the world, and on a daily basis radio listeners heard the world news and commentary from conservative newsmen like Upton Close. *Radio KGER Presents*, KGER-Brown Radio File, JBC.

29. "Wallbank Opens World Affairs Lecture Series," *TG*, September 24, 1948, 1, "Rotary Panel to Discuss UN At Next Forum" and "This Week Devoted to United Nations," *TG*, October 22, 1948, 1; "James Roosevelt Is to Be Main Speaker at Junior-Senior Banquet," *TG*, February 13, 1948, 1; "Governor Warren Will Be Speaker at Annual Commencement Program on June 6, Announces Haalboom," *TG*, April 2, 1948, 1. On Pepperdine's views of Bryan: Pepperdine, *Faith Is My Fortune*, 16. On Pepperdine's relationship with Kershner: Howard Kershner to George Pepperdine, May 11, 1954, and George Pepperdine to Howard Kershner, November 8, 1954, both letters in Peo-Peterson Folder, Box 13, HEK.

30. Clinton Davidson to J. Howard Pew, July 1, 1946, and George Benson to J. Howard Pew, July 8, 1946, H Folder 1946, Box 9, JHP; Hicks, *"Sometimes in the Wrong, but Never in Doubt,"* 29–30, 47.

31. George S. Benson, "Should the Public School System Be Subsidized by Federal Funds?" *Congressional Digest* 25 (January 1946), 47. Benson on federal aid quoted in Hicks, *"Sometimes in the Wrong, but Never in Doubt,"* 29-30, 47, 49–50.

32. George Benson to Honorable Secretary Snyder, August 25, 1947, H Folder 1947, Box 13, JHP.

33. J. Howard Pew to George Benson, November 3, 1949, H Folder 1949, Box 22, JHP; Hicks, *"Sometimes in the Wrong, but Never in Doubt,"* 50.

34. Guy Rush to J. Howard Pew, February 24, 1947, H Folder 1947, Box 13, George Benson to J. Howard Pew, June 24, 1949, H Folder 1949, Box 22, JHP; Hicks, *"Sometimes in the Wrong, but Never in Doubt,"* 52–53. Belding quoted in Thayer, *Farther Shores of Politics*, 276. Belding carried out his own patriot program in 1949, when, in

conjunction with Edward F. Hutton and Kenneth D. Wells, he established the Freedoms Foundation in Valley Forge, Pennsylvania, an institution that would become famous during the cold war for granting awards to "those who excel in selling the American way of life."

35. Hicks, *"Sometimes in the Wrong, but Never in Doubt,"* 62–63; Harold V. Knight, "Whooping It Up for Adam Smith," *TN* 175 (August 2, 1952), 87–89.

36. Jean Vandruff interview.

37. Koenig interview. Details of Marie King's experiences are also drawn from Michelle Nickerson, *Mothers of Conservatism: Women and the Postwar Right* (Princeton, NJ: Princeton University Press, forthcoming), manuscript draft, chap. 2. On Hollywood's labor wars: Starr, *Embattled Dreams*, 286–88.

38. *Radio KGER Presents*, KGER-Brown Radio File, JBC.

6. Plain-Folk Preaching Mainstreamed

1. J. Vernon McGee, *The Country Preacher Who Came to Town* (Pasadena, CA: Thru the Bible Radio Network, n.d.), 6–7, 24, in TTB.

2. John Pollock, *Billy Graham: The Authorized Biography* (Grand Rapids, MI: Zondervan, 1966), 50; Marshall Frady, *Billy Graham: A Parable of American Righteousness* (Boston: Little, Brown, 1979), 197–204.

3. Pollock, *Billy Graham*, 56–57; William Martin, *A Prophet with Honor: The Billy Graham Story* (New York: William Morrow, 1991), 117. "Puff Graham" and "headlines screamed again" quoted in John Pollock, *To All the Nations: The Billy Graham Story* (New York: Harper and Row, 1985), 39–48.

4. Robert Shuler, "The Spiritual Upheaval in Los Angeles," *PE*, February 4, 1950, 3, 12.

5. Elliott Smith, "Shapers of the California Southern Baptist Heritage: R. W. Lackey, Executive Secretary," *CSB*, March 6, 1980, 13; James O. Combs, ed., *Roots and Origins of Baptist Fundamentalism* (Springfield, MO: Baptist Bible Tribune Publications, 1984), 93; "Dr. Billington's Temple," *Newsweek*, April 11, 1949, 16; "Happy Visit to Akron Baptist Temple," *TF*, June 17, 1949, 1, 4–5. Akron Baptist Temple was also profiled by *Collier's* and *Life*; both articles are mentioned in correspondence between Norris and Billington in Folders 142–46, Box 4, JFN.

6. Records of the Southern California District Council of the Assemblies of God reveal a concerted effort to improve the ordination requirements of district pastors. See F. C. Woodworth to J. Roswell Flower, August 17, 1945, J. Roswell Flower to F. C. Woodworth, August 22, 1945, J. Roswell Flower to Rev. William E. Long, August 1, 1947, Southern California District Executive Files, 1941–1974, AGR. See also Edith L. Blumhofer, *Restoring the Faith: The Assemblies of God, Pentecostalism, and American Culture* (Champaign, IL: University of Illinois Press, 1993), 189, 196–97.

7. W. E. Long to J. R. Flower, July 20, 1947 and J. R. Flower to W. E. Long, August 1, 1947, Southern California District Executive Files, 1941–1974, AGR.

8. Jonathan Perkins to J. Roswell Flower, August 12, 1949, Jonathan Ellsworth Perkins File, AGR. Perkins's meeting with David Weissman is described in "The Making of an Anti-Semite," from Perkins's unfinished autobiography, JEPB.

9. "Jesus Christ Was Not a Jew—Gerald L. K. Smith," *TF*, October 31, 1947, 1.

10. J. Frank Norris to Rev. John R. Waters, October 29, 1947, and "J. Frank Norris Sells Out to the Pope?" *The Truth*, December 20, 1947, 1, Folder 1894, Box 42; J. Frank Norris to Dwight D. Eisenhower, July 13, 1952, Dwight Eisenhower to J. Frank Norris, August 4, 1952, Folder 1531, Box 34, JFNC.

11. MacArthur quoted in David Oshinsky, *A Conspiracy So Immense: The World of Joe McCarthy* (New York: Oxford University Press, 2005), 192.

12. Ibid., 98–100, 102–3, 108–9.

13. Ibid., 194; William Manchester, *The Glory and the Dream: A Narrative History of America, 1932–1972* (New York: Bantam Books, 1973), 561–62; "1945 Death of Macon Officer Called Chinese Red Atrocity," clipping from unidentified newspaper, 1950, Folder 153, Box 4, JFNC; Smith, "John Birch, the Missionary-Patriot," 25.

14. Starr, *Embattled Dreams*, 296–98, 306–7, 328–29; Rick Perlstein, *Nixonland: The Rise of a President and the Fracturing of America* (New York: Scribner, 2008), 34–35.

15. Nash, *Conservative Intellectual Movement*, 157–58; Jonathan Schoenwald, *A Time for Choosing: The Rise of Modern American Conservatism* (New York: Oxford University Press, 2001), 25.

16. Ibid., 28–29; Thayer, *Farther Shores of Politics*, 154–55.

17. Nash, *Conservative Intellectual Movement*, 135; *Freedom Club News*, April, 1952, Folder 4, Box 118, *Freedom Club News*, October, 1953, 8, Folder 4, Box 118, JIP.

18. Hargis's and McIntire's personal and professional dealings in Southern California are gleaned from series of correspondence and filed reports in LACRC, METP, CMSC, and, more generally, John H. Redekop, *The American Far Right: A Case Study of Billy James Hargis and Christian Crusade* (Grand Rapids, MI: William B. Eerdmans, 1968); Erling Jorstad, *The Politics of Doomsday: Fundamentalists of the Far Right* (Nashville, TN: Abingdon Press, 1970), 29–36.

19. "How long 'til Joseph Stalin is President of the United States?" *Freedom Club News*, October 1952, 1–7, Folder 4, Box 118, JIP. Thayer, *Farther Shores of Politics*, 260; *What Is the Church League of America?* (Wheaton, IL: Church League of America, n.d. [1959]), 2–3; Edgar Bundy, interview by author.

20. "Another Great Revival," *MC*, November 1948, 3–4; "Another Shuler Preacher," *MC*, November 1951, 12–15.

21. J. Vernon McGee, *The Country Preacher Who Came to Town* (Pasadena: Thru the Bible Radio Network, n.d.), 6–7, 24, TTB.

22. Details of McGee's life drawn from Gertrude L. Cutler, ed., *The Whole Word for the Whole World: The Life and Ministry of J. Vernon McGee* (Pasadena, CA: Thru the Bible Radio Network, 1991).

23. Ibid., 8, 40.

24. J. Vernon McGee and Wilbur Smith corresponded regularly, often with respect to special speaking engagements at Fuller Seminary or Church of the Open Door. These letters appear in the WSC.

25. McGee quoted in G. Michael Cocoris, *70 Years on Hope Street: A History of the Church of the Open Door, 1915–1985* (Los Angeles: Church of the Open Door, 1985), 81; Minutes for Board of Elders Meeting, February 8, 1949 and November 8, 1949, Board of Elders Minutes Folder, Committees Minutes, A–L Box; Minutes for Executive Board Meeting, January 18, 1949, Executive Board Minutes 1949 Folder, Board

Minutes Box, COD. McGee's predecessor, Louis Talbot, attended less than half of all COD Executive Board meetings: Executive Board Minutes, 1944–1948 Folder, Board Minutes Box, COD. On McGee and KGER: "Dr. Cole Interview, 1991," Dr. McGee's Memorabilia File, TTB; Bill George, interview by author. COD growth statistics from Cocoris, "The Rise, Decline, and Renewal of a Megachurch,"122.

26. Unsigned letter from Seattle, Washington, to McGee in J. V. McGee History File, TTB; "Radio Reactions from Burleson, Texas," *Open Door News*, June 1969, *Open Door News* File, COD; News Release for the *LAE*, 50th Anniversary Folder, "A" Miscellaneous Box, COD; Cutler, *Whole Word for the Whole World*, 55.

27. On McGee's simple preaching style: "Dr. Cole Interview, 1991" and "Advice to a Young Preacher," Dr. McGee's Memorabilia File, TTB. On Thru the Bible: "The New Look at the Old Book; Over 2,000 Registered for 'Thru the Bible' Study," *Open Door News*, October 1953, COD; "'Thru the Bible' Reaches Around the World," *Trans World Radio* (undated), 18–19, and "Radio's Great Trailblazer," *Worldwide Challenge*, March 1978, 34–36.

28. J. Vernon McGee, *Guidelines for the Understanding of the Scriptures* (Pasadena, CA: Thru the Bible Radio Network, n.d.), n.p., McGee—Printed Sermons File, TTB.

29. *Open Door News*, October 1952; "Our Pastor's Vacation (?)," *Church of the Open Door Bulletin*, September 25, 1949, COD.

30. Transcript of McGee Sermon, September 12, 1965, 50th Anniversary Folder, "A" Miscellaneous Box, COD.

31. J. Edgar Hoover, "Communism's Offensive Against God," *PE*, January 7, 1951. On the pervasiveness of this belief: Richard Gid Powers, *Not Without Honor: The History of American Anticommunism* (New York: Free Press, 1995), 252–55, and Robert Alan Goldberg, *Enemies Within: The Culture of Conspiracy in Modern America* (New Haven, CT: Yale University Press, 2001), chaps. 2 and 3. J. Vernon McGee, "Origin of Communism," McGee Sermon Notes File, TTB.

32. "A Nation at the Crossroads," McGee Sermon Notes File, TTB.

33. Quoted from "Mystery of Lawlessness." See also "Turning Ploughshares into Swords," "The United Nations and Prophecy," McGee Sermon Notes File, TTB.

34. Quoted in "Turning Ploughshares into Swords" and "The United Nations and Prophecy," McGee Sermon Notes File, TTB.

35. "The United Nations and Prophecy," McGee Sermon Notes File, TTB.

36. Most of McGee's archived sermons have articles and editorials from his favorite newspapers and magazines attached. For instance: "A Nation at the Crossroads," "The United Nations and Prophecy," "Can America Survive," "The Crisis of this Present Hour," "Modern Man and the Moral Muddle," McGee Sermon Notes File, TTB.

37. "Is Romanism as Great a Menace as Communism to America?" "Will America Go Communist or Roman Catholic or Is There a Third Alternative," McGee Sermon Notes File, TTB. McGee was on the mailing list of the *Manion Forum*.

38. McGee expressed this sentiment in a 1960s sermon titled "The Millennium and the Great Society," McGee Sermon Notes File, TTB.

39. Bob Shuler, "Negroes, Ahead of Schedule," *MC*, October 1951, 7; "North and South," *MC*, October 1957, 6. "Gerald L. K. Smith, Et Al!" *MC*, July 1953, 7.

40. Bell quoted in David Chappell, *A Stone of Hope: Prophetic Religion and the Death of Jim Crow* (Chapel Hill: University of North Carolina Press, 2004), 119–20.

41. Here McGee quoted from *Manion Forum*, December 12, 1958, with clip attached to sermon transcript for "What Can Happen to the Christian in 1962." On McGee's call for a "New Age, not a New Deal": "'Foul Weather' or 'The Time of Tribulation'"; also "Can America Survive?" and "The Crisis of this Present Hour," McGee Sermon Notes File, TTB.

7. THE NEW GOSPEL OF WEALTH

1. "Year of Fulfillment," Church Annuals and Special Events File, CBA.

2. Cinderella Homes promotional material in author's possession. On Orange County's suburban "magic land": John M. Findlay, *Magic Lands: Western Cityscapes and American Culture After 1940* (Berkeley: University of California Press, 1993).

3. Preceding sketch is drawn from Jean Vandruff interview.

4. Southern California Research Council, *Migration and the Southern California Economy* (Los Angeles: Report Number 12 by the Southern Research Council, Occidental College, 1964), 19–32; Thompson, *Growth and Changes in California's Population*, 152; Kevin Starr, *Golden Dreams: California in an Age of Abundance, 1950–1963* (New York: Oxford University Press, 2009), 227–28.

5. Autonetics data from Chamber of Commerce's promotional booklet, *Anaheim, California* (Anaheim, CA: Windsor Publications, 1967), 47, ALHC.

6. Joel Garreau, *Edge City: Life on the New Frontier* (New York: Anchor, 1992), 3–5. On Los Angeles as a postmodern geography: Edward Soja, *Postmodern Geographies: The Reassertion of Space in Critical Theory* (New York: Verso, 1989), Mike Davis, *City of Quartz: Excavating the Future in Los Angeles* (London: Verso, 1990), Rob Kling, Spencer Olin, and Mark Poster, eds., *Postsuburban California: The Transformation of Orange County Since World War II* (Berkeley: University of California Press, 1991); Greg Hise, "Home Building and Industrial Decentralization in Los Angeles: The Roots of the Postwar Urban Region," *Journal of Urban History* (February 19, 1993), 98.

7. Thompson, *Growth and Changes*, 68, 168, also tables VII-2 and XIV-8; Center for Planning and Development Research, *Characteristics of Metropolitan Growth in California, Volume 1: Report* (Berkeley: Institute of Urban and Regional Development, University of California, Berkeley, 1965), 7; Southern California Research Council, *Migration and the Southern California Economy*, 9–12, 16.

8. Quoted from *Life* magazine, 1953, in Sides, *L.A. City Limits*, 59.

9. According to the 1960 census, Los Angeles was more segregated than any city in the south and had fewer minorities living in its suburbs than any northern city, with the exception of Chicago and Cleveland. See Kirse Granat May, *Golden State, Golden Youth: California Image in Popular Culture, 1955–1966* (Chapel Hill: University of North Carolina Press, 2002), 14.

10. Sides, *L.A. City Limits*, 101; Kurashige, *The Shifting Grounds of Race*, 208–9.

11. Miller, *Billy Graham and the Rise of the Republican South*, 34–35.

12. Allen interview. In the 1940s, Southern Missionary Baptist briefly changed its name to Emmanuel Baptist, prior to calling itself Bristol Street Baptist in the early 1950s. According to enrollment books, Bristol Street Baptist's membership increased from 334 to 525. See also 1953 Building Expansion Brochure, BSHF.

13. Growth rates of other plain-folk evangelical denominations were accessed through denominational records in FBCLB, FCNLB, and PC, the latter of which also houses copies of *The Informant* (*TI*), from which many of my conclusions about local Assemblies of God developments are drawn. On blue-collar suburban transformations: Nicolaides, *My Blue Heaven*, 228–30; "Success Story," *TI*, February 1957; Looney, *History of California Southern Baptists*, 366–67.

14. "Report on Revival in Maywood," *TI*, July 1956, "Available," *TI*, September 1959; *Groundbreaking*, 2–3; "H. Frank Collins: He Was Always Late; He Didn't Have the Nickel for the Trolley," *BBT*, May 19, 1972, 13.

15. "Where the Evangels Go," in *PE*, March 25, 1950; "Interesting Statistics," *TI*, May 1956, "Progressing in One of Our Fastest Growing Counties," *PE*, September 16, 1956.

16. "We Need You Badly," *MC*, November 1948, 12; "My Swan Song!" *MC*, July 1953, 9–10, 12.

17. "Where Prayer Meetings Grow Big," *The King's Business*, November 1953, 12–13; "Where Bible Study Is Thrilling," *SST*, October 31, 1959, Miscellaneous Biographical File, TTB; Minutes of the Executive Board Meeting, March 15, 1949 and September 20, 1949, Executive Board Minutes 1949 File, Board Minutes Box; 1949 COD Annual Report, Annual Meetings and Reports, 1940; 1946–1953 File, "A" Misc. Box; "'Small Church' Advantages for Large C.O.D. Constituency," *Open Door News*, August–September 1953, 1–2, COD.

18. On the parachurch movement and religious realignments, see Wuthnow, *Restructuring of American Religion*.

19. Michael Richardson, *Amazing Faith: The Authorized Biography of Bill Bright* (Colorado Springs, CO: Waterbrook Press, 2000), 1–2, 15–20.

20. Demos Shakarian, *The Happiest People on Earth: The Long-Awaited Personal Story of Demos Shakarian as Told to John and Elizabeth Sherrill* (Old Tappan, NJ: Chosen Books, 1975), 49–75, 87–91, 117–20.

21. Richard Quebedeaux, *The New Charismatics: The Origins, Development, and Significance of Neo-Pentecostalism* (Garden City, NY: Doubleday, 1976), 91; Billy Graham, *Just As I Am: The Autobiography of Billy Graham* (New York: HarperCollins, 1997), 174–76.

22. Bill C. Malone, *Country Music U.S.A.* (Austin: University of Texas Press, 1968), 65–67, 155, 196–97, 291; Robert Byrd, interview by author.

23. Pat Boone, interview by author; Pat Boone, *Pat Boone's America: 50 Years* (Nashville, TN: B&H Publishing Group, 2006).

24. Ted Ownby, "Unpaid Debts: Metaphors and Millennialism in Southern Sectarian Movements," in Larry Eskridge and Mark A. Noll, eds., *More Money, More Ministry: Money and Evangelicals in Recent North American History* (Grand Rapids, MI: William B. Eerdmans, 2000), 251; quoted in Gary Scott Smith, "Evangelicals Confront Corporate Capitalism: Advertising, Consumerism, Stewardship, and Spirituality, 1880–1930," in Eskridge and Noll, *More Money, More Ministry*, 74.

25. Larry Eskridge, "Money Matters: The Phenomenon of Financial Counselor Larry Burkett and Christian Financial Concepts," in Eskridge and Noll, *More Money, More Ministry*, 329.

26. See *TI*, January 1956.

27. Phrase drawn from Michael Hamilton, "More Money, More Ministry: The Financ-

ing of American Evangelicalism Since 1945," in Eskridge and Noll, *More Money, More Ministry*, 104, 112-13.

28. Shakarian, *Happiest People on Earth*, 121–22; Quebedeaux, *New Charismatics*, 53, 79–80, 100–102; Allan Anderson, *An Introduction to Pentecostalism* (New York: Cambridge University Press, 2004), 145–46. Bright's "four spiritual laws" quoted in Richardson, *Amazing Faith*, 64–68. On the circular logic of evangelicals' economic thought: Hamilton, "More Money, More Ministry," 134.

29. *Anaheim, California* (Anaheim, CA: Windsor Publications, 1967); Walter Knott, "The Enterprises of Walter Knott," interview conducted by Donald J. Schipper, 1965, UCLA-OHC.

30. "Catalogue of Materials Designed to Strengthen and Safeguard the Structure of American Freedom," and "Your Grass Roots Report, January 1957," in National Education Binder, MKC; Hicks, *"Sometimes in the Wrong, but Never in Doubt,"* 62–66.

31. "The Millennium and the Great Society," McGee Sermon Notes File, TTB.

32. McGee quote from "God's Prophetic Person Is a Program." See also "A Nation at the Crossroads," "The Crisis of the Present Hour," "Can America Survive," McGee Sermon Notes File, TTB.

33. "Suburban warriors" drawn from Lisa McGirr, *Suburban Warriors: The Origins of the New American Right* (Princeton, NJ: Princeton University Press, 2002). Membership records are unavailable. However, Wells's funeral service and transfer records provide a glimpse at church demographics. See "Death File" and "D Church Letters File," Standing Cabinet, CBA.

34. Wilbur Smith, "A Survey of Religious Life and Thought," *SST*, January 11, 1958; "Dr. Bob Shuler Speaks Sunday," *CN*, May 13, 1959, Church Notes file; "14th Anniversary," *CBNL*, October 8, 1970, News Letters File, CBA.

35. "Bob Wells, and Orange County leader since 1956," *BBT*, October 24, 1985, 12; "Down Through the Years, 1956–1985: A Tribute to Our Pastor-Founder," Church Annuals and Special Events File, CBA.

36. *VTF*, April 1967, CBA; "Evangelistic Series Begins Sunday Night," *TR*, August 4, 1956; "Inter-City Evangelistic Crusade," *AB*, August 11, 1956; Paul Liefeld, "Let's Keep It on a . . . Miracle Basis," "Central Baptist Church Starts New Construction February 18th," *AB*, February 2, 1957; *CN*, June 3, 1959, CBA *CN*, April 14, 1960, CBA.

37. Central Baptist Church Bulletin, October 12, 1958, CBA.

38. Phillips-Fein, *Invisible Hands*, 121–27; Elizabeth Tandy Shermer, "Origins of the Conservative Ascendancy: Barry Goldwater's Early Senate Career and the De-legitimization of Organized Labor," *Journal of American History* 95 (December 2008), 703.

39. Schoenwald, *Time for Choosing*, 31, 40–41, 63–64, 79–82; Bundy, quoted in Donald Critchlow, *The Conservative Ascendancy: How the GOP Right Made Political History* (Cambridge, MA: Harvard University Press, 2007), 43; Welch quoted in Critchlow, *Phyllis Schlafly and Grassroots Conservatism*, 86–87.

40. Kurt Schuparra, *Triumph of the Right: The Rise of the California Conservative Movement, 1945–1966* (Armonk, NY: M. E. Sharpe, 1998), 30–31, and quoted, 33; Matthew Dallek, *The Right Moment: Ronald Reagan's First Victory and the Decisive Turning Point in American Politics* (New York: Oxford University Press) 13–15, 151; Ethan Rarick, *California Rising: The Life and Times of Pat Brown* (Berkeley: University of California Press, 2005), 54.

41. "The Enterprises of Walter Knott," CSUF-OHC; James Ingebretsen to Mr. W. M. Bennett, December 13, 1961, Spiritual Mobilization Correspondence, Allyn R. Bell–George C. S. Benson Folder, Box 67, JIP.

42. Central Baptist Church Bulletin, October 12, 1958. CBA.

8. DECLARATION OF INDEPENDENCE

1. "Declaration of Independence," AV, January/February 1960, 5.

2. Review of inaugural ceremony in AV, December 1958, 3–14.

3. Quoted in "Pasadena Revisited," Time, May 7, 1951; "Man Out of a Job," Life, December 11, 1950, 95–96; "Quandary in Pasadena," Time, November 27, 1950, 85–87.

4. Wayne J. Urban and Jennings L. Wagnor Jr., American Education: A History, 3rd ed. (Boston: McGraw-Hill, 2004), 290–91; Joel Spring, The American School: 1642–2004, 6th ed. (Boston: McGraw-Hill, 2005), 384–87; Ellen Herman, The Romance of American Psychology: Political Culture in the Age of Experts (Berkeley: University of California Press, 1995), 246–49, 255–57.

5. Lawrence A. Cremin, Transformation of the School: Progressivism in American Education, 1876–1957 (New York: Alfred A. Knopf, 1962), 216–17, 279; Diane Ravitch, The Troubled Crusade: American Education, 1945–1980 (New York: Basic Books, 1983), 50; Urban and Wagnor Jr., American Education, 291.

6. On fear of brainwashing: Abbott Gleason, Totalitarianism: The Inner History of the Cold War (New York: Oxford University Press, 1995), 90–105. On fear of "group dynamics": Ravitch, The Troubled Crusade, 53–54.

7. Nickerson, Mothers of Conservatism, chaps. 3 and 4.

8. "The Pacific Regional Conference on UNESCO: Tentative Pattern of Sectional Meetings, 1948" and Guy Halferty, "California Starts Move to Popularize UNESCO," CSM, July 31, 1948, Los Angeles County Government; Relations; International Folder, Box 74, JAF; Nickerson, Mothers of Conservatism, chap. 3.

9. "The California Church Tax Oath," Folder 9, Box 16, and correspondence and published material filed in Folders 5, 8, 11, Box 16, ACLUP; "Resolution of the California Christian Citizens Association" in Miscellaneous File and Bob Wells, "If the Pepper Tree Could Talk," VTF, November 1966, CBA; On Shuler's opinions about Brown: G. Archer Weniger, "Lifelong Democrat Shuler Opposes Brown," BP, August 19, 1958, 1.

10. "Educators Back UNESCO," MC, August 1954, 8.

11. Until the early 1950s California enforced state tax on private schools. The 1952 ruling, therefore, was a reversal of prior law. See "What About Proposition 3?" and "Be a Good Citizen—Vote," CSB, October 23, 1952, 3; "Defend Your Protestant Tradition," filed in Folder 3, Box 16, ACLUP; "Taxation without Justification: Proposition 16," Church Bulletin, August 28, 1958, "No, No, a Thousand Times, No! Proposition 16," Church Bulletin, October 12, 1958, "No. 16 Defeated, 2 to 1," Church Bulletin, November 9, 1958, Church Bulletins Folder, CBA.

12. "Evangelical Christian School Movement" (1952), 6–12, "School Directory National Association of Christian Schools" (1965–1966), 3, and School Directory National Association of Christian Schools (1965–1966), NACS.

13. See following articles in the Christian Teacher filed in NACS: quotes from "The

Need of the Hour," September 1, 1951, "The Fourth 'R' in Education," May 1952, "The Present Educational Battle," July 1, 1952. Also, "The Modern Revolutionary War," March 1, 1951, "John Dewey Is Dead," August 1, 1952, "Tools to Combat Subversive Tendencies," April 1954. Numbers for California Association of Christian Schools in 1961 taken from Bulletin of Heritage High School, Promotional File, CBA.

14. "Heritage High School Far From 'Ordinary'!" *VTF*, November 1966, 6, and "Bulletin of the Heritage High School," in Promotional File, "One of the Finest School Systems in Orange County," News Release File, History and Past Events Box, CBA.

15. "Think Carefully . . . Are You Happy with Your Child's School Progress?" Church Promotional/Publications Box and "Why a School Uniform?" Heritage General; Sixties and Seventies File; sample applications in the Central Baptist School Board material, CBA.

16. "Heritage Schools Self-Evaluation," 38, and undated clipping, Central Baptist Church-Self Evaluation, General Heritage File; on Slater and Hall, see "Do-It-Yourself? F.A.C.E. Feature for Restoring Americanism," *VTF*, December 1966, "Foundation for American Christian Education," and attached file clipping from the *Tennessee Farm Bureau News*, *VTF*, February–March 1967; "Shirley Matthews Wins Sixth Grade," Press News-Essay Contest File, all in CBA.

17. "Walkin' Through the Land," History and Past Events Box; Patriotic Program File, CBA.

18. "Patriotic Program, 1968" and "God of Our Fathers," History and Past Events Box; Patriotic Program File, CBA.

19. "P.T.F. Notes," November 4, 1965, *CBNL*, News Letter File, CBA.

20. William F. Buckley Jr., *God and Man at Yale: The Superstitions of "Academic Freedom"* (Chicago: Henry Regnery Company, 1951), 113; Nash, *Conservative Intellectual Movement*, 40–41.

21. On the plight of private schools in this era: Fones-Wolf, *Selling Free Enterprise*, 193; on federal funds accessed by private schools: Axel R. Schäfer, "The Cold War State and the Resurgence of Evangelicalism: A Study of the Public Funding of Religion Since 1945, *Radical History Review* 99 (2007), 80–106.

22. Rushford, *Crest of a Golden Wave*, 115–17; Henegar and Rushford, *Forever Young*, 99–113, 124–33, and quoted, 140; "Religion: The Nondenomination," *Time*, August 5, 1957, 58–59.

23. Young interview.

24. *Crest of a Golden Wave*, 64–65; Guy Halferty, "California Starts Move to Popularize UNESCO," *CSM*, July 31, 1948; Pullias's views of Pepperdine College's relationship with church from correspondence with school officials, in Series 7, Box 2, EVP.

25. "Pepperdine Loses 25% of Faculty," *LAHE*, April 17, 1958; "Mass Exodus of Faculty Impends at Pepperdine" and "Teachers Quit at Pepperdine," *LAMDN*, April 16, 1958; Henegar and Rushford, *Forever Young*, 148.

26. Henegar and Rushford, *Forever Young*, 151, 162; "New Faculty," *AV*, Fall 1963, 26; "Bi-Weekly Devotions—An Important Part of Pepperdine Dormitory Living," *TG*, May 6, 1960, 4.

27. "17 to Speak in Bible Forum," *TG*, March 16, 1962, 6; "Our Founder Leaves Us," *AV*, July–August 1962, 1. George Pepperdine quoted in Henegar and Rushford, *Forever Young*, 164, 176.

28. Pepperdine, *Faith Is My Fortune*, 232–33, 236; Henegar and Rushford, *Forever Young*, 151, 156.

29. Quoted in Henegar and Rushford, *Forever Young*, 162.

30. George Benson to Norvel Young, August 12, 1958, Norvel Young to George Benson, November 7, 1958, Box 26, George Benson to Norvel Young, December 22, 1958, Box 26, NYP.

31. Other Church of Christ schools following Harding's example included Oklahoma Christian College, in Oklahoma City. See Thayer, *Farther Shores of Politics*, 276. On John Brown University's American Heritage Seminars: Ostrander, *Head, Heart, and Hand*, 126–28, 134; "American Heritage Seminar to Be Held at JBU Campus," *Southwest American*, November 18, 1961, Christian American Heritage Seminar File, JBC. On Paul Harvey, Walter Knott, and J. Vernon McGee: "Second Annual Christian American Heritage Seminar: Imperatives in Perspective," "Eighth Annual Christian American Heritage Seminar," Christian American Heritage Seminar File, and "Harvey's Speech Highlights Homecoming," *John Brown University Bulletin*, May–June 1965, John Brown University Bulletin File, JBC.

32. "Senator McClellan Reports to the Nation at Pepperdine College's Freedom Forum," *AV*, June 1959, 16, George Benson, "An American Citizen's Responsibility—1959," Pepperdine College Freedom Forum, June 22, 1959, distributed by the National Education Program, Box 26, NYP.

33. Edward C. Gilbert to Mr. Glenn Green of the National Education Program, copied to Norvel Young, July 2, 1959, and Norvel Young to George Benson, June 30, 1959, August 7, 1959, September 5, 1959, and October 16, 1959, Box 26, NYP.

34. *Forever Young*, 278; Norvel Young to Henry Salvatori, June 28, 1963, NYP; "A New Year's Challenge," *AV*, Fall 1963.

35. Salvatori Profile, "Salvatori Center," and Novel Young to Henry Salvatori, May 1, 1975, Salvatori Folder, Box 26, NYP; Henegar and Rushford, *Forever Young*, 206–7; "Gulf Oil Presents Gift to Pepperdine," *AV*, March/April 1963.

36. Charles and Flora Laney Thornton profile in "A Woman Embracing the World," *PPM*, Fall 1984. For a profile of Thornton and Litton: *Fortune* magazine, May 1963, *Time*, October 4, 1963, *Dun's Review*, May 1966, *California Business*, June 1973. An edition of the *McGuffey Reader* was published under the auspices of Litton's Educational and Publishing division.

37. Henegar and Rushford, *Forever Young*, 272.

38. Boone, *Pat Boone's America: 50 Years*, 53; Boone quoted in Henegar and Rushford, *Forever Young*, 101; Young interview; "Chapel Visitor," *TG*, October 21, 1960; "Youth Forum Opens Today with Speech By Pat Boone," *TG*, April 7, 1961, 1.

39. "Declaration of Independence," *AV*, January/February 1960, 5; "President's Report to Alumni," *AV*, September/October 1959, 12–13.

40. "Columnists Laud Freedom Forum," *AV*, September/October 1961, 15.

41. "Third Annual Freedom Forum to Hear Senator Goldwater," *AV*, February/March 1961, 1; "Perils to United States Hit by Forum Conferees," *TG*, April 7, 1961, 2.

42. Norvel Young to Mr. Ted Kazy, Administrative Assistant to Senator Barry Goldwater, October 24, 1960, Barry M. Goldwater Folder, E–H Box, WBP.

43. "Perils to United States Hit by Forum Conferees," *TG*, April 7, 1961, 2.

9. SENTINELS OF FREEDOM

1. Barry Goldwater, *The Conscience of a Conservative* (Shepherdsville, KY: Victor Publishing Company, 1960), 14.

2. "Report on The Southern California School of Anti-Communism," Box 43, LACRC; Pat Boone, interview by author.

3. "Report on The Southern California School."

4. Rick Perlstein, *Before the Storm: Barry Goldwater and the Unmaking of the American Consensus* (New York: Hill & Wang, 2001), 3–16, 43–51; Barry Goldwater, *Why Not Victory? A Fresh Look at American Foreign Policy* (New York, 1962), 12–13; "Barry Goldwater . . . Would Carry the South," Box 3H505, SSBGP.

5. Aubrey B. Barker to Mr. Charles J. Roese, July 10, 1960 and July 18, 1960, and press releases from San Diego Barry Goldwater-for-President Committee, June 23, 1960 and June 27, 1960, Box 3H505, SSBGP; Robert Alan Goldberg, *Barry Goldwater* (New Haven, CT: Yale University Press, 1995), 144–46.

6. Goldberg, *Barry Goldwater*, xi.

7. Goldwater, *Conscience of a Conservative*, iii, 18–20, 22–23.

8. Ibid., 59, 62, 73–74.

9. Ibid., 77, 80, 82–85, 122–23.

10. Ibid., 34.

11. "Evangelical front," "hegemony of hope" in Central Baptist Church Bulletin, September 2, 1961, Heritage Files—Sixties and Seventies, Box 2, CBA.

12. Hicks, *Sometimes in the Wrong, but Never in Doubt*," 60, 76–79; "Pepperdine College Forum V," *AV*, November/December 1962; "Pro-American Forum at Pepperdine Monday," *LAT* April 15, 1962; Thayer, *Farther Shores of Politics*, 278.

13. "Report on The Southern California School of Anti-Communism," Box 43, and "Report on Billy James Hargis Meeting, February 12, 1962, Box 44, LACRC; Thayer, *Farther Shores of Politics*, 254; Allan Lichtman, *White Protestant Nation: The Rise of the American Conservative Movement* (New York: Atlantic Monthly Press, 2008), 197; Jorstad, *Politics of Doomsday*, 61; Redekop, *American Far Right*, 6, 21–23, 33.

14. "Report on Meeting of American Council of Churches of Christ," January 25, 1962, Folder 1962-14, Box 44, LACRC; Tim LaHaye to Reverend Archer Weniger, November 21, 1962, AWP. Bundy's textbook paraphrased in Thayer, *Farther Shores of Politics*, 259.

15. "Report on James Fifield Meeting," Folder 1952–71, Box 41, LACRC. On Marion Miller and other housewife spies: Mary C. Brennan, *Wives, Mothers, and The Red Menace: Conservative Women and the Crusade Against Communism* (Boulder, CO: University of Colorado Press, 2008), 10–11, 86–88. "The National Council at San Francisco," *BBT*, January 13, 1961; Dr. J. Kenneth Hutcherson letter to Archer Weniger, January 2, 1964, AWP.

16. "Eye Witness Account by a Group of Ministers of San Francisco Red Riots," *BP*, May 17, 1960; "Operation Abolition," *Time*, March 17, 1961; Schoenwald, *Time for Choosing*, 55–56; Louis L. Michael to Archer Weniger, March 9, 1961, AWP.

17. Raymond S. Richmond to G. Archer Weniger, October 26, 1963 and January 15, 1962; O. T. Gillam to Archer Weniger, December 9, 1961, AWP.

18. D.A. Waite, Assistant to Mr. Welch, to Archer Weniger, June 8, 1963, and Archer Weniger to D.A. Waite, June 24, 1963, AWP; See LaHaye's participation in "The John Birch Society Chapters of San Diego County Present Mr. Robert Welch, Founder," John Birch Society–San Diego County Folder, SDLHSF. On LaHaye's fight with the local JBS: Nicholas Guyatt, *Have a Nice Doomsday* (New York: Harper Perennial, 2007), 220–21.

19. *The Tidings*, March 30, 1962, 2; "Disarmament: Exposing the Appeasers' Plans to Destroy the Army, Navy, and Air Force of the U.S.A.," *VTF*, Voice of Truth and Freedom Folder, FC.

20. Quoted in Schoenwald, *Time for Choosing*, 106.

21. Orval Faubus to Perry Moore, August 11, 1961, Folder III, Subject Correspondence 1961 Box, STP. Context for the muzzling hearings drawn from Joseph Crespino, "Strom Thurmond's Sunbelt: Rethinking Regional Politics and the Rise of the Right," in Michelle Nickerson and Darren Dochuk, eds., *Sunbelt Rising: The Politics of Space, Place, and Region* (Philadelphia: University of Pennsylvania Press, forthcoming).

22. "Kennedy Asserts Far-Right Groups Provoke Disunity, *NYT*, November 19, 1961, 1; "Thurmond Assails Army 'Muzzling'; Senator Defends Military's Right to Speak Against Communism," *LAT* November 29, 1961; "Coast Cities Freedom Program presents Senator Strom Thurmond" and "Thurmond Says Russia 'Ordered' U.S. Muzzling," Folder 1961-189, Box 44, LACRC; "Sen. Tower Hits False Gods in Sermon Here," *LAT*, December 4, 1961.

23. Crespino, "Strom Thurmond's Sunbelt."

24. "12,894 Hear Walker Hit at U.S. in U.N.," *LAT*, January 1, 1962; "Gen. Walker Tours, Assails," *LAHE*, February 28, 1963; Redekop, *American Far Right*, 33.

25. Report on McIntire Meeting at Central Baptist Church, Folder 1964-28, Box 45, LACRC; "Hargis Speaking at Central, Wednesday," Church Bulletin, March 1, 1964, Bound Bulletin Collection, CBA; Bundy interview.

26. "Fraudulent Disarmament," *CBNL*, May 15, 1963, "Freedom: More Important Than Peace!" *CBNL*, May 22, 1963, Church News Letters Box, CBA; "World Dictatorship Sermon Said, 'Taken Out of Context,'" *TR*, May 19, 1965.

27. "Why We Dare Not Trust Arms Control," *CBNL*, May 20, 1965, "Sinister Arms Control Plot Exposed!" *CBNL*, May 13, 1965, "Special Rallies," *CBNL*, May 20, 1965, Church News Letters Box; "Arms Control," Letter to the Editor, *TR*, undated, Newspaper Clipping File, CBA.

28. Hargis quoted in William Martin, *With God on Our Side: The Rise of the Religious Right in America* (New York: Broadway Books, 1996), 77–78.

29. On Becker Amendment: Edwin Scott Gausted and Leigh Eric Schmidt, *The Religious History of America* (New York: Harper Collins, 2004), 359. "Response to Becker Amendment," *CBNL*, May 1964, News Letter File, CBA; J. Vernon McGee, "America Needs Declaration of Dependence," McGee Sermon Notes File, TTB; "Your Letter Is a Ballot," *PE*, August 6, 1961, 14, "Tragedy in New York," *PE*, August 12, 1962, 7; "The Supreme Court's Supreme Blunder," *PE*, August 25, 1963, 14–15, 23; "NAE Comments on Prayer Ruling, Warns Against Secularism Trend," *PE*, August 19, 1962, 23.

30. "Darwin Evolution Theory Ban Sought," *LAHE*, April 27, 1963; "Prayer Issue

454   NOTES TO PAGES 241-46

Unseats 3 on La Mesa School Board," *LAHE*, September 23, 1964; "Proposition 16," *CSB*, October 20, 1966, 4.

31. Dr. Bob Jones to Strom Thurmond, May 29, 1963, and Strom Thurmond to Dr. Bob Jones, June 5, 1963, Personal 10-1-2 (Bob Jones University) Folder, Subject Correspondence 1963 Box, STC; Summer Program for 1963, "For God and Country," AWP.

32. Mrs. Vera B. Patten to Strom Thurmond, August 3, 1961, Mrs. Mary E. Golden to Strom Thurmond, August 4, 1961, Folder II; Mr. James A. Martin to Strom Thurmond, August 19, 1961, Mr. Hervery B. Bailey to Strom Thurmond, August 22, 1961, Mr. W.E. Lyn to Strom Thurmond, August 29, 1961, Mr. Sidney S. Watts to Strom Thurmond, September 3, 1961, Folder IX; Mr. Doyle T. Swain to Strom Thurmond, August 11, 1961, Trent Devenney to Strom Thurmond, September 24, 1961, Folder XII, Subject Correspondence 1961 Box, STC.

33. D. B. Lewis to Strom Thurmond, March 12, 1964, Folder 1; Sam Jaffe to Strom Thurmond, March 3, 1964, Folder 1, Correspondence Series, Box 21, STC.

34. Daniel HoSang, "Remaking Liberalism in the Sunbelt West: California's 1964 Fair Housing Ballot Measure and the Politics of Racial Innocence," in Nickerson and Dochuk, *Sunbelt Rising*.

35. "What Is Happening to Freedom?" *CSB*, July 25, 1963, 2; "Ninety-nine New Churches in Five Years," *PE*, June 26, 1960, 6; "The Supreme Court Upholds Zoning Laws; The Planners Can Now Keep You Out," *BBT*, May 29, 1959, 1; Jean Vandruff interview.

36. "Southern California Sets a Great Record in Missionary Giving!" *TI*, March 1960, "Ten Highest Churches in Missionary Giving in the Nation," *TI*, April 1960; "Annual of The Southern Baptist General Convention of California" and "25th Anniversary Session Book of Reports," Southern Baptist General Convention of California Annuals, SBCR; "Texas Laymen Help Establish Mission in Orange County," *CSB*, June 8, 1961, 2, "Bristol Street, Santa Ana Celebrates Silver Anniversary," *CSB*, April 23, 1964, 12.

37. "Churches in the Midst of the Multitudes," "Outline for Canvas," Sunday School Promotional Material File; "A Wonderful Summer," *CBNL*, August 26, 1965, Church Notes File; "Project '67," 7, Church Promotional and Publication File, CBA; "Central Baptist Ambassador Ringing Bells in God's Name," *TR*, September 25, 1971; "News from California," *BBT*, June 18, 1971.

38. "Goldwater Organization," Box 3H514, SSBGP. Correspondence reveals Manion's ability to communicate with and mobilize evangelicals along the southern rim. See, for instance, Folders 62-7 to 62-9, Box 62, and letter from Mel and Norma Gabler to Manion in Folder 67-7, Box 67, CMP. On Goldwater's recruitment of Christian youth organizations: Undated memo, Box 4, CWP, also detailed in Phillips-Fein, *Invisible Hands*, 144.

39. Kurt Schuparra, "Barry Goldwater and Southern California Conservatism: Ideology, Image and Myth in the 1964 California Republican Presidential Primary," *Southern California Historical Quarterly* 74 (Fall 1992), 277–78; Richard A. Viguerie and David Franke, *America's Right Turn: How Conservatives Used New and Alternative Media to Take Power* (Chicago: Bonus Books, 2004), 83; "A Choice . . . Not an Echo! Barry Goldwater for President," Box 3H507, and "Footsoldier Program Instructions," Box 3H510, SSBGP.

40. Koenig interview; Young interview.

41. "Pepperdine Fights Communism" and "Coe Fellowships," *AV* September/October 1961; "Devenney New Y.R. Leader," *TG*, April 19, 1963; "Devenney Official Group Prexy," *TG*, May 3, 1963; "Demos are Coming; To Oppose YR 'Right,'" *TG*, September 13, 1963.

42. James Redden, interview by author. There is some discrepancy in the oral record whether the Central Baptist caravan proceeded to the Knott's Berry Farm rally or the Goldwater rally held months earlier in Dodger Stadium. For details on Knott's rally: McGirr, *Suburban Warriors*, 136; "Eyes on California: Its Voters Display Rising Anti-Goldwater Feeling," *WSJ*, May 29, 1964.

43. Schuparra, "Barry Goldwater and Southern California Conservatism," 290–91. Hargis quoted in Jorstad, *Politics of Doomsday*, 102–3.

44. "The Housing Initiative," Miscellaneous Folder; "The Political Arena," Southern California Committee of Christian Laymen Folder; "Orange County Citizens Against Proposition 14," October 30, 1964, Orange County Citizens Against Proposition 14 Folder, Proposition 14 Box, FC; "Property Rights Taken Is Issue with Churches," *AB*, December 28, 1963.

45. "Proposition 14 Confusion," *CSB*, September 10, 1964, 4; "From the Mailbag," *CSB*, October 8, 1964, 2.

46. "Speakers Handbook for Opposition to the Segregation Amendment," "Proposition 14—Fact Sheet," Miscellaneous Folder; "No Mississippi Here!" Californians Against Proposition 14 Folder, Proposition 14 Box, FC; Dallek, *Right Moment*, 6.

47. HoSang, "Remaking Liberalism in the Sunbelt West"; "Churches Say 'No' on 14," Orange County Committee Against Prop 14 Folder; David Collins, Transcript of speech to the Anaheim Board of Realtors, June 17, 1964, David S. Collins Folder, Proposition 14 Box, FC.

48. Shadegg, *What Happened to Goldwater?* 166–67. Schoenwald, *Time for Choosing*, 148; Joseph E. Lowndes, *From the New Deal to the New Right: Race and the Southern Origins of Modern Conservatism* (New Haven, CT: Yale University Press, 2008), 74; Gary Donaldson, *Liberalism's Last Hurrah: The Presidential Campaign of 1964* (Armonk, NY: M. E. Sharp, 2003), 20.

49. See Daniel Bell, ed., *The Radical Right: The New American Right, Updated and Expanded* (New York: Doubleday, 1963), as quoted in Schoenwald, *Time for Choosing*, 154; Goldberg, *Barry Goldwater*, 224.

50. Goldberg, *Barry Goldwater*, 224; "News and Views," vol. 27, no. 12 (November 1964), 3, Box 3H514, SSBGP; "The 1964 Religious Issue," *CC*, October 7, 1964, 1228; Jorstad, *Politics of Doomsday*, 99.

51. Goldberg, *Barry Goldwater*, 208, 229, quoted in Donaldson, *Liberalism's Last Hurrah*, 255, 257; clip from *Valley News*, September 27, 1964, Folder 1964-160, Box 44, LACRC.

52. "Transcript of 'Brunch with Barry' Nationwide Television Program NBC Network," October 23, 1964, and "Nationwide TV Address on 'Morality and Government' over the CBS Network," Box 3H514; Script for Campaign Promotion, Box 3H507, SSBGP.

53. "The City-Cage," *SEP*, October 10, 1964, "Opponents of Prop. 14 Shift Gears," *PW*, September 19, 1964, Miscellaneous Folder, Proposition 14 Box, FC; "Decision on Housing Initiative," *LAT*, February 2, 1964.

54. Goldwater brochure quoted in Schuparra, *Triumph of the Right*, 107.

55. Goldberg, *Barry Goldwater*, 232; Haas quoted in Dallek, *Right Moment*, 60–61.

56. Pundits quoted in Goldberg, *Barry Goldwater*, 234–35; William G. McLoughlin, "Is There a Third Force in Christendom?" *Daedalus* 96 (Winter 1967): 45, 60–61.

10. CREATIVE SOCIETY

1. "The Creative Society," The Creative Society Folder, Box C31, RRG.

2. W. S. McBirnie to Ronald Reagan, November 30, 1965, "The Creative Society" Folder, Box C31, RRG.

3. Carey McWilliams, "California Revolution," *TN*, January 30, 1967, 133.

4. Ronald Reagan, "A Time for Choosing," Box 3H514, SSBGP; Dallek, *Right Moment*, 69.

5. Unsigned letter to Friends of Ronald Reagan, June 28, 1965, 1966, J. L. Tillery to Ronald Reagan, June 7, 1965, Strom Thurmond to Ronald Reagan, January 12, 1966, and June 17, 1966, 1966 Campaign Correspondence Folder: Thompson, Millard-Tipton, Box C25; Letter from Draft Nixon-Reagan in 1968 to Ronald Reagan, April 21, 1966, 1966 Campaign Correspondence Folder: Boenish–Bork, Box C3, RRG.

6. *Oakland Tribune*, March 25, 1967, excerpted in *BP*, April 14, 1967; Ronald Reagan to Reverend Darwyn Hassert, Olivet, Michigan, May 29, 1968, AWP. On Moomaw and Reagan: John Turner, *Bill Bright and Campus Crusade for Christ: The Renewal of Evangelicalism in Postwar America* (Chapel Hill: University of North Carolina Press, 2008), 44.

7. Ronald Reagan to Marth Hansford, August 24, 1966, 1966 Campaign Correspondence Folder: Haaf–Henderson, Box C10, RRG.

8. Dallek, *Right Moment*, 14, 17–18; Rarick, *California Rising*, 71; LAT, March 21, 1976; Lou Cannon, *Governor Reagan: His Rise to Power* (New York: Public Affairs, 2003), 346.

9. Estimates of JBS membership: Schuparra, *Triumph of the Right*, 49–50, 57, and McGirr, *Suburban Warriors*, 76; "Welch Calls Houston Stronghold of John Birch Society," *Houston Chronicle*, April 18, 1961, 14–15, John Birch Society Folder, HMSF; "Statement of Ronald Reagan Regarding the John Birch Society," September 24, 1965, Birch Society Folder, Box C31; Mr. and Mrs. Arthur F. Bolint to Ronald Regan [sic], September 28, 1965, 1966 Campaign Correspondence Folder: Boenish–Bork, Box C3; Ronald Reagan to Hazel Blank, October 5, 1965, 1966 Campaign Correspondence Folder: Blakney–Bodel, Box C3, RRG. Reagan's eleventh commandment quoted in Schoenwald, *Time for Choosing*, 200.

10. Quoted in Dallek, *Right Moment*, 119, 210.

11. Ibid., 88.

12. Michael W. Flamm, *Law and Order: Street Crime, Civil Unrest, and the Crisis of Liberalism in the 1960s* (New York: Columbia University Press, 2005), 58–59; Dallek, *Right Moment*, 151–53, 158, 169–70.

13. "Ronald Reagan, Extremist Collaborator: An Expose" and "Extremists on the Left," editorial by Robert P. Sutton, Birch Society Folder, Box C31, RRG.

14. "Ronald Reagan, Rev. McBirney and the Creative Society," News Report by Tom Brokaw, The Creative Society Folder, Box C31, RRG.

15. Schuparra, *Triumph of the Right*, 135; "McBirnie Says Slavery on Increase in World," *Glendale News Press*, September 15, 1961; "Reagan Charges Democrats Stole McBirnie Letter; Candidate Admits Pastor Conceived His Campaign Slogan 'Creative Society,'" *LAT*, October 14, 1966. All endorsements in Endorsements Folder, Box C33, RRG. On Reagan stumping in Los Angeles County: Bill Boyarsky, *The Rise of Ronald Reagan* (New York: Random House, 1968), 132–34.

16. Reagan quoted in Cannon, *Governor Reagan*, 173–74; Boyarsky, *Rise of Ronald Reagan*, 164; correspondence between Ronald Reagan and Jack Blankenship, pastor of Centinela Southern Baptist Church in Los Angeles, September 27, 1966, and October 10, 1966, 1966, Campaign Correspondence Folder: Blakney–Bodel, Box C3, RRG.

17. Boone interview; Bob Slosser, *Reagan Inside Out* (Waco, TX: Word Books, 1984), 50–51; Graham, *Just as I Am*, 528–29. On Graham's political connections: Miller, *Billy Graham and the Rise of the Republican South*, 35–37, 202–6.

18. See, for instance, Oregon senator and evangelical statesman Mark Hatfield's foreword to Redekop, *American Far Right*.

19. Robert Booth Fowler, *A New Engagement: Evangelical Political Thought, 1966–1976* (Grand Rapids, MI: William B. Eerdmans, 1982), 11; "The Los Angeles Ecumenical Crusade," *BP*, September 10, 1963, 1; editorial on Los Angeles Revival, *CSB*, September 19, 1963.

20. Oscar T. Gillan to Archer Weniger, July 17, 1963 and August 17, 1963; J. Vernon McGee, "Labels" in Thru the Bible Radio Newsletter, August 1980, McGee, J. Vernon file, AWP.

21. Fowler, *New Engagement*, 45, 49.

22. Archer Weniger to Dr. I.D.E. Thomas, May 2, 1979, AWP.

23. On McBirnie's isolation: Cannon, *Governor Reagan*, 173. On McBirnie's endeavors: "In 7 Years," "American Research Center Opened," Voice of Americanism Folder, FC; "A New 'All-American' Center," *EO*, March 24, 1967; "California Graduate School of Theology" and "The Bible and National Affairs," McBirnie material, MKC and RRC.

24. This analysis draws from N.D.B. Connolly, "Sunbelt Civil Rights: Urban Renewal and the Follies of Desegregation in Greater Miami," in Nickerson and Dochuk, *Sunbelt Rising*, and Matthew Lassiter, *The Silent Majority: Suburban Politics in the Sunbelt South* (Princeton, NJ: Princeton University Press, 2006), 4–5.

25. Connolly, "Sunbelt Civil Rights"; Jesse Unruh Press Conference, July 17, 1968, 3, in Researcher file-Education—RR Memos from ACS Folder, Box 165, RRG.

26. Reagan Circular, Folder 20, Box 817, JTP; "Special Voters" Report filed by the Republican State Central Committee, 1974, in Republican State Central Committee of California Folder, Box 123, RRG.

27. On Wallace: Boyarsky, *Rise of Ronald Reagan*, 134; Dan Carter, *The Politics of Rage: George Wallace, the Origins of the New Conservatism, and the Transformation of American Politics* (New York: Simon & Schuster, 1995), 307–14, 341–44; William B. Hixson Jr., *Search for the American Right Wing: An Analysis of the Social Science Record, 1955–1987* (Princeton, NJ: Princeton University Press, 1992), 122–23, 154–55. Of 500 fundamen-

talist Baptist pastors surveyed in 1968, 40 percent picked Wallace as their candidate of choice. See "500 Baptist Pastors Surveyed, Nixon, Wallace Favored by Most," *BBT*, September 27, 1968. Bob Wells, "If Reagan Wins What Then?" *VTF* , December 1966, *The Voice* file; "L.A. Riots—Who is to Blame?" *CBNL*, September 9, 1965; "Sins of the White Man," *CBNL*, May 12, 1966, Church News Letter Box; "An Interview with . . . Abraham Lincoln," *VTF*, February–March 1967, 10–14, all in CBA.

28. "Orange County California: A Little Piece of America," *Newsweek*, November 14, 1966; Eleanor Vandruff, interview by author.

29. "Racism Not An Issue in California Southern Baptist Churches," *CSB*, June 25, 1964, 4. On Christian Life Commission and Criswell: Mark Newman, *Getting Right with God: Southern Baptists and Desegregation, 1945–1995* (Tuscaloosa, AL: University of Alabama Press, 2001), 63, 82–83. On Criswell: Paul Harvey, *Freedom's Coming: Religious Culture and the Shaping of the South from the Civil War through the Civil Rights Era* (Chapel Hill: University of North Carolina Press, 2005), 245.

30. Porter Routh to J. Terry Young, August 14, 1968, California Baptist Convention Executive Correspondence file, Executive Committee of the Southern Baptist Convention Records, SBCR.

31. Graham quoted in Miller, *Billy Graham and the Rise of the Republican South*, 128, 180. See also Taylor Branch, *At Canaan's Edge: America in the King Years, 1965–1968* (New York: Simon & Schuster, 2006), 294–97; Fowler, *New Engagement*, 49.

32. Jack O'Neal, "Race Relations Sunday," *CSB*, January 27, 1966, 5; "Survey Discloses 'Positive' Responses to Race Relations," *CSB*, February 29, 1968, 8.

33. "Fundamentalists Get Blunt Warning," *OT*, September 10, 1969; "New Evangelical Espouses Radical Ideas of Revolution in His Latest Book," Skinner, Tom Folder, AWP.

34. "Riot Commission Report," *CSB*, April 4, 1968, 4.

35. Acts 2:1–4 (New International Version), quoted in Vinson Synan, *The Holiness-Pentecostal Tradition: Charismatic Movements in the Twentieth Century* (Grand Rapids, MI: William B. Eerdmans, 1997), 229; "Pike Brands 'Speaking in Tongues' Heretical," *LAT*, May 7, 1963.

36. Quebedeaux, *New Charismatics*, 57–58.

37. "George Otis to Speak at MST Commencement Dinner," Ralph Wilkerson file, DDP; "Hollywood Faithful: Pat Boone's Home Becomes Mission for Stars," *DMN*, April 1, 1970, 22A; Rev. Lester Kinsolving, "A Star Is Put Out" (undated, from unidentified publication); "Boone Labeled 'Sin Carrier'?" *The Tennessean*, June 12, 1972, Pat Boone file, AWP.

38. "Faith not Liberal but Literal: Boone," *Globe and Mail*, April 6, 1971, PBPF; Quebedeaux, *New Charismatics*, 5, 10; J. Vernon McGee, "Labels" in Thru the Bible Radio Newsletter, August 1980, McGee, J. Vernon file, AWP.

39. Scott Billingsley, *It's A New Day: Race and Gender in the Modern Charismatic Movement* (Tuscaloosa, AL: University of Alabama Pres, 2008), 8–9; Craig Turner, "The Gospel (with Glitter) According to Rev. Wilkerson," *LAT*, Orange County Edition, April 8, 1979, 1; 10–14; Quebedeaux, *New Charismatics*, 105–6, 122.

40. Michael Harper quoted in Quebedeaux, *New Charismatics*, 138, also 106.

41. E.V. Hill, *A Savior Worth Having* (Chicago: Moody Press, 2002), 40–42, 61.

42. Ibid., 46–47; Reverend Edward Victor Hill tribute pamphlet, MZM.

43. "Highlights of Ministry" in "A Salute to Pastor Hill," MZM; Hill, *A Savior Worth Having*, 158.

44. Hill, *Savior Worth Having*, 98–99; transcript of interview of Pastor E. V. Hill by Mark Joseph, 1994, www.mjmgroup.com/EV_Hill.htm, accessed December 5, 2009.

45. Barbara Dianne Savage, *Your Spirits Walk Beside Us: The Politics of Black Religion* (Cambridge, MA, and London: Belknap Press of Harvard University Press, 2008), 9; transcript of interview of Pastor E. V. Hill by Mark Joseph, 1994.

46. Mervyn M. Dymally to Samuel W. Yorty, July 2, 1965; Edward V. Hill to Samuel Yorty, December 28, 1965; Edward V. Hill to Samuel Yorty, April 22, 1972; "News," March 26, 1973, all in Rev. E. V. Hill Folder, Box D28, SYP.

47. "Credentials, Biography, and Personal Data, Dr. Edward V. Hill," Edward V. Hill to Samuel Yorty, April 22, 1972, Rev. E. V. Hill Folder, Box D28, SYP; Hill, *Savior Worth Having*, 106. On criticism of Hill from other black evangelicals like Skinner and William Pannell, see taped interviews in WPI, and especially Tape 6, Collection 498, BGEA.

48. Hill quoted in Gerald Horne, *Fire This Time: The Watts Uprising and the 1960s* (Charlottesville, VA: Da Capo Press, 1997), 319; Hill, *Savior Worth Having*, 120.

49. "A Salute to Pastor Hill," MZM; Miller, *Billy Graham and the Rise of the Republican South*, 128.

50. "Vacation-Bible-School-Workshop: National Baptist and Southern Baptist Join Hands Again," A.C.C. Church news, in "25th Anniversary Celebration of Letha Mae Logan"; Jack O'Neal, "Watts Burned Again," *CSB*, October 26, 1967, 6–7.

51. "Anaheim Crusade: At Home with the Angels," *CT*, October 24, 1969, 40–41.

52. Reagan Circular, Folder 20, Box 817, JTP. Reagan singles out the Fellowship of Christian Athletes, a program under Campus Crusade authority, as an example of his vision.

11. JESUS PEOPLE

1. William Banowsky, "The Jesus Revolution," Transcript for *Sunday Show*, June 27, 1971, Series 5, Box 4, file 7, WBP.

2. "Boy Killed in Shooting at College," *LAHE*, March 13, 1969; "Pepperdine Reopens; 'Won't Be Coerced,'" *LAHE*, March 19, 1969, in Series 1, Box 1, file 6, WBP.

3. Letter, "Dear White Racist," Series 2, Box 1, file 5; "Pepperdine: A Changing Scene," *Daily Breeze*, in Series 1, Box 1, file 8, WBP.

4. Henegar and Rushford, *Forever Young*, 187; 196–97.

5. "Nation's Campus Turmoil Outlined During Wilshire C of C Address," *Wilshire Press*, June 25, 1970.

6. "It's Time for a Backlash!" *CSB*, January 5, 1967, 10–11.

7. Edmund Morris, *Dutch: A Memoir of Ronald Reagan* (New York: Modern Library, 1999), 336.

8. Ibid., 271; Flamm, *Law and Order*, 73; Bruce Schulman, *The Seventies: The Great Shift in American Culture, Society, and Politics* (New York: The Free Press, 2001), 3; Reagan quoted in Dallek, *Right Moment*, 193–94.

9. Boyarsky, *Rise of Ronald Reagan*, 280, 292.

10. Reagan quoted in Cannon, *Governor Reagan*, 287–95.

11. "Threat of Revolution and Violence at National Black Convention in Berkeley," *BP*, November 26, 1969; "Bishop Pike Drops a Bombshell," *BP*, December 27, 1960. 464. "Answering Bishop Pike's Latest Heresy," February 20, 1966, Bound Bulletin Collection; "The Coming World Crisis: Spirit of Antichrist—The 'Teach-In,'" *VTF* (April 1967); "Hippies, Beatniks, Mini-Skirted Exhibitionists and Other Assorted Nuts and Crackpots!!!" Church Notes Files, CBA.

12. On growth of Christian schools in the South: Crespino, *In Search of Another Country*, 250. Quoted in Richard Vetterli, *Storming the Citadel: The Fundamental Revolution Against Progressive Education* (Costa Mesa, CA: Educational Media Press, 1976), 4; 7, in MKC.

13. "The Church Cares: Central Baptist Church of Orange County," promotional brochure, Church Annuals and Special Events File; "Shall We Teach Sex in Public School?" March 24, 1966, "Sex Education in Public Schools—A Curse or a Blessing?" January 30, 1969, "Is Sex Training Sin Training?" March 20, 1969, *CBNL*, Newsletter File, CBA. School official quoted in Martin, *With God on Our Side*, 105, 111–13.

14. "Christian Heritage College; 1978–79 General Catalogue," Christian Heritage College Folder, FC; . "LaHaye Leaves His Church for TV," *SDU*, September 13, 1981, LaHaye File, SDLHSF. El Cajon's demographic profile drawn from Lending Activity in the City of San Diego, San Diego County Human Relations Committee Minutes, August 10, 1977, Folder 7, Box 1, Human Relations Commission Administrative Files, SDHRCP.

15. Schuparra, *Triumph of the Right*, 136–37; "Christian Heritage College; 1978–79 General Catalogue," Christian Heritage College Folder, FC; "Henry M. Morris, 87, Dies; A Theorist of Creationism," *NYT*, March 4, 2006, Henry Morris File, SDLHSF.

16. CACS Newsletter, January 1966, CACS Christian School Comment Folder, CBA.

17. "CACS Is Still Growing," Christian School Comment, March 1972; CACS News Notes, June 1968, CACS Christian School Comment Folder, CBA.

18. Dale Buss, *Family Man: The Biography of Dr. James Dobson* (Wheaton, IL: Tyndale House Publishers, 2005), 11–16, 27–30, 45; James Dobson, *Dare to Discipline* (New York: Bantam Books, 1977), 3.

19. Richard Viguerie, *The New Right: We're Ready to Lead* (Falls Church, VA: The Viguerie Company, 1981), 34–35; "Senator John G. Schmitz Reports Evidence of a Crisis in Public Higher Education in California," John G. Schmitz Folder, FC; "Grass Roots Campaign for Senate Bill No. 2," *CACS Quarterly Report* (January, February, March, 1970), "California Has First Tax Credit for Tuition," *CACS Quarterly Report* (Winter 1973), CACS Folder, CBA.

20. "Governor Reagan: 'God Is Not Dead on Your Campuses,'" *CACS Quarterly Report* (April, May, June, 1969), CACS Folder, CBA.

21. Memorandum to Key Issues Committee from Don Webster, September 4, 1968, Folder 8, Box 816, JTP; "Youth," Republican State Central Committee of California—1972, and "Special Voters," Republican State Central Committee of California—1974, Fact Book Folder, Box GO 123, RRG.

22. "An Urgent Report from J. Edgar Hoover" and "If You and I Could Have a Thoughtful Conversation," Steuart McBirnie Newsletter (undated); "In 7 Years," Voice

of Americanism Newsletter; "Youth Seminars," Voice of Americanism Newsletter (undated); "What Now . . . for Your Voice of Americanism?" and "One Thrilling New Major Step," in Voice of Americanism Folder, FC.

23. "Address by U.S. Senator Strom Thurmond, Accepting Honorary Degree from the California Graduate School of Theology"; "Thurmond Faces UCLA Hecklers," EO, November 10, 1970; "'Party' No Fun for Thurmond," undated newspaper clip, all in Folder 196, Box 16, STP.

24. Turner, Bill Bright and Campus Crusade for Christ, 109–11.

25. Braun quoted in ibid., 119–20.

26. Quoted in ibid., 122–25.

27. Ibid., 127–29; CT, May 8, 1970, 40.

28. "'Fire Insurance' Evangelism Big in America, Skinner Says," The Alabama Baptist, April 6, 1978, 1; Program for "Urbana 70" and "New Evangelical Espouses Radical Ideas of Revolution in His Latest Book," AWP.

29. Turner, Bill Bright and Campus Crusade for Christ, 123, 131; Robert Ellwood, One Way: The Jesus Movement and Its Meaning (Englewood Cliffs, NJ: Prentice Hall, 1973), 23–25.

30. Synan, Holiness-Pentecostal Tradition, 256.

31. "Thousands Attend Teen Challenge Rallies," TI, December 1964; "Christ on the Campus," TI, February 1968; "Teen Challenge," TI, May 1968. "Boy from New York Slums Finds His Role in 'Cross 'n Switchblade,'" AB, June 13, 1970.

32. Arthur Blessitt, Tell the World: A Jesus People Manual (Old Tappan, NJ: Fleming H. Revell, 1972), 9. Blessitt quoted in Eileen Luhr, Witnessing Suburbia: Conservatives and Christian Youth Culture (Berkeley: University of California Press, 2009), 78, 80.

33. "The 25th Anniversary Celebration of Letha Mae Logan," MZM; Letha Trammell, interview by author.

34. David Diggs, interview by author; "The Jesus Revolution," Time, June 21, 1971, 56–63; "The Jesus Movement Is Upon Us," Look, February 9, 1971, 15–21.

35. Maranatha: Goodnews Paper, vol. 1, no. 2 (1973), 1, Maranatha Evangelical Association Folder, FC.

36. Ibid., 3; Chuck Girard, "Things are Getting Better"; Maranatha: Goodnews Paper.

37. Diggs interview; Jean Vandruff interview.

38. Elliott Smith, "Shapers of the California Southern Baptist Heritage: The Presidents (1961–1970)," CSB, September 11, 1980, 13.

39. Henegar and Rushford, Forever Young, 203–5.

40. "The Church of Christ," CT, July 16, 1965, 28.

41. "'Clash' with Playboy Makes Impact," CCH, November 3, 1967, and "In a 'Playboy' World," CS (undated), Series 1, Box 1, File 2, WBP.

42. Larry Lynch to Norvel Young, November 27, 1968; James D. Bales to Bill Banowsky, October 24, 1968; William Banowsky to Bishop James Pike, December 11, 1968, Series 2, Box 1, File 6, WBP.

43. "Sex Morality Debate on Campus: Pike Ran into a Formidable Foe," IPT, January 11, 1969; "The 'Debate' That Never Was," CCH, January 13, 1969, 2; "Pike-Banowsky Discussion Gets Nation-Wide Attention," clip from unidentified newspaper, Series 2, Box 1, File 6, WBP.

44. "The 'Debate' That Never Was" "Pike-Bonowsky [sic] Sex-Ethics Debate Drives Antagonists to Compromise," Series 2, Box 1, File 6, WBP.

45. "Reaction to Pike-Banowsky Debate Wide, Varied, Unexpected," *CCH*, February 3, 1969, Series 1, Box 1, File 5; Mrs. J. Verna Luck to William Banowsky, January 5, 1969; Donald Irvin to William Banowsky, January 18, 1969, Series 2, Box 1, File 6, WBP. "The 'Debate' That Never Was"; "Sex Morality Debate on Campus: Pike Ran into a Formidable Foe"; Archie Luper to William Banowsky, January 7, 1969, Series 2, Box 1, File 6, WBP.

46. Rushford, *Crest of a Golden Wave*, 180; "A Case for Malibu," Series 2, Box 1, File 2, WBP.

47. Rushford, *Crest of a Golden Wave*, 163; Norvel Young to Henry Salvatori, September 10, 1969; Henry Salvatori to Mrs. Blanche Seaver, February 25, 1970, Folder 1, Box 2, NYP; "Private Colleges Win Reagan's Praise for Spirit of Freedom" and "State's Private Colleges Praised by Reagan," undated newspaper clips from *LAT* and *LAHE*, Series 1, Box 1, File 1, WBP.

48. William Banowsky, "A Spirit of Place," Series 2, Box 2, File 3, WBP.

49. "Rough Draft of Pepperdine College Statement to Be Made by President Young at Press Conference," Series 2, Box, File 5; "Pepperdine: A Changing Scene," *Daily Breeze*, December 20, 1970, in Series 1, Box 1, File, WBP.

50. "Pepperdine at Malibu; Dedication and Installation of Founding Chancellor, May 23, 1970," *EO*, Series 2, Box 2, File 3; Program for Dedication Ceremony, The Center for American Studies, Series 1, Box 1, File 10, WBP; quoted in *Crest of a Golden Wave*, 163.

51. William Banowsky, "An Unwitting Score for Tolerance," *LAT*, April 5, 1970; Herbert Marcuse, "The True Nature of Tolerance," *LAT*, April 12, 1970.

12. MORAL MAJORITY

1. Hill, *Savior Worth Having*, 49.

2. Tape 1171, Collection 191, BGEA; Turner, *Bill Bright and Campus Crusade for Christ*, 138–46; "Explosion to Change the World," *MM*, July–August 1972, 8.

3. Turner, *Bill Bright and Campus Crusade for Christ*, 144; See *DMN*, June 15 and 18, 1972; *NYT*, June 16, 1972; *Life*, June 30, 1972; Edward Plowman, "'Godstock' in Big D," *CT*, July 7, 1972; John Egerton, *The Americanization of Dixie: The Southernization of America* (New York: Harper's Magazine Press, 1974), xx, 24–25, 192–96.

4. Kirkpatrick Sale, *Power Shift: The Rise of the Southern Rim and Its Challenges to the Eastern Establishment* (New York: Random House, 1975), 5–7, 15; C. Vann Woodward, "The South Tomorrow," *Time*, September 27, 1976.

5. On Nixon's southern strategy and "calculated inattention" to race: Miller, *Billy Graham and the Rise of the Republican South*, 135. Perlstein, *Nixonland*, 88.

6. Harry Dent to Peter Flanigan, July 22, 1970, Folder 214, Box 7; Patrick Buchanan to President Richard Nixon, July 7, 1970, Folder 214, Box 7, HDP. This discussion draws from Lassiter, *Silent Majority*, 239–41.

7. Quoted in Lassiter, *Silent Majority*, 241; Remarks of the President to Southern Regional Reception, Atlanta, Georgia, October 12, 1972, Folder 375, Box 13, HDP.

Quotes from strategy papers of the Middle America Committee: "First Meeting of the Middle America Committee," October 16, 1969, and "Attracting the Middle Class," Folder 49, Box 2, HDP.

8. Kevin Phillips paid special attention to Southern California's foundational role in the "Sun Belt Phenomenon" and the rise of a southern Republican majority. See Kevin P. Phillips, *The Emerging Republican Majority* (New Rochelle, NY: Arlington House, 1969), chap. 5.

9. Graham quoted in Miller, *Billy Graham and the Rise of the Republican South*, 141–42. Graham's importance to Nixon highlighted in memo dated October 23, 1969, Folder 26, Box 1; H. R. Haldeman to Mr. Klein, November 30, 1970, Folder 117, Box 4; Harry Dent to Billy Graham, October 27, 1971, Folder 490, Box 20, HDP. Also White House Conversation, 31-85, October 16, 1972, NPM, detailed in Miller, *Billy Graham and the Rise of the Republican South*, 185–87; Perlstein, *Nixonland*, 500–502.

10. "Nation Feels Its Freedom, Singer Says," *Wichita Eagle and Beacon*, July 5, 1970, 1, PBPF; Tape 1069, Collection 191, BGEA. On Graham's first exposure to Southern California's "one way youth"—Jesus people: Larry Eskridge, "'One Way': Billy Graham, the Jesus Generation, and the Idea of an Evangelical Youth Culture," *Church History* 67 (March 1998), 83–106.

11. "Editor Interviews Bill Hartman" and "Program for the 1970 Republican National Leadership Conference," Sound Generation Folder, JBC; Wallace Henley to Bill Bright, October 25, 1972, Folder 336, Box 11, HDP; Turner, *Bill Bright and Campus Crusade for Christ*, 141.

12. Tape 13, Collection 176; Video 308, Collection 113, BGEA.

13. Harry Dent, *The Prodigal South Returns to Power* (New York: John Wiley & Sons, 1978), 159, 180–81; Wallace B. Henley to Harry Dent, Bob Brown, Paul Jones, December 30, 1971, Folder 238, Box 7, HDP; "The Black Silent Majority Committee: A Statement of Beliefs," Black Churches File, AWP.

14. Wallace Henley to Dr. Jack Terry, October 23, 1972, Jimmy G. Phillips to Wallace Henley, October 31, 1972, Gil A. Stricklin to Wallace Henley, October 25, 1972, Folder 336, Box 11; Wallace B. Henley to Dr. Hughes, May 18, 1972, Folder 335, Box 11, HDP.

15. "Summary, La Costa Conversations, July 25, 1970," Series 3, Box 1, File 2, WBP; James Wilburn, interview by author.

16. List of Attendees, Folder 124, Box 4, HDP. On Pew's sponsorship of Honor America Day, see correspondence in Honor America Day Folder, Box 105, JHP. Billy Graham to William Banowsky, November 13, 1972, Billy Graham File, WBP.

17. "Appointee Sees Bright GOP Future," clip from unidentified publication, Series 1, Box 2, File 1, WBP.

18. On Nixon's troubled relationship with conservatism: Schuparra, *Triumph of the Right*, chap. 4; Critchlow, *Conservative Ascendancy*, 92, 95–97; Patrick J. Buchanan to H. R. Haldeman, January 14, 1971, and John. D. Ehrlichman to Bob Haldeman, January 16, 1972, Folder 240, Box 7, HDP.

19. "Be Sure to Vote Right in the Election," Church Newsletter October 31, 1968, "The Red China Fiasco—Nixon's Covenant with Death and Agreement with Hell," Church Newsletter, July 22, 1971, Newsletter Box; "Should the U.S. Disarm," Taped Sermon;

Bob Wells, "If Reagan Wins What Then?" *VTF*, vol. 1, no. 2 (December 1966), The Voice File, CBA; Cannon, *Governor Reagan*, 389.

20. Schoenwald, *Time for Choosing*, 230; American Conservative Union strategy quoted in Lichtman, *White Protestant Nation*, 304–5; Phillips-Fein, *Invisible Hands*, 172; Viguerie, *New Right*, 28–35.

21. "Program for Freedom Forum XIII, 1971," Banowsky Political Material, Box E–H and the Great Issues Series, Series 1, Box 2, File 1. Sampling from editorials published in the *LAHE* between 1972 and 1973, all in Series 4, Box 2, Files 5 and 6. "Banowsky to Get GOP Post," *TG*, June 8, 1973, 1–2, "Banowsky Assumes State GOP Position," *PN*, July 7, 1973, 2, "Who's Who," *Time*, July 15, 1974, 8. "The Right Report," vol. 2, no. 8 (April 23, 1973), Series 1, Box 2, File 1, WBP.

22. On shift to "majoritarian" thinking: Nash, *Conservative Intellectual Movement*, 392.

23. Douglas W. Johnson, Paul R. Picard, and Bernard Quinn, *Churches and Church Membership in the United States: An Enumeration by Region, State and County* (Washington, D.C.: Glenmary Research Center, 1971), table 2, 13; table 3, 28–29. On the southern evangelical surge in California after 1970: Mark A. Shibley, *Resurgent Evangelicalism in the United States: Mapping Cultural Change since 1970* (Columbia, SC: University of South Carolina Press, 1996). On Dean Kelley's and Peter Wagner's scholarship: Carl S. Dudley, "Measuring Church Growth," *CC*, June 1979, 635.

24. "Melodyland News Release,'" Jerry Falwell-Charismatic Movement File, AWP; Annual of the Southern Baptist General Convention of California, 1975, SBCR.

25. Heather Hendershot, *Shaking the World for Jesus: Media and Conservative Evangelical Culture* (Chicago: University of Chicago Press, 2004), 180–82; Schulman, *Seventies*, 95.

26. Jim Montgomery, "The Electric Church," *WSJ*, May 19, 1978, 1; Craig Turner, "The Gospel (with Glitter) According to Rev. Wilkerson"; "Degrees Conferred upon MST Graduates," "'Who's Who' In Religion on MST Regents Board," Ecumenical Research Academy brochure, and weekly schedules for Melodyland, in Ralph Wilkerson File, DDP; "Whither the Wind?" *Melodyland in Motion*, August 1973, 2–3, Melodyland School of Theology File, AWP.

27. "10 Years of God's Miracles" and "Praise the Lord" Newsletter (April 1991), Trinity Broadcasting Folder, Box 28; Mark Ward Sr., "Chronology of Religious Broadcasting," *Directory of Religious Media* (1994), National Religious Broadcasters Directory Folder, Box 27, SDC.

28. Smith, "Shapers of the California Southern Baptist Heritage: The Presidents (1961-1970)," *CSB*, September 11, 1980, 13; "Moral Concerns in California," *CSB*, March 18, 1976, 4; untitled editorial, *CT*, December 3, 1976, 57–58.

29. "Christian Heritage College: 1978–79 General Catalogue," Christian Heritage College Folder, FC; McBirnie material, MKP and RRC; Christian Research Institute Pamphlet, Walter Martin Folder, and "Institute of Applied Christianity," *FEANV* (September–October 1972), AWP.

30. Beilenson quoted in Cannon, *Governor Reagan*, 209–10, 213. In 1973, Reagan would single out this decision as the most difficult of his career. Evangelicals forgave him after he tried to make amends in 1970 by joining Senator John Schmitz and Assemblyman Bob Burke in publicly opposing "further liberalization of abortion laws." See "Ease of Abortions Is Hit by Reagan," *SB*, June 9, 1970, and Rocklin School inter-

view, March 8, 1973, Research File—Legal Affairs—Abortion Folder, Box GO188, RRG.

31. Cannon, *Governor Reagan*, 210; Critchlow, *Conservative Ascendancy*, 135; Quebedeaux, *New Charismatics*, 72–80.

32. "Hollywood Community Fights Smut," *LAT*, January 15, 1971, PBPF.

33. "SOS: Stamp Out Smut," 2.49.1, and Los Angeles Lettergram to Kenneth Hahn, September 18, 1972, 2.49.2: Obscenity and Pornography Commission Folder, Box 223, KHP; Ronald Reagan press release, October 6, 1972, Research File—Legal Affairs—Pornography Folder, Box GO191, RRG.

34. Joseph Tuman, "Miller v. California," in Richard A. Parker, ed., *Free Speech on Trial: Communication Perspectives on Landmark Supreme Court Decisions* (Tuscaloosa, AL: University of Alabama Press, 2003), 187–202; "News for Good Neighbors," undated, in Christian Family Renewal Folder, FC.

35. California Republican Assembly Board of Directors Meeting, June 26–28, 1970, Folder 14, Box 1, and California Republican Assembly Board of Directors Meeting, January 23–24, 1971, Folder 15, Box 1, CRA; W. Barry Garrett, "High Court Holds Abortion to Be a Right of Privacy," *CSB*, February 15, 1973, 10; Michael McGuire, "Disappointed," *CSB*, March 15, 1973, 2.

36. "Christian Family Renewal Newsletter," "Dear Friend of the Unborn," Christian Family Renewal Folder, FC; claim drawn from Ethan Persoff's Web site at www.ep.tc/junior, accessed September 28, 2009.

37. "Family Bill of Rights," "Creed of Women For Home And Family," and "From Me to You," Christian Family Renewal Folder, FC.

38. Bob Jones to Mrs. E. R. Richardson, March 31, 1977; Archer Weniger to Tim LaHaye, December 4, 1974 and Tim LaHaye to Archer Weniger, September 27, 1978, AWP.

39. "A Word About the National Alliance for Family Life Foundation," December 1974, National Alliance for Family Life File, Box L–O, WBP; "People Panorama," *MM*, November 1974, 20; Fowler, *New Engagement*, 192–93.

40. R. Marie Griffith, *God's Daughters: Evangelical Women and the Power of Submission* (Berkeley: University of California Press, 1997), 4, 44–45; Vonette Bright to Wilbur Smith, January 26, 1972, WSC; Turner, *Bill Bright and Campus Crusade for Christ*, 156, 209–12. These women appeared together at a pro-family rally advertised by Christian Family Renewal. See undated newsletter, Christian Family Renewal Folder, FC.

41. Betty J. Coble, "Woman Needs Equal Rights?" *CSB*, March 8, 1973, 6.

42. Critchlow, *Conservative Ascendancy*, 100–102.

43. Phillips quoted in ibid., 103; Martin, *With God on Our Side*, 146–47; Miller, *Billy Graham and the Rise of the Republican South*, 184–85; "Party Must Admit Nixon Was a Threat, GOP Official Says," *LAT*, November 19, 1974, clip in Series 1, Box 2, File 2, WBP.

44. Canon, *Governor Reagan*, 386–89.

45. "Executive Order R 51-74" and "Your Prayers Can Change This Nation's History," State of California Committee National Day of Fasting and Prayer, Proclamations 1974–Prayer Folder, Box 73, RRG; Prayer Day, April 4, 1974, and Governor Reagan Appreciation Dinner Committee, May 6, 1974, Series 2, Box 3, File 3, WBP.

46. Schulman, *Seventies*, 48–52.

47. William F. Buckley, "Of Conservatives and Populists," *LAT*, December 9, 1974, and "Reply to Mr. Buckley," draft dated December 12, 1974, Series 3, Box 1, File 1, WBP.

48. "Secret Fund Paid $247,100 to Top Pepperdine Officials," *LAT*, March 13, 1975, "Pepperdine Critics Exposed," *TG*, March 21, 1975, "Younger Facing Decision on Late Vote Fund Report Involving Top Republicans," *LAT*, June 14, 1975, "Banowsky Rules Out Bid for Senate," *EO*, May 15, 1975, "Banowsky Resigns National GOP Post," *LAT*, November 5, 1975, Series 1, Box 2, File 3, WBP.

49. Schulman, *Seventies*, 51.

50. "Here's Life, America" brochure, E. V. Hill Folder, AWP; Turner, *Bill Bright and Campus Crusade for Christ*, 160–61, 168–69.

51. "Others Say . . . Economic Recession," *CT*, June 20, 1975, 21–22.

52. John Conlan, "Occupy Until He Comes: An Address by Hon. John B. Conlan, Christian Booksellers Association, Anaheim, Convention, 1975," *Bookstore Journal*, October 1975, 18–20.

13. BORN AGAIN

1. "Reagan's Pitch to Fundamentalists," *SFC*, August 23, 1980, 8.

2. Tape 4 and Tape 13, Collection 176, BGEA. Criswell's sermon did not detail his father's move to Fresno; those specifics are drawn from W. A. Criswell, *Standing on the Promises: The Autobiography of W. A. Criswell* (Dallas, TX: Word Publishing, 1990), 170–71.

3. Robert Wuthnow, "The Political Rebirth of American Evangelicals," in Robert C. Liebman and Robert Wuthnow, eds., *The New Christian Right: Mobilization and Legitimation* (New York: Aldine Publishing Company, 1983), 177; "Born Again! The Year of the Evangelicals!" *Newsweek*, October 25, 1976.

4. Schulman, *Seventies*, 93; Martin, *With God on Our Side*, 156; Wuthnow, "The Political Rebirth of American Evangelicals," 177.

5. Boyer, *When Time Shall Be No More*, 5–7; Schulman, *Seventies*, 82, 93; "The Late Great Planet Earth" press release, Hal Lindsey Folder, AWP.

6. Dr. M. H. Reynolds Jr., "Suddenly, Almost Everyone's an Evangelical," *F.E.A. News and Views* (July–August 1976), 1; "A Cloud in The Fundamentalists' Sky," *Focus on Missions*, December 1976, 1, Pat Boone Folder, AWP; Gary Wilburn, "The Doomsday Chic," *CT*, January 22, 1978, 22–23; "When Pat Boone Shows Up at a Synagogue, the Surprised Worshipers Ask Why," article from unidentified magazine, clip in PBPF.

7. Fowler, *New Engagement*, 236–37; Carey McWilliams, "The Evangelical Bloc," draft of article for *TN*, The Evangelicals Folder, Box 46, CWC; Chancellor as quoted in Martin, *With God on Our Side*, 150.

8. McWilliams, "The Evangelical Bloc"; Criswell quoted in Martin, *With God on Our Side*, 150, 154–55, 157–58;

9. Smith quoted in Martin, *With God on Our Side*, 157; Fowler, *New Engagement*, 237; John Maust, "The Growing Pains of Overexposure," *United Evangelical Association*, Summer 1978, 8–10.

10. "Jesus California Style '80," Walter Martin Folder, AWP; untitled clips from *Jerusa-*

lem Post, April 11, 1973, and "Attestation of Pilgrimage" and "Singer, Author Slate Tour of Holy Land," November 28, 1975, PBPF.

11. McWilliams, "The Evangelical Bloc," The Evangelicals Folder, Box 46, CWC.

12. Boone interview; Slosser, *Reagan Inside Out,* 13–15.

13. Craig Shirley, *Reagan's Revolution: The Untold Story of the Campaign That Started It All* (Nashville, TN: Nelson Current, 2005), xxviii; Robert T. Hartmann, *Palace Politics: An Inside Account of the Ford Years* (New York: McGraw-Hill, 1980), 101; Critchlow, *Conservative Ascendancy,* 144.

14. Quoted in Shirley, *Reagan's Revolution,* 245, also 192–95; James R. Dickenson, "Ford Walloped as Challenger Gains New Life," *WS,* May 2, 1976.

15. Sara Diamond, *Spiritual Warfare: The Politics of the Christian Right* (Boston: South End Press, 1989), 18; "Reagan's Religious Commitment," *CSB,* June 10, 1976, 4; "There's No Business Like Politics," *LAT,* August 11, 1976; Dent, *The Prodigal South Returns to Power,* 48–49.

16. Critchlow, *Conservative Ascendancy,* 148–50; quoted in Shirley, *Reagan's Revolution,* xxii–xxiii.

17. Critchlow, *Conservative Ascendancy,* 151.

18. "Nation's Spotlight on Southern Baptists," *CSB,* July 29, 1976, 4; "Reagan's Religious Commitment," *CSB,* June 10, 1976, 4; "Gray Matter: Strange Bedfellows," *CSB,* June 24, 1976, 4.

19. Lindsay, *Faith in the Halls of Power,* 16–17; Wilentz, *Age of Reagan,* 75–77; Lichtman, *White Protestant Nation,* 333.

20. Statistics cited in Robert Kuttner, *Revolt of the Haves: Tax Rebellions and Hard Times* (New York: Simon & Schuster, 1980), 55; Thomas Byrne Edsall with Mary D. Edsall, *Chain Reaction: The Impact of Race, Rights, and Taxes on American Politics* (New York: W. W. Norton, 1991), 130–31.

21. Trombley, "Pepperdine U. Torn by Tragedy, Internal Dissent."

22. "The Founding Four Hundred," Series 1, Box 3, File 2, WBP; Rushford, *Crest of a Golden Wave,* 169–70; "Friedman Guest at Pepperdine Fete," *LAHE,* February 11, 1977.

23. Sale, *Power Shift,* 5–7; Rushford, *Crest of a Golden Wave,* 170.

24. William S. Banowsky, "Conservative Shift Seen for Country," *LAHE,* June 19, 1976; William Banowsky, "Homeowner Digs Deeper and Deeper," undated clipping in Series 4, Box 3, File 1, WBP.

25. W. S. McBirnie, "What Are the Real Aftereffects of Prop. 13," in W. S. McBirnie material, MKC; Edsall and Edsall, *Chain Reaction,* 131.

26. Critchlow, *Conservative Ascendancy,* 164–65; McBirnie, "What Are the Real Aftereffects of Prop. 13.

27. Jerome L. Himmelstein, *To the Right: The Transformation of American Conservatism* (Berkeley: University of California Press, 1990), 90–92.

28. 1975 Minutes, Orange County Southern Baptist Association, 25–26, California-Orange County Association Annuals, SBCR; "'Public Decency' Initiative," *CSB,* March 11, 1976, 2; "Group to Lobby in California Against Hiring Homosexuals," *CSB,* October 14, 1976, 15.

29. "Group to Lobby in California Against Hiring Homosexuals," *CSB,* October 14, 1976, 15; John Keasler to Mr. George D. Williams, April 9, 1978, Folder 2, Box 5, SDHRCP;

"San Diego Surveys Gay Community," *Contact*, June 30, 1978, and Petition against Metropolitan Church, Folder 2, Box 5, and Letter from Gay Pride Parade committee to San Diego Human Relations Committee, June 8, 1977, Folder 7, Box 1, SDHRCP.

30. This discussion draws from Randy Shilts, *The Mayor of Castro Street: The Life and Times of Harvey Milk* (New York: St. Martin's Press, 1982), 153–57; Martin, *With God on Our Side*, 197–98.

31. Context and quotes drawn from Shilts, *Mayor of Castro Street*, 216, 230–31.

32. Pomona woman quoted in ibid., 215; Murray Norris, "The Blighted Eye That Is Never Satisfied," Christian Family Renewal Folder, FC; Timothy LaHaye, *Battle for the Mind* (Grand Rapids, MI: Baker Book House, 1980), 208.

33. Quoted in Shilts, *Mayor of Castro Street*, 243.

34. LaHaye quoted in Martin, *With God on Our Side*, 189.

35. Diggs interview; Christian Family Renewal newsletter, undated, Christian Family Renewal Folder, FC; Fowler, *New Engagement*, 206; "Pastor's Wife Takes Up Anti-Feminist Crusade," *Daily Review*, October 11, 1980, 6.

36. LaHaye, *Battle for the Mind*, 199; "Coast Moral Majority Keeps a Low Profile and Likes It That Way," *RNS*, March 17, 1981, 4; "Kick Off Rally SALT Committee," Californians for Biblical Morality, January 17, 1980; Timothy LaHaye to Michael Kirst, April 2, 1980; "Californians for Biblical Majority: The Sex Educators Are at It Again!" in Timothy LaHaye Folder, AWP. Robert Zweir, *Born-Again Politics: The New Christian Right in America* (Downers Grove, IL: InterVarsity Press, 1982), 21, 25, 31; Diamond, *Spiritual Warfare*, 62–63; Margaret Ann Latus, "Ideological PACs and Political Action," in Liebman and Wuthnow, *The New Christian Right: Mobilization and Legitimation*, 50–52, 77.

37. Diamond, *Spiritual Warfare*, 171, 173–75, 179; James L. Guth, "The New Christian Right," in Liebman and Wuthnow, *The New Christian Right: Mobilization and Legitimation*, 50–52; Wilentz, *Age of Reagan*, 92–93; Lichtman, *White Protestant Nation*, 342–44.

38. "Unlimited Fields to Plow," *JC*, January 26, 1979, 2, "Why Fundamentalists are Conservative," *JC*, October 13, 1978, 2, "America: Still the Best," *JC*, July 21, 1978, "A No-Growth America," *JC*, December 22, 1978, "Goodbye to the Goodtimes," *JC*, August 4, 1978, in AWP.

39. Simon quoted in Alice O'Connor, "Financing the Counterrevolution," in Bruce J. Schulman and Julian E. Zelizer, eds., *Rightward Bound: Making America Conservative in the 1970s* (Cambridge, MA: Harvard University Press, 2008), 158–59; William Simon, *A Time for Truth* (New York: McGraw-Hill, 1978), 230–33; Phillips-Fein, *Invisible Hands*, 193, 202–5; Himmelstein, *To the Right*, 141.

40. Phillips-Fein, *Invisible Hands*, 185–88; Pat Robertson, "A Christian Action Plan to Heal Our Land in the 1980s," Pat Robertson's Perspective: A Special Report to the Members of the 700 Club, Fall 1979, Folder 6, Box 29, Collection 309, BGEA; "The Roundtable Is Not a Cause?" and "Stop the Liberals from Rewriting the Bible: A Project of the Religious Roundtable," in Religion and Politics Files, DDP; "Christian Voice The Nation's Largest Christian Conservative Lobby" and "National Opinion Survey on Federal Government and the American Family," Christian Voice Folder, FC.

41. Viguerie, *New Right,* 52–53.

42. Historians agree that this purported shift from Old Right to New Right was one of style and emphases at most. Allan Lichtman quips that Viguerie's New Right was in fact the "seventh 'new right' in thirty years." Lichtman, *White Protestant Nation*, 308.

43. Cannon, *Governor Reagan*, 437, 446–47, 214. In 1979, Reagan advocated a constitutional amendment that would return the national abortion law to standards practiced prior to California's Beilenson bill of 1967.

44. "Christians for Reagan: A Project of Christian Voice Moral Government Fund," Reagan, Ronald (Campaign) U.S. President 1980 Folder, FC.

45. Tim LaHaye to Archer Weniger, April 1980, AWP; LaHaye, *Battle for the Mind*, 51, 141, 150–56, 165, 170, 188–91, 197–99.

46. "My People," PBPF; Turner, *Bill Bright and Campus Crusade for Christ*, 191.

47. Proverbs 31:26–28, King James Version; Joel 2:7, 8; "My People," PBPF.

48. Quoted in Cannon, *Governor Reagan*, 476–77.

49. Ibid., 465; Phillips-Fein, *Invisible Hands*, 238–50.

50. John Conlan to William Casey, April 24, 1980, Christians—File 1 of Folder 2, Box 307, MHP; John Conlan to Select Christian Leaders, September 27, 1979, Ronald Reagan to Ben Armstrong, August 16, 1979, and Ben Armstrong to John Conlan, October 8, 1979, Folder 1, Box 13, NRB; Robert Billings to Max Hugel, May 23, 1980, and letters to Hugel from LaHaye and Falwell in Evangelical/Born Again Folder, Box 309, MHP; Turner, *Bill Bright and Campus Crusade for Christ*, 193.

51. "Evangelist Says Carter Shuns Leadership Forum," *RNS*, Monday, June 30, 1980, and "Evangelical Politics Briefing Opens and Quickly Turns Right," *RNS*, Friday, August 22, 1980, James Robinson [*sic*] Folder, AWP; "10,000 Cheer Mix of Conservative Politics, 'Born Again' Religion," in *Tribune*, Friday, August 22, 1980, PBPC; "Preachers in Politics: Decisive Force in '80?" *USNWR*, September 15, 1980, 24.

52. Bill Stall, "Evangelicals Pin Their Faith on Political Action," *LAT*, August 24, 1980; "Kathy Sawyer, "Linking Religion and Politics," *WP*, August 24, 1980; Howell Baines, "Reagan Backs Evangelicals in Their Political Activities," *NYT*, August 23, 1980; Martin, *With God on Our Side*, 217–18;

53. "Religious Conservatives Launch Bid to Influence Presidential Politics," Monday, August 25, 1980, *RNS*, James Robinson [*sic*] Folder, AWP; Herbert Ellingwood to Ronald Reagan, August 26, 1980, 1980 Campaign Files, Box 148, EMP.

54. Congressman Robert K. Dornan form letter, August 29, 1980, Ronald Reagan (Campaign) U.S. President 1980 Folder, FC; "America's Pro-Family Conference" brochure, Tim LaHaye Folder, AWP; Martin, *With God on Our Side*, 173–89; Turner, *Bill Bright and Campus Crusade for Christ*, 194–95.

55. Quoted in Cannon, *Governor Reagan*, 487–88, 490–91, 505; Crespino, *In Search of Another Country*, 1; Wilentz, *Age of Reagan*, 124–25; Critchlow, *Conservative Ascendancy*, 179.

56. "Reagan 'Job Hunting' at Fair," *The Times: Shreveport—Bossier City—The Ark-La-Tex*, October 22, 1980, 20, PBPF; Cannon, *Governor Reagan*, 508–9.

57. Boone, *Pat Boone's America: 50 Years*, 101–2.

58. Quoted in Wilentz, *Age of Reagan*, 127–29.

59. Jerry Falwell, *Strength for the Journey: An Autobiography* (New York: Simon & Schuster, 1987), 366.

Epilogue: Wilderness Again

1. Smith, "Shapers of the California Southern Baptist Heritage," 13; Ola Brister, "Our Trip to California and Starting a Church in Long Beach," *CSB*, November 6, 1980, 3.

2. "1978 World Convention and Silver Anniversary Celebration," *FGBMV*, September 1978, 18–19; advertisement for Central Baptist Anniversary Celebration in News Release for Central Baptist Anniversary Celebration, History and Past Events Box, CBA.

3. "American Preaching: A Dying Art?" *Time*, December 31, 1979; "A Salute to Pastor Hill," "A Few Highlights of Pastor Hill's Ministries," Voting Guide, and White House press release, July 16, 1985, MZM.

4. "Secretary Regan Explains 'Reaganomics' at Dinner Honoring Justin Dart," *Pepperdine People* magazine, Winter 1981; on Wilson and Pepperdine's centers, see *Pepperdine People* magazine, Spring 2005; Rushford, *Crest of a Golden Wave*, 213–20.

5. "House of Worship, Drama," *Prospect '77*, in W. S. McBirnie loose material, MKC; Diamond, *Spiritual Warfare*, 23–24; Turner, "The Gospel (with Glitter) According to Rev. Wilkerson"; "Dissonance Jars the Melodyland Harmony," *CT*, December 1, 1978, "Seminary Opens with Only 12 Students," *LAT*, January 13, 1979; David duPlessis to Ralph Wilkerson, November 9, 1978, DPP.

6. Billingsley, *It's A New Day*, 109–11.

7. Frank Halbeck, "Strategy for Christ: A Prospectus for Orange County," *CSB*, May 29, 1980, 8.

8. Frank Halbeck, "Laguna Hills Church Grows Rapidly," *CSB*, June 5, 1980, 6–7.

9. "Bob Wells, an Orange County Leader Since 1956," *BBT*, October 24, 1986, 12; Jean Vandruff interview. On Central Baptist Church, Huntington Beach, see "History" in CBCHB; on Allen's and Rohrabacher's attendance and overview of this church: Vandruff interview and Robert Knutson, interview by author.

10. "Jerry Falwell at Lassen Pines Youth Camp," August 13–18, 1973, Falwell Folder, AWP; "Falwell Becomes Church Co-Pastor in Orange, Calif.," *BBT*, March 9, 1973; Melodyland News Release, undated, in Falwell, Jerry—Charismatic Movement Folder, AWP; G. Archer Weniger, "Jerry Falwell and the Charismatic Movement," April 28, 1978, AWP.

11. Knutson interview; Frances FitzGerald, *Cities on a Hill: A Journey Through Contemporary American Cultures* (New York: Simon & Schuster, 1986), 129, 132–34; Falwell, *Strength for the Journey*, 345–46, 313, 334–37, 345; Falwell quoted in Susan Friend Harding, *The Book of Jerry Falwell: Fundamentalist Language and Politics* (Princeton, NJ: Princeton University Press, 2000), 22.

12. Council for National Policy membership list in Series 2, Box 3, File 1, WBP; for appraisal of the "Christian Right" in California: J. Christopher Soper and Joel S. Fetzer, "The Christian Right in California: Dimming Fortunes in the Golden State," in John C. Green, Mark J. Rozell, and Clyde Wilcox, eds., *The Christian Right in American Politics: Marching to the Millennium* (Washington, D.C.: Georgetown University Press, 2003), 210–15.

13. William K. Stevens, "A New Culture Emerges in the Oil Patch," in John B. Boles, ed., *Dixie Dateline: A Journalistic Portrait of the Contemporary South* (Houston, TX:

Rice University Studies, 1983), 137; see Republican Party of Texas Report from 1985 in Series, Box 3, File 2, WBP.

14. Bush makes little mention of a conversion experience with Blessitt, preferring instead to stress his meeting in 1985 with Billy Graham. Alan Cooperman, "Openly Religious, to a Point: Bush Leaves the Specifics of His Faith to Speculation," WP, September 16, 2004.

15. William S. Banowsky to Richard M. Scaife, August 17, 1978, and William S. Banowsky to Dr. Willard Collins, September 6, 1978, Series 2, Box 4, File 3; William Banowsky to George Strake, June 14, 1985, Series 2, Box 3, File 2, WBP.

16. Vandruff interview.

SELECTED BIBLIOGRAPHY

The following is a list of secondary sources that contributed to the interpretive framework of this book.

Books

Allitt, Patrick. *Catholic Intellectuals and Conservative Politics in America, 1950–1985.* Ithaca, NY: Cornell University Press, 1993.

Avila, Eric. *Popular Culture in the Age of White Flight: Fear and Fantasy in Suburban Los Angeles.* Berkeley: University of California Press, 2004.

Barkun, Michael. *Religion and the Racist Right: The Origins of the Christian Identity Movement.* Rev. ed. Chapel Hill: University of North Carolina Press, 1997.

Bennett, David H. *The Party of Fear: From Nativist Movements to the New Right in American History.* Chapel Hill: University of North Carolina Press, 1988.

Berman, William C. *America's Right Turn: From Nixon to Bush.* Baltimore: Johns Hopkins University Press, 1998.

Bernard, Richard M., and Bradley R. Rice, eds. *Sunbelt Cities: Politics and Growth Since World War II.* Austin, TX: University of Texas Press, 1983.

Billingsley, Scott. *It's A New Day: Race and Gender in the Modern Charismatic Movement.* Tuscaloosa, AL: University of Alabama Press, 2008.

Black, Earl, and Merle Black. *The Rise of Southern Republicans.* Cambridge, MA: Harvard University Press, 2002.

Blum, Edward J. *Reforging the White Republic: Race, Religion, and American Nationalism, 1865–1898.* Baton Rouge, LA: Louisiana State University Press, 2007.

Blumhofer, Edith Waldvogel. *Restoring the Faith: The Assemblies of God, Pentecostalism, and American Culture.* Champaign, IL: University of Illinois Press, 1993.

Boles, John B, ed. *Dixie Dateline: A Journalistic Portrait of the Contemporary South.* Houston, TX: Rice University Studies, 1983.

Boyer, Paul S. *When Time Shall Be No More: Prophecy Belief in Modern American Culture.* Cambridge, MA: Harvard University Press, 1992.

Branch, Taylor. *At Canaan's Edge: America in the King Years, 1965–68*. New York: Simon & Schuster, 2006.

Brattain, Michelle. *The Politics of Whiteness: Race, Workers, and Culture in the Modern South*. Princeton, NJ: Princeton University Press, 2001.

Brennan, Mary C. *Wives, Mothers, and the Red Menace: Conservative Women and the Crusade Against Communism*. Boulder, CO: University Press of Colorado, 2008.

———. *Turning Right in the Sixties: The Conservative Capture of the GOP*. Chapel Hill: University of North Carolina Press, 1995.

Brinkley, Alan. *Liberalism and Its Discontents*. Cambridge, MA: Harvard University Press, 1998.

———. *End of Reform: New Deal Liberalism in Recession and War*. New York: Vintage, 1996.

———. *Voices of Protest: Huey Long, Father Coughlin, and the Great Depression*. New York: Vintage, 1983.

Buenger, Walter L. *Path to a Modern South: Northwest Texas between Reconstruction and the Great Depression*. Austin, TX: University of Texas Press, 2001.

Cannon, Lou. *Governor Reagan: His Rise to Power*. New York: Public Affairs, 2003.

Carpenter, Joel A. *Revive Us Again: The Reawakening of American Fundamentalism*. New York: Oxford University Press, 1997.

Carter, Dan T. *The Politics of Rage: George Wallace, the Origins of the New Conservatism, and the Transformation of American Politics*. New York: Simon & Schuster, 1995.

Chappell, David L. *A Stone of Hope: Prophetic Religion and the Death of Jim Crow*. Chapel Hill: University of North Carolina Press, 2004.

Cobb, James C. *A Way Down South: A History of Southern Identity*. New York: Oxford University Press, 2005.

Cobb, James C. *Redefining Southern Culture: Mind and Identity in the Modern South*. Athens, GA: University of Georgia Press, 1999.

Cohen, Lisabeth. *Making a New Deal: Industrial Workers in Chicago, 1919–1939*. New York: Cambridge University Press, 1990.

Creech, Joe. *Righteous Indignation: Religion and the Populist Revolt*. Champaign, IL: University of Illinois Press, 2006.

Crespino, Joseph. *In Search of Another Country: Mississippi and the Conservative Counterrevolution*. Princeton, NJ: Princeton University Press, 2007.

Critchlow, Donald T. *The Conservative Ascendancy: How the GOP Right Made Political History*. Cambridge, MA: Harvard University Press, 2007.

———. *Phyllis Schlafly and Grassroots Conservatism: A Woman's Crusade*. Princeton, NJ: Princeton University Press, 2005.

Dallek, Matthew. *The Right Moment: Ronald Reagan's First Victory and the Decisive Turning Point in American Politics*. New York: Free Press, 2000.

Davis, Mike. *City of Quartz: Excavating the Future in Los Angeles*. New York: Vintage, 1990.

DelFattore, Joan. *The Fourth R: Conflicts over Religion in America's Public Schools*. New Haven, CT: Yale University Press, 2004.

Denning, Michael. *The Cultural Front: The Laboring of American Culture in the Twentieth Century*. New York: Verso, 1997.

Diamond, Sara. *Spiritual Warfare: The Politics of the Christian Right.* Boston: South End Press, 1989.

Dinnerstein, Leonard. *Anti-Semitism in America.* New York: Oxford University Press, 1994.

Donaldson, Gary. *Liberalism's Last Hurrah: The Presidential Campaign of 1964.* Armonk, NY: M. E. Sharpe, 2003.

Edsall, Thomas Byrne, with Mary D. Edsall. *Chain Reaction: The Impact of Race, Rights, and Taxes on American Politics.* New York: W. W. Norton, 1991.

Egerton, John. *The Americanization of Dixie: The Southernization of America.* New York: Harper's Magazine Press, 1974.

Eskridge, Larry, and Mark Noll, eds. *More Money, More Ministry: Money and Evangelicals in Recent North American History.* Grand Rapids, MI: William B. Eerdmans, 2000.

Evans, Thomas W. *The Education of Ronald Reagan: The General Electric Years and the Untold Story of His Conversion to Conservatism.* New York: Columbia University Press, 2006.

Fenster, Mark. *Conspiracy Theories: Secrecy and Power in American Culture.* Minneapolis: University of Minnesota Press, 1999.

Findlay, John M. *Magic Lands: Western Cityscapes and American Culture After 1940.* Berkeley: University of California Press, 1992.

FitzGerald, Frances. *Cities on a Hill: A Journey Through Contemporary American Cultures.* New York: Simon & Schuster, 1986.

Flamm, Michael W. *Law and Order: Street Crime, Civil Unrest, and the Crisis of Liberalism in the 1960s.* New York: Columbia University Press, 2005.

Flamming, Douglas. *Bound for Freedom: Black Los Angeles in Jim Crow America.* Berkeley: University of California Press, 2005.

Fogelson, Robert M. *The Fragmented Metropolis: Los Angeles 1850–1930.* Berkeley: University of California Press, 1993 [1967].

Foley, Neil. *The White Scourge: Mexicans, Blacks, and Poor Whites in Texas Cotton Culture.* Berkeley: University of California Press, 1997.

Fones-Wolf, Elizabeth. *Selling Free Enterprise: The Business Assault on Labor and Liberalism, 1945–1960.* Champaign, IL: University of Illinois Press, 1994.

Ford, Lacy K. *Origins of Southern Radicalism: The South Carolina Upcountry, 1800–1860.* New York: Oxford University Press, 1988.

Formisano, Ronald P. *For the People: American Populist Movements from the Revolution to the 1850s.* Chapel Hill: University of North Carolina Press, 2008.

Fowler, Robert Booth. *A New Engagement: Evangelical Political Thought, 1966–1976.* Grand Rapids, MI: William B. Eerdmans, 1982.

Fraser, Steve, and Gary Gerstle, eds. *The Rise and Fall of the New Deal Order, 1930–1980.* Princeton, NJ: Princeton University Press, 1989.

Frederickson, Kari. *The Dixiecrat Revolt and the End of the Solid South, 1932–1968.* Chapel Hill: University of North Carolina Press, 2001.

Friedman, Murray. *The Neoconservative Revolution: Jewish Intellectuals and the Shaping of Public Policy.* New York: Cambridge University Press, 2005.

Garcia, Matt. *A World of Its Own: Race, Labor, and Citrus in the Making of Greater Los Angeles, 1900–1970*. Chapel Hill: University of North Carolina Press, 2001.

Gilmore, Glenda Elizabeth. *Defying Dixie: The Radical Roots of Civil Rights, 1919–1950*. New York: W. W. Norton, 2008.

Glass, William R. *Strangers in Zion: Fundamentalists in the South, 1900–1950*. Macon, GA: Mercer University Press, 2001.

Goldberg, Robert Alan. *Enemies Within: The Culture of Conspiracy in Modern America*. New Haven, CT: Yale University Press, 2001.

———. *Barry Goldwater*. New Haven, CT: Yale University Press, 1995.

Green, John C., Mark J. Rozell, and Clyde Wilcox, eds. *The Christian Right in American Politics: Marching to the Millennium*. Washington, D.C.: Georgetown University Press, 2003.

Gregory, James N. *The Southern Diaspora: How the Great Migrations of Black and White Southerners Transformed America*. Chapel Hill: University of North Carolina Press, 2005.

———. *American Exodus: The Dust Bowl Migration and Okie Culture in California*. New York: Oxford University Press, 1989.

Griffith, Barbara S. *The Crisis of American Labor: Operation Dixie and the Defeat of the CIO*. Philadelphia: Temple University Press, 1988.

Griffith, R. Marie. *God's Daughters: Evangelical Women and the Power of Submission*. Berkeley: University of California Press, 1997.

Hahn, Steven. *The Roots of Southern Populism: Yeoman Farmers and the Transformation of the Georgia Upcountry, 1850–1890*. New York: Oxford University Press, 1983.

Hale, Grace Elizabeth. *Making Whiteness: The Culture of Segregation in the South, 1890–1940*. New York: Pantheon Books, 1998.

Hangen, Tona J. *Redeeming the Dial: Radio, Religion, and Popular Culture in America*. Chapel Hill: University of North Carolina Press, 2002.

Hankins, Barry. *Uneasy in Babylon: Southern Baptist Conservatives and American Culture*. Tuscaloosa, AL: University of Alabama Press, 2002.

Harding, Susan Friend. *The Book of Jerry Falwell: Fundamentalist Language and Politics*. Princeton, NJ: Princeton University Press, 2000.

Harrell, David Edwin, Jr. *Varieties of Southern Evangelicalism*. Macon, GA.: Mercer University Press, 1981.

Harvey, Paul. *Freedom's Coming: Religious Culture and the Shaping of the South from the Civil War through the Civil Rights Era*. Chapel Hill: University of North Carolina Press, 2005.

———. *Redeeming the South: Religious Cultures and Racial Identities Among Southern Baptists, 1865–1925*. Chapel Hill: University of North Carolina Press, 1997.

Heineman, Kenneth J. *God Is a Conservative: Religion, Politics, and Morality in Contemporary America*. New York: New York University Press, 1998.

Hendershot, Heather. *Shaking the World for Jesus: Media and Conservative Evangelical Culture*. Chicago: University of Chicago Press, 2004.

Hicks, L. Edward. *"Sometimes in the Wrong, but Never in Doubt": George S. Benson and the Education of the New Religious Right*. Knoxville, TN: University of Tennessee Press, 1994.

Hill, Samuel S., Jr., ed. *Varieties of Southern Religious Experience*. Baton Rouge, LA: Louisiana State University Press, 1988.

Himmelstein, Jerome L. *To The Right: The Transformation of American Conservatism*. Berkeley: University of California Press, 1990.

Hise, Greg. *Magnetic Los Angeles: Planning the Twentieth-Century Metropolis*. Baltimore: Johns Hopkins University Press, 1997.

Hixson, William B. *The Search for the American Right Wing: An Analysis of the Social Science Record, 1955–1987*. Princeton, NJ: Princeton University Press, 1992.

HoSang, Dan. *Racial Propositions: Genteel Apartheid in Postwar California*. Berkeley: University of California Press, 2010.

Hughes, Richard T. *Reviving the Ancient Faith: The Story of Churches of Christ in America*. Grand Rapids, MI: William B. Eerdmans, 1996.

Hunter, James Davison. *Culture Wars: The Struggle to Define America*. New York: Basic Books, 1991.

Hyde, Samuel C., Jr., ed. *Plain Folk of the South Revisited*. Baton Rouge, LA: Louisiana State University Press, 1997.

Jacobs, Meg. *Pocketbook Politics: Economic Citizenship in Twentieth-Century America*. Princeton, NJ: Princeton University Press, 2005.

Jeansonne, Glen. *Gerald L. K. Smith: Minister of Hate*. New Haven, CT: Yale University Press, 1988.

Johnson, Ben, III. *Arkansas in Modern America, 1930–1999*. Fayetteville, AR: University of Arkansas Press, 2000.

Katznelson, Ira. *When Affirmative Action Was White: An Untold History of Racial Inequality in Twentieth-Century America*. New York: W. W. Norton, 2005.

Kazin, Michael. *A Godly Hero: The Life of William Jennings Bryan*. New York: Alfred A. Knopf, 2006.

———. *The Populist Persuasion: An American History*. New York: Basic Books, 1995.

Kirby, Jack Temple. *Rural Worlds Lost: The American South, 1920–1960*. Baton Rouge, LA: Louisiana State University Press, 1987.

Klatch, Rebecca. *A Generation Divided: The New Left, the New Right and the 1960s*. Berkeley: University of California Press, 1999.

Klein, Jennifer. *For All These Rights: Business, Labor, and the Shaping of America's Public-Private Welfare State*. Princeton, NJ: Princeton University Press, 2003.

Kling, Robert, Spencer Olin, and Mark Poster, eds. *Postsuburban California: The Transformation of Orange County Since World War II*. Berkeley: University of California Press, 1991.

Kruse, Kevin. *White Flight: Atlanta and the Making of Modern Conservatism*. Princeton, NJ: Princeton University Press, 2005.

Kurashige, Scott. *The Shifting Grounds of Race: Black and Japanese Americans in the Making of Multiethnic Los Angeles*. Princeton, NJ: Princeton University Press, 2008.

La Chapelle, Peter. *Proud to Be an Okie: Cultural Politics, Country Music, and Migration to Southern California*. Berkeley: University of California Press, 2007.

Lahr, Angela M. *Millennial Dreams and Apocalyptic Nightmares: The Cold War Origins of Political Evangelicalism*. New York: Oxford University Press, 2007.

Lassiter, Matthew. *The Silent Majority: Suburban Politics in the Sunbelt South.* Princeton, NJ: Princeton University Press, 2006.

Lichtenstein, Nelson. *Labor's War at Home: The CIO in World War II.* New York: Cambridge University Press, 1982.

Lichtman, Allan J. *White Protestant Nation: The Rise of the American Conservative Movement.* New York: Atlantic Monthly Press, 2008.

Liebman, Robert C., and Robert Wuthnow, eds. *The New Christian Right: Mobilization and Legitimation.* Hawthorne, NY: Aldine, 1983.

Lienesch, Michael. *Redeeming America: Piety and Politics in the New Christian Right.* Chapel Hill: University of North Carolina Press, 1993.

Lindsay, D. Michael. *Faith in the Halls of Power: How Evangelicals Joined the American Elite.* New York: Oxford University Press, 2007.

Lipsitz, George. *Rainbow at Midnight: Labor and Culture in the 1940s.* Champaign, IL: University of Illinois Press, 1994.

Lotchin, Roger W. *Fortress California, 1910–1961: From Warfare to Welfare.* New York: Oxford University Press, 1992.

Loveland, Anne C. *American Evangelicals and the U.S. Military, 1942–1993.* Baton Rouge, LA: Louisiana State University Press, 1996.

Lowndes, Joseph E. *From the New Deal to the New Right: Race and the Southern Origins of Modern Conservatism.* New Haven, CT: Yale University Press, 2008.

Luhr, Eileen. *Witnessing Suburbia: Conservatives and Christian Youth Culture.* Berkeley: University of California Press, 2009.

MacLean, Nancy. *Behind the Mask of Chivalry: The Making of the Second Ku Klux Klan.* New York: Oxford University Press, 1994.

Markusen, Ann, Peter Hall, Scott Campbell, and Sabina Deitrick. *The Rise of the Gunbelt; The Military Remapping of Industrial America.* New York: Oxford University Press, 1991.

Marsden, George M. *Reforming Fundamentalism: Fuller Seminary and the New Evangelicalism.* Grand Rapids, MI: William B. Eerdmans, 1987.

———. *Fundamentalism and American Culture: The Shaping of Twentieth-Century Evangelicalism, 1870–1925.* New York: Oxford University Press, 1980.

Martin, William. *With God on Our Side: The Rise of the Religious Right in America.* New York: Broadway Books, 1996.

May, Kirse Granat. *Golden State, Golden Youth: California Image in Popular Culture, 1955–1966.* Chapel Hill: University of North Carolina Press, 2002.

McGirr, Lisa. *Suburban Warriors: The Origins of the New American Right.* Princeton, NJ: Princeton University Press, 2001.

McGreevy, John T. *Parish Boundaries: The Catholic Encounter with Race in the Twentieth-Century Urban North.* Chicago: University of Chicago Press, 1996.

Miller, Donald E. *Reinventing American Protestantism: Christianity in the New Millennium.* Berkeley: University of California Press, 1997.

Miller, Robert Moats. *Bishop G. Bromley Oxnam: Paladin of Liberal Protestantism.* Nashville, TN: Abingdon Press, 1990.

Miller, Steven P. *Billy Graham and the Rise of the Republican South.* Philadelphia: University of Pennsylvania Press, 2009.

Mohl, Raymond A., Robert Fisher, Carl Abbott, Roger W. Lotchin, Robert B. Fairbanks, and Zane I. Miller. *Essays on Sunbelt Cities and Recent Urban America*. College Station, TX: Texas A&M University Press, 1990.

Moore, Deborah Dash. *To the Golden Cities: Pursuing the American Jewish Dream in Miami and L.A.* Cambridge, MA: Harvard University Press, 1994.

Moran, Jeffrey P. *Teaching Sex: The Shaping of Adolescence in the 20th Century*. Cambridge, MA: Harvard University Press, 2000.

Moreton, Bethany. *To Serve God and Wal-Mart: The Making of Christian Free Enterprise*. Cambridge, MA: Harvard University Press, 2009.

Morgan, Dan. *Rising in the West: The True Story of an "Okie" Family in Search of an American Dream*. New York: Vintage Press, 1992.

Nash, George H. *The Conservative Intellectual Movement in America Since 1945, Thirtieth Anniversary Edition*. Wilmington, DE: ISI Books, 2008.

Nash, Gerald D. *The American West Transformed: The Impact of the Second World War*. Bloomington, IN: Indiana University Press, 1985.

Nelson, Bruce. *Divided We Stand: American Workers and the Struggle for Black Equality*. Princeton, NJ: Princeton University Press, 2001.

Newman, Mark. *Getting Right with God: Southern Baptists and Desegregation, 1945–1995*. Tuscaloosa, AL: University of Alabama Press, 2001.

Nickerson, Michelle. *Mothers of Conservatism: Women and the Postwar Right*. Princeton, NJ: Princeton University Press, forthcoming.

Nicolaides, Becky. *My Blue Heaven; Life and Politics in the Working-Class Suburbs of Los Angeles, 1920–1965*. Chicago: University of Chicago Press, 2002.

Oldfield, Duane Murray. *The Right and the Righteous: The Christian Right Confronts the Republican Party*. London: Rowman and Littlefield, 1996.

Oshinsky, David M. *A Conspiracy So Immense: The World of Joe McCarthy*. New York: Oxford University Press, 2005.

Ownby, Ted. *Subduing Satan: Recreation and Manhood in the Rural South*. Chapel Hill: University of North Carolina Press, 1990.

Perlstein, Rick. *Nixonland: The Rise of a President and the Fracturing of America*. New York: Scribner, 2008.

———. *Before the Storm: Barry Goldwater and the Unmaking of the American Consensus*. New York: Hill & Wang, 2001.

Phillips, Kevin P. *The Emerging Republican Majority*. New Rochelle, NY: Arlington House, 1969.

Phillips-Fein, Kim. *Invisible Hands: The Making of the Conservative Movement from the New Deal to Reagan*. New York: W. W. Norton, 2009.

Postel, Charles. *The Populist Vision*. New York: Oxford University Press, 2007.

Powers, Richard Gid. *Not Without Honor: The History of American Anticommunism*. New York: Free Press, 1995.

Quebedeaux, Richard. *The New Charismatics: The Origins, Development, and Significance of Neo-Pentecostals*. Garden City, NY: Doubleday, 1976.

Rarick, Ethan. *California Rising: The Life and Times of Pat Brown*. Berkeley: University of California Press, 2005.

Reed, John Shelton. *Southern Folk, Plain and Fancy: Native White Social Types*. Athens, GA: University of Georgia Press, 1986.

Ribuffo, Leo P. *The Old Christian Right: The Protestant Far Right from the Great Depression to the Cold War*. Philadelphia: Temple University Press, 1983.

Richardson, Peter. *American Prophet: The Life and Work of Carey McWilliams*. Ann Arbor, MI: University of Michigan Press, 2005.

Rogin, Michael Paul, and John L. Shover. *Political Change in California: Critical Elections and Social Movements, 1890–1966*. Westport, CT: Greenwood Press, 1970.

Rosell, Garth M. *The Surprising Work of God: Harold John Ockenga, Billy Graham, and the Rebirth of Evangelicalism*. Grand Rapids, MI: Baker Academic, 2008.

Rossinow, Doug. *The Politics of Authenticity: Liberalism, Christianity, and the New Left in America*. New York: Columbia University Press, 1998.

Rymph, Catherine E. *Republican Women: Feminism and Conservatism from Suffrage Through the Rise of the New Right*. Chapel Hill: University of North Carolina Press, 2006.

Sale, Kirkpatrick. *Power Shift: The Rise of the Southern Rim and Its Challenge to the Eastern Establishment*. New York: Random House, 1975.

Savage, Barbara Dianne. *Your Spirits Walk Beside Us: The Politics of Black Religion*. Cambridge, MA: Belknap Press of Harvard University Press, 2008.

Schoenwald, Jonathan M. *A Time for Choosing: The Rise of Modern American Conservatism*. New York: Oxford University Press, 2001.

Schneider, Gregory L. *Cadres for Conservatism: Young Americans for Freedom and the Rise of the Contemporary Right*. New York: New York University Press, 1999.

Schulman, Bruce J., and Julian E. Zelizer. *Rightward Bound: Making America Conservative in the 1970s*. Cambridge, MA: Harvard University Press, 2008.

Schulman, Bruce J. *From Cotton Belt to Sunbelt: Federal Policy, Economic Development, and the Transformation of the South, 1938–1980*. New York: Oxford University Press, 1991.

Schuparra, Kurt. *Triumph of the Right: The Rise of the California Conservative Movement, 1945–1966*. Armonk, N.Y.: M. E. Sharpe, 1998.

Self, Robert O. *American Babylon: Race and the Struggle for Postwar Oakland*. Princeton, NJ: Princeton University Press, 2003.

Shafer, Byron E., and Richard Johnston. *The End of Southern Exceptionalism: Class, Race, and Partisan Change in the Postwar South*. Cambridge, MA: Harvard University Press, 2006.

Shibley, Mark A. *Resurgent Evangelicalism in the United States: Mapping Cultural Change since 1970*. Columbia, SC: University of South Carolina Press, 1996.

Shilts, Randy. *The Mayor of Castro Street: The Life and Times of Harvey Milk*. New York: St. Martin's, 1982.

Shirley, Craig. *Reagan's Revolution: The Untold Story of the Campaign that Started It All*. New York: Nelson Current, 2005.

Sides, Josh. *L.A. City Limits: African American Los Angeles from the Great Depression to the Present*. Berkeley: University of California Press, 2003.

Sitton, Tom, and William Deverell, eds. *Metropolis in the Making: Los Angeles in the 1920s*. Berkeley: University of California Press, 2001.

Smith, Christian. *American Evangelicalism: Embattled and Thriving*. Chicago: University of Chicago Press, 1998.

Soja, Edward W., and Allen J. Scott. *The City: Los Angeles and Urban Theory at the End of the Twentieth Century.* Berkeley: University of California Press, 1996.

Starr, Kevin. *The Dream Endures: California Enters the 1940s.* New York: Oxford University Press, 1997.

———. *Endangered Dreams: The Great Depression in California.* New York: Oxford University Press, 1996.

Stephens, Randall J. *The Fire Spreads: Holiness and Pentecostalism in the American South.* Cambridge, MA: Harvard University Press, 2008.

Sugrue, Thomas J. *The Origins of the Urban Crisis: Race and Inequality in Postwar Detroit.* Princeton, NJ: Princeton University Press, 1996.

Sutton, Matthew Avery. *Aimee Semple McPherson and the Resurrection of Christian America.* Cambridge, MA: Harvard University Press, 2007.

Svelmoe, William. *A New Vision for Missions: William Cameron Townsend, the Wycliffe Bible Translators, and the Culture of Early Evangelical Faith Missions, 1917–1945.* Tuscaloosa, AL: University of Alabama Press, 2008.

Svonkin, Stuart. *Jews Against Prejudice: American Jews and the Fight for Civil Liberties.* New York: Columbia University Press, 1997.

Synan, Vinson. *The Holiness-Pentecostal Tradition: Charismatic Movements in the Twentieth Century.* Grand Rapids, MI: William B. Eerdmans, 1997.

Tindall, George Brown. *The Ethnic Southerners.* Baton Rouge, LA: Louisiana State University Press, 1976.

Turner, John G. *Bill Bright and Campus Crusade for Christ: The Renewal of Evangelicalism in Postwar America.* Chapel Hill: University of North Carolina Press, 2008.

Wacker, Grant. *Heaven Below: Early Pentecostals and American Culture.* Cambridge, MA: Harvard University Press, 2003.

Wagner, Melinda Bollar. *God's Schools: Choice and Compromise in American Society.* New Brunswick, NJ: Rutgers University Press, 1990.

Wilcox, Clyde. *God's Warriors: The Christian Right in Twentieth-Century America.* Baltimore: Johns Hopkins University Press, 1992.

Wild, Mark. *Street Meeting: Multiethnic Neighborhoods in Early Twentieth-Century Los Angeles.* Berkeley: University of California Press, 2005.

Wilentz, Sean. *The Age of Reagan: A History, 1974–2008.* New York: HarperCollins, 2008.

Wilson, Charles Reagan. *Judgment and Grace in Dixie: Southern Faiths from Faulkner to Elvis.* Athens, GA: University of Georgia Press, 1995.

Wuthnow, Robert. *The Restructuring of American Religion: Society and Faith since World War II.* Princeton, NJ: Princeton University Press, 1988.

Journal Articles and Chapters in Books

Brauer, Jerald C. "Regionalism and Religion in America." *Church History* 54 (1985): 366–78.

Brinkley, Alan. "The Problem of American Conservatism." *American Historical Review* 99 (April 1994): 409–29.

Etulain, Richard W. "Regionalizing Religion: Evangelicals in the American West,

1940–1990." In *Religion and Culture: Historical Essays in Honor of Robert C. Woodward*, edited by Raymond M. Cooke and Richard W. Etulain, 79–103. Albuquerque: Far West Books, 1991.

Gerstle, Gary. "Race and the Myth of the Liberal Consensus." *The Journal of American History* 82, no. 2 (September 1995): 579–86.

Goff, Phillip. "Fighting Like the Devil in the City of Angels: The Rise of Fundamentalist Charles E. Fuller." In *Metropolis in the Making: Los Angeles in the 1920s*, edited by Tom Sitton and William Deverell, 220–53. Berkeley: University of California Press, 2001.

Gregory, James N. "The Southern Diaspora and the Urban Dispossessed: Demonstrating the Census Public Use Microdata Samples." *Journal of American History* 82 (June 1995): 111–34.

Heale, M. J. "Red Scare Politics: California's Campaign Against Un-American Activities, 1940–1970." *Journal of American Studies* 20 (1986): 5–32.

Hill, Samuel S. "Religion and Region in America." *The Annals of the American Academy of Political and Social Science* 480 (1985): 132–41.

Hise, Greg. "Home Building and Industrial Decentralization in Los Angeles: The Roots of the Postwar Urban Region." *Journal of Urban History* 19 (February 1993): 95–125.

Jordan, Terry G. "The Imprint of the Upper and Lower South on Mid-Nineteenth-Century Texas." *Annals of the Association of American Geographers* 57 (December 1967): 667–90.

Jordan, Terry G. "Forest Folk, Prairie Folk: Rural Religious Culture in Northern Texas." *Southwestern Historical Quarterly* 80 (1976): 135–62.

Kazin, Michael. "The Grass-Roots Right: New Histories of United States Conservatism in the Twentieth Century." *American Historical Review* 97 (February 1992): 136–55.

Kirby, Jack Temple. "The Southern Exodus, 1910–1960: A Primer for Historians." *The Journal of Southern History* 49 (November 1983): 585–600.

Pritchard, Linda K. "The Burned-Over District Reconsidered: A Portent of Evolving Religious Pluralism in the United States." *Social Science History* 8 (Summer 1984): 243–65.

Schäfer, Axel R. "The Cold War State and the Resurgence of Evangelicalism: A Study of the Public Funding of Religion Since 1945. *Radical History Review* 99 (2007): 80–106.

Schermer, Elizabeth Tandy. "Origins of the Conservative Ascendancy: Barry Goldwater's Early Senate Career and the De-legitimization of Organized Labor." *Journal of American History* 95 (December 2008): 678–709.

Schultz, Kevin M. "The FEPC and the Legacy of the Labor-Based Civil Rights Movement of the 1940s," *Labor History* 49 (February 2008): 71–92.

Schuparra, Kurt. "Barry Goldwater and Southern California Conservatism: Ideology, Image and Myth in the 1964 California Republican Presidential Primary." *Southern California Quarterly* 74 (Fall 1992): 281–98.

Sitton, Tom. "'Direct Democracy vs. Free Speech': Gerald L. K. Smith and the Recall Election of 1946 in Los Angeles." *Pacific Historical Review* 57 (August 1988): 285–304.

Tindall, George B. "The Benighted South: Origins of a Modern Image." *Virginia Quarterly Review* 40 (Spring 1964): 281–94.

Toy, Eckard V. "Spiritual Mobilization: The Failure of an Ultra-Conservative Ideal." *Pacific Northwest Quarterly* 61 (April 1970): 77–86.

Wacker, Grant. "Uneasy in Zion: Evangelicals in Postmodern Society." In *Evangelicalism and Modern America*, edited by George Marsden, 17–28. Grand Rapids, MI: William B. Eerdmans, 1984.

Zimmerman, Tom. "'Ham and Eggs, Everybody!'" *Southern California Quarterly* (Spring 1980): 77–96.

Dissertations and Theses

Bernstein, Shana. "Building Bridges at Home in a Time of Global Conflict: Interracial Cooperation and the Fight for Civil Rights in Los Angeles, 1933–1954." PhD diss., Stanford University, 2003.

Connolly, Nathan. "By Eminent Domain: Race and Capital in the Building of an American South Florida." PhD diss., University of Michigan, 2008.

Gloege, Timothy. "Consumed: Reuben A. Torrey and the Creation of Corporate Fundamentalism, 1880–1930." PhD diss., University of Notre Dame, 2007.

Graybill, Stuart Dean. "Bending the Twig: Conservative Educational Criticism and the Revival of the Right, 1900–1966." PhD diss., University of California, Davis, 1999.

Grem, Darren. "The Blessings of Business: Corporate America and Conservative Evangelicalism in the Sunbelt Age, 1945–2000." PhD diss., University of Georgia, 2010.

Griffith, Duff Witman. "Before the Deluge: An Oral History Examination of Pre-Watergate Conservative Thought in Orange County, California." Master's thesis, California State University, Fullerton, 1976.

Leonard, Kevin Allen. "Years of Hope, Days of Fear: The Impact of World War II on Race Relations in Los Angeles." PhD diss., University of California, Davis, 1992.

Manes, Sheila Golding. "Depression Pioneers: The Conclusion of an American Odyssey, Oklahoma to California, 1930–1950, a Reinterpretation." PhD diss., University of California, Los Angeles, 1982.

Martinez, G. Ted. "The Rise, Decline, and Renewal of a Megachurch: A Case Study of Church of the Open Door." Doctor of Ministry diss., Talbot School of Theology, Biola University, 1997.

Roche, Jeff. "Cowboy Conservatism: High Plains Politics, 1933–1972." PhD diss., University of New Mexico, 2001.

Still, Mark Sumner. "'Fighting Bob' Shuler: Fundamentalist and Reformer." PhD diss., Claremont Graduate School, 1988.

Stookey, Stephen Martin. "The Impact of Landkmarkism upon Southern Baptist Western Geographical Expansion." PhD diss., Southwestern Baptist Theological Seminary, 1994.

Williams, Daniel. "From the Pews to the Polls: The Formation of a Southern Christian Right." PhD diss., Brown University, 2005.

PHOTOGRAPH CREDITS

Nonstriker bloodied during Hollywood's "labor wars":
Los Angeles Times, October 6, 1945. Courtesy of UCLA Charles E. Young Research Library, Department of Special Collections, *Los Angeles Times* Photographic Archives

Mobilization for Democracy activists protesting Gerald L. K. Smith and Ham and Eggs:
From the Dorothy Healey Collection, Special Collections and University Archives, California State University, Long Beach

The Church of the Open Door, circa 1950:
Courtesy of the Church of the Open Door

Interior of the Church of the Open Door:
Courtesy of the Church of the Open Door

Billy Graham and Bob Shuler:
Courtesy of the Security Pacific Collection, Los Angeles Public Library

J. Vernon McGee preaching at the Church of the Open Door:
Courtesy of Thru the Bible Radio Network

Sign announcing the arrival of southern evangelist Doug Winn:
Courtesy of the Security Pacific Collection, Los Angeles Public Library

Heritage students in patriotic costumes:
Courtesy of Victory Baptist Church, Anaheim

Norvel and Helen Young in the early 1960s:
From the University Photographs Collection, Pepperdine University Special Collections and Archives

Southern California School of Anti-Communism, 1961:
Courtesy of the Security Pacific Collection, Los Angeles Public Library

Senator Barry Goldwater at Pepperdine's third freedom forum:
Photo by Hanson Williams, from the University Photographs Collection, Pepperdine University Special Collections and Archives

Pepperdine College students marching for Goldwater:
From the University Photographs Collection, Pepperdine University Special Collections and Archives

Young boy watching events unfold at a Goldwater rally:
Los Angeles Times, September 17, 1963. Courtesy of UCLA Charles E. Young Research Library, Department of Special Collections, *Los Angeles Times* Photographic Archives

Billy Graham and Ronald Reagan shaking hands:
Courtesy of the Billy Graham Evangelistic Association

Billy Graham preaching at Mount Zion Missionary Baptist Church:
Courtesy of Mount Zion Missionary Baptist Church, Los Angeles

Ruth Graham speaking to eleven thousand evangelical women gathered in Anaheim:
Courtesy of the Billy Graham Evangelistic Association

Youth at Billy Graham's Anaheim crusade in 1969:
Courtesy of the Billy Graham Evangelistic Association

William Banowsky confronts black protestors on campus:
Los Angeles Times, December 11, 1970. Courtesy of UCLA Charles E. Young
Research Library, Department of Special Collections, *Los Angeles Times* Photographic
Archives

William Banowsky and Bishop James Pike debate 1960s "new morality":
From the University Photographs Collection, Pepperdine University Special Collections and Archives

Jesus People praying and singing praise at Explo '72:
Courtesy of the Billy Graham Evangelistic Association

E. V. Hill applauding Richard Nixon in Knoxville, 1970:
Courtesy of the Billy Graham Evangelistic Association

Pat Boone working for Ronald Reagan at the 1976 Republican National Convention:
Courtesy of Pat Boone

Arthur Blessitt walking his wheeled cross on Sunset Strip:
Los Angeles Times, June 10, 1977. Courtesy of UCLA Charles E. Young Research
Library, Department of Special Collections, *Los Angeles Times* Photographic Archives

Gay rights activists marching against the Briggs initiative in Los Angeles, 1978:
Courtesy of the Security Pacific Collection, Los Angeles Public Library

E. V. Hill prepares for a "People's March" through South Central Los Angeles:
Courtesy of Mount Zion Missionary Baptist Church

Pepperdine University at dusk:
Courtesy of Pepperdine University

INDEX